THE RIGHT TO HEALTH AT THE PUBLIC/PRIVATE DIVIDE

Through a comparative global study of countries from all continents representing a diversity of health, legal, political, and economic systems, this book explores the role of health rights to advance greater equality through access to health care. Does pursuing a right to health care promote equality, or does it in fact advance the opposite result? Does inserting the idea of "the right to health" into health systems allow the reinsertion of public values into systems that are undergoing privatization? Or does it allow for private claims to be rearticulated as "rights," in a way that actually reinforces inequality? This volume includes studies from countries such as the United States, the United Kingdom, Brazil, Canada, the Netherlands, China, and Nigeria, as well as authors with expertise regarding both the legal and health systems of their countries, making this a seminal study that allows readers to see the differing role of rights in various health systems.

Colleen M. Flood is a Professor and Canada Research Chair at the Faculty of Law, University of Toronto, and is cross-appointed to the School of Public Policy and the Institute of Health Policy, Management, and Evaluation.

Aeyal Gross is an Associate Professor in Tel-Aviv University's Faculty of Law. He is also a Visiting Reader at the School of Oriental and African Studies, University of London.

The Right to Health at the Public/Private Divide

A GLOBAL COMPARATIVE STUDY

Edited by

COLLEEN M. FLOOD

University of Toronto, Faculty of Law and
The School of Public Policy

AEYAL GROSS

Tel-Aviv University, Faculty of Law

CAMBRIDGE
UNIVERSITY PRESS

CAMBRIDGE
UNIVERSITY PRESS

32 Avenue of the Americas, New York NY 10013-2473, USA

Cambridge University Press is part of the University of Cambridge.

It furthers the University's mission by disseminating knowledge in the pursuit of
education, learning and research at the highest international levels of excellence.

www.cambridge.org
Information on this title: www.cambridge.org/9781107038301

© Cambridge University Press 2014

First published 2014

A catalogue record for this publication is available from the British Library

Library of Congress Cataloguing in Publication data
The right to health at the public/private divide : a global comparative study / Colleen M. Flood,
University of Toronto, Faculty of Law; Aeyal Gross, Tel-Aviv University, Faculty of Law.
    pages cm
Includes bibliographical references and index.
ISBN 978-1-107-03830-1 (hardback)
1. Medical care – Law and legislation.   2. Right to health.   I. Flood, Colleen M., editor of
compilation.   II. Gross, Aeyal, editor of compilation.
K3601.R525   2014
362.1–dc23   2013042458

ISBN 978-1-107-03830-1 Hardback

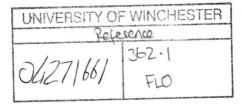

Contents

Contributors

Oscar A. Cabrera is the Executive Director of the O'Neill Institute for National and Global Health Law and Visiting Professor of Law at Georgetown University Law Center. In Venezuela, Oscar worked as an Associate at a Venezuelan law firm (d'Empaire Reyna Bermúdez). After earning his LLM at the University of Toronto, he worked as a Research Associate with Professor Colleen M. Flood, at the University of Toronto, Faculty of Law, and the Institute of Health Services and Policy Research (CIHR-IHSPR). Oscar has worked on projects with the World Health Organization, the Centers for Disease Control and Prevention, and the Campaign for Tobacco-Free Kids, among other organizations. His research interests focus on health and human rights, sexual and reproductive rights, global tobacco litigation and health systems law and policy. Oscar holds a law degree from his home country of Venezuela (Universidad Católica Andrés Bello, Caracas) and a LLM, with concentration in Health Law and Policy, from the University of Toronto (he was awarded a Canadian Institutes of Health Research Health Law and Policy Fellowship to attend this program).

Y. Y. Brandon Chen is an SJD candidate at the University of Toronto, Faculty of Law. He is currently a Vanier Canada Graduate Scholar and a Canadian Institutes of Health Research Fellow in Health Law, Ethics and Policy. Between 2012 and 2013, he was also named a Lupina Senior Doctor Fellow in the Comparative Program on Health and Society. Y. Y. holds a BSc from Emory University as well as MSW and JD degrees from the University of Toronto. He worked at the Canadian Civil Liberties Association from 2010 to 2011 as a Law Foundation of Ontario Public Interest Articling Fellow and was called to the Bar of Ontario in 2011. Y. Y.'s current research explores the intersection of global justice with health law and policy and examines topics such as medical tourism and international migrants' health care entitlement in developed countries.

André den Exter is a Lecturer in Health Law at the Institute of Health Policy and Management, Erasmus University Rotterdam, the Netherlands. Since returning to Erasmus University Rotterdam in 2008, his research has focused on international and European health law. The title of his dissertation was "Health Care Law-making in Central and Eastern Europe: Review of a Legal-Theoretical Model" (EUR 2002). His research topics include health care and human rights, access to health care, EU law and health care, and pharmaceutical law. Recent publications include *International Trade and Health Care: In Search of Good Sense* (2011) and *Human Rights and Biomedicine* (2010), both of which André edited. He has authored 150 other book contributions and articles.

Colleen M. Flood is a Professor and Canada Research Chair at the Faculty of Law, University of Toronto, and is cross-appointed to the School of Public Policy and the Institute of Health Policy, Management, and Evaluation. From 2006 to 2011 she served as the Scientific Director of the Canadian Institute for Health Services and Policy Research. Her primary areas of scholarship are in comparative health care law and policy, administrative law, public/private financing of health care systems, health care reform, and accountability and governance issues more broadly. She is the author or editor of seven books, including multiple new editions: *Data, Data, Everywhere: Access and Accountability?* (editor) (2011); *Canadian Health Law and Policy* (4th edition) (coedited with J. Downie and T. Caulfield) (2011); *Administrative Law in Context* (2nd edition) (coedited with Lorne Sossin) (2012); *Exploring Social Insurance: Can a Dose of Europe Cure Canadian Health Care Finance?* (coedited with Mark Stabile and Carolyn Tuohy) (2008); *Just Medicare: What's In, What's Out, How We Decide* (editor) (2006); *Access to Justice, Access to Care: The Legal Debate over Private Health Insurance* (coedited with Kent Roach and Lorne Sossin) (2005); and *International Health Care Reform: A Legal, Economic and Political Analysis* (2000).

Mária Éva Földes holds a PhD and a Master of Arts degree from Central European University, Hungary, and an International Master degree from the University of Leuven, Belgium. Her research interests include the influence of European integration on health policy and health systems, social determinants of health, regulation of medicinal products and medical devices, health-related rights of vulnerable groups, and healthy ageing. Since March 2014 she has been working as postdoctoral researcher at the University of Vienna's Institute for European Integration Research, Austria. Between 2010 and 2013 she worked as researcher at the University of Tilburg, the Netherlands, Faculty of Law, and Tilburg Law and Economics Center. Before moving to the Netherlands in 2010, she worked in Hungary for the Open Society Institute's Public Health Program where she coordinated a project promoting the health rights of vulnerable groups in Central and Eastern Europe with specific focus on the Roma minority.

Lisa Forman is the Lupina Assistant Professor at the Dalla Lana School of Public Health and Director of the Comparative Program on Health and Society at the Munk School of Global Affairs at the University of Toronto. Her research focuses on the contribution of international human rights law to remediating global health inequities, focusing on access to medicines in low- and middle-income countries and the post-2015 health development agenda. She has written widely on the right to health, access to medicines, trade-related intellectual property rights, human rights impact assessment, and global health policy, and she is coeditor of *Access to Medicines as a Human Right: Implications for Pharmaceutical Industry Responsibility* (2012). Lisa qualified as an attorney of the High Court of South Africa, with a BA and LLB from the University of the Witwatersrand. Her graduate studies include a Masters in Human Rights Studies from Columbia University and an SJD from the University of Toronto's Faculty of Law.

Fanny Gómez is an Adjunct Professor of Law at Georgetown University Law Center and a Human Rights Specialist with the Inter-American Commission on Human Rights (IACHR). Previously she was an independent consultant for Human Rights Watch and worked with the Canadian HIV/AIDS Legal Network in drafting model legislation on violence and discrimination against women in Sub-Saharan Africa. In 2009–2010, she participated in the Women's Law and Public Policy Fellowship Program at the Georgetown University Law Center. Her scholarly and research interests include women's human rights, sexuality and human rights, sexual and reproductive rights and health law, and the inter-American human rights system. She has lectured on these subjects at the Georgetown University Law Center and the Bloomberg School of Public Health at Johns Hopkins University. Fanny holds a law degree from the Andres Bello Catholic University in Caracas, Venezuela, and an LLM, with concentration in international law, from McGill University.

Aeyal Gross is a member of the Faculty in Tel-Aviv University's Faculty of Law. He is also a Visiting Reader at the School of Oriental and African Studies (SOAS) in the University of London. He holds an LLB from Tel-Aviv University (1990) and an SJD from Harvard Law School (1996). In 1998 he was awarded the Diploma in Human Rights from the Academy of European Law, European University Institute, in Florence. Aeyal serves as a member of the Board of the Association for Civil Rights in Israel. He also served as a Research Fellow at the Institute of Advanced Legal Studies at the University of London, as a Visiting Fellow at the Stellenbosch Institute for Advanced Studies in South Africa, and as a Joseph Flom Global Health and Human Rights Fellow at Harvard Law School. Additionally he taught as a visiting lecturer at Columbia University and the University of Toronto.

Anand Grover is a senior advocate practicing in the Supreme Court of India; the Director of the Lawyers Collective, India; and the UN Special Rapporteur on the Right to Health.

Christina S. Ho is an Associate Professor of Law at Rutgers University, having joined the faculty in 2010 from the O'Neill Institute for National and Global Health Law at Georgetown University Law Center, where she was a Senior Fellow and Project Director of the China Health Law Initiative. She was previously Country Director and Senior Policy Advisor for the Clinton Foundation's China program. During the Clinton administration she worked on the Domestic Policy Council at the White House and later led Senator Hillary Rodham Clinton's health legislative staff. Her teaching and research interests include administrative law and health law and policy. Christina received her AB magna cum laude from Harvard College, an MPP from Harvard's John F. Kennedy School of Government, and JD cum laude from Harvard Law School.

Allison K. Hoffman is Assistant Professor of Law at the UCLA School of Law. Her work focuses on U.S. health care law and policy. She currently teaches health care law and policy, torts, and a seminar on health insurance and reform. Allison is a Faculty Associate at the UCLA Center for Health Policy Research. Her research explores the role of regulation and the welfare state in promoting health and well-being. She received her AB summa cum laude from Dartmouth College and law degree from the Yale Law School, where she was submissions editor for the *Yale Journal of Health Policy, Law, and Ethics*. She previously practiced health care law at Ropes & Gray, LLP, where she counseled academic medical centers, insurers, pharmaceutical companies, and private equity firms on a wide range of health care regulatory matters. She has also provided strategic advice to health care companies and to nonprofit organizations and foundations as a management consultant at the Boston Consulting Group and the Bridgespan Group. Immediately prior to joining the faculty at UCLA, she was a Fellow at Harvard Law School's Petrie-Flom Center for Health Law Policy, Biotechnology, and Bioethics.

Everaldo Lamprea is a Professor at Los Andes Law School, Bogotá. He received his LLB from Los Andes Law School. Additionally, he completed a JSM and a JSD at Stanford Law School. In 2011 he coordinated a team at Colombia's Constitutional Court in charge of analyzing health-related public policy and regulation. His current research focuses on the regulation of public services and on how this interacts with socioeconomic rights adjudication in developing countries, with a focus on the regulation of health systems.

Anna-Sara Lind, LLD, is a Senior Lecturer of Public Law at Uppsala University, Sweden. Her research interests focus on fundamental rights in a national as well as in a European constitutional context and how these rights are communicated between these levels. Her latest articles have focused on the constitutional dimension of the right to health and the social rights of illegal immigrants in the European Union. Her current research projects deal with integrity rights and social security law, respectively. Although being quite different in comparison, these projects have some points in common. One is the constitutional dimension of the national legal order being tested and challenged by international law and/or EU law and how the power of lawmaking is fragmented between several constitutional actors. Another point is the possibility for the individual to be able to access and be part of the realization of their stated rights.

Joanna Manning is Associate Professor at the Faculty of Law, University of Auckland, where she teaches and has published widely on issues of health law, policy, ethics, torts, and accident compensation. She is a contributing author to *Medical Law in New Zealand* (2006), which won the Legal Research Foundation's J. F. Northey Annual Book award for 2006, and, most recently, the editor of *The Cartwright Papers: Essays on the Cervical Cancer Inquiry 1987–88* (2009). She was the consumer representative on the Medical Practitioners Disciplinary Committee for close to ten years. Formerly she worked as a prosecuting lawyer.

Maitreyi Misra is a Research Officer to Mr. Anand Grover, UN Special Rapporteur on the Right to Health. She is also managing the Global Health Rights Project, a Lawyer's Collective initiative. She has also worked on the Global Health and Human Rights Database Project, a Lawyer's Collective initiative in collaboration with the O'Neill Institute. She completed her LLM at the New York University School of Law in 2011 and was a Student Fellow at the Association for Civil Rights in Israel, Tel Aviv, before she joined Mr. Grover.

Christopher Newdick is a barrister and the Professor in Health Law at the University of Reading. He is an Honorary Consultant to National Health Service (NHS) health authorities and a member of the South Central Priorities Committee, which makes difficult decisions about the cost and affordability of new treatments in the NHS. He has given evidence to the House of Commons Health Committee, written position papers for the NHS Confederation and the NHS National Prescribing Centre, and was an expert witness to the National Inquiry into the Mid-Staffordshire NHS Foundation Trust (2011). His book, *Who Should We Treat? Rights, Rationing and Resources* (2nd ed.) (2005) considers the law, ethics, economics, and politics of health care rationing and builds on work over many years developing understanding of the macro – or public health – ethics that are fundamental to the legitimacy of health care systems.

Remigius N. Nwabueze is a Senior Lecturer at the Southampton School of Law, having joined the faculty in 2005 from an Assistant Professor position at the Faculty of Law, University of Ottawa. His research focuses on law, ethics, and the regulation of biomedical research in developing countries, especially African countries. His doctoral thesis focused on the conceptual and theoretical challenges to property law posed by biomedical technologies. He has published more than thirty-four articles and book chapters on these subjects as well as presenting at national and international conferences. His book, *Biotechnology and the Challenge of Property* (2007), stemming from his doctoral work, is considered pathbreaking. Remigius is internationally recognized as a leading authority on law relating to biotechnology, dead bodies and body parts, and the ethics of biomedical research in developing countries. His publications have gained international recognition, and one was recently cited by the U.S. Court of Appeals, Second Circuit, in *Abdullahi v Pfizer, Inc.*, 562 F.3d 163 (2nd Cir. CA, 2009), a case concerning the clinical trial of Trovan in Nigeria by Pfizer in 1996. Remigius received his LLB from the University of Nigeria in 1991, LLMs from the University of Lagos and the University of Manitoba, and his SJD from the University of Toronto.

Mariana Mota Prado is an Associate Professor at the Faculty of Law, University of Toronto. Her scholarship focuses on law and development, regulated industries, and comparative law. Her recent publications include a book (coauthored with Michael Trebilcock) entitled *What Makes Poor Countries Poor? Institutional Determinants of Development.* A Brazilian national, she regularly teaches intensive courses at Getulio Vargas Foundation in Rio de Janeiro, and she often collaborates with Brazilian scholars on projects related to institutional reforms in Brazil. Mariana received her LLB from the University of Sao Paulo and her LLM and JSD from Yale.

Lubhyathi Rangarajan is currently a Junior Consultant for the High Level Committee at the Ministry of Tribal Affairs, government of India. She was previously Guest Faculty at National Law School, Bengaluru, teaching human rights and international humanitarian law. In 2013 she graduated with a LLM in International Law from the University of California, Berkeley, School of Law, before which she was a Researcher for the Global Health Rights Project – a Lawyer's Collective initiative. She was also a practicing lawyer before the Bombay High Court while employed with Vidhii Partners, Mumbai. Her areas of interest include human rights and social justice.

Jerome Amir Singh (BA, LLB, LLM, MHSc, PhD) is Head of Ethics and Law at the Centre for the AIDS Programme of Research in South Africa, Nelson R. Mandela School of Medicine, University of KwaZulu-Natal (UKZN). He is also Adjunct Professor in the Dalla Lana School of Public Health Sciences and Joint Centre for Bioethics at the University of Toronto, Canada, and Course Director for Bioethics at Howard College School of Law, UKZN. He is a Senior Bioethics Researcher at the Sandra Rotman Centre, Toronto, Canada, where he advises the Bill and Melinda Gates Foundation on ethical, social, and cultural issues. He currently serves on several research bodies, including the International Research Ethics Board of Médecins Sans Frontières, the Research Ethics Committee of the South African Human Sciences Research Council, and the Scientific Advisory Board of the Aurum Institute of Health Research. He is an ad hoc consultant to the World Health Organization, and is a member of the Critical Path for TB Drug Regimens high-level Advisory Panel. He is the Co-Chair of the HIV Prevention Trial Network's

Ethics Working Group, and serves as a Special Advisor to the Biomedical Research Ethics Committee of the Nelson Mandela School of Medicine. He is an elected Founding Member and inaugural Co-Chair of the South African Young Academy of Science (SAYAS). He has previously served as the Co-Director of the Ethical, Social, and Cultural Issues Advisory Services to the Bill and Melinda Gates Foundation's Grand Challenges in Global Health Initiative, as a member of the World Health Organisation's Ethics Task Force on TB Management, the U.S. NIH's African Data and Safety Monitoring Board, the Health Law Advisory Committee to the South African Law Reform Commission, and as a Rapporteur for UNAIDS. He is an invited member of the International Association for Humanitarian Medicine, and he was a previous guest faculty member of the International Committee of Military Medicine.

Acknowledgments

We would like to thank the people who helped us convene such a fabulous group of scholars and facilitated our rich discussions and the production of this manuscript. In Toronto, thanks go to Bryan Thomas, Lorian Hardcastle, and Arthur Wilson who served as research managers over this time and helped us with our due diligence in locating the best possible contributors, organizing workshops and meetings, researching, editing and formatting papers, and so forth. Colleen M. Flood benefited from the support of both the Canadian Institutes of Health Research and the Canada Research Chair program.

In Tel Aviv, thanks to Sharon Bassan who served as research assistant and manager and helped in research, editing, and formatting, and to Michal Locker-Eshed who facilitated our workshop at Tel-Aviv University on behalf of the Minerva Center for Human Rights. Thanks to Professor Shai Lavi, director of the Minerva Center, and to Professor Daphane Barak-Erez, Dean of the Law School, and to Tel-Aviv University for their support of the Tel Aviv workshop. Aeyal Gross benefited from invaluable funding and support from the Israel National Institute for Health Policy Research and from the Joseph H. Flom Global Health and Human Rights Fellowship at Harvard Law School. At Harvard he is grateful to the Human Rights Program, which hosted him during the Fellowship, and in particular to its academic director Mindy Roseman and to his co-Fellow Alicia Ely Yamin. Special thanks also go to Dean Hanoch Dagan at Tel-Aviv University for supporting Aeyal's research leave, which allowed him to pursue the Fellowship and this project. We also thank John Berger and the team at Cambridge University Press for their fabulous work and support through the production of this manuscript.

It proved enormously challenging to convene the group of scholars we identified as having the requisite skills, but nonetheless this has been a fantastic project to work on – we have not always agreed on everything, but the debates have been rich and exciting. We would like to thank our eighteen authors for their superb contributions and we hope you enjoy reading their scholarship as much as we did.

A final note of thanks and love to our respective partners; first, Matthew, who kept calm and cool and provided huge amounts of support through the birth and first year of Conor as we simultaneously finished this manuscript; and to Ofer, who endured many hours of work spilling into nights and weekends.

Introduction: Marrying Human Rights and Health Care Systems

Contexts for a Power to Improve Access and Equity

Colleen M. Flood and Aeyal Gross

Marriage is a matter of more worth
Than to be dealt in by attorneyship.

1 Henry VI 5.5.50–51

In this volume, we explore the power of health care rights in diverse health care systems. Does a right to health care serve to advance greater equity or does it in fact advance the opposite result? Does the recognition of a right to health care help sustain public values (like equality) in systems that are undergoing privatization? Or, to the contrary, does a focus on rights-based norms foster individualism and exacerbate inequalities brought about by privatization? Does the legal means by which health care rights are established make a difference (whether in a constitutional document, in a statute, etc.)? How do courts balance the rights of an individual against collective needs in the distribution of health care? Has this differed depending on the wording of health rights protections? To what extent are broader legal, economic, and political considerations taken into account in the courts' reasoning about health rights? Does the interpretation of the right to health vary depending on the model of health system involved (e.g., private insurance, social insurance, single payer [public/tax-financed])?

WHY WE WROTE THIS BOOK

Many of us who teach or practice human rights law believe as an article of faith that pursuing the realization of health rights will result in public welfare improvements and, in particular, will improve the plight of some of the most vulnerable in society. But increasingly we are pressed to question this assumption, as statistics continue to underscore widespread inequities in health and access to health care. In colloquial terms then, we address whether the creation and judicialization of health rights is a force for good or ill. We also deeply appreciate that law is part of a larger

1

socioeconomic, political, and cultural context, and we are interested in how these contextual factors influence health care rights, for better or for worse.

A variety of social, political, and philosophical factors culminated in the framing of health as a human right. As Eleanor Kinney describes it, notions of a positive right to health originated in the nineteenth century, when public health reformers advocated government involvement in public health.[1] Pointing to the Enlightenment, the Latin American philosophy of human rights, and the rise of the modern welfare state, John Tobin suggests that the health and human rights approach indicates "an embrace of liberal values with an acceptance of the need for states to take measures to mitigate the harm caused by excessive liberalism and capitalism."[2]

But while the right to health as discussed later was included in the Universal Declaration of Human Rights (UDHR) from 1948, the rights in the UDHR were split into two separate covenants in 1966, one including civil and political rights and the other social and economic rights.[3] Jack Donnelly notes that Cold War tensions further bifurcated the development of human rights, with the West focusing on civil and political rights, while leaders in the East (particularly those in the Soviet bloc) focused on economic and social rights.[4] In dominant human rights discourse, the right to health care, as part of the framework of social and economic rights, was relegated to a second-class status.[5]

Seven factors contributed to the reemergence of rights to health and health care since the 1990s at both the national and international levels:

1. To some extent, the end of the Cold War reduced the ideological divide between civil and political rights and economic and social rights, as apparent in the Declaration adopted by the Second World Congress on Human Rights, referring to the two sets of rights as "universal, indivisible, and interdependent and interrelated."[6]

2. The growing critique of the international human rights movement, especially from postcolonial countries, arguing that the West's focus on civil and political

---

[1] Eleanor D. Kinney, The International Human Right to Health: What Does This Mean for Our Nation and World?, 34 Ind. L. Rev. 1457, 1459 (2001).

[2] John Tobin, The Right to Health in International Law 42 (2012).

[3] For a discussion, *see* Daphne Barak-Erez & Aeyal M. Gross, *Do We Need Social Rights? Questions in the Era of Globalisation, Privatisation and the Diminished Welfare State*, in Exploring Social Rights: Between Theory and Practice 3 (Daphne Barak-Erez & Aeyal Gross, eds., 2007).

[4] Jack Donnelly, Universal Human Rights in Theory and Practice 27 (2002).

[5] *Id.* at 7–8.

[6] Vienna Declaration and Programme of Action, U.N. General Assembly World Conference on Human Rights, A/CONF/157/23 (1993). On the effect of the end of the Cold War, *see also* Mindey Jane Roseman & Siri Gloppen, *Litigating the Right to Health: Are Transnational Actors Backseat Driving?*, in Litigating Health Rights: Can Court Bring More Justice to Health? 246, 249 (Alicia Ely Yamin & Siri Gloppen, eds., 2011); Tobin, *supra* note 2, at 1; For a discussion of this and some of the other factors, *see also* Helena Nygren-Krug, *The Right to Health from Concept to Practice*, in Advancing the Human Right to Health 39 (Jose M. Zuniga, Stephen Marks & Lawrence Gostin, eds., 2013).

rights ignored the harsh social distress experienced by much of the world's population, whose lack of access to housing, food, health care, and other material living conditions is no less detrimental than violations of rights such as freedom of speech or religion. The human rights movement recognized that it could not remain relevant while ignoring or downplaying social rights.[7]

3. Growing demands for health services spurred by technological developments and (in many developed countries) an aging population in combination with a neoliberal imperative to reduce public spending/privatize. Neoliberal economic measures emanating from the Washington Consensus, the International Monetary Fund, and the World Bank have encouraged policies that inadequately respond to the growing demands for health services. In some countries, especially those in Latin America, the result was the forced adoption of structural adjustments programs, involving reduction of government services and privatization, which had a particularly detrimental impact on health care.[8]

4. Also in the context of globalization, the Trade-Related Aspects of Intellectual Property Rights agreement created global patents in drugs, pitting a conflict between international trade law and access to medicines in poor countries.[9] The global campaign for universal access to antiretroviral therapies was grounded in the idea of health as a human right.

5. The wave of health care reforms enacted since the middle of the 1980s – internal market reforms, managed competition reforms, and the rise of managed care – has sought to control the cost, volume, and quality of health services supplied.[10] Patients facing denial or delays in care often turn to the courts, invoking the right to health.

---

[7] *See* Barak-Erez & Gross, *supra* note 3, at 5.

[8] *See* Roseman & Gloppen, *supra* note 6, at 249; David Harvey, A BRIEF HISTORY OF NEOLIBERALISM (2007). In the context of health, *see* Sue L. T. McGregor, *Neoliberalism and Healthcare*, 25 INT'L J. CONSUMER STUD. 82 (2001); Dani Filc, *The Health Business under Neo-Liberalism: The Israeli Case*, 25 CRITICAL SOC. POL'Y 180 (2005); Paul O'Connell, *The Human Right to Health in an Age of Market Hegemony*, in GLOBAL HEALTH AND HUMAN RIGHTS: LEGAL AND PHILOSOPHICAL PERSPECTIVES 190 (J. Harrington & M. Stuttaford, eds., 2010). *See also* Alicia Ely Yamin, *Power, Suffering and Courts: Reflections on Promoting Health Rights through Judicialization*, in LITIGATING HEALTH RIGHTS, *supra* note 5, at 333, 340; Jonathan Wolff, THE HUMAN RIGHT TO HEALTH 94 (2012).

[9] See Phillipe Cullet, *Patents and Medicines: The Relationship between TRIPS and the Human Right to Health*, in PERSPECTIVES ON HEALTH AND HUMAN RIGHTS 179 (S. Gruskin et al. eds., 2005); E 't Hoen, *TRIPS, Pharmaceutical Patents, and Access to Essential Medicines: A Long Way from Seattle to Doha*, in PERSPECTIVES ON HEALTH AND HUMAN RIGHTS, id at 100; Wolff, supra note 8, at 100–108; Lisa Forman & Jillian Clare Kohler, eds., ACCESS TO MEDICINES AS A HUMAN RIGHT: IMPLICATIONS FOR PHARMACEUTICAL INDUSTRY RESPONSIBILITY (2012). On the relevance of globalization generally, *see also* Audrey R. Chapman & Salil D. Benegal, *Globalization and the Right to Health*, in THE STATE OF ECONOMIC AND SOCIAL RIGHTS: A GLOBAL OVERVIEW 61 (Lance Minkler ed., 2013).

[10] Colleen M. Flood, INTERNATIONAL HEALTH CARE REFORM: A LEGAL, ECONOMIC AND POLITICAL ANALYSIS 1–9 (2003); Tobin, *supra* note 2, at 351–370.

6. The process of democratization has entailed drafting new constitutions, which often include an explicit justiciable right to health as part of the idea of transformative constitutionalism – a factor apparent in South Africa and Latin America.[11]

7. The rise of AIDS, which played a major role as advocates turned to human rights in order to both tackle discrimination and guarantee access to medications. Many of the groundbreaking cases relate to access to antiretroviral drugs.[12]

All of these factors contributed to a renewed interest in the right to health from the 1990s and into the 2000s. This growing recognition of health as a human right led to its articulation in myriad legal instruments, both international and domestic. Health rights, both general and specific, now appear in numerous international agreements,[13] as well as domestic state constitutions and statutes.[14] But for all these formal declarations of human health at the global level, we continue to see extreme inequalities – health care spending per capita for the top 5 percent of the world population is nearly 4,500 times that of the lowest 20 percent; 2.5 million people die annually from vaccine-preventable diseases;[15] and close to 7 million children younger than the age of five died in 2011 from malnutrition and mostly preventable diseases.[16] These sad but familiar statistics force us to take stock: What difference has law, particularly the judicialization of health rights, made?

The Office of the U.N. High Commission for Human Rights reports that at least 115 constitutions around the world speak to the right to health or health care,[17] but they can have varying degrees of legal force. Eleanor Kinney reports that 68 percent

---

[11] Yamin, *supra* note 8, at 339–340. On this role of social rights in the South African Constitution, *see e.g.*, Aeyal Gross, *The Constitution in Reconciliation and Transitional Justice: Lessons from South-Africa and Israel* 40 STAN. J. INT'L L. 47 (2004).

[12] *See* Yamin, *supra* note 8, at 338–339, 348–350; Wolff, *supra* note 8, at 39–91; Paul Hunt, *The Right to Health: From the Margins to the Mainstream*, 340 THE LANCET 1878 (2002).

[13] *See e.g.*, International Covenant on Economic, Social and Cultural Rights, G.A. Res. 22001 (XXI), U.N. GAOR, 21st Sess., Supp. No. 16, U.N. Doc A/6316, 993 U.N.T.D. 3 (1996); CESCR General Comment No. 14, The Right to the Highest Attainable Standard of Health, U.N. ESCOR, 22nd Sess., U.N. Doc. E/C.12/2000/4 (2000); Constitution of the World Health Organization, pmbl., 62 Stat. 6349, 14 U.N.T.S. 185. On the right to health in international law, *see* Brigit Toebes, THE RIGHT TO HEALTH AS A HUMAN RIGHT IN INTERNATIONAL LAW (1999); Tobin, *supra* note 2.

[14] *See e.g.*, Brazil Const. tit. II, ch. II, art.6 & tit.VIII, ch. II, art.196–197; South Africa Const. ch. II, art. 27–28.On the right to health, *see generally* Andrew Clapham & Mary Robinson, eds., REALIZING THE RIGHT TO HEALTH (2009); Stephen P. Marks, *The Emergence and Scope of the Human Right to Health*, *in* ADVANCING THE HUMAN RIGHT TO HEALTH, *supra* note 6, at 3. See also, Courtney Jung, Ran Hirschl and Evan Rosevear, Economic and Social Rights in National Constitutions (October 16, 2013) at 9, available at http://ssrn.com/abstract=2349680

[15] Lawrence Gostin, *The Unconscionable Health Gap: A Global Plan for Justice*, 375 THE LANCET 1504 (2010).

[16] World Health Organization Fact Sheet No. 178, *Children: Reducing Mortality* (Sept. 2012), *available at* http://www.who.int/mediacentre/factsheets/fs178/en/index.html.

[17] Office of the U.N. Commissioner for Human Rights, Fact Sheet No. 31, *The Right to Health: Fact Sheet* (June 2008), *available at* http://www.ohchr.org/Documents/Publications/Factsheet31.pdf.

of countries have a provision addressing health or health care (including "statements of aspiration" and "programmatic statements") in their constitutions, with 40 percent including a right to health care and 38 percent providing an affirmative duty for the state to provide care. However, her research shows that those with the greatest nominal commitment to health in their constitutions spend less than half as much per capita on health care as do countries with no formal constitutional declarations with respect to health.[18] One could conclude from this that there is a distinct lack of correlation between words on paper and actions on the ground. But that would be too simplistic. As we discuss in the Conclusion, there is indeed some degree of correlation between the constitutional recognition of a right to health and the existence of a weak (or nascent) public health care system. But this is likely attributable to the fact that establishment of a constitutional right to health is part of so-called second-generation rights, which appear mostly in newer constitutions of emerging democracies. By contrast, countries with stronger public health care systems are often established and richer democracies in which the health care system is part of a welfare state, developed historically without explicit reference to health rights.

OUR CHOSEN COUNTRIES

Our story of the power of health rights involves sixteen countries, each represented by a chapter. In selecting countries for study, we sought to capture a range of approaches to the legal recognition of health rights:

1. Specific health care rights are articulated in the constitution;
2. Constitutional rights (e.g., the right to life) have or could be interpreted to include rights to health care;
3. Health care rights are contained in domestic statutes and regulations; or
4. No legal rights to health care are recognized at all.

We classify our country chapters into three groups that, loosely understood, fall on a spectrum from more to less private. Our typology is as follows:

1. Public/Tax-Financed – these are countries in which public financing, based on taxation revenues, is a defining feature of the health care system. Our representative countries here are the United Kingdom, New Zealand, Canada, and Sweden.
2. Social Health Insurance/Managed Competition – these countries have universal coverage for health care and, like Public/Tax-Financed countries, redistribute (at least to some extent) from the rich to the poor and from the healthy to the sick. But in place of tax revenues, these systems are financed primarily through mandatory contributions from employers and employees to either

---

[18] Eleanor D. Kinney, *The International Human Right to Health in Domestic Constitutional and Statutory Law*, in LAW AND ETHICS, IN RATIONING ACCESS TO CARE IN A HIGH-COST GLOBAL ECONOMY 171, 175 (Wendy K. Mariner & Paula Lobato de Faria, eds., 2008).

non-profit social health insurers or competing private not-for-profit or for-profit insurers (managed competition). The representative countries we include in this category are Colombia, Israel, the Netherlands, Hungary and Taiwan.

3. Mixed Private/Public[19] – these are countries in which a private health system fulfills a central role alongside a public system. In these countries health care is not universal (e.g., the United States) or, alternatively, a universal public scheme exists but is so impoverished that private finance/delivery plays a very significant role (e.g., India). The representative countries we include in this section are China, South Africa, Brazil, the United States, Nigeria, Venezuela, and India.

The allocation of countries into these three categories is not cut-and-dried, and we have made judgment calls on categorization in consultation with our contributors. For example, in Hungary (which we classify as a Social Health Insurance country), there is a significant role for extra payments (bribes, etc.) made to doctors and other providers, which undoubtedly distorts the fair allocation of care. Nonetheless, we consider as an overall judgment that Hungary is better situated in the middle of our spectrum of public-private funding.

This framing puts heavy emphasis on the extent to which different mixes of public and private financing interact with health care rights, yielding differing levels of access and equity in health care. In developed countries, the maturation of public health systems and concerns about growing health care costs result in tensions over the inclusion of new technologies, drugs, and services – leading, it seems, to ever-more frequent attempts to privatize existing systems of redistribution. In middle-income and developing countries, issues focus more on developing universal health care systems to ensure access to some minimum of care for all citizens, but also can involve efforts on the part of some to access expensive new drugs and devices at public expense. This text looks at the role that legal rights to health care can and should play in these respective processes, and what is the broader impact on equity in health.

The health care systems considered in the text cover a blend of public, private, and public/private approaches to the funding and delivery of health care, with some systems transitioning toward increased privatization. Beyond formal laws and court actions, the realization of health care rights is impacted by the larger political, economic, and social context of the state; thus two systems with similar rights provisions but different social/political systems may – we hypothesize – show dramatic differences in their realization of health rights.

A further note here on our emphasis on the public/private mix: we also examine whether asserting "rights" can combat further privatization of health care and discuss

---

[19] "Public" in this context includes systems that are partially funded by tax finance as well as those partially funded by mandatory social health insurance or mandatory private insurance (the managed competition model).

whether health human rights are successful in this regard or not. For example, in 2008, an Egyptian court overturned a significant move on the part of the government to privatize the delivery of health care, finding that the privatization of the health care system would violate the government's obligations to affirm/protect citizens' right to health.[20] This can be contrasted with Canada, where the Supreme Court in *Chaoulli*, held that individuals have a legal right to buy private health insurance but have yet to find any positive obligation on the part of governments to provide public health care.[21]

SOURCES OF HEALTH CARE RIGHTS

Before going further, we need to provide a little more context on the sources of health and health care rights, which include international law (treaties, conventions, etc.), domestic states' constitutions, and domestic statutes. Rights can also emerge from long-term patterns of public policy, whereby rights, though not formally articulated, are acknowledged to exist (de facto rights). In what follows we discuss the differential impact of litigation of international rights versus the impact of rights contained in domestic legislation (constitutions and statutes) and as a matter of public policy.

International Rights

According to Article 25.1 of the Universal Declaration on Human Rights,[22] "[e]veryone has the right to a standard of living adequate for the health of himself and of his family, including food, clothing, housing and medical care and necessary social services." This concept was affirmed and expanded by Article 12.1 of the International Covenant on Economic, Social and Cultural Rights (ICESCR),[23] which recognizes "the right of everyone to the enjoyment of the highest attainable standard of physical and mental health." Further, Article 12.2 of the ICESCR strengthens the right by outlining the obligations of states to "achieve the full realization of this right."[24] Of the states considered in later chapters, all except South Africa and the United States are parties to this covenant.[25] Following ICESCR, several international instruments included provisions addressing the right to health, for

---

[20] Nabieh Taha Muhammad al-Bahyetors. vs. The President of the Republic et ors., Case no. 21550/61st judicial year/2008/State Counsel, Court of Administrative Justice (First circuit) (Egypt). (English translation on file with authors).

[21] Chaoulli v. Quebec (Attorney General), 2005 SCC 35 (Can.).

[22] G.A. Res. 217A(III), U.N. GAOR, 3d Sess., U.N. Doc. A/810 (1948).

[23] International Covenant on Economic, Social and Cultural Rights, *supra* note 13.

[24] Id.

[25] United Nations Treaty Collection, UN, http://treaties.un.org/Pages/ViewDetails.aspx?src=TREATY &mtdsg_no=IV-3&chapter=4&lang=en (last visited July 19, 2013). In 2009, Taiwan, while not a signatory to the agreement, passed legislation giving domestic legal effect to the ICESCR.

example, the 1978 Declaration of Alma-Ata.[26] This document is notable in its emphasis on the availability of primary care services and on "unacceptable" health disparities both within countries and between developed and developing countries.

In addition to these general declarations, many international instruments exist that attempt to address a specific global health concern. For example, UN Millennium Development Goal 5 and UN CEDAW Article 12(2) are focused on reducing maternal mortality, whereas the Framework Convention on Tobacco Control focuses on reducing tobacco usage. Another important document is the Doha Declaration, in which the World Trade Organization responded to the high price of AIDS medication by clarifying that patent protections in the Trade-Related Aspects of Intellectual Property Rights Agreement do not preclude member states from taking measures to protect public health.[27]

Although many of these international instruments are several decades old, there is a resurgence of interest in health and human rights. For example, in 2000, the UN Committee on Economic, Social and Cultural Rights issued a comprehensive document ("General Comment 14"), intended to elucidate the right to health, putting an emphasis on issues of equity, equality, and accessibility[28] and developing the "AAAQ" model of availability, accessibility, acceptability, and quality.[29] General Comment 14 reiterates important principles developed in social economic rights interpretation including the tripartite nature of state obligations, which includes the obligations to respect, protect, and fulfill.[30] The Comment also specifies that states have "core obligations" under the ICESCR, notwithstanding the accompanying principle of "progressive realization"[31] – meaning states must ensure, at the very least, minimum essential levels of each of the rights enunciated in the Covenant, including essential primary health care.[32] Finally, the Comment contains a presumption against retrogressive measures.[33] In 2002, the UN Commission on Human Rights appointed a Special Rapporteur on the right to health.[34]

---

[26] *Declaration of Alma-Ata*, WORLD HEALTH ORGANIZATION (Sept. 1978), *available at* http://www.who. int/publications/almaata_declaration_en.pdf.

[27] Doha Ministerial Declaration on the TRIPS Agreement and Public Health, WT/MIN(01)/DEC/2, art. 4 (Nov. 14, 2001), *available at* http://www.wto.org/english/thewto_e/minist_e/min01_e/mindecl_trips_ e.pdf.

[28] General Comment No. 14, *supra* note 13.

[29] For a discussion, *see* Aeyal Gross, *The Right to Health in an Era of Privatization and Globalization*, *in* Barak-Erez & Gross, *supra* note 3, at 300–305; A. Clapham & S. Marks, INTERNATIONAL HUMAN RIGHTS LEXICON 207 (2005).

[30] General Comment No. 14, *supra* note 13, at para. 33; Tobin, *supra* note 2, at 185–197.

[31] General Comment No. 14, *supra* note 13, at paras. 30, 43.

[32] Id. at para. 43; Tobin, supra note 2, at 238–252; Wolff, supra note 8, at 9–12; Lisa Forman, *What Future for the Minimum Core? Contextualizing the Implications of South African Socioeconomic Rights Jurisprudence for the International Human Right to Health*, *in* GLOBAL HEALTH AND HUMAN RIGHTS, supra note 8, at 66–80.

[33] General Comment No. 14, *supra* note 13, at para. 32.

[34] For a description on the role of the Rapporteur, *see* Paul Hunt, *The UN Special Rapporteur on the Right to Health: Key Objectives, Themes and Interventions*, 7 HEALTH & HUM. RTS. 1 (2003);

But as inspiring and influential as these developments may be, the nature of public international law can limit their impact. State sovereignty is invoked by a number of nations as a type of universal trump card to the articulation of health rights in international instruments, and thus an individual's health rights are usually determined by the domestic laws of their state and not by international conventions. In domestic courts, internationally ratified agreements may be used to interpret the meaning of domestic laws – in other words, the court will, if possible, assume that the government intended its domestic laws to be interpreted in a way that would comply with ratified international agreements. Thus, judicial interpretation of international instruments can prove to be an important normative force. In this regard, Andre den Exter notes in Chapter 7 that international human rights law has played an important role in interpreting the Dutch constitution to include a right to health care. Also, as Aeyal Gross notes in Chapter 6, Israeli courts have held that domestic laws should be interpreted to the extent possible so as to be compatible with international obligations. Venezuela offers another example, as its domestic constitution provides that international human rights treaties become part of domestic law immediately following ratification by the government.

Domestic Constitutional Rights

As previously noted, 68 percent of countries make some reference to health in their constitutions. Health care rights may be expressly articulated, as, for example, in Brazil or South Africa, or may be read in or inferred as part of other fundamental rights; thus, for example, in India, the courts have interpreted the right to life as including a right to health.

On the face of it, an obvious benefit of having health rights articulated in a state constitution is that (usually) a constitution is the supreme law of the land with which all other laws must comply. Further, constitutions transcend elected terms of government and tend to be more difficult to change or repeal than ordinary legislation is.

Statutory Rights

A third model arises where health rights do not exist in a domestic constitution but are created by statute. An example here would be Israel, where health rights are articulated in two statutes: the National Health Insurance Law and the Patient Rights Law (although on occasion, similar to India, Israeli courts have grounded a right to health in the constitutional right to life and body). While rights not enshrined

Paul Hunt & Sheldon Leader, *Developing and Applying the Right to the Highest Attainable Standard of Health: The Role of the UN Special Rapporteur (2002–2008)*, in GLOBAL HEALTH AND HUMAN RIGHTS, supra note 8, at 28.

in a state constitution would seem to be more fragile than constitutional rights, some note that the right to health now forms part of customary international law, which serves to strengthen the right domestically.[35] Another example is found in the Netherlands where high-level state obligations to "promote public health" are found in Article 22(1) of the constitution, but the formal articulation of specific entitlements to care is found in the country's 2006 Health Insurance Act. A statutory enactment of health rights may allow for a more detailed enumeration of rights (e.g., a patient's bill of rights), as opposed to very abstract and open-ended guarantees common in constitutions. Among other things, open-ended provisions may provide more latitude for judicial interpretation, resulting in very regressive readings of health rights (e.g., *Chaoulli*).

De Facto Rights

Is a formal expression of a positive right to health (domestic or international) a necessary component of such a right existing? It seems this is not necessarily so, particularly in older, established welfare state systems where entitlements to health care have been well entrenched as a result of public policy. Examples here would include Sweden, Canada, New Zealand, and the United Kingdom. While one might expect de facto health rights to be the most fragile of all, these four countries have historically shown some of the strongest, pragmatic affirmation of these rights, based both on the availability of care and the health of their populations.

But despite most of the countries in this category having relatively strong health care systems, there are ongoing structural inequities, and new challenges are on the horizon. In Canada, for example, aboriginal populations have less access to care and a significantly lower standard of health than the non-aboriginal populace does. Further, recent moves by the Canadian government will "delist" many refugee claimants from insured medical care in Canada even in emergency situations.[36] The government's unilateral decision, made without consultation with the public, health professionals, or provincial governments, shows the risk of not having a formal declaration of a right and the resulting need for judicial oversight of government.[37] Moreover, recent fiscal pressures associated with global economic downturns, an aging population, new medical technologies of questionable benefit, and a culture of individualism are pushing a privatization agenda that will test these systems and their lack of articulated health care rights.

---

[35]   Clapham & Marks, *supra* note 29, at 197; E. D. Kinney & B. A. Clark, *Provisions for Health and Health Care in the Constitutions of the World*, 37 Cornell Int'l L. J. 285 (2004).

[36]   Order Respecting the Interim Federal Health Program, 2012, SI/2012–26 (Can.).

[37]   Canadian Medical Association Bulletin, *Continue Coverage for Refugees: CMA*, 184 Can. Med. Ass'n J. 1212 (2012); *Government Information on Refugee Healthcare Changes is Misleading, May be Fatal*, Canadian Council for Refugees (May 3, 2012), http://ccrweb.ca/en/bulletin/12/05/03 (last visited July 19, 2013); Mark Tyndall, Op-Ed., *An Attack on Vulnerable Refugees*, Ottawa Citizen, May 9, 2012, at A15.

FROM HERE TO THERE AND THE STRUCTURE OF EACH CHAPTER

We turn now to explain the approach each country chapter follows and the themes we sought to explore. First, however, a note on the process we followed to determine the structure and themes. After conceptualizing the overall thesis of this book, we met together over a number of months to discuss the range of countries to be covered and possible contributors, employing a global network of scholars to identify the best person for each of the country chapters. We then organized two in-person meetings of our chosen contributors, first in Toronto and, eighteen months later, in Tel Aviv. With our colleagues we workshopped multiple drafts of the country chapters and developed a rich array of common themes and discussion points, which we discuss later. With respect to the basic mechanics of each chapter, we asked each of our authors that they clearly and coherently describe the dynamics of their respective health care system, describe the role of health rights and/or health rights litigation, and then analyze the dynamic between the two. To this end, and to better facilitate comparison between countries, we asked each author to follow a common four-part structure (described later in this chapter), addressing the issues we have identified as being crucial to the question equity in health care and to the public/private divide.

In the first section of each country chapter we describe the important features of the health care system in the country: how it is financed; the presence/absence of a national public health care/insurance system, and if such exists, what is its standing vis-à-vis private health systems (and insurance); who has access to health care and how health care services are allocated to different needs; how the most vulnerable groups in society fare in terms of access to health care services and to health more broadly; who, how, and at what level decisions are being made about which services and goods are provided; and whether there is a prescribed "basket" of services and goods provided.

In a bid to diagnose current or emerging equity gaps, the first section of each chapter identifies the source(s) of the most significant access gaps. Those gaps include, for example, extremely high informal payments to providers (Hungary), very high levels of user charges (Israel), or the poor state of Aboriginal people and the failure to include pharmaceuticals in the universal public plan (Canada). In some countries, the threat of a significant equity gap lurks on the horizon, with market-like reforms on the verge of implementation (England).

The theme of the "equity gap" is revisited throughout the other three sections of each chapter: the extent to which litigation of health care rights is helping ameliorate or address the gap (or not); how equity gaps map onto the public/private divide within the system; and how the collection of funding in the system is regressive or progressive – for example, a flat premium or fixed copayment is superficially fair but adversely discriminates against those on lower incomes.

The second section of each chapter discusses the legal instruments (provisions in international law, constitutions, statutes, etc.) that regulate access to health, and more specifically the right to health care in the country; what the concept of the right to health includes; whether the right to health is limited to health care or encompasses broader determinants of health; and how the scope of health rights, if such exist, have been defined/recognized by the courts and in state practice.

In the third section, each of our authors describes and analyzes litigation that has taken place in their respective country concerning access to health care. Each chapter addresses the following issues (as appropriate):

1. Litigation over access to services or goods that are not regularly provided/funded by the public health care system (and thus available only privately) but are asked for by patients (and their doctors).
2. Issues at the intersection of public and private, such as the legality and the scope of private (or semi-private) insurance, the regulation of the interaction between the systems, the provision of private services in public hospitals, and so forth.
3. Issues pertaining to services and goods provided by the public health system but financed partly through copayments that are charged out of pocket, thus partially privatizing the financing of these services.

Finally, for the content of the fourth section of their respective chapters, we asked each of our contributors to provide an overall assessment of the consequences of litigation of health care rights– notably whether litigation is associated with greater equity in health care access and health itself. In doing so we asked our authors to be aware that in testing whether rights litigation is progressive or regressive, several factors may contextualize their findings. In some countries, there is a huge amount of litigation concerning these issues. In others, the volume of litigation is significantly smaller, making it difficult to reach general conclusions about its impact overall. There may also be significant temporal issues; what may seem regressive or progressive at first may over time transpire not to be so. A further complicating factor is that the terms "progressive" and "regressive" and "rich" and "poor" and even "public" and "private" are laden with subjectivity. In any case, we have selected each of the contributors for their specialized knowledge of both the legal and health systems in their respective countries and rely on each of them to explain why in their expert opinion, and in the context of their country's political, legal and health systems, a decision should be viewed as regressive or progressive.

Clearly we have asked a great deal of our authors and to frame the discussion, let us identify two ways in which we have attempted to narrow the remit.

First, although discussions regarding the state of world health can be framed either in terms of health outcomes (life expectancy, maternal mortality rates, etc.) or in terms of access to care, we focus largely on the latter. There are many other contributing factors to health (geographic, sociopolitical, etc.), and it is very difficult to attribute specific cause and effect to each contributing factor. While our focus on access to health care may implicate us in the "medicalization" of the right to health – that is, the frequent focus on health care rather than on social determinants of health such as education, nutrition, and housing[38] – we do this because access to care is certainly a contributing factor to health outcomes. Moreover, issues of access to care are important independent of health itself because of issues associated with dignity and security. For example, access to end-of-life care contributes comparatively little to aggregate health outcomes, but most would prioritize this kind of care as an important function of health systems. Further, from a pragmatic perspective, access to health is more likely to be the subject of litigation; people bring court actions to argue that they were denied care (a discrete identifiable benefit) that they had a legal right to receive. Thus by focusing on access to care and the litigation that surrounds it we are able to present a contained and manageable topic for analysis. This is not to negate the need, however, in future studies to examine litigation relating to broader determinants of health.

Second, when prioritizing what to discuss, we have asked our authors to focus where possible on how the structure of their system impacts access and how access barriers can have especially detrimental effects for more vulnerable populations, particularly the poor. Here we focus, in part, on how problems of access to care may conspire with problems of access to justice. Where a vulnerable person is denied care they may lack the financial ability to bring litigation to assert their rights. Thus an important part of the context of health rights is the extent to which pro bono cases are brought by rights groups and the extent to which class action suits help offset the costs of litigation for the poor. A related issue is whether rulings for a given plaintiff are generalized/enforced across the system – a problem highlighted in the Canadian case of *Eldridge* discussed in Chapter 3.

THEMES AND ISSUES

A rich array of issues and themes arose through the process of workshopping draft chapters. Our authors emphasize or discuss many of the following themes and issues throughout this text – and in the Conclusion we return to these for a fuller analysis.

One important theme concerned the extent to which health rights litigation may serve to undermine a fair allocation of resources within a health care system. This theme is part of a broader problem of the limits of invoking individual rights in systems of mutual dependence, rationing, and priority setting. Frequently, human rights litigation is assumed to be progressive: the realization of rights will improve the position of the most vulnerable in society. Law is seen as rectifying injustice that results in the most vulnerable in society being allocated an unfair share of resources

---

[38] On "medicalization" in this context, *see* Benjamin Mason Meier, *The World Health Organization, The Evolution of Human Rights, and the Failure to Achieve Health for All, in* GLOBAL HEALTH AND HUMAN RIGHTS, *supra* note 8, at 163. On social determinants, *see* Audrey R. Chapman, *The Social Determinants of Health, Health Equity and Human Rights*, 12 HEALTH & HUM. RTS. 1 (2010).

because of economic inequality, prejudice, discrimination, racism, homophobia, sexism, and other factors. However, rights litigation that challenges allocation decisions in health care can destabilize the allocation of scarce public resources to the disadvantage of the more vulnerable in society. Thus, for example, litigation that results in successful claims to access expensive new drug therapies could result in limited public resources being spent on new drugs rather than preventative and primary care of greater benefit to poorer patients and communities. Authors discuss what it is that people are being given or seeking access to, including a discussion of medicalization and how commercial interests may drive perceptions of "need." Litigation can be used to promote those interests rather than the interests of the poor.

Various contributors, for example, Christopher Newdick in the context of the UK system and Mariana Prado in the context of the Brazilian health care system, explore whether issue-specific litigation undermines the fairness of overall allocation of health care resources. As others have pointed out, a focus on upholding individual rights may camouflage the distributive nature of the decision and encourage disregard for the needs of others. It may impede the larger social and political processes through which difficult distributive choices are made. The challenge – especially given the need for priority setting and rationing[39] – is to articulate health rights in a way that advances mutual social dependence while giving due consideration to the health needs of individuals.

Along with this concern about distorting overall allocations within health budgets is a more expansive concern: governments may not be spending enough on health care even if one assumes that the redistribution within that limited resource cap is fair. The chapter on Israel thus addresses this larger issue regarding the fairness of the overall health budget and the failure, for the most part, of health rights litigation to succeed in challenging the erosion of the public budget for health care. Authors throughout the text consider to what extent health care rights litigation has been or could be used in their jurisdiction to challenge the fairness of the total budget allocated to health care, the risks of distributing limited resources away from those in greatest need, and the need to hold government's feet to the fire regarding a fair determination of the public health care budget.

A second recurring theme, alluded to already, concerns the fact that the progressivity of human rights litigation cannot be readily disentangled from access to justice issues. Litigation is often extremely expensive. Frequently those who are most disadvantaged in the allocation of health and health care are not represented in case law. For example, the Aboriginal peoples of Canada have, on average, far worse health care outcomes than do others, yet to date they are poorly represented in health rights litigation. Access-to-justice issues are thus a core theme in this volume, with contributors exploring the costs of litigation, the ability for NGOs and other organizations to bring actions on the part of vulnerable populations, the ability

---

[39] Gross, *supra* note 29, at 297–300; Clapham & Marks, *supra* note 29, at 207–208.

to bring class actions, and other procedural impediments and facilitators for those without means. However, unmitigated access to justice is not always a solution. For example, Colombians can realize their constitutional rights to health care through a low-cost mechanism, a "tutela" action. However, these decision makers, without the discipline of a budget, largely approved every claim before them. As Everaldo Lamprea writes in Chapter 5, this significantly challenged the stability of the public health care system, although a subsequent court decision has attempted to address this problem.

A third theme explored in this volume, as mentioned, concerns how law and judicial decisions operate within a larger sociopolitical context. Each of the contributors to this volume has been selected for their overall understanding of their country's relevant health care and legal systems, particularly the interface of public and private, and how health care resources are allocated to the rich and the poor. Many of these systems are very complex; for example, as den Exter explains, the Dutch health care system is an amalgamation of public and private, where what looks like private effectively functions like public as a result of layers of detailed regulation. Each author, in addition to their expertise in health care systems, has also been selected for their ability to analyze judgments and legal reasoning and thus highlight the unique context of their country's legal system and its impact on the health care system. In some countries, for example Hungary, the legal system is refracted through health care systems that are rife with corruption. To understand the impact of human rights litigation in these countries, it is important to first understand the impact of corruption on the allocation of medical resources. In other countries, the health care system faces challenges from globalization. In India, for instance, alongside a robust medical tourism industry that boasts the capacity to perform some of the most advanced surgeries in the world, tuberculosis and diarrheal diseases together continue to claim the lives of more than one million people each year.[40]

In understanding the real impact of law as part of the larger sociopolitical context, it is also important to look past the point, for example, of a particular court ruling to examine the decision's impact over time. Thus, for example, a decision that is on its face progressive, ensuring access to health care services of high impact for vulnerable populations, may indeed have little real impact if the decision is not enforced. Similarly, a decision that is prima facie regressive, perhaps denying access to essential treatment, may mobilize political action and result in government(s) moving to fund the treatment despite the court's finding that they need not do so. Consequently, where possible, contributors to this volume explore what happens past the point of the judicial decision itself. An example here is the Canadian case of *Auton*.[41] Here the courts held that the government did not have a legal

[40] Amit Sengupta & Samiran Nundy, Editorial, *The Private Health Sector in India*, BRIT. MED. J. 1158 (2005).
[41] Auton v. British Columbia (Att'y.Gen.), [2004] 3 S.C.R. 657 (Can.).

obligation to fund a particular treatment for autism. However, the publicity generated by the case and the groundswell of support for the cause prompted provincial governments across Canada to eventually include this treatment within their public health insurance schemes. In Israel, while the Court in the *Israeli*[42] judgment rejected the legal argument against the huge copayment imposed on cochlear implants, the government did abolish it shortly thereafter.

A fourth theme explored concerns the impact of litigation of constitutional rights versus the impact of rights contained in domestic legislation. Do entrenched constitutional rights result in better and more frequent litigation that benefits the more vulnerable? In exploring this question we find that the mode of enactment is endogenous to other contextual factors. What emerges is that developing/emerging countries with progressive aspirations will entrench a constitutional right to health, while for the time being having poor public health systems. At this point, we cannot know whether a constitutional right to health care will have the desired impact of accelerating gains in access and equity.

Finally, a theme that emerges from a review of the country case-studies is that courts may not be the best venue if one hopes to *improve* equity or fairness, although they may suffice for simply protecting existing standards of equity (with some notable exceptions). Thus where there is an equitable system in place, the courts are more likely to protect it from challenges that would see resources distributed away from the most vulnerable. On the other hand, courts seem less capable of "producing" equity – that is, insisting that resources are redistributed to those most in need. Related to this, courts seem, overall, reluctant to interfere with the legislative/executive branches of government. Courts are most willing to intervene where a claim can be construed as a private law claim – a one-off dispute between private parties. From the perspective of equity, this trend may be unfortunate as it favors those with the resources to litigate their personal health rights claims. There are, however, some exceptions, where the courts are willing to act more boldly (e.g., as Lisa Forman and Jerome Amir Singh discuss, the Treatment Action Campaign case in South Africa,[43] a collective and not an individual petition, in which the Court interpreted the constitution to require the government to expand programs addressing mother-to-child transmission of AIDS in public clinics).

Our authors explore these five themes in the unique context of their country of study. In the concluding chapter we reflect on their rich explorations and weave together conclusions, some tentative and some stronger, to inform a better understanding of the powerful and complex marriage of human rights and health care systems.

---

[42] HCJ 2974/06 Israeli v. Committee for the Expansion of the Health Basket [2006] The Judicial Authority Website (Isr.).

[43] Minister of Health & Another v. Treatment Action Campaign & Others 2002 (5) SA 721 (CC) (S. Afr.).

PART I

National Public Health Systems (Tax Financed)

1

Litigating a Right to Health Care in New Zealand

Joanna Manning

INTRODUCTION

In 2006, a World Health Organization (WHO) survey found evidence of a substantial increase in patient-led litigation against health authorities and funders/insurers over access to medicines around the world.[1] New Zealanders have seldom litigated denials of access to health care. Part of the explanation lies in the fact that New Zealand has a legislated patients' "bill of rights,"[2] with enforcement through a complaints mechanism. Although the separate regime does not afford patients substantive legal protection in respect of complaints about lack of access to care, this form of alternative, low-level resolution of health care disputes does condition disgruntled patients not to turn to the courts for legal redress in relation to their rights. But given the increasing need for prioritization arising from serious concern about the sustainability of the public health system,[3] as well as a trend toward greater explicitness when it occurs, increased disappointment on behalf of patients and the public when care is denied or limited seems inevitable. This may well translate into increased patient-led litigation against health authorities and funders/insurers.

Section 1.1 provides an overview of the New Zealand health system, with a focus on the points at which resource allocation decisions are made, the identity of the decision maker, and the methods by which priority-setting occurs. Subsection 1.1.1 describes inequalities between population groups in New Zealand, both in health outcomes and in access to health care. Section 1.2 describes the legal

---

[1] See Hans V. Hogerzeil et al., Is access to essential medicines as part of the fulfillment of the right to health enforceable through the courts?, 368 LANCET 305, 305 (2006).

[2] New Zealand's Code of Health and Disability Services Consumers' Rights was prescribed in regulations, as a Schedule to the Health and Disability Commissioner (Code of Health and Disability Services Consumers' Rights) Regulations 1996 (reprint Sept. 14, 2006) (N.Z.), *available at* http://www.hdc.org.nz/theact/theact-thecode [hereinafter the Code of Rights].

[3] In this work I treat "rationing" and "prioritization" as synonymous terms, with "prioritization" or "priority-setting" often being the more politically palatable version.

framework surrounding the health and disability sector and discusses the lack of legislated rights to health and the limited right of access to health care in legislation, despite the existence of a legally enforceable Code of Health and Disability Services Consumers' Rights. While they cannot vindicate legal entitlements to care, Subsection 1.2.1 considers how the Code and Commissioner are nevertheless able to contribute to improvements in resource allocation decision making and to insist on providing patients with proper information about the basis for decisions, their options, and waiting times. As elsewhere, low litigation rates challenging care-limiting decisions are notable, explicable by access to justice concerns as well as the existence of the alternative dispute resolution pathway (Subsection 1.2.2). Section 1.3 describes and analyses the (only) two New Zealand cases where patients have challenged rationing decisions in health care before courts, and discusses their significant features.

1.1 FEATURES OF NEW ZEALAND'S PUBLIC HEALTH SYSTEM: LOCUS OF ALLOCATION DECISIONS

New Zealand's public health care system is one of universal coverage. Access to publicly available services is intended to be equal, based on need and ability to benefit rather than ability to afford treatment. Rationing is necessary in such a universal system committed to equality but faced with the reality of scarcity. This section describes key features of New Zealand's health care system: the locus and level of decision making about what services and goods are provided and the process by which these decisions are made. Originally based on the Beveridge model for the National Health Service, the system is still strongly hierarchical, with a significant degree of central command and control, despite moves toward greater decentralization more recently.

The country spends 10.3 percent of gross domestic product (GDP) on health, higher than the Organization for Economic Cooperation and Development (OECD) average,[4] although its total per capita health expenditure, public and private, is less than the OECD average.[5] It is a mixed system, permitting thus allowing a role for private finance for services that are covered by the public system. Government is the main financing source, funding 82.7 percent of health spending in 2011, which covers most personal care for the population. The share of total spending from private insurance is minor (approximately 5 percent), and the share of out-of-pocket payments is also low (at 10.9 percent).[6] Public health spending is largely financed

---

[4] *See* OECD, HEALTH DATA 2013: HOW DOES NEW ZEALAND COMPARE 1 (2013), *available at* http://www.oecd.org/els/health-systems/Briefing-Note-NEW-ZEALAND-2013.pdf.

[5] New Zealand's total health expenditure, public and private, per capita in 2011 was US$3,182 PPP. The OECD average is US$3,339 PPP; Australia's in 2010 was US$3,800 PPP, *see id.* PPP refers to the use of economy-wide adjusted purchasing power parities, which are based on a broad basket of goods and services chosen to be representative of all economic activity, and provides a means of comparing spending between countries on a common base.

[6] *See* OECD, HEALTH DATA 2013: FREQUENTLY REQUESTED DATA 157 (2013), *available at* http://www.oecd.org/els/health-systems/oecdhealthdata2013-frequentlyrequesteddata.htm.

from general tax revenues. An additional 8.4 percent of total funding comes from the accident compensation scheme, which provides no-fault insurance coverage and compensation for accidental injuries.[7]

An individual's first contact with the system is most often at the primary care level with a general practitioner (GP) or a practice nurse. GPs operate as private businesses, and patients are generally able to choose their preferred GP. Primary care is fully or partially subsidized, supplemented by copayments.[8] Publicly funded secondary care is free, accessed by GP referral. Patients are assigned to a specialist or hospital for publicly funded secondary care. The main hospitals are public and account for about 43 percent of public health expenditure. There is ongoing public concern, and thus political sensitivity and significant media attention, about lengthy public hospital waiting lists for elective services. The private system exists principally because of people's desire to gain faster access to surgery or treatment in smaller private hospitals or by specialists of their choice. Private treatment is funded either out of pocket or by medical insurance. About one-third of children and almost 40 percent of adults had private health insurance in 2006–2007,[9] but the proportion is likely to have reduced since then.

Access to publicly funded pharmaceuticals is regulated by means of a pharmaceutical management agency, Pharmac. Its objective is to ensure that public money spent on pharmaceuticals is invested efficiently and achieves best value for the money. A key role is to manage the Pharmaceutical Schedule, which is a list of subsidized prescription drugs and related products. Pharmac makes the final decision on subsidy levels and prescribing guidelines and conditions by balancing evidence of effectiveness with cost, within a fixed annual budget. It receives independent expert medical advice to inform its decisions from the Pharmacology and Therapeutics Advisory Committee (PTAC) and other specialist subcommittees. It uses cost-utility analyses to assess the important, often decisive cost-effectiveness criterion, which is one of nine decision criteria, for its prioritization decisions.[10] Compared to many overseas countries, which have experienced significant growth in pharmaceutical expenditure, New Zealand has been highly successful in curbing the

---

[7] *See* Ministry of Health, Improving the System: Meeting the Challenge – Improving Patient Flow for Electives (2012). The scheme is funded by compulsory employer, self-employed, employee, and motor vehicle levies; non-work injuries are subsidised by the government out of general taxation.

[8] Patient copayments are not statutorily regulated, although there are local agreements between District Health Boards and Primary Health Organizations (PHOs), and systems for arbitrating if practices appear to be charging excessively. (PHOs are the local structures which deliver and coordinate the wide range of services provided in primary health care by health professionals. Most GPs belong to a PHO); *see* OECD, OECD Economic Surveys: New Zealand 126 (2009).

[9] *See* Sarah Gerritsen, Niki Stefanogiannis & Yvonne Galloway, A Portrait of Health: Key Results of the 2006/07 New Zealand Health Survey, Chap. 6 (2008).

[10] *See* Pharmac, *Operating Policies and Procedures of the Pharmaceutical Management Agency*, Art. 2.2 (3rd ed., 2006), *available at* http://www.pharmac.govt.nz/2005/12/22/231205.pdf for Pharmac's decision criteria.

relentless growth in the rate of pharmaceutical spending.[11] Despite this, an expert panel concluded in 2010 that there does not appear to be evidence that health outcomes in New Zealand are worse overall than for other comparable counties, largely because it pays lower prices for medicines than do most comparable countries, and so achieves relatively good value for the money.[12] This has enabled investment in new medicines and expanded access to existing ones.[13] It remains controversial, however, whether Pharmac's success at containing costs has been at the expense of better access to new and more effective medicines.[14] Its role in allocating public funding for medicines has led on occasion to disappointment and challenge from patients and the public, the media, clinicians, and suppliers. Its decision to approve nine weeks of public funding for Herceptin for use in early breast cancer in 2006–2009, rather than a twelve-month regimen that many patients and lobbyists sought, is the most high-profile and controversial funding decision in its history, and provides a vivid example. It produced the first patient-initiated court challenge to a Pharmac decision, discussed in Subsection 1.3.1.

New Zealand does not have a prescribed minimum "basket" or "core" of health services that are publicly funded, despite an attempt, ultimately abandoned, to define one in the 1990s. Instead, the mix of goods and services provided in the public system is determined by allocation decisions made at all levels of the system. Ashton considers that the single most important strategy for containing public health expenditure in New Zealand has been the setting of a capped, global budget by government.[15] The Minister of Health with Ministry of Health advice divides

---

[11] New Zealand is a low pharmaceutical spender by OECD standards. Its per capita spending on pharmaceuticals (US$284 PPP) in 2011 was the fifth-lowest in OECD countries; the OECD average was US$483 PPP. Average spending on pharmaceuticals across OECD countries rose almost 50% in real terms between 2000 and 2009, and accounted for approximately 19% on average of total health spending in 2009, although in the two years since average per capita spending has become negative (0.9%); see OECD, HEALTH AT A GLANCE 2011: OECD INDICATORS 157 (2011), Available at http://www.oecd.org/health/healthpoliciesanddata/49105858.pdf; OECD, HEALTH AT A GLANCE 2013: OECD INDICATORS 160 (2013).

[12] The High Cost Medicines Review concluded that for the money it spends on pharmaceuticals, New Zealand gets "exceptional value," certainly relative to the likely counterfactual if Pharmac did not exist; see P. MCCORMACK, J. QUIGLEY & P. HANSEN, REVIEW OF ACCESS TO HIGH-COST, HIGHLY-SPECIALISED MEDICINES IN NEW ZEALAND 1, 45 (2010) [hereinafter "the High-Cost Medicines Review"].

[13] Since it was created, Pharmac has added more than 200 new medicines to the funded list. It estimates that its real buying power has increased threefold since 1993, so that it can now subsidize about three times the amount of medicines that could have been bought with the same money in 1993; see id. at 46.

[14] See M. Richards, Extent and Causes of International Variations in Drug Usage: A Report for the Secretary of State for Health (2010), available at http://www.dh.gov.uk/en/Publicationsandstatistics/Publications/PublicationsPolicyAndGuidance/DH_117962. (New Zealand ranked lowest in comparison of fourteen countries on use of range of fourteen selected medicines, including in usage of cancer drugs).

[15] See Toni Ashton, New Zealand, in COST CONTAINMENT AND EFFICIENCY IN NATIONAL HEALTH SYSTEMS: A GLOBAL COMPARISON 817 (J. Rapoport, P. Jacobs & E. Jonsson, eds., 2009).

the budget across the broad categories of public health, personal health care services, and disability services. Some services are funded nationally (for example, maternity care, mental health services, public health services). The budget for personal health services is allocated to twenty regionally based District Health Boards (DHBs) according to a predetermined risk-adjusted, weighted, demographically based formula. DHBs are responsible for providing or arranging the provision of all publicly-financed, personal health services in their geographically defined regions. They own the public hospitals in their region, through which they directly provide secondary care. They are also responsible for purchasing primary care services from nongovernment community and primary care providers via "service agreements." A large proportion of their primary care budgets is devolved to Primary Health Organisations (PHOs), which in turn pass it to their GP members through capitation payments.

Each DHB's District Annual Plan, negotiated annually with the minister and made public, specifies "the intended outputs of the DHB for the year" and "the expected performance of the DHB's hospital and related services during the year."[16] The minister can give directions relating to government policy, with which DHBs must comply, and, by written notice, can require a DHB to provide or arrange for the provision of any specified health services.[17] There are also overarching health strategies developed by the minister and ministry, stating broad objectives and priorities. These are designed to guide DHBs as to the goals they are to pursue, and to ensure that they act consistently with government policy and overall public health strategy.[18] From 2007–2008 onward, the ministry has introduced health targets, intended to better reflect and focus providers, especially DHBs, on government priorities in the area of health. The ministry reviews target areas annually to ensure they align with government health priorities.[19] Progress toward achieving each target, according to a specific, defined indicator, is reported quarterly.[20] DHBs are ranked against each target according to performance, and the results are publicly available. These mechanisms all provide the minister and the ministry with direct levers to determine national spending priorities and give strong direction to DHBs about which services

[16] New Zealand Public Health and Disability Act 2000, Sec. 39 (N.Z.).

[17] *Id.* at sec. 31, 33.

[18] Three have been developed: the New Zealand Health Strategy, the Disability Strategy, and the Primary Care Strategy. The priorities in the Health and Disability Strategies are incorporated by the Minister into the Funding Agreements with the DHB's, and the DHB's District Strategic Plans must reflect the overall direction set out in, and not be inconsistent with these strategies (Sec. 38(7)).

[19] The six 2010–2013 Health Targets are: shorter stays in emergency departments, improved access to elective surgery, shorter waits for cancer treatment, increased immunization, better help for smokers to quit, and better diabetes and cardiovascular services; *see Welcome to the New Zealand Ministry of Health*, MINISTRY OF HEALTH, *available at* http://www.moh.govt.nz/moh.nsf/indexmh/healthtargets-targets.

[20] For example, the indicator for Target 1 (Shorter Stays in Emergency Departments) is "95 percent of patients will be admitted, discharged, or transferred from an Emergency Department (ED) within six hours."

and goods are to be provided. Thus, as Toni Ashton and colleagues state, "although responsibility for purchasing services has been decentralised to the DHBs, their activities and decisions continue to be steered from the centre."[21]

Although DHBs would appear to have significant scope to determine spending priorities for their populations, their ability to do so is in fact quite limited. To decide how to allocate their budgets, they must assess the health needs of their local population, determine spending priorities, decide which services to provide themselves and which to purchase, and negotiate service agreements with providers for the latter.[22] They are encouraged to come up with their own set of guiding principles and processes for allocating their budgets, although there is considerable variation in the extent of public consultation and the degree of rigor in approaches to setting priorities.[23] One of the aims of the latest structural reform of the public health system in 2001 was to introduce a more decentralized system, under which funding was devolved to twenty-one (now twenty) DHBs.[24] The aim was to make the system more responsive to local needs and preferences, by providing for a majority of elected members on DHBs. Ashton and colleagues report, however, that in practice, the ability of DHBs to respond to consumer preferences and reallocate spending to reflect local needs has been limited to date, because their budgets are largely committed to existing services and contracts, there is strong central control exerted over them, and an overall focus on deficit reduction and the need to operate within budget.[25]

Access to elective surgery is rationed by a booking system – a radical approach introduced in 1996–1997. The system – as originally conceived – was replacing lengthy public hospital waiting lists with a system giving priority for treatment, determined by criteria agreed by clinicians based on need and ability to benefit. After a GP referral, patients are booked for an appointment for first specialist assessment (FSA), to occur within six months. Specialists then assess patients according to the agreed criteria and give them a clinical priority assessment criteria (CPAC) score. Those with a score above an agreed threshold are given a firm date ("booked") for their operations, which theoretically means they will receive treatment within six months of assessment. The clinical threshold is set as a function of available resources, to ensure that the patients above the threshold can realistically receive treatment within the promised six months. Those below the threshold are referred back to their GP for ongoing care. The aims were to move from implicit rationing

---

[21] Toni Ashton, Tim Tenbensel, Jacqueline Cumming & Pauline Barnett, *Decentralising resource allocation: Early experiences with District Health Boards in New Zealand*, 13 J. HEALTH SERVICES RESEARCH & POL'Y 109, 110 (2008).

[22] Id.

[23] Ashton, *supra* note 15, at 196–197.

[24] *See* New Zealand Public Health and Disability Act 2000, Sec. 3(1)(c) (N.Z.); Ashton et al., *supra* note 21, at 110.

[25] Id. at 111–112.

(chronological queueing) to an explicit, transparent form of rationing; to promote national consistency and equity of access, by allocating resources to those with greatest need and ability to benefit; and to provide patients with certainty about their relative priority and when they will receive treatment.[26]

Numerous problems, however, have persisted in implementing the booking system in practice. These include:[27]

- inconsistent selection of patients for first specialist assessments;
- a lack of correlation between CPAC scores and either health status before surgery measured using other measures or benefit obtained from surgery;
- a lack of clinical validity and hence limited acceptance by clinicians of the CPAC tools;
- inconsistent prioritization of patients for treatment;
- surgeons' gaming of scores;
- modest correlation only between CPAC scores and actual priority assigned for surgery;
- DHBs' ignoring six months' waiting times for both FSA and treatment, which are exceeded for significant numbers of patients;[28]
- wide regional variations in waiting times between patients with same level of need; and
- large regional variations in the CPAC process.[29]

There is also concern about the unmet need of patients not booked for surgery because their score is below the cutoff required for treatment, despite having significant clinical need. They are removed from waiting lists and returned to their GP with no hope of treatment unless their condition deteriorates or funding increases.[30] At a system level, this hides the true extent of the problem of waiting lists in

---

[26] Kevin Dew, Jacqueline Cumming, Deborah McLeod, Sonya Morgan, Eileen McKinlay, Anthony Dowell & Tom Love, *Explicit Rationing of Elective Services: Implementing The New Zealand Reforms*, 74 HEALTH POL'Y 1, 9 (2005).

[27] Many of the problems referred to in the text were found in an audit by the Auditor-General; *see* L. Provost, PROGRESS IN DELIVERING PUBLICLY FUNDED SCHEDULED SERVICES TO PATIENTS 16 (2011). See also Jacqueline Cumming, *New Zealand, in* WAITING TIMES POLICIES IN THE HEALTH SECTOR: WHAT WORKS? 208–212 (L. Siciliana, M. Borowitz & V. Morgan, eds., 2013).

[28] Ongoing audits of hospital waiting lists are periodically carried out, and financial penalties introduced where six-month waiting times are exceeded, creating a perverse incentive whereby DHBs culled waiting lists just prior to the end of each six-month period; *see* Martin Johnson, *Hospitals Cull Waiting Lists by Thousands*, THE N.Z HERALD, January 29, 2007, *available at* http://www.nzherald. co.nz/nz/news/article.cfm?c_id=1&objectid=10421381; Ashton, *supra* note 15, at 198–200.

[29] See Mary Seddon et al., *Coronary Artery Bypass Graft Surgery in New Zealand's Auckland Region: A Comparison between the Clinical Priority Assessment Criteria Score and the Actual Clinical Priority Assigned*, 119 N.Z.M.J. 1230 (2006); Sarah Derrett et al., *Prioritising Patients for Elective Surgery: A Prospective Study of Clinical Priority Assessment Criteria in New Zealand*, 19 INT'L J. TECH. ASSESSMENT IN HEALTH CARE 91 (2003); Dew et al., *supra* note 26, at 1.

[30] One small study found that for the 130 patients taken off the Auckland list for coronary artery bypass graft surgery, there was significant morbidity, transformation to emergency status, and mortality, *see*

New Zealand, deflecting political accountability and hence blunting the political will to confront them.

Under the sponsorship of the National Health Committee, the New Zealand Guidelines Group played an important role in initiating and promoting the development and implementation of evidence-based clinical guidelines.[31] These guidelines are useful as a nonbinding means of assisting clinicians when deciding priority for treatment between patients *within* a service area in the public system, rather than as a means of allocating funding *between* services. They are premised on the existing resource levels for a service. The Group is now defunct and guideline development has stalled. Application of the guideline for access to dialysis treatment for end-stage renal failure resulted in the decision to withdraw treatment from the patient in the *Shortland* case in 1998, one of the two judicial decisions where patients have litigated a right to access health care, discussed later.

The government injected a significant amount of new money to meet the aims of its reforms introduced in 2001. Between 2002 and 2007, primary health care received a large funding increase, pursuant to its 2001 Primary Health Care Strategy. Much of that funding was used to reduce the cost of prescriptions to patients, and given to PHOs to reduce copayments for GP visits for enrolled patients. As a result, the rate of growth in health spending was around 10 percent per annum over the period 2002–2008, although it has slowed more recently. Growth in health spending exceeded growth in national income by 30 percent.[32] Given the global financial crisis and likely nominal rates of growth in GDP, maintaining this rate of spending growth is now considered by government to be unsustainable. It is intent on bringing the rate of health spending growth down to match that of national income, and health budgets will be under more pressure than in previous years. At the same time, New Zealand faces many of the same pressures as other countries: an aging population with more people with chronic medical conditions requiring greater health care; new and improved health technologies and medicines becoming available all the time, making more interventions possible; growing professional health workforce shortages; and an increasingly informed and assertive public with high expectations of what the health system can and should deliver.

The mismatch between supply and demand for health care thus seems about to become more acute than ever. Projections done for the next twenty years suggest

---

John Neutze & David Haycock, *Prioritisation and Cardiac Events While Waiting for Coronary Bypass Surgery in New Zealand*, 113 N.Z.M.J. 69 (2000).

[31] This began in 1992–1993 with the development of guidelines in a range of "high-cost, high-use" areas. From 1996, government funded an extended guidelines program, accelerating the process of guidelines development and implementation.

[32] Ministerial Review Group, Meeting the Challenge: Enhancing Sustainability and the Patient and Consumer Experience Within the Current Legislative Framework for Health and Disability Services in New Zealand, para. 34 (2010), *available at* http://www.nzdoctor.co.nz/media/6430/MRG%20Report%20Meeting%20the%20Challenge.pdf.

that, assuming 2010 levels of care, real health care costs will nearly double. The new emphasis is on value for the money and "doing more with what we have." All of this will sharpen the debate about the range of health services publicly provided. There is a greater need than ever for funders to analyse carefully the cost-effectiveness of new therapies and focus on effective prioritisation.[33] This is likely to result in increased disappointment and challenge on behalf of patients and the public when care is denied or limited, which may translate into increased patient-led litigation against DHBs and other public funders.

1.1.1 *Disparities in Health Status*

One purpose of the legislation governing the public health system is "to reduce health disparities by improving the health outcomes of Māori (New Zealand's indigenous people) and other population groups,"[34] albeit within available funding. DHBs are also required to develop and implement services and programs, in consultation with the groups concerned, designed to raise their health outcomes to those of other New Zealanders."[35] This reflects the existence of social and ethnic inequalities in health status in New Zealand, which, as elsewhere, are manifestations of inequalities in per capita incomes and other sociocultural factors. Despite some recent progress, the 2006–2007 Health Survey showed large disparities across a range of risk factors and health outcomes for Māori and Pacific peoples compared to New Zealanders of Asian and European descent, and also for children and adults living in neighborhoods of high socioeconomic deprivation compared to those living in neighborhoods of low deprivation.[36] Māori and Pacific Island New Zealanders have a lower life expectancy, experience worse health outcomes, and demonstrate higher risk factors for chronic disease compared to the total population.[37]

Some of the findings of the Ministry of Health's 2006–2007 Health Survey in relation to access to primary care have shown recent improvement. This is explained in part by the success of the Primary Health Care Strategy in reducing the costs of GP visits for patients.[38] However, the survey found greater disparities in access to

---

[33] For instance, the government is in the process of implementing a recommendation of the 2010 Report of its Ministerial Review Group to set up a single national agency based on the Pharmac model to undertake the role assessing and prioritizing all significant new diagnostic procedures and treatment interventions for public funding; *see id.*, at para. 70–78.

[34] New Zealand Public Health and Disability Act 2000, Sec. 3(1)(b) & 3(2) (N.Z.). Public concern during the Act's passage about race-based preferential access to services were intended to be assuaged by the statutory doubt-avoiding injunction in Sec. 3(3) that "nothing in the Act entitles a person to preferential access to services on the basis of race."

[35] New Zealand Public Health and Disability Act 2000, Sec. 22 (1)(f) (N.Z.).

[36] Gerritsen et al., *supra* note 9, at XIV.

[37] Life expectancy at birth for European and Asian New Zealanders in 2005–2007 was 79 years for males and 83 for females, but 70.4 years and 75.1 for Māori males and females, respectively; *see* OECD, OECD ECONOMIC SURVEYS, *supra* note 8, at 108.

[38] *See* Gerritsen et al., *supra* note 9, at Chap. 5.

secondary services. For example, children of European descent were significantly more likely than those in the total population to have seen a medical specialist in the previous twelve months, whereas Pacific boys, Asian boys and girls, Pacific and Asian men and women, Māori women, and women in the most deprived neighborhoods were all significantly less likely. Adults of European descent were significantly more likely to have used private hospital services in the previous twelve months than those in the total adult population, while Māori and Asian men and women, Pacific women, and women in the most deprived neighborhoods were significantly less likely to have used such services. Māori and Pacific people have significantly lower rates of private health insurance compared to the total adult population,[39] used by wealthier people to avoid lengthy public hospital waiting lists for nonurgent elective surgery. Medical insurance cover decreases with increasing deprivation. As a result, low-income and minority groups have been disproportionately heavy users of public hospital emergency departments, where services are free and available at all hours.[40] Even though the Health Survey showed significant improvements in access to health care, particularly primary care, it concluded that reducing health inequalities remain an important unfulfilled challenge for both the health system and wider society in New Zealand.

1.2 LEGAL STRUCTURE

Despite passing a Code of Rights for patients, the New Zealand parliament has been extremely reluctant to create a legally enforceable right to health or the more limited right of access to health services, such as, for example, access without charge to a minimum core of publicly funded health services, or for their provision within specified or "reasonable" timeframes. As discussed in section 1.2.1, Code rights are concerned with rights in care once provided, rather than any right to access health care in the first place.

Conversely, parliament has been open about the fact of scarce resources and authorized rationing for publicly funded health care. There is no duty to provide treatment in the current statute regulating the funding of the public health system. The purpose of the New Zealand Public Health and Disability Act 2000 is "to provide for the public funding of personal health services, public health services and disability support services... in order to pursue" various objectives. These objectives include a population health focus, equity, community participation, and "to *facilitate* access to *appropriate*, effective, and timely health services."[41] The word "facilitate" avoids guaranteeing access, and the reference to "appropriate" services

---

[39] *See* Gerritsen et al., *supra* note 9, at 131, Fig. 6.64.

[40] The trend may be lessening, as a decline in the use of emergency departments was seen in all men and Māori men between 1996–1997 and 2006–2007; *see* Gerritsen et al., *supra* note 9, at Chap. 6.

[41] New Zealand Public Health and Disability Act 2000, Sec. 3(1)(d) (N.Z.).

is deliberately vague as to their specific nature and suggests variation according to individual circumstances and available resources. The statute goes on to acknowledge scarcity and explicitly authorize rationing, stating that these objectives "are to be pursued to the extent that they are reasonably achievable within the funding provided."[42] Parliament was similarly explicit in the same statute about Pharmac's role in rationing access to publicly funded drugs. Its statutory objective is "to secure for eligible people in need of pharmaceuticals, the best health outcomes that are reasonably achievable from pharmaceutical treatment and from within the amount of funding provided."[43] Similarly, the Accident Compensation Act 2001, which within the definition of coverage for treatment of injury includes "failure to provide treatment, or to provide treatment in a timely manner," but excludes, however, "personal injury that is solely attributable to a resource allocation decision."[44]

In making rationing decisions, Pharmac, DHBs, and other health care providers cannot discriminate on the basis of prohibited factors in antidiscrimination legislation, including age, race, and disability. The two relevant statutes are the Human Rights Act 1993 and the New Zealand Bill of Rights Act 1990. The Human Rights Act applies to private actors in various spheres (such as the supply of goods and services, employment, accommodation, and partnerships), whereas the New Zealand Bill of Rights Act applies to persons or bodies performing "any public function, power, or duty conferred or imposed . . . by or pursuant to law."[45] Section 44(1)(b) of the Human Rights Act makes it unlawful for a provider of services to the public "to treat any . . . person less favourably in connection with the provision of those . . . services than would otherwise be the case, by reason of any of the prohibited grounds of discrimination." Section 19 of the Bill of Rights Act is the right to be "free from discrimination on the grounds in the Human Rights Act 1993." Those grounds include "age" and "disability." It is an everyday occurrence in the health sector to take into account factors such as age and comorbidities (disability) to inform need and ability to benefit to decide priorities between patients. There may well be grounds for complaint that doing so is prima facie discriminatory.[46] The New Zealand Bill of Rights Act affirms fundamental rights and freedoms, albeit largely civil and political rights.

---

[42] *Id.* at sec. 3(2) (N.Z.). In *Shortland*, the High Court held that a similarly worded provision in the predecessor legislation did not impose an absolute duty to treat, but was subject to clinical judgment and available resources; *see Shortland v. Northland Health Ltd.* (unreported), M75/95, 20 Sept. 1997 (N.Z.).

[43] *See* New Zealand Public Health and Disability Act 2000, Sec. 47(a) (N.Z.).

[44] Accident Compensation Act 2001, Sec. 32(1)(2)(b) (N.Z.).

[45] *See* Human Rights Act 1993, Sec. 20J(1)(b) (N.Z.); New Zealand Bill of Rights Act 1990, Sec. 3(b) (N.Z.).

[46] The Human Rights Act 1993 permits defenses of "genuine justification" and "good reason" to be made out. And in respect of publicly funded health care, it is defense to a breach the antidiscrimination right in sec. 19 of the New Zealand Bill of Rights Act 1990, if the act or omission is a justified limitation on the right "prescribed by law" and "demonstrably justified in a free and democratic society" under section 5 of the New Zealand Bill of Rights Act 1990; *see* Human Rights Act 1993, Sec. 20L(2) (N.Z.).

While it affirms the right to refuse to undergo any medical treatment,[47] for example, there is no right to health or to access health care. It does affirm the fundamental "right not to be deprived of life," sometimes invoked in cases of rationing where life itself may be at stake.[48] An unsuccessful challenge was made on this basis in *Shortland v Northland Health Ltd*.[49]

New Zealand is a signatory to international instruments such as the International Convention on Economic, Social and Cultural Rights, which "recognises the right of everyone to the enjoyment of the highest attainable standard of physical and mental health" and covenants "to undertake steps, to the maximum of its available resources, with a view to achieving progressively the full realisation of the [right] . . . by all appropriate means."[50] However, the rights affirmed have not been directly incorporated into domestic law.[51]

1.2.1 *A Code of Rights and Commissioner*

A legacy of the notorious "unfortunate experiment at National Women's Hospital"[52] is New Zealand's legislated code of patients rights passed into law in 1996. While not constitutionally protected, as in South Africa, the rights in the Code are legislated in regulations and enforced via a complaints regime under the jurisdiction of an independent Health and Disability Commissioner.[53] The Commissioner's statutory function is "to promote and protect consumers' rights" and "to that end, to facilitate the fair, simple, speedy and efficient resolution of complaints relating to infringements of those rights."[54] The system provides for relatively low-level resolution of disputes, and is one of "low" rather than "no blame."[55] As such, it mitigates access to justice concerns, as described in section 1.2.2.

---

[47] *See* New Zealand Bill of Rights Act 1990, Sec. 11. Also s. 10 (N.Z.).

[48] See *R. v. Cambridge District Health Authority ex parte B* [1995] 1 W.L.R. 898 (Can.); *Chaoulli v. Quebec (Attorney-General)* [2005] 1 S.C.R. 791 (Can. S.C.).

[49] *Shortland v Northland Health Ltd.* [1998] 1 NZLR. 433 (CA) (N.Z.).

[50] *See* International Covenant on Economic, Social and Cultural Rights, Dec. 16, 1966, S. Treaty Doc. No. 95-19, 6 I.L.M. 360 §2 & §12 (1967), 993 U.N.T.S. 3.

[51] The courts have, however, suggested that domestic statutes should be interpreted consistently with obligations in applicable international instruments where possible, and that rights recognized in international instruments may be mandatory relevant considerations for decision makers exercising a public function (e.g., allocating public funding), thereby opening up the possibility of judicial review absent such consideration or interpretation; *see Tavita v. Minister of Immigration* [1994] 2 NZLR. 257 (CA) (N.Z.); *Puli'uvea v. Removal Review Authority* [1996] 2 HRNZ 510 (CA) (N.Z.); *Ye v. Minister of Immigration* [2010] 1 NZLR 104, at Para 24 (SC) (N.Z.)

[52] *See* Silvia r. Cartwright, The Report of the Cervical Cancer Inquiry 1988 (1988), *available at* http://www.cartwrightinquiry.com/wp-content/uploads/2011/11/The_Cartwright_Inquiry_Introduction.pdf; *see generally* The Cartwright papers: Essays on the Cervical Cancer Inquiry, 1987–88 (Joanna Manning ed., 2009).

[53] On the Code and the complaints regime generally, *see* Peter Skegg, *A Fortunate Experiment?* 19 Med. L. Rev. 235 (2011).

[54] *See* Health and Disability Commissioner Act 1994, Sec. 6 (N.Z.).

[55] See Joanna Manning, Access to Justice for New Zealand Health Consumers, 18 J. L. & Med. 39 (2010).

The Code of Rights states ten rights possessed by health and disability services consumers and correlative obligations on providers. Consumers are able to make a complaint to the Commissioner alleging any action of a provider in breach of the Code, as measured against the yardstick of rights in the Code. A key right is the right to have services provided of an appropriate standard, which includes with reasonable care and skill.[56] The Code's rights extend much further, such as to rights to be treated with respect, to be free from discrimination, coercion, and harassment, and from sexual, financial, or other exploitation, and to receive appropriate information and give informed consent. However, the exclusion of any kind of right to access health or disability services was insisted on by government at the outset.[57] There was political nervousness about the potential of the Code being used to attack macro-level funding decisions, and about giving a nonlegally or nonmedically qualified Commissioner the ability to intervene in individual cases to ensure an individual patient's access to services ahead of other patients. However, Commissioners remain unpersuaded by the case for amending the Code to include a broad right of access to, for example, publicly funded services or a defined core of such services. To the extent that the Code is enforceable against individual health providers, it seems unfair to visit statutory liability on them for a breach of the Code that stems from resource allocation decisions over which they have no control. However, providers would have a defence if they took "reasonable actions in the circumstances to give effect to the rights."

Given that the Code binds organizational providers, such as DHBs and public hospitals, the Commissioner could hypothetically impose guarantees of access, thus providing a degree of accountability for providers' resource allocation decisions. However, not only does the Code not contain a general right to access health care; the difficulty in using the Code to challenge decisions denying or limiting care on resource grounds is exacerbated by the "reasonable actions in the circumstances" defense, with "the circumstances" defined to include "the provider's resource constraints."[58]

Nevertheless, even though the Code excludes access issues, a Commissioner can still utilize it to advance patients' interests in relation to access issues. The Code supports a transparent and accountable process for decision making regarding access to care. The Commissioner has been prepared to assess DHBs' policies and processes for prioritizing patients and decide whether they meet an acceptable standard in terms of Right 4(1).[59] The Commissioner can make sure that a provider has properly

---

[56] *See* The Code of Rights, Right 4(1).

[57] One right does come close to an access right. Right 4(3), "to have services provided in a manner consistent with [the consumer's] needs," could be interpreted liberally as giving a right of access to "needed" services, but has been carefully interpreted as confined to the quality of care once provided. Complaints alleging failures to provide treatment in the first place or unacceptable delays in receiving treatment because of limited resources are rejected as outside the Commissioner's jurisdiction.

[58] *See* the Code of Rights, cl 3(1)-(3).

[59] Right 4(1) is the right to have services provided with reasonable care and skill.

applied a policy to an individual's case, and require that patients receive appropriate care and information while they are waiting for treatment.[60]

In several decisions on complaints about patient referrals to public hospitals for assessment for elective services, Commissioner Paterson[61] has emphasized that a patient has a right under Right 4(1) to an appropriate assessment and prioritization of his/her level of need, using relevant standards and guidelines. DHBs owe the patient a duty of care to ensure that referrals for specialist assessment and diagnostic or elective services are managed appropriately. "Prioritization systems should be fair, systematic, consistent, evidence-based and transparent."[62] In one decision, the Commissioner was determined to clarify the relative roles and responsibilities of specialists, general practitioners, and DHBs in prioritizing patients accessing elective services.[63]

The Commissioner also decided that a DHB must appropriately manage its waiting lists. It has the primary responsibility for ensuring that patients and GPs are clear about when a patient can expect to be seen for a FSA and, if booked, when treatment will be provided. The DHB had a duty to advise patients and GPs that either the patient would be seen for a FSA within six months or that the service was unable to do so, and about the option of seeking private assessment and treatment. A DHB cannot simply leave matters to the specialist, knowing that time frames are not being met. It must have a system to alert staff when referrals are not receiving their FSAs within specified time frames.

The Commissioner has also made adverse findings in cases where patients have been improperly triaged for prioritization purposes or the policy prioritizing treatment was wrongly applied to their case. For example, in one case, the Commissioner held a DHB breached Right 4(1), where a patient's priority was inappropriately downgraded from semi-urgent to routine, overriding a specialist's assessment of greater urgency because important clinical information was overlooked, such that she was denied access to a publicly funded MRI.[64]

---

[60] *See e.g.*, Health and Disability Commissioner, Northland Health Board, Case 09HDC00836 (February 3, 2010), *available at* http://www.hdc.org.nz/media/102594/09hdc00836dhb.pdf; *see* http://www.hdc.org.nz/decisions-case-notes for the Health and Disability Commissioner's decisions.

[61] New Zealand has had three Commissioners: Robyn Stent (1994–2000); Ron Paterson (2000–2010) and Anthony Hill (2010–present).

[62] *See* Health and Disability Commissioner, Nelson Marlborough District Health Board, Case 09HDC00891 (March 31, 2010), *available at* http://www.hdc.org.nz/media/128729/09hdc00891dhb.pdf; Health and Disability Commissioner, Roles and Responsibilities in Prioritisation for First Specialist Assessment, Case 04HDC13909 (April 4, 2006), *available at* http://www.hdc.org.nz/media/65824/04hdc13909casenote.pdf.

[63] Roles and Responsibilities in Prioritisation for First Specialist Assessment, *supra* note 62.

[64] *See* Nelson Marlborough District Health Board, *supra* note 62; *See also* Health and Disability Commissioner, Management of Referrals for Specialist Urological Services, Case 09HDC01040 (April 23, 2010), *available at* http://www.hdc.org.nz/media/131157/09hdc01040casenote.pdf; Northland Health Board, *supra* note 60.

The Code[65] also has been used to insist on scrupulous disclosure to patients of clear, accurate, and timely information about the priority decision and the reasons for it, about waiting times and when treatment is likely to be provided,[66] and about their options and the risks of each, including the risks (if any) of no or delayed treatment.[67] Patients may need information about their options, such as to be treated in the public system free of charge or the option to have treatment privately if publicly funded services are not available or involve long waiting times, and of the additional costs of private treatment.[68] This is especially important when a doctor has a responsibility for a patient's position on the public waiting list and also has a private practice, and the potential for a conflict of interest arises.[69]

The Commissioner has also made use of decisions to highlight and express broader concerns on issues of public concern to patients in cases where access issues are complained about, such as national inconsistency of access and the inequities of the postcode lottery, and the practice of queue-jumping by private patients whereby FSAs are undertaken in private.[70] In this way, while not able to actually adjudicate complaints about limitations on access under the Code, the Commissioner is able to act as an advocate on behalf of patients and urge for improvements at a systemic level.

In conclusion, parliament's reluctance to legislate rights of access to health care means that statute law offers little substantive assistance to a patient seeking to litigate a decision denying or limiting access to health care. Although confined to their rights once patients gain access, the Code does enable the Commissioner to insist on good

---

[65] Right 6(1) of the Code is the right to the information that a reasonable consumer, in that consumer's circumstances, would expect to receive, and includes an explanation of the condition, the options available, including an assessment of the risks, side effects, benefits, and costs of each, as well as advice of the estimated time within which the services will be provided.

[66] ROLES AND RESPONSIBILITIES IN PRIORITISATION FOR FIRST SPECIALIST ASSESSMENT, *supra* note 62 (in booking system for publicly funded elective services, DHB has a duty to provide information to patients and referring GPs either that they will be seen within six months or not, and of option to seek private treatment, where patients outnumber available resources); NORTHLAND HEALTH BOARD, *supra* note 60 (failure to provide information about why surgery was postponed or when it was likely, or of additional risk of more invasive surgery entailed in delay).

[67] NELSON MARLBOROUGH DISTRICT HEALTH BOARD, *supra* note 62 (five-month delay in advising patient that publicly funded treatment is unavailable); ROLES AND RESPONSIBILITIES IN PRIORITISATION FOR FIRST SPECIALIST ASSESSMENT, *supra* note 62 (urologist allocated urgent priority to all patients for an FSA, when it was clear that all could not be seen in a timely manner, in breach of Right 4(1)).

[68] NELSON MARLBOROUGH DISTRICT HEALTH BOARD, *supra* note 62 (patient should have been told that a publicly funded MRI was not available and of her right to seek a private MRI, and of the risks of not receiving treatment for a semi-urgent condition).

[69] *See* HEALTH AND DISABILITY COMMISSIONER, OPHTHALMOLOGIST, DR C SOUTHLAND DISTRICT HEALTH BOARD, Case 05HDC12122 (June 29, 2007), *available at* http://www.hdc.org.nz/media/14743/05hdc12122ophthalmologist.pdf (a specialist failed to ensure that a patient understood options of fully public or part public/part private treatment and of her liability to pay for additional costs of private consultations; exploitation of patient when the specialist charged the patient for preoperative and postoperative serves to which she was entitled free of charge).

[70] NELSON MARLBOROUGH DISTRICT HEALTH BOARD , *supra* note 62.

standards in the process of allocative decision making, and ensure transparency and adequate information for patients. Common law judicial review on the traditional grounds of illegality, procedural unfairness, and irrationality is available in respect of publicly funded care. However, there have only been two legal decisions in which patients have challenged decisions limiting care. The next section discusses access to justice issues, which partially explain the paucity of cases.

1.2.2 *Access to Justice*

All the cases in which New Zealand patients have litigated rights to health care have been brought since 1990, after which more explicit forms of rationing became more prevalent. Before that, as elsewhere, the tradition of implicit rationing meant that patients were often unaware of the rationing basis of care-limiting decisions.

Nevertheless, New Zealanders are not litigious in relation to their health care. This is explained, in large part, by issues surrounding access to justice. Many patients would require legal aid to mount legal challenges, yet civil legal aid is the most difficult type of legal aid to obtain. It is means-tested, and the eligibility criteria, which involve complex considerations of the applicant's assets and income, are restrictive.[71] It addresses the needs of people with very limited financial means only, leaving a significant proportion of low- and middle-income people ineligible. Conditions on grants requiring applicants to make interim payments, repayments, and authorizing caveats or registered charges over property as security for repayment can also operate as a significant disincentive on bringing proceedings. Legal aid must also be refused if the applicant has not shown reasonable grounds for taking the proceedings, and the Ministry of Justice – the body that administers legal aid – has a broad discretion to refuse a grant where the applicant's prospects of success are considered insufficient or a grant not justified or unreasonable.[72] As a result, legal aid may well be refused in judicial review proceedings where rights to health care are asserted, in which, traditionally at least, the prospects of success have been low.[73] The government has tightened up the availability of and the criteria for legal aid recently, principally for criminal legal aid, amid much publicity.[74] The strong message given is that it is available as a last resort to those in dire straits.

However, the cost of litigating a right to health care may not be the only – or even the dominant – explanation for the small number of cases brought. It seems

---

[71] Legal aid must be refused where an applicant's income *or* disposable capital exceeds maximum thresholds set in regulations, unless special circumstances are shown. *See* Legal Services Regulations 2011, S.R. 2011/144, reg. 5 & 6 (N.Z.).

[72] *See* The Legal Services Act 2011 sec. 10(3) & 10(4)(d)(i) (N.Z.).

[73] Although commentators suggest that these cases are currently more likely to succeed than ever before, *see* Hogerzeil et al., *supra* note 1 (patients successful in 83% of cases of medicines access litigation around the world).

[74] Implementing the recommendations of a law reform report, *see* Margaret Bazely, Transforming the Legal Aid System: Final Report and Recommendations (2009).

that New Zealand patients have a low propensity to bring legal claims in any event, despite the system being one in which access to justice issues might be expected to be less of a barrier. An accident compensation scheme replaces the tort action for damages in New Zealand. The other functions of the civil action – corrective justice (vindication and professional accountability) and deterrence – are intended to be fulfilled principally by the complaints regime. A free, less formal, largely lawyer-free complaints process should pose few barriers to the bringing of complaints. Thus, one might expect that New Zealand patients who have suffered an adverse event would be more able and willing to make complaints to the Commissioner than are their tort counterparts to sue. However, a study of the proportion of complaints lodged by patients after an adverse event in public hospitals revealed the converse to be the case. Marie Bismark and colleagues found that complaints are rare, in the sense that the vast majority of preventable adverse events never trigger a complaint.[75] Elderly patients were 25 percent less likely to complain following an adverse event, and patients from the most socioeconomically deprived areas and of Pacific ethnicity – both groups with a worse health status, as noted earlier – were significantly less likely to complain.[76] One reason for not complaining may be that injured patients are interested in monetary redress only, available via the separate compensation scheme. However, as outlined, there is no possibility of a legal remedy from either the compensation scheme or the complaints regime in respect of lack of access to health care. Litigation offers these patients the only hope of legal redress. Yet the legal challenges remain few in number. There may be cultural factors at work here. Perhaps New Zealand patients have been conditioned by abolition of the damages remedy for personal injury such that they no longer look to the courts for redress for perceived injustices in the health sector.

1.3 LEGAL CHALLENGES TO RATIONING DECISIONS IN HEALTH CARE

There have been three patient challenges to rationing decisions in health care in New Zealand. Two were successful, the patients ultimately gaining access to expensive treatments previously denied them. In the first, threatened litigation amid media publicity was all it took to achieve access. The second patient claimed violation of a duty under the criminal law and asserted a quasi-constitutional "right to life," whereas the patients in the third case raised more traditional judicial review grounds through administrative law. All cases were accompanied by media attention, but it

---

[75] Only one in 200 (0.4 per cent) of patients who suffered an adverse event later lodged a complaint. Among patients who suffered a serious, preventable injury or death, only 4% complained – about the same percentage as those who bring a civil damages action in other common law jurisdictions; *see* Marie Bismark et al., *Relationship between Complaints and Quality of Care in New Zealand: A Descriptive Analysis of Complainants and Non-Complainants Following Adverse Events*, 15 QUALITY & SAFETY IN HEALTH CARE 17, 18–19 (2006).

[76] *Id.* at 7, 21.

was explicitly employed as part of an overall strategy, which included litigation, in the third case.

The first two cases involved the withholding of dialysis from patients with end-stage renal failure. Both occurred during the 1990s, and were attended by intense public and media interest because they galvanized public concern about perceived dwindling access to publicly funded health care. In the first case, threatened litigation was all it took for the provider to capitulate and provide access. In the second case, the patient died of kidney failure early on the morning after the Court's decision upholding the denial of care.

The first case, *South Auckland Health*, illustrates the potential for patients to invoke the Human Rights Act when alleging that a failure to provide a treatment is discriminatory. In 1995, seventy-six-year-old James McKeown was initially denied dialysis treatment for his end-stage renal failure by renal physicians at Middlemore Hospital. His family laid a complaint of age discrimination with the Human Rights Commission, alleging that, in applying a guideline that "in usual circumstances, persons over 75 years are not likely to be accepted onto a . . . dialysis programme," South Auckland Health had breached the Act. Ultimately South Auckland's resolve crumbled. It ordered its clinicians to reassess the patient ignoring his age, and promptly provided the dialysis treatment. Mr. McKeown enjoyed another eighteen months of life. The decisive factor appears to have been the allegation of age discrimination. The hospital was understandably wary of the opprobrium attached to a finding of unlawful discrimination.[77]

1.3.1 *Shortland v Northland Health Ltd*[78]

In the second case, *Shortland v Northland Health Ltd*, the hospital refused to back down despite pressure, and the case ended up in court. The patient, Rau Williams, a sixty-three-year-old Māori man, had a long history of Type 2 diabetes.[79] He was admitted to Northland Health's Whangarei Hospital and placed on interim dialysis to enable assessment of his suitability for acceptance to the hospital's renal replacement program – specifically his suitability for long-term, home-based peritoneal dialysis (CAPD). An interdisciplinary team considered his suitability clinically and socially over a ten-week period, during which they held five or six meetings, attended by family members. Northland Health then advised the family of its decision to discontinue dialysis. The decision was made in part by applying an evidence-based

---

77 An unsatisfactory aspect of *Shortland v Northland Health Ltd.* [1998] 1 NZLR. 433 (CA) (N.Z.) was that there was no consideration of the Human Rights Act. The guideline was possibly discriminatory on the ground of disability. This aspect is not discussed here, *but see* Joanna Manning & Ron Paterson, *"Prioritization": Rationing Health Care in New Zealand*, 33 J. L. MED. & ETHICS, 681 (2005).

78 *Shortland v Northland Health Ltd.* [1998] 1 NZLR. 433 (CA) (N.Z.).

79 After adjusting for age, Māori men and women have twice the prevalence of diagnosed diabetes than men and women in the total population; *see* Gerritsen et al., *supra* note 9, at Chap. 3.

access guideline for entry to the program developed by the regional health authority responsible for funding the treatment. The guideline allocated the resource on the basis of ability to benefit from treatment, providing that in the usual case, a prognosis of more than two years' life was required for automatic admission to the program. Williams's prognosis was that continued dialysis would extend his life by about a year. Of those patients not expected to derive the two-year benefit, some also fell into Group A of the guideline, which listed factors that in isolation were likely to result in a decision of unsuitability, and for whom admission to the program was then exceptional. The relevant section of the guideline read:[80]

Group A

Factors which in isolation are likely to determine that an individual is not suitable for treatment of End Stage Renal Failure

. . .

CNS / Mental Function

Dementia (moderate to severe), very low IQ, a disabling psychiatric disorder which is unlikely to respond to further therapy, previous major stroke with persisting severe functional disability.

Basis: There must be the ability to co-operate with active therapy."

Williams had moderate dementia, a complication of the diabetes that had caused his renal failure and need for dialysis. Attempts to teach him to perform CAPD during the assessment period were unsuccessful, and he disconnected his CAPD on two occasions, on one occasion causing life-threatening peritonitis. The treating renal physician concluded that he would be incapable of living independently and of performing any form of home dialysis, though family members indicated their willingness to supervise.[81] He was considered unable to "co-operate with active therapy" due to his dementia, in terms of Group A of the guideline, and hence considered unsuitable for entry on to the program. As a result of the family's protests, opinions were obtained from five renal physicians from major centers around the country, all of whom concurred that discontinuing dialysis in the circumstances was appropriate and consistent with national practice. The applicant, a nephew representing the family, challenged the withdrawal of dialysis on judicial review, seeking an interim order requiring Northland Health to continue or resume dialysis until a full judicial review proceeding could be heard. The patient's evidence was

[80] This section of the guidelines is quoted in the High Court decision of Salmon J.; *see Shortland v. Northland Health Ltd.* (unreported), M75/95, 20 Sept., 1997, 7 (N.Z.).
[81] The evidence indicated, however, that it had proved impossible to ensure a family member took responsibility for his care during the assessment period when efforts had been made to train Williams in the procedure; *see Shortland v. Northland Health Ltd.* (unreported), M75/95, 20 Sept. 1997, 5 (N.Z.).

that he did not wish to die; he enjoyed some quality of life on dialysis, including pleasure from seeing his family. After the High Court rejected the first application for judicial review, the family brought a second application two weeks later, raising various fresh grounds. The Court rejected that too, and the same day an urgent appeal was brought, heard, and determined by the Court of Appeal.

The applicant made two arguments that the decision to discontinue dialysis was unlawful. The first was that Northland Health's refusal to provide dialysis amounted to breach without lawful excuse of its duty in criminal law to provide the necessaries of life to Rau Williams.[82] The second was that withdrawing and withholding of dialysis constituted a breach of Mr. Williams' right not to be deprived of life in s 8 of the New Zealand Bill of Rights Act. In relation to the first argument, the applicant submitted that withholding dialysis was without lawful excuse, because it was in breach of the requirements of "good medical practice" as defined in *Auckland Area Health Board v Attorney-General (AAHB)*.[83] That was a case where doctors had applied to the Court seeking a declaration that they would not be criminally responsible if they withdrew artificial ventilation from a patient with extreme Guillain-Barré syndrome, in which the family agreed that the proposed course of action was in the patient's best interests. The High Court in *AAHB* held that medical and nursing staff were under no duty to provide the life-support system and would be acting with "lawful excuse" in withdrawing it and so attract no criminal responsibility, if the discontinuance was in accordance with "good medical practice," defined as comprising:

(1) a decision in good faith that withdrawal of the life support system was in the best interests of the patient;

(2) conformity with prevailing medical standards and with practices, procedures, and traditions commanding general approval within the medical profession;

(3) consultation with appropriate medical specialists and the medical profession's recognised ethical body; and

(4) the fully informed consent of the family.[84]

The Court considered that medical staff had complied with the first two *AAHB* criteria. There could be no doubt that the decisions to first withdraw and later withhold dialysis were "made in good faith in the belief that they were in the best

---

[82] The Crimes Act 1961 Sec. 151(1) (N.Z.), states that "[e]very one who has charge of any other person unable, by reason of . . . sickness . . . to withdraw himself from such charge, and unable to provide himself with the necessaries of life, is . . . under a legal duty to supply that person with the necessaries of life, and is criminally responsible for omitting without lawful excuse to perform such duty if the death of that person is caused, or if his life is endangered or his health permanently injured, by such omission."

[83] *Auckland Area Health Board v Attorney-General (AAHB)* [1993] 1 NZLR 235 (HC) (N.Z.).

[84] *Shortland v Northland Health Ltd.* [1998] 1 NZLR. 433, 442 (CA) (N.Z.).

interests of Mr Williams."[85] Failure to comply with the second was "simply not arguable,"[86] given that the evidence overwhelmingly demonstrated a unanimous view among those consulted in New Zealand that the case was unsuitable for long-term dialysis. Medical staff had not complied with the third and fourth criteria: there was no formal consultation with an ethics committee, nor did the decision to cease dialysis have the fully informed consent of the patient's family. The Court stated that these were not mandatory requirements in all cases, and neither was appropriate or applicable in the circumstances of this case, which was an entirely different situation to that in *AAHB*. Formal consultation with an ethics committee was not necessary in this case, because the decision-making process conformed to the framework and processes recommended in the guideline. The guideline itself was the product of extended consideration by a representative committee (including ethicists) and was in line with practice nationally; and, the Court asserted, "the present case did not raise significant ethical issues as such. The issues arising were essentially ones of clinical judgment, not ethics."[87] The Court also held that consent from the family was not required for the cessation of treatment from Mr. Williams in the circumstances of this case. Only reasonable consultation with the patient and available family members, and taking their views into account, where circumstances permit, was required. Otherwise, the family would be given the power to require the treatment to be given or continued, irrespective of the clinical judgment of the doctors involved. While this proposition may be "appropriate in the context of the proposed removal of a life-support system," it was one "the law could not countenance" in the different situation of a decision to put a patient on long-term dialysis when such a course was considered clinically inappropriate.[88] "Those responsible for the patient's care . . . ultimately . . . must decide what in clinical terms and within available resources is best for their patient," and, the Court continued, "we are satisfied that this is exactly what happened in Mr Williams' case, albeit there was no resource dimension in the present case."[89]

Shortland proceeded on the basis that *AAHB* and *Shortland* were both "best interests" cases. The issue in each case was whether the clinical judgment – that a patient's imminent death was better than his life prolonged by life support – was legally defensible. As at the date of the Court of Appeal hearing, it was possible to justify this view of the case, because arguably at that time, it was unlikely that it was in Mr. Williams's best interests that dialysis be resumed. The evidence then was that his life expectancy was only a few days, and that further dialysis was very risky and highly unlikely to have a favorable outcome for his quality of life. However, a month

---

[85] *Id.*
[86] *Id.*
[87] *Id.* at 443.
[88] *Id.*
[89] *Id.*

earlier when dialysis was first removed, it was much harder to sustain that claim, especially given that Mr. Williams wished to proceed with dialysis.

The Court in *Shortland* repeatedly asserted that the circumstances of *AAHB* and *Shortland* were entirely different, without ever explaining why. The key distinction was that in *AAHB* the doctors, with family's agreement, were seeking the Court's sanction to *withdraw* life support, based on a judgment about the patient's best interests, thereby liberating scarce, expensive ventilation technology, while Mr. Williams and his family were insisting on *continued* provision of scarce, expensive treatment. The Court perhaps realized the potential difficulties in permitting families to dictate the provision of expensive, life-prolonging therapies. However, it would countenance no suggestion that *Shortland* was a case in which clinicians had concluded, applying the guidelines, that to accede to the patient's wish for continued treatment was an unjustifiable use of scarce resources. Rather than acknowledging that care was being rationed, the Court instead preferred to portray the episode as a clinical decision about best interests. It is unclear why the Court felt it necessary to make the remarkable claim that there was no resource dimension in the case,[90] and that it raised no significant ethical issues. It is widely acknowledged that there is no consensus on the principles that would dictate how to allocate resources fairly, and that allocative choices in health care involve ethical and subjective judgments, to which there are no straightforward answers. The case coincided with widespread public suspicion of the 1990s health reforms, so perhaps the Court sought to provide reassurance about the nation's health system, and preserve the "fiction of [a health system capable of] meeting everyone's needs."[91] Such speculation aside, it is my view that the key factor in the decision is limited resources. The guidelines were an explicit rationing tool, premised on demand for the treatment exceeding supply, aimed at making fairer, more consistent, and transparent allocation decisions as between patients who could derive varying levels of benefit from treatment. Ironically, the clinical decision was reached by applying an explicit rationing tool, but the Court's decision fell back on the discredited practice of implicit rationing, obscuring a denial of care based on a resource allocation decision (where life itself was at stake) as a clinical judgment about the patient's best interests.

Finally, the Court rejected the argument that the withholding of dialysis constituted a breach of Mr. Williams's right not to be deprived of life. Taking what has been referred to as a definitional approach to fundamental rights, the Court considered that Northland Health's actions of refusing to provide dialysis treatment would not "deprive" Mr. Williams of his life in terms of s 8. The reasoning was

---

[90] Northland Health's evidence, in an attempt to counter a suggestion that its decision was resource-driven, had been that to admit Williams to the program would not have impinged on its budget as it was reimbursed on a per-case basis by the funder. Even if the hospital's budget was not capped, it is hard to imagine that admitting an additional patient would not impact on the regional or national dialysis budget.

[91] See Stephen Harrison, The Politics of Evidence-based Medicine in the United Kingdom, 26 POL'Y & POLITICS 15, 18 (1998).

as follows. The careful process of assessment on the basis of the guideline, which included reasonable consultation of the patient and family, amounted to a "lawful excuse" in terms of the criminal provision imposing the duty to provide the necessaries of life. "Equally," the Court continued, "it could not be said that [Northland Health's] actions... would 'deprive' Mr Williams of his life."[92] However, the one (that withholding dialysis would not deprive Mr Williams of his life) simply does not follow from the other (a lawful excuse for not providing him with the necessaries of life). After all, the Court accepted that if Mr. Williams received treatment, his life would have been extended. It may have made for more compelling reasoning to focus the real debate around whether the lawful excuse satisfied the requirements of the qualification to the right to life or the balancing considerations in the "justified limitations" provision in the Bill of Rights Act.

1.3.2 *Walsh v Pharmaceutical Management Agency*[93]

In the third case, *Walsh v Pharmac*, patients disappointed by an allocation decision limiting care successfully challenged it, this time not pursuant to quasi-constitutional litigation but through judicial review in administrative law. In December 2005, Roche applied for public funding to extend the listing of Herceptin (trastuzumab) on the Pharmaceutical Schedule for use in HER-2 positive, early breast cancer. It sought funding for a twelve-month sequential treatment regimen, relying on evidence of promising preliminary results from three major international Phase III trials of Herceptin in HER-2 positive early breast cancer, principally its own sponsored international study, HERA.[94] HERA showed that patients on Herceptin for one year were 46 percent less likely to die or have a recurrence of their cancer after follow-up of twelve months, compared to non-Herceptin treated patients. Around the same time, the preliminary results of a much smaller,[95] publicly funded Finnish study called Finland Herceptin (FinHer) became available,[96] which showed a benefit in terms of recurrence-free survival after only nine weeks of Herceptin treatment comparable with the health gain seen after twelve-month treatment in HERA.[97]

---

[92] *Shortland v Northland Health Ltd.* [1998] 1 NZLR. 433, 445 (CA) (N.Z.)

[93] *Walsh v Pharmaceutical Management Agency* [2010] NZAR 101 (HC) (N.Z.).

[94] Martine J. Piccart-Gebhart, et al., *Trastuzumab after Adjuvant Chemotherapy in HER2-Positive Breast Cancer*, 353 NEW ENG. J. MED. 1659 (2005).

[95] A small subgroup of 232 women with HER-2 positive breast cancer were randomly assigned to post-surgery treatment with nine weeks of trastuzumab concurrently with chemotherapy (115 women), compared to treatment with chemotherapy alone (115 women), whereas the HERA trial comprised some 5,090 patients, of whom 1994 were provided with the twelve-month sequential trastuzumab treatment following chemotherapy.

[96] The study was published in February 2006; *see* Heikki Joensuu et al., *Adjuvant Docetal or Vinorelbine with or without Tratuzumab for Breast Cancer*, 354 NEW ENG. J. MED. 809 (2006).

[97] After a three-year follow-up, the FinHer data indicated that those who received trastuzumab for nine weeks were 48% less likely to die or have a cancer recurrence than those who had not, compared with

Some 350 to 400 New Zealand women are diagnosed annually with HER-2 positive early breast cancer and could benefit from treatment. After negotiation with Roche, the cost of twelve months' funding was estimated at approximately NZ$20–25 million (US$16–20 million) annually, including service costs. Pharmac had not budgeted for the funding of Herceptin, so DHBs would have to come up with additional funds if it was to be funded. This would potentially increase the budget for pharmaceutical cancer treatments in public hospitals by about 45 percent.

Over the next approximately eighteen months, Roche's application was extensively considered by Pharmac's board, its committees, and in-house staff. A cost-utility analysis undertaken by Pharmac staff indicated a cost-per-QALY of between $70,000 and $80,000 for a twelve-month treatment.[98] Most treatments that Pharmac had invested in at the time had a cost per QALY of below $40,000, with an average of $13,700 per QALY in 2004–2005. In July 2006, Pharmac's Board decided to decline Roche's application "at this time" but resolved to keep the issue under review as new information emerged.[99]

Pharmac became aware of the FinHer data in April 2006. The oncologist members of Pharmac's Cancer Treatments Subcommittee, an advisory subcommittee comprising oncologists and hematologists to the Pharmaceutical Treatments Advisory Committee (PTAC)[100] and the board, all strongly supported twelve months' funding, but the hematologists were opposed. Its carefully drafted recommendation to the board was that, in the absence of the availability of funding for a twelve-month treatment, a nine-week treatment based on the weaker FinHer data was reasonable. The subcommittee stated that they "wished to emphasise that this recommendation was strongly based on financial considerations, since it had more confidence in the validity of the 12 months treatment results."[101] For the subcommittee, a compromise

---

46% in HERA. The absolute risk of Disease Free Survival for Herceptin treated patients at three years in FinHer was 89% compared to 78% in the control group, as opposed to 86% at one year in HERA compared to 77% in the control group.

[98] First developed in 1968, QALYs or Quality-adjusted Life Years (QALYs) are used in health sectors worldwide to inform resourcing decisions and provide information about the opportunity costs of decisions. For an explanation of QALYs, *see* CHRISTOPHER NEWDICK, WHO SHOULD WE TREAT? RIGHTS, RATIONING AND RESOURCES IN THE NHS 28, (2nd ed., 2005).

[99] *See* Pharmac DHB joint Media Release, *Herceptin Not Funded, under Continuing Review*, SCOOP HEALTH INDEPENDENT NEWS (July 28, 2006, 1:41PM), *available at* http://www.scoop.co.nz/stories/GE0607/S00116.htm.

[100] PTAC is an expert clinical advisory committee whose purpose is to provide the board with objective, independent, free and frank, and high-quality advice and recommendations on pharmaceuticals. If the board or PTAC considers it needs specialist input into its advice, it can seek advice from more than fifteen specialist subcommittees of PTAC. One of these, the Cancer Treatments Subcommittee, was heavily involved in the Herceptin funding issue.

[101] *Cancer Treatments Subcommittee of PTAC Meeting Held 18 November 2011*, Para. 4.13 (Nov. 2011), *available at* http://www.pharmac.govt.nz/2012/04/20/2011-11-18%20CaTSoP%20Subcommittee%20minutes%20-%20web%20version.pdf; *Walsh v Pharmaceutical Management Agency* [2010] NZAR 101, para 23 (HC) (N.Z.) affidavit of Vernon Harvey from Nov. 30, 2007.

of nine weeks' funding was better than none at all. PTAC's ultimate recommendation to the board was in support of a nine-week funded treatment.

During March 2007, Pharmac consulted on a proposal to fund a nine-week regimen.[102] Nearly all patients who made submissions, as well as Roche (unsurprisingly), supported a funded treatment regimen of twelve months. They noted that twenty-three other OECD countries had twelve months as the standard treatment, making it the "international standard of care." The oncology community unanimously preferred funding therapy for twelve months.

Pharmac's staff prepared a Cost Utility Analysis for the concurrent nine-week regime. At a cost-per-QALY of less than $20,000, it showed the regimen was highly cost-effective when compared with other pharmaceuticals being funded or awaiting funding, and four times more cost-effective than the twelve-month sequential regimen. On April 24, 2007, the board agreed to fund the nine-week concurrent treatment, relying on the FinHer study as evidence of its effectiveness and the regimen's much superior cost-effectiveness and affordability.[103] The board also agreed to contribute to participation in a proposed international "head to head" study comparing nine weeks' and twelve months' duration Herceptin treatment (the Short or Long Duration or SOLD study)[104] estimated at $23.55 million.

In June 2007, eight patients filed judicial review proceedings against three Pharmac decisions:

  (i) the July 2006 decision not to list Herceptin for 12 months treatment "at this time";
 (ii) the Board's second decision in April 2007 to fund the nine weeks' concurrent regimen;[105] and
(iii) Pharmac's decisions declining each plaintiff's application for individual funding of a 12-month regimen under Pharmac's Cancer Exceptional Circumstances policy.[106]

---

[102] See, Jackie Evans, Therapeutic Group Manager, Consultation on a Proposal to Widen Access to Trastuzumab (Herceptin) and Docetaxel (Taxotere) for Adjuvant Treatment of HER 2 Positive Early Breast Cancer, PHARMAC (March 20, 2007), *available at* http://www.pharmac.govt.nz/2007/03/19/200307.pdf.

[103] *See* Pharmac and DHBNZ Media Release, 350 *Women Each Year to Benefit from Herceptin Funding Decision*, SCOOP HEALTH INDEPENDENT NEWS (May 3, 2007 10:38 AM), *available at* http://www.scoop.co.nz/stories/GE0705/S00034.htm.

[104] SOLD was a planned Phase III randomized controlled trial of 3,000 patients, comparing nine weeks of Herceptin concurrently with docetaxel followed by a further chemotherapy regimen with the same regimen followed by twelve months of Herceptin-alone treatment.

[105] This challenge failed, as there was no procedural error, because Pharmac consulted widely, and the decision was not unreasonable or irrational, as there was ample evidence to support it being reasonable. Even if it was flawed, Gendall J would not set it aside, because 150 women on the nine-week regimen, who were not before the Court, would be adversely affected; *see Walsh v Pharmaceutical Management Agency* [2010] NZAR 101, para. 215–216 (HC) (N.Z.).

[106] The plaintiffs' claimed bias, in that the process involving "appeal" by a panel and the medical director's review set up by Pharmac were not independent of Pharmac. The Court held that Pharmac was

The Court was concerned that many of the plaintiffs' arguments directly challenged the merits of Pharmac's decisions. Because it was abundantly clear that there was room for more than one view as to which side of the factual argument was correct or to be preferred, such a challenge was beyond the Court's jurisdiction on judicial review. The Court stated: "The decision to fund the nine weeks regime was not unreasonable or irrational in any legal sense. There was ample evidence to support it as being reasonable, though many may have disagreed."[107]

In relation to Pharmac's first "decision" of July 2006 not to fund the twelve-month treatment, the applicants argued that PTAC had acted *ultra vires* in taking account of funding considerations in providing its advice to Pharmac. The Court held that because the board was required to perform its functions "within the amount of funding provided," PTAC, as well as its subcommittees, could lawfully give and receive advice on both the benefits of drugs and their associated costs.[108] This attempt to restrict PTAC to considering the efficacy and safety of medicines only and to exclude it from considering cost-effectiveness and affordability in formulating its advice to the board was fortunately rejected. Had the attempt succeeded, the effect would be to disconnect PTAC from the resource implications of its recommendations – an essential reality check in any prioritization model – and to skew PTAC's recommendations in favor of more expensive drugs.

However, the plaintiffs succeeded on their second argument that the decision was unlawful because of a failure to consult interested parties before reaching it. Pharmac contended that it was not obliged to consult at this stage, given a statutory requirement to consult only when it considered it "appropriate" to do so.[109] It did not reasonably consider it "appropriate" to consult before its decision, because the board's resolution of July 2006 was not a final decision to decline funding of the twelve-month regimen, but rather one step in a continuing process of assessment and a resolution not to list it "at this time." The later decision to fund the nine-week treatment, before which there was full consultation, was in fact also the decision to decline funding for the twelve-month treatment. The Court disagreed. Pharmac had taken two decisions: first, a stand-alone decision to decline funding for twelve months, and the second one to approve nine weeks' funding in April 2007. After the July 2006 meeting, the twelve months' funding application had been declined. All considerations thenceforth by Pharmac and its committees related to the nine weeks' funding proposal.

---

charged with managing the process, that it did not have to be a judicial process, and the administrative process it established was lawful; *see Walsh v Pharmaceutical Management Agency* [2010] NZAR 101, para. 218–256 (HC) (N.Z.).

[107] *Id.* at Para. 215.

[108] *Id.* at Para. 160–161.

[109] *See* The New Zealand Public Health and Disability Act 2000, Sec. 49 (N.Z.).

Pharmac then argued that it was not required to consult before the first decision, relying on a "standard practice [not] to consult on past decisions that were recommending a decline."[110] The Court disagreed. Pharmac did not have unlimited freedom to decide when to consult as it felt inclined. While it was not obliged to consult on every decision to decline funding, neither could it have a standard practice or policy not to do so. That was not a proper exercise of discretion. It does indeed seem indefensible for Pharmac to have a blanket practice not to consult on decisions declining funding, given the potentially serious adverse effect on people who might benefit from a medicine that Pharmac decides not to fund. Thus, after *Walsh*, Pharmac is legally required to undertake consultation on proposals to decline to list a pharmaceutical, "where there is a known wide and continuing public interest by groups, organisations or individuals likely to be considerably affected by a decision."[111] It had a duty to consult on this decision to decline, which it knew was a significant, sensitive, and high-profile issue that would clearly affect groups and patients.

Pharmac's failure to consult before the first decision was not "cured" by extensive consultation before the second decision to fund the nine-week treatment. The second decision was effectively a choice between nine weeks' funding or no funding at all, rather than a reopening and genuine reconsideration of the proposal for twelve months' funding, as to which there was no chance of Pharmac's decision being revisited.[112] The Court set aside the decision not to fund the twelve-month treatment and ordered Pharmac to consult on and determine it afresh. It acknowledged that Pharmac could reach the exactly same decision after consultation, but it had to approach the consultation with an open mind. The decision is legally unremarkable. It illustrates the well-recognized phenomenon that reviewing courts are much more comfortable upholding legal challenges based on procedural errors, such as failure to consult and breach of fairness, than grounds relevant to the merits, such as the irrationality of a decision.[113]

Pharmac then consulted on a proposal to decline the funding of the twelve-month treatment, ending in early June 2008, with more than 300 submissions received. Once again, a majority considered that it should fund the twelve-month regimen in preference to the nine-week regimen. In August 2008, the board announced its decision to reaffirm its earlier decision to decline funding for the twelve-month

---

[110] *Walsh v Pharmaceutical Management Agency* [2010] NZAR 101, para. 183 (HC) (N.Z.).

[111] *Id.* at Para. 189.

[112] *Id.* at Para. 201.

[113] *See* Keith Syrett, *Health Technology Appraisal and the Courts*, 6 HEALTH ECON. POL'Y & L. 469, 479–80, (2011). The traditional reticence to uphold irrationality arguments may well be changing, however, as courts, especially in the United Kingdom, are less deferential and more ready to take a more critical, "high intensity" approach to judicial review; *see* NEWDICK, *supra* note 98, at 100–107, 128.

regimen and affirmed funding for the nine-week concurrent regimen.[114] A similar public furor followed.[115]

Pharmac may have won the battle, but it was ultimately to lose the war. By this time, as a result of patient lobbying, a media portrayal generally sympathetic to the patients, and the high-profile litigation, the issue had become highly politicized. New Zealand was in the midst of a national election campaign, in which Herceptin had become a prominent issue.[116] The National opposition, in a populist move to appeal to voters' sympathies, particularly those of middle-class women, promised that it would fund the twelve-month regimen if it won the election later in the year.[117] On being elected to government in November 2008, one of its first acts was to deliver on its promise to put in place funding for the twelve-month treatment regimen.[118] Funding was provided directly from the health budget generally via a separate scheme, rather than out of Pharmac's budget,[119] because of advice that the government was legally unable to direct Pharmac to approve a specific funding application.[120] Although this sidestepped Pharmac, the special funding arrangement at least forced the government to appropriate funding for its own promise, rather than requiring Pharmac to disinvest or exceed its budget. The effect was to expand the budget for prescription medicines, but at the expense of a diversion of resources from spending on other health services such as elective surgery or primary care.

Throughout the decision-making process Pharmac was kept under sustained pressure. Breast cancer patients formed themselves into a well-organized and effective

[114] See Notification of a Decision Regarding The Funding of 12 Months Treatments with Trastuzumab (Herceptin) for Her2-Posive Early Breast Cancer, PHARMAC, 2 (Aug. 7, 2008), *available at* http://www.pharmac.govt.nz/2008/08/07/Notification%20Letter%20August%202008.pdf.

[115] BCAC called the decision "inhumane"; see Craig Borley, *Women's Groups Split on Herceptin Decision*, N.Z. HERALD (August 8, 2008), *available at* http://www.nzherald.co.nz/nz/news/article.cfm?c_id=1&objectid=10525897; Editorial, *Pharmac Drug Decision Is a Pill That Must Be Swallowed*, N.Z. HERALD, 10 (Aug. 10, 2008), *available at* http://www.nzherald.co.nz/opinion/news/article.cfm?c_id=466&objectid=10526182.

[116] *Herceptin 'Now an Election issue'*, STUFF.CO.NZ (Aug. 8, 2008), *available at* http://www.stuff.co.nz/national/herceptin-debate/569826/Herceptin-now-an-election-issue.

[117] Martin Johnson, *National Would Fund Year of Herceptin*, N.Z. HERALD, July 31, 2008. The policy was fronted by the prime ministerial aspirant as well as its Associate Health spokeswoman, Dr. Jackie Blue.

[118] Tony Ryall, *12-Month Herceptin Treatment Now Available*, SCOOP HEALTH INDEPENDENT NEWS (December 10, 2008), *available at* http://www.scoop.co.nz/stories/PA0812/S00083.htm. Pharmac issued a statement stating that it fully respected the democratic process that led to the government's decision to fund the twelve-month treatment; *see* Maggie Tait, *Govt Dodges Pharmac to Fund Full Herceptin Courses*, N.Z. HERALD (Dec. 10, 2008), *available at* http://www.nzherald.co.nz/nz/news/article.cfm?c_id=1&objectid=10547373.

[119] *See* Maggie Tait, *id.* Pharmac continued to administer and fund the nine-week regimen, so that women were provided with a choice of funded treatment regimens.

[120] *See* interview with Matthew Brougham, CEO, PHARMAC, in Wellington, N.Z. (Jun 12, 2009).

lobby group, BCAC.[121] Bald-headed, pink-clad, and calling themselves Herceptin Heroines, patients made themselves highly visible publicly in parliament, in street parades,[122] and on national television describing selling or mortgaging their homes, going into debt, and organizing fund-raising activities to fund private treatment at a cost of, on average, $110,000 a year.[123] There were three petitions to parliament, a select committee report, and a complaint to the Human Rights Commission. Opposition MPs, one a breast cancer physician,[124] campaigned for funding of the longer treatment regimen and criticized Pharmac's decision publicly. The issue split women's groups.[125] There was a powerful and uncritical media campaign, much of which focusing on pushing the benefits of the medicine,[126] sometimes in misleading terms.[127] As elsewhere, the dominant narrative was of women being denied access to a potentially life-saving "wonder drug"[128] by a heartless, bureaucratic agency because of cost.[129] Positive decisions to fund the twelve-month treatment by public agencies

[121] Formed in 2004, BCAC is an umbrella lobby group representing breast cancer survivors and (later) some nineteen breast cancer organizations. Its chairwoman, Libby Burgess, is an articulate and experienced scientist and breast cancer survivor, and spearheaded the campaign on its behalf.

[122] Martin Johnson, *Herceptin Campaigners Protest in Aotea Square*, N.Z. HERALD, July 31, 2007; Martin Johnson, *"Funeral March" Protest against Herceptin Ruling*, N.Z. HERALD, July 31, 2006; NZPA, *"Biking for Boobs" Delivers Breast Cancer Drug Message*, N.Z. HERALD, March 13, 2008; Sophie Hazelhurst, *Crowd of Pink-Clad Bikies Rolls into Parliament*, N.Z. HERALD, March 12, 2008.

[123] Deborah Coddington, *Instead of Spending $150,000 on a House, I'll Spend It on My Life*, N.Z. HERALD, Feb. 19, 2006; *Treatment Cost Stuns Herceptin Patient*, THE DOMINION POST, Sept. 10, 2007.

[124] Opposition MP, associate spokeswoman for health and former breast physician Jackie Blue spearheaded National's campaign in support of the patients to extend funding to its use in early breast cancer. Blue tabled the petition in parliament.

[125] BCAC campaigned strenuously for public funding for the longer-duration treatment. Two other women's groups broke ranks to publicly support Pharmac's decision to fund a shorter course of treatment, and were attacked by BCAC for betraying women; see Craig Borley, *Women's Groups Split on Herceptin Decision*, N.Z. HERALD, Aug. 8, 2008; Editorial: *Brave Voices Deserve to Be Heeded*, N.Z. HERALD, Aug. 6, 2006.

[126] The medicine was consistently described in positive and uncritical terms, with few media articles mentioning potential adverse side effects. See, e.g., *Young Mother with Cancer Begs for a Chance to Live*, N.Z. HERALD, Feb. 9, 2006 ("life-saving wonder drug," "huge breakthrough"); Rebecca Walsh, *Cancer Drug to Cost $104,000*, N.Z. HERALD, October 17, 2005 ("a monumental aid in the fight against an aggressive form of breast cancer"). Coverage seldom cited the more modest estimated absolute risk reduction (approximately 8%), more often quoting the much more impressive-sounding relative risk reduction figure of around 50%.

[127] Pharmac's complaint to the Broadcasting Standards Authority about a *60 Minutes* item on TV3 on October 16, 2006, which examined the differences in early HER-2 positive breast cancer treatment in Australia and New Zealand, asking why Herceptin was publicly funded in Australia but not in New Zealand, was upheld as amounting to a "serious departure from broadcasting standards" as unbalanced and misleading. See Broadcasting Standards Authority, *Pharmac v. CanWest TV Works Ltd*, Decision No. 2006–127, Sept. 11, 2007.

[128] The drug was promoted internationally as an exciting and important "wonder drug," a "magic bullet," and a "must have" medicine in the fight against this aggressive form of breast cancer; see Sarah Boseley, *The Selling of a Wonder Drug*, THE GUARDIAN, March 29, 2006; and Lisa Hitchen, *Primary Care Trusts Must "Challenge the Fiction of the Wonder Drug"*, 337 BMJ 197 (2008).

[129] See, e.g., Deborah Coddington, *Drug "Madness" Puts Lives at Risk*, N.Z. HERALD, March 18, 2006.

in Britain and Australia were highlighted.[130] There was little consideration of the opportunity costs of funding the drug.[131] In this climate, both Pharmac's decisions were widely greeted with anger and dismay.

The Herceptin funding case is a striking example of the triumph of the Rule of Rescue – an approach that accords significant priority to potentially life-saving interventions – to which the patients appealed. They made forceful individualistic claims and emphasized the urgent need of patients facing an increased risk of premature death from a life-threatening condition. This contrasts with the scientific rationality of the agency, which placed overriding priority on the careful stewardship of scarce resources and based its decision on utilitarian considerations of maximizing the benefit from a finite resource. It also attached importance to promoting the public good of advancing scientific knowledge about the efficacy and safety of unproven therapies through randomized clinical trials. Both ethical perspectives – Pharmac's community-based approach and the patients' individualistic focus – are defensible as different, but entirely respectable, theories of distributive justice.

The government's overruling of Pharmac's decision raises concerns about undermining of Pharmac and compromise of its independence. Politically dictated access created a high-profile precedent, inevitably raising public expectations that disappointed patients could circumvent Pharmac by approaching government, which might be prepared to intervene routinely to bypass Pharmac's processes.[132] The Herceptin case might be tolerable as a relatively rare case of value-laden politics trumping "neutral science" on the basis of the Rule of Rescue; political intervention to override Pharmac's funding decisions has occurred once before in strikingly similar circumstances.[133] After all, cost-effectiveness is only one decision criterion, and is not determinative of allocation decisions. However, if the Herceptin case signaled a more permanent move toward greater politicization, there is a real danger of the process of funding medicines becoming arbitrary and unfair, and of funding decisions deteriorating into a competition in which scarce resources are won by "whoever screams the loudest."[134] Those with a stigma attached to their disease, or

---

[130] Martin Johnson, *Cancer Drug Too Expensive*, N.Z. HERALD, July 29, 2006; Ben Hirschler, *UK Bows on Breast Cancer Drug*, N.Z. HERALD, June 11, 2006; Martin Johnson, *NZ Cancer Toll Worse Than Australia*, N.Z. HERALD, Jan. 8, 2008. *But see* NZPA, *Australia Having Second Thoughts Over Herceptin*, N.Z. HERALD, Aug. 4, 2006.

[131] *But see* Tapu Misa, *Putting Prices on Loved One's Lives*, N.Z. HERALD, Aug. 18, 2008.

[132] *Funding of Cancer Drug 'Bad' Precedent*, THE PRESS (Dec. 11, 2008), *available at* http://www.pressbrowser.com/days/nz/20081210/topnews/161637.htm.

[133] The case also involved a new government keeping a promise made in opposition to specific groups to fund a medicine in the context of a general election campaign. In December 1999, the incoming minister of health, Annette King, directed Pharmac to fund interferon beta for multiple sclerosis, after a pledge by the Labour party to fund it as part of its successful 1999 general election campaign; *see* Jacqueline Cumming, Nicolas Mays & Jacob Daubé, *How New Zealand Has Contained Expenditure on Drugs*, 340 BMJ 1224 (2010).

[134] This memorable phrase was used by the Chief Executive of Pharmac in the aftermath of the Herceptin case; *see Opposition Politicians Criticise Herceptin Decision*, N.Z. HERALD (Aug. 8, 2008), *available at* http://www.nzherald.co.nz/pharmac/news/article.cfm?o_id=332&objectid=10525972.

without the means or willingness to thrust themselves into the media to attract public sympathy, could well miss out in such a process. After the Herceptin case, the government was warned about the importance of maintaining Pharmac's independence and the strong undesirability of interfering in its funding decisions.[135] It appears to have heeded the warning to date, preferring to increase Pharmac's budget rather than to intervene in its processes. However, it is surely only a matter of time before another "must have" medicine becomes available and, given the inevitability of patient disappointment and challenge in this contentious field, Pharmac's processes and allocative choices again become subject to challenge.[136]

1.4 CONCLUDING REMARKS

Because of its small number of cases, the New Zealand experience does not allow for any definitive conclusions in respect of the key theme of this collection. It is unclear whether litigating health care rights in this jurisdiction has been potentially redistributive, in terms of being associated with ensuring greater equality in access to health care and to health itself by those with lower health status and therefore most in need health care – what the collection's editors term a "progressive" outcome. Nor is it clear whether the cases have served to exacerbate inequality, for example, by creating channels that allow "queue jumping" for those with better access to lawyers and courts – a "regressive" outcome. Nonetheless, one can make some observations about the distributional effects of the particular cases.

There is no evidence from the New Zealand experience that litigation has benefited the health or improved access to health care of the most vulnerable. In *Shortland*, the patient was Māori, elderly, poor, and from a rural area. The circumstances could not have been more dramatic, in that the highly publicized litigation concerned life-prolonging treatment and was decided as the patient was close to death. The challenge was unsuccessful; indeed, the Court disavowed that the case concerned allocation of health care in the context of scarce resources at all. The second case, *Walsh*, might be characterized as of the second, "regressive" kind. The plaintiffs brought a test case. They were highly committed and visible advocates for their cause. They were apparently well-resourced, represented by leading counsel,

---

[135] *See* OECD, OECD ECONOMIC SURVEYS, *supra* note 8, at 130; MCCORMACK et al., *supra* note 12, at 52.

[136] For example, in June 2011, PHARMAC was again the subject of patient and lobby group criticism and media pressure in relation to its refusal to fund some high-cost medications for the treatment of some rare metabolic lysosomal disorders; *see* Interview with Dr Peter Moodie, PHARMAC Medical Director, in Radio New Zealand: Nine to Noon (June 7, 2011), *available at* http://www.radionz.co.nz/national/programmes/ninetonoon/audio/2490732/pharmac-funding-decisions. In 2013 Pharmac's public consultation over its proposal to decline public funding for Eculizumab (Soliris), the world's most expensive drug, for the treatment of paroxysmal nocturnal haemoglobinuria generated considerable media attention and patient pressure, which included the possibility of legal challenge; *see* Proposal to decline a Funding Application for Eculizumab, PHARMAC (May 21, 2013), *available at* http://www.pharmac.health.nz/ckeditor_assets/attachments/362/consultation-2013-05-21-eculizumab.pdf.

and backed by a highly organized, effective lobby group. Litigation was used as a part of an overall strategy, which included political and media pressure, and was ultimately successful in achieving access to an expensive medicine, even though the Court did not itself grant that access. The work of the Herceptin Heroines paid off and their victory was acclaimed.[137] While the outcome in effect added considerably to spending on pharmaceuticals, it diverted spending from other health services with no consideration of the opportunity costs of doing so, and at the risk of undermining the established process and the legitimacy of the public agency created to make these allocative choices. Norman Daniels and James Sabin's description of an American episode relating to disputes over insurers' coverage of ABMT for advanced breast cancer in the 1990s could just as easily have been written in relation to the Herceptin funding issue in New Zealand nearly two decades later:[138]

> [T]he social climate – including well-organised women's groups, a crusading media, committed practitioners, suspicious courts, and opportunistic legislators – clearly made the standard "technology assessment" approach to holding the line against coverage for last chance . . . therapies untenable.

---

[137] Chris Walsh, the named plaintiff in *Walsh v Phamac*, was made an Officer of the New Zealand Order of Merit in the 2010 New Year's Honours List.

[138] *See* Norman Daniels & James Sabin, SETTING LIMITS FAIRLY: LEARNING TO SHARE RESOURCES FOR HEALTH, 71 (2nd ed., 2008).

2

The Right to Health in Sweden

*Anna-Sara Lind**

INTRODUCTION

With a population of nine million inhabitants, Sweden is the largest of the five Nordic countries. The population is generally healthy and has high life expectancy, but is aging rapidly. Total Swedish health care spending is about 10 percent of the gross domestic product (spending per capita US$3,758 in 2010).[1] The public health care sector is founded on the principle of good health care to everyone on equal conditions. However, as I discuss further throughout this chapter, this principle is under significant challenge in today's Sweden.

The private health care sector has traditionally been quite small in Sweden, but has grown considerably during the past decade. It has done so in two ways. First, *within* the publicly funded system there are many private health care providers, especially in primary care. The twenty-one county councils (which have primary responsibility for the delivery of public health care) spend part of their budget on services provided by private providers. For example, in some county councils more than half of the providers in primary care are private. The majority of the health care provided is financed by taxes, even though the percentage of private health care providers has grown over the last years. The increased presence of private health care providers has triggered debates over the need to legislate against profit-making in health care. Today, there is no such legislation. Second, in addition to the growing role for private delivery within the public system and the concerns raised by this, there is also a growing share of completely privately funded health care. Private

* The author wishes to thank Elisabeth Rynning, former Professor of Medical Law at the Faculty of Law, Uppsala University and LL.M. Febe Westberg, former research assistant in Medical Law at the Faculty of Law, Uppsala University, for valuable advice and comments on this article.

[1] OECD Health Data 2012, http://www.oecd.org/els/health-systems/oecdhealthdata2012.htm (last visited March 13, 2013).

health insurance still covers less than 5 percent of the population, but has been increasing in the past few years. The main motivation for those seeking privately financed care is to avoid long waiting times, a long-standing problem in the public system.

The Swedish Constitution states that public institutions shall *promote good conditions for health* (Instrument of Government, Chapter 1, Section 2). These "good conditions" are understood to include access to health care as well as other aspects of public health promotion, such as safe environment and good living conditions.[2] In contrast to other Nordic countries, Sweden still does not have any specific legislation on the status and rights of patients. In fact, the UN Special Rapporteur on the Right to Health has expressed his surprise at finding that explicit reference to the right to health remains absent from Sweden's domestic health policies. Swedish health legislation is based on stipulating duties for health care providers and professionals, and with few exceptions does not offer individuals any justiciable rights. The legislation is characterized as framework regulation, allowing regional and local governments considerable freedom in how they organize and prioritize health services. Even though the principle of equality is strongly emphasized in the preparatory works and also expressed directly in the Health and Medical Services Act (HMSA),[3] inequalities in health services provided by different regions constitute a problem (see the further discussion in Subsection 2.2.2). Moreover, there are a number of vulnerable patient groups who are not fully included in the public system or protected by the principle of equality in health care, such as asylum seekers and irregular immigrants.[4] Although not specifically included in the constitution, rights to health care have acquired a semi-constitutional status in Sweden by a backdoor route. As discussed later in Sections 3.2 and 3.4, these rights have been incorporated into law as a result of a commitment to uphold the European convention on human rights and fundamental freedoms.

---

[2] *See* the preparatory works: Proposition [Prop.] 2001/2002:72 Ändringar i regeringsformen – samarbetet i EU m.m. [Changes in the Instrument of Government – The Cooperation in the EU] [government bill] 49 (Swed.); Statens Offentliga Utredningar [SOU] 2001:19 Vissa grundlagsfrågor [Some Constitutional Questions] [government report series] (Swed.); Statens Offentliga Utredningar [SOU] 2008:125 En reformerad grundlag [A Reformed Constitution] [government report series] 749 (Swed.).

[3] HÄLSO- OCH SJUKVÅRDSLAG [Health and Medical Services Act] (Svensk Författningssamling [SFS] 1982:763) (Swed.).

[4] In Statens Offentliga Utredningar [SOU] 2011:48 Vård efter behov och på lika villkor – en mänsklig rättighet [Care According to Needs and on Equal Terms – A Human Right] [government report series] (Swed.) it was proposed that asylum seekers and irregular immigrants should have access to medical care on the same conditions as Swedish citizens. A political agreement was then achieved stating that irregular immigrants will have access to medical care on the same conditions as asylum seekers, that is emergency care (*vård för tillstånd som inte kan anstå*). According to the agreement, children will also get access to preventive and dental care. The new rules were planned to be in force July 1, 2013. *See infra,* II2.1 & III4.

2.1 BASIC FEATURES OF SWEDISH HEALTH CARE

2.1.1 *Local self-governance as a point of departure*

The Nordic welfare state model is characterized by universal, residence-based social entitlements, with equal access to the highest standard, promoted by extensive public participation.[5] This is true also for the Swedish health care system, which is based on general, tax-funded coverage. Most of the responsibility for delivery of health care rests at the regional level in 21 county councils; however, certain services are the responsibility of the (smaller) 290 local municipal governments. Within the publicly funded system, patients thus have access to health care in the form of subsidized benefits-in-kind, for a small fee, with an annual high-cost protection limit. Prescription of pharmaceuticals falls under separate legislation, with a similar high-cost protection. For most adult Swedish patients, dental care is the most costly type of health services, also regulated separately but with more limited public subsidies.[6]

From a constitutional point of view, it is important to underline that the main constitutional Act, the Instrument of Government (IoG), is built on the principle that the people are sovereign and that the will of the people shall be expressed in every field of the public sphere.[7] Thus, all public power proceeds from the people. The classical horizontal separation of powers, where the power has been divided between institutions hierarchically at the same level (the legislative, the executive, and the judiciary) is not clearly present in the Swedish constitution. To realize the will of the people at every level of government and in all functions of the public, the IoG prescribes that the people's will is realized through representative elections to the parliament (when it concerns the state) and to municipalities and county councils (local self-government).[8] As we shall see, consequently there is no individual and justiciable right to health care in Sweden, and to understand the Swedish system, it is crucial to understand the ideological choices that have formed the Swedish welfare state. One of these choices is the use of local self-government to express the people's will.

---

[5] Mette Hartlev, *The raison d'être of Nordic Health Law*, in NORDIC HEALTH LAW IN A EUROPEAN CONTEXT – WELFARE STATE PERSPECTIVES ON PATIENTS' RIGHTS AND BIOMEDICINE, 29 (Elisabeth Rynning & Mette Hartlev eds., 2011).

[6] TANDVÅRDSLAG [DENTAL SERVICES ACT] (Svensk Författningssamling [SFS] 1985:125) (Swed.); Tandvårdsförordning [Dental Services Ordinance] (Svensk Författningssamling [SFS] 1998:1338) (Swed.); Lag om statligt tandvårdsstöd [National Dental Care Subsidy Act] (Svensk Författningssamling [SFS] 2008:145) (Swed.); Förordning om statligt tandvårdsstöd [National Dental Care Subsidy Ordinance] (Svensk Författningssamling [SFS] 2008:193) (Swed.).

[7] Regeringsformen [RF] [Constitution] 1:1 (Swed.).

[8] One could, however, argue that there is a vertical separation of powers guaranteed in the Constitution, for example, between the different levels of government. *See* Thomas Bull, *Självständighet och pluralism – om vertikal maktdelning i Sverige [Independence and Pluralism – About Vertical Separation of Powers in Sweden]*, in FESTSKRIFT TILL FREDRIK STERZEL, 107 (Lena Marcusson ed., 1999).

The Swedish health care system is based on universal coverage and it also aims at realizing the idea of nondiscrimination. In principle, for a small fee, everyone has access to health care in the county where they live.[9] Moreover, as underlined in the Discrimination Act,[10] this entitlement extends to the most vulnerable groups in society. However, as I discuss in Subsections 2.2.1 and 3.3.2, good intentions with regard to providing health care to everyone fade when it comes to providing access to some of the most vulnerable in society, specifically irregular immigrants and asylum seekers.

2.1.2 *A Focus on Patient Needs*

In the Swedish system there is no statement of a minimum level of health care or a prescribed "package" of certain minimum services. Instead, health care should be tailored to the particular medical need of the patient. Health and medical care is defined in Article 1 of the HMSA as actions to medically prevent, diagnose, and cure diseases and injuries. According to the law and established practice, treatments that do not match this criterion do not fall within the scope of the public obligation to provide health care. Thus, treatments such as in vitro fertilization and plastic surgeries *not diagnosed as medically necessary* do not fall within this scope.[11] A gray zone concerns treatment motivated from a religious point of view, such as circumcision. The latter is covered in some cases where the Act on the Circumcision of Boys is applicable.[12] A further issue relating to access is wait lists, which recently has been the subject of much public debate.

---

[9] These fees are decided by the counties, within the framework of an organization called Swedish Association of Local Authorities and Regions (in Swedish the organization is called Sveriges Kommuner och Landsting, SKL). The fee for an appointment with a primary care doctor varies between 100 SEK and 300 SEK (for the year 2013); *see* Sveriges Kommuner och Landsting, *Patientavgifter i öppen hälso- och sjukvård år 2013* [*Patient fees in outpatient health care in 2013*] (Jan. 1, 2013), *available at* http://www.skl.se/MediaBinaryLoader.axd?MediaArchive_FileID=b501d6b5–1513–4399-a537–0d9c47521725&FileName=patientavgifter+2013_2.pdf. When a patient has paid 1,100 SEK, the health care is free for the rest of the twelve-month period that starts at the first visit. *See* 26 & 26a §§ Hälso- och sjukvårdslag [Health and Medical Services Act] (Svensk författningssamling [SFS] 1982:763) (Swed.); *see also* 5 § Lag om läkemedelsförmåner [Act on Pharmaceutical Benefits] (Svensk Författningssamling [SFS] 2002:160) (Swed.). Pharmaceutical products are regulated in Läkemedelslag [Act on Pharmaceutical Products] (Svensk Författningssamling [SFS] 1992:859) (Swed.), Läkemedelsförordning [Ordinance on Pharmaceutical Products] (Svensk Författningssamling [SFS] 2006:272) (Swed.) and other statutes. According to the Act on Pharmaceutical benefits, it is the Dental and Pharmaceutical Benefits Agency who decides if a pharmaceutical product is to be considered as a benefit and thus covered by the amount of 1,100 SEK; *see* Act on Pharmaceutical Benefits, 7–20 §§. The decision from the Agency can be appealed to the administrative court (Act on Pharmaceutical Benefits, 26 §).

[10] Diskrimineringslag [Discrimination Act] (Svensk Författningssamling [SFS] 2008:567) (Swed.).

[11] However, denied treatment in these cases can be appealed to the NBHW.

[12] Lag om omskärelse av pojkar [Act on Circumcision of Boys] (Svensk författningssamling [SFS] 2001:499) (Swed.); Förordning om omskärelse av pojkar [Ordinance on Circumcision of Boys] (Svensk Författningssamling [SFS] 2009:1240) (Swed.).

2.1.3 *A Shared Responsibility for Health Care Rights*

The responsibility for health and medical services is shared between the state, the counties, and municipalities. The HMSA, a piece of framework legislation, lays out the responsibilities of counties and municipalities, providing a significant degree of latitude to these actors on how to organize health and medical care delivery. The state has the overall responsibility for the formulation of the political choices concerning health care and it is the Ministry of Health and Social Affairs that, together with state agencies, puts forward new legislation as needed, monitors how counties and municipalities deal with issues of health care, and negotiates with the counties and municipalities on how to realize different health care goals. The state transfers funds to both the municipalities and the counties, as required by the HSMA.[13] The major part of health care funding at the regional and local level comes from taxes.

The most important state agencies (all of which are at arm's length from government) implicated in controlling the delivery of health care are the National Board of Health and Welfare, NBHW (Socialstyrelsen),[14] the Medical Responsibility Board, MRB (Hälso-och sjukvårdens ansvarsnämnd), and since June 2013, the Health and Social Care Inspectorate, HSCI.[15] The NBHW is responsible for enacting national guidelines in relation to public and private care providers and developing health care through standard setting procedures. In January 2011, the task of receiving complaints from patients was transferred to the NBHW from the MRB. Today, the MRB examines particular complaints on the part of the NBHW, the Parliamentary Ombudsmen, and the Chancellor of Justice, and does not direct complaints from patients. The MRB is accordingly responsible for overseeing the licensing and regulation of health and medical care staff. The newest of these agencies, the Health and Social Care Inspectorate, has taken over the responsibility of supervising the realization of health and medical care from the NBHW.

The public health care sector is also supervised by the Parliamentary Ombudsmen (Justitieombudsmannen, JO).[16] Recently (2012), the Swedish Agency for Health and

---

[13] In 2011, 70% of the county councils' income came from taxes and 18% from the state. *See* the report from the Swedish Association of Local Authorities and Regions (Sveriges Kommuner och Landsting, SKL): SVERIGES KOMMUNER OCH LANDSTING, STATISTIK OM HÄLSA- OCH SJUKVÅRD SAMT REGIONAL UTVECKLING 2011 [STATISTICS ON HEALTH AND HOSPITAL CARE AND ON REGIONAL DEVELOPMENT 2011] 10, *available at* http://webbutik.skl.se/bilder/artiklar/pdf/7164-695-8.pdf?issuusl=ignore.

[14] The tasks of the NBHW are many and cover a vast area. In addition to what was mentioned earlier in the chapter, the National NBHW also enacts agency ordinances that health care providers should respect. Agency ordinances are a result of the delegation of powers stated in REGERINGSFORMEN [RF] [CONSTITUTION] Chap. 8 (Swed.), according to which the government has the means to delegate to an agency the power to decide and enact certain rules.

[15] Proposition [Prop.] 2012/13:20 Inspektionen för vård och omsorg – en ny tillsynsmyndighet för hälso-och sjukvård och socialtjänst [Inspectorate for Health and Social Care – A New Supervisory Agency for Health and Medical Care and Social Services] [government bill] (Swed.).

[16] Between July 1, 2010 to June 30, 2011, 254 cases concerning medical care were brought to the attention of the Parliamentary Ombudsmen. Eighty-four of these were examined and in 24 cases, the Ombudsmen

Care Services Analysis[17] was created and its main task is to follow up and analyze, from a patient, user, and citizen perspective, activities and conditions in health and medical care and in dental care. This new actor's main mission is to assist the Swedish government with reviews and reports analyzing how health and care services work and the effectiveness of different governmental activities in the field of health care. Accordingly, the agency gives advice to the government and makes recommendations on how the state's institutions could be more effective in the area of health.

2.2 THE LEGAL STRUCTURE OF THE RIGHT TO HEALTH CARE AND QUESTIONS OF ACCESS TO HEALTH

2.2.1 *Constitutional Perspectives*

In the Swedish Constitution, the Instrument of Government (IoG), Chapter 1 Section 2, the right to health is stated as a goal that public institutions should promote:

> The personal, economic and cultural welfare of the private person shall be fundamental aims of public activity. In particular, it shall be incumbent upon the public institutions to secure employment, housing and education, and to promote social care and social security and good conditions for health.[18]

The constitution thus does not contain an individual, justiciable right to health. To illustrate why this is the case, we need to look more closely at the development of constitutionally granted rights in Sweden. The present IoG came into force in 1975 and was the culmination of a long transformation of constitutional structures that had started with the affirmation of parliamentary sovereignty in the beginning of the 1920s. Through a series of reforms in the 1950s and 1960s, the parliament (Riksdag) was explicitly granted the position of supreme power, as the position of the king had for decades been diminished. This development concluded with the enactment of the present IoG – a constitutional law that was intended to lay down the most important features of how public power should be organized – and with the increased power given to elected politicians. During the twentieth century, judicial interpretation of the constitution did not played a crucial role, and from the 1920s

---

pronounced criticism; *see* JO:s ämbetsberättelse 2011/12 [The Swedish Parliamentary Ombudsmen Report for the period July 1, 2010 to June 30, 2011], *available at* http://www.jo.se/Global/%c3% 84mbetsber%c3%a4ttelser/2011–12.pdf (summary in English at the end of the report, at 709).

[17] Förordning med instruktion för Myndigheten för vårdanalys [Ordinance with Instruction for the Agency for Health and Care Services Analysis] (Svensk Författningssamling [SFS] 2010:1385) (Swed.).

[18] Health was introduced in REGERINGSFORMEN [RF] [CONSTITUTION] 1:2 (Swed.) in 2002. *See* Proposition [Prop.] 2001/2002:72 Ändringar i Regeringsformen – Samarbetet i EU m.m. [Changes in the Instrument of Government – The Cooperation in the EU] [government bill] 23–26 (Swed.); ANNA-SARA LIND, SOCIALA RÄTTIGHETER I FÖRÄNDRING, [SOCIAL RIGHTS UNDERGOING CHANGES] 52–55 (2009).

and on, most of the political divergences were handled through dialogue and political compromises. This period of constitutional stability was likely a result of the dominance of the Social Democratic Party, who through a series of majority governments had great scope to steer societal development. The imperative was to develop and affirm the welfare state through different political actors using legislative measures. Indeed, the dominant political party expressed on several occasions concerns about the impact of justicializing the constitution in terms of individual rights. The Social Democratic Party feared that such rights could threaten the strong expansion of the welfare state and leave too much power to the courts. This stance may also have reflected a general social consensus given that no political party had as part of its political platform the judicialization of health or social rights, or promised to guarantee a certain minimum level or core of rights. The result is that in the Swedish constitution there are social rights formulated as goals, to be pursued through the democratic process as opposed to enforced by the judiciary. That being said, over the last few decades, individual and justiciable social rights have been granted in various pieces of legislation, such as the right to social and medical assistance that falls within the scope of the Social Care Act, Chapter 4.[19] These rights can be subject to appeal to the administrative courts and are also formulated as individual rights. But the constitutional protection is still very weak.

Sweden is a dualist country,[20] and the way international agreements concluded by Sweden become part of its legal order differs from the monistic approach. This means that for the international rules to become legally binding within the national legal order, the parliament has to implement them by enacting a law that incorporates or transforms the international agreement.[21] It is only after this formal Act of Parliament that courts and other authorities are obliged to apply the rules. If the international rules are not made part of the national legal order, they can only be used as a source of interpretation by the courts and the authorities. As a consequence, the vast majority of international agreements Sweden has ratified are not enforceable by courts and do not guarantee individual rights. However, as a source of interpretation and supportive tool in the process of enacting legislation, international rules are currently mentioned and referred to much more frequently.

Sweden is a member of the Council of Europe and has ratified the European Convention on Human Rights and Fundamental freedoms (ECHR) and the Revised European Social Charter (ESC). Both these conventions are important in securing and defining the content of the right to health. The ECHR has a special status in the

---

[19] SOCIALTJÄNSTLAG [SOCIAL CARE ACT] (Svensk författningssamling [SFS] 2001:453) (Swed.).

[20] This was expressed by the two Supreme Court decisions in the beginning of the 1970s. *See* Nytt Juridiskt Arkiv [NJA] [Supreme Court] 1973–10–20 p. 423 (Swed.); Regeringsrättens årsbok [RÅ] [Supreme Administrative Court] 1974–06–06 ref 61 (Swed.).

[21] For the constitutional rules concerning concluding international agreements, compare with REGERINGSFORMEN [RF] [CONSTITUTION] chap. 10 (Swed.). There is no specific statement in the Instrument of Government that Sweden is a dualist legal order.

Swedish legal order. Sweden ratified the ECHR at the beginning of the 1950s and decided to incorporate the convention in the 1990s after being much criticized by the European Court of Human Rights.[22] Consequently, the Riksdag passed legislation in 1994 specifically incorporating the ECHR.[23] But the ECHR also has a special semi-constitutional status; since 1995 it is stated in the Instrument of Government that no legislation shall be promulgated that does not respect the ECHR (including the case law of the European Court of Human Rights).[24] As a consequence, the scope of the Convention rights defined by the European Court must be respected by all public institutions at all levels (state, regional, and local). During the last decade, Swedish courts have begun applying the Convention in their decision making.[25]

2.2.2 *The Content of the Right to Health in Swedish Statutes*

2.2.2.1 The Health and Medical Services Act (HMSA)

In Sweden, the right to health care is regulated in statutes and it is the HMSA that most clearly articulates their content and scope. The HMSA is a goal-oriented framework legislation, which states that its goal is to provide good health and care on equal terms for the entire population (Section 2), and sets out that need will determine priority in accessing health care services. Dignity, need, and solidarity are the governing principles of the Act, which requires that for everyone, care shall be provided with respect for the equal dignity of all human beings and for the

---

[22] Sweden has signed, but not yet ratified, the Convention on Biomedicine and Human Rights of the Council of Europe. In the last few years, the Swedish government has on several occasions stated that the convention ought to be ratified by Sweden, but noted that their reluctance primarily lies with rules concerning people who are incapable of consenting to treatment (Convention on Human Rights and Biomedicine, April 4, 1997, 36 I.L.M. 817, art. 6). The Biomedicine Convention does not include any specific remedies (*cf.*, *id.* at art. 23, 25). However, it is important to remember that the Convention is used as a source of interpretation by the European Court of Human Rights even if the respondent state has not ratified the convention. *See* Glass v. the United Kingdom, App. No. 61827/00, Judgment of 9 March 2004, 2004-II, Eur. Ct. H.R.; Vo v. France, App. No. 59324/00, Judgment of 8 July 2004, A318-B Eur. Ct. H.R. (2004); Evans v. the United Kingdom, App. No. 6339/05, Judgment of 10 April 2007, 2007-I, Eur. Ct. H.R. A full analysis of how the Swedish legislation today gives full protection for the rights stated in the Biomedicine Convention has not yet been done.

[23] The Convention has the status of law (act). *See* Införlivandelagen [Implementation Act] (Svensk författningssamling [SFS] 1994:1219) (Swed.); Proposition [Prop.] 1993/1994:117 Inkorporering av Europakonventionen och andra fri- och rättighetsfrågor [Implementation of the European Convention and Other Questions Regarding Freedoms and Rights] [government bill] 29–30 (Swed.).

[24] Regeringsformen [RF] [Constitution] 2:19 (Swed.).

[25] Anna-Sara Lind, *Folkrätten i den svenska konstitutionen* [*Public International Law in the Swedish Constitution*], in FOLKRÄTTEN I SVENSK RÄTT, 153 (Rebecca Stern & Inger Österdahl eds., 2012). The judgments from the European Court in the 1980s have led to numerous reforms of the Swedish legal order. One example is the right to a fair trial (Convention for the Protection of Human Rights and Fundamental Freedoms, Nov. 4, 1950, 213 U.N.T.S. 222. Art. 6), which has changed the structure of complaints within Administrative Law and even changed the Instrument of Government (REGERINGSFORMEN [RF] [CONSTITUTION] (Swed.)) in the beginning of 2011.

dignity of the individual (Section 2, Para. 2).[26] The definition of health and medical services refers to measures for the medical prevention, investigation, and treatment of disease and injury, including ambulance services, and how to handle deceased persons (Section 1).[27] In practice, economic aspects are crucial to the realization of the right to health, as several constitutional "actors" (the state, the counties, and the municipalities) are responsible for financing and for realizing good health care for everyone. These economic realities also require that priorities are set and choices made on what is to be considered most important.

The right to health care is recognized as a statutory right, inasmuch as the public sector has an *obligation* to provide health care. Recently, several reforms have been undertaken to strengthen access to health care. However, whereas other Nordic countries have enacted Patients' Rights legislation, this has not yet occurred in Sweden.[28] The character of the legislation to focus on duties and obligations is, however, more strongly emphasized. For example, the duties of health care personnel are strongly emphasized in the Patient Safety Act, Chapter 6, and so are the duties of the health care providers.

Even though the goal of the HMSA is clear – to provide health care to everyone on equal terms – there are nevertheless certain groups of patients that have difficulties in accessing health care. This is attributable to lack of knowledge and lack of financial means; moreover, in the case of irregular immigrants to date, there is also difficulty associated with a lack of a formal legal status. Asylum seekers' and irregular

---

[26] Proposition [Prop.] 1996/1997:60 Prioriteringar inom hälso- och sjukvården [Priorities in Health and Hospital Care] [government bill] 31–35 (Swed.).

[27] The responsibility to deceased persons was added to the HMSA in 1992, since it is always a medical doctor who should certify the death of a person; *see* Proposition [Prop.] 1991/1992:152 Om Hälso- och sjukvårdens ansvar vid dödsfall m.m. [The Responsibility of Health Care and Hospital Care Regarding Death] [government bill] (Swed.). Additionally, a number of people do die at health care institutions, and the government wanted to clarify the responsibility of the health care institutions. Dental care is not covered by the HMSA, but in specific statutes; *supra* note 4. Nevertheless, the aim of the rules regarding dental care is similar to the rules on health care in the HMSA, that is, good dental health for all and on equal terms for the whole population. The counties have the main responsibility for reaching this goal. Dental care is free for children and adolescents, but adults have to pay a cost that is decided by the county board. These fees are quite burdensome for many people as 60% of the total cost for dental care is paid by patient fees; *see* Statens Offentliga Utredningar [SOU] 2012:2 Framtidens högkostnadsskydd i vården [The Future Cost Protection of Care] [government report series] 25 (Swed.). *See also* Erik Grönqvist, *The Demand for Dental Care: Analyses of the Importance of Price and Income* (Swedish Social Security Agency, Working Papers in Social Insurance, no. 2012:1, 2012).

[28] In March 2011, a commission was appointed with the task of drafting such an act; terms of reference Dir. 2011:25 Stärkt ställning för patienten genom en ny patientlagstiftning [Stronger position of the patient through a new patients' act]. A first step toward a Swedish Patient Act was taken in the beginning of 2013 when the commission presented a first draft of this act; *see* Statens Offentliga Utredningar [SOU] 2013:2 Patientlag [Patient Act] [government report series] (Swed.). This draft focuses mostly on the patient's rights to information, participation, and second opinion. *See also* Elisabeth Rynning, *Still No Patients' Act in Sweden – Reasons and Implications, in* Nordic Health Law in a European Context – Welfare State Perspectives on Patients' Rights and Biomedicine, 122 (Elisabeth Rynning & Mette Hartlev eds., 2011).

immigrants (*sans papiers*) are especially vulnerable.[29] This has been criticized at the international level,[30] and the legislation concerning these persons' right and access to health care has been subject to evaluation by the government, which recently suggested a new Act giving irregular immigrants the same right to access to health care as asylum seekers.[31]

It is expressly stated in the HMSA that dental care is regulated separately, and the Dental Services Act requires each county to provide dental care for the persons that reside therein.[32]

2.2.2.2 Reforms Aimed at Strengthening Patients' Rights

2.2.2.2.1 THE CARE GUARANTEE In the Swedish context, the right to health care and hospital care is part of a legally recognized guarantee of care (*vårdgaranti*), which, interestingly, is not justiciable. This guarantee has been in place since the beginning of 2010 prescribed by Sections 3 g-h of the HMSA.[33] This guarantee is built on the same principles that were earlier part of the agreement between the state and the organization of municipalities and counties. According to the guarantee, the patient is entitled to have access to a primary care institution the same day as she tries to get hold of the institution and she has the right to meet a doctor within seven days. If there is a need for it, this doctor shall organize an appointment with a specialist within a guaranteed maximum of ninety days, and within another ninety days the

---

29 LAG OM HÄLSO- OCH SJUKVÅRD ÅT ASYLSÖKANDE M.FL. [ACT ON HEALTH AND HOSPITAL CARE FOR ASYLUM SEEKERS] (Svensk författningssamling [SFS] 2008:344) (Swed.); *See also* Press Release *Sveriges HIV/AIDS-vård och stödinsatser behöver förbättras radikalt* [*Sweden's Health Care for HIV and AIDS Needs to be Radically Improved*] (on Euro HIV Index), HEALTH CONSUMER POWERHOUSE (Oct. 13, 2009), *available at* http://www.healthpowerhouse.com/images/stories/ehivi_2009_press_release_sweden.pdf.

30 Report of the Special Rapporteur on the Right of Everyone to the Enjoyment of the Highest Attainable Standard of Physical and Mental Health, Paul Hunt Addendum Mission to Sweden, United Nations A/HRC/4/28/Add. 2, 28 February 2007, *available at* http://daccess-dds-ny.un.org/doc/UNDOC/GEN/G07/111/82/PDF/G0711182.pdf?OpenElement.

31 Terms of reference Dir. 2010:7 Hälso- och sjukvård åt asylsökande, personer som håller sig undan verkställighet av ett beslut om avvisning eller utvisning samt personer som befinner sig i Sverige utan att ha ansökt om nödvändiga tillstånd för att vistas i Landet [Health Care and Hospital Care for People in Sweden Without Having Permissions to be in Sweden]; Statens Offentliga Utredningar [SOU] 2011:48 Vård efter behov och på lika villkor – en mänsklig rättighet [Care According to Needs and on Equal Terms – A Human Right] [government report series] (Swed.). As well, Ministry Report, Ds 2012:36 Hälso- och sjukvård till personer som vistas i Sverige utan tillstånd [Health Care and Hospital Care for People Residing in Sweden Without Permission] includes the recently suggested act on access to health care for irregular immigrants.

32 Statens Offentliga Utredningar [SOU] 2011:48 Vård efter behov och på lika villkor – en mänsklig rättighet [Care According to Needs and on Equal Terms – A Human Right] [government report series] (Swed.).

33 FÖRORDNING OM VÅRDGARANTI [ORDINANCE ON CARE GUARANTEE] (Svensk Författningssamling [SFS] 2010:138) (Swed.). *In* Statens Offentliga Utredningar [SOU] 2013:2 Patientlag [Patient Act] 229–238 (Swed.), it is suggested that the guarantee should also be stated in a new Patient Act and include diagnoses.

patient shall receive the necessary treatment.[34] In Sweden, the waiting times have been excessive, and to some extent, these measures seem to have reduced wait times. But from an international perspective, Sweden still has a problem with long waiting periods.[35] At the same time, the quality of health care is very good, when compared to other countries.[36] The number of patients waiting for an appointment or medical treatment in specialist care decreased between 2009 and 2011, and fewer patients than before had to wait for more than ninety days. Ninety percent of the patients visiting a care center waited not more than a week and 90 percent of the phone calls to the care centers were answered the day the call was made.[37] The reforms designed to address concerns about waiting times are, however, quite recent, and to have a solid empirical basis for firm conclusions, one should follow how the results of the reforms develop over the coming years.

The NBHW has concluded that the counties' supervision of the waiting lists has improved and that the care guarantee reform has been successful as it has improved accessibility for new patients.[38] However, this has been partly achieved at the expense of other patient groups, for example patients in need of consecutive medical appointments.[39] Accessibility varies from county to county, and it has been proven that in counties with high accessibility – for example, through counseling over the phone – the patients are more content with waiting times.[40] This is not the case for specialist health care, for which patients all over the country consider waiting times too long.[41] Regional differences in waiting times and accessibility are not acceptable considering the goal of having a good and equal health and medical care in the whole country.[42] Over the last three years, the government has provided one billion SEK extra per year to the counties in order to enable them to take measures to shorten the waiting times for patients and strengthen the care

---

[34] For specialist treatment, there is accordingly a time limit of six months; *see* Proposition [Prop.] 2009/2010:67 Stärkt ställning för patienten – vårdgaranti, fast vårdkontrakt och förnyad medicinsk bedömning [Stronger Position for the Patient – Care Guarantee, Care Contract and Renewed Medical Assessment] [government bill] 36–40 (Swed.).

[35] *Cf.* Statens Offentliga Utredningar [SOU] 2008:127 Patientens rätt. Några förslag för att stärka patientens ställning [The Patient's Right. Suggestions for Improving the Position of the Patient] [government report series] 165–167 (Swed.). *See also* ARNE BJÖRNBERG, ET. AL., EURO HEALTH CONSUMER INDEX 2009 (2009), *and* press release *Sverige tappar mark i årlig EU-ranking av sjukvården* [Sweden is Losing Positions in the Annual EU Ranking of Hospital Care], HEALTH CONSUMER POWERHOUSE (Sept. 25, 2009), *available at* http://www.healthpowerhouse.com/files/Sweden.pdf; OECD, HEALTH AT A GLANCE 2011: OECD INDICATORS 131 (2011) where it is shown that Sweden does have a problem with waiting times compared to other EU Countries.

[36] Arne Björnberg, et. al., *id*, at 8–9.

[37] National Board on Health and Welfare, Vårdgarantioch kömiljard – uppföljning 2009–2011 [Care Guarantee and Billion – A Follow-Up 2009–2011], 24–30 (2012).

[38] *Id.* at 78–90.

[39] *Id.*

[40] *Id.* at 27–28.

[41] *Id.* at 29.

[42] *Id.*

guarantee reform. This has been successful to some extent, but in the meantime the extra resources demand certain measures to be taken and that, in turn, can lead to different priorities and different routines in handling referrals between and within the counties. Patients needing several appointments with a doctor risk being put aside in the quest of shorter waiting lists. The criteria to be fulfilled in order to get the additional resources have increasingly become harder, meaning that it has become more difficult for the counties to live up to the demands put forward by the government.[43] In addition, patients with low priority health concerns can easily be put before those with a more complicated and high-priority health situation when the treatment of a patient belonging to the former group has passed the time limits set up for treatment in general.

Measures taken to shorten waiting lists can be classified both as short term and long term in terms of the ultimate payoff. In the latter regard, the county boards have started to take measures aimed at changing organizational structure over the longer term. In regard to short-term measures, in response to a lack of health care personnel, a common solution adopted by many counties is to hire doctors for short periods of time. In many cases, however, what was intended as a stop-gap solution has become the new normal and threatens both the quality and continuity of care received by patients.

To conclude, reforms geared toward reducing wait times have resulted in all counties buying more health and medical care services from other counties and private care providers to manage the demands put forward in the guarantee reform.[44] Consequently, more patients are forced to go to other counties to get the care they are entitled to in a timely fashion.

2.2.2.2.2 THE "FREE CHOICE" REFORM Another recent reform is that of "free choice" of primary health care provider (*fritt vårdval i primärvården*). If a private health care provider can meet the conditions required by the county, then this care provider has the right to establish in the primary care sector and be reimbursed by public means. This has opened up the possibility for patients to choose between several different health care providers.[45] Since 2010, the counties are obliged to have a system of free choice of health care in primary care and must accordingly comply with the Act on free choice systems.[46] The Act aims to strengthen choice on the part of an individual patient who can choose his or her health care provider and the public reimbursement flows according to the patient's choice of provider, ensuring that providers have an incentive to compete for patients. But there are problems with

---

43 In 2011, the added money varied from 11 SEK to 590 SEK per person between the different counties.
44 National Board on Health and Welfare, *supra* note 38, at 99, 105.
45 Proposition [Prop.] 2008/09:74 Vårdval i primärvården [Care Choices in Primary Care] [government bill] (Swed.).
46 LAG OM VALFRIHETSSYSTEM [FREE CHOICE SYSTEM ACT] (Svensk Författningssamling [SFS] 2008:962) (Swed.).

this concept of free choice for it is meaningless in the absence of providers to choose from, which is the case in some parts of Sweden where the number of habitants is low.[47] The patient must also have the strength and ability to act as a consumer or client within the market of health care services or have assistance to do so.[48] In some municipalities there are large numbers of health care providers, and that can also create difficulties for the individual to know how to differentiate between them, even though patients may value the concept of choice itself. It can also be difficult, and sometimes emotionally hard, to change providers if the patient has feelings of loyalty toward the health care provider.[49]

Well-informed choices require that patients have adequate, accessible, and easy-to-understand information regarding quality and efficacy. From this point of view, the information that is presently available to assist a patient's choice is limited, and health care providers have not yet found a suitable and appropriate way to promote their services. The possibility of choice has also not proved as popular among patients as first envisaged; this could mean that the goal of the reform, namely improved quality, might not be realized.[50]

2.2.2.2.3 THE PATIENT INJURY ACT[51] It is compulsory for care providers to have insurance covering economic compensation for physical damages that may occur to patients in a health care setting. The rules governing compensation for these damages are provided for in the Patient Injury Act and are applicable to all injuries that occur to patients when receiving care in Sweden.[52] This is a no-fault insurance scheme; the patient does not have the burden of proving that an injury is the result of a specific action performed by the care provider or associated personnel, and it is enough that an injury has occurred to grant compensation. The compensation sum can, however, be reduced if it has been shown that the patient has not taken steps to mitigate his or her injury.

The Patient Injury Board[53] handles patient claims for compensation, and courts are not involved in handling the compensation for a patient's injury, unless the patient prefers turning to the court with a claim for compensation according to

---

[47] National Board on Health and Welfare, Report Valfrihetssystem ur ett befolknings-och patientperspektiv – slutredovisning [Freedom of Choice From a Population Perspective and a Patient Perspective], 13 (2012), *available at* http://www.socialstyrelsen.se/Lists/Artikelkatalog/Attachments/18595/2012-2-9.pdf.

[48] *Id.* at 34.

[49] *Id.* at 42.

[50] *Id.* at 41.

[51] PATIENTSKADELAG [PATIENT INJURY ACT] (Svensk författningssamling [SFS] 1996:799) (Swed.).

[52] If a county has contracted a foreign care provider or sent a patient abroad, PATIENTSKADELAG [PATIENT INJURY ACT] (Svensk Författningssamling [SFS] 1996:799) (Swed.) is also applicable, but not when EC Regulation 883/2004 1–123 (OJ L 166, 30.4.2004) is applied. In that case, the compensation system of the host state is applicable to the Swedish citizen.

[53] Förordning om Patientskadenämnden [Ordinance on the Patient Injury Board] (Svensk Författningssamling [SFS] 1996:992) (Swed.).

the tort rules. The reason for this is that it was considered that the process with a board would be shorter, less expensive for the individual, and more effective than a similar process in the courts. The Association of Patient Insurers funds compensation payments.

2.2.2.2.4 THE PATIENT SAFETY ACT[54] Care providers have the duty to undertake active and continuous work on matters relating to the safety of patients. The Patient Safety Act states that a provider must start an investigation if something has happened in the care of a patient that has led to an injury of some sort or if the patient has been exposed to a risk of suffering an injury or illness. The act also stipulates that patients and their relatives have the right to information about the safety issues in the care situation. If authorized personnel could be considered as a risk to patient safety, the care provider is obliged to report this to the HSCI.

The Patient Safety Act comprises rules governing withdrawal of the personnel's authorization, disciplinary measures, and rules relating to the right to act as a care provider. Chapter 6 of the Act also states the duties of the personnel vis-à-vis the patient, for example to respect patient integrity. Accordingly, health care personnel are obliged to perform their work in accordance with science and proven medical experience, and the personnel and the patient shall together, as far as possible, discuss and decide the individual care of the patient.

2.2.2.2.5 THE POSSIBILITY TO CHOOSE PLANNED HEALTH CARE IN SWEDEN – IMPLICATIONS FOR EQUAL HEALTH CARE For more than ten years, a Swedish patient has been able to choose his or her health care provider (either as a result of agreements entered into by counties[55] or through statute). However, in its quest for health care on equal terms for everyone, Sweden faces ever-increasing challenges. At the time the welfare state was established, Sweden was quite homogenous. Today, Sweden is a heterogeneous country, and accordingly the right to health has to be seen in a new light.[56] If a patient does not have access to health care that corresponds to his or her personal wishes founded on cultural or religious beliefs, the patient might choose to renounce the care. In such a situation the individual's right to health has not been fulfilled.

Freedom of choice in relation to health care is an important part of one of the most fundamental principles in health care, namely the respect for the patient's autonomy

---

[54] PATIENTSÄKERHETSLAG [PATIENT SAFETY ACT] (Svensk författningssamling [SFS] 2010:659) (Swed.).

[55] Swedish Association of Local Authorities and Regions, Rekommendation om valmöjligheter i vården [Recommendation on Choice Options in Health Care], Agreement A 00:56 between the County Councils, *available at* http://www.skl.se/vi_arbetar_med/halsaochvard/ersattning/valmojligheter_inom_halso-_och_sjukvard.

[56] Statistiska centralbyrån, Integration – en beskrivning av läget i Sverige [Integration – A Description of the Situation in Sweden], 18 (2008), *available at* http://www.scb.se/statistik/_publikationer/LE0105_2008A01_BR_BE57BR0801.pdf.

and integrity. This is also expressed in the HMSA[57] and the Patient Safety Act.[58] One basic feature of the right to autonomy is to have the right to refuse care. Health care is accordingly not obligatory for the patient; he or she has the right to decline treatment, even if it would be damaging to his or her health.[59] The possibilities for patients to realize their own personal and individual choices have, as indicated earlier, increased over the last few years, especially in primary care.[60]

The Equality Ombudsman has noticed that discrimination in health care is a matter of the behavior of the personnel toward the patient and not a question of resources. Accordingly, questions relating to power, lack of knowledge, attitudes, and so forth are relevant.[61] A recent study also confirms that among persons living in Sweden, the ones who believe that they have the least access to health and medical care are those who were born outside the Nordic countries.[62] When planning health care, it is thus very important to bear in mind that different cultural groups will have different concerns and different ways in which they wish to engage with health care providers and the health care system. As a result, rules applied in the same way to different groups or individuals might inadvertently result in inequalities and discrimination. The demands put on the health care provider are that every provider should have the personnel necessary to provide health care of good quality, and that the county is obliged to plan health and medical care so that the needs of the population are met.[63] Chapter 1, Sections 4 and 13 of the Discrimination Act prohibits direct and indirect discrimination in the field of health and medical care.[64]

However, it might be difficult to draw the line between the respect for a patient's wishes, which might be based on cultural or religious beliefs, and the duty of the

---

[57] 2a § HÄLSO- OCH SJUKVÅRDSLAG [HEALTH AND MEDICAL SERVICES ACT] (Svensk Författningssamling [SFS] 1982:763) (Swed.).

[58] Ch. 6, 1 § PATIENTSÄKERHETSLAG [PATIENT SAFETY ACT] (Svensk Författningssamling [SFS] 2010:659) (Swed.).

[59] *See, e.g.*, Convention for the Protection of Human Rights and Fundamental Freedoms, art. 6; Pretty v. the United Kingdom, 2002-III Eur. Ct. H.R. (2002).

[60] 3a § HÄLSO- OCH SJUKVÅRDSLAG [HEALTH AND MEDICAL SERVICES ACT] (Svensk Författningssamling [SFS] 1982:763) (Swed.); Ch. 6, 7 § PATIENTSÄKERHETSLAG [PATIENT SAFETY ACT] (Svensk författningssamling [SFS] 2010:659) (Swed.).

[61] The Equality Ombudsman Office, Rätten till sjukvård på lika villkor [The Right to Hospital Care on Equal Terms], 18, 31 (2012).

[62] Swedish Association of Local Authorities and Regions, Vårdbarometern – Befolkningens attityder till, kunskaper om och förväntningar på hälso- och sjukvården, [Health Barometer – The Population's Knowledge About and Expectations on Health Care and Hospital Care] 15 (2012), *available at* http://www.vardbarometern.nu/PDF/Årsrapport%20VB%202011.pdf; *see also* Fundamental Rights Agency (FRA) Fact Sheet 2011 on Inequalities and multiple discrimination in healthcare, *available at* http://fra.europa.eu/sites/default/files/fra_uploads/1947-FRA-Factsheet_InequMultDiscrimination_EN.pdf.

[63] *See* Sec. 2a, 7 respectively HÄLSO- OCH SJUKVÅRDSLAG [HEALTH AND MEDICAL SERVICES ACT] (Svensk Författningssamling [SFS] 1982:763) (Swed.).

[64] *See also* Statens Offentliga Utredningar [SOU] 2010:55 Romers rätt [Rights of the Romas] [government report series] (Swed.).

health care personnel to provide high-quality and effective health care. Patient integrity, cultural values, and discrimination might very easy merge together.[65] And these questions are not often discussed. In early 2012, several counties in southern Sweden introduced limitations on the right of women to request a woman gynecologist. These limitations were attributable at least in part to an increased number of patients that refused to be examined by male gynecologists because religious and/or cultural beliefs. The Association of Gynecologists does not approve of this, warns that discrimination toward male doctors might occur, and is of the view that individual demands for woman gynecologists should not be permitted.[66] This is just one recent example, but if the standards of availability, accessibility, acceptability, and quality are to be respected, one has to make sure that health and medical services are constructed so that they can meet cultural demands (from individuals, groups, minorities, and societies) as well as needs related to gender and age.[67]

2.3 LITIGATION AND HEALTH CARE

2.3.1 *Administrative Law and Health Care*

Respect for regional and local self-governance has been considered a strong argument against justiciable individual health rights. There is normally no appeal available against decisions with respect to individual access to health care, and litigation is thus not common in this field. The available legal "remedies" are limited to the patient complaint system administered by the HSCI, unless the care denied has compromised a patient's health and falls under the Patient Insurance Scheme. A patient may also claim that he or she has been discriminated against on the grounds of, for example, gender, ethnic origin, or religious belief, before the Equality Ombudsman. This can then be tried by court if the Ombudsman decides there are grounds for the court to review. The Parliamentary Ombudsman might criticize cases of incorrect administrative procedures, but all in all, the main responsibility for protecting the right to health in Sweden rests with the primary supervisory agencies, the NBHW and the HSCI. The activities of these two agencies, however, are more focused on patient safety than on equal access to health care.

---

[65] *Cf.* Oddný Mjöll Arnardóttir, *Cultural Accommodation in Health Services and European Human Rights*, in NORDIC HEALTH LAW IN A EUROPEAN CONTEXT – WELFARE STATE PERSPECTIVES ON PATIENTS' RIGHTS AND BIOMEDICINE, 181 (Elisabeth Rynning & Mette Hartlev eds., 2011).

[66] Elisabeth Rynning, Patientautonomi och diskriminering – om valfrihet och kulturell anpassning i hälso- och sjukvården [Patient Autonomy and Discrimination – Freedom of Choice and Cultural Adaptation in Health and Hospital Care], in FESTSKRIFT TILL ASBJØRN KJØNSTAD (Ketscher et al. eds., forthcoming 2013). In primary care, the patient has the right to freely choose his or her doctor, regardless of whether the choice is based on sex, ethnicity, religion, and so on.

[67] *Id.*

The role of the courts in relation to health care is thus secondary. Therefore, it is important to understand how Swedish administrative law works in relation to the courts, but also to remember the constitutionally guaranteed independence of the administration vis-à-vis the government. To be able to appeal to a higher administrative authority or to a court, a decision that can be subject to appeal must have been addressed to the individual. It is the decision that can be subject to legal review with reference to the legal merit stated in the statute. A doctor's decision on how to treat a patient is not an administrative decision, and the HMSA does not provide the individual patient a right to appeal. Nor is it stated that the treatment given by a doctor starts an administrative procedure that leads to an individual decision that could be appealed. One usually explains this by making a comparison with higher education.[68] A professor who is lecturing is working in the administrative field, pursuing a task regulated by law. When the professor is grading a student's work, he or she is handling an administrative task that culminates in a grade – a decision that is based on law. That decision can be appealed. But the medical treatment of a patient is *not* a decision. The payment for the care that a patient receives is a formal decision that can be appealed, but not the care received as such. Accordingly, there is no possibility for the patient to appeal the care or the lack of care received.

The right to health care as such is thus not justiciable in Sweden.[69] However, there are some enforceable rights; the right to abortion and the right to sterilization. A negative decision – that is, the patient is not entitled to receive any care or not the care he or she asked for – can be overruled by the HSCI.[70] In the Compulsory Psychiatric Act (1991:1128), the right to refuse treatment is protected to some extent, and it is possible for a patient to ask for judicial review from the administrative courts.[71] There is, however, as pointed out earlier in the chapter, no legislation on the status and rights of the patients. The patient's right to access his/her own medical

[68] Statens Offentliga Utredningar [SOU] 2010:29 En ny förvaltningslag [A New Administrative Act] [government report series] 96–97 (Swed.); Statens Offentliga Utredningar [SOU] 2008:117 Patientsäkerhet Vad har gjorts? Vad behöver göras? [Patient Safety. What Has Been Done? What Needs to be Done?] [government report series] (Swed.); Proposition [Prop.] 2009/2010:210 Patientsäkerhet och tillsyn [Patient Safety and Supervision] [government bill] (Swed.).

[69] *See infra* sec. 2.1 in regards to the Socialtjänstlag [Social Care Act] (Svensk Författningssamling [SFS] 2001:453) (Swed.); see Lag om stöd och service till vissa funktionshindrade [Act on the Assistance and Service for Persons with Disabilities] (Svensk Författningssamling [SFS] 1993:387) (Swed.) which also states individual and justiciable rights; *cf.* sec. 3.3.1.

[70] 4 § Abortlag [Abortion Act] (Svensk Författningssamling [SFS] 1974:595) (Swed.); 2 § Steriliseringslag [Sterilisation Act] (Svensk Författningssamling [SFS] 1975:580) (Swed.).

[71] So does Smittskyddslag [Protection against Communicable Diseases Act] (Svensk Författningssamling [SFS] 2004:138) (Swed.). In very few cases treatment can be forced upon the patient; *see* Lag om psykiatrisk tvångsvård [Compulsory Psychiatric Act] (Svensk Författningssamling [SFS] 1991:1128) (Swed.). The rules of necessity in Brottsbalk [Criminal Act] (Svensk Författningssamling [SFS] 1962:700) (Swed.) are the only exceptions to the rule of consent.

records is also a right that can be legally enforced; see Chapter 8 Section 1 and 2 of the Patient Data Act.[72]

Although the HMSA sets out the respective obligations of the state, the counties, and the municipalities, there is no possibility for an individual to employ this as a platform to make an appeal. What *is* justiciable, however, is the right not to be discriminated against in a situation of health care, guaranteed in Section 13 of the Discrimination Act.[73] In relation to this Act and to the work of the Equality Ombudsman, there is the prospect of litigating health care rights in court. The few cases in which the Equality Ombudsman has been involved are discussed in this section. Prior to this, however, I outline challenges of European law to the Swedish administrative system in relation to health law.

2.3.2 *EU Law and Swedish Health Care*

Sweden has been a member of the European Union since 1995. The principle of nondiscrimination has been a major tool in creating access to social benefits and rights for union citizens in Sweden. This principle is stated in the Treaty of the Functioning of the European Union, TFEU (article 18), but also in secondary legislation such as Regulation 883/2004 (former Regulation 1408/71) and Directive 2004/38. Even though EU law does not per se guarantee a right to health care, because the European Union has not been given competence in that field, an additional possibility has been provided by EU law, allowing patients a legal right of access to health care in another Member State, under certain circumstances. If certain conditions are met, patients then have a justiciable right at least to be reimbursed for such cross-border health care. This additional possibility is now propelling change in Swedish national statutes.

The possibility for Swedish citizens to access health and medical care in another Member State has increased significantly since Sweden joined the EU.[74] Such opportunity is guaranteed both through secondary legislation and the TFEU. The

---

[72] PATIENTDATALAG [PATIENT DATA ACT] (Svensk Författningssamling [SFS] 2008:355) (Swed.). Private health care providers are expressly included; see 2 § PATIENTDATALAG [PATIENT DATA ACT] (Svensk Författningssamling [SFS] 2008:355) (Swed.) with reference to TRYCKFRIHETSFÖRORDNINGEN [FREEDOM OF THE PRESS ACT] (Svensk Författningssamling [SFS] 1949:105) (Swed.) and OFFENTLIGHETS-OCH SEKRETESSLAG [SECRECY AND TRANSPARENCY ACT] (Svensk Författningssamling [SFS] 2009:400) (Swed.).

[73] This section has not yet been tried by the Swedish courts. According to the *travaux préparatoires*, the possibilities for making exceptions and thus "discriminating" in accordance with the law relates to vulnerable persons, such as special housing and emergency health care for women that are or have been victims of violence in family relations. *See* Proposition [Prop.] 2007/2008:95 Ett starkare skydd mot diskriminering [A Stronger Protection Against Discrimination] [government bill] 521–525 (Swed.).

[74] Bilateral conventions and contracts on health care provided in another country are not treated here.

Swedish Social Insurance Agency (*Försäkringskassan*) is the coordinating national authority under two options. The first option, provided pursuant to Regulation 883/2004, applies to planned treatment in another Member State by those individuals covered by the regulation (e.g., all Swedish citizens). The Swedish Social Insurance Agency makes a decision prior to a patient receiving care and reimburses the foreign health care provider the costs occurred. When deciding on an application, the agency is required to take into account whether the treatment in question is a benefit given according to Swedish law,[75] and whether the patient can receive the treatment in Sweden in a reasonable time with regard to the patient's health conditions and the characteristics of the illness. If all the necessary conditions are met, the Swedish health insurance plan will pay for the costs.[76] According to the same regulation, a Swedish citizen has the right to emergency health care accessed in public institutions in another Member State when staying in another member state for a period of up to one year.[77] Upon return to Sweden, the agency reimburses the costs except for the fees that patients in the host state would normally pay in order to get health care.

Alternatively, applicants may refer to the TFEU. Because health care is considered to be a service according to EU law, Articles 56 and 57 of the same treaty are applicable. Sweden's Social Insurance Agency has proven relatively reluctant in applying the treaty in cases where individuals have asked to be reimbursed for care in another Member State, and did not initially discuss or provide guidance to patients on this possibility until the Supreme Administrative Court ruled on the matter in 2004.[78] However, since then, a Swedish citizen has the right to be reimbursed for costs, including emergency health care, in both public and private institutions,[79] after the treatment has been given.[80]

---

[75] Permission can be denied only if an identical or just as efficient treatment can be given in Sweden on time; *cf.* European Court of Justice of the European Union Judgment of 12 July 2001, Smits and Peerbooms (C-157/99, ECR 2001 p. I-5473), para. 103, *and* Judgment of 23 October 2003, Inizan (C-56/01, ECR 2003 p. I-12403), para. 45.

[76] In 2010, 1,780 people applied for reimbursement for planned health care based on the TFEU, and 770 of these applications concerned dental care. Of these, 1,384 people were granted such reimbursement. There were 9,877 applications for reimbursement after receiving care abroad, and of these, 7,833 people were granted reimbursement; *see* Ministry Report, Ds 2012:6 Patientrörlighet i EU [Free Movement of Patients in the EU] 39–40 (Swed.). *See also* Statens Offentliga Utredningar [SOU] 2007:95 Tjänster utan gränser [Services Without Borders] [government report series] 89 (Swed.).

[77] See Ersättning för kostnader för vård i annat EES-land [Reimbursements for Care Costs in Another EEC Country] (Referral from the Government to the Council on Legislation for an opinion, Jan. 18, 2007).

[78] Regeringsrättens årsbok [RÅ] [Supreme Administrative Court] 2004–01–30 ref. 41 (Swed.).

[79] *See* Statens Offentliga Utredningar [SOU] 2007:95 Tjänster utan gränser [Services Without Borders] [government report series] 89 (Swed.).

[80] *See* Kammarrätten i Stockholm [Stockholm Administrative Court of Appeal], 2007–03–28 case 2762–06 (Swed.).

In 2007, the European Commission commenced the process of a Directive on patients' rights[81] that was enacted in May 2011.[82] To implement the Directive, a Governmental Bill to the Swedish parliament was presented in March 2012.[83] The new Swedish statute respects the demands of EU law, namely that the rules should not hinder nor make it less attractive to fulfill the rights and freedoms granted by the Treaty and that such rights and freedoms should not be applied in a discriminatory way. Further, the rules must meet the EU requirement that they be necessary in the light of a public interest and, finally, the rules should realize the goal that the legislator strives for and not go beyond what is necessary for achieving this goal.[84] Because the Directive clearly states the situations when prior authorization is required (Articles 7–9), the suggested legislative changes aim at implementing the Directive.[85]

2.3.3 *Litigation or Supervision and Complaints*

2.3.3.1 National Board of Health and Welfare (NBHW) and the Health and Social Care Inspectorate (HSCI)

The NBHW has a broad remit and supervises health and medical care, dental care, health protection, infectious disease control, social care, support and service to some persons with disabilities, questions relating to alcohol and drugs and, lastly, the institutions of the National Board of Institutional Care.[86] Every year, the NBHW publishes a report that summarizes performance in different areas of health and medical care.

2.3.3.1.1 COMPLAINTS FROM INDIVIDUALS RELATING TO HEALTH CARE In 2011, the NBHW received 6,689 complaints relating to health care.[87] The board rendered

---

[81] Proposal for Directive 2008/0142 of the European Parliament and of the Council on the Application of Patients' Rights in Cross-Border Healthcare, COM(2008) 414 final (July 2, 2008), *available at* http://ec.europa.eu/health/ph_overview/co_operation/healthcare/docs/COM_en.pdf. *See also* Communication from the Commission, Consultation regarding Community action on health services, SEC(2006) 1195/4 (Sept. 26, 2006), *available at* http://ec.europa.eu/health/ph_overview/co_operation/mobility/docs/comm_health_services_comm2006_en.pdf; Communication from the Commission, A Community Framework on the Application of Patients' Rights in Cross-Border Healthcare, COM(2008) 415 final (July 2, 2008), *available at* http://ec.europa.eu/health-eu/doc/com2008415_en.pdf.

[82] Directive 2011/24/EU of the European Parliament and of the Council of 9 March 2011 on the Application of Patients' Rights in Cross Boarder Health Care, 2011 O.J. (L 88) 45–65.

[83] Ministry Report, Patienttörlighet i EU [Free Movement of Patients in the EU], Ds 2012:6 (Swed.)

[84] Lotta Vahlne Westerhäll, Regeringsrättens domar om ersättning för vårdkostnader i annan medlemsstat i Europeiska unionen, [Supreme Administrative Court's Rulings on Reimbursement for Costs Relating to Health Care in Another Member State] EUROPARÄTTSLIG TIDSKRIFT, 2, 282 (2004).

[85] The Directive was scheduled to be implemented at the latest on October 25 2013. The suggested legislative changesentered into force on October 1, 2013.

[86] National Board on Health and Welfare, Tillsynsrapport 2012 – Hälso- och sjukvård och Socialtjänst, [Supervision Report 2012 – Health and Hospital Care and Social Services].

[87] The 2,312 complaints that the NBHW took over from HSAN on January 1, 2011 are not included in these numbers.

decisions in relation to 3,250 of these complaints, was critical of provider performance in 200 of these cases, and asked the relevant care provider to take specific measures to improve performance.[88] Receiving complaints from individuals is today a task of the HSCI. The complaints to the HSCI, and before that to the NBHW, are limited in that they do not lead to a change of treatment in the individual case since the Inspectorate only has the power to retroactively criticize performance and can never order specific treatments, and because it is not possible for patients to appeal a board decision.

2.3.3.1.2 LEX MARIA Owing to severe malpractice resulting in the death of patients at a hospital in Stockholm in the 1930s, a special law called Lex Maria was enacted in 1937.[89] Today, Lex Maria is included within the Patient Safety Act, Chapter 3, Sections 5 and 6. This law states that it is the duty of all personnel to report to the care provider risks of injuries and incidents that have or could have led to injuries. The care provider then has the duty to investigate these risks and incidents and report to the HSCI any findings that are severe in character. It is then the task of the Inspectorate to make sure that the necessary investigations have been carried out and that the care provider has taken measures needed to achieve a high level of patient safety. But the Inspectorate should also inform all health care providers about the incidents reported and take other measures needed to secure a high level of patient safety.[90]

2.3.3.1.3 LEX SARAH Lex Sarah was enacted as a result of shortages in the field of geriatric care that were the subject of extensive commentary by the media in 1997,[91] and was to a large extent based on Lex Maria. This legislation imposes a duty on the care provider to report poor conditions and deficiencies in the care provided to geriatric and disabled patients.[92]

---

[88] National Board on Health and Welfare, Tillsynsrapport 2012, *supra* note 86.

[89] Ewa Axelsson, Patientsäkerhet och kvalitetssäkring i svensk hälso- och sjukvård. En medicinrättslig studie [Patient Security and Quality Assessment in Swedish Health and Medical Care], 22 (2011). The incidents mentioned earlier took place at the hospital Maria sjukhus in Stockholm, hence the name Lex Maria.

[90] In 2011, 2,093 incidents were reported to the NBHW. The board has underlined that a great majority of severe incidents are not reported, and at the time of writing, the board was working on new rules aimed at enforcing Lex Maria, specifically strengthening the reporting procedure.

[91] The first name of the nurse who contacted the media on the events at the time is Sarah and therefore the Act is called Lex Sarah.

[92] Lag om stöd och service till vissa funktionshindrade [Act on The Assistance and Service for Persons with Disabilities] (Svensk Författningssamling [SFS] 1993:387) (Swed.). *See also* Proposition [Prop.] 2004/2005:39 Kvalitet, dokumentation och anmälningsplikt i lagen (1993:387) om stöd och service till vissa funktionshindrade (LSS), m.m. [Quality, Documentation and Duty to Report According to the Act (1993:387) on the Assistance and Service for Persons with Disabilities (LSS), etc.] [government bill] (Swed.). For the care of the elderly the duty is expressed in Ch. 14, 2 § SOCIALTJÄNSTLAG [SOCIAL CARE ACT] (Svensk Författningssamling [SFS] 2001:453) (Swed.), and for the care of the disabled it is

Lex Sarah is today applicable to the delivery of most social services, and the term "social services" is to be interpreted expansively; all activities covered by the social care legislation are included, for example decisions relating to benefits and care given without the informed consent of an individual.[93] Both private and public care providers have a duty to investigate existing poor conditions or risks that may subsequently result in poor conditions. Prior to 2011 this was only a requirement for public care providers, but today it applies to both public and private providers. There is, in addition, a clear demand that all documentation concerning these investigations be archived, which will help facilitate the supervision of health care providers. Poor conditions should be documented, investigated, and resolved. If there is a clear risk of serious harm, there is also a duty to report it to the Inspectorate. The Social Board of the municipality is always obliged to investigate, according to Chapter 11 Section 1 of the Social Care Act.

Everyone who fulfills a task within the various social service systems in Sweden has a duty to contribute to ensuring the delivery of a high-quality service.[94] Lex Sarah is accordingly an expression of a long-term commitment to improve the quality of care in the field of social services. Most of the complaints in 2011 relate to geriatric care and the situation of the disabled.

2.3.3.2 The Equality Ombudsman

The Equality Ombudsman has to date considered claims with respect to two forms of discrimination: discrimination in a provider's encounter with a patient, and discrimination in relation to access to health care. The former set of claims related to discrimination on the grounds of disability[95] and on the grounds of

---

included since 2005 in 24a § Lag om stöd och service till vissa funktionshindrade [Act on the Assistance and Service for Persons with Disabilities] (Svensk Författningssamling [SFS] 1993:387) (Swed.); Proposition [Prop.]. 1997/1998:113 Nationell handlingsplan för äldrepolitiken [National Action Plan for the Elderly] [government bill] (Swed.).

93 *See* Proposition [Prop.] 2009/2010:131 Lex Sarah och socialtjänsten – Förslag om vissa förändringar [Lex Sarah and the Social Services – Suggestions on Changes] [government bill] (Swed.); National Board on Health and Welfare regulation SOSFS 2011:5 (S) Lex Sarah (Swed.). *See also* National Board on Health and Welfare, *Information om nya bestämmelser om lex Sarah* [*Information About the New Rules of Lex Sarah*], (communication nr 6/2011, July 2011), *available at* http://www.socialstyrelsen.se/Lists/Artikelkatalog/Attachments/18393/2011-7-5.pdf.

94 Ch. 14, 2–3 §§ Socialtjänstlag [Social Care Act] (Svensk författningssamling [SFS] 2001:453) (Swed.); 24 a, 24 b §§ Lag om stöd och service till vissa funktionshindrade [Act on the Assistance and Service for Persons with Disabilities] (Svensk författningssamling [SFS] 1993:387) (Swed.). Excluded are voluntary workers and family homes; *see* Proposition [Prop.] 2009/10:131 Lex Sarah och socialtjänsten – Förslag om vissa förändringar [Lex Sarah and the Social Services – Suggestions on Changes] [government bill] 50 (Swed.).

95 Landstinget i Kalmar: Ärende [Reconciliation with the County Council of Kalmar], ANM 2009/1877 (July 7, 2011) (Swed.), *available at* http://www.do.se/sv/Om-DO/Forlikningar-domstolsarenden/kalmar/. The patient received compensation of 60 000 SEK.

ethnicity,[96] and in both cases, the patients were totally denied care. The Equality Ombudsman resolved these cases using alternative dispute resolution so the general courts did not review the cases.[97] As to the second group of cases, discrimination in access to health care, the discrimination related to denied care or health care performed on less favorable conditions through higher fees or partial medical evaluation.[98] Three of these cases concern the rights of lesbian couples seeking in vitro fertilization (IVF) treatment.[99] In two of these cases, the Equality Ombudsman lost the case because the courts concluded that the Ombudsman did not manage to show that a similar situation would be handled in a different way.

In a third case, from the Stockholm District Court,[100] a homosexual woman was denied an appointment at her local care center for tests necessary to start an IVF treatment. The personnel explained to the patient that she should turn to a center specializing in receiving homo-, bi-, and transsexuals. She was accordingly denied treatment on the basis of her sexual orientation. The county argued in court that the patient had not been treated unfairly; on the contrary, she was assigned a better care provider. Not surprisingly, the court did not accept that reasoning, or the claim that the care center did not have enough knowledge about the social and legal matters relating to donor insemination. The court underlined the importance of care providers having knowledge about the law and their duties.[101] The court concluded that the woman had been directly discriminated against and that she had the right to a compensation of 15,000 SEK. In the Court of Appeal, the amount was raised to 30,000 SEK.[102] At the time of writing, the case has been appealed to the Supreme Court and no judgment has yet been rendered.

Two cases concerning the conduct of a psychiatrist in Stockholm should be added to the second group of cases.[103] The doctor made generalized statements based on the ethnic origins of different patients. The patients were offended and furthermore received a partial medical assessment that resulted in serious financial consequences

---

[96] Landstinget i Värmland [Reconciliation with the County Council of Värmland], ANM 2009/337 (Feb. 24, 2011) (Swed.), *available at* http://www.do.se/sv/Om-DO/Forlikningar-domstolsarenden/Forlikning-landstinget-i-Varmland/; Primärvården i Södra Bohuslän [Reconciliation with the County Council of Södra Bohuslän], ANM 2009/720 (Dec. 20, 2010) (Swed.), *available at* http://www.do.se/sv/Om-DO/Forlikningar-domstolsarenden/Forlikning-Primarvarden-i-Sodra-Bohuslan/. In the first case, the patient received compensation of 30,000 SEK and in the second case, 25,000 SEK.

[97] When mediation is successful, the parties agree and the courts do not try the case.

[98] The Equality Ombudsman Office, rätten till sjukvård på lika villkor [The Right to Hospital Care on Equal Terms], 31 (2012), *available at* http://www.do.se/Documents/rapporter/R%c3%a4tten%20till%20sjukv%c3%a5rd%20p%c3%a5%20olika%20villkor.pdf.

[99] Svea Hovrätt (HovR) (Court of Appeals) 2009–11–5, T 9187–08 (Swed.); Umeå tingsrätt (TR) (District Court), 2009–11–6, T 1795–08 (Swed.).

[100] Stockholms tingsrätt (TR) (District Court), 2011–10–13, T 7473–10 (Swed.).

[101] Homosexual female couples have had the right to insemination and IVF treatment since 2005.

[102] Svea Hovrätt (HovR) (Court of Appeals) 2012–11–12, T 9222–11 (Swed.).

[103] Stockholms Tingsrätt (TR) (District Court) 2009–12–10, T 16183–06 & T 25395–06 (Swed.).

for them because they lost their sickness benefits. The court underlined that general pronouncements and declarations relating to ethnic origins from health care personnel have nothing to do with competent and careful care. The discrimination was even more serious considering that the patients were extremely dependent on the doctor in question.

2.3.4 *Toward a Universal Right to Health in Sweden? Recent Proposals Covering Vulnerable Groups*

The government of Sweden has recently addressed the situation of vulnerable or marginalized groups and their access to care.[104] Recently a much welcome agreement on how to strengthen the right to health for irregular immigrants and persons hiding to avoid deportation from Sweden was presented.[105] According to the proposed act, these persons will have the same right to health care as asylum seekers. This means that irregular immigrants who are not yet eighteen years old will have the right to health care, dental care, and pharmaceutical products.[106] Adult irregular immigrants and "hidden persons" will be given right to urgent health and dental care and to care related to pregnancy. They will also be given a right to pharmaceutical products needed for treatment in such cases and to health examination. The act entered into force on July 1, 2013.[107] One can conclude that this agreement is welcome by the health personnel in many counties, because in enacting this law, Sweden will more effectively respect the demands of the international community and the international conventions regarding the right to health, foremost the International Covenant on Economic, Social and Cultural Rights (Art. 12) and the European Social Charter (Art. 12 and 13).

Patients falling within the scope of the Compulsory Psychiatric Act have the right to (and may be obliged to undergo) treatment. Recently, the fact that it has been difficult for this group to get care of the appropriate quality, and sometimes even to access care at all, has been highlighted and a proposal to legislate has been presented in order to provide clearer regulation regarding the responsibility and duties toward this group. For addicts, it has been known for many years that it can be hard to get access to care. The Parliamentary Ombudsmen has on several occasions underlined

---

[104] *Cf.* Committee on Economic, Social, and Cultural Rights, *General Comment No. 14, The Right to the Highest Attainable Standard of Health,* U.N. Doc. E/C.12/2000/4 (Aug. 11, 2000), reprinted in Compilation of General Comments and General Recommendations Adopted by Human Rights Treaty Bodies, U.N. Doc. HRI/GEN/1/Rev.6, para. 18–29 (2003), *available at* http://www.unhchr.ch/tbs/doc.nsf/%28symbol%29/E.C.12.2000.4.En.

[105] Hälso- och sjukvård till personer som vistas i Sverige utan tillstånd [Health Care and Hospital Care for Persons Residing in Sweden Without Permission] (Ministry Report, Ds 2012:36, 2012).

[106] At the time of writing, "hidden" children already have the same rights as children of asylum seekers.

[107] Lag om hälso- och sjukvård till vissa utlänningar som vistas i Sverige utan nödvändiga tillstånd [Act on Health care and hospital care for some foreigners esiding in Sweden without Necessary permissions] (Svensk Författningssamling [SFS] 2013:407) (Swed.).

that there is a societal duty to provide everyone health care and that it is not correct to deny health care to addicts because of their addiction.[108]

Finally, the government has asked the Committee on the Patients' Rights to closely study the rights of children in relation to health and medical care.[109] There is also hope for new rules regarding the situation of people not capable of giving consent to treatment, a group whose situation has not been regulated explicitly yet.[110] Such an act would be welcome and would allow Sweden to ratify the Biomedicine Convention.

2.3.5 *Collective Health Care Rights versus Individual Ones: A Changing Landscape?*

The role for private health care insurance has increased over the last years, even though one does not need private insurance to access the best health care in Sweden. Though private insurance has doubled I recent years, only 0.2 percent of the total health care expenditure in Sweden is covered by private insurance.[111] In 2012, 522,000 persons had a private health care insurance and 80 percent of which was purchased by employers on behalf of employees.[112]

The phenomenon of private health insurance is a new one in the Swedish context and raises several interesting questions. The positive aspect of private insurance is that patient waiting time is shorter. Private insurance is thus a good way for the employer to make sure that employees return to work more quickly than may be possible if left to public health insurance alone.[113] At the same time, the increasing

---

[108] Decisions by the Swedish Parliamentary Ombudsmen: JO 1988/89 p. 191 and JO 1984/85 p. 227.

[109] Terms of reference Dir. 2011:25 Stärkt ställning för patienten genom en ny patientlagstiftning [Stronger Position of the Patient Through a New Patients' Act] (Swed.); Terms of reference Dir. 2012:24 Tilläggsdirektiv till utredningen om stärkt ställning för patienten genom en ny patientlags-tiftning [Additonal Directives to the Commission on a Stronger Position for the Patient Through a New Patients' Act] (Swed.). Statens Offentliga Utredningar [SOU] 2013:2, 184–198 Patientlag [Patient Act] [government report series] (Swed.) highlights the situation of children and suggests that the age and maturity of the child should be taken into consideration when medical care is given to the child patient.

[110] Terms of reference Dir. 2012:72, Beslutsoförmögna personers ställning i hälso- och sjukvård, tandvård, socialtjänst och forskning [The Position of Persons Unable to Consent to Health Care and Hospital Care, Dental Care, Social Care and Research] (Swed.).

[111] For the year 2011, *see* Statens Offentliga Utredningar [SOU] 2012:2, 25 Framtidens högkostnadsskydd i vården [The Future Cost Protection of Care] [government report series] (Swed.).

[112] Statistics from the Organisation Swedish Insurance (Branschorganisationen Svensk försäkring), Antalet privata sjukvårdsförsäkringar fortsätter att öka [The Number of Private Health Care Insurance Continues to Increase], Svensk Försäkring (March 7, 2013), available at http://www.svenskforsakring.se/Huvudmeny/Fakta–Statistik/Forsakringens-roll-i-samhallet/Undersidor/Sjukvardsforsakringsstatistik-2012/.

[113] Although part of the public sector in Sweden, several municipalities (!) have acquired private insurance for their personnel. Today this is also a way for the unions in Sweden to gain (and keep) members.

amount of private insurance also indicates that the fundamental idea behind the Swedish system of high-quality health care for all is under challenge. Not every Swedish citizen can benefit from private health insurance. To get a private health care insurance contract, one has to be healthy. Thus, for example, diabetics are often denied private insurance and most insurers do not insure persons older than sixty-five years, and the older the insured person is, the more expensive the premium. Moreover, private health insurance does not cover emergency health care or, in general, prenatal care, birth, psychiatric care, and plastic surgery.

2.4 CONCLUSION

The right to health in Sweden can be considered a "soft" right, from a legal perspective. It is also different from other social rights such as the right to social assistance in the Act on Social Care. The reason for this is to be found in the historical development of the welfare state in Sweden and its resulting constitutional implications. The right to health in the MHSA has been formulated as a duty on the part of providers and not as a right for the patients themselves. Notwithstanding this rather weak articulation of a right to health in Swedish law, we see today that there is quasi-constitutional protection emerging around health rights as a result of the impact of European law.

The extent to which social rights can be considered rights depends on several factors. In particular, Swedish public law suggests that the following factors are of assistance in assessing the content and judicial strength of a social right. First, one has to consider if the right in question is formulated as a right or if it has a more general meaning (goal oriented). As I have discussed, the right to health is not formulated as a justiciable "right for the individual," in contrast to the rights contained in the Act on Social Care. Second, the conditions an individual must fulfill to receive the social right or benefit should be sufficiently precise and included within a statute. With respect to health, a general right is articulated within a statute but the specifics of what is covered by that right are rarely articulated in legislation. Third one has to consider if the right is dependent on public funding – which is clearly the case for much of health care in Sweden. The fourth factor is whether or not an individual can appeal a determination with respect to the right or benefit. In this regard, the Swedish system is relatively weak, even though there have been a number of reforms in the last few years. Finally, one has to consider if the benefit is the object of supervision by state authorities and if it is possible to seek judicial review of the authority in charge of the social right. The last two criteria have been strengthened lately, with the increased importance of European law and also by the newer reforms implemented in Swedish law discussed earlier.[114] It can also be noted

---

[114] *See also* Lind, *supra* note 19, at 455.

that European law has strengthened the first three criteria, contributing to a stronger foothold for the right to health within Sweden.

As we have seen, historically a Swedish patient has had a very limited ability to appeal a decision concerning his or her medical treatment. New possibilities with respect to the right to appeal would strengthen the position of patients.[115] In this context, European law is also of relevance, and in the face of various EU court decisions it remains to be seen if Swedish administrative law can continue to deny a stronger individualization of the right to health. Taking a broader European perspective into account, one might question if the collective orientation of the Swedish approach to the right to health is preferable to more individualistic alternatives. Studying the case law of the European Court of Human Rights, one can conclude that the legal landscape is changing. The Court now includes benefits that are financed through tax-based systems in the sphere of property.[116] Also, when considering Art. 6 of the ECHR, one has to keep in mind that the expectations of the individual regarding what the right to health comprises can change according to how the legislator handles the right. A stronger emphasis on a rights discourse, from the political power, will leave traces in the legal texts and the steering documents indicating that a more individual right to health is emerging.

Another point I have made in this chapter is that there are strong legal mechanisms for oversight and governance of health and medical services in Sweden, and that there are numerous indicators, questionnaires, and regulations about how to evaluate health and medical services. This phenomenon strengthens both the collective as well as the individual aspects of the right to health and could be used in a more rights-oriented way, referring to the criteria included in General Comment no. 14.

To the foreign reader, the Swedish system can seem strange when it comes to the lack of litigation. In my view, this paucity is attributable to the fact that the legal possibilities to litigate have, until recent times, been very narrow and pressure to change this has not been strong because, until recently, health care was generally considered adequate. Situations that have been debated in Sweden, such as irregular immigrants' right to health care, have not been taken to court, because Swedish law (administrative as well as private) did not offer any possibilities for challenge

To conclude, there has been a historical reluctance on the part of legislators (and other political decision bodies) to involve courts in health care decision making. This reluctance is rooted in the belief that democracy and the will of the people are the best way of realizing the welfare state and guaranteeing a high-quality, universal right to health. Thus the emphasis is on the collective dimension of the right to health.

---

[115] Elisabeth Rynning, Patientens rättsliga ställning – två steg fram och ett tillbaka?[The Legal Position of the Patient], in FESTSKRIFT TILL LOTTA VAHLNE WESTERHÄLL, 307 (Erhag et al. eds., 2011); Rynning, Still No Patients' Act in Sweden -Reasons and Implications, supra note 29.

[116] Moskal v. Poland, App. No. 10373/05, Judgment of 15 September 2009, para. 38, (2009), *available at* http://www.echr.coe.int; Stec and Others v. The United Kingdom, App. No. 65731/01, 65900/01, Judgment of 6 July 2005, 2005-X, Eur. Ct. H.R. (2005).

This resistance to judicialization is also an expression of concern that government may lose its control over public expenditures and over choices regarding the design of the welfare state. Would the creation of a justiciable health right be a positive development? In my view, strengthening the patient's legal status would complement, not diminish, the strong emphasis put on the collective dimension of the right to health in Sweden. But at the same time, it is crucial that for this complex right to be accessible and affordable for everyone the state must proactively assume responsibility.

3

Litigating Health Rights in Canada

A White Knight for Equity?

Colleen M. Flood*

3.1 AN OVERVIEW OF CANADIAN HEALTH CARE

Canada is often held up as exemplifying the "single-payer" model of health care financing. The label is somewhat misleading, because government is by no means the only "payer" for health care in Canada: roughly 30 percent of health care spending is *privately* financed, which puts Canada below the OECD average in its ratio of public-to-private financing.[1] Close to 65 percent of Canadians hold private insurance for a wide swath of medical goods and services not covered by the public system, notably for prescription drugs taken outside of hospitals, and care deemed not medically necessary, such as routine dental care.[2]

Canadian Medicare provides first-dollar public funding for all "medically necessary" hospital care and "medically required" physician services.[3] Surprisingly, however, there is no legal definition or clearly established criteria for deciding what counts as medically necessary. Decisions as to what treatments are included in the Medicare basket are left to the provinces and territories ("provinces"), and are normally the by-product of annual fee negotiations between provincial Medical Associations and the relevant provincial Ministries of Health.[4] These negotiations tend to focus mainly on whether the coming year's fees for the established basket of

---

* This paper is based in part on an earlier publication – "Charter Rights & Health Care Funding: A Typology of Canadian Health Rights Litigation" (with Y.Y. Brandon Chen) (2010) 19 Annals of Health Law 479–526. Grateful thanks to my associates, Bryan Thomas and Arthur Wilson, for their excellent research assistance.

[1] OECD, *OECD Data 2010: How does Canada Compare*, OECD (2012), *available at* http://www.oecd.org/dataoecd/46/33/38979719.pdf.

[2] F. Colombo & N. Tapay, *Private Health Insurance in OECD Countries: The Benefits and Costs for Individuals and Health Systems* 11 (OECD Health Working Papers no. 15, 2004), *available at* www.oecd.org/dataoecd/34/56/33698043.pdf.

[3] Canada Health Act, R.S.C. 1985, c. C-6.

[4] Colleen M. Flood & Sujit Choudhry, *Strengthening the Foundations: Modernizing the Canada Health Act* (Commission on the Future of Health Care in Canada, Discussion Paper No. 13, 2002).

services will be raised or lowered relative to the year past; year to year, there is no systematic reassessment of which services should be included in the basket. This creates a bias toward preserving the status quo, leading to concerns about whether the funding tracks the most effective treatments for the most pressing medical needs.[5] As we shall see, the framework legislation for Canadian public health care, the Canada Health Act,[6] focuses coverage on physician/hospital services. This focus is to the exclusion of, for example, autism therapies delivered in schools, to say nothing of the whole range of goods and services linked to social determinants of health, such as access to clean water, income, housing, employment status, and working conditions.

Where a treatment is deemed *not* to be medically necessary, it is left largely to the free market to determine who has access, leading to serious inequalities in access and quality of care. As mentioned, prescription drugs fall largely outside of the Medicare basket, although pharmaceuticals delivered in hospitals are publicly financed, and the provinces offer varying levels of public coverage for seniors and low-income patients. Unequal access to prescription drugs has a regressive effect on the public health care system as a whole, as those who lack drug coverage are less likely to make use of physician services.[7] Private financing must also cover dental care, home care, ambulance services, and medical equipment used outside of hospitals.

These limitations on the comprehensiveness of public coverage often have dire consequences. Studies have shown, for example, that the disabled, the chronically ill, and the poor routinely face difficulties acquiring needed prescriptions, owing to problems of affordability.[8] Likewise, the 32 percent of Canadians who lack private insurance often forgo routine dental care, or sometimes seek it out in cut-rate underground facilities.[9] While there has been a move recently toward treating people with mental illnesses in a community setting rather than in an institution, the lack

---

[5] Colleen Flood, Mark Stabile & Carolyn Tuohy, *What Is In and Out of Medicare? Who Decides?*, in READINGS IN COMPARATIVE HEALTH LAW & BIOETHICS (Timothy Stoltzfus Jost ed., 2nd ed., 2007). *See also* Lisa Priest, *Ontario, B.C. Want to Cut Fees for Cataract Surgery*, THE GLOBE AND MAIL (July 11, 2011), http://www.theglobeandmail.com/life/health/new-health/health-news/ontario-bc-want-to-cut-fees-for-cataract-surgery/article2092994/.

[6] Canada Health Act, at c. C-6.

[7] Sara Allin & Jeremiah Hurley, *Inequality in Publicly Funded Physician Care: What Is the Role of Private Prescription Drug Insurance*, 18 HEALTH ECONOMICS 1218 (2009). The interplay between drug coverage and utilization of physician/hospital service is complex. There is evidence, for example, that cost-sharing schemes for prescription drugs – whereby, for example, patients are obliged to pay out of pocket up to a maximum of $200 annually – may lead to an *increase* in the utilization of physician services. *See* Aslam H. Anis et al., *When Patients Have to Pay a Share of Drug Costs: Effects on Frequency of physician Visits, Hospital Admissions and Filling of Prescriptions*, 173 CAN. MED. ASS'N J. 1335 (2005). *See also* M. Stabile, *Impacts of Private Insurance on Utilization* (Paper prepared for the IRPP conference "Toward A National Strategy on Drug Insurance," Sept. 23, 2002), *available at* http://www.irpp.org/events/archive/sep02/stabile.pdf.

[8] Joel Lexin, A NATIONAL PHARMACARE PLAN: COMBINING EFFICIENCY AND EQUITY (2001).

[9] Michele Henry, *Bogus 'Dentists' Prey on Immigrants*, TORONTO STAR (June 10, 2010), www.thestar.com/news/article/821527–bogus-dentists-prey-on-immigrants. *See also* William H. Ryding, *The 2-Tier Dental Health Care System*, 72 J. CAN. DENTAL ASS'N 47 (2006).

of comprehensive coverage for home care means that many who suffer from mental illnesses are denied necessary home care and support.[10]

These limits on the comprehensiveness of public coverage are compounded by disparities in the regulation of care across the public/private divide. For reasons that are unclear, provincial regulators have mostly focused their attention on guarding patient safety within the realm of publicly financed care, making comparatively little effort to regulate privately financed care. For example, a recent study found that among the roughly 15,000 clients of the Winnipeg Regional Health Authority's Home Care program, approximately 800 clients experienced an adverse event in 2004, more than 500 of which were potentially preventable or ameliorable.[11] A 2010 undercover report on the treatment of residents and the quality of conditions at a Toronto private retirement home further underscored these concerns. A *Toronto Star* reporter posing as a new resident at the retirement home observed appallingly poor sanitary conditions and in some cases profound neglect – residents left for hours in diapers, or left stranded on the floor after a fall.[12] Peering beyond the boundaries of what is deemed, somewhat arbitrarily, to be medically necessary, one finds profound inequalities, with vulnerable populations denied access or receiving substandard care.[13]

There is ample evidence that health outcomes are not solely, or even primarily, a function of access to health care, but rather depend on social determinants of health, such as income, housing, employment status, and working conditions.[14] Public spending across a range of social services relating to these social determinants of health will promote health equality. Thus, it is worth noting that recent OECD estimates found Canada to have one of the *lowest* levels of net public social spending among developed nations. OECD nations on average commit 23 percent of Net National Income to public social spending. At 19.6 percent, Canada ranks near the bottom, between the United States (18.2 percent) and Australia (19.9 percent).[15]

---

[10] Commission on the Future of Health Care in Canada, BUILDING ON VALUES: THE FUTURE OF HEALTH CARE IN CANADA – FINAL REPORT 179 (2002).

[11] Keir G. Johnson, *Adverse Events among Winnipeg Home Care Clients*, 9(Sp) HEALTHCARE Q. 127, 132 (2006).

[12] Dale Brazao, *Reporter's Diary Reveals Substandard Conditions at Retirement Home*, THE TORONTO STAR (Oct. 1, 2010), *available at* http://www.thestar.com/news/gta/article/869047; Dale Brazao & Moira Welsh, *Seniors at Risk in Retirement Home, Investigation Reveals*, THE TORONTO STAR (Oct. 1, 2010), *available at* http://www.thestar.com/news/investigations/article/869045–seniors-at-risk-in-retirement-home-investigation-reveals.

[13] See Colleen M. Flood et al., *Cosmetic Surgery Regulation and Regulation Enforcement in Ontario*, 36 QUEEN'S L. J. 31 (2011).

[14] World Health Organization, *Losing the Gap in a Generation: Health Equity Through Action on the Social Determinants of Health, Final Report of the Commission on Social Determinants of Health* (2008), *available at* http://whqlibdoc.who.int/publications/2008/9789241563703_eng.pdf; J. Mikkonen & D. Raphael, *Social Determinants of Health: The Canadian Facts* (2010), *available at* http://www.thecanadianfacts.org/The_Canadian_Facts.pdf.

[15] OECD, *Social Expenditure – Aggregated Data*, OECD.STATEXTRACTS, http://stats.oecd.org/Index.aspx?DataSetCode=SOCX_AGG.

In particular, within Canada's aboriginal population[16] one finds considerably higher rates of chronic disease, obesity, hypertension, alcoholism and drug addiction, and suicide.[17] Life expectancies for Aboriginals in Canada tend to be five or more years less than for the non-aboriginal population,[18] or roughly equivalent to the average life expectancy of Mexico.[19] Problems of access to health care are one root cause here, although current and historical inequalities along with other social determinants of health – income, education, employment, living conditions, and the availability of social supports – also play a key role.[20] Canada's sullied history of action – and inaction – toward Aboriginal peoples is a key contributor to the health problems faced by these populations today. "Mental health problems faced by aboriginals arise from a long history of colonization, residential school trauma, discrimination and oppression, and losses of land, language and livelihood."[21] This historic and ongoing cultural devastation has further contributed to dysfunctional families, residential instability, and problems with addiction – all factors that conspire to produce these poorer health outcomes.[22] Suicide is a particularly acute problem for Aboriginals in Canada. Among Aboriginals between the ages of ten and forty-four, suicide is the leading cause of death, and suicide rates in Aboriginal youth populations are five to six times higher than for non-aboriginal youth in Canada.[23] The failure of Canada to take *real* action to ameliorate these issues continues to blight the nation's collective conscience and international reputation with respect to human rights.

To this point we have seen how inequalities manifest themselves within the Canadian health care system as it now stands: public coverage is not as comprehensive as it might be, the private sector is not adequately regulated, and the country's broader socioeconomic inequalities yield unacceptable disparities in health outcomes. However, Canadian debate over equitable access to health care very often centers not

---

[16] *See* ABORIGINAL HEALTH IN CANADA: HISTORICAL, CULTURAL, AND EPIDEMIOLOGICAL PERSPECTIVES (J. B. Waldram et al. eds., 2006) for a historical overview.

[17] M. King, *Chronic Diseases and Mortality in Canadian Aboriginal Peoples: Learning from the Knowledge*, 31 CHRONIC DISEASES IN CANADA 2 (2010).

[18] Statistics Canada, CANADIAN INSTITUTE FOR HEALTH INFORMATION, HEALTH CARE IN CANADA, FIRST ANNUAL REPORT (2000).

[19] *The World Factbook, Country Comparison: Life Expectancy at Birth*, CENTRAL INTELLIGENCE AGENCY, *available at* http://www.cia.gov/library/publications/the-world-factbook/rankorder/2102rank.html.

[20] Malcolm King et al., *Indigenous Health Part 2: The Underlying Causes of the Health Gap*, 374 THE LANCET 76 (2009).

[21] National Aboriginal Health Organization, *Addressing Mental Illness* (National Aboriginal Health Organization Fact Sheet, Feb. 2011), *available at* http://www.naho.ca/documents/naho/english/factSheets/mental_Health.pdf.

[22] Statistics Canada, *supra* note 17.

[23] National Aboriginal Health Organization, *The Facts on Youth Suicide* (National Aboriginal Health Organization Fact Sheet, Apr. 2009), *available at* http://www.naho.ca/documents/naho/english/factSheets/suicidePrevention.pdf.

on these issues, but instead on the sustainability of the "single-payer" system. There is a common perception, real or imagined, that Canadians face unacceptable wait times for health care, and that the panacea is to allow private financing of medically necessary care. There is also justified concern that health care spending is crowding out other vital government services, such as education and social assistance. Under these circumstances, it becomes a quixotic undertaking, politically, to define and defend a robust role for public health care, especially where that involves *prohibiting* the private purchase of care.[24] What we see as a result are increasing numbers of ostensibly "necessary" health goods and services silently falling into the privately financed basket, in a process some have dubbed "passive privatization."[25] In recent years, for example, numerous clinics have popped up across the country, delivering diagnostic services, such as MRI and CT scans, and in some cases even "medically necessary" physician and hospital services to patients paying out of pocket.

This growing infrastructure of privatized care may threaten the public system. For one, it risks blurring the status distinction between public- and private-sector physicians – a regulatory distinction that is arguably essential to the integrity of the public system.[26] Moreover, policing these private clinics to ensure they do not become a back channel for queue jumping is a difficult and thankless task, for which governments have shown little enthusiasm in recent years. One very salient question for defenders of equal access to health care, then, is whether the increased recognition of "health rights" will ameliorate or exacerbate these systemic concerns. Before turning to that question, let us first set out the basic legal instruments governing access to health care in Canada.

3.2 LEGAL INSTRUMENTS REGULATING ACCESS TO HEALTH/HEALTH CARE

Canada has a federalist system of government, with both levels of government, federal and provincial, sharing responsibility for the regulation and financing of health care. Under the division of powers set out in the Constitution Act,[27] the provinces are assigned the lion's share of responsibility for health, but the federal government uses its broad spending powers to induce the provinces to participate in a national Medicare scheme. In theory, to receive federal transfer payments for

---

[24] *See* Colleen M. Flood, *Chaoulli's Legacy for the Future of Canadian Health Care Policy*, 44 OSGOODE HALL L.J. 273 (2006) for a discussion of the problems associated with allowing a duplicate private tier.

[25] Raisa Deber, *Thinking Before Rethinking: Some Thoughts about Babies and Bathwater*, 1(3) HEALTH-CARE PAPERS 25, 25–31 (2000).

[26] See Marie-Claude Prémont, *Wait-Time Guarantees for Health Services: An Analysis of Quebec's Reaction to the Chaoulli Supreme Court Decision*, 15 HEALTH L.J. 43, 53–56 (2007) for a more detailed discussion; see also Colleen M. Flood & Bryan Thomas, *Blurring of the Public/Private Divide: The Canadian Chapter*, 17 EUR. J. HEALTH L. 257 (2010).

[27] The Constitution Act, 1867, 30 & 31 Vict., c. 3 (U.K.).

health care, the provinces must comply with five principles set out in the federal
Canada Health Act (CHA):

(i) public administration;
(ii) comprehensiveness;
(iii) universality;
(iv) portability; and
(v) accessibility.[28]

The requirement of *public administration* refers to the insurance system for medically necessary care, but does not preclude private *delivery* of health care services,
as is often mistakenly believed. In fact, most Canadian physicians are independent
professionals, billing government on a fee-for-service basis. The principle of *comprehensiveness* requires that a province's public insurance scheme cover "all insured
health services provided by hospitals, medical practitioners or dentists."[29] However,
given that the Act leaves it largely to the provinces to themselves determine the basket
of health services to insure, the comprehensiveness requirement packs a relatively
light punch. The principle of *universality* requires that all insured persons receive
uniform coverage. This would appear to preclude, for example, means testing for
public coverage. The principle of *portability* ensures that Canadians retain coverage
when moving from one province to another. Lastly, the principle of *accessibility*
forbids employment of user fees (out-of-pocket payment at point of service) and
extra billing (physicians charging an additional fee above the public subsidy they
receive), which might block people of limited means from making use of Medicare.
The CHA has an in-built mechanism for enforcing the principle of accessibility,
mandating dollar-for-dollar withholding of federal funding to provinces that allow
extra billing or user fees. For every dollar patients or private insurers are billed for
medically necessary care, the federal government must withhold a dollar from the
transfer payment to the relevant province.

   The CHA holds a kind of talismanic power over progressive Canadians, and
is viewed as the Magna Carta of universal health care. The reality, as hinted at
already, is that the CHA may be partly to blame for some of the previously described
inequalities. Drafted to protect a system of public health care originating in the 1960s,
the CHA focuses entirely on health care delivered by physicians and in hospitals.[30]
This has meant, for example, that the CHA does nothing to ensure public coverage
for the growing spending on pharmaceuticals consumed outside of hospitals, or
spending on long-term care. The "passive privatization" of health care abides by the
letter, but not the spirit, of the CHA.

---

[28] Canada Health Act, R.S.C. 1985, c. C-6.
[29] *Id.* § 9.
[30] *See id.* § 2 for the definition of "insured services."

As indicated, supplementary private health insurance is common in Canada, but it has long been thought that allowing a *duplicative* private tier – that is, private insurance for medically necessary care – would threaten the quality and sustainability of the public system. For example, there is a worry that a private tier would siphon health professionals from the public system, exacerbating wait times, and there is a further concern that the political will to sustain the public system would be lost if the well-to-do were allowed to migrate to a privately financed tier. In response, each province has enacted regulations to prevent the private sale of medically necessary care, involving permutations of the following measures:

(i) a ban on private health insurance for services covered by Medicare;
(ii) a requirement that physicians who sell medically necessary care privately must wholly opt out of billing the public system;
(iii) forbidding physicians from charging private payers more than the public payer pays for a given service (thus eliminating incentives); and
(iv) banning extra billing; and banning direct billing.[31]

These prohibitions are thought by some to be draconian and – as described at greater length later in the chapter – are now under sustained constitutional attack. This form of litigation of health care "rights" – that is, the right to access private services – has garnered more success[32] than litigation of rights to publicly funded health care, even though the latter would arguably improve overall equity and be far more in keeping with Canadian Charter of Rights and Freedoms (Charter)[33] values.

To be clear, the CHA does not itself entrench rights to health or health care. As indicated, where a province violates the principle of accessibility by allowing extra billing, the federal government must respond by withholding a portion of transfer payments. However, on a plain reading, the CHA does not issue *citizens* a right to challenge their provincial government's noncompliance with the five principles.[34] Canadian patients have nevertheless found legal avenues for securing access to health care – for example, by launching mass tort claims, requesting administrative reviews, and bringing constitutional challenges. In *Cilinger*,[35] a class action was certified against twelve Quebec hospitals for having allowed breast cancer patients to wait longer than the medically recommended eight weeks for radiation therapy.

---

[31] Colleen M. Flood & Tom Archibald, *The Illegality of Private Health Care in Canada*, 61 Can. Med. Ass'n J. 825, 825–830 (2001). See Colleen M. Flood & Amanda Haugan, *Is Canada Odd? A Comparison of European and Canadian Approaches to Choice and Regulation of the Public/Private Divide in Health Care*, 5 Health Econ., Pol'y & L. 319 (2010) for a comparative overview of regulation of the public/private divide.

[32] Chaoulli v. Quebec (Att'y Gen.), [2005] 1 S.C.R. 791 (Can.).

[33] Canadian Charter of Rights and Freedoms, Part I of the Constitution Act, 1982, *being* Schedule B to the Canada Act, 1982 c. 11 (U.K.).

[34] But cf. Sujit Choudhry, *The Enforcement of the Canada Health Act*, 41 McGill L. J. 462 (1996).

[35] Cilinger c. Centre hospitalier de Chicoutimi, [2004] R.J.Q. 2943 (Can. Que. C.A.), *aff'g* [2004] R.J.Q. 3083 (Can. Que. Super. Ct.).

In *Stein*,[36] a Quebec man successfully argued that the refusal by an administrative tribunal to pay for his out-of-country cancer treatment was patently unreasonable, given the amount of time he would have waited to receive the procedure in the province. In *Lalonde*,[37] the Ontario government's decision to restructure a franco-phone hospital was challenged by area residents and quashed by courts on grounds that it violated the constitutional principle of protection of minorities.

In keeping with the overall theme of this volume, my discussion focuses on *rights-based* challenges. Since 1982, the Constitution has included the Charter, which protects Canadians' basic rights and freedoms against infringement by laws or state actions.[38] Section 24(1) of the Charter stipulates that anyone whose rights are violated "may apply to a court of competent jurisdiction to obtain such remedy as the court considers appropriate and just in the circumstances."[39] While the Charter does not provide any explicit guarantee of a right to health, Canadians are increasingly using other Charter rights to contest governmental limits on publicly funded health care, notably the right to "life, liberty and security of the person" guaranteed under s. 7 and the equality rights under s. 15.

As explained in Section 3.3, health rights litigation has to date had mixed success in Canadian courts, making it hard to neatly encapsulate the content of the "right" to health. Charter litigation might *in principle* yield a positive right to a given treat-ment, or to publicly funded care without excessive wait times, although unqualified successes of this sort are very rare. The closest, it seems, that Canadian plaintiffs have come is to successfully litigate a positive right to care, only to see that right go unenforced on the ground. Another potential outcome of Charter-based health rights litigation is the establishment of a negative right, where courts are asked to invalidate a law or a government action that allegedly *blocks* access to medical treatments – for example, a criminal prohibition of medical marijuana, or a ban on private insurance for medically necessary care. Most health rights challenges that have succeeded in Canada fall into this category of negative rights. Thus, it appears in the Canadian context that Charter rights have been successfully used to challenge restrictions within the health care system, but not to meaningfully expand or improve it, and as I elaborate later in the chapter, there are concerns about what this dynamic portends for equality within Canadian health care.

In Section 3.3 of this chapter, I layer in a further wrinkle to my discussion of the impact of health care rights and elaborate on how health rights discourse and litigation may have positive or negative consequences that are not captured in the

---

36 Stein v. Quebec (Tribunal administratif), [1999] R.J.Q. 2416 (Can. Que. Super. Ct.).

37 Lalonde v. Ontario (Health Services Restructuring Commission) (2001), 208 D.L.R. 4th 577 (Can. Ont. C.A.), *aff'g* (1999), 181 D.L.R. 4th 263 (Can. Ont. Div. Ct.).

38 Canadian Charter of Rights and Freedoms, § 52(1). This provision affirms the supremacy of the Con-stitution of Canada and stipulates "any law that is inconsistent with the provisions of the Constitution is, to the extent of the inconsistency, of no force or effect."

39 *Id.* § 24(1).

tally of courtroom victories and losses. Health consumers can fail in their legal pursuit of a right but, by drawing attention to an issue, galvanize public support for their cause, or at least soften resistance. In some cases, public sympathy toward the plaintiffs' circumstances has pressured government into policy changes. In other cases, however, health rights claimants come up empty-handed in the courts, and lose public support for their cause in the process.

3.3 A REVIEW OF HEALTH RIGHTS LITIGATION IN CANADA

Section 7 of the Charter provides that "[e]veryone has the right to life, liberty and security of the person and the right not to be deprived thereof except in accordance with the principles of fundamental justice."[40] On a narrow reading, s. 7 might be interpreted as merely guaranteeing a right to *due process* in individuals' interactions with the legal system, and indeed much of s. 7 jurisprudence relates to this theme. However, when read more expansively, s. 7 is interpretable as conferring substantive rights – either *forbidding* the state from interfering with citizens in certain fundamental aspects of life (i.e., negative rights), or *positively obliging* the state to assist citizens in securing the necessities of a secure and autonomous life (i.e., positive rights). Courts have for the most part been reluctant to read substantive rights into s. 7, particularly positive rights, although there have been victories in this vein, some relating to health care.

3.3.1 *Prospects for Positive Health Rights under Section 7*

To date, the majority of successful Charter claims relating to health have involved negative rights, which by their nature do not necessarily advance equality. However, one might read s. 7 as imposing a *positive* obligation on government to ensure that Canadians have access to the necessities of a secure and autonomous life, such as a minimal income or basic health care. To date, the courts have been reluctant to read s. 7 in this way, although theoretically they remain open to the possibility. In *Gosselin*[41] – a case challenging the province of Quebec's policy of drastically reducing social assistance for individuals under the age of thirty who refuse to participate in work training programs – the Supreme Court of Canada wrestled with whether s. 7 encompassed positive socioeconomic rights. Justice Arbour, writing in dissent, with L'Heureux-Dube J. concurring on point, argued that "in certain contexts the state's choice to legislate over some matter may constitute state action giving rise to a positive obligation under s. 7."[42] The majority in *Gosselin* agreed, in principle, that s. 7 "could be read to encompass economic

---

[40] *Id.* § 7.
[41] Gosselin v. Quebec (Att'y Gen.), [2002] 4 S.C.R. 429 (Can.).
[42] *Id.* para 328.

rights"[43] and that "one day s. 7 may be interpreted to include positive obligations,"[44] but concluded that the facts in *Gosselin* did not warrant breaking ground in this way. Canadian courts have since cited *Gosselin* as authority for the proposition that s. 7 *may*, under the right circumstances, confer positive duties on government, but never have those right circumstances been found to exist. Although acknowledging the possibility, courts have consistently rejected positive rights claims grounded in s. 7. For example, in *Flora*,[45] the Ontario Court of Appeal ruled that s. 7 did not impose a positive obligation on government to fund out-of-country medical treatments, even when the procedures were considered life saving.

This reluctance to recognize positive rights under the Charter may be explained, among other things, by a philosophy among many judges that sees the complex balancing involved in spending decisions as properly falling within the jurisdiction of the executive rather than the judiciary. As a case in point, Binnie and LeBel JJ. cautioned in *Chaoulli* against founding a positive right to health care on s. 7, because to do so would necessitate that courts determine the scope of health services and the length of wait times reasonably required by the Charter.[46] While some legal scholars contest,[47] it remains one of the most significant hurdles to infusing s. 7 with positive state obligations.

3.3.2 *Prospects for Positive Rights under Section 15 (The Charter's Equality Guarantee)*

Another avenue for Canadians seeking access to medical services not normally provided is to allege an infringement of s. 15 equality rights. In *Andrews*, the Supreme Court of Canada explained that s. 15 is intended "to ensure equality in the formulation and application of the law."[48] The Supreme Court later explained in *Law* that s. 15(1) aims at "assuring human dignity by the remedying of discriminatory treatment."[49] As such, one cannot invoke s. 15 to demand that government proactively address existing inequalities in society. However, once government has elected to take certain actions or enact legislation, s. 15 requires that it do so without discrimination.

Regarding health resource allocation, s. 15 may be triggered if a province makes a medical treatment available but denies it to some group in a way that violates

---

43 *Id.* para 81.
44 *Id.* para 82.
45 Flora v. Ontario Health Insurance Plan (2008), 91 O.R. 3d 412 (Can. Ont. C.A.).
46 Chaoulli v. Quebec (Att'y Gen.), [2005] 1 S.C.R. 791, para. 163 (Can.).
47 *See e.g.,* Lorne Sossin, *Towards a Two-Tier Constitution? The Poverty of Health Rights, in* ACCESS TO CARE, ACCESS TO JUSTICE: THE LEGAL DEBATE OVER PRIVATE HEALTH INSURANCE IN CANADA 161, 171–173 (Colleen M. Flood et al. eds., 2005).
48 Andrews v. Law Soc'y of British Columbia, [1989] 1 S.C.R. 143, 171 (Can.).
49 Law v. Canada (Minister of Employment & Immigration), [1999] 1 S.C.R. 497, para. 52 (Can.).

dignity, or instead ostensibly makes the treatment available to all but *fails to take into account* the unique needs or circumstances of some minority group – what has been termed "adverse effect discrimination."[50] In *Eldridge*, deaf patients alleged that the failure to provide sign language translation in hospitals infringed s. 15. In a unanimous judgment, the Supreme Court found an infringement of the plaintiff's equality rights, which could not be "demonstrably justified in a free and democratic society," under s. 1 of the Charter.[51] The thrust of the Court's ruling with respect to s. 1 was that offering sign language interpretation for the entirety of British Columbia would cost only $150,000, or approximately 0.0025 percent of the province's health care budget at the time.[52] The Court gave the government of British Columbia six months to explore its policy options and implement the necessary changes.

One might have hoped that *Eldridge* would trigger a rush, nationwide, to ensure that hospitals have adequate translation services.[53] However, to date, British Columbia and Ontario remain the only provinces that have adhered to the ruling. David Lepofsky, a legal activist whose writings La Forest J. quoted in *Eldridge*, sums up the decision's impact: "It was a big court breakthrough but the impact has been weak because governments have never lived up to their obligations."[54] Even in the two provinces where free medical interpreting services are available, there have been concerns with timely access to sign language interpreters. The Canadian Hearing Society contends that to provide effective translation services, Ontario would need to double its current funding.[55] British Columbia has also experienced similar interpreter shortages.[56]

Since the enactment of the Charter, there appear to have been only twelve cases where the Supreme Court of Canada has ruled a state action or some legislation unconstitutional on the ground of breaching s. 15.[57] Of these, *Eldridge* appears to

---

[50] Eldridge v. British Columbia (Att'y Gen.), [1997] 3 S.C.R. 624, para. 64 (Can.).

[51] Canadian Charter of Rights and Freedoms, Part I of the Constitution Act, 1982, *being* Schedule B to the Canada Act, 1982 c. 11 (U.K.), § 1, which reads: "The Canadian Charter of Rights and Freedoms guarantees the rights and freedoms set out in it subject only to such reasonable limits prescribed by law as can be demonstrably justified in a free and democratic society."

[52] *Eldridge*, para 87.

[53] Kent Roach, *Remedial Consensus and Dialogue under the Charter: General Declarations and Delayed Declarations of Invalidity*, 35 U.B.C. L. Rev. 211, 230 (2002).

[54] Helen Enderson, *In the Shadows No More; After 25 Years of Activism, the Emphasis Is Finally on Ability Not Disability*, The Toronto Star, Mar. 15, 2008, at L1.

[55] *Deaf Rights Victory Paves the Way for Change*, The Toronto Star, Sept. 16, 2000, at RL02. See also Anna Piekarski, *Deaf Lack Help in Crises; Deaf Need a Voice in Crisis Ontario's Hard of Hearing Are Lacking Others to Speak for Them in Emergencies*, The Toronto Star, July 25, 2006, at B01.

[56] Allison Cross, *Phone Service Lures Away Deaf Interpreters; U.S.-Based Video Service Offers Better Pay, Hours Than Sign-Language Jobs, Interpreters Say*, The Vancouver Sun, May 9, 2008, at B5.

[57] Mary Hurley, *Charter Equality Rights: Interpretation of Section 15 in Supreme Court of Canada Decisions* 17–31 (Law and Government Division, Background Paper BP-402E, 2007), *available at* http://www.parl.gc.ca/content/LOP/ResearchPublications/bp402-e.htm. Hurley compiled a list of section 15 cases decided by the Supreme Court of Canada as of March 2007. There were a total of fifty-two cases, of which twelve were successful. A review of Supreme Court of Canada cases post-March

be the only one that deals directly with health resource allocation. The aftermath post-*Eldridge* suggests that even a successful juridical recognition of a positive right to health services is not in and of itself sufficient to effect the sought-after changes in practice. The Supreme Court of Canada's preferred remedy in such cases appears to be a declaration of invalidity or a declaration of entitlement, rather than an injunction that details the exact measures required of the governments to correct the illegality.[58] As we have just seen, this approach to remedies runs the risk of non- or under-compliance.[59]

3.3.3 *Discrimination Claims Pursuant to Human Rights Acts/Codes*

As an alternative to challenging government health care policy under the Charter, litigants may be able to challenge policy as discriminatory under provincial or federal human rights legislation before a human rights tribunal. However, even when discrimination is made out prima facie, provisions in this legislation generally further shield a law or decision. This is similar to s. 1 of the Charter, which states that rights are guaranteed "subject only to such reasonable limits prescribed by law as can be demonstrably justified in a free and democratic society." However, the rights protections and the limitations on those protections in other human rights legislation are not identical to the Charter, and thus there is at least the possibility that a claim would succeed if based on the former even if it would fail if based on the latter. Consider the following two cases.

In *Cameron*,[60] a couple successfully claimed that denying provincial funding for intra-cytoplasmic sperm injection (ICSI), a specialized in vitro treatment, discriminated against the infertile. However, the Nova Scotia Court of Appeal ruled that the provincial government's funding scheme was justified under s. 1 of the Charter. The Court said of the specialized in vitro fertilization (IVF) procedures that, "in the order of priorities . . . having regard to costs, the limited success rate and the risks do not, at this time, rank sufficiently high to warrant payment for them from public funding," and that "this [was] the real explanation why these procedures were considered not medically necessary."[61]

2007 revealed another nine cases where alleged violations of section 15 were at issue. In all nine cases, the Court dismissed the section 15 claims.

58 Roach, *supra* note 53, at 228–229.

59 *See* Little Sisters Book and Art Emporium v. Canada (Minister of Justice), [2000] 2 S.C.R. 1120, para. 258. (Can.), Iacobucci J., dissenting ("[D]eclarations are often preferable to injunctive relief because they are more flexible, require less supervision, and are more deferential to the other branches of government. However, declarations can suffer from vagueness, insufficient remedial specificity, an inability to monitor compliance, and an ensuing need for subsequent litigation to ensure compliance.").

60 Cameron v. Nova Scotia (Att'y Gen.) (1999), 204 N.S.R. (2d) 1, (Can. N.S. C.A.).

61 *Id.* para. 87.

Cameron can be contrasted with another case – this time before a human rights tribunal – involving access to IVF with ICSI: *Buffett v. Canadian Forces.*[62] Unlike *Cameron*, *Buffett* was ultimately successful in challenging the lack of funding for ICSI by alleging discrimination. Mr. Buffett claimed that the Canadian Forces' (CF) coverage policy, which provided IVF treatment for infertile female members, discriminated against men by failing to also provide coverage for IVF and ICSI for male members and their spouses. The Canadian Human Rights Tribunal found that there had been discrimination, and that funding should be provided to allow "the couple the opportunity to conceive and have a child that is biologically theirs,"[63] thereby allowing both Mr. Buffett and his wife, who was not covered by the CF plan, to receive infertility treatments. The Tribunal dismissed CF's claim that the financial burden posed undue hardship, finding a lack of evidence and that CF had inflated the costs it presented.[64] At judicial review, the Federal Court found that the tribunal had mischaracterized the purpose of the fertility treatments as enabling a *couple* to have their own children—leading to the mistaken conclusion that the CF was obliged to finance IVF treatments for Buffett's wife. Rather, the court reasoned, the purpose of fertility treatments is to "remove roadblocks to conception."[65] The CF was obliged to remove roadblocks faced by Officer Buffett by funding ICSI, but it was not required to finance the couple's goal of conceiving by funding IVF treatment involving the wife. When the matter was handed back to the Canadian Human Rights Tribunal for reconsideration in 2008, it was ordered that, as long as CF provided IVF funding for females, males should receive funding for ICSI.[66]

Cameron and *Buffett* reflect the two channels available to claimants alleging discrimination in the provision of health care: court challenges under s. 15 Charter, or challenges before human rights tribunals, under anti-discrimination provisions in provincial and federal human rights legislation. Whether one channel is more promising than the other is an open question. The Charter guarantees only equality "under the law," and as we have seen, the content of the Medicare basket is largely determined by non-legal processes (e.g., negotiations between provincial funders and provincial medical associations). As we will see later, in *Auton,*[67] the Supreme Court rejected demands for public funding for autism therapies, by noting that the Canada Health Act[68] only requires coverage of "medically necessary" care. By contrast, federal and provincial Human Rights acts protect broadly against discrimination with respect to services, goods, and facilities in the public and private sectors. Where an infringement is established, both the Charter and human rights legislation allow

---

[62] Canada (Att'y Gen.) v. Buffett, 2007 FC 1061 (Can.).
[63] *Id.* para. 48.
[64] *Id.* para. 101.
[65] *Id.* para. 55.
[66] Buffett v. Canadian Forces, 2008 CHRT 4, para. 4 (Can.).
[67] Auton v. British Columbia (Att'y.Gen.), [2004] 3 S.C.R. 657 (Can.).
[68] Canada Health Act, at c. C-6.

government to proffer a justification, under s.1 proportionality analysis or an "undue hardship" test respectively. Again, it is unclear whether courts or human rights boards provide a more hospitable venue for claimants at this stage: in both, where funding of health services is at issue, government justifications will focus on resource constraints.

Overall, while discrimination claims may seem appealing to litigants because of the ability to identify as disadvantaged by aligning oneself with an identifiable group (e.g., the disabled), courts and tribunals appear well attuned to the distinction between discrimination on its face and discrimination in substance. Although vulnerable and identifiable groups may not be able to access certain treatments, this may be both a necessary and inevitable result of fair health care rationing and prioritization. As explicit decision making grows, so too will the volume of decisions that are potentially contestable, but as rationing bodies become more open and transparent, with clearer guidelines and processes, the relative risk of a successful challenge seems likely to decline.

3.3.4 *Litigation over Negative Rights of Access to Health Care*

Most successful litigation vis-à-vis health care rights have been in the form of "negative" claims – that is, that government should not interfere with, for example, one's ability to access an abortion, consume medical marijuana, or obtain medical assistance to commit suicide in the face of terminal illness or unbearable suffering. The case of *Morgentaler*,[69] where the constitutionality of the criminal ban on abortion came under challenge, is the paradigmatic example of the successful assertion of negative rights in health. Section 251 of the Criminal Code at the time prohibited abortions unless a therapeutic abortion committee at an approved hospital determined that the continuation of pregnancy would endanger the woman's life or health.[70] The Supreme Court struck down this criminal provision as an infringement of the Charter right to security of the person. *Morgentaler* was a 5-to-2 ruling, and those in the majority penned three concurring decisions, making its precedent somewhat unclear. Chief Justice Dickson held that the impugned provision threatened women's physical integrity by denying their reproductive autonomy, and also imposed serious psychological stress; the approval process was deemed to be arbitrary, and to cause unnecessary delays.[71] Justice Beetz, in his concurring reasons, explained that the guarantee of security of the person "must include a right of access to medical treatment for a condition representing a danger to life or health, without fear of criminal sanction."[72] Wilson J., again concurring, staked out the most

---

[69] R. v. Morgentaler, [1988] 1 S.C.R. 30 (Can.).
[70] Criminal Code, R.S.C. 1970, c. C-34, § 251 (Can.).
[71] *Morgentaler*, paras. 22–34.
[72] *Id.* para. 78.

expansive position, finding that "the right to liberty contained in s. 7 guarantees to every individual a degree of autonomy over important decisions intimately affecting their private lives."[73]

By their nature, of course, negative rights do nothing to ensure equal access to treatments in the sense of securing public funding thereof. Indeed, in the case of abortion, there is evidence suggesting that accessibility of services actually *declined* after the *Morgentaler* decision.[74] In 1986, two years before *Morgentaler*, there were 643 hospitals in Canada with obstetrics capacity, of which 225 (i.e., 35.0 percent) provided therapeutic abortions.[75] By contrast, in 2003, a study by the Canadian Abortion Rights Action League found that only 123 of Canada's 692 hospitals (i.e., 17.8 percent) offered abortion services.[76] The percentage of Canadian hospitals with abortion services further decreased to 15.9 percent in 2006.[77] Currently, there are no hospitals or clinics in the province of Prince Edward Island that would perform the procedure.[78] Women in that province must obtain the procedure out of province, and seek reimbursement from the public health insurance plan.[79]

Even at hospitals where abortion services are ostensibly available, access is sometimes restricted to those having received physician referrals[80] and those who are

---

[73] *Id.* para. 298.

[74] *See, e.g.,* Nancy Bowes, et al., Access Granted, Too Often Denied: A Special Report to Celebrate the 10th Anniversary of the Decriminalization of Abortion, Canadian Abortion Rights Action League (CARAL) Report (1998); Timothy Wilson, Protecting Abortion Rights in Canada: A Special Report to Celebrate the 15th Anniversary of the Decriminalization of Abortion, CARAL Report (2003).

[75] Raymond Tatalovich, THE POLITICS OF ABORTION IN THE UNITED STATES AND CANADA: A COMPARATIVE STUDY 211 (1997).

[76] WILSON, *supra* note 73, at 13, 61. According to the Canadian Abortion Rights Action League, there are various reasons for the decreasing number of abortion providers. To some extent, the decline can be explained by the fact that since *Morgentaler* abolished the legally required therapeutic abortion committees in hospitals, there is no longer an obligation for hospitals to have at least one trained abortion doctor on staff. Also contributing to the decline is the trend to amalgamate religious and secular hospitals, which has left publicly funded Catholic institutions as the sole provider of reproductive health services in many communities across Canada. In many cases, these Catholic hospitals do not provide abortion services. For example, it was observed that of 127 hospital mergers that took place between 1990 and 1998, half led to the elimination of at least some, if not all, reproductive health services that had previously been available.

[77] Jessica Shaw, REALITY CHECK: A CLOSE LOOK AT ACCESSING ABORTION SERVICES IN CANADIAN HOSPITALS 15 (2006).

[78] *Abortion Information Line Disconnected,* CBC NEWS (Jan. 29, 2008), *available at* http://www.cbc.ca/canada/prince-edward-island/story/2008/01/29/abortion-line.html. *See* Tamsin McMahon, *No Change to Abortion Funding on PEI: Minister,* NATIONALPOST (Dec. 15, 2011), *available at* http://news.nationalpost.com/2011/12/15/no-change-to-abortion-funding-on-p-e-i-minister/.

[79] SHAW, *supra* note 76, at 32 (a woman who wishes to have her abortion publicly funded must first receive approval from a PEI doctor who deems such procedure as medically necessary, and subsequently have the doctor submit a request for funding to the province's Department of Health and Social Services).

[80] Sanda Rodgers, *Women's Reproductive Equality and the Supreme Court of Canada, in* HEALTH LAW AT THE SUPREME COURT OF CANADA 189, 214 (Jocelyn Downie & Elaine Gibson, eds., 2007). In New Brunswick, for instance, the referrals of two physicians are required to access abortion services.

within the gestational limits.[81] As such, many women have to travel to find a medical facility able and willing to perform an abortion, incurring significant travel and accommodation expenses. In provinces that do not publicly fund abortions performed at clinics (e.g., New Brunswick), women who cannot access abortions at hospitals are left to pay for the procedure out of pocket, at costs ranging between $500 and $750.[82]

3.3.5 *Using Charter Rights Litigation to Attack One-Tier Medicare and Equity*

Although litigants have had little success in arguing for access to publicly funded care, advocates of privatization have successfully used the Charter to attack universal one-tier health care.

In *Chaoulli*,[83] the validity of Quebec's ban on private health insurance was challenged by Dr. Chaoulli and Mr. Zeliotis – the former a physician who had unsuccessfully applied for a license to open an independent private hospital in the province, the latter a Quebecker who had suffered from numerous health conditions and encountered difficulties accessing timely care in the public health care system. The co-plaintiffs alleged that the ban on private insurance was in breach of patients' rights to life and security of the person, under both s. 1 of Quebec's Charter of Human Rights and Freedoms[84] and s. 7 of the Canadian Charter. In a 4–3 decision, the Supreme Court agreed with the petitioners and repudiated the prohibition of private insurance on the basis of the Quebec Charter. Justice Deschamps, for the majority, ruled that the prohibition on private insurance forced patients to endure long wait times in the public system, putting their life and personal security in jeopardy. In their reasoning, the justices relied on a crude international comparison of health systems and concluded that the presence of a parallel private sector would not necessarily undermine the quality of the public health care regime.[85] The decision afforded Quebeckers a negative right against government prohibitions of private health insurance. Three of the four majority judges in *Chaoulli* also found the legislative prohibition in question to have infringed on the right in s. 7 of the Canadian Charter.

---

[81] SHAW, *supra* note 76, at 15 (a national survey of hospitals found that, among those that responded, one would only perform abortions up to ten weeks of gestation, nine would do so up to twelve weeks, three up to thirteen weeks, six up to fourteen weeks, one up to fifteen weeks, three up to sixteen weeks, one up to eighteen weeks, and two up to twenty weeks).

[82] *Id.* at 24.

[83] Chaoulli v. Quebec (Att'y Gen.), [2005] 1 S.C.R. 791 (Can.).

[84] Charter of Human Rights and Freedoms, R.S.Q. c. C-12, § 1 (Can.) ("Every human being has a right to life, and to personal security, inviolability and freedom.").

[85] *See* Colleen Flood, *Chaoulli: Political Undertows and Judicial Riptides,* HEALTH L. J. (SPECIAL EDITION) 211 (2008) for a thorough discussion on the flaws of the Supreme Court's international comparative exercise.

Nationally, the main effect of the *Chaoulli* decision has been to legitimize in a political sense two-tiered health care as a policy option.[86] In a legal sense, however, its true impact was much more limited for as *Chaoulli* was decided on the basis of the Quebec Charter, its legal application does not extend beyond the province of Quebec. Consequently, similar prohibitions of private health insurance in other provinces remain in force. Even within Quebec, the negative and contextualized nature of the right established in this case has provided the provincial government some room for policy maneuver. In 2006, the Quebec legislature passed Bill 33: An Act to Amend the Act respecting health services and social services and other legislative provisions,[87] which provides for a range of measures to facilitate the fulfillment of wait time targets in the public system.[88] The bill also allows the sale and purchase of insurance for hip, knee, and cataract surgeries.[89] However, if the Quebec government delivers on its promise of a shorter wait time for these procedures,[90] it will undermine any demand by the public for private insurance coverage in these three areas. Thus one can see that the Quebec government has not responded to *Chaoulli* by allowing private health insurance across the board, and where it has allowed some private health insurance (hip, knee and cataract), it has put in place measures to effectively quell demand.

In any event, some of those keen to acquire private insurance may have difficulty finding an insurer willing to sell them an affordable policy.[91] Ironically, at sixty-five years of age and with preexisting heart and hip conditions, Mr. Zeliotis, the patient at the center of the *Chaoulli* case, would have likely been unable to access private

---

[86] *See, e.g.,* Douglas Thomson & Dennis Jeanes, *Info – One Year after Chaoulli – Uncertainty and Clinical Gridlock,* 73 Can. Orthopaedic Assoc. Bull. 4 (2007). ("Quebec's formal response, in terms of an expected huge increase in private services, hasn't come to pass and isn't likely to in the near future.").

[87] Nat'l Assemb. Bill 33, An Act to amend the Act respecting health services and social services and other legislative provisions, 37th Leg., 2nd Sess., (Que. 2006), S.Q. 2006, c. 43 (Can.).

[88] *Id.* §§ 7, 8, 17(1). Sections 7 and 8 of the Act create a centralized mechanism for the management of wait lists by hospitals for specialized and super-specialized services. The Director of Professional Services is responsible for ensuring that each clinical department manages its wait times accordingly. If there are long wait times for specific specialized medical services in a region, section 17(1) of the Act empowers the Health Minister to take measures to implement alternative procedures to alleviate the strain and ensure reasonable standards are maintained. *See also* Marie-Claude Premont, *Crunch Time for Public Health Care in Quebec,* The Toronto Star, Nov. 17, 2006, at A21.

[89] *Id.* § 42.

[90] In a discussion paper published in the wake of *Chaoulli* and before the enactment of Bill 33, the Quebec government sets out a wait time guarantee of six months for hip, knee, and cataract surgeries. The same document also provides that if a patient waits for more than six months, the government will pay for treatment in a private clinic. If the wait exceeds nine months, then the patient may receive care out-of-province at public expense. *See* Ministère de la Santé et des Services Sociaux (Quebec), Guaranteeing Access: Meeting the Challenges of Equity, Efficiency and Quality (2006).

[91] Barbara Sibbald, *Questions Raised about Private Insurance,* 173 Can. Med. Assoc. J. 585 (2005).

insurance.[92] As with abortion services and medical marijuana, courtroom success in securing negative rights will often ring hollow on the ground.

Chaoulli, however, was the first battle in a larger campaign to create opportunities for more private financing of medically necessary care, and similar litigation is now occurring across Canada. In Alberta, William Murray is presently pursuing a class action against the province for the damage he allegedly sustained from the denial of access to a special form of hip replacement procedure by the public health insurance plan. He argues, inter alia, that the denial of public coverage, in conjunction with sections of the Alberta Health Care Insurance Act[93] that effectively prevent treatment access outside of the government-run regime, violates his rights under s. 7 of the Charter.[94] In Ontario, an ongoing case initiated by Lindsay McCreith and Shona Holmes (who now appears as a spokesperson for the Republican Party's opposition to universal health care)[95] points to wait time problems and calls into question the constitutionality of provincial regulations designed to suppress the expansion of the private health care sector.[96] A private for-profit clinic, Cambie Surgical Corporation (Cambie), is contesting the constitutional validity of similar provisions under British Columbia's Medicare Protection Act.[97] Cambie is represented by Dr. Brian Day, a past president of the Canadian Medical Association (CMA).[98] I examine this latter challenge later in the chapter, in the context of discussing de facto privatization in Canada.

3.3.6 *User Fees, Extra Billing, and Privatization*

In Section 3.1 above we saw some of the dynamics giving rise to the "passive privatization" of Canadian health care, for example, the fact that an increasing percentage of health care spending is devoted to pharmaceuticals, which fall partly outside the

---

[92] Colleen M. Flood, *Chaoulli's Legacy for the Future of Canadian Health Care Policy*, 44 Osgoode Hall L. J. 273, 309 (2006).

[93] Alberta Health Care Insurance Act, R.S.A. 2000, c. A-20 (Can.).

[94] Murray v. Alberta (Minister of Health) (2007), 76 Alta. L.R. 4th 118, paras. 21–22. (Can. Alta. Q.B.) *See also* Tatalovich, *supra* note 744, at 224–25.

[95] See Daniel Tencer, *Shona Holmes, Canadian Woman Who Went for Treatment in U.S., Appears in Koch Brothers' Anti-Obama Ad*, The Huffington Post Canada (April 9, 2012), *available at* http://www.huffingtonpost.ca/2012/09/04/shona-holmes-koch-brothers-ad_n_1854773.html.

[96] Statement of Claim, McCreith v. Ontario (Att'y Gen.), No. 07-CU-339454PD3 (Can. Ont. Super. Ct. filed Sept. 5, 2007), *available at* http://www.canadianconstitutionfoundation.ca/files/1/McCreith%20Issued%20Statement%20of%20Claim%20pdf.pdf. *See also* Tatalovich, *supra* note 744, at 226–229.

[97] Medicare Protection Act, R.S.B.C. 1996, c. 286 (Can. B.C.).

[98] Cambie Surgeries Corp. v. British Columbia (Med. Serv. Comm'n), 2010 BCCA 396 (Can.). This case is part of an early round of this constitutional battle concerning the ability of the Medical Service Commission to audit Dr. Day's clinic. The audit sampled 468 services provided by two private clinics (Cambie and Specialist Referral Clinic) and found that almost half were illegally billed. See Audit & Investigations Branch, Ministry of Health, Specialist Referral Clinic (Vancouver) Inc. and Cambie Surgeries Corporation Audit Report (2012), *available at* http://www.health.gov.bc.ca/msp/legislation/pdf/srccsc-audit-report-2012.pdf.

Medicare basket; or the fact that private-pay MRI clinics are cropping up nation-wide, enabling those with the financial means to gain faster diagnoses and potentially expedite treatment.[99] A somewhat distinct privatization threat occurs where user fees or extra billing are allowed for publicly insured care. As we have seen, the CHA's commitment to accessibility should, in principle, stand in the way of privatization, were it not for two problems: one legal, the other political. The legal problem is that, in the wake of *Chaoulli*, provincial bans on user fees and extra billing are vulnerable to constitutional challenge. The political problem is simply the federal government's laxity in enforcing the CHA's principle of accessibility.

Of the three post-*Chaoulli* challenges just mentioned, Dr. Brian Day's claim, launched in British Columbia, presents the most direct assault on the single-payer system for medically necessary care. Dr. Day, along with a team of private investors, opened the Cambie Surgery Centre in 1996, with the stated aim of providing faster access to operations, outside of the public health insurance system. The initial plan was to serve patients whose care was financed outside of the province's general public insurance scheme: workers' compensation claimants and RCMP officers, for example.[100] Over time, however, Cambie began to provide care to any patient facing "an unacceptable waiting period for surgery" under the public system, provided they could afford the clinic's extra billing.[101] In September 2008, the BC Medical Services Commission gave notice that it would audit Day's clinic on suspicion of unlawful billing practices, in violation of s. 17 of the province's Medicare Protection Act. As a preemptive move, Cambie – along with four other private clinics and the Canadian Independent Medical Clinics Association (a lobby group formed by Dr. Day) – filed a counterclaim with the British Columbia Supreme Court on January 28, 2009. They allege, inter alia, that British Columbia's ban on extra billing infringes patients' Charter right to personal security and does not accord with principles of fundamental justice.[102] The basic contention is that the ban on extra billing leads to a decrease in the health care system's overall capacity, putting patients in jeopardy.[103]

It is hard to predict whether this challenge will succeed. For better or for worse, the *Chaoulli* decision does invite courts to weigh in on highly complex and contested questions concerning the structural features of the health care system. In *Chaoulli*, the majority's conclusion was strengthened – rhetorically at least – by the factual finding that Canada is the *only* country in the developed world to rely (in some

[99] Eduard Bercovici & Chaim M. Bell, *How Busy Are Private MRI Centres in Canada?*, 4 HEALTHCARE POL'Y 59 (2008).

[100] *From Beatles and Castro to the CMA: Dr. Brian Day: Likely New Head of Physicians' Group Has Colourful Past*, NATIONAL POST (Feb. 18, 2006), *available at* http://www.nationalpost.com/news/story. html?id=5ff7b7b8-ce38–453d-b90c-c5c8e5b25770&p=1.

[101] Rod Mickleburgh, *CMA Chief Defends Letting Patients Jump Queue*, THE GLOBE AND MAIL, Aug. 14, 2007, at A6.

[102] Statement of Claim para. 28, Canadian Independent Medical Clinics Ass'n v. Medical Services Comm'n of British Columbia, No. S-090663 (B.C. Sup. Ct. filed Jan. 28, 2009).

[103] *Id.* para. 14.

provinces) on a complete prohibition of private insurance (for medically necessary care). The same cannot be said of the ban on extra billing. France, for example – whose health care system is very well regarded – controls extra billing so as to assure that patients in the country's universal program have access to timely, quality care.[104] To meet this constitutional challenge, the BC government will need to show convincing social science evidence that allowing patients with financial means to queue-jump will have a deleterious effect on the public health care system. The difficulty the BC government faces is that unless and until this kind of privatization occurs, it is difficult to conduct the kind of empirical research required, and then, of course, if privatization does occur, it will be next to impossible to put the genie back in its bottle.

Even if regulations safeguarding equal access survive constitutional challenge, the CHA's principle of accessibility may fade into irrelevance because of a lack of enforcement by the federal government. In the spring of 2010, the province of Quebec floated the idea of a $25 user fee for doctor visits. This seems a clear violation of the CHA, yet the response from the federal government was one of studied ambivalence, with the federal Health Minister dispatching an aide to proclaim that, "The Canada Health Act is the law of the land. We expect the provinces and territories to abide by the act."[105] The minister's statement left Canadians speculating as to whether the federal government would declare that the user fees violated the CHA, and withhold funding accordingly. Leading pundit Andrew Coyne offered this explanation of the *realpolitik* at play: "With the cost of health care nearing 50 percent of provincial budgets, no federal government has any intention of withholding federal transfers in retaliation, from Quebec or any other province. The *Canada Health Act* is a dead letter."[106] It is not clear that a move to enforce the CHA's principle of accessibility would resound with voters, as polls at the time indicated that nearly half of Canadians are willing to accept user fees in a bid to contain health care spending.[107]

3.3.7 *The Broader Political Impact of Health Rights Litigation*

To this point, we have seen that health rights litigation has done little to advance equality of access to health care, let alone to equalize broader social determinants of health. However, litigation can have an impact on broader political dynamics.

---

[104] Flood & Haugen, *supra* note 31.

[105] *Quoted in* Robert Silver, *The Canada Health Act Is Dead*, THE GLOBE AND MAIL (Apr. 9, 2010), *available at* http://www.theglobeandmail.com/news/politics/second-reading/the-canada-health-act-is-dead/article4352673/.

[106] Andrew Coyne, *It's Like Putting a Puzzle Together*, MACLEAN'S MAGAZINE (Apr. 9, 2010), *available at* http://www2.macleans.ca/2010/04/09/it%E2%80%99s-like-putting-a-puzzle-together/.

[107] *Canadians Warming to Controversial Medical User Fees, Poll Finds*, THE GLOBE AND MAIL (June 6, 2010), *available at* http://m.theglobeandmail.com/commentary/munk-debates/canadians-warming-to-controversial-medical-user-fees-poll-finds/article598676/?service=mobile.

Occasionally, there have been cases that involved particularly sympathetic factual circumstances, and the publicity surrounding the defeat of these Charter challenges has generated considerable public backing for the litigants' causes. In some cases, this public pressure has led government to fund therapies even after courts have held that they were not legally obliged to do so. One example here is the move to gain Medicare coverage for Intensive Behavioural Intervention (IBI) – a form of autism treatment that incorporates a special technique termed Applied Behavioural Analysis (ABA).

In *Auton*,[108] four preschoolers with autism and their parents launched a Charter challenge against the province of British Columbia for failing to fund a comprehensive, universal ABA/IBI program. The plaintiffs argued that intensive, early-intervention ABA/IBI programs were medically necessary for autistic children and should be universally funded by the public health insurance plan akin to health services similarly required by children with other forms of disabilities or illnesses. The government's failure to do so, they alleged, unjustifiably discriminated against children with autism on the basis of disability and therefore contravened s. 15(1) of the Charter. Both the Supreme Court of British Columbia and the province's appellate court agreed.[109]

The Supreme Court of Canada, however, overturned the lower courts' rulings and held that the plaintiffs' equality rights were not engaged in this instance. In a unanimous decision written by McLachlin C.J.C., the Court emphasized that s. 15(1) of the Charter merely guaranteed Canadians, inter alia, "equal benefit of the law without discrimination."[110] Given that the CHA and the provincial Medicare Protection Act only required British Columbia to finance medically necessary services performed at hospitals or provided by physicians, public funding for ABA/IBI programs – which were delivered by therapists outside of hospitals – did not amount to a benefit conferred by law and therefore did not trigger s. 15 of the the Charter.[111] Furthermore, the Court noted that when compared to autistic children, non-disabled persons or individuals suffering from a disability other than autism were equally denied public funding for medical procedures that were emergent in nature and fell outside of the core health services defined by law notwithstanding how important such procedures might be to their health. Therefore, the Court held that the plaintiffs failed in establishing differential treatment by the government.

---

[108] Auton v. British Columbia (Att'y.Gen.), [2004] 3 S.C.R. 657 (Can.).

[109] *Auton* (2000), 78 B.C.L.R. 3d 55 (Can. B.C. Sup. Ct.), aff'd (2005), 6 B.C.L.R. 4th 201 (Can. B.C. C.A.). *But see* Donna Greschner & Steven Lewis, *Auton and Evidence-Based Decision-Making: Medicare in the Courts*, 82 CAN. BAR REV. 501 (2003). Greschner and Lewis criticized both trial and appellate courts' decisions in *Auton*, arguing that public funding for ABA/IBI was not supported by empirical evidence concerning the cost-effectiveness of the treatment.

[110] Canadian Charter of Rights and Freedoms, Part I of the Constitution Act, 1982, *being* Schedule B to the Canada Act, 1982 c. 11 (U.K.), §. 15.

[111] *Auton* was distinguished from *Eldridge* in that the latter dealt with differential access to health care services that were prescribed by law.

According to a survey conducted by Ipsos-Reid approximately one month after the release of the Supreme Court's decision, a staggering 89 percent of Canadians believed that Medicare should cover the cost of IBI treatment.[112] This level of support echoed the views expressed in the opinion editorials, columns, and letters to the editors published in the print media in the wake of *Auton*, most of which voiced a sense of disappointment, and at times even outrage, with the Supreme Court's ruling.[113] One columnist, however, offered a more positive perspective by observing that "a lot [had] been gained by the failed legal action" as the *Auton* case had "raised public sensibility with respect to autism to a level that governments now [would] be hard-pressed to ignore."[114]

Indeed, notwithstanding the *Auton* ruling, the general trend in Canada has been for the provincial governments to finance ABA/IBI programs, at least partially. Even before the *Auton* case went to trial, public funding for IBI therapy was available in Alberta, Ontario, Prince Edward Island, Newfoundland, and Manitoba.[115] In British Columbia, at the time *Auton* reached the Supreme Court of Canada, the province's autism programs offered up to $20,000 per year to families with autistic children under age six to help them purchase ABA/IBI therapy. For families with autistic children between the ages of six and eighteen, the province provided up to $6,000 per year per child.[116] While the outpouring of public support for government-funded ABA/IBI programs subsequent to the *Auton* decision did not contribute to these policy developments, it arguably played a role in preventing provincial governments from rolling back these ABA/IBI-related benefits after the Supreme Court absolved them of legal obligations to provide such services.

In fact, across Canada, not only has the existing public funding for ABA/IBI continued post-*Auton*, but in some cases, governments have allocated new resources to these treatment programs. For example, less than two weeks following the release of the Supreme Court's decision, the government of Nova Scotia announced that it would direct $4 million toward early-intervention IBI therapy.[117] In Ontario, government spending on services for children and youth with autism more than doubled between 2003 and 2006, allowing the number of children receiving IBI to increase

---

[112] *Canadians Support Autism Treatment*, THE VANCOUVER SUN, Dec. 21, 2004, at B3.

[113] *See, e.g.*, John Ivison, *Ottawa Must Now Address Another Injustice*, NATIONAL POST, Nov. 23, 2004, at A6; Justin Himmelright, *Autistic Kids Deserve Better*, NATIONAL POST, Nov. 23, 2004, at A19; Jennifer Ralph, *Cowardly Ruling*, THE OTTAWA CITIZEN, Nov. 24, 2004, at A13.

[114] Janice Harvey, *Funding Autism Therapy Is the Right Thing to Do*, TELEGRAPH-JOURNAL (Saint John, N.B.), Nov. 24, 2004, *available at* ProQuest, Doc. No. 423225915.

[115] Auton v. British Columbia (Att'y.Gen.), [2004] 3 S.C.R. 657, para. 11 (Can.).

[116] Vikram Dua, *Autism Spectrum Disorders in British Columbia: A Short History of the Creation of a New Program*, 8 NADD BULLETIN 3 (2005), *available at* http://thenadd.org/modal/bulletins/v8n1a3~.htm.

[117] Department of Health, *Good News for Children with Autism*, NOVA SCOTIA NEWS RELEASE (Dec. 2, 2004), available at http://www.gov.ns.ca/news/details.asp?id=20041202004.

by approximately 70 percent during this time.[118] By the end of 2006, all Canadian jurisdictions, with the exception of Nunavut, provided some public funding toward ABA/IBI therapies.[119]

Notwithstanding the move to public funding in all provinces, in the absence of a national strategy, the extent of funding for ABA/IBI therapies remains at the discretion of provinces and territories, and there are significant disparities from province to province. Whereas Alberta offers each child with autism up to $60,000 a year for ABA/IBI treatment until the age of eighteen, in most provinces ABA/IBI is partially funded and only for children younger than six.[120] For example, up until 2005, Ontario's Intensive Early Intervention Program only provided IBI for children with autism aged two to five. In *Wynberg*,[121] thirty-five autistic children and their families challenged the constitutionality of this age-based funding scheme in Ontario under ss. 7 and 15 of the Charter. The Ontario Court of Appeal rejected the petitioners' age-based discrimination claim, holding that the age cutoff in this instance was based on expert findings that suggested autistic children between the ages of two and five would benefit from the ABA/IBI therapy the most. The plaintiff's second argument – a disability-based s. 15(1) claim – was dismissed for lack of evidence that the existing education services were inadequate for students with autism and that ABA/IBI constituted the only appropriate special education program for this population. Lastly, the petitioners' s. 7 claim was dismissed as the Court reiterated that Canadian jurisprudence had not yet founded a positive right to health care upon this section of the Charter. However, echoing developments surrounding the *Auton* decision, the provincial government decided to remove the age limit from its publicly funded ABA/IBI programs before the Court released its decision in *Wynberg* decision. Responding to public confusion post-*Wynberg* over the government's commitment to autism funding, the government said it "[would] continue to provide services and support to autistic children regardless of age."[122] As such, the *Wynberg*

---

[118] *Ontario Expanding Supports for Children and Youth with Autism*, CAN. NEWSWIRE, June 16, 2006, at 1.

[119] Odette Madore & Jean-Rodrigue Pare, *Provincial and Territorial Funding: Programs for Autism Therapy* (Parliamentary Information and Research Service, PRB 06–22E, 2006), *available at* http://www.autismsocietycanada.ca/DocsAndMedia/KeyReports/Library_of_Parliament_ASD_Treatment_Summary_2006.pdf. *See also* THE STANDING SENATE COMMITTEE ON SOCIAL AFFAIRS, SCIENCE AND TECHNOLOGY, FINAL REPORT ON THE ENQUIRY ON THE FUNDING FOR THE TREATMENT OF AUTISM: PAY NOW OR PAY LATER – AUTISM FAMILIES IN CRISIS 7 (2007), *available at* http://www.parl.gc.ca/Content/SEN/Committee/391/SOCI/rep/repfinmar07-e.htm. *But see* Kristen Yu, *The Words Within*, CTV NEWS (Mar. 22, 2008), *available at* http://www.goqsoftware.com/fr/nouvelles/latest-news/ctv-news/ (in addition to Nunavut, the news article listed Northwest Territories as having no formal ABA/IBI programs, either, citing sources from Autism Society of Canada).

[120] Yu, *supra* note 118.

[121] Wynberg v. Ontario (2006), 82 O.R. 3d 561 (Can. Ont. C.A.), *rev'g* (2005), 252 D.L.R. 4th 10 (Can. Ont. Super. Ct. J.), leave to appeal to Can. Sup. Ct. refused, 31713 (Apr. 12, 2007).

[122] Mary Anne Chambers, *Ontario Committed to Helping Autistic Children*, THE TORONTO STAR, July 12, 2006, at A23.

case represents another example of health rights litigation that failed in the court-room but nonetheless played a part in instigating policy changes sought by health consumers.

This chain of events – where unsuccessful Charter challenges have triggered public support for the health services in question – is not limited to the context of autism treatment. The *Rodriguez* case,[123] which dealt with the issue of end-of-life care, arguably followed a similar pattern of juridical and political outcomes. Sue Rodriguez was a forty-two-year-old mother who suffered from amyotrophic lateral sclerosis (ALS), a neurodegenerative illness commonly known as Lou Gehrig's disease. During the course of the disease, most patients become bedridden and gradually lose the ability to speak and to ingest food. In most instances, the illness is terminal within two to three years of first diagnosis as it causes wasting of the muscles used in respiration. With her health rapidly deteriorating, Ms. Rodriguez sought to take control of the circumstances surrounding her death. She hoped to have an intravenous device installed by a medical practitioner that would allow her to end her life at a time of her choosing. To do so, she launched a Charter challenge to invalidate the criminal prohibition against aiding or abetting a person to commit suicide, arguing that the blanket ban violated her rights under ss. 7 and 15(1).

In a 5–4 decision, the Supreme Court of Canada denied Ms. Rodriguez's request. Although the majority agreed that the right to security of the person under s. 7 of the Charter encompassed the right to make choices regarding one's own body and to control one's physical and psychological integrity, it held that the limitation of this right by the criminal provision in question was in line with the principles of fundamental justice. That is, according to the majority of the Court, the prohibition against assisted suicide served the important function of preserving the sanctity of life and protecting the vulnerable in society. As for Ms. Rodriguez's equality rights argument, the Court held that even if the criminal sanction contravened s. 15 of the Charter, such infringement was justified under s. 1 as it properly struck a balance between the right to personal autonomy and society's respect for human life.

Despite this courtroom loss, supporters of assisted suicide and voluntary euthana-sia concluded that Rodriguez had "won an incredibly important victory in single-handedly putting this question of the right to death with dignity on the national political agenda."[124] Media attention surrounding the case generated support for the cause: a 1993 poll by Angus Reid found that 76 percent of Canadians supported the right to die for terminal patients who wished to end their lives.[125] Although no government-initiated bills on the subject of end-of-life care have ever been intro-duced in parliament, a number of private member's bills have been tabled over the

---

[123] Rodriguez v. British Columbia (Att'y Gen.), [1993] 3 S.C.R. 519 (Can.).

[124] Robin Brunet, *In the Court of Public Opinion: The Rodriguez Case Could Lead to Softer Laws on Assisted Suicide*, 5(7) B.C. Rep. 33 (1993). *See also* Margaret Otlowski, Voluntary Euthanasia and the Common Law 382 (1997).

[125] Otlowski, *supra* note 123, at 262.

years, including several by Svend Robinson, who has become one of the strongest supporters of Sue Rodriguez's endeavor.[126] Although these attempts at legislative change have remained unsuccessful to date, as in the case of *Auton*, they nevertheless reflect the significant pressure faced by parliament to act on the issue of assisted dying post-*Rodriguez*. This political momentum and the passage of time has allowed for another constitutional challenge to be brought to the provisions of the criminal code that bar assisted suicide – succeeding at trial but overturned at the appellate level.[127]

While cases such as *Auton*, *Wynberg*, and *Rodriguez* illustrate how political victories can flow from courtroom defeats, there are contrary examples. The issue of whether to cover assisted reproductive technologies under Canadian Medicare, which was at the center of the *Cameron* case,[128] discussed above in Subsection 3.3.3, is one such example.

Alex Cameron, a lawyer, and Cheryl Smith, a medical doctor, were a married couple who had had difficulties conceiving. As a result, Mr. Cameron took part in four cycles of intra cytoplasmic sperm injection (ICSI) – a specialized form of in vitro fertilization (IVF) – while Ms. Smith underwent two frozen embryo transfers. After incurring approximately $40,000 in medical costs, the couple remained unsuccessful in their attempts at conception.[129] In 1997, they launched a Charter challenge against the province of Nova Scotia, contending that IVF and ICSI should be considered medically necessary procedures under the Canada Health Act and the province's Health Services and Insurance Act,[130] and alleging that the denial of coverage violated s. 15(1) of the Charter by discriminating against infertile individuals.

The Nova Scotia Court of Appeal rejected the Camerons' claim. Relying on the testimonies of medical experts, the Court held that IVF and ICSI were not medically necessary because of their high costs, limited success rates, and the health risks involved therein. With respect to the plaintiffs' Charter challenge, the majority ruled that the government's refusal to fund IVF and ICSI did constitute a violation

---

[126] Marlisa Tiedemann & Dominique Valiquet, Parliamentary Info. & Research Serv., 91–9E, Euthanasia and Assisted Suicide in Canada 17–20 (2008). Mr. Robinson introduced a bill calling for the legalization of physician-assisted suicide in December 1992 and again in February 1994 upon Ms. Rodriguez's death. In 1997, he introduced a motion to have a special committee established for the preparation of a bill on euthanasia and assisted suicide. In 2005 and again in 2008, Francine Lalonde tabled another private member's bill that would have removed criminal sanctions against assisted suicide under certain circumstances.

[127] *See, e.g.*, Carter v. Canada (Att'y Gen.), 2012 BCSC 886 (Can. B.C. Sup. Ct.). The Court held that the provisions of the *Criminal Code* barring assisted suicide violated ss. 7 and 15 of the Canadian Charter of Rights and Freedoms. The court suspended the effect of its declaratory ruling for twelve months to allow parliament time to consider new legislation. The decision was overturned at the British Columbia Court of Appeal, with the majority finding that *Rodriguez* remains a binding precedent. *See* Carter v. Canada (Att'y Gen.) 2013 BCCA 435.

[128] Cameron v. Nova Scotia (Att'y Gen.) (1999), 204 N.S.R. 2d 1 (Can. N.S. C.A.).

[129] *Id.* paras. 8–9.

[130] Health Services and Insurance Act, R.S.N.S. 1989, c. 197 (Can. N.S.).

of the plaintiffs' equality rights, but went on to hold the infringement was justifiable, under s.1, on grounds of cost containment.

As the plaintiffs' request for leave to appeal the decision was denied by the Supreme Court of Canada in 2001,[131] the appellate court's ruling in *Cameron* has become the leading Canadian case law on the right, or lack thereof, to publicly funded IVF and ICSI procedures. Post-*Cameron*, whereas other jurisdictions such as England, New Zealand, and others have moved to provide funding for IVF treatments, it is only in 2011 that Quebec announced a program of public funding for IVF services[132] – no other province has yet moved to do so except in an extremely limited way.[133] This

[131] *Cameron*, leave to appeal to Can. Sup. Ct. refused, 27584 (Nov. 15, 2001).

[132] Prior to the policy change, Quebec had been offering a refundable tax credit of up to $6,000 per annum to couples for costs associated with IVF. *See* Edward Hughes, *Access to Effective Fertility Care in Canada*, 30 J. OBSTET. GYNAECOL. CAN. 389 (2008). After years of advocacy campaign – which has significantly benefited from the support of Julie Snyder, a high-profile TV personality in Quebec – during the 2008 provincial election campaign, Premier Jean Charest pledged to expand Quebec's health care coverage to include two cycles of IVF if reelected. According to his campaign platform, couples who require more IVF treatments after the two publicly funded attempts would continue to receive the tax credit. *See* Ingrid Peritz, *Kissing Babies Isn't Enough*, THE GLOBE AND MAIL, Nov. 22, 2008, at F3. After having won the election, in April 2009, the Quebec government sought to fulfill its campaign promise by introducing Nat'l Assemb. Bill 26, An Act Respecting Clinical and Research Activities Relating to Assisted Procreation, 39th Leg., 1st Sess. (Can. Que. 2009), *available at* http://www2.publicationsduquebec.gouv.qc.ca/dynamicSearch/telecharge.php?type=5&file=2009C30A.PDF. According to the government announcement, the new Quebec program will pay for up to three cycles of IVF treatments. *Ontario Standing Still While Quebec Meets Election Promise by Funding In-Vitro Fertilization: Quebec Couples to Get 3 IVF Cycles Funded*, CAN. NEWSWIRE, Apr. 24, 2009, *available at* http://www.newswire.ca/fr/story/464083/ontario-standing-still-while-quebec-meets-election-promise-by-funding-in-vitro-fertilization.

[133] Through a program that predates *Cameron*, Ontario pays for IVF through its public health insurance plan, but only for women with complete blockages in both fallopian tubes and for a maximum of three cycles. *See* Elizabeth Payne, *OHIP Falls under the Knife*, THE OTTAWA CITIZEN, Feb. 18, 1994, at A1. The legality of Ontario's IVF funding scheme, however, is currently being contested. In August 2009, Amir Attaran and his wife Ana Ilha filed a complaint with the Human Rights Tribunal of Ontario. They alleged that the IVF funding restrictions in Ontario discriminates against infertile individuals and therefore violates the provincial human rights code. *See* Natalie Alcoba, *The Right to Bear Children; Politics, Ethics Muddy Couple's Fight for Fertility Treatment*, NATIONAL POST, Aug. 22, 2009, at A1. In an editorial published in September 2009, the Canadian Medical Association Journal (CMAJ) – of whose Editorial-Writing Team Attaran is a member – came out in support of Attaran's human rights complaint, arguing that public funding of IVF would reduce the need for infertile women to have multiple embryos implanted at once and therefore would decrease the costs associated with multiple births. *See* Jeff Nisker, *Socially Based Discrimination against Clinically Appropriate Care*, 181 CAN. MED. ASSOC. J. 764 (2009). Similar economic arguments have been cited by the Ontario Expert Panel on Infertility and Adoption in its August 2009 report, which recommended the provision of "public funding for three cycles of IVF under certain conditions." *See Expert Panel Releases Report on Infertility and Adoption in Ontario*, CAN. NEWSWIRE, Aug. 26, 2009, *available at* http://www.cnw.ca/en/releases/archive/August2009/26/c7687.html. Judging from these recent developments, it would appear that, a decade after *Cameron*, advocacy efforts to have IVF publicly funded are finally picking up momentum again. However, as noted in the CMAJ editorial, public support on this issue seems to have remained questionable. Given such lackluster public sentiment, it begs the question whether Attaran's legal action, if it turns out to be unsuccessful, may run the risk of setting back the political movement as *Cameron* did.

low level of state funding for assisted reproductive technologies sets Canada starkly apart from most other countries that also have a universal health care system.[134]

The *Cameron* case did not appear to be as successful as *Auton* and *Rodriguez* in regards to enlisting public support for the plaintiffs' plight. In fact, in comparison to the outpouring of public sympathy in the wake of *Auton* and *Rodriguez*, the public response to the *Cameron* case seemed relatively mute. A review of the print media yielded only a handful of opinion editorials and letters to editors that commented on the lawsuit, most of which questioned the medical necessity of infertility treatments and disapproved of the Camerons' demand for public IVF funding.[135] Consequently, provincial governments have been under little pressure to deviate from the status quo and have relied on the *Cameron* ruling as the bottom line concerning IVF and ICSI funding.

3.4 CONCLUSION: AN OVERALL ASSESSMENT OF WINNERS AND LOSERS

Section 1.1 of this chapter surveyed the Canadian health care landscape, highlighting the public system's limitations in achieving health equality. I noted, for example, that the CHA centers myopically on physician services and care delivered in hospital; moreover, the criterion used in determining whether a therapy is subject to first-dollar public coverage – *medical necessity* – is not clearly defined. As more and more health care spending is devoted to goods and services failing outside this envelope (e.g., pharmaceuticals, long-term care, private diagnostics), the overall scheme of health care allocation becomes more regressive. I also noted the great disparities in health outcomes that arise out of inequalities in social determinants of health, and cited evidence showing that Canada ranks near the bottom of OECD nations in its levels of public social spending. Lastly, we saw that there is concern about the very sustainability of Canadian Medicare in the face of legal and political efforts to undo regulations blocking two-tiered care. Now I turn to the question that animates this volume: Has health rights discourse and litigation served to combat or exacerbate these inequalities?

Much of Canada's health rights litigation is centered on securing public coverage for particular therapies (ICSI treatments for infertile couples, ABA/IBI therapy for autistic children, etc.), and in an optimistic mood one might see this litigation as expanding and patching holes in universal Medicare – a boon for overall equality. Any such optimism should be tempered. As explained, *Eldridge* is the

---

[134] Jeff Nisker, Distributive Justice and Infertility Treatment in Canada, 30 J. OBSTET. GYNAECOL. CAN. 425, 426 (2008). See also Edward Hughes & Mita Giacomini, *Funding In Vitro Fertilization Treatment for Persistent Subfertility: The Pain and the Politics*, 76 FERTIL. STERIL. 431, 432 (2001).

[135] *See e.g.*, J. J. Forrestal, *In Vitro Not a Necessity*, THE GLOBE AND MAIL, July 29, 1998, at A14; Naomi Lakritz, *Infertile Couples Not Covered under the Charter; Governments Do Not Owe Couples Babies, No Matter How Much the Couples Think They Deserve Them*, CALGARY HERALD, Feb. 18, 1999, at A16.

only case where plaintiffs have successfully litigated a positive right to a health service. A main sticking point is that the courts are reluctant to direct government on
questions of resource allocation. Thus even in *Eldridge*, the chosen remedy was
under-prescriptive, allowing provincial governments across the country to persist in
underfunding sign language translation services in hospitals.

Whether successful or not, health rights litigation can draw public attention
to gaps in Medicare, with an overall effect that promotes equality. Optimism on
this score should again be tempered. In the sampling of cases examined in this
chapter, we have seen that public opinion is not uniformly sympathetic to health
rights claimants. While plaintiffs in cases such as *Rodriguez* and *Auton* appear to
have generated public support and galvanized political momentum through high-
profile (but ultimately unsuccessful) litigation, the similarly unsuccessful litigation in
Cameron exemplifies the opposite dynamic, stalling any momentum toward public
insurance coverage for IVF and ICSI.

Regarding the impact of health rights on broader political discourse, a deeper
question is whether overall health equity is advanced by having public attention
rapt with the struggles of individual rights claimants. From the standpoint of health
equity, the lack of public coverage for IVF treatments does not seem quite so grave a
failing as, for example, the aboriginal population's deprivations across various social
determinants of health. Yet, at present, there appears to be little hope that health
rights litigation can or will be used ameliorate the social determinants that drive
inequalities in health. Litigation currently stands as a tool available only to those
who can best afford to use it, and thus remains unavailable to those who suffer most
from the inequalities in our society. Absent some form of wealthy "white knight"
to bring the concerns of the disadvantaged before the courts, an alternate method
needs to be found to ensure that the Canadian "single-payer" model of health care
is transformed to ensure an equitable delivery of health services (both direct and
indirect) in Canada.

4

Promoting Access and Equity in Health

Assessing the National Health Service in England

Christopher Newdick

This chapter assesses the National Health Service (NHS) in England and the extent to which it promotes access and equity among its patients. I explain the structure of the NHS, how it works, and the courts' role in improving resource allocation systems. The NHS was founded in 1946 on principles of solidarity, citizenship, security, and fairness. It expresses a political willingness to engage with distributional ethics in which collective resources may be shifted from the well to the ill and from the rich to the poor. It has much in common with many other European health care systems. Since the 1990s, this centralized model has been modified by commercial and consumer levers introduced to improve performance. I discuss how significant progress has been made with respect to accountability surrounding access to *acute* care, but that serious socioeconomic challenges remain as regards *chronic, noninfectious* diseases caused by modern patterns of living. As we discuss, the cost implications of these trends are beyond judicial competence. Although well understood, they are yet to generate the policy responses they deserve.

For consistency, the sequence of the analysis adopts the pattern used in the other contributions to this volume, as follows: (1) the system of finance and access to health care, (2) legal documents governing the NHS, (3) an analysis of litigation over rights to NHS care, and (4) whether litigation has promoted equality of access.

4.1 FINANCE AND ACCESS: SALIENT FEATURES OF THE NHS

The NHS is financed from general taxation rather than individual insurance premiums. NHS doctors may not charge for providing NHS care, and treatment in hospital and in the community is normally provided free of charge. However, NHS charges may be imposed for prescription drugs provided in the community (but not in hospital), prescribed eyewear, and community dentistry services.[1] Actually,

---

[1] The National Health Service Act, 2006, c. 41(Eng.) (which contains many of the principles contained in the original National Health Service Act 1946) provides that NHS services shall be free of charge,

so many sections of the community are exempt from these "community" health charges that, in practice, almost 90 percent of drug prescriptions are provided without charge to patients.[2] Access to NHS care is available to those who are "ordinarily resident" in the United Kingdom, including overseas nationals who have settled in the country.[3] The following section discusses the salient features of the NHS.

4.1.1 *Duty to Promote a Comprehensive Health Service*

The Secretary of State must "promote" a "comprehensive health service,"[4] and general practitioners (GPs) must provide patients with the care that is "needed" under terms set down by statutory regulations.[5] Thus, rights and duties in the NHS are described by concepts[6] rather than a defined "basket" of benefits.[7] As we discuss later, this "conceptual" approach gives decision makers considerable discretion and leads to variations between different parts of the country. There is no suggestion that a defined list might be introduced to the NHS.[8] The only marginal exception to this general approach is with respect to a long "black list" of treatments that GPs may not provide in primary care and a short "grey list" of treatments that may be provided in limited circumstances only.[9] Although the black list is lengthy, it does not stop GPs from prescribing the care needed by patients. Instead, it includes over-the-counter products like retail cough mixtures, soaps, toothpastes, and even Flora margarine.

except as directed otherwise by the Secretary of State. Thus, charges may be made for prescription drugs outside hospital and for dental and optical care. The current charge is £7.65 per prescription, which may be for a single item or a course of medicine over a period of months.

2 Excluded from charges are children younger than sixteen, pregnant women, people older than sixty, young people in full-time education, people in receipt of certain benefits such as Income Support or Jobseekers' Allowance, and people suffering from specific conditions, such as certain types of physical disability, diabetes, or epilepsy, for which they hold a valid exemption certificate.

3 The test of "residence" means that British nationals who have paid taxes all their lives and contributed to the NHS lose their rights to NHS care as soon as they move abroad and cease to be ordinarily resident. But those who move here to work, and have made no such contribution, immediately become entitled to free NHS care. Proposals to reform these laws in 2004 came to nothing.

4 National Health Service Act, sec. 1.

5 The National Health Service (General Medical Services Contracts) Regulations, 2004, S.I. 2004/291, Sched. 6, Para 42 (U.K).

6 *See generally* Christopher Newdick, WHO SHOULD WE TREAT? RIGHTS, RATIONING AND RESOURCES IN THE NHS (2d ed, 2005). As Andre den Exter, Mária Éva Földes, and Elizabeth Rynning, respectively, describe in this volume, this "conceptual" approach has also been adopted in Holland, Hungary, and Sweden.

7 Defined treatment lists have the advantage of certainty, but the disadvantage of inflexibility. For example, how often is it updated, by whom, on the basis of what clinical evidence (given that knowledge is often evolving), and what about patients with multiple conditions whose circumstances are not covered?

8 *See* J. Schreyögg et al., *Defining the "Health Benefit Basket" in Nine European Countries – Evidence from the European Union Health BASKET Project*, 6(Suppl 1) EUR. J. HEALTH ECON. 2 (2005). Israel adopts a "health care basket" approach; *see* Aeyal Gross, Chapter 6 in this volume.

9 The lists are contained *in* The National Health Service (General Medical Services Contracts) (Prescription Drugs) Regulations, 2004, S.I. 2004/629 (U.K.).

The grey list, by contrast, is a very short list of treatments that should be prescribed with caution. It includes sildenafil (trade name Viagra) as, perhaps, the only example of a treatment restricted for "rationing" (rather than clinical safety) reasons.

4.1.2 *Delegation of Powers to Local Health Commissioners*

Since its creation in 1946, the NHS has kept a reasonably consistent structure. The Secretary of State's duties are delegated to an intermediate tier of statutory management lying between the central Department of Health and clinicians. This intermediate tier of organization "commissions" (or purchases) care under the National Health Service 2006 (and its predecessor Acts) by planning and organizing health care for their local communities. These intermediate bodies are currently called Clinical Commissioning Groups (CCGs), which are arm's length bodies with statutory duties to exercise the Secretary of State's duties to promote a comprehensive health service.[10] The size of these intermediate bodies has varied over time, reflecting the organizational balance of advantages and disadvantages between larger numbers of health authorities responsible for smaller numbers of patients (which are more responsive to local need but lack negotiating power with hospitals and suppliers) and fewer authorities with larger numbers of patients, greater economies of scale, and bargaining power (but less sensitive and reactive to local circumstances). Reflecting this tension, from 1996 to 2002, there were 100 health authorities. From 2002 to 2006, 303 primary care trusts (PCTs) were reduced to 150 after national reorganization. From 2013, CCGs will probably exceed 200.[11] Each reorganization presents its own pros and cons, but this continual disruption must undermine continuity and the accumulation of experience and, ultimately, the quality of NHS services.

4.1.3 *The NHS "Market" for Services*

NHS services are provided by a "mixed economy" of public or private providers.[12] For example, most hospitals belong to the NHS, but GPs are private contractors who contract their services to the NHS. However, since the 1980s, successive governments have favored market forces in the NHS as a lever to improve value for money. Today, NHS hospitals compete with each other for patients and with *private* contractors that may also bid for business from NHS commissioners. Correspondingly, patients are

---

[10] Clinical Commissioning Groups replaced Primary Care Trusts as commissioners under the Health and Social Care Act, 2012, c. 7 (Eng.). The statutory names and functions of these bodies is subject to too much change, and analogous functions have previously been performed by, for example, area health authorities, regional health authorities, family health services authorities, health authorities, and primary care trusts.

[11] At the time of writing (August 2012), the number was not finalized.

[12] Because the National Health Service Act, sec. 12, enables the Secretary of State to "arrange with any person or body to provide, or assist in providing, any service under this Act."

regarded as "consumers" with rights to choose where they will receive their hospital care, on the principle that this will improve the quality of the NHS. The impact of market competition on the NHS is difficult to assess. Comparing the quality of services between different providers is difficult, and the data is not easily accessible to patients. In any case, patients often wish to be treated locally near their family and not to travel long distances from home. Government is increasing the comparative data available to patients,[13] but it is yet uncertain whether this policy will succeed, or whether patients' preferences for high-quality local hospitals will always blunt its impact.

4.1.4 *NICE and Post Code Rationing*

As we have noted, commissioning decisions about NHS funding allocations are delegated to individual commissioners (i.e., CCGs). Given the number of NHS commissioners, there is a danger of differing funding policies generating "post code rationing" (as the press call it), in which patients in one area may be denied access to care available elsewhere. For this reason, the National Institute for Health and Clinical Excellence (NICE, renamed the National Institute for Health and Care Excellence [still known as NICE]) was created in 1999 to encourage greater consistency of practice between commissioners. NICE has power to issue *Technology Appraisal Guidance* (TAG), which has mandatory impact in the sense that commissioners are obliged to pay for the medicines it recommends. The *mandatory* force of TAGs derives from the power of the Secretary of State to issue "Directions" to NHS bodies, and he has done so in relation to the powers of NICE.[14] As of August 2012, NICE had issued about 260 TAGs. Although this is helpful for treatments covered by a TAG, there are, of course, many more treatments that NICE has not considered and that remain subject to the commissioning discretion of CCGs.

An exception to this general rule about local commissioning exists in respect of specialist care for rare conditions, which are commissioned centrally. Specialist commissioning is necessary when services need to draw from a larger population base in order to focus a critical mass of patients in one hospital unit and so foster and preserve adequate expertise. Specialist commissioning is now undertaken by the National Commissioning Board.

4.1.5 *Regional and Demographic Variations: Equity Issues*

Do current resource allocation policies respond to the needs of various groups fairly and equally? At a macro level, there is no absolute calculation by which to

---

[13] See *NHS Hospital Episode Statistics*, HES ONLINE, *available at* http://www.hesonline.nhs.uk/Ease/servlet/ContentServer?siteID=1937&categoryID=1295.

[14] See *Funding of Technology Appraisal Guidance from the National Institute for Health and Clinical Excellence (NICE)*, DEPARTMENT OF HEALTH (March 17, 2010), *available at* http://www.dh.gov.uk/en/Publicationsandstatistics/Legislation/Directionsfromthesecretaryofstate/DH_4075685.

judge which groups should obtain what proportion of the health care budget. For example, how should need for obstetric care be assessed against neonatal, pediatric, orthopedic, cancer, or mental health care? As a result, there are considerable differences between the funding of clinical specialties, illuminated in the *Atlas of NHS Services*.[15] Also, unexplained variations exist, for example, as to the proportion of patients admitted to hospital, the time spent there, the expenditure set aside to treat them, and rates of mortality and morbidity after treatment. This suggests that care in some places is less effective and efficient than in others, perhaps for reasons of poor clinical and managerial habit. To some extent, this can be addressed by NICE and national guidelines, but changing clinical practice is notoriously difficult, and clinical variations remain a significant challenge for the NHS.

More generally, the burden of illnesses suffered by the poorest in society is a concern (in common with many other countries). Despite reasonably clear policy commitments to respond to disadvantaged groups, the health divide between richest and poorest in society continues to widen. Since 1998, successive governments have attempted to redress the systemic pattern of health inequality in the NHS, but although *aggregate* standards of health have increased, health *inequalities* between rich and poor have become more marked. As the House of Commons Health Committee said in 2009:

> Health in the UK is improving, but over the last ten years health inequalities between the social classes have widened – the gap has increased by 4% amongst men and by 11% amongst women. . . . Inequalities have worsened not because the health of the poor is getting worse or even staying the same, but because the rate of gain amongst more advantaged groups.[16]

Four causes bear disproportionate responsibility for these inequalities. They are tobacco, physical inactivity, excess alcohol consumption, and poor diet. They are responsible for 42 percent of deaths from leading causes and 31 percent of all disability-adjusted life years (DALYs). "Avoidable" diseases account for close to £9.4 billion annually in direct costs to the NHS, out of a total budget of approximately £100 billion, and the costs are increasing steadily.[17] The escalating financial implications of failure to reduce health inequalities are severe because the burden of

---

[15] NHS, *The NHS Atlas of Variations in Healthcare* (2010) *available at* http://www.rightcare.nhs.uk/atlas/qipp_nhsAtlas-LOW_261110c.pdf.

[16] House of Commons Health Committee, HEALTH INEQUALITIES, HC 286–1, Third Report of session 2008–09, (Feb. 26, 2009), *available at* http://www.publications.parliament.uk/pa/cm200809/cmselect/cmhealth/286/286.pdf. Within each social class, differentials of health status exist between gender (men worse than women), age (old worse than young), and ethnic subgroups (South Asians worst); *see id.*, at 18, 59. It is estimated that 80–85% of variation in PCTs' mortality statistics are caused by socioeconomic factors outside the control of health care, such as poverty, intelligence, and ethnicity. *See* House of Commons Health Committee, TACKLING INEQUALITIES IN LIFE EXPECTANCY IN AREAS WITH THE WORST HEALTH DEPRIVATION, HC 186, Third Report of session 2010–11 (Oct. 26, 2010), *available at* http://www.publications.parliament.uk/pa/cm201011/cmselect/cmpubacc/470/470.pdf.

[17] Howard Bernstein, Paul Cosford & Alwen Williams, ENABLING EFFECTIVE DELIVERY OF HEALTH AND WELLBEING 21 (2010).

treating diabetes, coronary heart disease, stroke, and cancer will increasingly reduce the resources available for other people.

Lack of *access* to NHS care is not the primary reason for these health inequalities. True, there are fewer GP practices in the poorest neighborhoods, but all NHS patients have a right to be registered with a GP practice and so have reasonable access to primary care and a right to be referred to hospital. It is also true that patients who pay for *private* treatment may secure care more quickly. However, most NHS treatment is provided within eighteen weeks,[18] so the advantages of paying for care are less marked than they were previously, when NHS waiting lists were longer. More important drivers of health *inequality* are modern patterns of living, which incline people to drink, eat, and smoke more and to take less exercise. Clearly, in an era of austerity in public funding, this steep increase in "avoidable" illness presents a substantial challenge to policy makers. Close to 96 percent of the current funding of the NHS responds to health need *after* patients have fallen ill. As lifestyle diseases increase and demographic trends of "greying" populations exacerbate these pressures, the failure to redress this trend will make current expectations of the NHS unsustainable. More energy is required to find ways of stopping people falling ill. However, shifting spending from those who are ill to preserving and promoting standards of public health involves hugely sensitive issues of liberty and autonomy and will cause much anxiety and debate.

4.2 NHS LEGAL DOCUMENTS

As we have seen, since 1946, the Secretary of State has had a duty to "continue the promotion of a comprehensive health service"[19] and "the services so provided must be free of charge except in so far as the making and recovery of charges is expressly provided for by or under any enactment."[20] The Secretary of State's policies are developed and disseminated in collaboration with the National Commissioning Board (created by the Health and Social Care Act 2012).

4.2.1 *The National Health Service Act 2006*

Note that the duty is to "promote" (but not *provide*) the service, and the word "comprehensive" is not defined. The rights conferred are statutory in character (rather than constitutional, or common law). As the courts acknowledge, they are imprecise, and the Secretary of State and commissioners have wide discretion both as to the objectives identified for the NHS and the policies by which they should be

---

[18] Under government undertakings made *in The NHS Constitution* NHS (March 8, 2012), *available at* http://www.nhs.uk/choiceintheNHS/Rightsandpledges/NHSConstitution/Documents/nhs-constitution-interactive-version-march-2012.pdf.

[19] National Health Service Act, sec. 1 as amended by Health and Social Care Act, sec. 1.

[20] National Health Service Act, sec. 1(4), as amended by the Health and Social Care Act. This enables charges to be made for prescription drugs, spectacles and dental services.

achieved. As we discuss later, they are sometimes referred to as target duties and are more easily understood as conferring *procedural* rights only, rather than substantive rights to tangible treatments.[21] This means that individual claims are not divorced from the community context in which they arise, and the courts' intervention is limited to referring the decision back to the CCG to be reconsidered and requiring it to be taken again in the light of the court's guidance.[22]

4.2.2 *Regulations, Directions, and Guidance*

Many of the rights and duties imposed by the 2006 Act are set down more fully in statutory regulations and Secretary of State's mandatory "Directions" to NHS bodies. For example, as we have seen, the duties imposed on GPs are set down in statutory regulations, and the duty to fund treatments recommended in a NICE TAG is contained in "Directions." Statutory regulations are commonly used to govern the NHS, especially as regards the functions and membership of statutory bodies such as NHS hospital boards, CCGs, NICE, and the National Commissioning Board.

Central influence may also be exercised by means of Department of Health *guidance*. In legal theory, unlike regulations and directions, guidance is not mandatory. CCGs are obliged to take guidance into account in decision making, but are not bound to follow it. This is because *local* CCGs, not the Secretary of State, are responsible for local priority setting. However, the national press finds the Secretary of State an attractive target to blame for complaints arising in the NHS. As a result, government often imposes severe informal political pressure on local health commissioners. Hostile headlines can result in an urgent telephone call from the Department of Health in London to the local commissioner with uncompromising instructions to get a difficult story out of the news by funding a treatment. In practice, therefore, this informal pressure often has more direct impact than do statutes, regulations, and directions. Indeed, in 2001, government was criticised in a report it had itself commissioned for falsely blaming everyone else when hard decisions attracted adverse publicity.[23]

---

[21] This contrasts with the *substantive* rights arising from NICE TAGs, *see infra* Sec. 2–3. This "procedural" response contrasts with Columbia and Brazil (discussed by Everaldo Lamprea [Chapter 5] and Marianna Prado [Chapter 12] in this volume) where the courts order "substantive" remedies which provide tangible access to treatments. Such an approach causes opportunity costs of those unable or unwilling to litigate for their care.

[22] Contrast the South African courts, which have used a "substantive" approach and ordered government to provide social welfare benefit (*see* the *Treatment Action Campaign* case, discussed by Lisa Forman and Jerome Amin Singh in Chapter 11 of this volume). Equally, they have done so cautiously. Thus, the difference between the English and South African approach may be less dramatic than it appears, because English "procedural" review may be so intense that the public authority collapses and provides the treatment to the patient. By contrast, the Colombian and Brazilian approaches use the courts as the usual means of accessing treatment, and there the contrast with English law is stark.

[23] "Governments of the day have made claims for the NHS which were not capable of being met on the resources available. The public has been led to believe that the NHS could meet their legitimate needs, whereas it is patently clear that it could not. Healthcare professionals, doctors, nurses, managers,

4.2.3 *The NHS Constitution*

Belatedly perhaps, government has acknowledged the fact of NHS priority setting by publishing the NHS Constitution in 2010. This was brought about by judicial review litigation that criticized the poor quality of decision making in respect of commissioning (which we outline later). The NHS Constitution is a bill of rights for patients, which has statutory recognition and applies to all NHS bodies including the Secretary of State.[24] The Constitution covers a broad range of rights and duties.[25] Significantly, it acknowledges that the NHS works within a limited budget and that hard choices are unavoidable. For example, it states: "The NHS is committed to providing best value for taxpayers' money and the most effective use of finite resources."[26] An explanatory document that accompanies this candor explains: "Like all public authorities, PCTs are required to operate within finite budgets and, therefore, have to prioritise some treatments over others according to the needs of local communities .... Disinvestments should be considered along with investments."[27]

The Constitution confirms the "substantive" status of NICE TAGs.[28] Thereafter, it describes patients' rights to NHS treatment as "procedural." For example, it says: "You have the right to expect local decisions on funding of other drugs and treatments [ie not subject to NICE TAGs] to be made rationally following a proper consideration of the evidence. If the local NHS decides not to fund a drug or treatment you and your doctor feel would be right for you, they will explain that decision to you."[29] It continues:

and others, have been caught between the growing disillusion of the public on the one hand and the tendency of governments to point to them as scapegoats for a failing service on the other . . . The NHS was represented as "a comprehensive service which met all the needs of the public. Patently it did not do so . . ."

Learning From Bristol: The Report of the Public Inquiry into Children's Heart Surgery at the Bristol Royal Infirmary 1984–95 57, para 31 (2001).

[24] *See* National Health Service Act, sec. 2 as amended by Health and Social Care Act, sec. 3. The NHS Constitution is not a statute, but statutes require NHS bodies to have regard to it. Also, new statutory regulations The National Health Service Commissioning Board and Clinical Commissioning Groups (Responsibilities and Standing Rules) (2012, S.I. 2012/2996, Pt. 7 (U.K.)), effective from April 1, 2013) have been made under the NHS Act 2006. These regulations will give specific force to the parts of the NHS Constitution on "transparency" in priority setting. So, in this respect, the NHS Constitution will have statutory force.

[25] Including: "You [the patient] should recognise that you can make a significant contribution to your own, and your family's, good health and well-being, and take some personal responsibility for it." *See* Principle 2b. the NHS Constitution.

[26] THE NHS CONSTITUTION, *supra* note 18, at principle 1(6)

[27] Department of Health, *Defining Guiding Principles for Processes Supporting Local Decision Making about Medicines* 3, 14 (2009), *available at* http://www.dh.gov.uk/prod_consum_dh/groups/dh_digitalassets/documents/digitalasset/dh_093433.pdf.

[28] THE NHS CONSTITUTION, *supra* note 18, at principle 2a.

[29] Id.

[E]ach PCT must have in place arrangements for making decisions and adopting policies on whether particular healthcare interventions are to be made available for patients for which the PCT is responsible.... Each PCT must compile and publish clear written information outlining the arrangements specified.... Where a PCT makes a decision to refuse a request for the funding of a healthcare intervention, where the PCT's general policy is not to fund that intervention, the PCT must provide that individual with a written statement of its reasons for that decision.[30]

Although this is concerned with individual access to treatment, the context is obviously community-based. Health authorities should develop accountability mechanisms that describe how the "macro" resource allocation decisions have led to an individual treatment decision. To this extent, in encouraging the link between individual patient rights and the wider duties to the community, the NHS Constitution may make a significant contribution to public health.

4.2.4 *Paying for Private Care*

We have noted that NHS care is provided free of charge to everyone (i.e., at the point of use, because funding is provided from general taxation)[31] based on the principle of *equality of access* to care. Recently, however, this principle has given rise to a dilemma. Like all health care systems, the NHS has to identify priorities. Some expensive treatments may not be funded if they are likely to have only marginal therapeutic benefits, otherwise funding would be exhausted before the end of financial year. What if a patient wishes to have access to treatment that is not normally commissioned because of cost and limited clinical evidence? Her doctor explains that it is unlikely to have significant therapeutic impact, but the patient wishes to try it anyway. Should she be permitted to "top up," or supplement her NHS care in order to have it, or does this offend the principle of equality of access?

Take a patient who suffers from cancer. He has received the treatment normally funded by his health authority, but it has not been successful and his prognosis is poor. His doctor recommends a new drug as a last resort which is expensive and about which there is limited evidence of efficacy. The CCG refuses to pay because of the poor evidence it will work and it would divert resources from other patients. Therefore, the patient volunteers to pay for the drug himself provided he can remain in an NHS hospital for medical, nursing, and other care (including monitoring and supervision) – in other words, to share the costs of his care with the NHS. He can afford the drug costs, provided the NHS continues to pay for his hospital bed and clinical care. Should the patient have the right to this extra treatment and remain

---

[30] National Health Service, England, *Directions to Primary Care Trusts and NHS Trusts Concerning Decisions about Drugs and Other Treatments* (March 31, 2009), *available at* http://www.nyypct.nhs.uk/AdviceInformation/MakingDecisions/docs/F3%20-%20Decision%20Making.pdf.

[31] *See infra* regs. 1–3.

an NHS patient, or could this undermine equality by diverting NHS hospital beds, staff time and equipment away from NHS-only patients?

Previously, the Department of Health forbade patients from making contributions to the cost of their NHS care on the ground that it would dilute the commitment to equality of access. Thus, until 2009, there was a clear presumption that once a patient paid for care privately, concurrent NHS care had to stop.[32] The patient was treated either entirely within NHS or privately. However, in 2009, the Secretary of State published new guidance on *NHS Patients who wish to Pay for Additional Care*.[33] Reversing the previous policy, it says:

> Patients may pay for additional private healthcare while continuing to receive care from the NHS. However, in order to ensure that there is no risk of the NHS subsidising private care, the guidance insists that it should always be clear whether a treatment is privately funded or NHS funded, private and NHS care should be kept as clearly separate as possible, and private care should be carried out at a different time and place to the NHS care that a patient is receiving.[34] Privately funded patients should meet any additional costs associated with the private element of care, such as additional treatment needed for the management of side effects.[35]

This is a compromise between top-down, central control and bottom-up, individual choice; between *equality* and *liberty*. Notice that the private treatment should be provided at "a different time and place to NHS treatment" because it would be unacceptable to have patients with similar needs having rights to different standards of treatment in the same hospital wards. But there will be cases in which additional private treatment must be delivered concurrently, or where the patient is too frail to be moved. Responding to this concern, the guidance says: "Departing from these principles of separation should only be considered where there are overriding concerns of patient safety, rather than on the basis of convenience."[36] The delicate

---

[32] Previous guidance said: "A patient cannot be both a private and a NHS patient for the treatment of one condition during a single visit to a NHS organization.... Patients referred for a NHS service following a private consultation or treatment may join any NHS waiting list at the same point as if the consultation or treatment were a NHS service."

Department of Health, *A Code of Conduct for Private Practice* (2004), *available at* http://www.nhsemployers.org/SiteCollectionDocuments/DH_085195.pdf. Although one suspects, however, that doctors would often have treated patients as both NHS patients and privately.

[33] *See id.*; Department of Health, *Guidance on NHS Patients Who Wish to Pay for Additional Private Care* (2009), *available at* http://www.rcn.org.uk/__data/assets/pdf_file/0005/228839/RCN_response_to_additional_private_care_consultation_FINAL.pdf.

[34] *Id.*, at Para. 4.2. Examples of cases in which these principles apply are suggested in the *guidelines*.

[35] *Id.*, at Para. 8.2. However, where the same diagnostic, monitoring, and other procedures have been undertaken in the NHS, they may be available to assist the private element of care without charge.

[36] And that such a departure should normally have been agreed with the hospital medical director. *Id.*, at Para. 4.3.

balance between these competing objectives have not yet been considered by the courts, and difficult distinctions are bound to arise.[37]

4.2.5 *NHS Care or Social Care?*

Lastly, the National Health Service Act 2006 sets down duties in respect of *health care* only. Social care is dealt with by the National Assistance Act 1948. The distinction is crucial because NHS care is provided free of charge; social care is subject to means testing. This is especially important for elderly people receiving long-term care in nursing and residential homes who need help washing, dressing, toileting, and feeding, yet it is extremely difficult to apply in practice.[38] In England, there never has been a satisfactory way of distinguishing the two. In Scotland, "personal" social care is not subject to charging, but the "residential" aspect of care is paid for out of pocket. The NHS/social care divide has troubled patients, policy makers, and caregivers since the 1950s. Government consultations and proposals for reform are constantly in the air, yet the practical complexity of introducing fair, transparent, and *affordable* distinctions between free NHS care and chargeable social care continues to confound government.[39]

4.3 ANALYSIS OF LITIGATION: "HARD LOOK" PROCEDURAL RIGHTS

How do patients enforce their rights under the National Health Service Act 2006? Unlike some European Constitutional courts, the UK courts have developed judicial review principles in administrative law to supervise NHS resource allocators.[40] The right of action is normally against the local commissioner because the duty to improve the effectiveness, safety, and quality of care is imposed on CCGs.[41] As we have said, given the large numbers of CCGs, differences may exist between them. Some of these differences are inevitable; the needs of an inner city community will

---

[37] In Canada, the "choice" v. "equity" dilemma has been resolved in favor of choice; *see Chaoulli v. Quebec* (Attorney General) [2005] 1 SCR 791 (Can.), discussed by Colleen Flood in Chapter 3 of this volume. The case demonstrates the inclination of courts to favor "individualistic" solutions to social problems.

[38] See Christopher Newdick, *Patients, or Residents?: Long-term Care in the Welfare State*, 2 MED. L. REV. 144 (1996).

[39] Current reform proposals are contained *in* Andrew Dilnot, Norman Warner & Jo Williams, AIRER CARE FUNDING – THE REPORT OF THE COMMISSION ON FUNDING OF CARE AND SUPPORT (2011).

[40] New Zealand courts demonstrate equal willingness to scrutinize and review; *see* Joanna Manning, Chapter 1 in this volume. Compare the reluctance to become involved in resource allocation litigation of the Constitutional courts in Hungary, The Netherlands, and Sweden, discussed by Mária Éva Földes (Chapter 8), Andre den Exter (Chapter 7), and Anna-Sara Lind (Chapter 2), respectively, in this volume.

[41] The new duties are set out in the National Health Service Act, sec. 14 (inserted by the Health and Social Care Act, sec. 25).

differ from those of a seaside resort popular with retirees. However, not all post code differentials between commissioners are easily explained. Add to this the role of the press promoting "personalized" accounts of illness and our increasing willingness to voice complaint, and one understands the growth in litigation.

Judicial review tests the lawfulness of commissioning decisions under the NHS Act 2006. We have remarked on the "target" and *procedural* nature of NHS rights in which courts may refer decisions back to commissioners to be taken again, but which do not require judges to allocate resources themselves. Let us see how this works by first distinguishing between "weak" and "hard look" judicial review.

4.3.1 *"Weak" Judicial Review*

Surprisingly perhaps, the first case to challenge funding decisions in the NHS was not heard until 1980,[42] more than thirty years after the NHS commenced. Two cases followed in 1987 and 1988.[43] Each failed on the grounds that the courts were not the proper forum in which to test matters of health care resource allocation. Responsibility for decisions of this nature were properly delegated to public representatives with expertise to do so and, unless their decisions were "outrageous," they could not be subject to judicial review. Obviously, this erected an extremely high hurdle for litigants to climb. This passive phase of judicial review was not unique to NHS law. It applied equally to other challenges against government departments and represents an era when the courts were more hesitant in encroaching on areas of policy making considered the proper domain of legislators accountable to the electorate. However, this judicial deference to decision-makers made judicial review so weak that the procedural "right" it protected was rendered, for practical purposes, ineffective.

4.3.2 *"Hard Look" Judicial Review*

"Hard look" judicial review evolved in the mid-1990s.[44] It describes a general change in attitude about the proper balance of power between the judiciary and legislature. In this more active stage of judicial review, the remedy is normally *procedural*, not substantive, in the sense that judicial review enables the court to overturn such a decision and to refer it back to the decision maker to be reconsidered. Even now, some challenges are so "political" that they are difficult to conceive, for example a challenge to government's *overall* funding policy for the NHS. However, in respect of funding decisions about individual patients, there has been considerable development. Although the court has no power to make substantive funding

---

[42] R. v. Secretary of State, ex p Hincks [1992] 1 BMLR 93 (decided in 1980) (U.K.).

[43] R v. Secretary of State, ex p Walker [1992] 3 BMLR 32 (U.K.); R. v. Central Birmingham HA, ex p Collier [1988] (unreported, Court of Appeal) (U.K.).

[44] *See* Christopher Newdick, WHO SHOULD WE TREAT? RIGHTS, RATIONING AND RESOURCES, Chap. 5 (2nd ed, 2005) for comparison of "weak" and "hard look" judicial review.

decisions,[45] judicial review has clarified the procedural duties of commissioners. Resource allocation principles were first described in 1999 by the Court of Appeal in *ex p A, D & G*[46] in an application by three litigants for trans-gender surgery. The claim challenged a *refusal* to fund gender reassignment surgery (when understanding of gender dysphoria was less developed – clinical attitudes have changed considerably since then). The Court of Appeal generated clear guidance as to the procedural safeguards that should accompany these decisions and these principles have been developed by subsequent cases. In outline, they can be summarized as follows:

First, as we have said, local resource allocation decisions are for each local health commissioner to make within the framework of the statutes governing their powers and duties. There is no all-embracing definition of what the "promotion" of a "comprehensive health service" requires; it is a matter of discretion for each CCG. This means that priority setting is lawful (other than in respect of NICE TAGs) and there may be variation between commissioners about the same treatments. Sympathizing with the need for health care rationing, the Court said:

> The precise allocation and weighting of priorities is clearly a matter of judgement [for] each authority. . . . It makes sense to have a policy for the purpose – indeed, it might well be irrational not to have one – and it makes sense that an Authority would normally place treatment of transsexualism lower in its scale of priorities than, say, cancer or heart disease or kidney failure.[47]

Second, however, the manner in which this discretion is exercised is subject to close judicial scrutiny. Decision making must adhere to principles of procedural fairness, be consistent, consider relevant factors, and exclude irrelevant ones. For example, the framework for decision making should consider the:

(1) nature and seriousness of the illness,
(2) cogency of the evidence that the treatment works,
(3) extent and likelihood that it will work in *this* patient,
(4) extent of improvement it might be expected to provide,
(5) absolute cost of the treatment,

---

[45] Although legal theory permits decision makers to reconsider the decision and come to the same conclusion by a different route, once the patient succeeds in judicial review, legal, political, and media pressures invariably force the authority to concede the point and treat the patient. Although health care should be allocated according to fair, transparent, and consistent principles, sometimes those who shout loudest get the most.

[46] *See* R. v. NW Lancashire Health Authority, ex p A, D & G [1999] Lloyds Rep. Med. 339 (U.K.).

[47] *Id.*, at 408. *See also* R v. Cambridge DHA, ex p B [1995] 2 All ER 129, 137 (U.K.) in which the judge said: "I have no doubt in a perfect world any treatment which a patient, or a patient's family, sought would be provided if doctors were willing to give it, no matter how much it cost, particularly when a life was potentially at stake. It would however be shutting one's eyes to the real world if the court were to proceed on the basis that we do live in such a word."

(6) numbers that might benefit, and

(7) its relative cost and effectiveness by comparison to other effective treatments.[48]

Decision makers must, therefore, have a robust system for priority setting and be ready to defend the hard choices that may be required because "the more important the interests of the citizen that the decision effects, the greater will be the degree of consideration that is required of the decision-maker. A decision that, as is the evidence in this case, seriously affects the citizen's health will require substantial consideration, and be subject to careful scrutiny by the court as to its rationality."[49]

Third, what happens when there is incomplete or disputed clinical evidence surrounding a treatment (as was the case with respect to transgender surgery in 1999)? For example, what if specialists support the treatment, but there are no reliable trials demonstrating its effectiveness? The Court said:

> [T]he mere fact that a body of medical opinion supports the procedure does not put the health authority under any legal obligation to provide the procedure.... However, where such a body of opinion exists, it is ... not open to a rational health authority simply to determine that the procedure has no proven clinical benefit while giving no indication of why it considers that is so.[50]

The view of individual doctors is a relevant consideration, but it is not decisive. The CCG must weigh and balance this together with the other relevant factors. In this case, one of the reasons for rejecting the request for funding was the absence of a randomized controlled trial. This, the court said, was unreasonable, first because it was unreasonable to expect large-scale trials to be available when the total numbers of patients having had transgender surgery was very small, and second because the health authority failed to consider sufficiently the views of the doctors involved in these cases.

Fourth, balancing community interests with the needs of individuals, these procedures must respond to patients with *exceptional* clinical merit who will derive much more benefit from the treatment than other patients will. As with general purchasing questions, commissioners may come to differing conclusions about similar cases, provided they have weighed and balanced all the relevant factors. This means that "blanket bans" on certain treatments are unlikely to survive judicial

---

[48] *Id.* Such a system is used by the South Central Ethical Framework. *See* South Central Priorities Support Unit, *South Central Ethical Framework,* NHS (Feb. 12, 2008), *available at* http://www .oxfordshirepct.nhs.uk/about-us/how-the-pct-works/documents/SOUTHCENTRALETHICAL FRAMEWORKFeb08.pdf.

[49] *Id.,* at 412; *Contra,* applying the South Central Ethical Framework and the policies made thereunder, *see* AC v. Berkshire West PCT and the EHRC [2011] 119 BMLR 135 (U.K.) the claimant, a transgender patient, requested cosmetic breast implants to enhance her sense of body image. The PCT refused to fund the treatment because its policy on cosmetic surgery normally denied such treatment to natal women. The court upheld the fairness of the PCT's refusal to create an exception in these circumstances.

[50] R v. NW Lancashire HA, Lloyds Rep Med 399, 412.

review.[51] This rule on blanket bans forces decision makers to confront the difficult balance between community and individual interests, which we consider next.

4.3.3 *Balancing Community and Individual Interests*

How is this balance between exceptional individuals and community interests to be achieved? For example, take the common example of a cancer treatment which is (a) expensive, (b) can prolong a patients' life by a small number of months only, and (c) may make some patients worse. Commissioners may prefer to use that money to support palliative cancer care services instead and, therefore, refuse to fund it. How do courts resolve contested clinical evidence of this nature? What if a well-respected oncologist gives evidence that his cancer patient is "exceptional"? Understandably, judges often respond with sympathy to these cases,[52] but there is a danger of responsible priority setting being undermined by exceptional cases. Courts must acknowledge the differences in persuasive weight of, at one end of the spectrum, individual clinical opinion about a single patient and, at the other, the results of multi-center randomized controlled trials involving thousands of patients (and the gradations in between). This enables the court to accord appropriate weight to clinical opinion about the potential benefits of, perhaps, experimental treatment, but does not give individual experts disproportionate influence.[53] Unless this process is managed responsibly, "exceptional" cases will obtain an unfair advantage over others and so undermine the principle of equality and fairness.

4.3.4 *Clinical "Need" and "Social" Circumstances*

Should social circumstances ever qualify as "exceptional"? Take the example of a mother with a terminal illness who has young children who must be resettled before she dies of her illness. Should this fact entitle her to greater resources to

---

[51] *Id.*, at 408.

[52] See cases discussed in Christopher Newdick, *Exceptional Circumstances: Access to Low Priority Treatments after the Herceptin Case*, 1 Clinical Ethics 205 (2006); Christopher Newdick, *Judicial Review: Low-Priority Treatment and Exceptional Case Review*, 15 MED. L. REV. 236 (2007). Compare the "substantive" responses of the courts in Columbia and Brazil discussed in this volume, where such cases have greater prospects of success. English lawyers might express concern about the "opportunity cost" to non-litigants of having resources diverted to successful litigants.

[53] The numbers of judicial review applications for "exceptional" access remains small. The courts have not attempted to define what is exceptional. For this reason, there is a danger of inconsistency of response in both health authorities and courts. The National Prescribing Centre has clarified the position by reminding clinicians of the "hierarchy of clinical evidence," which gives proportionately more priority to treatments as the evidence of effectiveness becomes more robust. It is yet to be reviewed by the courts. *See* National Prescribing Centre, SUPPORTING RATIONAL LOCAL DECISION-MAKING ABOUT MEDICINES (AND TREATMENTS): A HANDBOOK OF GOOD PRACTICE GUIDANCE 42, Box XI (2009) for "hierarchy of evidence" that distinguishes: well-conducted meta-analysis of several, similar, large, well-designed RCTs; large well-designed RCT; meta-analysis of smaller RCTs; case-control and cohort studies; case reports and case series; consensus from expert panels; and individual opinion.

extend her life for as long as possible for the benefit of her children? Or could nonclinical factors discriminate against, for example, single people who are not carers, elderly patients (by comparison to the young), and unemployed people (by comparison to those in work)? Unless otherwise recommended by NICE, this question belongs to local commissioners and is subject to judicial review. "Need" is a famously elastic word that has both biological and sociological perspectives.[54] For example, some health authorities have refused to permit *nonclinical* circumstances to be recognized as health "needs." In *Condliff v. North Staffordshire PCT*,[55] the claimant's body mass index (BMI) was higher than 40, and he was referred for stomach-reducing surgery. However, the commissioner refused his request for funding because its policy considered patients for such surgery only at BMI 50 and higher (as a way of regulating demand for a service that could divert resources from other patients). He argued that he was suffering such unhappiness and discomfort that he had exceptional "social" circumstances that deserved funding. However, the health authority's "exceptionality" policy was restricted to *clinical* circumstances only. It excluded "social" circumstances because they are too imprecise to be measurable and, if permitted, likely to cause inconsistency and unfairness between patients. In judicial review, the Court of Appeal accepted the legitimacy of this policy as a reasonable response to the challenge of maintaining a system fair to everyone. This is clearly an extremely sensitive ethical problem.

Each of these "procedural" developments was generated piecemeal by the courts. The number of cases was limited and, at least at first, their impact on the NHS as a whole was small. However, from the case of A, D & G on, as the cases accumulated, they exercised greater influence collectively. As the consistency of the courts' response made the giving of legal advice to health authorities more straightforward (and the legal cases became increasingly newsworthy), the government responded by publishing the NHS Constitution, which, as we discussed earlier, reduces the cases to a single code of good practice and cements patients' rights. So, although no single case was significant in isolation, the persuasive weight imposed by a number of cases has had a profound impact on priority setting in the NHS.[56]

4.3.5 *Impact of European Law – the ECHR and ECJ*

What has been the effect of European Law on UK law? Some litigants have attempted to engage the Human Rights Act 1998 (which gives the European Convention on Human Rights statutory force), but they have not been very successful. A number of cases from the European Court of Human Rights have dismissed claims for

---

[54] The literature is vast. *See, e.g.*, Lyn Payer, Medicine & Culture (1988).

[55] R (Condliffe) v. North Staffordshire PCT [2011] EWCA Civ 910.

[56] No cases have yet argued the NHS Constitution on this point. This is not to say that it has not been influential. Many health authority's faced with a claim based on the Constitution would be advised to settle.

access to care, which would have had the effect of rearranging existing patterns of resource allocation and could have adversely affected the rights of others. Even with respect to reductions in expenditure on hemodialysis services[57] and the treatment of HIV/AIDS,[58] the Human Rights Court generally considers that decisions about "positive" entitlements to social and economic rights do not trigger articles 3, 6, and 8 of the Convention and remain within the discretion of national decision makers.[59]

However, EU law is having a different impact. The European Court of Justice has used the free-movement-of-services rules to say that individual patients are entitled to obtain the health services "normally available" within their own systems in any other EU country if the services cannot be provided within a "reasonable time" at home. Exceptions are made only where granting the right would undermine the financial stability of the health care system involved (which, of course, is unlikely).[60] This approach has led to so much confusion that the European Commission has had to pass an EU directive on access to health care.[61] Why does this provoke difficulty?

The difficulty is illuminated by the problems presented by the unequal burden of ill health suffered by the poorest in society. As we have discussed, a plausible public health response is to shift the distribution of health resources away from acute care in hospitals and toward *health promotion and preventive care* in the community (especially for children). The advantage will be less morbidity and mortality overall, but the downside is that waiting times for hospital treatment may increase. The decision is one of judgment based on clinical, financial, social, and political considerations. The *procedural* response of the UK courts has been to demand a proper framework of reasoning for these decisions but not to determine which patients should be given

---

[57] Pentiacova v. Moldova [2005] 40 EHRR 209 (U.K.).

[58] N v. United Kingdom [2008] (App no 26565/05)[2008] 47 EHRR 39 (U.K.), *but see* D v. United Kingdom [1997] 42 BMLR 149.

[59] The UK Supreme Court has considered the position in two analogous cases involving social services care. *See*Tomlinson v. Birmingham City Council [2010] UKSC 8 (U.K.) para. 49 Lord Hope said: "the award of services or benefits in kind is not an individual right of which the applicant can consider himself the holder, but is dependent upon a series of evaluative judgments by the provider as to whether the statutory criteria are satisfied and how the need for it ought to be met, do not engage article 6(1). . . . They do not give rise to 'civil rights' within the autonomous meaning that is given to that expression for the purposes of that article"; *see* R (McDonald) v. Royal Borough of Kensington and Chelsea [2011] UKSC 33 (U.K.) para. 16 where Lord Brown said: "[T]he clear and consistent jurisprudence of the Strasbourg Court establishes 'the wide margin of appreciation enjoyed by states' in striking 'the fair balance . . . between the competing interests of the individual and of the community as a whole' and 'in determining the steps to be taken to ensure compliance with the Convention', and indeed that 'this margin of appreciation is even wider when . . . the issues involve an assessment of the priorities in the context of the allocation of limited state resources' – *Sentges*, . . . *Pentiacova*, and *Molka v Poland*. . . . The complaints in all three cases were unanimously held to be manifestly ill-founded and thus inadmissible."

[60] *See* Case C-157/00, Gareats-Smits v. Stichting Ziekenfonds Vgz, Peerbooms v. Stichting Cz Groep Zorgverzekeringen, 2004 E.C.R. I-5473. *See also* the chapter by Mária Éva Földes, considering the case of Hungary.

[61] Council Directive 2011/24, 2011 O.J. (L 88/45) on the Application of Patients'Rrights in Cross-Border Healthcare.

priority. By contrast, the ECJ has created a *substantive* right. Once the conditions of access are satisfied (i.e., "normal treatment" and "reasonable time"), the patient may seek treatment elsewhere in the EU, pay for it there, and seek reimbursement from their health authority at home. This has implications for the ethical integrity of national systems. It undermines the democratic right of parliaments to manage health care and threatens the legitimacy of national priority setting. In our preventive care example earlier in the chapter, say the NHS decided to reallocate NHS resources in the way described and, in so doing, agreed that hospital waiting times for some treatments would lengthen. Accordingly, patients facing longer waiting times for hospital admission bring actions before the ECJ to challenge their delayed treatment. The ECJ's approach is to re-divert resources from the "public health" policy and give it back to litigants seeking hospital treatment. The ECJ did not consider – and may not have understood – that by "favoring" patients who are relatively fit and able to travel and who need acute *hospital* care, it risks ignoring poorer members of society who cannot afford to pay for their care and those in need of *preventive* care.[62]

The ECJ failed to recognize the challenges of public health. It appears to have grasped only the "micro," individualistic and market-based dimension of health care ethics and ignored the challenges of fairness, solidarity, and redistributive policies that are the bedrock of European public health systems. It gives the impression of making judicial policy without knowledge of the public consequences of doing so, perhaps to pursue interests and agendas of its own.[63] Recent jurisprudence from the ECJ suggests that it may now be recognizing the difficulties presented here and be adopting a "procedural" approach similar to that of the ECHR.[64] It is clearly desirable for the ECJ to accommodate the historical commitment of European nation states to the politics of distributional welfare and social solidarity.[65]

4.4 CONCLUSION: DOES LITIGATION PROMOTE EQUALITY?

There are a number of problems with litigation as a driver of equality and fairness in health care systems. Litigation often focuses on individual rights rather than public

---

[62] *See* Christopher Newdick, *Citizenship, Free Movement and Health Care: Cementing Individual Rights by Corroding Social Solidarity*, 43 *CMLR* 1668 (2006) for the author's criticism of the ECJ. Patients are required to pay out of pocket in the "host" state and seek reimbursement at "home." However, unless the reimbursement is delayed for as long as the treatment would otherwise have been provided, earlier payment is likely to disrupt forward budgetary planning and affect other patients' access to care. Like in Canada and the United States, this individualistic preference may undermine the interests of patients whose interests are not before the court.

[63] *See* Scott Greer, The Politics of European Union Health Policies 3 (2009).

[64] *See* Case C-512/08, Commission v. France, 2010 E.C.J., I-8833, upholding the right of national authorities to regulate access of patients to expensive diagnostic procedures in other member states.

[65] *See, e.g.*, Peter Baldwin, THE POLITICS OF SOCIAL SOLIDARITY – CLASS BASES OF THE EUROPEAN WELFARE STATE 1875–1975 (1993).

interests. It arises at random from the strength of feeling, funding, and fortitude of individuals, rather than as part of any coherent program. Litigation looks backward to problems from the past rather than solutions for the future (although, as we have seen, it can encourage planning). Courts have limited expertise to adjudicate over claims by one patient or group to receive "priority" treatment over others. Threats of litigation often encourage "defensive" policy making, in which decisions are made more out of fear of complaint and criticism than as a result of proper balancing of community interests. "Community" interests are more comfortably dealt with by "politics" and accountable policy makers than by judges. Indeed, there is concern that if judges were to routinely absorb this political role, the function and legitimacy of democratic institutions could be undermined.[66] Often, litigation is a distraction from public health policies that promote fair distribution of health care services. It generates anxiety among health authority decision makers and may divert attention from more pressing public health concerns.

To these general misgivings, however, should be added a number of specific comments.

4.4.1 *Benefit of the "Hard Look" Procedural Judicial Review*

First, the preference for *procedural* remedies in the United Kingdom should not hide the significant change in the practice of NHS commissioners as a result of judicial review. Previously, judicial review was passive and deferential to public authorities. Individual rights were not well balanced in the decision-making process because the courts considered the matter beyond their authority. However, especially since 1999 and the case of *ex p A, D & G*, a very different approach has developed in which the courts have adopted a proactive role by subjecting public authority discretion to close scrutiny under a "hard look" approach. Although the remedy remains procedural, the effect has been to hold public authorities to higher standards of accountability, to establish proper systems within which to make decisions, and to encourage consistent decision making and a capacity to explain the reasons for decisions. As we have discussed, the courts have clarified the procedural duties of public authorities and the commensurate rights of patients,[67] and the NHS Constitution has given practical force to judicial requirements by expressing in a uniform code the principles developed by the courts. Clearly, UK courts regard NHS resource allocation as a democratic, not judicial, function. Nevertheless, their restrained activism has done much to improve the quality and transparency of decision making in the NHS.

---

[66] Fritz Scharpf, *Legitimacy in the Multilevel European Polity* (MPIfG Working Paper, Paper no. 09/1, 2009).

[67] *See* Keith Syrett, Law Legitimacy and the Rationing of Health Care (2007).

4.4.2 *Can Judicial Review Regulate Private Organizations?*

However, while judicial review is transforming the behavior of *public* authorities, what will be the impact on accountability rights of policies that encourage private companies to run public services? This was promoted by the Labour government in 2000, has been continued ever since, and is common in many other health care systems. In the NHS, the policy has been largely restricted to private *providers* of care, for example clinics and hospitals. However, it may be extended to private *commissioners* of care for populations of people.[68] This has special significance in the United Kingdom because of the particular function of judicial review. Judicial review is available only against *public* authorities. For example, in respect of a private nursing home, private companies have argued successfully that they are engaged under a private contract for commercial gain, which is not subject to Human Rights Act review and public accountability.[69] If this is also correct in respect of the commissioning of NHS services, judicial review litigation will be powerless to hold private bodies accountable, or to control the fairness and transparency of their decision making. This problem has not gained traction in politics,[70] but it is a significant and unresolved challenge for accountability in future.[71]

4.4.3 *Access, Equity, and "Avoidable" Illness*

Third, in the United Kingdom, the major concern is less about *access* to health care and more about inequality of health *status*.[72] In other words, equal rights of access to the NHS have not reduced the systemic inequalities in noncommunicable diseases, which most burden poorer parts of the community. Can litigation be effective here? These deep-seated problems, which are greatly influenced by culture and societal norms, are probably beyond the competence of the courts. For example, if we agree that *equality* of health status is a fundamental objective of public health systems,

---

[68] Indeed, the policy may be required by the European Court of Justice, which, as we have seen, has promoted market freedoms between member states.

[69] *See* YL v. Birmingham City Council, [2007] UKHL 27, [2007] 3 W.L.R. 112 (appeal taken from Eng.).

[70] See Christopher. Newdick, The NHS in Private Hands – Regulating Private Providers of NHS Care, in Current Legal Problems 2000, 1–25 (2000).

[71] The issue has arisen in social care (where private contractors were not amenable to judicial review); *see* R (on the appl. of Heather) v. Leonard Cheshire Foundation, [2002] 2 All ER 936, [2002] EWCA Civ 366; YL v. Birmingham City Council [2007] UKHL 27 (U.K.) but is yet to be fully explored in respect of NHS treatment organized by private bodies. The question has also arisen in Israel; *see* Daphne Barak-Erez, *Three Questions of Privatisation*, in Comparative Administrative Law, chap. 29 (Susan Rose-Ackerman & Peter Lindseth eds., 2010); *see also* discussion by Andre den Exter in this volume regarding the Netherlands health care system.

[72] "Internationally, England is the only country with a broad, cross-government strategy to tackle health inequalities." *See* Report by the Comptroller and Auditor General, *Tackling Inequalities in Life Expectancy in Areas with the Worst Health and Deprivation*, National Audit Office, HC 186 Session 5 (July 2, 2010), *available at* http://www.nao.org.uk/publications/1011/health_inequalities.aspx.

should we promote *paternalistic* policies committed to equality even if they conflict with ideas of individuality and negative rights "to be let alone"? When does equality overstep the boundary that protects individual liberty? Which institution is best able to balance individual rights with community interests – parliaments or the judiciary? The solution to these problems is probably more susceptible to democratic decision making than litigation.[73] Indeed, as we saw with the ECJ, there is a danger of courts encouraging an individualistic approach to health care claims blind to the adverse consequences for others.

4.4.4 *Recognizing Social and Economic Rights*

There has been some limited response to concerns about socioeconomic equality by the Equality Act 2010. This imposes a duty on public authorities with strategic decision-making powers that they "must. . . have due regard to the desirability of exercising them in a way that is designed to reduce the inequalities of outcome which result from socio-economic disadvantage."[74] The duty to "have due regard," rather than to take positive steps, is procedural only. Judicial review may scrutinize the factors considered (or ignored) and the relative weight given to them in the balancing exercise, the proportionality of the result, or the time scale within which policies are introduced.[75] Bearing in mind the problems of judges assessing the competing socioeconomic claims, and indeed, identifying the proper target for litigation (e.g., the NHS, education system, housing, etc.), the impact of the new provision will probably be limited. Nevertheless, a procedural, or "accountability" rights approach to issues of socioeconomic disadvantage is likely to ensure they become more prominent on the decision-making agenda. In the United Kingdom, the 2010 Act may require public authorities to satisfy the courts that relevant factors have been given proper consideration. In this way, the voices of "hard to reach" groups may be heard more clearly.

To conclude, the NHS has made significant improvement with respect to transparency and accountability for individual patients, but it has done little to narrow the health divide between rich and poor. This challenge is not unique to the

---

[73] Supporting the role of the courts, *see* Sandra Fredman, Human Rights Transformed – Positive Rights And Positive Duties, Chap. 5 (2009), balancing the arguments in respect of Public Interest Litigation in the Indian courts. Although broadly supportive of PIL in India, *see* a discussion of the difficulties it brings in Surya Deva, *Public Interest Litigation in India: A Critical Review*, 28 Civ. Just. Q. 19 (2009).

[74] Equality Act, 2010, c. 15, sch. 1 (Eng.); See Sandra Fredman, *Positive Duties and Socio-economic Disadvantage: Bringing Disadvantage onto the Equality Agenda*, 3 Eur. Hum. Rts. L. Rev 290 (2010).

[75] Can we develop common indices by which to compare how different data has been weighed and considered by different departments of state? *See* Colin Harvey & Eoin Rooney, *Integrating Human Rights? Socio-Economic Rights and Budget Analysis*, 3 Eur. Hum. Rts. L. Rev. 266 (2010) for tentative suggestions.

United Kingdom.[76] The potential economic impact of this challenge is immense and threatens the viability of many public health care systems. Policy makers rarely discuss these issues explicitly, but as lifestyle diseases absorb a larger share of our limited resources, they concern us all. Litigation has been effective in day-to-day complaints, but the longer-term challenges presented by avoidable diseases are often beyond judicial competence. The solution is more likely to lie in the "politics" of compromise which requires a very different response.[77]

[76] *See* The Commission on Social Determinants of Health (WHO), *Closing the Gap in a Genera-tion: Health Equity through Action on the Social Determinants of Health* (2008), *available at* http://whqlibdoc.who.int/publications/2008/9789241563703_eng_contents.pdf.

[77] John Coggon, WHAT MAKES HEALTH PUBLIC? (2012).

PART II

Social Health Insurance Systems

5

Colombia's Right-to-Health Litigation in a Context of Health Care Reform

Everaldo Lamprea

INTRODUCTION

During the early 1990s, two transformative events overlapped in Colombia. One was the introduction by the 1991 Constitution of judicial institutions that led to the judicial enforceability of the right to health in thousands of individual lawsuits – whereby plaintiffs demand from private insurance companies and from the government concrete health services like medications, exams and medical procedures. The other was the implementation in 1993 of an ambitious health care overhaul (crystallized in Law 100 of 1993) based on the regulated competition of private insurance companies.

The thesis I advance in this chapter is that this overlap produced a number of unexpected effects. One of the most consequential has been the dramatic escalation of right-to-health litigation in Colombia, which, according to a recent comparative literature, is unparalleled among middle-income countries.[1]

This chapter aims at providing a process-tracing account of the problematic overlap in Colombia during the past two decades (1991–2013) between the trajectories of health care as a *right* and as a *system*. Focusing on several critical junctures of this encounter between the two trajectories, I reconstruct how a set of stakeholders (policy makers, judges, and litigants) interacted among themselves to spur the surge of right-to-health litigation. I close this chapter by discussing the two bills presented on June 2013 by the Santos administration aimed at revamping some key elements of the 1993 health care overhaul.

---

[1] A recently published study shows that Colombia has, by far, the highest per capita rate of right-to-health litigation among comparable middle-income countries. *See* Ottar Moestad, Octavio Luiz Ferraz & Lise Rakner, *Assesing the Impact of Health Rights Litigation: A Comparative Analysis of Argentina, Brazil, Colombia, Costa Rica, India and South Africa, in* LITIGATING HEALTH RIGHTS: CAN COURTS BRING MORE JUSTICE TO HEALTH? 273 (Alicia Yamin & Siri Gloppen eds., 2011).

5.1 COLOMBIA'S HEALTH CARE SYSTEM

5.1.1 *Colombia's Health Care System before the 1993 Reform*

Before the 1993 overhaul, Colombia's health care sector rested on three pillars. The first was the "official" or public sector steered by the Ministry of Health. This first subsector received approximately 21 percent of the total of public health expenditure. The ministry's own network of public hospitals and medical facilities was supposed to offer health care services to 66 percent of Colombia's population. However, estimates indicated that only 39 percent of that population had some kind of real access to health care services provided by the government-owned facilities.[2] According to some studies, prior to the 1993 reform, at least 27 percent of Colombians did not have access to any kind of formal health care.[3]

The second pillar was the social security sector, composed of the civil servant's social insurance institute (CAJANAL), the Social Insurance Institute for the formally employed (ISS), and a set of corporatist-like health care regimes for employees of the National Petroleum Company, the National Teachers' Association, the Central Bank, the Military, the Banking Superintendence, the Ministry of Communication, and others. This second pillar absorbed approximately 32 percent of the total of public health expenditure. Both the ISS and CAJANAL operated their own network of hospitals and health care providers, although in some parts of the country they had contractual arrangements with the Ministry of Health's facilities. By 1989, the allocation of per capita health expenditure was markedly favorable to public servants: the US$134 allocated per capita for CAJANAL beneficiaries offered a stark contrast with the US$15 and US$66 allocated per capita for Ministry of Health and ISS beneficiaries, respectively. It is estimated that before the 1993 reform, the state's social security system offered health care to only 21 percent of Colombia's population.[4]

Finally, the third pillar was the subsector that provided private health care to those willing to pay out of pocket or through insurance packages. During the first half of the 1990s, prepaid private health insurance was growing markedly, but only a very limited sector of the population was capable of paying its costly fees and deductibles.[5]

5.1.2 *The Enactment of the Health Care Overhaul: Law 100 of 1993*

In 1993, the Ministry of Health proposed an ambitious reform of the social security system – that is, pensions and health care. Anchored to the model of "managed

---

[2] Carmelo Mesa-Lago, CHANGING SOCIAL SECURITY IN LATIN AMERICA: TOWARD ALLEVIATING THE SOCIAL COSTS OF ECONOMIC REFORM 136 (1994).

[3] Gerard La Forgia, *Health Sector Reform: A Financial-Service Flow Model and the Colombian Case*, in DO OPTIONS EXIST?: THE REFORM OF PENSION AND HEALTH CARE SYSTEMS IN LATIN AMERICA 225 (María-Amparo Cruz-Saco & Carmelo Mesa Lago eds., 1998).

[4] MESA-LAGO, *supra* note 1.

[5] La Forgia, *supra* note 3.

competition," the section of the bill devoted to the health system was a crystallization of the 1991 Constitution's intended balance between health care privatization and governmental regulation. Colombia's Minister of Health Juan Luis Londoño and Harvard's Julio Frenk coined the term "structured pluralism" to describe the reforms' particular interpretation of the managed competition model. Under "structured pluralism," governmental regulation was an essential mechanism for ensuring that the new private health insurers and providers ushered in by the health care reform were guided in the direction of public interest.[6]

After months of deliberations in which health sector unions clashed with interest groups favoring Chilean-style privatization[7] (although less vehemently than in the case of pensions reform), the Colombian legislature enacted Law 100 of 1993. Largely grounded on the Ministry of Health's proposals, Law 100 overhauled Colombia's health care system, with a view to providing universal coverage by means of a comprehensive and mandatory social insurance system in which private health insurers and providers were to compete for patients not only among themselves but also with traditional public insurers such as the ISS. In addition to universality, the social insurance system introduced by Law 100 was built on principles of efficiency, quality, and equity, as explicitly mentioned in the text and also in article 49 of the 1991 Constitution.

Law 100 intended to liberate individuals from a highly monopolistic and ineffective health sector, creating a new institutional arrangement where they would operate as rational decision makers. In theory, allowing individuals to choose the best health services from a diverse assortment of health insurance companies and providers would unleash an upward spiral of efficiency and quality. This would occur in a regulated market, in which effective governmental agencies would set and enforce the rules of the game.

Another key aspect of Law 100 was that the creation of two different insurance regimes would level the playing field, resulting in greater equity. On the one hand, Law 100 created the "contributory regime." Within the contributory regime, employees, employers, and independent workers who earn more than twice the minimum wage contribute with part of their incomes. The formally employed and independent workers contribute payroll taxes totaling 12.5 percent, collected by the insurance

---

[6] J. L. Londoño & J. Frenk, *Structured Pluralism: Towards an Innovative Model for Health System Reform in Latin America*, 41 HEALTH POL'Y 1 (1997).

[7] Chile's reforms during the 1980–1990 decade are considered to be the most comprehensive and radical Latin American adoption of the model of managed competition championed by the World Bank and by the Interamerican Development Bank (IDB). According to this model, low- or middle-income countries should advance toward more efficient and equitable health care systems. This was to be accomplished through the instauration of private schemes and by fostering competition in the delivery of health services. *See* Kamran Abbasi, *The World Bank and world health: Changing sides*, 318 BMJ 865 (1999); Tony Groote & Jean-Pierre Unger, *Colombia: In Vivo Test of Health Sector Privatization in the Developing World*, 35 INT'L J. HEALTH SERVICES 125–141 (2005); Nuria Homedes & Antonio Ugalde, *Why Neoliberal Health Reforms Have Failed in Latin America*, 71 HEALTH POL'Y 83 (2005).

company of their choice. On the other hand, the contributory scheme coexists with a "subsidized regime." Within this regime, the health insurance of the neediest stratum of Colombians is financed through a solidarity-based percentage of the payroll contribution paid by the formal employees (1.5 percent) and through matching funds from general taxation.[8]

The policy makers who designed the two-tiered insurance scheme of Law 100 assumed that the government would progressively reduce and eventually lift the barriers to what Norman Daniels calls "equitable access to needed services," and provide a unified basket of health services.[9] The integration of the contributive and subsidized baskets depended heavily on the progressive incorporation of the population working in the informal and nontaxable employment sector into the formal sector and then into insurance schemes built on tax revenues, social security payments, or employer-based contributions. Nonetheless, for most of the population the benefits of the subsidized basket of health services have been limited by comparison to the contributive regime's basket, despite Article 153 of the Law 100 explicitly stating that "the General Social Health Insurance System will gradually provide health services of equal quality to all the inhabitants of Colombia, independent of their capacity to pay." Only in July 2012, eleven years after the initial deadline set by Law 100 of 1993,[10] did the Ministry of Health announce the unification of both baskets of health services for all Colombian citizens. Yet it is still uncertain how the government is going to finance the unification of the two baskets.

Decisions about coverage under the subsidized regime relied on the procedure set out in Law 60 of 1993. Law 60 obliged the government to replace horizontal social subsidies – including health care subsidies – which benefited the totality of the population, with subsidies targeted at the poorest. As a result of this, focalized and demand-centered subsidies were to be allocated using an instrument designed for identifying beneficiaries of governmental programs according to a nationwide survey known as SISBEN. The SISBEN survey classified the population's socioeconomic strata into six different levels, with level one being the most vulnerable individuals. Colombians classified in levels one and two of the SISBEN compose nearly 70 percent of the subsidized regime.[11]

---

[8] Law 100 preserved a set of special health regimes for employees of the National Petroleum Company, the National Teachers' Association, the Central Bank (Banco de la Republica), and the Military. *See* Rosa Rodríguez-Monguió & Alberto Infante, *Universal Health Care for Colombians 10 Years after Law 100: Challenges and Opportunities*, 68 HEALTH POL'Y 129 (2004).

[9] Norman Daniels, JUST HEALTH: MEETING HEALTH NEEDS FAIRLY 258 (2008).

[10] Article 162 of the Law 100 set 2001 as the year when both regimes' baskets of health services would integrate.

[11] Fifteen percent belong to level 3 and the remaining 15% have not been properly classified by the SISBEN. *See* Francisco Yepes, LUCES Y SOMBRAS DE LA REFORMA DE LA SALUD [LIGHTS AND SHADOWS OF THE HEALTH REFORMS] 24(2010).

5.1.3 *Law 100's Financing Mechanisms*

The Law 100 reform created a host of new private actors that were supposed to be incorporated into highly intricate financing mechanisms. The organizational scheme of Colombia's health sector soon became very complex. Ancillary legislation and regulation made the picture even more obscure. The organizational intricacy of the health sector, combined with the lack of conflict resolution bodies and low technical standards shown by regulatory agencies, opened Colombia's health sector to all kinds of loopholes.

According to Law 100, health insurance entities in charge of administering the contributory regime were Health Promoting Entities or *Entidades Promotoras de Salud* (EPS). Since 1993, private corporations have owned most EPSs.[12] Both private and public EPSs are in charge of guaranteeing the delivery of the basket of health services accorded to the members of the contributory regime. They delivered health services either through their own network of health providers or, indirectly, through Institutional Health Service Providers or *Instituciones Prestadoras de Salud* (IPS).

Law 100 also introduced a separate kind of EPSs for the subsidized regime, called EPS-Ss. The main function of EPS-Ss is to deliver the less inclusive basket of health services awarded to the subsidized regime.[13] They do so by organizing a network of health providers, also called IPS. As is the case with EPS in the contributory regime, most EPS-Ss are private, and users are permitted to "shop" among them.

The taxpayer-financed fund used to pay health insurance companies for the delivery of health services is the Fondo de Solidaridad y Garantía (FOSYGA), managed by a private equity fund.[14] The FOSYGA's main function is geared toward paying all insurance entities a risk-adjusted premium for the services included in the contributory and subsidized regimes' baskets.

The FOSYGA equity fund has four accounts: (1) the "compensation" account for the contributive regime; (2) the "solidarity" account for the subsidized regime; (3) the "catastrophic" account; and (4) the "public health" account. The compensation account functions as a risk pool for the contributory regime; it is funded by the 12.5 percent payroll tax contribution paid by the formally employed. However, only 11 percent of the payroll contribution becomes individual risk-adjusted premiums paid to insurers. The remaining 1.5 percent goes to the solidarity account, which – along with general taxation – finances the insurance premiums for those in the subsidized

---

[12] In 2011, the largest and oldest public health insurance entity (ISS) was completely absorbed by a partially public EPS (Nueva EPS).

[13] With the unification of the baskets of health care services announced by the government on July 2012, all Colombian citizens – regardless of whether they belong to the subsidized or contributive regimes – would receive the same health care services. However, it is far from clear whether the health system's finances are solid enough to deliver the same basket of health care services – updated and expanded in 2011 – to all Colombians.

[14] In September 2011, the Ministry of Social Security chose a new "mixed" – publicly and privately funded – equity fund (SAYP) to manage the public funds previously entrusted to a private equity fund.

regime. The third and fourth accounts pay for expenses such as ER treatment for people hurt in car accidents, and for public health activities, respectively.[15]

The actual functioning of the health care system's financing is beset by a number of intricacies introduced by the Law 100 and by subsequent regulations. It is difficult to offer a simple illustration of what in reality is a mesh of contributions, subsidies, and governmental transfers flowing at the local and national level.[16] At the core of the scheme is a per capita payment, the *Unidad de Pago por Capitación* (UPC). The FOSYGA uses the UPC to pay to all insurance entities for the delivery of health services included in both baskets of health services. Drawing from epidemiological, economical, and risk-based variables, the value of the UPC was supposed to be defined and readjusted by the National Social Security Health Board or *Consejo Nacional de Seguridad Social en Salud* (CNSSS), and since 2007 by the Health Regulatory Commission or *Comisión de Regulación en Salud* (CRES).[17] Yet, the CNSSS and the CRES have readjusted the value of the UPC according to the yearly recalibrations of the minimum wage sanctioned by the government, excluding any other economic or epidemiological considerations.[18] Since its inception, the value accorded to the UPC of the contributory regime has been considerably higher than the subsidized regime's UPC. By 2010, the UPC for the subsidized regime was worth only 60 percent of the contributory UPC.[19] Following the government's update and unification of the baskets of health care services on July 2012, it is still unclear how the UPC should be readjusted in order to pay insurance companies for the expanded list of health care services included in the unified basket.

The procedure by which insurance entities in the contributory regime (EPSs) obtain per capita payments (UPC) from the FOSYGA fund is also fraught with difficulty. The back-and-forth operations start with EPSs acting as *financial intermediaries* that collect the obligatory premiums paid by the insured population. From this pool of resources, EPSs discount the value of the UPC for the delivered health services

---

[15] Amanda Glassman, Maria-Luisa Escobar & Ursula Giedion, From Few to Many: Ten Years of Health Insurance Expansion in Colombia 162 (2009).

[16] For a description of the health care system's financial schemes, *see* Rodríguez-Monguió & Infante, *supra* note 8.

[17] In December 2011, the CRES produced, for the first time, a substantive update of the baskets of health services following the orders handed down by Constitutional Court's ruling T-760 of 2008. *See* Corte Constitucional [C.C] [Constitutional Court], julio 31, 2008, Sentencia T-760/08 (Colom.), *available at* http://www.http://www.corteconstitucional.gov.co/relatoria/2008/t-760-08.htm. However, in July 2012, the Santos government announced that because of its underperformance, the CRES was going to be terminated; according to the government, by the end of 2012, all of CRES's regulatory faculties are going to be assigned to the Ministry of Health.

[18] Using the minimum wage to calculate the UPC is, of course, a poor policy choice. It is argued that the minimum wage is the only available proxy, because the government lacks a reliable "epidemiological profile" of Colombia's population.

[19] Yepes, *supra* note 11. Assigning different values for the UPC is explained by the fact that the basket of health services awarded to the contributory regime is more complete than the subsidized basket is, and thus is more expensive.

and then proceed to transfer the rest of the money to the FOSYGA fund. If the difference is negative, the FOSYGA compensates the EPSs. In addition to UPC-based payments flowing from the FOSYGA, EPSs are financed by copayments, profits, and financial investments of their own.[20] Finally, an EPS may be ordered by a judicial ruling (*Tutela*) to provide a service otherwise "excluded" from coverage; these costs are in turn reimbursed by FOSYGA. As explained later in the chapter, Tutela litigation has had a negative financial impact on Colombia's health care sector.

There are three main sources of financing for the EPS-Ss of the subsidized regime: national and local general taxation; the 1.5 percent share of the payroll contributions' pool from the contributory regime; and the FOSYGA payments, which (prior to the unification of the baskets of health services on July 2012) were based on a lower per capita payment unit (UPC) than that used for the contributive regime.

5.2 CONSTITUTIONAL AND LEGAL FRAMEWORK OF COLOMBIA'S HEALTH CARE SECTOR

5.2.1 *The National Constituent Assembly (NCA) and the 1991 Constitution*

The 1993 health care reform was the culmination of a broader process of "State modernization" in Colombia focusing on decentralization.[21] Law 100 of 1993 was also the crystallization of the agreements on social security, the health system, and the right to health, reached by the 1991 National Constituent Assembly (NCA) appointed by popular vote to draft a new constitution.

Echoing the guidelines of Law 10 of 1990,[22] the 1991 NCA defined health care and social security as public services regulated by the decentralized state, and open to the participation of private capital. Deliberations within the NCA's Commission V set the benchmark for the elaboration of the Constitution's articles, which defined Colombia's social security and health care systems. Among others, the following themes guided the NCA's deliberation in the areas of health care and social security:

(i) the crisis of the social security system, and more particularly, the dire situation of the public institution in charge of social security in Colombia (the ISS);
(ii) the low coverage of health care and social security services in Colombia;
(iii) the need to design – either at the Constitutional Assembly or through ordinary legislative procedures – unified, structured, and decentralized health and social security systems based on the principle of solidarity;
(iv) the incorporation of private capital in the insurance and provision of health care and social security services;

---

[20] Rodríguez-Monguió & Infante, *supra* note 8.
[21] *See* generally, Tulia Falleti, DECENTRALIZATION AND SUBNATIONAL POLITICS IN LATIN AMERICA (2010).
[22] L. 10/90, enero 10, 1990, Diario Oficial [D.O.] (Colom.). Law 10 was a groundbreaking statute that pioneered the decentralized provision of health services in Colombia.

(v) the inclusion of the "right to health" within the "right to social security"; and

(vi) the fiscal consequences of framing social security and health care as rights of the citizenry and duties of the state.[23]

Articles 48 and 49 of the 1991 Constitution – drafted by the ANC's Commission V – respectively describe the rights to health care and social security in sufficiently loose terms. Article 48 states, for instance, that social security is a

> Mandatory public service that will be provided under the direction, coordination and control of the state, according to the principles of efficiency, universality and solidarity.... The *inalienable right* to social security will be guaranteed to all citizens. Social security may be provided, according to the law, by the state or by private parties. (emphasis added)

Health care services are almost identically defined in Article 49 of the Constitution. However, unlike social security, the Assembly decided not to define health as a right, but as a public service:

> Health care services and environmental sanitation are public services assigned to the state. Every person has guaranteed access to services that promote, protect and improve health. The state is expected to organize, direct and regulate the delivery of health and sanitation services according to the principles of efficiency, universality and solidarity. The State is also expected to establish the policies for the delivery of health services by private entities, and to control and oversee them.

Additionally, Article 365 of the Constitution defined social security, health care, education, and public utilities such as water and electricity as public services guaranteed by the state and open to the participation of private capital. While Article 365 states that public services are "inherent to the state's social purpose; it is the state's duty to guarantee the efficient delivery of public services to all the inhabitants of the land," it also states that "private parties" can be public services providers on the same footing with governmental agencies. Yet what at first blush seems like an outright concession to privatization is later moderated by Article 365's assertion about the indispensable role of the State as the ultimate umpire of public services: "In any event, the State will be still in charge of public services' regulation, control and overseeing."

Articles 48, 49, and 365 of the 1991 Constitution form part of a wide-ranging consensus, reached within the frame of the Constituent Assembly, as to the role of free market and interventionist approaches to the economy. The consensual definition of public services such as social security and health care is "capable [in the words of Constituent Assembly's delegates Serpa, Perry and Verano] of keeping

---

[23] *See* Everaldo Lampera, La Constitucion de 1991 y la Crisis de la Salud: Encrucijadas y Salidas [The 1991 Constitution and the Health Crisis: Crossroads and Exits] (2011) (an in-depth analysis of the NCA's deliberations about the health system, the right to health, and social security).

economic freedoms within the limits of the common good while retaining the state's steerage of the economy."[24]

5.2.2 *Health Care as a Right: The Tutela Claim and the Constitutional Court*

Colombia's 1991 Constitution introduced a new form of political organization based on the basic precept of *new constitutionalism*, which is that human or constitutional rights are basic to the democratic legitimacy of the state.[25] The 1991 NCA introduced the Tutela claim, an informal and expedited injunction that allows any citizen to seek judicial protection when their basic rights are threatened by the state or by a third party, which opened the door to increased health rights litigation – among many other rights. According to Article 85 of the 1991 Constitution, following the filing of a Tutela injunction by a plaintiff, the judge or Court assigned to the case has less than ten days to hand down a final decision on the matter. Unlike ordinary litigation, the Tutela eliminates most of the usual legal formalities and is a fast-track judicial procedure that does not require the involvement of lawyers.

In addition, the introduction by the 1991 Constitution of a Constitutional Court endowed with exclusive constitutional review powers and with faculties for selecting and annulling any number of Tutela rulings handed down by Colombian judges created a "super-Court" with enough clout to bolster and enforce a vigorous precedent on the justiciability of the right to health.[26] According to Bruce Wilson, the Tutela and the Constitutional Court's "abandonment of high levels of judicial formality, the adoptions of broad definitions of standing, the removal of many barriers to access, and the relatively quick resolution of their cases" created the conditions for what he calls *Colombia's rights revolution*.[27]

The Constitutional Court's T-484 of 1992 decision set a key precedent, borrowing from jurisprudence of the German Constitutional Court, to infer a right to health from the right to life. This rationale proved to be an enduring precedent, later evolving into a full-fledged recognition of the right to health as a basic right.[28]

---

[24] Unijus & Ministerio de Justicia Y Derecho, Servicios Publicos Domiciliarios: Calidad de Vida y Construcción del Estado Social de Derecho [Domestic Public Services Quality of Life and Social State Building Law] (1997).

[25] Rodolfo Arango, *Basic Social Rights, Constitutional Justice, and Democracy*, 16 Ratio Juris 141 (2003); Alec Stone Sweet & Jud Mathews, *Proportionality Balancing and Global Constitutionalism*, 47 Colum. J. Transnat'l L. 73 (2008).

[26] Rodrigo Uprimny, *The Enforcement of Social Rights by the Colombian Constitutional Court: Cases and Debates, in* Courts and Social Transformation in New Democracies 127 (Roberto Gargarella ed., Ashgate ed. 2006).

[27] Bruce M. Wilson, *Institutional Reform and Rights Revolutions in Latin America: The Cases of Cost Rica and Colombia*, in 2 J. Pol. Latin America 59 (2009).

[28] *See* Corte Constitucional [C.C] [Constitutional Court], Sentencia T-760/08 (Colom.).

Additionally, a more expansive appeal to a dignified and flourishing human life helped bolster the justiciable right to health in Colombia. Decision T-484 of 1992 also ruled that the right to health ought to be protected "whenever such protection is necessary to preserve threatened fundamental rights, such as the right to life and personal integrity (concerning diagnose services, medicines, treatment, surgeries, etc.), or the right to human dignity." With a handful of sweeping decisions in the early 1990s, the Constitutional Court set broad precedents for health rights litigation, which have since been enhanced in response to a sharp increase in health rights litigation and the poor institutional performance within the health care sector.[29]

5.3 LITIGATION TRENDS

5.3.1 *Right to Health Litigation and Conflict Resolution Deficit*

After the progressiveness of the "foundational period" (1992–1993), the Court's precedent encountered the harsh realities brought about by the problematic implementation of the 1993 health care overhaul. This encounter teemed with tensions and contradictions. A growing tide of Tutela-based litigation propelled by the shortcomings of key executive and regulatory agencies buffeted the Constitutional Court's initial precedent. The Court reacted by expanding and invigorating the original precedent on the justiciability of the right to health.

The intense use of Courts and the Tutela for health-related cases was largely the result of the underperformance of the Ministry of Health and the Superintendancy of Health, the governmental regulatory agency – independent from the Ministry of Health – that is supposed to operate as the watchdog of Colombia's health sector. These governmental agencies have refrained from disciplining health insurance companies (both EPSs and EPS-Ss) and providers that systematically refuse pharmaceuticals and medical procedures included in the baskets of health services in the contributory and subsidized regimes. For instance, even though magnetic resonance imaging (MRI) is part of the contributory regime's basket, many health

---

[29] In this first period the Constitutional Court's jurisprudence on the right to health brought into sharp relief the principles of solidarity and universality of health systems foreshadowed by the 1978 WHO's Declaration of Alma Ata. *See* Corte Constitucional [C.C] [Constitutional Court], agosto 11, 1992, Sentencia T-484/92 (Colom.), *available at* http://www.corteconstitucional.gov.co/relatoria/1992/T-484-92. htm for an illustration of this early precedent. These rulings are also part of what López calls the "foundational period" of the Court's precedent on the right to health. Albeit of short duration, the "foundational" precedent of the Court casted a long shadow over the subsequent Court's decisions on the right to health. Over a period of nearly twenty years (1993–2012), the founding 1992 precedent branched out as the Court tried to address the steep escalation of litigiousness on the right to health and the poor institutional performance within the health care sector. Diego López, Sistema de Salud y Derecho a la Salud: Historia de su Interrelación en la Jurisprudencia Constitucional [Health System and the Right to Health: The History of Its Interrelation in the Constitutional Court] (2008).

insurance companies commonly refuse to deliver MRI scans, arguing that they involve the administration of a contrast agent "excluded" from the basket.[30] Costly anti-hemophilic pharmaceuticals offer another example. Despite their being part of the contributive basket of health services, health insurance companies refuse to deliver anti-hemophilic medication to patients. Even more disturbing is the fact that during 2009, the FOSYGA public fund paid more than $US 8 million to health insurance companies for anti-hemophilic pharmaceuticals that were already included in the contributory basket, and that insurance companies were therefore obliged to provide.[31] The set of studies produced by the Human Rights Ombudsman Office (*Defensoría del Pueblo*) show this trend: most Tutela plaintiffs demand the delivery of a health service (surgical operation, pharmaceutical, procedure, etc.) that already is included in the baskets of health services and that health insurance companies unlawfully refuse to provide.[32] However, the Superintendancy and the Ministry of Health have proved ineffectual in chastising health insurance companies that customarily deny "included" health services. It is reasonable to suppose that a vigorous enforcement of disciplinary measures against rogue health insurance companies would have deterred the enactment of unlawful barriers to access and avoided much of right-to-health litigation.

Patients who are refused treatment, exams, pharmaceuticals, and surgeries included in both baskets of health services are left with no better alternative than to launch a Tutela claim. There are no other effective conflict resolution mechanisms to solve these types of disputes; for instance, procedures at the Superintendancy of Health are highly ineffective and dilatory.

Several studies point to the lack of conflict resolution mechanisms and bodies that, on the one hand, could have addressed these types of conflicts and, on the other, would have prevented the escalation of litigation. Studies by Rodolfo Arango,[33] Aquiles Arrieta,[34] and the Public Prosecutor's Office (Procuraduría General de la Nación)[35] have stressed the fact that within the Law 100's framework, a specialized jurisdiction for the resolution of this kind of conflict between patients and health insurance companies is conspicuous in its absence.

---

[30] Procuraduría General de la Nación, COLOMBIA, EL DERECHO A LA SALUD EN PERSPECTIVA DE DERECHOS HUMANOS [THE RIGHT TO HEALTH IN HUMAN RIGHTS PERSPECTIVE] 59 (2008).

[31] *See* Una Muestra de Factores Antihemofílicos, OBSERVAMED (Oct. 25, 2010), *available at* http://www.medinformatica.net/BIS/BisBcm44de2010_25a31octio.htm.

[32] Defensoría del Pueblo, COLOMBIA, LA TUTELA Y EL DERECHO A LA SALUD [THE TUTELA AND THE RIGHT TO HEALTH] (2013).

[33] Rodolfo Arango, *El Derecho a la Salud en la Jurisprudencia Constitucional* [*The Right to Health in the Constitutional Court*], *in* TEORÍA CONSTITUCIONAL Y POLÍTICAS PÚBLICAS: BASES CRÍTICAS PARA UNA DISCUSIÓN (Alexei Julio, Manuel José Cepeda, & Eduardo Montealegre eds., 2008).

[34] Aquiles Arrieta, *Justo Formalismo – La Aplicación Formal del Derecho, Casos y Límites* [*Just Formalism – The Formal Application of Law, Cases and Limits*], 1 REVISTA PRECEDENTE 164 (2003).

[35] Procuraduría General de la Nación, Colombia, *supra* note 30.

Although Law 100 instituted a particular kind of committee within health insurance companies – called a Scientific Technical committee or CTC – as a mechanism to solve conflicts between patients and EPS regarding medical services and pharmaceuticals "excluded" from the basket of health services, they proved to be less a solution than a problem. Reformed in 1997 by a governmental act,[36] these committees were ascribed to all health insurance companies and endowed with decisional faculties regarding patients' demands for the delivery of medications and health treatments "excluded" from the baskets of health services. Perhaps the two most important features of CTCs are, on the one hand, that their decisions denying "excluded" health services are not final because they are subject to Tutela review, and, on the other, that EPS-employed doctors and officials sit on CTCs. Not surprisingly, their decisions usually advance the EPS interests. Accordingly, for most plaintiffs, it is clear that a CTC or a Superintendancy-based procedure does not respond as swiftly and fairly as Tutela procedures do to demands for health services that patients consider they are entitled to obtain. As a result, the judicial branch absorbed most of the hundreds of thousands of patients' demands for access to "included" and "excluded" pharmaceuticals and medical treatments.

5.3.2 *The Constitutional Court's Precedent on "Excluded" Health Services*

The Constitutional Court created and enforced a vigorous precedent on access to pharmaceuticals and medical procedures "excluded" from the baskets of health services of both the contributive and subsidized regimes. During the first half of the 1990s – when this precedent began to take form – it was clear that Law 100 of 1993 did not offer any hint about whether health insurance companies had to provide such "excluded" pharmaceuticals and health services.[37] In 1994, the Ministry of Health published a resolution clarifying that the prescription and delivery of medications was confined only to those explicitly included in the contributory and subsidized baskets of health services. According to Articles 13 and 49 of the Constitution, health insurers are under no circumstances obliged to provide an "excluded" medication. Thus, patients in need of "excluded" medications had to use their own resources to purchase them.

As a result of the Ministry's resolution, for a period of more than one year (1994–1995), health insurance companies denied access to most medications and treatments "excluded" from the baskets of health services. They made exceptions only in some cases where the "excluded" medication or treatment would "cure" the patient's condition. No exceptions were made for a wide range of medications and treatments used for what health insurance companies considered "terminal" or non-curable medical conditions, such as cancer, HIV/AIDS, and kidney or hepatic dysfunction.

---

[36] Ministerio de Salud, Colombia [Colombian Ministry of Health], Resolución 5061 (1997).
[37] Arrieta, *supra* note 34.

Nonetheless, in a 1995 decision, the Constitutional Court ruled that neither public nor private health insurance companies could argue that only individuals with "curable" medical conditions are entitled to life-saving medications "excluded" from the baskets of health services.[38] According to this ruling, in cases of gravely ill or terminal children, medication "excluded" from the baskets of health services must be delivered by the state at public institutions. Building on this precedent, in ruling T-271 of 1995, the Court decided that this rule extended to all individuals living with an incurable medical condition such as HIV/AIDS. Ruling T-271 was the Court's reaction to the critical situation of people living with HIV/AIDS in Colombia, where health insurance companies were customarily denying their demands for medication.

However, it was only in 1997 that the Constitutional Court articulated in detail the basic features of its precedent on "excluded" medication and health services. In SU-480, the Court ruled that a private insurance company had to provide "excluded" antiretroviral medication to a plaintiff living with HIV/AIDS, because his life was at stake. The Court laid down the prerequisites for the provision of "excluded" medications or health services:

1. The lack of medication or treatment "excluded" from the baskets of health services threatened the plaintiff's basic right to life and corporeal integrity.
2. The medication or treatment could not be substituted by one already included in the baskets of health services.
3. The plaintiff lacked the economic means to acquire the medication or medical treatment and was not part of a medical plan that may provide the good.
4. The medication or medical treatment was prescribed by a doctor affiliated to the plaintiff's health insurer.

Finally, in this ruling the Court decided that once the health insurance company provided the "excluded" pharmaceutical, the company was entitled to demand a reimbursement from the FOSYGA fund.

Arrieta's study shows that in 1997, the National Social Security Health Board CNSSS adopted the precedent on "excluded" pharmaceuticals and medical treatments spelled out by the Court in ruling SU-480 of 1997. Through a 1997 ordinance,[39] the CNSSS explicitly acknowledged that when the patient's right to life was at stake, private health insurance companies were required to provide medications and treatments "excluded" from the baskets of health services. The CNSSS's ordinance also endowed the FOSYGA with funding to reimburse private health insurance companies after they have delivered the "excluded" medication or treatment to the patient.

---

[38] *See* Corte Constitucional [C.C] [Constitutional Court], febrero 9, 1995, Sentencia SU-43/95 (Colom.), *available at* http://www.corteconstitucional.gov.co/relatoria/1995/SU043–95.htm.

[39] *See* Consejo Nacional de Seguridad Social en Salud [CNSSS], Acuerdo 83 (1997) (Colom.).

After the CNSSS's 1997 ordinance, the Constitutional Court's precedent on "excluded" pharmaceuticals and medical treatments branched out. Cancer pharmaceuticals and chemotherapy, dialysis, neurological medications, transplants, plastic surgery, and overseas medical treatments, among many others, joined the list of "excluded" health services that could be demanded using the Tutela.

Despite its sheer size, the financial impact of this precedent on "excluded" health care services was mostly overlooked by the Constitutional Court. Only in 2008[40] did the Court address the structural causes and dire financial consequences – for the government and taxpayers – of the escalation of this type of litigation.

5.3.3 *The Escalation of Right-to-Health Litigation*

Against a background where the Constitution endowed citizens with a set of basic rights and Tutela claims provided an effective mechanism to protect and promote those rights, it is not at all surprising that Tutela litigation rapidly became the most common judicial proceeding in Colombia.[41] In just the past decade (1999–2010), close to 3 million plaintiffs have used the Tutela claim process to assert their rights.[42] Furthermore, the rate of success of Tutela plaintiffs is remarkably high. For instance, in right-to-health cases, more than 85 percent of rulings are in favor of the plaintiff.[43]

It is worth noting that Tutela rulings only apply to the individual case before the judge or the court. This is the case even where the Constitutional Court rules on Tutela claims, although these decisions are supposed to become the benchmark for the adjudication of health-related cases for all judges and courts across the country. Yet every year the Constitutional Court reviews and overturns hundreds of lower courts' rulings that flatly contradict the Constitutional Court's precedent on the right to health.

Propelled by the growing tide of basic-rights litigation brought about by Tutela claims, the Constitutional Court expanded and diversified its docket.[44] Among the overwhelming number and diversity of basic-right cases spurred by Tutela litigation, right-to-health cases stand out. A set of four studies published by Colombia's Human Rights Ombudsperson Office show that between 1999 and 2012, the right to health

---

[40] *See* Corte Constitucional [C.C] [Constitutional Court], Sentencia T-760/08 (Colom.).

[41] Defensoría del Pueblo, Colombia, La Tutela y el Derecho a la Salud [The Tutela and the Right to Health], Periodo 2003–2005 (2007).

[42] Defensoría del Pueblo, Colombia, *supra* note 32.

[43] Defensoría del Pueblo, Colombia, La Tutela y el Derecho a la Salud [The Tutela and the Right to Health], Periodo 2006–2008 (2009).

[44] This basic rights precedent includes sweeping decisions about racial minorities, indigenous peoples, environmental rights, gender, same-sex couples, euthanasia, basic-subsistence rights and extreme poverty, sexual orientation, personal drug consumption, abortion, gender equality and women's rights, freedom of religion, freedom of the press, and protection of persons with disabilities, among many other subjects. *See* Manuel José Cepeda, *Judicial Activism in a Violent Context: The Origin, Role, and Impact of the Colombian Constitutional Court*, 3 Wash. U. Glo. Stud. L. Rev. 529 (2004).

TABLE 5.1. *Growth of tutela claims relating to the right to health, 1999–2012*[45]

| | Tutela claims | | | Annual growth/last year | |
Year	Health	Total	Participation	Health	Total
1999	21,301	86,313	24.68%	–	–
2000	24,843	131,764	18.85%	16.63%	52.66%
2001	34,319	133,272	25.75%	38.14%	1.14%
2002	42,734	143,887	29.70%	24.52%	7.96%
2003	51,944	149,439	34.76%	21.55%	3.86%
2004	72,033	198,125	36.36%	38.67%	32.58%
2005	81,017	224,270	36.12%	12.47%	13.20%
2006	96,226	256,166	37.56%	18.77%	14.22%
2007	107,238	283,637	37.81%	11.44%	10.72%
2008	142,957	344,468	41.50%	33.31%	21.45%
2009	100,490	370,640	27.11%	−29.71%	7.60%
2010	94,502	403,380	23.43%	−5.96%	8,83%
2011	105,947	405,359	26,14%	12,11%	0,49%
2012	113,313	424,400	26,94%	7,90%	4,70%
TOTAL	1.089.864	3.555.120	30,66%		

was the most litigated basic right in Colombia, with an aggregate of 1,089,864 cases out of a total of 3,555,120.[46] In 2008, 1 in every 300 Colombians lodged a Tutela claim in order to demand a health-related good such as pharmaceuticals, medical procedures, surgical interventions, medical appointments, or prosthetic devices. During the 1999–2010 period, 177,755 plaintiffs lodged a Tutela claim to demand a surgical procedure, followed closely by 176,806 pharmaceutical-based claims.

A recently published study suggests that Colombia has the highest per capita rate of right-to-health litigation among middle-income countries.[47] Using 2008 data, this study concluded that the number of right-to-health legal actions in Colombia, for each 1 million individuals, was 3,289. Brazil, Costa Rica, Argentina, South Africa, and India come below Colombia with 206, 109, 29, 0.3, and 0.2 cases, respectively.

Table 5.1 illustrates the growth of Tutela litigation in Colombia between 1999 and 2012. It reflects the total aggregate of litigation on the right to health, which means it includes both plaintiffs in the contributory and subsidized regimes. Several studies – reviewed by Rodríguez – show that the majority of right-to-health litigants belong to the contributory regime.[48] According to the most reliable figure available, in 2003, the

---

[45] Taken from Defensoría del Pueblo, Colombia, *supra* note 32.
[46] Defensoría del Pueblo, Colombia, *supra* note 32.
[47] Moestad, et.al, *supra* note 1.
[48] See César Rodriguez-Garavito, *Justicia y Salud en Colombia: Retos y Oportunidades Creadas Mediante la Intervención de los Jueces [Justice and Health in Colombia: Challenges and Opportunities Intervention Produced By Judges]*, in LIBRO BLANCO EN SALUD: LOGROS, RETOS Y RECOMENDACIONES (Oscar Bernal & Catalina Gutiérrez eds., 2012) (a synthesis of these studies).

number of Tutela claimants who belonged to the contributive regime was six times greater than the number in the subsidized regime.[49] These studies suggest that right-to-health litigation may be at loggerheads with equity. This is so because those who belong to the contributive regime were not only endowed with a more robust basket of health services than the subsidized population, but also because the contributive population belongs to the middle and upper socioeconomic strata of Colombia's population.[50] Accordingly, it is likely that access to judicial mechanisms to protect the right to health is unequally distributed among Colombia's population. However, the evidence is not conclusive on this point. It is likely that a poor person who is part of the subsidized regime has a more reliable social security safety net – in the form of subsidies, for instance – than a marginally richer person from the contributive regime who has a low-paid job but who is excluded from the subsidies assigned to the poorest sectors of the Colombian population. Additionally, Rodríguez's study suggests that there is not enough evidence to argue that in Colombia the higher the region's level of Human Development Index (HDI), the more likely it is to have a high volume of right-to-health litigation.

From 1999 to 2008, health care–related actions for the protection of constitutional rights in Colombia increased 300 percent, declining later in 2009 and 2010, largely as a result of the Constitutional Court's ruling T-760 of 2008. Yet, according to the Ombudsman's Office, right-to-health litigation peaked again in Colombia during 2011, reaching 105,947 cases, 12,11 percent more than in 2010. During 2012 the growing trend of right-to-health litigation continued.

In the following section I briefly address Ruling T-760 of 2008.[51] I describe some of the ruling's orders and the government's compliance with them.

5.3.4 *Ruling T-760 of 2008 and Its Aftermath*

Ruling T-760 of 2008 opened the Court's new "institutional" or "structural" precedent on the right to health care. The Court identified some of the institutional determinants that incentivize right-to-health litigation; it also outlined an institutional roadmap for the reforms that the legislative and executive branches ought to undertake in order to mitigate or eliminate the "structural" determinants of right to health litigation. Among the structural orders handed down by the Court in ruling T-760, there are several related to the updating of the baskets of health services, the unification of the subsidized and contributory regimes, and the improvement of the health system's financial arrangements and universal coverage of the social security system.

---

[49] Id.
[50] Id.
[51] See César Rodriguez-Garavito, *Latin American Constitutionalism: Social and Economic Rights: Beyond the Courtroom: The Impact of Judicial Activism on Socioeconomic Rights in Latin America*, 89 Tex. L. Rev. 1669 (2011) (a socio-legal analysis of this ruling).

As a result of ruling T-760/2008, the Court created a follow-up panel to oversee the government's policy compliance with T-760's structural orders. Furthermore, on July 7, 2011, the Court hosted a public hearing – broadcasted on TV and the Internet – in which the government and several regulatory agencies came together with civil society organizations, academics, NGOs, and patients' groups and debated the government's compliance with ruling T-760. A second public hearing took place on May 10, 2012. Amid the financial crisis of the health care sector, Colombia's mainstream and alternative media covered both public hearings, creating awareness about the government's lack of compliance with the Court's orders – encapsulated in ruling T-760. Following the first public hearing, the follow-up panel appointed several groups of independent experts and patients' organizations. The outcomes of the experts and patients workshops helped the Court obtain basic input conducive to a series of rulings whereby the governmental compliance with ruling T-760 was assessed.[52] Partly as a result of these rulings, in December 2011 (for the first time since 1993), President Santos's Ministry of Health produced a major update of the basket of health services, complying with some of the structural orders handed down by the Court in ruling T-760. Furthermore, in January 2012, the Ministry of Health decided to jump-start pharmaceuticals' price regulation in Colombia. Finally, in July 2012, the Ministry of Health announced the unification of the contributive and subsidized baskets of health services. The most important effect of having a unified basket of health services is that all Colombians are entitled to the same health care services, irrespective of their affiliation with the contributive or subsidized regimes. Nonetheless, the implementation of the government's unification policy seems to be beset by a number of problems: for instance, in July 2012, several health insurance companies from the subsidized regime have pulled out from large cities arguing that they are not financially capable of providing the updated basket of health care services to their affiliates.

Ruling T-760 of 2008 responded to the spiraling volume of rulings on the right to health and the fiscal costs that resulted. Consequently, one of the goals of decision T-760 was to funnel part of the health care litigation burden from courts and judges to CTCs (i.e., committees within private insurance companies). T-760 reaffirmed a rule introduced by a Ministry of Health's resolution (2933 of 2006), according to which EPSs would get only a partial reimbursement (50 percent) from the FOS-YGA fund when a Tutela claim overturned a CTC decision denying access to an "excluded" health service. In cases where a CTC accepted the patient's demand for an "excluded" service, the EPS obtained a full reimbursement from the government. Not surprisingly, this rule incentivized CTCs to approve the demands for "excluded" health services in order to avoid an adverse Tutela decision and obtain full reimbursement for "excluded" health services.

---

[52] *See* Corte Constitucional [C.C] [Constitutional Court], octubre 21, 2011, Auto 226/11 (Colom.), *available at* http://www.corteconstitucional.gov.co/T-760–08/Autos%20genericos/AutosGenericos.

By giving more leverage to CTCs, ruling T-760 of 2008 produced the desired effect of reducing health care–related Tutela claims; in 2009, there were 42,467 fewer cases than in 2008 (see Table 5.1). However, the number of cases decided by CTCs greatly increased during 2009. Additionally, during 2010, the number of right-to-health Tutela lawsuits escalated again, reaching levels similar to those reached in 2008. Likewise, because of the heavy caseload of CTCs, there was a dramatic increase in the costs of medication and health services paid by the government's FOSYGA fund to health insurance companies. During 2009, these payments were close to US$963 million, whereas in 2006 they were close to US$162 million.[53] This figure suggests that CTCs are even less optimal decisional bodies – in terms of cost containment – than normal Courts when it comes to assigning medical treatments "excluded" from the baskets of health services. One possible explanation is that CTCs are especially prone to overlooking the high costs of "excluded" medications and medical services that they approve on a case-by-case basis. In other words, CTCs have incentives to approve high numbers of costly "excluded" pharmaceuticals and medical services because, on the one hand, the government is paying for them – through the FOSYGA fund – and on the other, because the subsequent reimbursements paid by the FOSYGA fund to insurance companies for "excluded" health services and drugs offer attractive profit opportunities.

According to President Uribe's government (2002–2010), an overall paralysis of the Colombian health sector was imminent because of the fiscal strain brought about by health care rights litigation. Contradicting the structural reforms suggested by the Constitutional Court in ruling T-760 of 2008, Uribe's government decided to cut the Gordian knot for good. Using extraordinary provisions entrenched in the Constitution, in January 2010, the executive declared an economic state of emergency in order to issue a series of controversial decrees. Among other measures, the set of emergency decrees practically rendered the Tutela claim useless as a mechanism for obtaining "excluded" treatments. Following a public uproar and a number of doctors and patients demonstrations, the Constitutional Court decided that most of the decrees were unconstitutional.[54] The Court upheld only the tax measures that funneled more resources to the health sector.

However, the Santos Administration rekindled some of the mechanisms to reduce or eliminate Tutela litigation proposed by Uribe's failed decrees. In January 2011, the Santos government successfully passed reforms, encapsulated in Law 1438 of 2011. A centerpiece of the reforms was the establishment of a Peer Scientific Committee tasked with making decisions concerning "excluded" treatments, which would theoretically render the Tutela unnecessary. According to this statute, the committee's

---

[53] Departamento Nacional de Planeación, COLOMBIA, PLAN NACIONAL DE DESARROLLO [NATIONAL DEVELOPMENT PLAN] 2010–2014 302 (2011).

[54] *See* Corte Constitucional [C.C] [Constitutional Court], marzo 29, 2011, Sentencia C-225/11 (Colom.), *available at* http://www.corteconstitucional.gov.co/relatoria/2011/C-225–11.htm

members are drawn from a list of "specialist doctors and other professionals" (Art. 27) who review the decisions of the health insurance companies' CTCs. It appears that plaintiffs cannot lodge Tutela injunctions against the decisions of the Peer Scientific Committee, although this point is far from clear because the ministry has not yet implemented this new decisional body.

5.4 CONCLUDING REMARKS ON THE OVERLAP BETWEEN RIGHT TO HEALTH CARE LITIGATION AND HEALTH CARE SECTOR REFORM IN COLOMBIA

5.4.1 *The "Pharmaceuticalization" of Colombia's Public Health Care System*

The "pharmaceuticalization"[55] of public health discourse in Colombia coincides with a stagnation of the preventive elements of health care delivery and deterioration in key social determinants of health. Two reinforcing phenomena can depict the unfavorable "pharmaceuticalization" of Colombia's public health and the declining indicators of several social determinants of health.[56] On the one hand, since the 1993 health overhaul, there has been an increase in cervical cancer incidence and a worsening of vaccination rates, maternal and child mortality, and vector-transmitted diseases.[57] Additionally, the incorporation into the baskets of health care services of examinations that may prevent or detect pathologies has been faulty. For instance, several exams for the detection of cervical cancer (colposcopy and biopsy) and breast cancer (mammography and breast biopsy) were "excluded" from the subsidized basket during most of the past decade.[58]

On the other hand, Colombia's public expenditure on pharmaceuticals vis-à-vis its GDP has escalated in recent years. Whereas in the 2006–2008 public expenditure on pharmaceuticals was around 1.33 percent of GDP, in 2009 it increased to approximately 3.15 percent of GDP.[59]

---

[55] I am drawing the term "pharmaceuticalization" from anthropologist Adriana Petryna. According to Petryna, "pharmaceuticalization" implies an "over-fetishization" of medications inimical to a more robust public health approach. *See* Adriana Petryna & Arthur Kleinman, *The Pharmaceutical Nexus*, in GLOBAL PHARMACEUTICALS: ETHICS, MARKETS, PRACTICES (Andrew Lakoff, Adriana Petryna, & Arthur Kleinman eds., 2006); Adriana Petryna, WHEN EXPERIMENTS TRAVEL: CLINICAL TRIALS AND THE GLOBAL SEARCH FOR HUMAN SUBJECTS (2009).

[56] *See* the results of the "White Book on Colombia's Health Sector" published in 2012 by Los Andes Univeristy for a review of the waning public health indicators in Colombia. LIBRO BLANCO EN SALUD: LOGROS, RETOS Y RECOMENDACIONES (Oscar Bernal & Catalina Gutiérrez eds., 2012).

[57] Marion Piñeros, Gustavo Hernández & Freddie Bray, *Increasing Mortality Rates of Common Malignancies in Colombia*, 101 CANCER 2285 (2004).

[58] YEPES, *supra* note 11, at 34.

[59] Tatiana Andia, *The Invisible Threat: the Rise of Non-Intellectual Property and Non-Trade Pharmaceutical Regulations in Colombia*, in INTELLECTUAL PROPERTY, PHARMACEUTICALS AND PUBLIC HEALTH: ACCESS TO DRUGS IN DEVELOPING COUNTRIES 77 (Kenneth Shadlen ed., 2011).

The cost escalation associated with the burgeoning pharmaceutical expenditure is one of the most cited causes of the health care sector's crisis. Even more troubling is the fact that a large part of Colombia's public pharmaceutical expenditure is absorbed by high-end biotech pharmaceuticals.[60] For example, in 2008, 45 percent of the total public expenditure on pharmaceuticals went to pay health insurance companies for only twenty high-end pharmaceuticals produced (mostly) by Roche, Abbot, and Novartis.[61] These results suggest that in Colombia pharmaceutical expenditure is not only extremely high but badly allocated as well.

Colombia's mounting expenditure on pharmaceutical products attributable to right-to-health care litigation and CTC decisions went almost unchecked by the government and by regulatory agencies. A recent document from the government's Department for Economic Planning (DNP) illustrates that while in 2006 the FOS-YGA fund paid health insurance companies US$162 million in 2009 and 2010 the reimbursements increased to US$963 million and US$1,264 million, respectively. In 2009, 87 percent of the US$963 million was spent on reimbursing health insurance companies for "excluded" pharmaceuticals, with the remaining part of FOSYGA's reimbursements going to cover medical treatments, exams, and medical devices.[62]

The drastic deregulation of pharmaceutical prices accomplished by the regulatory agency in charge of pharmaceuticals' prices regulation (CNPM) in 2006 set the stage for a fiscal meltdown in Colombia's health care system. In a sweeping 2006 decision (Circular 04), the CNPM opted to move all commercialized pharmaceuticals to free market pricing. Hence, all types of pharmaceuticals – including the most expensive and specialized biotech products in the market – were "freed," thus allowing the market to allocate prices without any regulatory interference. Additionally, Circular 04 significantly raised the threshold for price regulation of monopolistic pharmaceuticals: only those pharmaceuticals with no competitors within their therapeutic class could have their prices regulated by the CNPM. Not surprisingly, under such a rule, only a limited number of pharmaceuticals are considered monopolistic and thus have their prices regulated by the CNPM.[63] It took the Ministry of Health until January 2012 to overturn Circular 04 of 2006 and reinstate a more robust regulation of pharmaceutical prices in Colombia. Under the leadership of Santos's minister of health (economist Alejandro Gaviria) and a team of experts, the government announced, on December 2013, a major overhaul of the regulation of pharmaceutical prices in Colombia. This new policy will allow the government to

---

[60] Id.

[61] Con Sólo Diez Medicamentos las Multinacionaleslas Vendieron Más de Col$ 380.000.000.000.- el 2008 [With Only Ten Medicines the Multinationals Sold More than 380,000,000,000 in 2008] Obser-vamed (Nov. 9, 2009), *available at* http://www.med-informatica.net/BIS/WebMail_09a15nov09.htm.

[62] Departamento Nacional de Planeación, Colombia, *supra* note 53. These figures include the reimbursements paid by the FOSYGA resulting from Tutela litigation and CTCs decisions.

[63] Andia, *supra* note 59.

regulate 334 medications, whose prices have to be equal to or lower than the prices paid by the health care systems of comparable middle-income countries.[64]

Yet, the fiscal harm inflicted by the deregulation of pharmaceuticals' prices during the period 2006–2013 was immense and had many ramifications. For instance, the overpricing of pharmaceuticals as a result of deregulation proved highly problematic when successful Tutela claims compelled the government to repay health insurance entities for the myriad high-end pharmaceuticals "excluded" from the baskets of health services. Using taxpayer money managed by the FOSYGA fund, the government's reimbursements to health insurance companies were made based on uncommonly high prices, all of which exacted a high toll on Colombia's public finances.

5.4.2 A Problematic Map of Rights and Duties

The Constitutional Court's precedent that allowed plaintiffs to circumvent the barriers of access to "excluded" pharmaceuticals created a "map of rights and duties." This map served as the blueprint for judicial cases in which plaintiffs argued that the lack of access to pharmaceuticals or medical treatments "excluded" from the basket of health services constituted a serious threat to their survival. As previously mentioned, the majority of right-to-health litigants belong to the contributory regime. This fact suggests that the most vulnerable population in the subsidized regime has had less access to Tutela claims as a mechanism to demand "excluded" health services. The impact on equality of the "hijacking" of right-to-health litigation by middle and higher socioeconomic strata remains a nagging problem in Colombia.

According to this map, three actors stand out as right-holders; contrastingly, only one actor is the duty-bearer. The right-holders are the following:

(i) the plaintiff who has the right to life-saving medication or medical treatments "excluded" from the basket of health services;

(ii) the health insurance company who has the right to be reimbursed for the pharmaceutical or medical treatment provided to the plaintiff following a judicial ruling; and

(iii) in drug-based judicial cases, the pharmaceutical company who has the right to the economic compensation for its prior research and development investment.

Conversely, the Colombian government is the only duty-bearer. Accordingly, the government has at least three duties with which to comply. The first is that of guaranteeing the patient's right to health by providing a pharmaceutical or medical

---

[64] See Regulación de Precios a Fármacos Llega a Dorguerías [Regulation of Drugs' Prices Reaches Drugstores] EL TIEMPO (December 18, 2013), *available at* http://www.eltiempo.com/vida-de-hoy/salud/ARTICULO-WEB-NEW-NOTA-INTERIOR-13297128.html

treatment "excluded" from the basket of health services. Despite its exclusion from the basket, the government has the duty to pay for the pharmaceutical or medical treatment to the extent that it is considered an indispensable means for the plaintiff's survival. The second duty is the reimbursement of health insurance companies that provide to successful plaintiffs pharmaceuticals or medical procedures "excluded" from the basket of health services. The third duty is imposed by a global set of rules envisaging monopoly rights in the form of patents and/or data exclusivity as the only mechanism to compensate the pharmaceutical industry for its R&D investment.[65] According to this duty, the government has the positive duty to pay for the full price of the pharmaceutical as defined by pharmaceutical companies operating in a heavily deregulated market. It also has the negative duty to avoid any infringement on the intellectual rights of pharmaceutical companies.

This map of rights and duties entrenched in the Constitutional Court's precedent on "excluded" pharmaceuticals is problematic on several levels. I highlight only two sore spots usually overlooked by the literature that has addressed Colombia's right to health care litigation.

The first problematic feature of the Court's precedent is the production of a hyper-individualization of the right to health care, which underemphasizes the social and institutional determinants behind individual demands for access to pharmaceuticals and medical treatments "excluded" from the baskets of health services. For instance, the Constitutional Court's precedent on the right to health is practically devoid of cases that address the constitutionality of the across-the-board deregulation of pharmaceutical prices that has caused a great fiscal havoc within the health sector. The escalation of health litigation in a context of deregulation of pharmaceutical prices transformed Colombia's hyper-individualized right-to-health litigation into a fiscal trap with detrimental effects on the financial stability of the health sector.

The second problematic feature of the Court's precedent on "excluded" health services is its low evidence standards. In most cases where a plaintiff demands an "excluded" pharmaceutical or medical procedure, judges take for granted that the pharmaceutical or medical procedure demanded by the plaintiff is a reasonable treatment both in medical and financial terms. In many cases, the Constitutional Court has awarded costly pharmaceuticals and procedures despite the fact that there is not enough medical or scientific evidence to conclude that they are the most effective medical treatments for the plaintiffs.[66] The negative financial impact

---

[65] Sarah Joseph, *Pharmaceutical Corporations and Access to Drugs: The "Fourth Wave" of Corporate Human Rights Scrutiny*, 25 HUM. RTS. Q. 425 (2003).

[66] *See, e.g.*, Corte Constitucional [C.C] [Constitutional Court], diciembre 5, 2008, Sentencia T-1214/08 (Colom.), *available at* http://www.corteconstitucional.gov.co/relatoria/2008/T-1214–08.htm. In this case the Court awarded a plaintiff an expensive biotech pharmaceutical (MABTHERA) even though this medication is not described by Colombia's Sanitary Authority (INVIMA) as the most therapeutically adequate treatment for the plaintiff's type of pathology – eye cancer.

produced by the aggregation of lower courts' rulings that follow this type of precedent is worrisome.

5.4.3 *Health Care Reform as Social Experimentation*

The health care sector overhaul included in Law 100 of 1993 is an example of policy making as a form of "social experimentation," based on trial and error.[67] The extent of that "error" is the subject of heated debate, exacerbated recently by the deepening of the financial crisis in Colombia's health care system.

The accomplishments of the Law 100 reform include: the marked growth of coverage of the social security system; the reduction of out-of-pocket payments and private health expenditure; the positive redistributive effects of targeted subsidies on poverty alleviation; and the growth of public health expenditures.

Regarding coverage, according to a 2010 poll conducted by the National Planning Department (DNP) and Profamilia, the social security system currently offers health care to more than 89 percent of the population.[68] On an even more optimistic note, the Ministry of Health argues that Colombia's health system reaches 94 percent of Colombia's population. Yet it is far from clear what part of that population has real access to health care and what part simply has a social security ID yet faces considerable difficulties to obtain health care. Arguably, destitute individuals and people living in isolated parts of the country, internally displaced populations, racial minorities, and groups hit hard by the internal armed conflict have more difficulty in accessing the social security system compared to the rest of the population. Nonetheless, the current coverage figures offer a striking contrast with the health care system before the 1993 reform, circumscribed to less than 21 percent of the population.

Furthermore, according to the latest WHO data on Colombia, private expenditure as a percentage of total expenditure on health decreased from 41.4 percent in 1995 to 27.3 percent in 2010. During the same period, per capita government expenditure on health grew from US$109 to US$343, and general government expenditure on health as a percentage of total expenditure on health increased from 50.6 percent to 72.7 percent. Whereas in 1993 total expenditure on health as a percentage of GDP was 6.2 percent, in 2010 it was 7.6 percent.[69] According to data by Glassman and colleagues, social insurance expenditure as percentage of GDP climbed from 1.6 percent in 1993 to 4.3 percent in 2003, whereas during the same period average per capita out-of-pocket expenditure shrank from US$57.02 to US$12.30. The proportion

---

[67] DANIELS, *supra* note 9.

[68] See *Encuesta Nacional de Demografía y Salud [ENDS]* [*National Demographic and Health*], PROFA-MILIA (2010), *available at* http://www.profamilia.org.co/encuestas/Profamilia/Profamilia/index.php? option=com_content&view=article&id=147&Itemid=117 Profamilia.

[69] See *Global Health Observatory Data Repository*, World Health Organization (2012), *available at* http://apps.who.int/ghodata/?vid=6500&theme=country#.

of household income spent on health services also decreased from 12.1 percent in 1977–1980 to 10.7 percent in 1997 and then to 7.24 percent in 2003.[70]

Additionally, several studies show that the targeting of subsidies on the lower socioeconomic quintiles is having a positive impact on poverty alleviation. The absolute value of subsidies and its percentage of overall household income are higher in the poorest strata of Colombian society.[71] For instance, according to Glassman and colleagues, in 1992, the poorest 20 percent of Colombia's population received health system benefits equal to 6.25 percent of their income; in 2003, the participation of these benefits climbed to 50 percent.[72]

Turning to the "errors" of the Law 100's implementation, three loom large as structural shortcomings of Colombia's health care sector. First, despite the growth of coverage, inequality is still a pervasive feature of Colombia's health care sector. The National Planning Department's (DNP) poll shows that while 16 percent of the lowest-income population remains unaffiliated with the social security system, only 7 percent of the highest-income population is currently unaffiliated.

Secondly, contrary to the estimations of the 1993 reformers, there has been a rapid growth of the subsidized population relative to the growth of the contributory population. By 2011, 21 million individuals – roughly 44.6 percent of Colombia's population – belonged to the subsidized regime. Contrastingly, the contributory regime covers 18.3 million people – 39 percent of Colombia's population.[73] This is counter to two core assumptions of the Law 100 reform: that the population laboring in the formal market would increase faster than the that working in the informal labor market, and that unemployment would decrease. In reality, informal labor has remained higher than formal labor.[74]

Thirdly, the projections included in Article 162 of the Law 100, according to which the baskets of health services of the contributory and subsidized regimes would integrate by 2001, proved to be wrong. Only in 2011 did Colombia's Ministry of Health approve the integration of the baskets for children and the elderly. In 2012, the Santos administration announced that the entire population would have access to an integrated basket of health services.

---

[70] GLASSMAN et al., *supra* note 15, at 164.

[71] YEPES, *supra* note 11.

[72] GLASSMAN et al., *supra* note 15, at 164.

[73] J. N. Méndez et al., LA SOSTENIBILIDAD FINANCIERA DEL SISTEMA DE SALUD COLOMBIANO – DINÁMICA DEL GASTO Y PRINCIPALES RETOS DE CARA AL FUTURO [FINANCIAL SUSTAINABILITY OF COLOMBIAN HEALTH SYSTEM DYNAMICS OF EXPENDITURE AND MAIN CHALLENGES OF THE FUTURE] (2012).

[74] According to governmental data (DANE), by April 2012, 50.2% of the employed population worked in the informal sector of the economy.
  Resumen Ejecutivo, Medicion del Empleo Informal y Seguridad Social [Executive Summary Measuring Informal Employment and Social Security], DANE (June 13 2012), *available at* http://www.dane. gov.co/files/investigaciones/boletines/ech/ech_informalidad/re_ech_informalidad_feb_abr2012.pdf.

Finally, deregulation of the health sector is surely one of the greatest institutional shortcomings of Colombia's health sector. The negative impact caused by governmental deregulation in the areas of pharmaceutical pricing and the updating of the baskets of health services was especially harmful to patients in need of examination, medical procedures, and pharmaceuticals. By all accounts, the Tutela claim system and the Constitutional Court's precedent on the right to health were instrumental in overcoming the unlawful barriers to health services brought about by deregulation.

5.4.4 *Winds of Reform (2013–2014): A New Round of Social Experimentation?*

Key elements of the current health care system are bound to be revamped by two governmental bills submitted to Congress on June 2013. The first bill already passed through Congress on June 2013 and is pending review from the Constitutional Court.[75] Two contributions of this first bill deserve to be highlighted: (1) it enshrines the protection of the right to health as the foundation of Colombia's health system; and (2) it seeks to de-incentivize the surge of litigation on costly health care services by controlling more effectively the prices of drugs and by forbidding the use of public funds to reimburse cosmetic and experimental medical treatments demanded by patients. It is evident that the drafters of the bill followed closely the recommendations laid down by the Constitutional Court's ruling T-760/08, according to which the right to health should be the founding block of Colombia's health sector. Because the government's bill bows down to ruling T-760/08, it is likely that the Court will uphold it.

However, the heart of the health care overhaul proposed by the Santos administration lies in a far more complex bill – bill 210 of 2013 – that is currently being – hotly – discussed by Congress and whose enactment is expected to take place sometime during the first semester of 2014. Yet, since President Santos will run for reelection on May 2014, the chances that the bill is finally approved by Congress remain uncertain.[76] According to this bill, health insurance companies (EPS) will be replaced by a new type of health-managing companies called GESs. These new companies will no longer collect or manage the obligatory premiums paid by the insured population. A new public agency – provisionally called My Health or *Salud*

[75] For a synthesis of the bill, *see* Ministerio de Salud y Protección Social [Ministry of Health and Social Protection], *Aprobada en Primer Debate la Ley Estatutaria de Salud [The Healthcare Reform Bill Is Approved by Congress]*, URNA DE CRISTAL (June 6, 2013), *available at* http://www.urnadecristal.gov.co/gestion-gobierno/ley-estatutaria-salud-colombia.

[76] For a description of this bill, see Ministerio de Salud y Protección Social [Ministry of Health and Social Protection], *Abecé del Proyecto de Ley que Redefine del Sistema de Salud [Nuts and Bolts of the Bill That Redefines the Health Care Sector]*, URNA DE CRISTAL (May 6, 2013), *available at* http://www.urnadecristal.gov.co/gestion-gobierno/abc-reforma-a-la-salud.

Mía – will take care not only of the financial intermediation between the insured population and GESs but also of the management of the social security information of all the Colombian population. More importantly, *Salud Mía* will pay GESs for each and every health service that they supply to insured patients across the country. Some critics argue that *Salud Mía* would be a self-defeating public agency because, on the one hand, it would demand far more state capacity than the Colombian government can actually provide, and on the other hand, it could easily fall prey to corrupt politicians and bureaucrats.[77] Yet the current minister of health, economist Alejandro Gaviria, argues that the government would only be able to stop the financial hemorrhage of Colombia's health care sector if it becomes the exclusive manager of the money that flows through it.[78]

Additionally, if the bill is approved by Congress, a new basket of health care services (provisionally called My plan or *Mi Plan*) will be instituted. Unlike the current POS – which specifies the medical treatments and drugs that Colombians have the right to demand from health insurance companies and the government – *Mi Plan* would consist of those medical treatments and medications that patients are *not* allowed to demand in any circumstance. In other words, whereas the current POS is a list of "included" medical services, *Mi Plan* is a list of "excluded" medical services. Accordingly, doctors and medical practitioners would decide more discretionally which treatments and medications they prescribe to patients. The Ministry of Health is adamant that the new mechanisms included in the bill to reduce the prices of pharmaceuticals and medical treatments will ensure that the discretional prescriptions of doctors do not bankrupt the health system. However, some experts remain skeptical about this point.

Another nagging question raised by the bill is the following: Does the new institutional arrangement proposed by the Santos administration preclude the use of the Tutela claim to demand pharmaceuticals and treatments specified in the list of exclusions of *Mi Plan*? Although Minister Gaviria has repeatedly emphasized that Tutela litigation on the right to health will remain untouched by the bill,[79] it is likely that the Court rules that some of the bill's sections are at loggerheads with the protection of the basic right to health given that they curtail the use of the Tutela claim to demand "excluded" health care services. As I showed in this chapter, a vast precedent of the Court indicates that if a patient demonstrates that the lack of an

77 See J. Gossain, *Esto dice la Letra Menuda del Proyecto de Reforma de la Salud* [*This Is What the Healthcare Reform Bill Means*], EL TIEMPO (May 8, 2013), *available at* http://www.eltiempo.com/politica/reforma-de-la-salud-por-juan-gossan_12787303-4.

78 See *La Creación de Salud Mía Genera Controversia* [*The Creation of Salud Mía is Met with Controversy*] LA REPUBLICA, (June 7, 2013), *available at* http://www.larepublica.co/economia/creaci%C3%B3n-de-salud-m%C3%ADa-genera-controversia_40297.

79 See *La Tutela no Saldrá Afectada con la Reforma* [*The Health Care Reform Will Not Curtail the Tutela Claim*], VANGUARDIA LIBERAL (May 15, 2013), *available at* http://www.vanguardia.com/actualidad/colombia/208220-la-tutela-no-saldra-afectada-por-reforma.

"excluded" pharmaceutical or medical treatment impairs her survival or well-being, then the Tutela proceeds. Yet it remains to be seen if the Court, facing a new institutional arrangement for the health system – which should be enacted in 2014 and fully implemented before 2016 – decides to modulate its precedent on "excluded" medications.

As it happened in the late 1980s and early 1990s, strong winds of reform are blowing in Colombia's health care sector. Influential policy makers and several sectors of Colombia's civil society and academia demand from the government a structural reform of the health system.[80] Unlike what happened then, a new actor, the Constitutional Court, is playing a decisive role in the reform of the health system. The Court has repeatedly emphasized that the restructuring of the health care system is indispensable for the protection of the basic right to health of all Colombians. Whereas some academics demand a new phase of social experimentation within the health care sector and contend that Congress should reintroduce a state-based social security system that precludes the participation of private health insurance companies,[81] other sectors – including the Ministry of Health – defend a more gradual approach to health care reform. According to this more gradualist approach, private health insurance companies should be preserved, but under a new and more stringent regulatory arrangement. According to the ministry, those health insurance companies incapable of insuring large and diverse pools of Colombians should disappear or be absorbed by more robust ones. Those insurance companies that survive the new regulatory demands should have enough financial muscle not only to administer the basket of health services in exchange of governmental payments but also to help the state further its public health goals and insure all Colombians against risks related to sickness.

According to some policy makers and scholars, Tutela litigation on the right to health is one of the driving forces of the current crisis of Colombia's health care system.[82] Consequently, proposals to overhaul the judicial system in order to prevent right-to-health litigation and adjudication are still popular among some sectors. For instance, in December 2013, Santos's minister of finance, economist

---

[80] During the first half of 2013, a group of civil society organizations held a number of colloquiums and round tables across the country during which several proposals to reform the health care system – including the government's – were discussed. For the conclusions of these roundtables, *see Continúa Debate Sobre Reforma a la Salud [The Debate About the Health-Care Reform Continues]*, Ası́ Vamos En Salud, (June 25, 2013), *available at* http://www.asivamosensalud.org/publicaciones/boletin-de-prensa/publicacion.ver/75.

[81] For a synthesis of these proposals, *see Las EPSs Generan Ganancias, Pero No Mitigan la Crisis de la Salud [EPSs Obtain Profit But Do Not Mitigate the Crisis of the Health Care System]*, Agencia De Noticias UN, (May 20, 2013), *available at* http://www.agenciadenoticias.unal.edu.co/ndetalle/article/las-eps-generan-ganancias-pero-no-mitigan-la-crisis-de-la-salud.html.

[82] *See* D. Cherminovsky, R. Guerrero & G. Martínez, *The Incomplete Symphony: The Reform of Colombia's Healthcare System* (The Inter-American Conference on Social Security (CISS), (Working Paper Sep., 26, 2012), *available at* http://www.proesa.org.co/proesa/images/docs/The%20Incomplete%20Symphony_DC_26sep2012_FINAL%20INGLES.pdf.

Mauricio Cárdenas, passed through Congress a bill (bill 326 of 2013) aimed at restricting the Constitutional Court's – and other higher courts' – rulings whose economic consequences could harm public finances. According to this bill, if the government considers that a ruling handed down by any higher Court is inimical to public finances, it can flatly ignore the orders included in the ruling. Albeit the chances that the Constitutional Court will strike down the government's bill are high because it obviously encroaches on the enjoyment of basic and social rights, it is nonetheless meaningful that a government that presents itself as progressive is currently taking decisive steps to restrict the scope of Tutela litigation.

Yet, as this chapter suggests, Tutela-based litigation on the right to health is the canary in the coal mine that signals deeper institutional dysfunctions within Colombia's health sector. Shooting the messenger would not change the bad news.

6

The Right to Health in Israel between Solidarity and Neoliberalism

*Aeyal Gross**

6.1 THE ISRAELI HEALTH CARE SYSTEM DESCRIBED

6.1.1 *The National Health Insurance Law and the Structure of the Public Health System*

The National Health Insurance Law (NHIL), which came into force on January 1, 1995, marked the transformation of the Israeli health system from a Bismarck-style social insurance model of health care to a mixed model in which Sick Funds[1] remained the providers of most health services, but the role of insurer was transferred to the state, which also assumed the responsibility for the funding of the Health Services Basket. The post-1995 Israeli health care system has been described as reflecting a hybrid Bismarck-Bevridge model.[2] Prior to 1995, both health insurance and health care services in Israel were for the most part provided by four Sick Funds. The 1994–1995 reform did not abolish the Sick Funds, but transferred the financial responsibility for health care to the state and made health insurance mandatory and universal.[3]

* I am grateful to The Israel National Institute for Health Policy Research and to the Joseph H. Flom Global Health and Human Rights Fellowship at Harvard Law School for their support of this research, to Sharon Bassan for her research assistance, and to Michael Prawer for the excellent editing work.

[1] The Sick Funds are nonproftis that provide the bulk of health care services in Israel. There are five recognized Sick Funds. *See* Gabi Bin Nun, Yitzhak Berlovitz & Mordechai Shani, Ma'arechet Habriut BeIsrael [The Health System in Israel], 71–94 (2010) (Isr.).

[2] The term "Bismarck model" is used to designate a social-insurance-based sick-fund-based health system, whereas the term "Bevridge model" designates a tax-funded national health system. *See* Gur Ofer & Baruch Rosen, *Ma'arechet Habriut BeIsrael: Hesegim, Beayot Vehashlamat Hareforma [The Health System in Israel: Accomplishments, Achievements, Problems and the Completion of the Reform]*, in Hareforma BeMa'arechet Habriut: Avar Veatid [The Reform in the Health System: Past and Future] 11, 20–22 (Reuven Gruneau ed., 2002) (Isr.). *See* Carmel Shalev & David Chinitz, *In Search of Equity and Efficiency: Health Care Reform and Managed Competition in Israel*, 20 Dalhouise L. J. 553 (1997) for an analysis of the law.

[3] Prior to the legislation, about 95% of the population was insured through the Sick Funds. *See* Bin Nun et al., *supra* note 1, at 73–74.

The NHIL created a triad relationship in which the state is responsible for the financing of the Health Services Basket, the Sick Funds are responsible for the provision of health services, and residents are entitled to the health services.[4] In theory this structure separates the financial relationship between the resident and the state (to which he or she pays the health tax) from the clinical relationship that exists between the resident and the Sick Funds that provide health services. Financial relationships exist between the Sick Funds and the state, and the latter is mandated by statute to finance the health basket. This triad relationship is premised on the statutorily guaranteed severance between the payment for health insurance and the receipt of health services. This premise, fully endorsed, would treat health, and specifically health care, as a right, insofar as it would create equal access to health services, based on need as opposed to graded access, based on the ability to pay. However, as discussed in Subsection 6.1.1.3, a number of legislative reforms enacted shortly after the adoption of the NHIL changed the financing structure of the health system in a manner that deviated from its original premise and promise. They reduced the state's responsibility and shifted much of the burden to patients in the form of direct out-of-pocket payments, thus creating a situation in which, despite the semblance of a "universal" system, access is often conditioned on payment. In addition, there are significant discrepancies between those who are legally deemed "residents" and those who are not, and even within the category of Israeli residents, there are center-periphery discrepancies and other discriminatory practices, discussed later in the chapter. It is against this background that the question of health rights litigation in Israel must be understood. In reality, the Israeli health insurance system is a three-tier system, consisting of the universal national insurance, supplementary insurance offered by the Sick Funds at an extra charge, and private insurance.[5] All of these issues became the subject of litigation concerning equal access to health care, discussed in Section 6.1.3.

Notwithstanding the three-tier system, national health insurance in Israel since 1995 is "universal" in the sense that all residents of Israel are entitled to health service under the NHIL scheme.[6] However, while article 1 of the NHIL determines that national health insurance in Israel is based on the principles of justice, equality, and solidarity,[7] these principles, as well as the principle of universality, were already undermined to an extent by the statute itself, and even more dramatically by a series of legislative amendments introduced shortly after its enactment.

---

4   There are, of course, other actors involved, most notably hospitals. *See* Ofer & Rosen, *supra* note 2, at 20–22.

5   Dana Schwartz Ilan, Bein Revacha Lehafrata: Hitpatchut Bituach Habriut BeIsrael [Between Welfare and Privatization: Development of Health Insurance in Israel] 37–53, 140–162 (2011) (Isr.). While all Israeli residents are covered by the NHIL, 73% are covered additionally by complementary insurance and 35% also by private commercial insurance. *Id.* at 162.

6   National Health Insurance Law, 5954–1994, 1469 LSI 156, art. 3(a) (1994) (Isr.).

7   In the Hebrew original, the third of these principles appears as "mutual assistance," which I translated here as solidarity.

The basic structure of the public health system is laid out in the NHIL, which establishes the state's responsibility for financing from the sources listed in the statute (which include a progressive health tax paid by residents)[8] and the Sick Funds' responsibility to provide their members the full range of health services to which they are entitled under the NHIL.[9] The NHIL also determines that the health services included in the health services basket will be provided according to reasonable medical discretion, within a reasonable period of time, and within a reasonable distance from the residence of the insured, all within the framework of the financial resources available to the Sick Funds in accordance with financing sources listed in the statute.[10] It further states that health services will be provided with respect for human dignity.[11]

6.1.2 *The Health Services Basket*

The NHIL establishes the Health Services Basket (HSB),[12] which is detailed in the schedules to the statute. The HSB is defined as comprising the "Basic Services Basket," which includes the services and medicines that Clalit, the largest of the Sick Funds, gave its members on January 1, 1994.[13] Any change in the HSB that involves an increase in costs requires the consent of the Minister of Finance and the cabinet, and is subject to the statutory requirement of finding a financial source for the addition to the HSB.[14] The list is periodically updated on a national level, and new services are added to the HSB based on recommendations from a non-statutory HSB Committee, which prioritizes new technologies and is dependent on the budgetary decision for each fiscal year.

The NHIL authorizes the Minister of Health and Minister of Finance to determine the cost of the HSB, and establishes a mechanism for updating the cost based on the "health cost index." However, this index is based wholly on the general and health-related prices index, and does not factor in new technologies and demographic changes.[15] The addition of new funding for new technologies is dependent on the annual budget decided by the government as part of the general budget.[16]

---

[8] National Health Insurance Law, art. 3(b); the financing sources are listed in art. 13.

[9] *Id.*, art. 3(c). The law did not change the fact that some categories of health services, including preventive medicine, geriatric and convalescent hospitalization, mental health, and provision of some rehabilitation equipment are provided by the Ministry of Health and not the Sick Funds; *see* art. 7(a)(2).

[10] *Id.*, art. 3(d).

[11] *Id.*, art. 3(e).

[12] *Id.*, art. 7(a).

[13] *Id.*, art. 7(a).

[14] *Id.*, art. 8(a).

[15] *Id.*, art. 9; National Health Insurance Law, 5954 – 1994, 1469 LSI 156, Fifth Schedule (1994) (Isr.).

[16] See David Chinitz, *Sal Hasherutim Habsisi Bemisgeret Hok Bituach Briut Mamlachti: Technocracy Leumat Politica* [*The Basic Health Basket as Part of the National Health Insurance in Israel: Technocracy vs. Politics Revisited*], 54 SOCIAL SECURITY 53 (1999) (Isr.); Sharon Asiskovitch, LACHAIM YESH MECHIR: HAKALKALA HAPOLITIT SHEL CHOK BITUACH BRIUT MAMLACHTI BEISRAEL [PRICE TAG FOR

The NHIL thus lacks a mechanism for updating the basket and its cost in light of new technologies and drugs, demographic changes, and the overall increased cost of health care. This shortcoming is demonstrated by the fact that since 1998, annual budgets have been allocated for the updating of the HSB[17] but have not necessarily covered all the required new technologies. As a result, thus far, certain new technologies have been omitted, being available only to those who could pay the full cost or hold private insurance.

6.1.3 *The Financing of the Health System and the Neoliberal Reforms*

Through a series of amendments to the NHIL, some of the financing of the HSB was shifted to patients by imposition of out-of-pocket user fees for services and medications. While a limited range of such payments was already recognized by the NHIL itself, the amendments significantly expanded their scope, creating a stronger connection between the ability to pay and access to health care services *within* the public system. Unlike the health tax, these payments are regressive: they are uniform (i.e., rich and poor pay the same flat fee) and are, with the exception of some existing waivers, charged to patients regardless of their financial capacity. This was the result of three major legislative amendments that overhauled the entire financing structure. The first was the abolishment in 1997 of the "parallel tax" paid by employers,[18] which had been a major source of funding and which accounted for approximately 40 percent of the Sick Funds' income.[19] The second, the 1998 amendment, allowed the Sick Funds to require patient payments (i.e., user charges and copayments) for services included within the HSB, departing from the far more limited copayment scheme that existed in the original law.[20] The statute stated that users' fees must be "uniform and non-discriminatory, and not dependent on members' income."[21] However, this wording is oxymoronic and belies the reality in which "uniform" and "non-discriminatory" payments actually discriminate against the poor and violate the imperative of substantive equality, inasmuch as the poor are denied access to required health services and medicines, which they cannot afford because of the additional payments. In spite of existing waivers and caps[22], copayments have become a major bar to accessibility. The third is the 2003 amendment that solidified the regressive nature of earlier reforms by limiting the eligibility for waivers and

---

Life: The Political Economy of the National Health Insurance Act in Israel], 154–170, 186–190 (2011) (Isr.).

[17]   Bin Nun et al., *supra* note 1, at 214.

[18]   Arrangements Law in the State Economy (Legislative Amendments to Achieve the Budget Destinations for 1997) 5967–1996, 260 LSI 16, art. 12(7)(a) (2006) (Isr.).

[19]   Bin Nun et al., *supra* note 1, at 253.

[20]   National Health Insurance Law, art. 8(A1)(1).

[21]   *Id.*, art. 8(A1)(2).

[22]   *Id.*, art. 8.

discounts in conjunction with user fees, notably by canceling the entitlements to waivers of people depending on income support from the state.[23]

These changes have significantly increased household expenses on medications, being particularly onerous for the poor, with a high percentage of their free income being spent on medications. Research shows that a significant part of the population has given up medical treatment or prescribed drugs because of their price, showing (with some variations between years) that between 11 percent and 17 percent of the population have waived medications and other medical treatments because of their inability to pay.[24]

The percentage of private financing of a health care system is a major indicator of inequality, and the percentage of private financing of the health system in Israel is among the highest in the Western world.[25] Whereas in the 1980s the ratio of public-to-private financing for health care in Israel was 75-to-25,[26] and in 1996 it was 69-to-31[27], in 2011 it was 58-to-42 (out of the private funding 29 percent was out-of-pocket expenses and 7 percent private insurance), in contrast to the average OECD ratio, in the same year, of 72-to-28 in favor of public expenses.[28] This rise reflects the growing percentage of household spending on health care, with a principal component of the expense being the purchase of supplementary insurance, dental expenses, and medications.[29] This data is augmented by research that has shown that the budget allocated by the state to the HSB eroded by 33 percent in real terms between 1995 and 2003.[30]

The changes described here violate the right to health, because financially based discrimination and the creation of financial barriers to accessibility to health care place a disproportionate burden on poor households and constitute a regressive measure in terms of the right to health. (While the right to health is not limited

---

[23] Arrangements Law in the State Economy (Legislative Amendments to Achieve the Budget Destinations and Economic Policy for 2003) 5953 – 2002, 1850 LSI 428 (2002) (Isr.).

[24] Bin Nun et al., *supra* note 1, at 247. See also Revital Gross, Shuli Brammli-Greenberg & Bruce Rosen, *Tashlumey Hishtatfut Atzmit: Hashlachot al Negishut Lesherutim Veal Shivioniut [Co-Payments: The Implications for Service Accessibility and Equity]*, 6 Mishpat Ve-Aksim 197, 213–220 (2007) (Isr.).

[25] Bin Nun et al., *supra* note 1, at 129.

[26] Bin Nun et al., *supra* note 1, at 125.

[27] Ministry of Health, Economy and Health Insurance department, *Hok Bituak Briut Mamlachti – Kobetz Netunim Statistiym 1995–2011 [National Insurance Health Law: Statistical Data 1995–2011]*, PPT. Presentation, Chart 37 (Jan. 2012), *available at* http://www.old.health.gov.il/Download/pages/stat2011_1995.pdf (for the purpose of using this chart, 2.6% that are based on contributions from outside Israel were adduced to the private expenditure).

[28] *See* OECD, Health at a Glance 2011: OECD Indicators (2011), *available at* http://www.oecd.org/health/healthpoliciesanddata/49105858.pdf.

[29] *Id.* at 125–126.

[30] Leah Achdut, Amir Shmueli & Miri Sabag-Andbler, *MiMun Sal HaSherutim BaAsor HaRishon LeHafalat HaChok – Megamot VeSugiuot [The Financing of the Services Basket in the First Decade of the Operation of the Law – Issues and Tendencies]*, in A Decade to the National Health Insurance Law 1995–2005, 219, 226–227 (Gabi Ben-Nun & Gur Ofer, eds., 2006). This data factors in demography, inflation, and the lack of required technological development.

to access to health care, this chapter focuses exclusively on this component of the right). The principle of accessibility articulated in General Comment 14 declares that the health cost burden for poor households must not be disproportionate to that borne by wealthier households.[31] Making health care financially inaccessible therefore violates the core obligations of the right to health as expressed in the Comment. In Israel's case, this has been effected through regressive measures and the adoption of legislation or policy that is incompatible with existing legal duties relating to the right to health.[32]

More generally, the changed financing structure represents a battle between the NHIL's principles of justice, equality, and solidarity and the adoption of a market-oriented neoliberal version of health care. As Filc notes, Israel has become a part of neoliberal globalization, having gradually abandoned the Keynesian socioeconomic model of the 1980s in favor of a neoliberal one in which privatized health is a central feature. This privatization was effected by abolishing public financing of health care services as a means of cutting public expenses. The current Israeli health system is a combination of a privatization process that started in the 1970s and the NHIL that sets out a public single-payer system.[33] So while the NHIL ostensibly went against the neoliberal trend by creating a universal health care system, its passage was accommodated by a unique confluence of political factors,[34] including a neoliberal desire to weaken the Histadrut, the biggest Federation of Trade Unions in Israel, by disassociating it from Clalit, the largest Sick Fund.[35] Moreover, as Asiskovich notes, the NHIL, while promising health coverage to all Israeli residents, joined the neoliberal trend by shifting much of the decision making to the bureaucracy of the Ministry of Finance, making health care dependent on budgetary decisions – a significant fact given the Ministry of Finance's role as a leading agent of neoliberalism in Israel.[36] Thus, the legislation of the NHIL, while "nationalizing" health care and strengthening the universality of access, in reality also strengthened the reliance of the Israeli health system on government-sponsored policy and measures guided by neoliberal logic.

6.1.4 *The* in personam *Scope of Coverage*

Another problem is the scope of coverage, or determining who is a resident. The NHIL states that "[e]ach resident is entitled to health services in accordance with this

---

[31] Committee on Economic, Social, and Cultural Rights, *General Comment No. 14, The right to the highest attainable standard of health*, ¶12, U.N. Doc. E/C.12/2000/4 (Aug. 11, 2000), reprinted in Compilation of General Comments and General Recommendations Adopted by Human Rights Treaty Bodies, U.N. Doc. HRI/GEN/1/Rev.6 at 85 (2003), *available at* http://documents-ddsny.un.org/doc/UNDOC/GEN/G00/439/34/pdf/G0043934.pdf?OpenElement.

[32] *Id.*, paras. 32, 48.

[33] Dani Filc, CIRCLES OF EXCLUSION: THE POLITICS OF HEALTH CARE IN ISRAEL (CULTURE AND POLITICS OF HEALTH CARE WORK) 58–60 (2009).

[34] *Id.* at 52–58.

[35] Asiskovitch, *supra* note 16, at 91–196.

[36] Asiskovitch, *supra* note 16, at 6, 34–36, 107–114, 150–154, 170–183, 207–212.

law."[37] The law does not cover three especially vulnerable groups: asylum seekers, migrant workers, and Palestinian residents of the Occupied Territories. While the law imposed on employers the duty to provide health insurance for migrant workers,[38] the private insurance companies through which these insurances were procured often tried to shirk their responsibility to workers who became ill.[39] Only children of migrant workers are insured through one of the Sick Funds by virtue of a special arrangement with the Ministry of Health, and even this coverage is lacking in that it depends on registration and paying of an insurance fee by the parents.[40] When it comes to the Occupied Territories, Palestinian residents do not have access to the Israeli system, but must instead rely on a weak Palestinian health system. The problems in this sphere pertain not only to questions of the existence and adequacy of the health care system, but also to violations of health care rights through physical restrictions on accessibility, which derive from restrictions on freedom of movement both within the Occupied Territories and in order to exit them.[41] Notably Israel applied the NHIL to Israeli Jewish settlers living in the Occupied Territories[42] but not to their Palestinian residents.

6.2 THE LEGAL FRAMEWORK FOR HEALTH RIGHTS IN ISRAEL

Israel lacks a full, comprehensive constitution. Its two basic laws on human rights, which serve as its incomplete constitution, do not include explicit recognition of the right to health. The scope of the general right to human dignity guaranteed under the Basic Law: Human Dignity and Liberty is contested,[43] with the hegemonic position being that the right to human dignity encompasses only the right to a minimal material existence, including "access to rudimentary medical services."[44] This minimum approach to social rights casts a shadow on the possibility for judicial review of legislation through the lens of the right to health. While the Israeli Supreme Court recently held that there should be no distinction between the protection of civil and political rights on the one hand and social and economic rights on the other hand, it did so while upholding the recognition of the right to existence in dignity as

---

[37] National Health Insurance Law, art. 3(a).

[38] Migrant Workers Law, 5951 – 1991, 1349 LSI 112, art. 1A, 1D (1991)(Isr.) and order issues in accordance with the law.

[39] Filc, *supra* note 33, at 111–116.

[40] Filc, *supra* note 33, at 119–123.

[41] Filc, *supra* note 33, at 129–152. Angelo Stefanini & Hadas Ziv, *Occupied Palestinian Territory: Linking Health to Human Rights*, 8 HEALTH & HUM. RTS. 161 (2004); Filc, *supra* note 33, at 129–152.

[42] Law extending emergency regulation on application of Israeli Law (Judea, Samaria and Gaza – Criminal Jurisdiction and Legal Assistance), 5927 – 1967, 517 LSI 20, art 6(b), schedule (1967).

[43] See Daphne Barak-Erez & Aeyal Gross, *Do We Need Social Rights, in Exploring Social Rights?: Questions in the Era of Globalization, Privatization, and the Diminished Welfare State, in* EXPLORING SOCIAL RIGHTS: THEORY AND PRACTICE 1 (Daphne Barak-Erez & Aeyal Gross eds., 2007).

[44] RAA. 4905/98 Gamzu v Yeshaiahu 55(3) PD 360, 375–376 [2001] (Isr.); HCJ 366/03 Association for Commitment to Peace and Social Justice v Finance Minister, 60(3) PD 464 [2005] (Isr.).

limited to the notion of "minimal human existence in dignity"[45] The consequences of this decision for the context of health rights remains to be seen. At the same time, the Israeli legal system has a long-standing tradition of recognizing non-written rights in a way that enables judicial review at least of administrative action, if not primary legislation.[46] Moreover, the Basic Law does include explicit references to the rights to life and to body, both of which can directly impact on issues of access to health care. The minimal approach to social rights generally and to health specifically was critical in some of the litigation and served to justify a restrictive approach to health rights. At the same time there were other cases in which lower courts gave the right to health a broader interpretation in order to justify a more expansive approach and considered the right to health as a constitutional social right.[47]

Apart from the constitutional framework and the NHIL discussed in Section 6.1.1, there is also the Patient Rights Law 1996, which determines the right to health care in accordance with law, and in accordance with the conditions and arrangements valid at the time in the Israeli health care system,[48] it prohibits discrimination,[49] includes the right to appropriate health care as far as professional level, medical quality, and interpersonal relationship,[50] and includes the duty to respect the dignity and privacy of patients.[51] As will be seen in Section 6.3, the Patient Rights Law's provision concerning a person's unconditional right to emergency medical care[52] played a role in some of the litigation concerning access to health care.[53] Also, the Israeli courts occasionally refer to international human rights norms. For example, Israel ratified the ICESCR in 1991 and courts often refer to international human rights law, holding that Israeli law should be interpreted as much as possible in a manner consistent with its international obligations.[54]

6.3 HEALTH RIGHTS LITIGATION IN ISRAEL

As the discussion in this section shows, health rights litigation in Israel has addressed a wide variety of issues relating to access to health care. Many of the cases discussed

---

45 HCJ 10662/04 Saleh Hasan v. National Insurance Institute (Feb. 28, 2012), Nevo Legal Database (by subscription) (Isr.).

46 *See* Aeyal M. Gross & Daphne Barak-Erez, *Social Citizenship: The Neglected Aspect of Israeli Constitutional Law, in* IMPLEMENTING SOCIAL RIGHTS 243 (Daphne Barak-Erez & Aeyal Gross eds., 2007).

47 *See e.g.,* NLC 575–09 Macabee Health Services v. Dahan (Jan. 6, 2011), Nevo Legal Database (by subscription) (Isr.).

48 Patients Rights Law, 5956 – 1996, 1591 LSI 327 art. 3(a) (1996) (Isr.).

49 *Id.*, art. 4.

50 *Id.*, art. 5.

51 *Id.*, art. 10.

52 *Id.*, art. 3(b), 11.

53 *See* Bin Nun et al., *supra* note 1, at 442–466 for a discussion of the legal framework for the health system in Israel, which addresses other relevant laws.

54 Daphne Barak-Erez, *The International Law of Human Rights and Constitutional Law: A Case Study of an Expanding Dialogue*, 2 I-CON 611 (2004).

were heard by the Israeli Supreme Court sitting as the High Court of Justice (HCJ), although numerous cases have also been filed by patients against the Sick Funds in the Labor Courts. As will be seen, in handling these issues the courts examined the rights arguments which were based on various sources: Israel's Basic Laws that enjoy constitutional status, statute-based rights, and international law.

6.3.1 *Financing/Updating and Structural Issues*

As mentioned, the NHIL contains no fixed mechanism for proper updating of the HSB, having only a limited health cost index. This generated a series of cases, originating in the fact that the Health Council, a statutory advisory body, recommended the establishment of an automatic updating system for the HSB. This update mechanism would reflect the real costs of the Israeli health system and take into account the growth and ageing of the population as well as technological advancement. After the ministers of health and of finance failed to adopt this recommendation, the Sick Funds petitioned the HCJ, requesting it to order them to act in accordance with it. The HCJ held that the ministers should consider the recommendation, draw conclusions, and then give their reasoned decision.[55]

Ultimately the ministers rejected the recommendation, leading to the filing of an additional petition. The HCJ rejected the petition, having been persuaded that the ministers had given the recommendations due consideration, and pointing out that the Health Council is only an advisory body. In this judgment the HCJ refrained from addressing the issue on its merits, emphasizing that discretion rests with the ministers.[56] It would take another decade for the HCJ to change its position. When the issue again came before the HCJ, it was stressed that the limited updating mechanism within the NHIL does not include the changing price of hospital days and the changing wages in the public sector. The result was that one decade later, in 2012, the HCJ finally held that the government had acted unreasonably in its protracted failure to address the recognized need for an update of the "health cost index." This index determines the cost of the HSB and, by extension, the adjustment of the budget allocated to it. The HCJ noted that the erosion of the budget of the Sick Fund effectively emptied the right to health of its content and ordered the ministers of health and of finance to expedite – within six months – the adoption of a mechanism for updating the health cost index.[57] This decision is of importance given its recognition of the connection between the question of the right to health and the health cost index mechanism, and its determination – the practical implications of which are still unknown at the time of writing – that the government must introduce some changes in this regard.

[55] HCJ 2344/98 Macabee Health Services v. Minister of Finance 54(5) PD 729, 778 [2000](Isr.).
[56] HCJ 9163/01 Clait Health Services v. Minister of Health 56(5) PD 521, 528 [2002](Isr.).
[57] HCJ 8730/03 Macabee Health Services v. Minister of Finance, para. 54 (June 21, 2012), Nevo Legal Database (by subscription) (Isr.).

6.3.2 *Access to Drugs and Services Not Provided*

Litigation concerning the scope of the HSB takes place in Israel in two formats. In the first format, the insurer's claims are brought to the Labor Courts against Sick Funds by Israeli residents covered under the NHIL, in cases in which individual patients request a treatment or medicine not provided within the HSB. The second format consists of petitions brought to the HCJ, in which petitioners seek judicial review of governmental decisions not to provide certain medication or treatments. As we will see, while some of the first kind of claims has succeeded, the claims of the second type have all failed.

6.3.2.1 Labor Courts: Insurers' Claims against the Sick Funds

Numerous petitions are brought before the Israeli labor courts, which are the courts with jurisdiction under the NHIL in suits against Sick Funds concerning denial of coverage for prescribed medications and services. The challenges faced by the courts can be classified under a few major headings: (1) the question of the scope of the treatments covered under the HSB (e.g., how many sessions of physical therapy a patient is entitled to); (2) eligibility for treatments or medications that are included in the HSB but for a different indication than the one for which it was prescribed; (3) medications and services completely excluded from the HSB, but which patients nonetheless request the Sick Funds to provide; (4) medications excluded from coverage but which are required in cases of emergency; and (5) medications and services that are excluded from the HSB but which the Sick Funds have in fact provided to certain patients, thus exposing themselves to discrimination-based claims.[58]

Generally, the labor courts' position in these cases has been that the health basket is limited and does not purport to include all of the medical services required by a person. The health services included in the basket, which the Sick Funds must provide, are the basic, essential services. The Sick Funds can, however, offer additional services or medications beyond those prescribed by law, in accordance with their financial resources and in light of their commitment to fulfilment of the goals and principles of the NHIL and their status as a public organ.[59] The lower courts have occasionally relied on the lack of recognition of the right to health as a constitutional right as the basis of their rejection of claims made by patients to

---

[58] See Aeyal Gross, *Briut BeIsrael: Bein Zchut Lemitsrach [Health in Israel: Between a Right and Commodity]*, *in* SOCIAL AND ECONOMIC RIGHTS IN ISRAEL 437, 502–528 (Yuval Shany & Yoram Rabin eds., 2004) (Isr.) for an elaborate discussion of the case law. *See also* Carmel Shalev & David Chinitz, *Joe Public v. The General Public: The Role of the Courts in Israeli Health Care Policy*, 33 J. L. MED. & ETHICS 650, 652 (2005) for a discussion of litigation concerning health rights in Israel.

[59] National Labor Court 5–7/97 Madzini v Klalit Health Services, 33 Labor Judgments 193, 203 [1999] (Isr.).

anything beyond the basic basket components.[60] On the other hand, in those cases in which courts have ruled in favor of the petitioners, they have relied mostly on three different forms of legal justification. All of them may be regarded as strategies for bypassing the "minimum" approach to the right to health[61]:

1. *The duty to provide emergency care unconditionally:* based on section 3(b) of the Patient's Rights Law,[62] which determines that "in a medical emergency a person is entitled to emergency medical care unconditionally."[63]
2. *Dynamic interpretation of the health basket:* cases holding that the basket must be interpreted in a flexible and dynamic way.[64]
3. *The duty to exercise discretion in specific cases:* In the past the regional labor court held that the Sick Fund could exercise discretion to provide services beyond those prescribed by law, and that as a public body, the fund *must* exercise its discretion and consider the issue.[65]

Later cases that resorted to the third form of legal justification focused on the Sick Funds' "exceptions committees." In one case, a holding that the right to health services is a legal social right with constitutional Characteristics was based on the inclusion of the rights to life and bodily integrity within the Basic Law. Accordingly,[66] the National Labor Court (NLC) rejected the position taken by a Sick Fund, that the exceptions committee must only consider medical irregularities, and held that it should examine "hard cases" and determine whether, given the recognition of the right to health and the right to life, it is possible, in cases where there is no solution within the HSB, to provide the required treatment to a patient. The NLC

---

[60] District Labor Court (TA) 22/99 Isaac v State of Israel [Dec. 10, 1999), Nevo Legal Database (by subscription) (Isr.).

[61] Additionally in one case the court exercised judicial review over a decision to exclude a service from the HSB, holding that the government's decision was defective by reason of its failure to take into account the various considerations in favor of including it, in addition to the financial considerations, giving due consideration to matters of human dignity as mandated by the Basic Law and the NHIL. District Labor Court (TA) 5360/01 Dekel v Klalit Health Services, para. 106 (Aug. 1, 2002), Nevo Legal Database (by subscription) (Isr.). It was later decided again, by the HSB Committee, not to include the device in the basket of health services. This case is unusual as regularly judicial review of noninclusion itself was litigated in the HCJ and not the labor courts.

[62] Patient's Rights Law, 5956 – 1996, 1591 LSI 327 (1994) (Isr.).

[63] District Labor Court (TA) 14339/99 Grundstein v Klalit Health Services, para. 7 (March 24, 1999), Nevo Legal Database (by subscription) (Isr.).

[64] National Labor Court 1557/04 Klalit Health Services v Kaftsan, Judge Rabinovich, para 5 (Dec. 29, 2005), Nevo Legal Database (by subscription) (Isr.). A Petition to the High Court against this judgment ended in a settlement where the principle of flexible interpretation was accepted, subject to budgetary considerations, *see* HCJ 3723/06 Klalit Health Services v Ministry of Health (July 23, 2006) Nevo Legal Database (by subscription) (Isr.).

[65] District Labor Court (Hi) 4037/01 Tabro v Klalit Health Services, (April 18, 2002), Nevo Legal Database (by subscription) (Isr.).

[66] NLC 575–09 Macabee Health Services v. Dahan, para 24 (Jan. 6, 2011), Nevo Legal Database (by subscription) (Isr.).

in this case held that the Sick Funds should examine a triad of considerations: (1) objective considerations vis-à-vis the requested treatment such as the international experience with it and its proved efficiency; (2) subjective considerations such as previous treatment given to the patient, and whether there are any considerations that bar providing the treatment normally indicated for the patient's condition in the HSB, in way that justifies giving the patient the requested medicine or treatment[67]; and (3) broad budgetary considerations, in accordance with the principle of equality, for which the Sick Fund must find a basis for in the concrete case at hand.[68] The principles outlined in the NLC judgments were incorporated into a memorandum issued by the Ministry of Health.[69] Both the NLC judgment and the memorandum are, at the time of this writing, under review by the HCJ.[70]

Judicial guidelines regarding determinations on the part of the exceptions committees are a promising development, as they require the committees to examine the data and evidence regarding technologies not included in the HSB generally, as well as in regard to the specific patient. This may reduce the risk of approving new technologies merely because of the pressure of interested parties such as pharmaceutical companies, while at the same time allowing the committee to take specific circumstances into account. For example in one case involving a cancer patient who, for medical reasons, could not undergo chemotherapy, the exceptions committee held that a drug indicated in the HSB as a second-line drug should only be provided if chemotherapy failed, given that the relevant indication stated "failure in previous treatment." The NLC, however, rejected this position, holding that a proven medical situation that prevents the first-line treatment amounts to "failure" even if the first-line treatment was not tried on the patient. It therefore ordered that the drug in question should be provided to her.[71]

Despite their positive trend, the NLC decisions in this regard raise certain problems. For example, why should the burden of supplying these technologies be on the Sick Funds and not on the state? How can one ensure equal access to the committees and avoid biases in favor of those with access to information and lawyers? Moreover, the NLC ruled that when considering the efficacy of the medicine in relation to the specific patient, successful experience with the drug in regard to the patient

---

[67] However, the economic situation of the specific patient should not be a consideration.

[68] Previous judgments held that if the Sick Funds provides drug not included in the HSB to a patient, they must provide it also to other similarly situated patients. This principle was upheld by the HCJ *in* HCJ 6637/03 Axelkov v. National Labor Court (Nov. 18, 2003), The Judicial Authority Website (Isr.).

[69] Deputy Director-General Memorandum to Supervision of the Sick Funds and Other Health Services, Memorandum 6/10, Matan Sherutim She'einam Basal Limvutahei Hakupa [The Accordance of Services Which Are Not in the Basket to the Insurers in the Fund], Ministry of Health, (10.5.2010) (Isr.).

[70] *See* NLC 575–09 Macabee Health Services v. Dahan, para 24 (Jan. 6, 2011), Nevo Legal Database (by subscription) (Isr.), currently under review, HCJ 5438/11 Macabee v. Minister of Health (pending) (Isr.).

[71] National Labor Court 45021–05–10 Eliav v Klalit Health Services, para. 26 (July 12, 2010), Nevo Legal Database (by subscription) (Isr.).

in question should be taken into account, even if the drug was funded privately.[72] The result of this ruling is that patients with access to private funds may have a better chance in front of the Exceptions Committee, meaning that access to private funds may eventually allow a patient more access to public funds. Also, research has shown that in spite of the fact that the exceptions committees are now regulated by a directive issued by the Ministry of Health, information about them is not widely available to patients, and the number of applications filed is very low. Nonetheless, between 45 percent and 65 percent of the applications submitted to the committees are approved, with variations among the different Sick Funds. The research also pointed to the very significant effect of the case law on the work of the committees.[73]

The developments described here indicate that whereas in some cases judges regard the health basket and its specific composition as an immutable reality that cannot be tampered with, leading to their rejection of petitioners' arguments, in other more recent cases they have been willing to engage in rights analysis, be it the right to life and bodily integrity explicitly recognized in the Basic Law, the right to health as a penumbral right, or the right to emergency health care guaranteed under the Patient's Rights Law.[74] Rights analysis, in conjunction with the principle of flexible and dynamic interpretation, has paved the way to judicial intervention in favor of patients in a way that arguably may broaden access to health care.

6.3.2.2 HCJ Petitions against the Government

In contrast to insurers' claims against the Sick Funds, where labor courts were on occasion prepared to intervene, petitions to the Israeli HCJ requesting judicial review of the government's decision concerning the scope of the HSB have been consistently unsuccessful. The most elaborate discussion and determination on these issues was made by the HCJ in the 2008 *Luzon* case.[75]

The dispute in this case focused on the Erbitux drug, which was prescribed for certain patients (who ultimately petitioned the HCJ) but was not rated sufficiently high in the prioritization of the HSB Committee and was hence excluded from the HSB even after an additional budgetary allocation by the government.[76]

The petitioners requested that the HCJ order the inclusion of the Erbitux drug in the HSB with an indication for colon cancer treatment. They argued that the

---

[72] NLC 575–09 Macabee Health Services v. Dahan, 39–42 (Jan. 6, 2011), Nevo Legal Database (by subscription) (Isr.).

[73] Daniel Sperling, Bchinat Dfusei Hachlata Be'Va'adot Hacharigim she Kupot Hacholim, Ma'amadan utrumatan Lenegishut ve'eichut Hatipul Harefui, Doch Madai Meforat [The Examination of the Patterns of Decision Making in the Exceptions Committees of the Sick Funds, Their Status and Their Contribution to the Accessibility and Quality of Medical Treatment, Detailed Scientific Report Submitted to The Israel National Institute for Health Policy Research] (2013) (Isr.).

[74] Gross, *supra* note 58, at 502.

[75] HCJ 3071/05 Luzon v. Government of Israel (July 28, 2008) Nevo Legal Database (by subscription) (Isr.).

[76] HCJ 3071/05 Luzon v. Government of Israel, para. 2–4.

exclusion of this drug violated the right to health, which is part of the right to life and bodily integrity, as well as the right to human dignity, all of which are anchored in the Basic Law. They also argued that the HSB Committee's decision did not give sufficient weight to the value of human life, and discriminated against them vis-à-vis other patients whose required medications were included in the HSB.[77]

The judgment's main determinations may be summarized as follows:

1. *Constitutional status of the right to health*

The HCJ determined that the scope of the constitutional right to health is difficult to define as it encompasses a very broad range of rights, some of which enjoy constitutional protection in Israel. Given the many aspects of the right, there is no point in examining the constitutional status of the right as a whole, but rather it is preferable to evaluate the underlying reasons for the different rights and interests they protect, in terms of their relative social importance and the intensity of their link to the constitutional rights enumerated in the Basic Law.[78] The right to health care, and specifically to publicly funded health care, is not explicitly mentioned in the Basic Law, which raises the difficult question of whether it amounts to a constitutional right, especially to the extent that its recognition imposes a positive duty on the state that encompasses its responsibility for financing of health services in Israel. The HCJ held that constitutional rights in the Basic Law may include elements touching on the area of social welfare and security, including the sphere of health, but it is unclear whether this means interpreting the Basic Law as including a constitutional right to health services, which is broader than the basic level necessary for human existence within society. The dilemma is between the centrality of health to human life and the ability to realize all other human rights, on the one hand, and the reality in which the right to public funded health services entails the imposition of a positive duty, and hence involves general distributional questions, on the other hand. Given the need of the HCJ to be wary of shaping economic policies and interfering with national priorities, it is doubtful whether one should read into the rights in the Basic Law a right that would impose a correlative duty to provide public health services on a level higher than the minimum required for human existence in society. Moreover, even under the assumption that the right is included within the constitutional rights, like all other rights, it is not absolute and would have to be balanced against competing rights and interests.[79] For the purposes of the case in question, President Beinisch ruled that it sufficed to determine that, given that the drug in question is a novel medicine for colon cancer, and there is no consensus regarding its ability to save or prolong

---

[77] HCJ 3071/05 Luzon v. Government of Israel, para. 5.
[78] *Id.* para. 9.
[79] *Id.*, para. 10.

life, it would seem that the medicine in question as well as other new and experimental medications are not part of the *basic* health services required for minimal human existence in society, and that given the limited public resources, it is doubtful if the demand for public funding of new medications may be anchored in the core of the Basic Law's protected constitutional rights. Furthermore, even in accordance with an interpretive position which would expand the constitutional dimension of the right to human dignity beyond the necessary minimum, only in exceptional circumstances would the state be constitutionally obligated to fund a specific drug – out of numerous drugs for which demands for public funding are raised.[80]

2. *Scope of the statutory right to health services*

After addressing the constitutional issue, the HCJ emphasized that the right to public health services does exist as a statutory right, regardless of the constitutional question, and this warrants an examination of whether this statutory right was violated.[81] The right itself is anchored in the Patient's Rights Law,[82] as well as by the NHIL. President Beinisch analyzed the structure of the NHIL, determining that the law is based on the principle of solidarity, its aim being for each insured person to pay in accordance with their ability and to receive according to their needs, having consideration for the weaker members of society, even if, she added, over the years a series of amendments to the NHIL had eroded the principle according to which the right to receive medical service is an independent right, irrespective of the ability to pay for the service.[83] After addressing the mechanism for updating the cost of the HSB and the widespread criticism thereof, and the ensuing litigation, Beinisch concluded that the government has wide discretion in determining the annual addenda to the cost of the HSB.[84] Based on the statutes, Beinisch ruled that while the Israeli legal system recognized a statutory right to health services that is broader than the core minimum of basic health services required for human existence in society, it is nonetheless clear that the HSB does not purport to include the full range of possible medical services that an individual may require. The statutory right, it was held, includes a core and a penumbra. The core of the statutory right to basic health services includes the health services that the state is committed to fund. In accordance with the NHIL, this includes the "basic services basket" that was in force in Clalit, the largest Sick Fund, before the NHIL entered into the picture,[85] and which served as the baseline

---

[80] *Id.* para. 12.
[81] *Id.* para. 13.
[82] *Id.* para. 14.
[83] *Id.* para. 15.
[84] HCJ 3071/05 Luzon v. Government of Israel, para. 15.
[85] This is according to the NHIL, which, upon coming into effect, established that basket as the starting point for the HSB.

under the statute, and the funding of which within the HSB is a statutory duty. At the penumbra of the statutory right are the health services not included in this baseline, and the right to expansion within the HSB beyond the baseline is a budget-dependent right, which derives from policy as determined in the annual budget law.[86] Thus, the scope of the statutory right to public health services beyond the "basic basket" derives from the annual budget law.

Having said that, Beinisch added one caveat: the budget limit is not "an impenetrable roof"; international law indicates the duty to act for the progressive realization of the right, and when the state takes retrogressive measures in relation to the right, it assumes the onus of showing that these measures are necessary given the maximum resources available to it:[87]

> [T]he question that is likely to arise in our legal system is whether a serious reduction in the funding of the health services basket – including by way of significant cumulative erosion of the funding of the basket in the absence of a substantive mechanism for a real adjustment of its cost – transfers the burden to the State to show that this reduction is indeed justified and dictated by reality.

This interpretive question, Beinisch added, would necessitate an examination of whether the statutory right for the expansion of the HSB, while budget-dependent, should be interpreted in accordance with international law and the principle of progressive realization. Beinisch noted, however, that this is not the question before the HCJ in the present case and should be left open.[88] This final comment relied on the fact that the petitioners in *Luzon* did not challenge the budgetary framework allocated by the state for the expansion of the HSB, but rather attacked the exercise of discretion by the basket committee. Given this analysis, Beinisch could conclude that Erbitux was not part of the baseline basket under the NHIL, and so access to it is not a statutory, but rather a budget-dependent right.

3. *The determination of the basket and the discretion of the basket committee*

In this part of the judgment Beinisch addressed the procedure for adding new technologies and described the process in which on an annual basis the Ministry of Health issues a call for requests to include new medications and technologies in the HSB. This is followed by an evaluation process of the various proposals, conducted by professional bodies in the ministry, which then pass the information to the HSB committee. The HSB committee prioritizes the new medications and technologies and presents its recommendations to the Health Council, a statutory body authorized to advise the Minister of Health. If the minister accepts the recommendations, then further consent is

---

[86] HCJ 3071/05 Luzon v. Government of Israel, para. 16.
[87] *Id.* para. 17. In this context Beinisch drew on the ICESCR and on Committee on Economic, Social and Cultural Rights (CESCR), *General Comment No. 14, supra* note 31.
[88] HCJ 3071/05 Luzon v. Government of Israel, para. 17.

needed from the Minister of Finance, to be followed by the consent of the government, which must also approve the financial resource to expand the HSB.[89] The committee, it was held, enjoys a wide range of discretion, and the HCJ will not intervene in its discretion as long as its recommendations were formulated in a proper procedure and as long as it does not substantially deviate from the relevant considerations it is obligated to take into account, or from striking an appropriate balance between them.[90]

The HCJ did not find any grounds for intervention, noting that the question of how to set priorities in the allocation of public resources is a controversial one, admitting of differing opinions, and that it is not the court's role to choose one prioritization system over another.[91] Having perused the protocols of the HSB committee's discussion, the HCJ ruled that the scientific evidence concerning the drug in question was still elementary and inconclusive. Accordingly, the committee's decision to give it a rating that was lower than the rating of proven life-saving technologies is not unreasonable to an extent that warrants judicial intervention.[92]

The HCJ's analysis in *Luzon* enables the following observations: regarding the constitutional status of the right, the HCJ adhered to the minimalistic approach; regarding the statutory right, the HCJ's distinction between the core and the penumbra may indeed have its parallel in the recognition of "core obligations" in the right to health,[93] but the HCJ chose to identify the core obligations with the 1994 baseline HSB, so that anything beyond it is within the scope of budget-dependent penumbra. This particular choice neglects a substantive test, which requires consideration to be given to the changing meanings of what is at the "core" in accordance with technological developments, thus confusing the "is" with the "ought."

The *combination* of HCJ's holdings in the three aspects of its judgment seems to close the door on the possibility of judicial review of decisions concerning the inclusion of new technologies. Even if new technologies or drugs are more established than Erbitux, the HCJ's analysis precludes their inclusion within the scope of the statutory right, and it would seem practically impossible to make claims on a constitutional or administrative level. Indeed, the state has allocated budgets for new technologies since 1998, but this budget has been declared to be insufficient for

---

[89] *Id.* para. 20.

[90] *Id.* para. 21–23. *See id.* para. 26 for a discussion of the relevant considerations as laid out by the committee before the court.

[91] HCJ 3071/05 Luzon v. Government of Israel, para. 27–28.

[92] *Id.* para. 29.

[93] See also Aeyal M. Gross, *The Right to Health in a Era of Privatization and Globalization: National and International Perspectives, in* EXPLORING SOCIAL RIGHTS, supra note 43, at 289, 303; Lisa Forman, *What Future for the Minimum Core? Contextualizing the Implications of the South African Socioeconomic Rights Jurisprudence for the International Human Rights to Health, in* GLOBAL HEALTH AND HUMAN RIGHTS 62, 67–70 (Harringron & Stuttaford eds., 2010).

purposes of covering all essential and life-saving drugs. It relies on the government's annual budgetary decision and is not guaranteed, and hence cannot be trusted, especially given the lack of an adequate regular updating mechanism described earlier.

As for the third aspect of the judgment, the criterion for intervention set by the HCJ may be a sound one as indeed the HCJ cannot be expected to replace the committee's discretion with its own discretion. Nonetheless, Luzon still reads like a missed opportunity. Consider the paragraphs in which Beinisch suggests that significant and cumulative erosion of the financing of the basket and the lack of a substantial mechanism for a realistic update of its cost may amount to a severe violation of the financing of the HSB ("retrogressive measures"[94]), which imposes a burden on the state to demonstrate that the said violation is indeed justified and necessary. Indeed, Beinisch determined that this was not the issue confronting the HCJ, and the petitioner did not challenge the budgetary allocation for health care but rather its determination of priorities therein. Nonetheless, it is arguable that on a factual level it was indeed the erosion of the financing of the health basket, as described, and the lack of a substantial mechanism for realistic update of its cost as discussed earlier, that formed the background to the litigation in *Luzon*. The reason is that these factors caused the exclusion from the HSB of technologies that do not rank sufficiently high on the committee's list, despite their life-saving or life-extending potential. Indeed the committee should have wide discretion, and as a rule it is difficult to justify intervention in the priorities it sets. However, the state's policies on health care may indeed justify a transfer of the onus to the state to explain and justify any significant reduction of public funding for health care. In that scenario, judicial intervention would be justified if the explanation were inadequate. Accordingly, while the petitioners in this case did not challenge the budget allocated for the health care basket but rather the way in which it was allocated, the HCJ could have seized on the opportunity to transfer the burden of proof and determine that the state's neglect of this issue creates a presumption against the propriety of its decisions. While litigation cannot replace policy making, which requires seeing the broad picture and making prioritization decisions, in cases like *Luzon* it may arguably serve as a catalyst for a review of the policy from a rights perspective. My critique of *Luzon* does not imply then that any drug requested by a patient or a doctor should be automatically provided within the HSB, but rather points to its reasoning that takes the mirror image position, that is, that one cannot make an argument for any drug not provided in 1994 (or added subsequently as part of budgetary additions). Erbitux itself was added to the HSB in 2012.[95]

---

94 HCJ 3071/05 Luzon v. Government of Israel, para. 17.
95 Director General Directive 1/12, *Harchavat Sal Sherutey Habriut LiShnat 2012* [*Expansion of the Health Services Basket for 2012*], MINISTRY OF HEALTH, (10.1.2012) (Isr.), *available at* http://www.health.gov.il/hozer/mk01_2012.pdf.

6.3.3 *Copayments*

The issues of copayments, mentioned earlier in the chapter, came before the HCJ in one significant case, which involved a petitioner who was losing her hearing, but for whom the process was reversible were she to undergo a cochlear implant operation. This operation was included in the HSB, but entitlement to the operation under the law was conditional on a self-contribution of 70 percent of the cost of the implant and the procedure, which, in this case, amounted to 70,000 NIS (about US$15,500). This sum was far in excess of the economic capacity of the petitioner, a teacher and single mother, and she based her petition not only on the right to health but also on the right to equality, the latter having been recognized as part of the right to human dignity under Israel's Basic Law: Human Liberty and Dignity. Although the Court queried whether a 70 percent self-contribution could really be regarded a "contribution," in *Israeli*[96] it refused to intervene, arguing that the question of deciding on the services to be included in the HSB and under what conditions, as well as the establishing of priorities, rests first and foremost with the committee authorized to recommend the scope of the HSB and to establish priorities, and ultimately with the government.

While expressing its hope that the issue would be revisited by the HSB committee in the future, the HCJ did not intervene in the matter but rather wished the petitioner a full recovery, and expressed its hope that she would find comfort in the fact that she had raised the problem and given it a voice. The latter hope was fulfilled: the litigation was part of a process that drew attention to the problem of the high self-contribution requirement for cochlear implant operations – a requirement that was cancelled by the government two months later.[97]

This judgment continues to exemplify judicial deference to the government's decision and a refusal to deliberate questions of accessibility, equality, and progressive realization of the right to health. As a matter of fact, in this case the HCJ could have relied on previous case law (albeit in a different context) where it held that requiring high payments that prevent accessibility to important services may constitute a violation of the right to equality.[98] It is also interesting to contrast the decision to one given a few months later where the HCJ held that making the granting of a demonstration permit conditional on the financing of the expenses of the demonstration's security by its organizers is illegal as it violates the right to

---

[96] HCJ 2974/06 Israeli v. Committee for the Expansion of the Health Basket [2006] The Judicial Authority Website (Isr.).

[97] *Alut Sal Sherutey Habriut* [*The Cost of Health Services Busket*], Government Resolution Number 406, Israel Sec'y of State (Aug. 27, 2006) (Isr.), *available at* www.pmo.gov.il/PMOEng/Secretarial/ decisions/.

[98] HCJ 5394/92 Hupert v Yad Vashem, 48(3) PD 35 [1994] (Isr.). *See* Gross, *supra* note 58, at 491–492 for a discussion of the relevance of this case to the legality of copayments.

freedom of speech.[99] Both cases involved a governmental fee imposed on people wishing to exercise a right. However, whereas in the context of the right to freedom of speech, such a fee was considered as illegally violating this right, the HCJ refused to make that determination in the context of the right to health care. Contrasting the two cases illustrates how the line and the hierarchy between civil rights and social rights is artificial, as both may require public funding to be exercised equally, but nonetheless, it is still maintained by the HCJ.

6.3.4 *Public/Private*

The term "Private Health Services" (PHS)[100] is used to refer to a program that enables patients to choose their doctor – specifically surgeons – within public hospitals, for an additional out-of-pocket payment by the patient. These programs have been promoted in governmental hospitals since 1996 by way of private companies that entered into agreements with the hospitals' research funds.[101] In 2002, the Attorney General declared the practice illegal. Petitions against his decision were filed in the HCJ by a group of doctors and a group of citizens, and in 2009 the HCJ decided to reject the petitions and uphold the Attorney General's decision concerning the illegality of the PHS (the *Kiryati* ruling). In addressing the matter, Justice Berliner noted that in reality, the PHS was limited to the selection through payment of surgeons in governmental hospitals. Nonetheless, the issue before the HCJ actually has far broader implications, because permitting PHS would also legitimate the provision of a wide array of health services by means of a payment on top of the health tax. This could have significant implications for the character of the public health system in Israel, which she described as national and public, with each citizen paying a fixed monthly sum from his or her salary regardless of his or her medical condition, and receiving treatment in accordance with his or her needs.[102] Berliner contrasted this system to the PHS regime under which the patient can choose the surgeon based on a private out-of-pocket payment, which is generally used to select the more senior doctors who naturally have greater expertise in their respective fields.[103] Health services in the hospitals should be provided exclusively in accordance with medical considerations, and under no circumstances should they be based on the enhanced ability to pay.[104] The service provided for citizens within

---

99 HCJ 2557/05 Majority Headquarters v Israeli Police (Dec. 12, 2006), The Judicial Authority Website (Isr.)

100 As per the Hebrew acronym = SHARAP.

101 For a discussion, *see* Bin Nun et al., *supra* note 1, at 131–137; Y Shuval & O Hanson, Ha'Ikar HaBriut [Most Importantly, Health] 307–314 (2000) (Isr.).

102 HCJ 4253/02 Kiryati et al. v the Attorney General, para 2 (March 17, 2009), Nevo Legal Database (by subscription) (Isr.).

103 *Id.* para. 3.

104 *Id.* para. 34, 41, 48.

state hospitals is a public service given for free, and any ability to buy an improved service within the public service that is normally given for free must be authorized by legislature.[105]

The petitioners in this case attempted to enlist rights arguments in making the case for allowing PHS, arguing that the prohibition of PHS violates the rights enumerated in the Patient's Rights Law as well as in the Basic Law, which protects the autonomy of the individual, including the individual's right to select the doctor and the hospital in which he or she is to be treated.[106] Judge Berliner rejected these arguments, relying on the previous HCJ rulings that recognized the right to dignity as including a minimum human existence but not a broader right to health. Accordingly, a right to choose a physician is not part of the core services required for the maintenance of human existence in dignity.[107] Additionally, if the right to choose a physician were to be considered a part of the personal autonomy recognized by the Basic Law, it would mean allowing every patient to select a physician without payment, as part of the HSB. Yet the protection of autonomy does not entitle the citizen to the realization of each and every one of their desires just because they can pay for it.[108]

Justice Berliner's ruling in *Kiryati* demonstrates a commitment to the principles of the NHIL and to a public health system in which medical services are provided in accordance with need and not just the ability to pay. Her rejection of the rights arguments made by the petitioners demonstrates a commitment to an egalitarian concept of health provided in accordance with need and not in accordance with ability to pay, and she justly held that if autonomy means the right to choose one's doctor, than it should be provided to all patients, and not just to those who can pay for it.

This ruling is in contrast with the Canadian Supreme Court decision in *Chaoulii,*[109] which protected access to private health insurance – in the name of the protection of the right to the security of the person – for those who can pay for it. Interestingly, in reaching her conclusion, Judge Berliner relied on the narrow, minimal recognition of the right to health as part of the right to human dignity as recognized in Israeli law. In this case it was a minimal construction of the right to health that served to justify equal access to health care rather than a broader construction. All the same, given Justice Berliner's rejection of the argument from autonomy, she could have rejected an argument made from the right to health even if the right had been given a broader construction in Israeli law. In other words, the

---

[105] HCJ 4253/02 Kiryati et al. v the Attorney General, para. 36. Justice Berliner based her decision also on a few statutory provisions (*See* id. para. 26–30).

[106] *Id.* para. 24.

[107] *Id.* para. 52.

[108] *Id.* para. 57.

[109] Chaoulli v. Quebec (Attorney-General), [2005] SCC 35, 1 S.C.R. 791 (Can. S.C.); *see* Aeyal Gross, *Is There a Human Right to Private Health Care?*, 41 J. L. Med. & Ethics 138 (2013).

rationale for rejecting the right to autonomy claim could also have been used for rejecting the claim based on the right to health. Both of them are rights to which all persons should have equal access regardless of ability to pay. Rejecting the argument made from the right to health on these grounds would have been a better response than the one given in the judgment. From reading *Kiryati* it is evident that rights discourse can be and was in fact used by the petitioners for the attempted promotion of privatization within the health care system in a manner that creates inequality. However a concept of rights grounded in a substantial concept of equality – which was adopted in this case by the HCJ – should reject these claims and point to the fact that for a rights argument to be justified, it must be shown that access to health care is equal and not dependent on the ability to pay.

At the same time, and as the petitioners justly argued, the principle of equality is already undermined by many other factors: recall that while *Kiryati* prohibited discrimination between patients within the public hospital in regard to choice of surgeon based on the ability to pay, *Israeli* upheld discrimination within the public hospital, based on the ability to pay, even where that ability determined the very possibility of undergoing an essential operation. This gap points to the limits of the HCJ's discourse. It may in fact indicate that it was easier for the HCJ to protect equality in *Kiryati*, where its decision was limited to the upholding of policy and did not require intervention. A similar position was taken by the HCJ when it de facto rejected, without a reasoned judgment, a petition arguing that the prohibition on including "life saving medicines" in supplementary insurance programs offered by the Sick Funds violated the rights of those who wanted to buy the supplementary program.[110]

On the other hand, and effectively retreating somewhat from the *Kiryati* ruling, the HCJ rejected a later petition that challenged the legality of PHS in publicly funded hospitals that provide public services but are operated by private companies and are not government hospitals in the same way as the hospitals addressed in *Kiryati* were. Writing for the Court, President Grunis based his reasoning mostly on

---

[110] HCJ 73/08 Levy v Knesset. I discuss this case in detail in Gross, *Is There A Human Right To Private Health Care?, id.* In another case, HCJ 7716/11 Assuta Medical Centers v. Minister of Health (March 17, 2013) (*available at* The Judicial Authority Website (Isr.)), the HCJ rejected a petition against a directive of the Ministry of Health, which determined that women who chose to undergo amniocentesis privately at an institution that charged more than what would be refunded under the National Health Insurance Law (usually the additional payment would be for the right to choose the specific physician who would conduct the test) would no longer be entitled to a refund. Before the directive they were entitled to a refund for the fixed cost of the amniocentesis. The result is that if a woman paid more because of a "top-up" such as choosing the practitioner who would conduct the test, she would not be refunded at all. Petitioners argued that the new regulation violates basic rights to autonomy, freedom of contract, freedom of occupation, and equality, and was issued ultra vires. The HCJ rejected the arguments holding that at stake was an issue of policy, which justified it. It deferred to the government policy choice and the fact that rights had not been violated. The Court stressed that the government adopted the policy in order to secure public funding for public health care and not for the purchase of private health care. It relied in its judgment on the *Kiryati* decision discussed above.

the laches doctrine, holding that the petition was submitted after a significant delay, but also distinguishing the case from *Kiryati* based on the difference between the types of hospitals involved. Addressing the question of whether, given the nature of the rights involved, the HCJ should consider the merits of the case notwithstanding the delay, the Court noted that even if the right to equal access to health care is to be recognized as derivative of the constitutional right to human dignity, the right is at the periphery and not at the core of the constitutional right.[111] This statement further points to the weak status of the right to health in Israeli constitutional law and to a position that is at odds with the need to integrate the concept of equal access into its analysis. In the absence of such a concept, health's status as a right will be further eroded, increasingly becoming a commodity, the availability of which is based on the ability to pay as opposed to need.[112]

6.3.5 *Discrimination among Residents*

There is litigation that addresses discrimination among residents protected by the NHIL on grounds other than ones of financial accessibility discussed so far. Palestinians who are Israeli citizens, unlike those in the Occupied Territories, are included in the NHIL, but still suffer from the underdevelopment of services in their towns and villages[113] and a history of inequality.[114] This issue is especially severe when it comes to Bedouins living in "unrecognized villages."[115] A few petitions concerning the lack of clinics in these villages did lead to the opening of some Sick Fund clinics, while at the same time the HCJ rejected the demand that the Minister of Health determine binding rules for the establishment of clinics, which he was authorized to do under the NHIL, with the agreement of the Minister of Finance.[116] Another case involved a three-year-old who suffered from a severe form of cancer, which required regular injections that had to be refrigerated. However, the toddler and her family lived in an "unrecognized village" in the Negev, where Bedouins live in villages that the state does not recognize and for which it fails to provide basic services.[117] The village was not connected to the electricity grid, and thus the family relied on a generator

---

[111] HCJ 2114/12 The Association for Civil Rights in Israel v. Government of Israel (Aug. 15, 2012), The Judicial Authority Website (Isr.).

[112] In two other cases related to the public/private divide, the HCJ upheld, and arguably encouraged, the privatization of preventive medical services given to children in school, even though the NHIL stated in Article 21A that those services will be provided by the Ministry of Health. *See* HCJ 5012/97 Matan Health Welfare and Nursing Services v. Ministry of Health (Jan. 19, 1998), Nevo Legal Database (by subscription) (Isr.); HCJ 1083/07 Israel Medical Association v. Ministry of Health (May 24, 2012), Nevo Legal Database (by subscription) (Isr.).

[113] FILC, *supra* note 33, at 31.

[114] SHUVAL & HANSON, *supra* note 101, at 296–303.

[115] FILC, *supra* note 33, at 75–99.

[116] HCJ 4540/00 Labar Abu Afash v. Minister of Health (May 14, 2006), The Judicial Authority Website (Isr.).

[117] Filc, *supra* note 33, at 75–99.

that belonged to a neighboring family and for which maintenance costs were very high. Based on these facts, the HCJ was asked to order that the house of the toddler and her family be connected to the national electricity grid or that they be provided regular electric services. The HCJ rejected the petition holding that based on the Israeli planning laws it was not possible to connect the petitioners to the electric grid. The HCJ further mentioned that various funds managed by the state had agreed to give the family some financial support that would help operate the generator for a few months. While this solution is far from optimal, Justice Levy noted, one cannot ignore the fact that the toddler's parents chose to live in an unrecognized village, knowing that they would thus be unable to connect to the electric grid.[118] The HCJ decision in this case represents a failure to guarantee basic conditions that would enable access to health care for one of the most vulnerable groups in Israeli society, instead blaming the toddler's parents for their "choice," and represents another facet of neoliberal approach that does not consider that people are entrenched in social conditions and relationships of power. Although litigation resulting from the cases discussed earlier in the chapter was useful in the opening of more clinics accessible to residents of unrecognized villages, the HCJ's record on this issue is tainted by its decision in this last case.

Health inequalities occur on many other levels, not all of which have been the subject of litigation. "[G]eographical periphery" in Israel, as Filc describes it, includes poorer and more excluded social groups, where geography, ethnicity, and class coverage, together with unequal distribution of material resources and political power, cause health care to be less developed in the geographical periphery, and health indicators as well as numbers of physicians and hospital beds per capita confirm this.[119]

6.3.6 *Discrimination Based on Residency Status*

As noted earlier in the chapter, only Israeli residents are covered by the NHIL. The HCJ rejected a petition against a statutory amendment providing that certain categories of people would not be considered "residents" for the purpose of national health insurance. These included any persons holding migrant workers visas.[120] It held that residency is an acceptable criterion for the allocation of social benefits.[121] Addressing the petitioners' argument that the statute violated the right to health insurance, the HCJ accepted that certain aspects of health insurance are part of the right to dignity under the Basic Law, and a social right to basic

---

[118] HCJ 8062/05 Inyias al-Atrash v. Minister of Health (Nov. 23, 2005), The Judicial Authority Website (Isr.).

[119] Filc, *supra* note 33, at 32–33.

[120] *See* HCJ 494/03 Physicians for Human Rights v. Minister of Finance, 59(3) PD 322, 328, [2004] (Isr.) for an analysis of the statute by the HCJ.

[121] *Id.* para 11–13.

health services can be anchored in the right to bodily integrity, also protected by the Basic Law. Nonetheless, the right to health insurance does not necessarily include the right to be insured within the national health insurance, and the denial of membership need not be viewed as a violation of a person's right to dignity or bodily integrity. The result of this case is a refusal by the HCJ to use the notion of the right to health in order to protect vulnerable groups of migrant workers and asylum seekers.

The HCJ's ruling in this case deviates from the objective of the NHIL as determined in Article 1 and views the latter purely as an instrument for the provision of health services. The problem is that by excluding asylum seekers, migrant workers, and others from this system it effectively denies them health care unless they can pay for it themselves. While it is true that current law requires that migrant workers be insured through private insurance purchased by their employers, and a more comprehensive arrangement was instituted for children of migrant workers, these arrangements are far from satisfactory.[122] Further exclusions pertain to Palestinians living under Israeli control in the OPT, to which the Israeli health care system does not apply. In this context, many of the problems that reached Israeli courts pertain to physical access to health care, often blocked because of checkpoints or the Israeli-built separation wall in the West Bank. These issues compel a separate discussion because of the unique nature of the questions they raise and the fact that they are not litigated under the framework of the NHIL. Indeed, the gap between the Israeli-Jewish residents of these areas, to whom the NHIL was applied in personam, and the Palestinian residents of the same territories, who depend on the weaker Palestinian health system and who are subject to severe restrictions on freedom of movement, amount to what Filc calls "The Ultimate Violation of the Right to Health" in Israel.[123]

6.4 ASSESSING THE ROLE OF RIGHTS IN THE ISRAELI HEALTH CARE SYSTEM

The NHIL Law reforms in 1995 ensured universal coverage and seemed on its face to be a progressive move toward greater equity. However, the cumulative effect of subsequent legislative reforms has shifted the balance from the principles of solidarity, stated in the law and embedded in its basic structure, to neoliberal policy that reduces public spending and expands private spending, creating growing pockets of privatization within the system. Health rights litigation in Israel is conducted against this background, as well as against the background of various forms of inequalities within society: the severe neglect of infrastructure in some of the Palestinians towns within Israel and especially the unrecognized Bedouin villages; the exclusion from

---

[122] *See supra* Section 6.1.4; *see also* Filc, *supra* note 33, at 100–128 for this issue in detail.
[123] Filc, *supra* note 33, at 129–152.

universal health care of migrant workers; and the severe problems concerning access to health care of Palestinians living in the occupied territories.

There has been much debate in recent years on whether law generally and human rights specifically can fulfill any important role in the area of public health care.[124] On the one hand, a human rights approach can help (re)instate public values, such as equality, into public health care systems that undergo privatization. On the other hand, rights arguments may reinforce privatization and increase inequality by disguising private interests in the cloak of rights. In a way, none of the above happened in the Israeli case, where the HCJ has generally been deferential to governmental decisions. As we have seen, with the exception of the most recent petition, in the series of cases concerning the health cost index update, the HCJ upheld the majority of government policies and decisions, even when they de facto restricted access to health care, being highly deferential, and sticking to a minimal concept of both the constitutional and statutory right to health, by holding that anything beyond the minimum is budget-dependent and at the state's discretion, and refusing to intervene when intervention could have a budgetary affect. The story is somewhat different in the labor courts, where trial courts, seeing an individual in front of them, sometime chose to intervene, and where the NLC developed criteria for the manner in which Sick Funds' exceptions committees should function.

The HCJ's rationale might have been more convincing were it not for its practice of intervening in civil rights cases, even where its intervention had budgetary ramifications.[125] Obviously the courts cannot replace policy decisions or priority setting. It is true that the health system requires prioritization and collective decision making that sees the "big picture." But what courts can and should do is review policy decisions relating to human rights. Do they increase inequality or reduce it? Does the state act to lift barriers to health care, which may cause discriminations between people and make access harder, especially for those who cannot afford it, or does it introduce additional barriers? Does the state show a commitment to progressive realization, or does it retreat from its obligations?

In the Israeli case, because many of the government's policies create increasing inequality in the form of retrogressive measures and increased access barriers, courts should exercise review according to these criteria, where state policies do not uphold human rights, or principles of equality in relation to health, understood as substantive equality or equity. Indeed, as discussed in Section 6.3, when the state did take measures to prohibit privatization steps that would have increased inequality, the court rejected the attempt to justify privatization using rights claims, emphasizing

---

[124] See Gross, *The Right to Health in an Era of Privatization, supra* note 93; Litigating Health Rights: Can Courts Bring More Justice to Health? (Alicia Ely Yamin & Siri Gloppen eds., 2011).

[125] HCJ 2974/06 *Israeli v Committee for the Expansion of the Health Basket* [2006] The Judicial Authority Website (Isr.)

the principles of equality, justice and solidarity, and rejecting the attempt to invoke rights discourse in order to justify demands for private care. However, the logic of these cases should have driven the court to confer greater weight to substantive equality in other cases such as the ones discussed here, and possibly, in consideration of the huge erosion in the budget allocated to health care by the state, toward shifting the burden on the state when it makes decisions – such as the denial of treatment – that violate the principles of substantive equality.

In examining individual petitions in the labor courts, we should recall the oft-voiced concern about judicial review that whereas health care policy decisions are polycentric, claimants evoke instant sympathy because of their needs. Thus, courts have "telescopic vision" with regard to the cases before them, which may blind them to almost anything else; a troublesome perspective from which to view a system with interlocking components. A further risk involved in judicial review in this context is that it could tilt the system in favor of those with the resources to initiate legal action.[126] Given these concerns, it has been argued that the courts should defer to government decisions in such matters and recognize that these decisions reflect the system's values.[127] But courts should examine whether state policy shows a commitment to progressive realization and to ensuring equity and accessibility in health care; if policy decisions fail to adhere to these standards, judicial review should be exercised, especially when the litigation concerns access to medication or treatment that is critical for saving or prolonging life or that has a significant effect on quality of life. While decision making in individual cases might, indeed, obscure the general picture, sometimes there can be an advantage to seeing the actual person involved. As I suggested before, following the work of Seyla Benhabib, there is a need to see both the "general other" (as required from an ethics of justice and rights) and the "concrete other" (as required from an ethics of care and responsibility).[128] Thus, in concrete instances like those deliberated by the labor courts, if there is any value to the human dignity and human rights discourse, the court cannot ignore the person standing before it; analysis based on general principles and rights must be combined with consideration of the concrete person and his or her specific circumstances and whether the general rules offer a satisfactory response to his or her case. Indeed, the general health scheme might not offer a solution to those whose only hope is a drug generally not indicated for their particular condition.

Consider, for example, the case where a patient could not, because of another condition, take the first-line drug indicated for a form of cancer he or she has, in

---

[126] D Greschner, *Charter Challenges and Evidence-Based Decision Making in the Health care System: Towards a Symbiotic Relationship, in* JUST MEDICARE: WHAT'S IN, WHAT'S OUT, HOW WE DECIDE 42 (Colleen M. Flood, ed., 2006).

[127] Id.

[128] Seyla Benhabib, SITUATING THE SELF: GENDER, COMMUNITY, AND POSTMODERNISM IN CONTEMPORARY ETHICS 102–148 (1992); *see* Gross, *The Right to Health in a Era of Privatization, supra* note 93.

which the NLC intervened.[129] In such cases, it is necessary to see the particular circumstance and allow the patient access to the second-line drug, even if the HSB generally prescribes it only as second line. In such cases, seeing not only the general other but also the concrete other requires seeking a solution that will effectively guarantee the particular patient's access to health care. From this perspective, the Israeli labor courts' decision requiring the Sick Funds to apply discretion in cases not covered in the health basket, along with the judicial review of the decisions made by the Sick Funds' exceptions committees, and the development of criteria the committees must consider, are examples of what rights analysis can achieve in the context of health. The approach advocated here does not ignore the budget issues or the need to set priorities. The state can set priorities within the existing health system and can prefer one treatment over another if it is more essential, effective, or cheap, as long as it upholds the core of the right to health, the principle of accessibility (including economic accessibility) and equality, and demonstrates a commitment to health and progressive realization of the right. Also, the courts should give careful consideration to the scientific evidence and should be convinced that the requested treatment or therapy is warranted by medical need and will significantly improve the quality of life, prolong life, or actually save life. Ideally, this would be conducted by the Ministry of Health, but the reality is that the ministry is part of a governmental system not always sufficiently committed to patients' welfare. Judicial intervention may, therefore, be justified in appropriate instances. This is especially so given the fact that the Israeli Medical Association has cautioned repeatedly that many crucial drugs are excluded from the basket under the existing process and in light of the government's shrinking contribution to financing health care and individual households' increasing share of the burden.[130]

At the same time, it is interesting to note that in Israel, generalized and principled petitions that sought to address the structural issues of health care usually failed, and success came mostly in some individual cases in the lower courts. While addressing the issue of the individual before the court may in *some* cases, as I mentioned earlier, be a welcome intervention, the overall picture is one where courts usually did not address the structural issues of inequality – which the HCJ could have done in a few of the cases before it – and judicial help was only given, in some cases, to individuals who could bring their cases to the labor courts. Another interesting development is the fact that losses in court sometimes were actually followed by change of policy by other branches of government, as happened with the cochlear implant and the Eributx drug. At the same time, victories at court, such as in the case of the PHS program, do not necessarily lead to the results expected, as is manifested in the reinstatement of the PHS in nongovernmental hospitals, which the HCJ upheld.

---

[129] National Labor Court 45021–05–10 Eliav v Klalit Health Services (July 12, 2010), Nevo Legal Database (by subscription) (Isr.).
[130] Gross, *supra* note 58, at 527.

The role of human rights litigation in addressing access to health care in Israel may therefore be smaller than it would seem given the number of cases. In assessing its impact, we should consider that at the HCJ level, the Court has usually upheld government's policies, both when those policies advanced equality and when they neglected equality. From this position its decisions had neither a progressive nor a regressive effect. Moreover, the Court employed a progressive discourse when upholding egalitarian policies, but a minimalist discourse on the right to health when upholding government's policies that were regressive. When it comes to the NLC, it seems that the most significant step in this history of its involvement with the NHIL are the recent cases that outline criteria for the exceptions committees. Given the novelty of these cases, it is too early to tell what will be their long-term effect on access to health care, but notwithstanding problems addressed in the discussion, they may open the door for an approach that sees both the general and the concrete others, who stand before the law, seeking its help in access to health care.

7

Health Care Access in the Netherlands

A *True Story*

*André den Exter**

INTRODUCTION

The Dutch health care system has undergone a shift toward a universal basic health insurance scheme for the entire population, but unlike most universal systems, the system is carried out by multiple private health insurers. Although based on the principles of competition – allowing providers and insurers to compete for consumers – it is also highly regulated to ensure the allocation of essential care according to need.

The Dutch system is an interesting marriage of tensions in that while it moved to expand insurance to all citizens, it simultaneously introduced a much greater role for the private sector in terms of relying on competing private for-profit health insurers. Although liberalizing and privatizing health care may be justifiable for economic and financial reasons (cost reduction, efficiency improvement, innovation), there are serious concerns about whether a system of regulated competition and emerging private health arrangements respects the basic human right of equal access to health care services. From a human rights perspective, combining competition and private initiatives in several health care markets with restrictive measures inspired by social values is an extremely difficult exercise. For example, as I discuss in more detail later in the chapter, several market-driven policies have undermined the right to equal access (e.g., preferential treatment arrangements, voluntary deductibles, discounts for group insurance schemes).

One might expect a strong response by the judiciary in striking the balance between market reforms and respect for human rights, including the right to equal access. However, as I discuss further later in the chapter, a review of the case law reveals a rather disappointing picture as a self-imposed conservative interpretation of

* Lecturer in Health Law, Institute of Health Policy and Management, Erasmus University Rotterdam, The Netherlands.

social rights hinders a more progressive approach in health care access litigation. On a brighter note, on several occasions supranational law – in the form of international treaties and covenants – has significantly strengthened claims for health human rights. In turn, however, such judicial decisions trigger heated political debate, with critics arguing for the restoration of Dutch sovereignty through reservations or even denouncing the challenged treaty. If successful, such arguments would deprive future plaintiffs of an effective remedy, and thus seem contrary to international human rights law.

By describing the main features of the health care system, explaining the relevant legal framework, and analyzing the role of the judiciary in health care access disputes, I reveal external and internal constraints that hamper the Dutch system's ability to address health inequalities.

7.1 HISTORY AND MAIN CHARACTERISTICS OF THE DUTCH HEALTH CARE SYSTEM

Prior to 2006, the Dutch health insurance system was characterized by a dual system of social (compulsory) and private or voluntary health insurance. Those who were too wealthy to qualify for the social health insurance scheme (essentially equivalent to a public health insurance system in a tax-financed regime) were free to purchase private health insurance. Social insurance was based on the notion of solidarity and regulated by statutory law. In health care, the solidarity principle means that there is no relationship between the premium paid and access to the insurance entitlements. Solidarity was institutionalized by means of social security legislation, and therefore accomplished by (legitimized) force. Its redistributive effect demonstrates that solidarity is based on the notion of social justice.

One of the main pillars of the Dutch health insurance system was the former Health Insurance Act (*Ziekenfondswet* 1966), establishing a statutory insurance scheme for curative care. Sickness funds were private entities operating on a non-profit basis (associations or foundations), which contracted with health care providers that delivered the insured care. Sixty-five percent of the population (all those earning less than €32,000 in 2005) was covered for curative care by sickness funds. A further 5 percent of the population was covered by a health insurance scheme for public servants. Dutch citizens earning above the sickness fund threshold (the remaining 30 percent of the population) were free to purchase private insurance for curative care.

The *Ziekenfondswet* 1966 defined in general terms the entitlements for those covered by sickness funds. More specific details of benefit provisions were regulated by bylaws and specific policies of sickness funds. By law, sickness funds were obligated to guarantee access to medical care under the insurance scheme. This obligation of result forms the essence of the benefit-in-kind health care scheme, for which the insurer is accountable and could be held liable for noncompliance. This is in contrast to national health care systems such as exist in England and New Zealand, for example, where there is no specific list of entitlements and no resulting contractual liability on the part of the public insurer to provide them.

In the Netherlands, the nature and scope of the packages covered by private medical insurance for the wealthier 30 percent of the population excluded from the social health insurance scheme were largely identical to those required to be provided by the sickness funds pursuant the *Ziekenfondswet*. Private medical insurance policies were, however, more flexible, allowing for free choice of provider, and permitting cash benefits instead of benefits-in-kind entitlements.

This dual approach (social and private insurance) caused inequality in health care access. Owing to the statutory regime, administrative courts ruled sickness funds litigation procedures, whereas civil courts adjudicated private insurance disputes using civil law principles. Civil courts proved willing to recognize patients' reimbursement claims with reference to general contractual norms such as reasonableness and fairness. Administrative courts, on the other hand, were inclined to reject patients' claims by defining health care benefits with reference to public law.[1] The divergence in judicial interpretation was one of the reasons given by government for health care reforms and eliminating the two-tiered health insurance scheme. What is important to note is that the insurance status (sickness fund or privately insured) did not affect the waiting time for a medical treatment. In other words, having private insurance did not allow those insured to jump queues for treatment, because treatment is based on objective medical criteria (medical necessity) only. Also, because hospitals charged similar tariffs for public and privately insured patients, there was no incentive to treat patients differently.

Since the introduction of the *Ziekenfondswet* in 1966, successive governments proposed a number of comprehensive health insurance reform plans, the 2006 reforms being the most radical. The current model is a regulated competitive health insurance market that nonetheless aims to provide universal access to health care to the Dutch population. The new Health Insurance Act, the *Zorgverzekeringswet*, came into force on January 1, 2006, replacing the *Ziekenfondswet*. Unlike the *Ziekenfondswet*, under the *Zorgverzekeringswet*, beneficiaries pay a flat-rate premium (€1,222 in 2012), and an income-dependent employer contribution is automatically deducted by the employer. In addition, a compulsory "own risk" payment was introduced for primary and secondary care providers (€220 per annum in 2012), which may be combined with a flexible system of voluntary own-risk payment ranging from €100 to €500 per annum. To offset the high fixed premium, lower income groups are partly compensated by means of a "health care allowance."

Long-term and disability care is excluded from the *Ziekenfondswet*/ *Zorgverzekeringswet* scheme but is covered by a separate health insurance program, the AWBZ

---

[1] H. Hermans & A. den Exter, *Priorities and Priority-Setting in Health Care in the Netherlands*, 39 CROAT. MED. J. 346, 353–354 (1998).

scheme. This mandatory insurance scheme is part of the social health insurance system and covers expenses that anyone faces through serious medical illness or long-term disability – notably mental illness requiring prolonged nursing and care, and physical or mental handicap – expenses that virtually no insurer is in a position to bear without help from the state or elsewhere. Similar to the former *Ziekenfondswet*, the AWBZ is funded by income-related contributions collected through taxation and a complicated means-tested system of payments by users.[2]

Finally, a third scheme consists of a voluntary health insurance (VHI) scheme that covers services excluded from social health insurance and out-of-pocket payments, except for the €220 mandatory deductible. VHI policies differ according to health insurer and may cover non-evidence-based health care services that can be reasonably afforded by the individual such as alternative medicine. Unlike social health insurance, health insurance companies are free to set the premium of the voluntary health insurance policy and may refuse potential beneficiaries for nonmedical reasons. Normally, patients enter into a basic and voluntary health insurance policy with the same health insurer, although they may also opt for different insurers for each.

7.1.1 *Health Care Providers*

Although the main focus of the 2006 health insurance reforms was on the new *Zorgverzekeringswet*, they also restructured the health care provider market and most notably hospital admission policies. Prior to 2007, the Hospital Provision Act (WZV) of 1971 strictly regulated hospital capacity planning. This planning regime enabled the government to regulate the supply of hospitals and health care institutions and made provincial health authorities responsible for implementing this plan. Hospitals were not constructed or renovated – wholly or partly – without successfully completing a declaration and licensing process. Project approval was based on a detailed plan for each hospital service affected in a specific geographic area.

The hospital planning process under the WZV was criticized for its complexity and lack of flexibility. The major revision of the WZV occurred in 2006, when it was replaced by the Law on Health Facilities Admission (*Wet Toelating Zorginstellingen*, or WTZi). The WTZi introduced a shift from central planning toward a decentralized, demand-driven system in which the governmental role is restricted to setting general conditions that govern hospital planning. These conditions attempt to ensure public interests such as accessibility, quality, and efficiency of inpatient care. As such, the WTZi sets requirements for hospital admission, organizational structure, and management and health care governance. The rationale is that consumer demand and market competition will determine the required hospital capacity. Withdrawal of governmental interference in capacity planning was replaced by promoting entrepreneurship, creating a level playing field between competitive

---

[2] In 2012, a contribution of 12.15% was levied from the salary of citizens.

health insurers contracting hospitals, and liberalizing health care prices, with the aspiration of achieving equilibrium between demand and supply.

A basic tool under the new regime is *admission*, which is a license to provide the health care services covered by health insurance legislation. To receive this license, hospitals guarantee the quality of care provided, accessibility of specific (emergency) services, financial transparency, and sound management. The Health Inspectorate, an independent advisory body to the Ministry of Health, supervises whether health care institutions comply with the law. If not, the ultimate sanction imposed is withdrawal of admission.

The WTZi also introduced a for-profit category of outpatient health care entities providing, inter alia, audiology services, intensive care for thrombotic patients, general practice, dental, pharmaceutical, obstetrics, and transportation services. Supported by public funds, these entities can be established on a for-profit basis.

For-profit health care providers raise concerns about the distribution of dividends funded by public means and shareholders' influence on health care decision making. According to the Minister of Health, this will be solved by making payments conditional; that is, distribution of profits over private investments are allowed but should be reinvested in the institution itself – a so-called *vermogensklem* – and shareholders will have limited powers as concerns strategic decision making.[3] However, such restrictive measures will not encourage private investors (pension funds, hedge funds, private equity funds) to invest in "corporate" hospitals: without the private sector's involvement in managing the clinical functions of the hospital, private investors will not generate risk-bearing capital for hospital innovation.[4]

Based on foreign experiences, however, commercial hospitals are not a panacea, because their market share remains limited. Even in countries with a relatively large for-profit sector in hospital care, such as the United Kingdom and Germany, bed capacity is limited compared to public and private not-for-profit hospitals.[5] Whether building and running hospitals in public-private partnerships is a long-term solution to public health care is debatable. Commentators claim that it is far from clear that the result is better health care; in fact, according to some, the results "are bitterly disappointing."[6] Its high costs may threaten the long-term financial viability of NHS trusts.

3 TK 32012, no. 1, Governance in de zorgsector, 31–32 (2008–2009); TK 32012, no 4, 6 (2009–2010), *available at* http://opmaatnieuw.sdu.nl/opmaat/. A proposal introducing a new legal entity Maatschappelijke onderneming will be submitted to parliament. The prohibition of distributing payments to shareholders does not exclude a "result-based compensation" over private capital.

4 As confirmed by the chair of one of the largest pension funds in the Netherlands (PGGM), M. van Rijn, *Pensioenfonds is geen Pinautomaat van de Gezondheidszorg [Pension Fund Is Not an ATM Machine of Healthcare]*, Financieel Dagblad [Daily Financial], Sept. 7, 2009, at Extra 26–27.

5 J. G. Sijmons, Maatschappelijk Ondernemen in het Bijzonder in de Zorg [Corporate Social Responsibility in Particular in Healthcare], 66 (2008).

6 M. Hellowell & A. M. Pollock, *The Private Financing of NHS Hospitals: Politics, Policy and Practice*, 1 Econ. Aff. 13 (2009); less outspoken are M. McKee et al., *Public–Private Partnerships for Hospitals*, 84 Bull. of the World Health Organization 890 (2006).

Apart from potential improvements in efficiency and innovation, there are general concerns about the accessibility and quality of for-profit hospital care. In its latest assessment the Dutch Health Inspectorate gave moderately positive reviews of the quality of care provided by for-profit private clinics.[7] But given that the reliability of quality indicators was not part of the assessment, doubts remain. In terms of timeliness, however, these private clinics have contributed to waiting list reduction for certain interventions (orthopaedics and ophthalmology) by extending capacity, and to considerable cost reduction resulting from lower fees (average 22 percent lower than hospitals).[8] However, because these clinics are only located in major cities, accessibility is limited to densely populated areas.

7.1.2 *Price Liberalization as the Final Step*

The final stage of the health care sector reforms, which first started in 2007, included a gradual shift toward deregulation of prices in health care. In competitive markets, price is based on the equilibrium between demand and supply, but because health care is for many reasons a unique market, price regulation was not removed entirely. Governmental supervision of health care price setting is delegated to the Health Care Authority (NZa). The NZa supervises both health care providers and insurers, ensuring that they provide high-quality and efficient health care to the consumer.

The NZa defines the tariffs of most inpatient health services, making any goal of a free market only aspirational in practice. This tariff is calculated using "hospital products" divided into "diagnosis-related" groups (DBCs), which are based on all types of procedures used during hospital admission.[9] Without NZa approval, it is forbidden to charge another tariff.

So far, most NZa decisions have related to the setting of these tariffs (e.g., policy rules, performance description, price ceilings, outpatient care), which is not altogether different from the previous practice of more uniform charges. On an experimental basis, however, the NZa liberalized tariffs (prices) on some health services (e.g., physiotherapy, remedial therapy, diet advice, and pharmaceuticals), which means that prices are set by the free market. In terms of hospital care, market tariffs have partly replaced budget financing negotiated between health insurers and hospitals. As expected, free hospital prices grew 50–70 percent in 2012 compared to 2011.[10] Whether, and to what extent, such a measure will contribute to cost reduction and more efficient purchasing of inpatient health care remains to be seen.

---

[7] Inspectie voor de Gezondheidszorg [The Dutch Healthcare Inspectorate]. *Het Resultaat Telt. Particuliere Klinieken 2008* [The Result Counts. Private Clinics 2008], Oct. 14, 2010.

[8] NZa [Dutch Healthcare Authority], *De rol van ZBC's in de ziekenhuiszorg* [The Role of ZBC's in Hospital Care], MONITORSPECIAL, 73–74. (2007).

[9] On January 1, 2012, DBCs were renamed DOTs, a simplified system for hospital services.

[10] TK 32620, no. 6. (2010–2011), *available at* http://opmaatnieuw.sdu.nl/opmaat/.

7.2 REGULATING HEALTH CARE ACCESS

Despite increased reliance on for-profit insurers and opening the for-profit hospital market, the system is heavily regulatde to achieve greater equity and access. The main legal instruments used to further these goals are the Constitution, statutory social health insurance law, and international treaty law. By analyzing the regulatory framework, the ongoing question is whether the goal of equity can be a bedfellow with the goal of efficiency through market-oriented reforms.

7.2.1 *A Constitutional Right to Health Care*

Under Article 22(1) of the Dutch Constitution, rewritten in 1983, "the authorities shall take steps to promote public health." This provision has generally been interpreted as a "mere" obligation of the government to establish health facilities and facilitate access to necessary health care.[11] This obligation has been achieved by way of a health insurance system that includes two schemes: a scheme for uninsurable risks (AWBZ) and a scheme for curative care (*Zorgverzekeringswet*).[12] Within these health insurance schemes, insurers purchase services from health care facilities and professionals. Apart from establishing a health insurance system, Article 22 has been interpreted to include obligations to regulate the entry of health care facilities into the market and to regulate the purchaser-provider relationship. As such, the constitutional obligations reflect the core elements of the right to health (availability, accessibility, and quality of individual health care services).

Owing to its "programmatic goals," the constitutional right to health care amounts only to very soft obligations, therefore having a weaker legal status than individual rights. Absence of constitutional judicial review (which is prohibited by the Constitution itself) makes it even more difficult to interpret this right. On an international and national level, however, there is a tendency to strengthen the legal status of a social right like the right to health care. For instance, international human rights law and international social security law further define the nature and scope of social rights. The Committee on Economic and Social Rights' (CESCR) *General Comment No. 14* outlines the right to health as contained in the International Covenant of Economic, Social and Cultural Rights (ICESCR) in terms of general and specific state obligations.[13] One general obligation is the concept of "progressive realization," which requires member states to advance the ICESCR's rights while acknowledging the difficulties states have in complying with these obligations. Accordingly,

---

[11] P. W. C. Akkermans et al., GRONDRECHTEN EN RECHTSBESCHERMING IN NEDERLAND [CONSTITU- TIONAL RIGHTS AND LEGAL PROTECTION IN THE NETHERLANDS] 134 (3d ed., 1999).

[12] Uninsurable risks include long-term care (e.g., nursing homes and residential care).

[13] United Nations, Committee on Economic, Social and Cultural Rights, U.N. ESCOR, 22d Sess., *The Right to the Highest Attainable Standard of Health*, U.N. Doc. E/C, (Dec. 4, 2000) ICESR General Comment 14 (2000), *available at* http://www2.ohchr.org/english/bodies/treaty/comments.htm.

although the right itself has immediate effect, progressive realization enables countries to take necessary measures to give effect to that right over a longer period of time. Such measures should still be concrete, deliberate, and targeted toward the full realization of article 12 ICESCR.[14] This flexibility device means that state parties have a "specific and continuing obligation" to move toward full realization of ICESCR rights, which creates a strong presumption that deliberately retrogressive measures are prohibited.[15] Combined with the (health-related) nondiscrimination principle, the progressive realization concept introduces elements traditionally reserved to classical freedom rights into social rights like the right to health.[16]

A further factor reinforcing the legal status of a right to health care is the differentiation of the specific legal obligations to respect, to protect, and to fulfill.[17] The obligation to respect prevents states from denying or limiting equal access to special groups (e.g., women, prisoners, children). The obligation to protect requires states to take necessary measures preventing third parties (health providers and insurers) from interfering with the right to health. For example, health insurers are obliged to accept new applicants and they are not allowed to differentiate their premiums according to the risk profile of the applicants. This obligation of protection means that regulatory steps must be taken to ensure availability, accessibility, acceptability, and quality of health care as the Dutch government seeks to introduce more private elements into the insurance and delivery of care.[18] The obligation to fulfill requires states to develop a national health policy with a detailed plan to realize the right to health, including regulatory and financial measures to facilitate the necessary infrastructure (public health facilities, professional training and education programs, promoting information campaigns with respect to sexual and reproductive health services, etc.).

Without a doubt, the CESCR's authoritative interpretation of state obligations contributes to understanding the meaning of the right to health. In addition, social security codes, such as ILO Convention C130 and the European Code of Social Security, further specify this right in terms of categories of persons entitled to health care services (e.g., employees, prescribed classes of economically active population, classes of residents), categories of entitlements (e.g., medical care, dental care, pharmaceutical care), and the maximum payments that patients can be required to pay out of their own pockets.[19]

---

[14] *Id.* at § 30.

[15] *Id.* at § 31.

[16] By virtue of articles 2.2 and 3 of the ICESCR, the Covenant prohibits any discrimination in access to health care, for example the introduction of substantial copayments that disproportionally affect vulnerable groups (e.g., chronically ill). Without adequate justification, such a deliberately taken retrogressive measure is not permissible because it breaches the progressive realization concept and results in health-related discrimination.

[17] *Id.* at § 33–37.

[18] *Id.* at § 35.

[19] Medical Care and Sickness Benefits Convention, (No. 130), June 25, 1969, U.N.T.S. 11829, *available at* http://www.ilo.org/dyn/normlex/ ; European Code of Social Security, April 16, 1964, 123 E.S.T 48, *available at* http://www.conventions.coe.int/Treaty/.

In the Netherlands, international human rights law plays an important role in interpreting access to health care as a constitutional right (Section 7.3). By contrast, constitutional review of the right to health care is absent in general health care litigation cases, because that type of review is the prerogative of the Dutch parliament. Beyond Article 22 of the Constitution, statutory law is the most important legal source incorporating the right to health care. Translated into health care *entitlements*, access to health care is effectuated in social health insurance law.

7.2.2 *Health Care Entitlements under the Health Insurance Act*

The 2006 Health Insurance Act (*Zorgverzekeringswet*) introduced a compulsory health insurance scheme for the entire population, carried out by for-profit insurance companies.[20] Health insurance agreements are private law contracts and are therefore based on principles such as freedom of contract. However, the legislature imposes certain restrictions to protect the principle of equal access to health care. The prohibition of risk selection by health insurers is one clear example of this. In addition, all health insurers must participate in a risk equalization system, which ensures that those insurers who cover individuals with a higher risk profile receive more funding. Such a leveling mechanism prevents direct or indirect risk selection of so-called high-risk insured (i.e., the chronically ill). Entitlements or benefits covered by health insurers are defined by law, but contracting parties can agree about where and who will deliver the insured health services. For reasons of public interest, freedom of contract is nonexistent in case of emergency care and highly specialized care. By law, health insurers are forced to cover both types of services. These and other restrictions of the *Zorgverzekeringswet*'s free contracting principle reflect the tension between promoting market-like competition while still attempting to ensure solidarity in accessing health care.

The *Zorgverzekeringswet* provides coverage for essential curative care tested against the criteria of necessity, proven efficacy, cost effectiveness, and collective or individual responsibility.[21] Under the scheme provided by the *Zorgverzekeringswet*, the insured may opt for a benefits-in-kind or reimbursement model or a combination of both models. Although both models guarantee a standard insurance policy, under the reimbursement model, the insured have free choice of provider. Under the benefits-in-kind variant, the insured are limited to a set list of health providers who have entered into contracts of delivery with the patient's chosen health insurer. In exceptional cases under this model, the insured may opt for a non-contracted provider abroad, for example, where there is a long waiting period.

---

[20] The Health Insurance Act (Zorgverzekeringswet, Zvw Stb. 2005, p. 358) came into force on January 1, 2006, replacing the Sickness Fund Act (ZFW of Oct. 15, 1964).

[21] Based on the method for priority setting by the Dunning Committee "Choices in Health Care" (1991). This framework of criteria basically functions as a series of sieves separating care that should be funded from that which should not be funded.

Although the *Zorgverzekeringswet* makes a commitment to equality in health care, in reality the Netherlands has retreated from that principle since 2006, which has caused a change in the public's commitment to equitable access. Prior to 2006, policy proposals that restricted access had no or little chance of assent and, consequently, were never placed on the policy agenda. Yet in March 2006, the Diaconessen hospital announced it had entered into an agreement with a health insurer, Zorg & Zekerheid, and that the waiting times for a cataract operation would be shorter for its policyholders than for those of other health insurers, and this development drew little attention.[22] Similarly, Groene Hart Ziekenhuis launched a plan for a "business club" giving preferential treatment to workers.[23] Prior to 2006, such preferential treatment in the provision of medically necessary care would have caused much more of a furor.

Another example of the retreat from equitable access to health services is an agreement between a local hospital Kennemer Gasthuis and a mediation agency. It was agreed that contracted patients/employees would receive necessary health care services ahead of other patients in need. In its assessment, the NZa concluded that such a *commercial* mediation initiative is forbidden by law.[24] Its reasoning was based merely on technical legal arguments: charging commercial tariffs violates Dutch tariff regulations.[25] On the merits, however, the NZa welcomed such an initiative for efficiency (better use of existing capacity) and quality (reduction in waiting times) reasons. The key problem of risk selection by health providers based on financial incentives instead of medical needs was not the responsibility of the NZa; instead, the Health Inspectorate, charged with supervising health care quality, should prevent this behavior.[26] Unfortunately the NZa ignores the fact that risk selection on nonmedical needs is *inherent* to commercial mediation. Otherwise, there is no incentive to health providers to treat contracted patients first.

In defense of preferential treatment schemes, advocates claim that an increase in supply will ultimately lead to an overall improvement in the fulfillment of health care needs. As the chair of the board of directors of Diakonessen Hospital stated, "while it is true that the health insurer's clients would receive care more quickly, this would also benefit the patients on the standard waiting list for cataract surgery."[27] The Rawlsian argument here is that with the added profits from the contract with the health insurer, the Diaconessen Hospital can expand its service capacity, making

---

[22] Editorial, DAILY NEWSPAPER TROUW, March 25, 2006, at 8.
[23] TK no. 314, *Aanhangsel van de Handelingen* [*Appendix*], OVERHEID.NL (2010–2011), *available at* https://zoek.officielebekendmakingen.nl/ah-tk-20102011–314.html.
[24] Letter from NZA to the Minister of Health (Feb.11, 2009) (Neth.).
[25] Wet Marktordening Gezondheidszorg [Healthcare Regulation Act] (WMG), Stb. 2006, p. 415, art. 35.
[26] So far, only two patients have applied this commercial intermediation procedure. However, any number undermines the medical-needs-based fundament of the Health Insurance Act.
[27] *See supra* note 22.

everyone better off.[28] Nonetheless, their benefit is less than patients in the preferential treatment scheme, *mutatis mutandis* patients excluded from commercial mediation.

Apart from altering the allocation of health services, the *Zorgverzekeringswet* scheme has caused a regressive shift in the distribution of the cost of health insurance premiums. First, while the premium was partially fixed during the final phase of the former health insurance act (*Ziekenfondswet*), the amount paid by insured persons was primarily based on income. Second, under the *Zorgverzekeringswet*, health insurers may offer insurance policy options with a limited number of *voluntary* deductibles (up to €500). Insured persons receive a discount on their premium in return for accepting a level of financial risk. Third, health insurers can now enter into group insurance schemes with employers for their employees and their dependents. The discount for employees may exceed 10 percent of the premium base for each employee or dependent. As a consequence, healthy individuals may now reduce their premiums by accepting a high deductible in the more unlikely event they require care.

The new health insurance system is designed to address the needs of those requiring health care (both the affluent and the more needy). However, the new system serves the wealthy more generously than it does the poor. For example, a €220 personal risk premium is unlikely to deter those who are relatively affluent and require health care. These individuals would presumably prefer and can afford a more expensive reimbursement policy. In addition, they will take out supplementary insurance coverage. Moreover, if eligible for group insurance, which is not unlikely given they are more likely to be part of a group insurance plan through their employer, they will receive the maximum premium discount. In contrast, those with limited financial means will be required to pay the compulsory health insurance contribution, will have to consider the impact of accepting a level of out-of-pocked payment in order to reduce their annual premium payment, will have to opt for a benefits-in-kind policy, and, moreover, may not be able to afford to take out supplementary insurance coverage. Additionally, it is less likely that they are eligible for a large discount as part of group insurance.

Whereas prior to 2006, under the income-related *Ziekenfondswet*, premium costs were determined according to the insured person's ability to pay, other factors now play a more decisive role. The waning support for the ability-to-pay principle is being replaced by the growing importance of factors such as freedom of choice and socioeconomic status. When claims are made that the individual cost of premiums under the *Zorgverzekeringswet* are determined by individual choices, it is important to remember that the income, health, and socioeconomic circumstances of individuals determine the range of health insurance options available to them. Under the *Zorgverzekeringswet*, unhealthy and more needy individuals enjoy less freedom of choice than their unhealthy and more affluent counterparts, regardless of how well

---

[28] J. Rawls, A Theory of Justice, 303 (1971).

informed their health insurance decision is. If any freedom of choice remains, their options are limited to choices that conflict with their health care interests. When discussing the right to health care as the right to access to effective care, the actual access for unhealthy and more needy residents of the Netherlands is now far more limited than that of their affluent neighbors.

7.2.3 *Long-Term Care under the AWBZ Insurance Scheme*

In addition to the *Zorgverzekeringswet*, the AWBZ scheme covers the whole population for uninsurable risks (e.g., nursing homes). The AWBZ provides a benefit-in-kind insurance for health care entitlements. Similar to the *Zorgverzekeringswet*, entitlements are determined according to functions. These functions are broadly defined in terms of the patients' needs (e.g., personal care regarding activities of daily living, nursing as regards a physical or mental disorder, treatment and accommodation in a health care institution). Instead of receiving a health care entitlement, the insured may opt for receiving a personal budget (*persoonsgebonden budget*) and purchase care individually from a health care provider. Otherwise, the insured is entitled to receive health care from a contracted provider. Before a person can qualify for care under the AWBZ, he must apply for a needs assessment (*indicatie*). Decisions as to whether care is necessary, which type of care is appropriate, and to what extent that care is required are made by an independent body established by the local government, the Center of Needs Assessment (CIZ).[29]

By law, health insurance companies implement the AWBZ scheme, a task delegated to regional care offices (*Zorgkantoren*) operated by the regionally dominant health insurer. As such, insurance companies may carry out a dual task: the private health insurance scheme under *Zorgverzekeringswet* as well as the public health insurance scheme under AWBZ. Although *Zorgkantoren* are responsible for purchasing AWBZ care, the CIZ decides on the entitlement. As such, the insurer cannot influence a decision-making process, which seems, from an insurance perspective, quite odd. This limited administrative role of health insurers under the AWBZ seems contrary to the notion of insurance, in which the insurer has the exclusive competence to determine entitlements. It has been argued that the AWBZ scheme has lost its insurance character and become a public service.[30]

7.3 ENFORCING HEALTH CARE ACCESS

In the Netherlands, courts have accepted individual claims seeking access to health care services framed in statutory law, international human rights law, and even EU law, both under the *Zorgverzekeringswet* and the AWBZ.

---

[29] Each local CIZ performs needs assessments, following the rules set by the AWBZ.
[30] J. M. van der Most, *De Zorgelijke Staat van de AWBZ* [*The Problematic Status of the AWBZ*], 4 TvGR 240 (2009).

7.3.1 *Litigating* Zorgverzekeringswet *Claims: The Impact of European Treaty Law*

As mentioned before, health care litigation under the *Zorgverzekeringswet* is mainly concerned with the denial of reimbursement of health care services provided (abroad).[31] One of the main reasons is the so-called functional approach of classifying health insurance entitlements. Instead of a preestablished list of types of treatment for which reimbursement is guaranteed, the *Zorgverzekeringswet* only includes a general description of the care covered by the insurance package (i.e., medical, dental, pharmaceutical). Although the law sets legal requirements for what entitlements include, it is up to the health provider and insurer to further define necessary care under the law. Thus, what constitutes necessary care is determined by "the state of medical science and practice."[32] The state of medical science and practice criterion follows the principles of evidence-based medicine (EBM). Although it is largely up to the discretion of the health insurer to decide which types of treatment satisfy that condition, in applying that criterion, the insurer must do so on the basis of what is sufficiently tried and tested by *international* medical science. Widening the state of medical science and practice criterion to what is considered as normal among *international* circles is a direct consequence of the *Smits-Peerbooms* and *Müller-Fauré* cases decided by the European Court of Justice (ECJ).[33] This could mean that where a certain treatment has been sufficiently tested by international science, the health insurer would not be able to refuse authorization on the grounds that it is not presently provided in the Netherlands.[34] The only justifiable reason to refuse approval is where, given the need to maintain an adequate supply

---

[31] E.g, A v. C, No. 2012.00070 (Kennisplein Ziektekostenverzekeringen, Aug. 29, 2012); A v. C, No. 2012.00216 (Kennisplein Ziektekostenverzekeringen 29 Aug., 2012) arbitral rulings concerning cross-border health insurance claims.

[32] Besluit Zorgverzekeringswet [Bylaw Health Insurance Act], Stb. 2008, p. 549, art. 2.1 sub. 2.

[33] Case C-157/99, Geraets-Smits v. Stichting Ziekenfonds VGZ and Peerbooms v. Stichting CZ Groep Zorgverzekeringen, 2001 E.C.R. I-5473; Case C-385/99, Müller-Fauré v. Onderlinge Waarborgmaatschappij OZ Zorgverzekeringen and Van Riet v. Onderlinge Waarborgmaatschappij ZAO Zorgverzekeringen, 2003 E.C.R. I-4409.

[34] Last year, the ECJ confirmed this interpretation in *Elchinov*, a claim challenging the denial of reimbursement of proton therapy in Germany. Although this treatment was not available in Bulgaria, the national health fund was forced to reimburse for its provision abroad because it fulfilled the international medicinal science test, even though not explicitly classified as an entitlement under the social health insurance scheme. Case C-173/09, Elchinov v. Natsionalna zdravnoosiguritelna kasa, 2010 E.C.R. I-8889. Given the similar functional approach under the Zvw, this would mean that such a treatment would also be available for Dutch insured. Recently, the Health Insurance Advisory body (CVZ) recommended that the Minister of Health recognize this proton therapy as an entitlement (under the category of medical-specialist care), because it fulfills the evidence-based criteria. CVZ, Protonentherapie Bij Model-Based Indicaties (Hoofdhalstumoren, Mammacarcinoom, Longcarcinoom En Prostaatcarcinoom) En Bij Overige Indicaties Proton-Therapy in Model-Based Indications (Head and Neck Cancer, Breast Cancer, Lung Cancer and Prostate Cancer) and in Other Diagnoses, Report no. 28030245 (2011089740), (Aug. 22, 2011), *available at* http://www.cvz.nl/binaries/live/cvzinternet/hst_content/nl/documenten/standpunten/2011/sp1108-protonentherapie.pdf.

of hospital care and to ensure the financial stability of the health insurance system, the "same or equally effective treatment can be obtained without undue delay."[35] It is important to note that in determining whether "the same or equally effective treatment can be obtained without undue delay, the mere fact that a person is on a waiting list does not necessarily mean that the treatment is unavailable."[36] Undue delay is defined as the period within which medical treatment is necessary with respect to the patient's medical condition, the history and probable course of the patient's illness, the degree of pain the patient is in, and/or the nature of the patient's disability.[37]

Although the ECJ rulings have restricted national sovereignty vis-à-vis denial of coverage for medical services sought abroad, this did not automatically extend the insured's right to cross-border care in national arbitral rulings. Except for the "undue delay" cases, proving that an alternative treatment satisfies the "international medical science" test remains extremely difficult for the complainant.[38] In most cases before the arbitral insurance body (SKGZ), complainants failed to meet this test, because scientific evidence was not available yet, or simply because of limited accessibility and understanding of scientific literature on new medical technologies.

Apart from the EU-internal market rules, Dutch citizens may also rely on the European Convention on Human Rights (ECHR) when claiming access to and/or the reimbursement for a certain medical intervention or medicine. On several occasions, particularly when the health service was not included in the social health insurance benefit package, the European Court of Human Rights has interpreted the private or family life provision (Article 8) of the ECHR to require an insurer to fund the service.[39] For instance, in *Sentges v. the Netherlands*, a teenage boy with multiple handicaps, Nicki Sentges, complained when his request for a robotic arm was denied.[40] He submitted that, under Article 8, the authorities were under

---

[35] Case C-372/04, The Queen, on the application of Yvonne Watts v. Bedford Primary Care Trust and Secretary of State for Health, 2006 E.C.R. I-4325, § 119.

[36] Here, the Central Appeals Tribunal (CRvB) refers to standards, so-called maximum acceptable waiting time limits for a specific medical intervention. The underlying idea is that hospitals, for planning and efficiency reasons, need a certain waiting time. *See* Stichting Ziekenfonds VGZ v. X, No. LJN: AP4731, § 92 (rechtspraak, June 18, 2004) (an eleven-month waiting period for a hip replacement is not considered "timely").

[37] Case C-372/04, The Queen, on the application of Yvonne Watts v. Bedford Primary Care Trust and Secretary of State for Health, 2006 E.C.R. I-4325, § 63.

[38] *See, e.g.,* A v. C No. 2011.02569 (Kennisplein Ziektekostenverzekeringen, Aug. 29, 2012); A v. C No. 2012.00025 (Kennisplein Ziektekostenverzekeringen Aug. 15, 2012).

[39] Marzari v. Italy, App. No. 36448/97, 28 Eur. Ct. H.R. 175, 179 (1999); Zehnalovà and Zehnal v. the Czech Republic, App. No. 38621/97, 2002-V Eur. Ct. H.R.; Pentiacova and others v. Moldova, App. No. 14462/03, Eur. Ct. H.R. (2005). *See* Convention for the Protection of Human Rights and Fundamental Freedoms, Nov. 4, 1950, E.T.S. No. 5, § 8 which, in so far as relevant, provides as follows: "everyone has the right to respect for his private . . . life; 2. There shall be no interference by a public authority with the exercise of this right except such as is in accordance with the law and is necessary in a democratic society in the interests of national security, public safety or the economic well-being of the country."

[40] Sentges v. Netherlands, App. No. 27677/02, Admissibility Decision (2003).

a positive obligation to provide him with this medical device, arguing that the concept of private life encompassed notions pertaining to the quality of life, including personal autonomy, and the right to establish and develop relationships with other human beings. Sentges argued that the constraints on him were unacceptable as he was never able to be alone and his total dependency on others "forced him to establish and develop friendships that he might not have chosen had he not been disabled." While the essential object of Article 8 is to protect the individual against arbitrary interference, the Court has held that this provision may also include positive obligations inherent in effective respect for private or family life.[41] These obligations may involve the adoption of measures designed to secure respect of private life.[42] But in order to find a positive obligation on the part of the state, there needs to be a "direct and immediate link" between the measures sought by the applicant and his private life.

Regrettably, the Court declined to decide whether such a link had been established. Instead, the Court concluded that with regard to issues involving the assessment of priorities of limited health care resources, national authorities enjoy a particularly wide margin of deference because they "are in a better position to carry out this assessment than an international court." This is also called the "fair balance" test of the competing interests of the individual and the community as a whole, which includes a consideration of the costs of health care. In the *Sentges* case, the Court considered that the provision of a robotic arm fell within the margin of deference to national authorities given that the applicant had access to the standard package of health care provided by the former ZFW, specifically an electric wheelchair with an adapted joystick. Only in case of manifestly unreasonable outcomes will the Court consider intervening. This could occur, for example, if an applicant was denied a life-saving medicine and it is possible for the state to meet the cost. In the case of life-essential treatment or medicines, one may also consider an appeal based on the right to life, Article 2 of the Convention.[43]

Thus, following *Sentges*, it is only in exceptional cases that a claim under section 8 will provide relief to an applicant; the Court's understandable hesitation to link the health care right with individual rights, and its "fair balance" test, means it is extremely difficult, if not impossible, to enforce health care claims on this basis.[44]

[41] *See also* Lopez Ostra v. Spain, App. No. 16798/90, 303C Eur. Ct. H.R. (Ser. A) 51, 58 (1994); Guerra and Others v. Italy, App. No. 14967/89, 1998 – I Eur. Ct. H.R. 7; Botta v. Italy, App. No. 21439/93, Eur. Ct. H.R. 12 (1998).

[42] *E.g*, Stubbings and Others v. the United Kingdom, App. No. 22083/93, 22095/93, Eur. Ct. H.R. 44, § 62 (1996).

[43] *See* Nitecki v. Poland, App. No. 65653/01, Eur. Ct. H.R., §1 (2002), where the Court considered that "it cannot be excluded that the acts of omissions of the authorities in the field of health care policy may in certain circumstances engage their responsibility under Article 2."

[44] In the past such claims have been mainly successful in the context of prisoners' right to health care, where states failed to guarantee access to adequate medical care to the detained, therefore violating article 3 of the Convention, which prohibits inhuman and degrading treatment. *See, e.g.,* McGlinchey

7.3.2 AWBZ Claims: Reliance on Human Rights and International Social Security Law

In terms of claiming AWBZ entitlements, disputes center on the denial of reimbursements, but also on questioning the revision of needs assessment (*indicatie*) decisions and cost-sharing decisions.[45] Prior to judicial review, the complainant submits a request for internal review by the health insurer or CIZ (the latter in case of the needs assessment decision). Finally, the *Centrale Raad van Beroep* (the Central Appeals Tribunal) or CRvB functions as the appeal court in social security (AWBZ) disputes.

The variety of AWBZ disputes brought before the CRvB reveal an emerging interest in international treaty law, both human rights treaty law (ECHR)[46] and international social security law (ILO Conventions and the European Code of Social Security),[47] whether or not combined with general nondiscrimination treaty provisions (e.g., International Covenant of Civil and Political Rights, Article 26).[48] In practice, such appeals based on international treaty norms are only successful in exceptional circumstances, but the impact can be considerable. In 2006, the CRvB reluctantly concluded that the European Code of Social Security included some self-executing treaty provisions (articles 32 and 34) that prohibit copayments for treatment associated with occupational health-related injuries.[49] As a direct consequence of this ruling, the Dutch parliament agreed to partially denounce the European Code (part VI) and simultaneously ratify the Revised Code, which allows more flexibility in terms of copayments.[50] A similar response was considered in 1996, when the CRvB held that the ILO-Convention 102/103 was self-executing, thereby prohibiting copayments in terms of in-patient maternity care.[51] The criteria used by the CRvB to determine whether norm-setting treaties or treaty provisions are self-executing

---

and Others v. The United Kingdom, App. No. 50390/99, 87 E.H.R.R. 41 (2003); Dybeku v. Albania, App. no. 41153/06, Eur. Ct. H.R. (2007).

[45] Dutch case law, rechtspraak, keywords: AWBZ indicatie; 646 hits (August 27).

[46] Breach of Art. 6 § 1 ECHR (reasonable time) of the Convention for the Protection of Human Rights and Fundamental Freedoms, Eur.T.S. No. 5, Nov. 4, 1950, 213 U.N.T.S. 221 on account of the length of the decision-making process, A v. Onderlinge Waarborgmaatschappij Centrale Zorgverzekeraars, LJN: BK8934 (rechtspraak, Jan. 12, 2010); A v. SVZ, No. AZ7262 (rechtspraak, Jan. 26, 2007); A and others v. UWV, LJN: BB6578 (rechtspraak, Oct. 18, 2007); A v. Zorgkantoor Noord-Oost Brabant, LNJ: BB6913 (rechtspraak, Febr. 10, 2011).

[47] A v. Achmea Zorgverzekeringen No. LJN: AY8221 (rechtspraak, Sept. 8, 2006).

[48] In case of differential treatment of cost sharing: A v. NUTS-AEGON, No. LJN AE8567 (rechtspraak Dec. 13, 2001).

[49] *See* Besluit Zorgverzekeringswet [Bylaw Health Insurance Act], Stb. 2008, p. 549.

[50] Opzegging deel VI Europese Code inzake sociale zekerheid [Termination Part VI European Code of Social Security], Stb. 2009, p. 474. Upholding ratification would cause an estimated loss of up to €80 million. TK 31 267, no 6, 4 (2007–2008), *available at* http://opmaatnieuw.sdu.nl/opmaat/. Ratification European Code on Social Security (revised), Stb. 2009.

[51] F v. Stichting Regionaal Ziekenfonds BAZ Nijmegen, No. LJN: AL0666 (rechtspraak, May 29, 1996). In this particular case, however, copayments were based on the former Health Insurance Act (ZFW).

include the nature (instructive or imperative) and specificity of the wording of the specific provision. Therefore, the reliance on the self-executing effect of ILO social security treaties provide Dutch citizens with a limited claim to enforce the social right to health care before national courts. Conversely, the judiciary rejected such reliance repeatedly in cases invoking the ICESCR, because its provisions are insufficiently precise, and the instructive nature provides states with considerable deference in realizing these rights.[52] So far, the judiciary has continued that line of reasoning and has not been willing to incorporate the concept of "progressive realization" of social rights.

In the case of immigrants without a residence permit (illegal immigrants), however, the CRvB seems more generous. By law, these individuals are excluded from the AWBZ scheme, but on several occasions the CRvB annulled that rule based on Article 8 of the European Convention (right to private life), but only in very exceptional cases, where the humanitarian grounds against the removal were compelling. These cases concern aliens with life-threatening diseases who are facing deportation, where it is clear that the necessary medical facilities and family support are not available in the individual's home country.[53] The Tribunal has confirmed the European Court of Human Rights' doctrine that the right to private life may create a positive obligation to provide access to necessary care (*D v. UK*).[54] Furthermore, inherent in the Convention is a search for a fair balance between the demands of the general interest of the community and the requirements of the protection of an individual's fundamental rights. Withholding necessary care under these exceptional circumstances cannot be considered a "fair balance."

The Convention's threshold is very strict ("critical stage in a fatal illness"; see the landmark case *D v. UK*). However, in cases of a Surinam patient suffering from a progressive muscle disease, as well as a mentally handicapped child (both facing no imminent death),[55] the CRvB used a more flexible interpretation, concluding that denial of rehabilitation care or day care, respectively, denies the person's development and therefore their private life; moreover, this, in turn, was held to constitute a violation of human dignity. These cases suggests that in cases involving illegal immigrants aliens, the Dutch judiciary accept a breach of Article 8 more easily than the European Human Rights Court did in *D v UK* based on Article 3.

Denunciation was allowed at the end of any successive period of five years after ratification and thereafter. Because that period expired, denunciation failed.

[52] J v. het Dagelijks Bestuur van het Werkvoorzieningschap Zwolle en Omgeving (WEZO), No. AK9520 (rechtspraak, Dec. 17, 1991).

[53] X v. Achmea, ECLI:NL:CRVB:2011:BT1738 (rechtspraak, September 9, 2011; X v. Agis, ECLI:NL:CRVB:2011:BR5581 (rechtspraak, August 4, 2011); X v. Agis, ECLI:NL:CRVB:2010:BO3581 (rechtspraak October 20, 2010); contrary: X v. Achmea ECLI:NL:CRVB:2012:BW7703 (rechtspraak June 6, 2012).

[54] See D v. UK, App. No. 30240/96 Eur. Ct. H.R. 25 (1997) (St Kitts) though the Court used Article 3 and not article 8 of the Convention.

[55] See *supra* n. 54.

Referring to the Tribunal's October 20, 2010 ruling in the case involving the mentally handicapped Nigerian immigrant, members of parliament asked the Minister of Justice whether this ruling would affect his policy concerning the protection of children without a residence permit.[56] The minister rejected this conclusion, arguing that the general rule of excluding illegal immigrants from health care services will remain valid. He did agree, however, to accept the outcome of a "fair balance" test made by the judiciary in each individual case.[57]

7.4 FINAL REMARKS

The shift to a universal system operationalized through regulation of private, for-profit health insurance in the Netherlands has caused human rights concerns, particularly regarding equal access to health care services. For instance, the new liberalized health insurance scheme has resulted in preferential health care arrangements that significantly challenge the notion of equity or solidarity within the Dutch health care system.

International law, however, offers little – if any – basis to justify preferential treatment in de facto access to health care on the basis of criteria other than objective medical need. The fact that Dutch health care providers have nonetheless introduced merit-based (instead of needs-based) criteria appears to be inconsistent with international law. The fact that those disadvantaged by such forms of preferential treatment, in principle, do not have the ability to domestically enforce international rights does not detract from the fact that the Dutch government is legally bound by these obligations.

Under the new health insurance regime, factors like freedom of choice, health care needs, and socioeconomic status have become more important principles in determining access, whereas the ability-to-pay principle has waned. Given the limited options of unhealthy and more needy individuals, a substantial inequality in access to health care between several socioeconomic groups will likely emerge over time in the Dutch system.

While privatizing health insurance seems to undermine equal access to health care, the impact of free prices and liberalizing the health care provider market is less pronounced. One of the reasons could be the step-by-step introduction of a less strict health care prices regime and the limited number of private for-profit institutional providers. So far, the efficiency improvement gained by introducing private capital in the competitive hospital market is primarily based on economic assumptions. While waiting lists have reduced in size, quality of care provided in private clinics still remains an issue of concern. At the same time, foreign experiences with

---

[56] TK no. 1581, Aanhangsel van Handelingen, (Parliamentary Questions) 1 (2010–2011), *available at* http://opmaatnieuw.sdu.nl/opmaat/ referring to Case CRvB LJN: BO3581.

[57] *Id.* at 2–3.

public-private partnership arrangements in health care paint an alarming picture. Distorting resource allocation and uncertainty about long-term affordability may lead to serious financial deficits and, subsequently, plans for further cuts to services under the basic insurance scheme. It does seem that a public-private partnership policy in health care further complicates the already difficult task of guaranteeing equality in access to health care.

Confronted with health care privatization, the judiciary must play its constitutional role of safeguarding health care rights and galvanizing more equitable access to health care. Yet domestic courts are very hesitant to wade strongly into the health care sector. One of the reasons is a reluctance to incorporate supranational social rights in their decision making, owing to a self-imposed conservative interpretation of their mandate. According to such an interpretation, the right to health in the ICESCR has no self-executing status and has therefore been excluded from judicial review, irrespective of doctrinal developments such as the tripartite typology of state obligations. More successful have been claims invoking international social security rights (under the ILO Conventions or ESC), or by equating the right to health to the European Convention on Human Rights (private life). But such claims are relatively scarce and rely on the interpretation of the judiciary. Also, these legal disputes caused heated debate vis-à-vis state sovereignty and in one case even led to denunciation of international treaty law.

Furthermore, there are no signs that the regime change of the *Zorgverzekeringswet* from public to private law leads to significantly different outcomes in the granting or denial of health insurance claims. Arbitral review is based on objective criteria – "the state of international science and practice" – which itself relies on evidence-based medicine. Particularly in cases of health-care-abroad issues, the state of science and medical practice gives reason for denial of reimbursement of the treatment. This is not necessarily problematic because it concerns health care claims for unproven treatments. Generally, the arbitral body accepts the outcomes of the research provided by the advisory body (Health Insurance Board), covering a search of international medical-scientific databases, (inter)national guidelines and advisory opinions, published opinions of medical experts, and the results of foreign health insurance companies or other relevant organizations. The analysis includes its methodological validity, focusing on research approach, research population, control group, randomizing, follow-up, and statistical analysis. By accepting this well-structured and transparent approach, which is open for judicial review, the arbitral rulings contribute to galvanizing equal access in the Netherlands.

Finally, judicial review of newly introduced health insurance priority arrangements is, so far, absent. Although this phenomenon has been defended on the basis that only a few patients have laid complaints, this defense fails to understand the essence of the nondiscrimination principle. It is expected that by challenging the inequality of priority arrangements, the reference to equality and nondiscrimination provisions may strengthen the justiciability of health care claims, protecting the rights of the most vulnerable and disadvantaged groups in society.

Overall, being confronted with the tensions between market reforms and equity, courts have appeared moderately successful in restoring equal access by referring to international and European treaty law. The price – triggering the political debate on sovereignty – however, can be high. But such considerations are out of the scope of judicial reasoning. Taking that into account, one may indeed conclude that landmark cases from the Central Appeal Tribunal and the relatively new arbitral insurance body have been successful in challenging market competition in health care by protecting equity and solidarity in the face of market reforms.

8

Addressing Equity in Health Care at the Public-Private Intersection

The Role of Health Rights Enforcement in Hungary

Mária Éva Földes

INTRODUCTION

All health systems in the European Union face the challenge of meeting rising costs with limited resources. Increasing health care costs put pressure on health systems, requiring cost-containment measures, usually involving several forms of rationing. Decision makers face the challenge of imposing these limits on health care coverage while also safeguarding the shared values of EU health systems: solidarity, universality, access to good quality care, and equity.[1] Such challenges are particularly pressing for EU members in Central and Eastern Europe, who must cope with the legacies of the state-socialist regime in trying to meet EU standards.

Patients challenge these decisions concerning resource allocation in health care and the limitations of coverage, and they increasingly rely on rights-based litigation.[2] Patients also rely sometimes on supranational rights, such as the freedom to provide services within the EU, to challenge limits placed on the domestic health system.[3]

---

[1] These shared values are stipulated in Council of the European Union, Conclusions on Common Values and Principles in European Union Health Systems 2006/C, 2006 O.J. (C 146) 1, 0001–0003 (EC). Equity is defined as access to care according to one's medical needs. Equitable distribution of resources in health care takes into account one's ability to pay for services, and it does not place a proportionally higher financial burden on lower-income groups.

[2] Aeyal M. Gross, *The Right to Health in an Era of Privatisation and Globalisation: National and International Perspectives*, in EXPLORING SOCIAL RIGHTS: BETWEEN THEORY AND PRACTICE 416 (Daphne Barak-Erez & Aeyal M. Gross eds., 2007); Colleen M. Flood & Brandon Y. Y. Chen, *Charter Rights & Health Care Funding: A Typology of Canadian Health Rights Litigation*, 19(3) ANN. HEALTH LAW 479 (2010).

[3] In the European Union, patients can rely directly on the freedom to provide services when seeking health care in a Member State other than where they are insured. The freedom to provide services is one of the four fundamental freedoms set forth in the EU Treaty and includes the freedom to provide and receive health care in another Member State. Extension of this freedom to health care has been done by a series of judgments delivered by the European Court of Justice. See for example the following judgments: Case C-158/96, Raymond Kohll v. Union des caisses de maladie, 1998 E.C.R. I-1931; Case C-120/95, Nicolas Decker v. Caisse de maladie des employés privés, 1998 E.C.R. I-1831; Case C-368/98,

Courts are willing to engage in rights-based review of health care, and intervene in issues concerning allocation of resources. However, commentators have raised concerns regarding the impact of rights-based litigation on equality and equity in health and health care.[4] Some contest the value of rights-based litigation in health care–related matters, arguing it is likely to protect individual interests in a way that reinforces rather than combats inequalities. They criticize courts for focusing only on the narrow perspective of the individual and not looking to the larger context in which a public health system operates.

This chapter examines the role of the rights-based litigation in addressing inequities in access to health care in an EU Member State located in Central Europe: Hungary. The goal of the analysis is to contribute to the debate about factors that bring about or sustain inequalities in health and health care at the public-private intersection. Toward this end, the chapter presents first an overview of the Hungarian health care system. It then analyzes the scope and content of the right to health by discussing Hungary's constitutional protection of health rights and the right to health care guaranteed within the public health system. Further to that, the chapter reviews the main mechanisms of rights enforcement in health care. It describes the health care litigation that has taken place in Hungary with the focus on equity issues at the public-private intersection. The analysis concludes by discussing the role of health rights enforcement in promoting equity in access to health care.

8.1 FEATURES OF THE HUNGARIAN HEALTH CARE SYSTEM

At the end of the state-socialist regime in 1989, the Hungarian health care system embarked on a road leading away from the highly centralized system in place during its state-socialist years. Features of the state-socialist health care system included centrally planned and administered health policy, tax-based financing, state-owned health facilities, and state-employed health professionals.[5] In 1990, Hungary opted to reestablish social health insurance and put in place a more pluralist system

---

Abdon Vanbraekel and Others v. Alliance nationale des mutualités chrétiennes (ANMC), 2001 E.C.R. I-5363; Case C-157/99, B.S.M. Geraets-Smits v. Stichting Ziekenfonds VGZ and H.T.M. Peerbooms v. Stichting CZ Groep Zorgverzekeringen, 2001 E.C.R. I-5473; Case C-385/99, V.G. Müller-Fauré v. Onderlinge Waarborgmaatschappij OZ Zorgverzekeringen UA and E.E.M. van Riet v. Onderlinge Waarborgmaatschappij ZAO Zorgverzekeringen, 2003 E.C.R. I-4409; Case C-56/01, Patricia Inizan v. Caisse primaire d'assurance maladie des Hauts-de-Seine, 2003 E.C.R. I-12403; Case C-8/02, Ludwig Leichtle v. Bundesanstalt für Arbeit, 2004 E.C.R. I-2641; Case C-145/03, Heirs of Annette Keller v. Instituto Nacional de la Seguridad Social (INSS) and Instituto Nacional de Gestión Sanitaria (Ingesa), 2005 E.C.R. I-2529; Case C-372/04, The Queen, on the application of Yvonne Watts v. Bedford Primary Care Trust and Secretary of State for Health, 2006 E.C.R. I-4325; Case C-466/04, Manuel Acereda Herrera v. Servicio Cántabro de Salud, 2006 E.C.R. I- 5341; Case C-444/05, Aikaterini Stamatelaki v. NPDD Organismos Asfaliseos Eleftheron Epangelmation (OAEE), 2007 E.C.R. I-3185.

[4] Gross, *supra* note 2, Flood & Chen, *supra* note 2.

[5] Similarly to most countries of Central and Eastern Europe, during the state-socialist years Hungary followed the health system model developed in the Soviet Union in the 1920s. For further details on the state-socialist system, *see* WHO REGIONAL OFFICE FOR EUROPE AND THE COUNCIL OF EUROPE

of health care governance with responsibilities divided between different bodies at various levels.[6] The first democratically elected government decided to transform the system from one financed predominantly from taxes during the state-socialist years to one based on compulsory, nonprofit social health insurance. The compulsory social health insurance scheme that funds the Health Insurance Fund – hereafter the HIF scheme – was created in 1993. The HIF is a single public fund separated from the central budget, operating nationwide and administered by a centralized public agency, the National Health Insurance Fund Administration (NHIFA).[7]

8.1.1 *Organization and Financing*

In the early 1990s, the Hungarian health care system underwent a decentralization process. Local governments – at the county and municipal levels – became important actors in planning and providing health care services. They became the owners of most primary care facilities, outpatient care facilities, and hospitals.[8] They took responsibility for funding the capital costs of the health services, the investment, and amortization costs (while the HIF scheme covered the operational costs on a contractual basis). Local governments could benefit from matching and conditional grants provided by the central government to supplement their funds for renovation and investment. They could contract out service delivery to private providers and have done so extensively in primary care and increasingly so in secondary care.[9] Privatization of hospital care has been very limited so far, with only a small share of hospitals owned by foundations, churches, or other private actors.[10] A large share of the hospital personnel is still publicly employed, with strictly regulated remuneration and low salaries compared to non-health care sectors of the economy and to West European countries. A recentralization process in hospital care was initiated at the end of 2011 by the Hungarian government.[11]

DEVELOPMENT BANK, HEALTH AND ECONOMIC DEVELOPMENT IN SOUTH- EASTERN EUROPE 43–44 (2006).

[6] In fact, sickness funds functioning on the basis of solidarity within professional groups already existed in Hungary between the 1840s and the Second World War. See also Péter Mihályi, BEVEZETÉS AZ EGÉSZSÉGÜGY KÖZGAZDASÁGTANÁBA [INTRODUCTION TO HEALTH ECONOMY], 261–263 (2003).

[7] By separating the HIF from the central budget, the government hoped to increase efficiency in financing and put an end to resource waste caused by the soft budget constraint in health care funding during the state-socialist years. See János Kornai, ECONOMICS OF SHORTAGE (1980) (on the consequences of the soft budget constraint).

[8] In 2009, local governments still owned 78% of all hospital beds. See Péter Gaál, Szabolcs Szigeti, Márton Csere, Matthew Gaskins & Dimitra Panteli, *Hungary: Health System Review*, 13(5) HEALTH SYSTEMS IN TRANSITION 1, xxii (2011).

[9] A widespread arrangement was that local governments remained the owners of health care facilities but outsourced the provision of services or management to private individuals or companies. This arrangement is known as functional privatization. See Gaál et al., *supra* note 8, at 171–173 (for details on ownership and management of health care providers).

[10] This concerns both ownership privatization and functional privatization.

[11] In January 2012, the government nationalized thirteen hospitals located in the capital of Hungary. The process was expected to continue in 2012 with hospitals owned by local governments.

In addition to the recently started recentralization process in hospital care, the central government has other direct responsibilities for health care delivery. This includes health service provision at national institutes for health, clinical departments of major medical universities, and special facilities owned by certain ministries. The central government is also responsible for providing emergency care through the National Emergency Ambulance Service, blood products through the National Blood Supply Service, and infectious disease control and public hygiene through the National Public Health and Medical Officer.[12] Furthermore, it finances directly a number of high-cost, high-tech interventions, health promotion, health education, and family planning services (notwithstanding the exceptions specified by law).

The HIF scheme finances different types of services through separate mechanisms, and thus has several sub-budgets for each service, capped overall by a national budget ceiling.[13] For example, general practitioners are predominantly financed through capitation fees adjusted to the patient's age and supplemented by a fixed fee based on the type of the practice (adult, child, or mixed) and the number of patients involved. Outpatient clinics are funded through a German-type fee-for-service point system.[14] Chronic inpatient care is financed through daily fees consisting of a fixed amount established per day per patient and adjusted according to the type of care.[15] Acute inpatient care is funded through a system called Homogeneous Disease Groups, similar to the American Diagnosis Related Groups (DRG).[16] Special rules apply to emergency patient transfer. The HIF is separated from the budget of the central government, which cannot use HIF funds for other purposes.

The HIF scheme was designed as a needs-based system based on solidarity, equity, and comprehensive coverage. Membership is mandatory and opting out is prohibited. Health insurance contributions are calculated as percentages of salary income and additional income,[17] which are taxed separately. Insured individuals are entitled to all health services and goods covered by the HIF. Salary-based health insurance contributions are divided between employees and employers and the rate is statutorily regulated.[18] It is the obligation of the employer to deduct the contribution from the employee's gross salary and transfer it to the national tax office, which in turn

---

[12] *See* 1997. évi CLIV. törvény az egészségügyröl [Act CLIV of 1997 on Health] (Hung.), Art. 142(2).

[13] *See* Gaál et al., *supra* note 8, at 59–100. *See also* Imre Boncz, Júlia Nagy, Andor Sebestyén & László Körösi, *Financing of Health Care Services in Hungary*, 5 Eur. J. Health Econ. 252 (2004) (for a detailed analysis of health care financing in Hungary).

[14] *See* Éva Orosz, Ellena Guy & Mellitta Jakab, *Reforming the Health Care System: The Unfinished Agenda*, in Public Finance Reform during the Transition: the Experience of Hungary 221, 239–241 (Lajos Bokros & Jean-Jacques Dethier eds., 1998) (for further details on this system and its implementation in Hungary).

[15] *E.g.*, care provided at a nursing department, rehabilitation, hospice care, tetraplegic patients care.

[16] *See* Orosz et al., *supra* note 14, at 239–241 (for details on the implementation of this system).

[17] *E.g.*, income generated from property renting, dividends.

[18] *See* 1997. évi LXXX. törvény a társadalombiztosítás ellátásaira és a magánnyugdíjra jogosultakról, valamint e szolgáltatások fedezetéről [Act LXXX of 1997 on Persons Entitled to Social Insurance Services and Private Pension and the Financing of These Services] (Hung.), para. 19(1)-(3).

transfers it to the HIF scheme. The central government transfers tax-based revenue to the HIF scheme to compensate for individuals who are entitled to health services but are not required to pay contributions. This concerns a wide range of population groups including minors, full-time students, persons on maternity leave, persons receiving sickness benefits, disability benefits, or social assistance for low income, persons placed in social care institutions, prisoners, war veterans, low-income pensioners, and homeless people.[19]

Health spending in Hungary has been unstable since the transition to social health insurance, with repeated budget cuts. Public expenditure on health decreased from 6.1 percent of GDP in 1995 to 5.2 percent in 2009, while private expenditure increased from 16 percent of total expenditure on health in 1995 to 30.3 percent in 2009.[20] Private spending consists mainly of out-of-pocket payments made by patients. The current share of private expenditure in total health expenditure is estimated to be above 30 percent and one of the highest in the EU.[21] The share of out-of-pocket payments is estimated to exceed the OECD average.[22]

In 2006, the Hungarian government launched a series of reforms with cost containment as a dominant objective. This has led to a number of technical improvements such as implementing a computerized information and reporting system for checking patients' entitlement status, introducing health technology assessments, and incentives to promote generic competition among medicinal products reimbursed by the NHIFA.[23] To increase transparency in health care rationing, the government also introduced regulation of publicly accessible waiting lists in the form of central waiting lists and provider-level waiting lists.[24] Currently, health care providers must make sure that waiting lists are publicly accessible online and must provide the services according to the order of placement on the waiting list. Jumping the queue is only allowed in "emergency situations," defined as conditions endangering life or causing lasting health damage. The government has also created a legal framework for the establishment of waiting list protocols that allow for a more sophisticated needs assessment and rationing process.

Salary-based contribution rates have been changed several times since the early 1990s. On January 1, 2011, this rate was set at 6% of the gross salary for employees with an additional 2% paid by employers.

[19] *Id.*, art. 16(1), 26(5) and 39(1). *See also* 2005. évi CXIX. törvény az adókról, járulékokról és egyéb költségvetési befizetésekröl szóló törvények módosításáról [Act CXIX of 2005 on the Amendment of Certain Acts concerning Taxes, Mandatory Contributions and Other Payments to the Central Budget] (Hung.), art. 130 and 134.

[20] *See* Gaál et al., *supra* note 8, at 60.

[21] OECD, *Healthcare Reform: Improving Efficiency and Quality of Care*, in REFORMS FOR STABILITY AND SUSTAINABLE GROWTH: AN OECD PERSPECTIVE ON HUNGARY 59 (2008).

[22] *Id.* at 59.

[23] *See also* Gaál et al., *supra* note 8, at 167–182 (on recent health reforms).

[24] Central waiting lists are lists of national application that regulate access to a number of high-cost services (e.g., PET/CT scans) and all forms of organ transplantation. Provider-level waiting lists regulate access to non-emergency care in case of limited human, infrastructural, or financial capacity.

Other government reforms have been less successful. Notably, its initiatives to introduce managed competition in social health insurance and replace the NHIFA with private, for-profit insurance companies (a reform which, as André den Exter shows in Chapter 7, has been implemented in the Netherlands) failed in 2008. The government has also failed to consolidate social health insurance and ensure a stable flow of revenues. Although the tax office reported in 2008 that computerized information and the reporting system on patient entitlement status had contributed to the enforcement of contribution payments,[25] the latter remains compromised in the context of relatively high rates of unreported employment and underreporting salaries and other income. The central government is responsible for covering the deficit of the HIF from tax revenues[26] – which in practice means a yearly injection of tax money.

8.1.2 *Standing of the Health System vis-à-vis Private Health Care and Insurance*

A system of private health insurance coexists in Hungary with the HIF scheme, encompassing voluntary complementary health funds and private, commercial insurance companies. The current legal framework for the establishment and functioning of voluntary complementary health funds was created in 1993 by adopting Parliamentary Act XCVI of 1993 on Voluntary Mutual Insurance Funds.[27] These health funds are based on the principles of solidarity, mutuality, independence, voluntary membership, self-governance, nondiscrimination, and nonprofit functioning. In 2010, there were thirty-seven of them operating in Hungary and encompassing 960,470 members (about 9.6 percent of the Hungarian population).[28] Membership is open to any person older than sixteen who is enrolled simultaneously in the HIF scheme. Membership fees are paid either directly by individual members or by their employers (fees are paid in addition to HIF scheme contributions). The initial risk-pooling element was abolished in 2003, and voluntary complementary insurance currently operates as an individual medical saving account scheme used solely by account holders for their own and their dependents' benefit. It can only be used to cover a limited range of health services listed in Act XCVI of 1993: (1) a

---

[25] Adó és Pénzügyi Ellenörzési Hivatal Sajtóanyag: Egészségbiztosítási Jogviszony – Tisztul A Kép, Csökken A Rendezetlen Jogviszonyok Száma [National Tax and Customs Administration: Press release: Entitlement to Health Insurance: The Picture Is Getting Clearer, the Number of Unclear Entitlements is Decreasing] (Sept. 12, 2008), *available at* http://nav.gov.hu/data/cms52645/Egeszsegbiztositasi_jogviszony–Tisztul_a_kep–csokken_a_rendezetlen_jogviszonyok_szama.pdf.

[26] *See* Act LXXX of 1997 (Hung.), art. 3(2).

[27] *See* 1993. évi XCVI. törvény az Önkéntes Kölcsönös Biztosító Pénztárakról [Act XCVI of 1993 on Voluntary Mutual Insurance Funds] (Hung.).

[28] Pénzügyi Szervezetek Állami Felügyelete, Aranykönyvek 2010 [Hungarian Financial Supervisory Authority, Golden Books 2010] (2010), *available at* http://www.pszaf.hu/bal_menu/jelentesek_statisztikak/statisztikak/aranykonyv_cikk.html.

number of services excluded from or only partially covered by the HIF scheme; (2) copayments charged for pharmaceuticals and medical aids in the HIF scheme; (3) income-replacing or complementing cash benefits in case of sickness or disability; and (4) services promoting a healthy lifestyle.[29] It is not possible to use voluntary health insurance to gain faster access to treatments for which waiting lists are in place. In this sense, voluntary insurance has a limited complementary and supplementary role.[30]

Private for-profit (commercial) health insurance also exists in Hungary, but it is very limited. Foreigners living in Hungary can use this insurance if they are not members of the HIF scheme. Hungarian residents can use it to cover services offered at certain private providers not contracted by the HIF if they are not satisfied with the publicly covered services. In certain cases they can also use it to purchase above-standard hospital accommodation services that are not covered by the HIF. Hungarians can also purchase private insurance to cover medical care that becomes necessary during a temporary visit abroad. This concerns mainly non-EU countries, because Hungarians can use the European Health Insurance Card to cover health care costs incurred during a temporary visit to an EU Member State.[31]

Non-contracted private providers operate alongside the public system mainly in outpatient specialist care, dental care, and, to a very small extent, in hospital care. They rely largely on out-of-pocket payments made by patients and to a lesser extent on private health insurance. This means that access to health services at non-contracted providers is effectively open only to patients who can afford to pay out of pocket the full price of services and/or take private health insurance. These providers have a predominantly market-oriented approach and try to attract patients by offering better, faster care and a more consumer-friendly attitude. In some cases they develop a complete service cluster in order to attract foreign patients who can afford higher prices than Hungarians can. As a result, there are private clinics for dental care, aesthetic surgery, and eye surgery that rely predominantly on foreign patients.[32]

---

[29] *See* Act XCVI of 1993, art. 51/B-E.

[30] See Sarah Thomson & Elias Mossialos, *Regulating Private Health Insurance in the European Union: The Implications of Single Market Legislation and Competition Policy*, 29 J. Eur. Integration 89, 94–95 (2007).

[31] The European Health Insurance Card was introduced in Hungary in 2005 following the country's EU accession. An instrument to ensure access to health care for persons exercising their freedom of movement within the EU, the card is issued free of charge to all persons insured within the HIF scheme. Individuals can use this card to obtain health care that becomes necessary during a temporary stay in another EU country. The physician providing the health services decides whether the treatment is planned or not; he/she should not accept the card to cover planned care.

[32] For example, the Hungarian towns situated near the Austrian border present a high concentration of health care providers offering services that are uncovered or only partially covered by the Austrian health system. These clinics attract Austrian patients by offering cheaper, faster, and comprehensive services. *See also* August Österle, *Health Care across Borders: Austria and Its New EU Neighbors*, 17 J. Eur. Soc. Pol'y, 112 (2007).

While patients need to cover out of pocket the cost of services obtained from private providers operating in Hungary, in certain cases they may be reimbursed for such services if the private provider operates in another EU Member State. This possibility stems from Hungary's membership in the EU and concerns predominantly outpatient services. Hungary has implemented European Court of Justice (ECJ) case law, extending the freedom to provide services to health care. This created a right for individual patients to get reimbursed by their domestic health fund for planned outpatient care obtained in another EU Member State.[33] In line with the ECJ case law, Parliamentary Act LXXXIII of 1997 stipulates that Hungarian patients do not need a prior authorization from the NHIFA to obtain planned outpatient care at public or private providers operating in another Member State.[34] The NHIFA reimburses such costs up to the level of reimbursement applied to the same or equally effective treatment provided within the HIF scheme (but not exceeding the actual amount paid abroad). EU accession has thus created an option for Hungarians to access treatment provided in private or public facilities located in another Member State; patients who are able to temporarily advance the cost of the treatment and then cover the difference in tariffs can make use of this option. At the same time, perversely, the NHIFA will not reimburse patients for services obtained at non-contracted private providers operating in Hungary.

8.1.3 *Equity at the Public-Private Intersection*

A number of measures have been implemented in the HIF scheme with the aims of ensuring equity in access to health care and promoting economic accessibility of services for low-income groups. The central government compensates from tax-based revenues for individuals who are entitled to health care services but are not required to pay contributions to the HIF scheme. This includes low-income groups as defined by means testing.[35] The state also covers their official copayments for certain services included in the insurance package (such as pharmaceuticals prescribed in outpatient care, medical aids, and rehabilitation services).

Nevertheless, equitable distribution of the burden of health care financing remains an unfinished agenda. Measures protecting low-income groups are present only in case of health care provided within the HIF scheme by contracted providers and do not extend to services obtained from non-contracted private providers. About 30 percent of total expenditure on health is private and consists mainly of out-of-pocket payments and to a smaller extent of private health insurance. Out-of-pocket payments constitute a strongly regressive element entrenched in the HIF scheme in

---

[33] See *supra* note 3 for the ECJ case law related to access to health care in another Member State.

[34] 1997. évi LXXXIII. törvény a kötelező egészségbiztosítás ellátásairól [Act LXXXIII of 1997 on Services of Compulsory Health Insurance] (Hung.), art. 27(6).

[35] See *supra* Para 1.1. See *also* Act LXXX of 1997, art. 16(1), 26(5) and 39(1).

the form of official copayments and unofficial, informal payments. Furthermore, voluntary complementary insurance operates as a system of individual medical saving accounts, which is also a regressive form of private financing in health care.

8.1.3.1 The Challenge of Informal Payments

Informal payments constitute a serious challenge to equity in the HIF scheme, and they likely form the bulk of out-of-pocket payments.[36] Informal payments are illicit and usually unreported payments made by patients to health care professionals for services or goods that are covered by the HIF scheme and should be provided free of charge at the point of delivery. There is a lot of ambiguity and controversy surrounding the characteristics and role of informal payments in health care. Based on a comprehensive review of the main theoretical debates in the Hungarian context, Gaál and McKee describe two hypotheses conceptualizing informal payments as either unofficial, illicit fees-for-service or voluntary donations/gifts to express gratitude.[37] The two hypotheses give very different responses to questions concerning the causes, role, and impact of informal payments. Moreover, there are different policy implications depending on whether informal payments are conceptualized as illicit fees or as voluntary gifts. On one hand, proponents of informal payments argue that there is no coercion associated with such voluntary payments and no net ill effects. In their view, such payments are rooted in tradition and culture. The opponents of informal payments argue that patients are forced to make these payments in order to access care, causing significant systemic ill effects. In their view, such payments place a proportionally higher financial burden on low-income groups and deter them from seeking health care.

The actual magnitude and characteristics of informal payments in Hungary are difficult to determine. A 1999 survey shows that informal payments are unevenly distributed among medical professionals; amounts paid vary considerably by medical specialty, with the highest being hospital-based surgeries and gynecology/obstetrics.[38] Results of a 2008 survey show that 72 percent of patients treated between 2005 and 2008 gave informal payments to health professionals.[39] The survey also illustrates

---

[36] According to HISA estimates: Egészségbiztosítási Felügyelet, *Az egészségbiztosítás helyzetének értékelése 2008* [*Assessment of health insurance situation in 2008*] 15 (December, 2009), *available at* http://www.ebf.hu. (The HISA was closed in 2010, and this publication is no longer available online.)

[37] Péter Gaál & Martin McKee, *Fee-for-service or Donation? Hungarian Perspectives on Informal Payment for Health Care*, 60 Soc. Sci. Med. 1445 (2005).

[38] Bognár Géza, Gál Róbert Iván & Kornai János, *Hálapénz a Magyar Egészségügyben* [*Informal Payments in the Hungarian Health System*], TÁRKI Társadalompolitikai Tanulmányok, Stud. 17 (1999), *available at* http://www.tarki.hu/kiadvany-h/soco/soco17.html; *see also* András L. Nagy, *Hálapénz a Magyar Egészségügyben: Ki, Kinek, Miért, Mennyit?* [*Gratitude Payments in the Hungarian Health Care System: Who Pays to Whom, Why, How Much?*] 10 LAM 726 (2000).

[39] Magyar Önkéntes Egészségpénztárak Szövetsége, Hálapénz: A Patika Egészségpénztár Reprezentatív Kutatása A Betegek Hálapénz-Adási Szokásairól [Hungarian Association of Voluntary Health Funds,

how informal payments can function as illicit fees: 66 percent of respondents claimed to pay informal charges with the aim to ensure extra attention on behalf of hospital personnel and 74 percent claimed to do so in ambulatory treatment.[40] In another 2008 survey, 31 percent of respondents claimed to pay informal charges to ensure the provision of appropriate health services.[41] Patients' motivations for paying informal charges include securing better-quality services delivered in better conditions, more patient-friendly attitude, better information, and shorter waiting times.

Informal payments raise important equity concerns in health care. A 2006 Hungarian study shows that low-income groups pay proportionally more for health care provided in the public health system through informal payments than higher-income groups do.[42] Using the Kakwani progressivity indices, the study revealed that the informal payments system in Hungary was one of the most regressive internationally. The authors concluded that the highly regressive way of funding health care services caused by informal payments affected all three types of health care examined: primary, outpatient, and hospital care. The entrenched system of informal payments made the overall system of health care funding more regressive than it would be had it been based solely on officially established contributions and copayments.[43]

8.2 THE SCOPE AND CONTENT OF THE RIGHT TO HEALTH

At the end of the state-socialist regime, economic necessity forced the Hungarian health care system to withdraw the regime's previous promise of free health care to all citizens as a state duty. Such promises by the state-socialist system were consolidated in the II/1972 Health Act, which stipulated that the state had to provide health care free of charge as a right of citizenship. Although the introduction of social health insurance had started before the regime change, the state was largely responsible for keeping the promise of free health care until the end of state-socialism. Small copayments were charged officially for certain pharmaceutical products, medical aids, and prostheses only. However, unofficial, informal payments for health services were widespread and tolerated despite the fact that the 1972 Health Act prohibited them explicitly.[44] The official rhetoric of free and universal health care provided as a citizen's right was in sharp contrast with the existence of informal payments causing nontransparent and unfair prioritization. Together with the introduction of the HIF

Representative Research of the Patika Health Fund on Patients' Habits concerning Informal Payments] 21 (2009), *available at* http://www.patikapenztar.hu/dok/halapenz_egyben.pdf.

[40] *Id*, at 17–18.

[41] The survey results were published by the Health Insurance Supervisory Authority (HISA) in 2009, *see* Egészségbiztosítási Felügyelet, *supra* note 36.

[42] Ágota Szende & Anthony J. Culyer, *The Inequity of Informal Payments for Health Care: The Case of Hungary*, 75 HEALTH POL'Y 262 (2006).

[43] Szende & Culyer, *supra* note 42, at 270.

[44] Ádám György, AZ ORVOSI HÁLAPÉNZ MAGYARORSZÁGON [GRATITUDE PAYMENTS FOR MEDICAL CARE IN HUNGARY] (1986).

scheme, the right to free health care based on citizenship was replaced by the right to health care based on HIF membership.

8.2.1 *Health Rights in the Hungarian Constitution*

Hungary adopted its first written constitution in 1949. Since then, the constitution has undergone two major changes. It was heavily amended in 1989 after the fall of the state-socialist regime, when a new catalog of fundamental rights was introduced. Then, a new constitution was adopted in 2011, named the Fundamental Law of Hungary. It came into force on January 1, 2012.

The constitution adopted in 1949 and in force until 1989 included a right to health for workers only. It based the right to health on the right to work and focused on occupational health.[45] The amendments introduced in 1989 included a right to the *highest possible level of physical and mental health* (Article 70/D), a right to a *healthy environment* (Article 18), and a *right to social security* (Article 70/E). Post-1989, the right to health imposed on the state an obligation to implement it through "institutions of labor safety and health care, through the organization of medical care and the opportunities for regular physical activity, as well as through the protection of the urban and natural environment" (Article 70/D). The broad formulation of the right to the highest possible level of health reflected the intention to place health among the top priorities of the new democratic state. Post-1989, the constitution also set forth a responsibility for the national government to "define the state system of social welfare and health care services and ensure sufficient funds for such services" (Article 35(1)(g)). The right to social security stipulated for individuals an entitlement to support required in case of sickness and a duty for the state to implement this right through the system of social security and social institutions (Article 70/E).

The Fundamental Law of Hungary in force since January 2012, removed the broad formulation of the right to health by omitting the "highest possible level" formulation. Article XX stipulates that "everyone has a right to physical and mental health." It broadens, however, the related state obligations by adding the duty to ensure an agriculture that is free from genetically modified organisms, as well as access to healthy food and drinking water. The Fundamental Law amended also the formulation of the right to social security, which now states in Article XIX:

> (1) Hungary shall strive to provide social security to all of its citizens. Every Hungarian citizen shall be entitled to statutory subsidies for maternity, illness, disability, widowhood, orphanage and unemployment not caused by his or her own actions.

---

[45] *See also* Judit Sándor, *Ombudspersons and Patients' Rights Representatives in Hungary, in* Protecting Patients' Rights? A Comparative Study of the Ombudsman in Healthcare 55, 55–76 (Stephen Mackenney & Lars Fallberg eds., 2004) (for the discussion of the right to health in the constitution adopted in 1949).

(2) Hungary shall implement social security for the persons listed in Paragraph (1) and other people in need through a system of social institutions and measures. (3) The nature and extent of social measures may be determined by law in accordance with the usefulness to the community of the beneficiary's activity.[46]

It is noteworthy that the new social security clause no longer includes the rights language, replaced with the much weaker language of aspirational goals. Interpretation of the constitutional right to health and to social security is discussed in detail in Section 8.3 of this chapter.

8.2.2 *The Right to Health Care in the HIF Scheme*

Various actors and instruments regulate the right to health care within the HIF scheme. Parliament determines the scope and content of the benefit package at the level of broad categories, specifies minimum standards and procedures and the provider payment methods, and establishes the final budget of the HIF. It also establishes on a yearly basis the income-related contribution rates in the HIF scheme. Decisions taken by parliament are stipulated in acts with national application. The most relevant parliamentary acts are:

1. Act CLIV of 1997 on Health, which sets forth the right to health care and patients' rights, determines broadly the scope and content of health services, and specifies minimum standards and procedures.
2. Act LXXXIII of 1997 on Services of Compulsory Health Insurance, which defines the benefit package and regulates exclusion or inclusion of services at the level of broad functional categories.
3. Act LXXX of 1997 on Persons Entitled to Social Insurance Services and Private Pension and the Financing of These Services, which regulates entitlement.
4. Act LXVI of 1998, which regulates health insurance contributions.

Both the central government and the President of the Republic, in addition to members and committees of parliament, can initiate amendments to these acts, and decrees of the central government and ministerial decrees regulate their detailed implementation. The detailed content of the health benefit package and the decision-making process concerning inclusion or exclusion of benefits are usually regulated at the level of ministerial decrees,[47] but lower-level regulations (resolutions, orders, policies, communications, and statements interpreting legislation) are also used sometimes to influence the implementation of the right to health care. The NHIFA is responsible for payment of health care providers and performance

---

[46] *See* Magyarország Alaptörvénye [The Fundamental Law Of Hungary], § XIX.
[47] See also the analysis of Péter Gaál, *Benefits and Entitlements in the Hungarian Health Care System*, 6 Eur. J. Health Econ. 37 (2005).

measurement and decides on inclusion or exclusion of pharmaceuticals in the benefits package. The Ministry of Health regularly consults its various advisory bodies and institutions for expert advice. In addition, national-level decision makers must consult relevant interest groups when preparing the laws, including professional organizations (chambers), patient organizations, health care provider associations, and NGOs.

Act CLIV of 1997 on Health defines the right to health care along several dimensions that reflect the elements of the right to health as set forth in the General Comment No. 14 of the UN Economic and Social Council. According to that Act, members of the HIF scheme have a right to quality health care that is:

5. medically necessary;
6. appropriate (i.e., in accordance with professional and ethical rules and guidelines);
7. continuously available (i.e., the health system functions twenty-four hours per day);
8. provided in accordance with the equal treatment principle;[48] and
9. provided in the shortest possible time, taking into account the patient's health condition.

The Act sets forth a comprehensive right to information among other patients' rights. The equal-treatment principle includes the prohibition of discrimination as well as the duty of the state to ensure access to health care for low-income groups. In terms of content, three types of service packages are distinguished:

1. a basic package financed from the central budget to which all Hungarian residents are entitled regardless of insurance status;
2. an insurance package contingent on membership in the HIF scheme; and
3. a supplementary package with services uninsured within the HIF scheme and covered by patients out-of-pocket payments or through private health insurance.

The basic package contains a limited range of health services provided as a state duty to everyone residing in Hungary without checking entitlement status.[49] It includes services related to infectious disease control (mandatory vaccinations, screenings, medical examination, isolation and transportation of patients) as well as emergency ambulance services and emergency care if irrecoverable from other resources. Hospitals provide emergency ambulance care unconditionally whenever a patient needs immediate care (i.e., in case of accidents, life-threatening conditions, danger of

---

48 The principle of equal treatment in health care is set forth also in 2003. évi CXXV. törvény az egyenlö bánásmódról és az esélyegyenlöség elömozdításáról [Act CXXV of 2003 on Equal Treatment and Promotion of Equal Opportunities] (Hung.), art. 4(k).

49 *See* 1997. évi CLIV. törvény az egészségügyröl [Act CLIV of 1997 on Health] (Hung.), art. 142(2).

lasting harm, pregnancy and childbirth, urgent need of pain relief or acute disorder of consciousness).

The insurance package covers health services and goods offered based on membership in the HIF scheme. The insurance package includes fully covered services, subsidized services, and partially covered services requiring copayment by insured persons. Fully covered services include:[50]

1. prevention and early detection services;
2. curative care, including general practitioner services, outpatient specialist care, inpatient care, and certain dental care services;
3. other services, including maternity care, medical rehabilitation, patient transportation, and emergency ambulance services; and
4. medically necessary health care obtained abroad.[51]

The insurance package is further defined and operationalized through benefit catalogs provided mainly by ministerial decrees and applied nationally (with the exception of general practitioner services and certain diagnostic services).[52] The most detailed benefit catalogs concern inpatient care and outpatient specialist care.

Subsidized services include pharmaceuticals prescribed in outpatient care, medical aids, and travel to the health care facility. Pharmaceuticals are subsidized at 50 percent, 70 percent, 90 percent, or 100 percent of the total price. Inclusion of pharmaceuticals and medical aids in the insurance package and the share of subsidy are regulated at the level of ministerial decrees, which also set forth the basic principles for making these decisions.[53] According to these principles, such

---

[50] *See* 1997. évi CLIV. törvény az egészségügyröl [Act CLIV of 1997 on Health]; 1997. évi LXXXIII. törvény a kötelezö egészségbiztosítás ellátásairól [Act LXXXIII of 1997 on Services of Compulsory Health Insurance] (Hung.).

[51] This includes both emergency care and planned care. For planned care obtained abroad prior authorization issued by the NHIFA is necessary – unless the patient seeks outpatient care in another EU Member State, which will be reimbursed without prior authorization up to the amount covered for the same treatment within the HIF scheme. Access to planned treatment abroad is regulated by a governmental decree. *See* 227/2003. (XII. 13.) Korm. r. a külföldi gyógykezelésekkel kapcsolatos egyes kérdésekröl [Governmental Decree No. 227/2003 (XII. 13.) on Certain Issues related to Medical Treatment Abroad] (Hung.). Access to emergency care abroad is ensured via the European Health Insurance Card in other EU countries and bilateral agreements in non-EU countries.

[52] Benefit catalogs are documents detailing the components of the given service category by listing the cases/services for payment purposes, specifying the broad functional categories or specifying professional requirements. *See also* Gaál, *supra* note 47, at S42–S43.

[53] *See* 32/2004. (IV. 26.) ESzCsM r. a törzskönyvezett gyógyszerek és a különleges táplálkozási igényt kielégítö tápszerek társadalombiztosítási támogatásba való befogadásának szempontjairól és a befogadás vagy a támogatás megváltoztatásáról [Decree No. 32/2004 (IV. 26) of the Minister of Health on Criteria for Inclusion in Social Insurance Coverage of Authorized Medicinal Products and Food Supplements and on the Changing of Inclusion or Coverage] (Hung.); 14/2007. (III. 14.) EüM r. a gyógyászati segédeszközök társadalombiztosítási támogatásba történö befogadásáról, támogatással történö rendeléséröl, forgalmazásáról, javításáról és kölcsönzéséröl [Decree No. 14/2007 (III. 14.) of the Minister of Health concerning Inclusion in Social Insurance Coverage of Medical Aids and Coverage of Their Prescription, Supply, Reparation and Borrowing] (Hung.).

decisions should be based on scientific professional evidence; they should ensure safety and efficacy, take into account the limits of budgetary resources, and aim at cost-efficiency. The decisions should be needs-based, transparent, verifiable, and reveal potential conflicts of interest. It is noteworthy that equity – defined as equal opportunity in access – was included as a basic principle in the draft ministerial decree but omitted from the final and adopted text.[54] The NHIFA determines whether a given pharmaceutical product is subsidized and the share of that subsidy, and publishes the regularly updated list of subsidized products.[55] Decisions on strategic issues (e.g., determining the share of subsidy applied to a certain group of substance) are the joint responsibility of the Minister of Health and the Minister of Finance.

Partially covered medical services requiring copayment include orthodontic devices for patients under eighteen, tooth replacement, certain sex reassignment surgeries, care provided in a sanatorium, inpatient nursing at designated facilities, and comfort-increasing services in hospital care such as single rooms, access to internet, and the like.[56] Copayments are charged when patients request alternative services involving additional costs.[57] Hospitals are entitled to charge copayments for patients' free choice of physicians except for pregnancy and maternity care. Patients are also charged copayments for hospital care obtained without a general practitioner referral or not in the hospital referred to, except in emergencies. According to a 2010 study published by the Hungarian Health Insurance Supervisory Authority (HISA), hospitals often ask patients to advance a significant share of the copayment.[58] Patients can use voluntary (nonprofit) health insurance to cover copayments for hospital services provided within the HIF scheme.

In 2007, a new type of flat-rate copayment was introduced for general practitioner care, specialized outpatient care, and hospital care services included in the insurance package. It was called "visit fee" for outpatient care and "hospital daily fee" for inpatient care.[59] Such copayments were estimated to account for 3.5 percent of total

---

54 Judit Jóywiak-Hagymásy, Dóra Hermann & István Udvaros, Értékválasztás, Prioritásképzés És Rangsorolás A Magyar Egészségügyben [Value Choice, Priority-Setting And Rationing In The Hungarian Health Care System] 47 (2006), *available at* http://www.eski.hu/new3/politika/zip_doc_2006/prioritas.pdf.

55 The NHIFA can also decide to subsidize the cost of allopathic medicines and medical devices that are not yet included in the insurance package.

56 *See* 1997. évi LXXXIII. törvény a kötelező egészségbiztosítás ellátásairól [Act LXXXIII of 1997 on Services of Compulsory Health Insurance] (Hung.), art. 23.

57 *E.g.*, certain types of prostheses and special, lighter orthopedic (surgical) casts.

58 On average, the amount charged in advance was 67% of the total copayment fee. Egészségbiztosítási Felügyelet, Térítési Díjak A Magyar Egészségügyben [Health Insurance Supervisory Authority, Copayments in the Hungarian Health Care System] (2010), *available at* http://weborvos.hu/adat/files/veraaprilis/terdij.pdf.

59 *See* 2006. évi CXV. törvény egyes, az egészségügyet érintő törvényeknek az egészségügyi reformmal kapcsolatos módosításáról [Act CXV of 2006 on Amendment of Certain Health Care Related Laws concerning the Health Care Reform] (Hung).

out-of-pocket spending in 2007.[60] Despite the relatively small financial burden[61] and the wide-ranging exemptions covering almost 40 percent of the population (i.e., low-income groups, minors and full-time students, patients seeking care for chronic conditions, etc.), the visit and hospital daily fees have become a major confrontation issue in the political arena.[62] A high-turnout national referendum initiated by the opposition party in 2008 reflected the strong public objection and voted for the elimination of the visit and hospital daily fees, which were abolished immediately.[63] The referendum was followed by a health care reform crisis, discharge of the Minister of Health, and collapse of the government coalition.

The supplementary package includes a limited group of services excluded from the insurance and the basic package. Such services must be paid for fully by the patient, either out of pocket or by means of private health insurance. They include non-curative treatments for aesthetic or recreational purposes, nonmandatory vaccinations, medical certifications not relevant to patient care,[64] abortion and sterilization without medical necessity, prostate-specific antigen for general screening, alcohol and illicit drug tests for forensic purposes, alcohol and illicit drug detoxification, and manual therapy.[65] In addition, patients must cover the services obtained from private facilities operating in Hungary that have no contract with the NHIFA.

In summary, the right to health care in the HIF scheme includes a comprehensive benefit package with few services left out. Nevertheless, the burden of copayments has increased during recent years, especially regarding certain pharmaceuticals and medical aids. Copayments and informal payments entrenched in the system are strongly regressive elements that pose equity challenges. The next section discusses the mechanisms available to individuals to address equity issues and provides an overview of the litigation that has taken place in Hungary concerning access to health services and goods.

---

[60] Éva Orosz, *The Political Economy of the "Reform-Crises" in the Hungarian Healthcare System*, Conference presentation, Eötvös Loránd University (2009), *available at* http://egk.tatk.elte.hu/index.php?option=com_content&task=view&id=69&Itemid=44.

[61] E.g., the amount of the visit fee was fixed at 300 HUF (approx. €1.20) per doctor visit and a maximum of 6,000 HUF (€24) per calendar year.

[62] It is noteworthy that other, more substantial copayments were also introduced as part of the 2006–2007 reform but did not become a political issue. For example, the increase of copayments on pharmaceuticals was nearly four times higher but received much less attention. *See also* Orosz, *supra* note 60.

[63] *See* 2008. évi IX. törvény a 2008. március 9-i országos ügydöntő népszavazásokon hozott döntések végrehajtásáról [Act IX of 2008 on the Implementation of the Decisive National Referendums Held on Mar. 9, 2008] (Hung.), art. 1–3.

[64] E.g., certificates required for obtaining driving license, or for possession of firearms. The cost of occupational health examinations must be covered by the employer. Medical certifications required from social benefit applicants are covered by the insurance package.

[65] *See* 1997. évi LXXXIII. törvény a kötelező egészségbiztosítás ellátásairól [Act LXXXIII of 1997 on Services of Compulsory Health Insurance] (Hung.); 46/1997. (XII. 17) NM r. a kötelező egészségbiztosítás terhére igénybe nem vehető ellátásokról [Decree of the Minister of Welfare No. 46/1997 (XII.17) on Services that Cannot Be Used at the Cost of the Mandatory Health Insurance] (Hung.).

8.3 CHALLENGING EQUITY ISSUES AT THE PUBLIC-PRIVATE
INTERSECTION

For the reasons described in the preceding sections, it is important to distinguish between theory and practice when discussing equity in access to health care in Hungary. In theory, the organization and financing of the health system safeguards equitable access to a comprehensive package of health services funded predominantly from public sources. In practice, however, approximately 30 percent of health system financing derives from private sources made up largely of out-of-pocket payments including official copayments and illicit informal payments. Individuals have challenged such regressive elements through a range of mechanisms.

8.3.1 *Constitutional Litigation*

In Hungary, individuals can turn to the Constitutional Court to challenge the constitutionality of laws and to appeal judicial decisions on constitutional grounds.[66] Individuals have attempted several times to challenge health care laws and decisions of public authorities based on the constitutional right to health. Decisions of the Constitutional Court have contributed to the clarification of the scope and content of the constitutional right to the health.

During the first half of the 1990s, following the replacement of the previous, tax-based health system by the system of social health insurance, a number of submissions to the Constitutional Court contested the elements of this reform on the basis of the constitutional right to health. Elements challenged included, among others, the newly introduced financing methods, division of responsibilities between the state, local governments and the HIF, and responsibilities of county-level public health officers. The Court collected several submissions concerning the right to health and addressed them together in Decision 54/1996.

Decision 54/1996[67] provides a synthesis of the Court's interpretation of the scope and content of the constitutional right to health, and the Court has upheld this view in subsequent rulings.[68] The Court made it clear that the constitutional right to the highest possible level of health *could not be interpreted as an individual right that was justiciable.* Instead, Article 70/D(2) of the Constitution in force until 2012 formulated a *constitutional obligation for the state* to organize medical care and ensure the functioning of a system of health care institutions. It is left for the legislator to establish the catalog of these individual rights and regulate their enforcement. The Court also emphasized that the concept of *highest possible level*

---

[66] The Constitutional Court was established in 1989. *See* 1989. évi XXXII. törvény az Alkotmánybíróságról [Act XXXII of 1989 on the Constitutional Court] (Hung.).

[67] Alkotmánybíróság (AB) [Constitutional Court], MK.1996.(105) 54/1996. (XI. 30.) (Hung.), at 173.

[68] *See* Alkotmánybíróság (AB) [Constitutional Court] Sept. 9, 1998, 261/B/1997 (Hung.); Alkotmánybíróság (AB) [Constitutional Court] Dec. 16, 1996, 1316/B/1995 (Hung.).

was not absolute because its implementation was contingent on available economic resources and the capacity limits of the state and the health insurance system. In other words, the decision maker can take into account economic, institutional, and organizational considerations in addition to medical and technical considerations. Despite the broad formulation of the constitutional right to health, its interpretation by the Court has made it clear that individuals could not rely on this right in order to challenge inequities faced in the health system.

At the same time, the Constitutional Court indicated that there were other constitutional rights providing the basis for individual rights related to health care. One of these is patients' right to self-determination derived from the constitutional right to human dignity.[69] Another is the right to health care within the HIF scheme derived from the constitutional right to social security[70] and the constitutional protection of property.[71] It is noteworthy that the Court interprets the right to health care solely within the framework of the HIF scheme. It emphasizes that health care based on social insurance is a "purchased entitlement"[72] that is guaranteed by the state according to the requirements of the constitutional right to social security and the right to property, and is conditioned on membership in the HIF scheme. The new techniques for health care financing, the funding constraints imposed on medical treatment, and the new system of resource allocation must comply with the constitutional rights to social security and property. The right to health care within the HIF scheme is no longer based on citizenship, but instead on fulfillment of entitlement conditions including payment of insurance contributions.

The Court interpreted the constitutional right to social security as an individual right that created an obligation for the state to guarantee health care for members. This included the duty to ensure that no member is left without health care owing to lack of financial capacity.[73] The health system is constitutional as long as the state implements its guarantee (i.e., by supplementing the resources of the HIF from tax revenues, a state duty set forth in Parliamentary Act LXXX of 1997).[74] It is not a constitutional issue to determine whether the choices made by the state to fulfill its obligation are the appropriate ones, and whether the adopted measures are efficient. The state is given wide discretion in deciding how to organize, finance, and deliver health services, and the courts cannot question the appropriateness of these decisions, provided a minimal threshold is met. To date, the Court has not defined

---

[69] A Magyar Köztársaság Alkotmánya [Constitution of the Republic of Hungary], art. 54(1) (in force until Jan. 1, 2012); Magyarország Alaptörvénye [The Fundamental Law of Hungary], art II (in force since Jan. 1, 2012).

[70] A Magyar Köztársaság Alkotmánya, art. 70/E. The social security clause Magyarország Alaptörvénye, art. XIX includes an aspirational goal for the state to provide social security to its citizens. *See supra* part. 2.1.

[71] A Magyar Köztársaság Alkotmánya, art. 13; Magyarország Alaptörvénye, art. XIII.

[72] Alkotmánybíróság (AB), MK.1996.(105) 54/1996. (XI. 30.), at 190.

[73] *Id.*, at 190.

[74] *See* Act LXXX of 1997, art. 3(2).

this minimal threshold. The only example it has given so far is that the complete lack of health care institutions and medical care in a given region of the country would be unconstitutional.[75] So, one can conclude that the Court interpreted the right to health care within the HIF scheme as an obligation on the part of the state to provide social security but with latitude as to the specifics. Since the Fundamental Law of Hungary came into force in January 2012, it is still unclear to what extent the reformulation of the social security clause and omission of the rights language will weaken further individuals' possibilities to challenge inequities under this clause (see the discussion on the new phrasing in Subsection 8.2.1).

The Court has also ruled on the constitutionality of limits on funding of certain medical goods. Decision 517/B/2003[76] concerned the limits placed by the NHIFA on the subsidy of certain medical aids for patients suffering from incontinence. Patients' submissions focused on the argument that the increased share of copayments required for these aids violated their constitutional right to the highest possible level of health and to social security. The Court dismissed the submissions relying on its earlier Decision 54/1996. In particular, it emphasized that the constitutional right to health was not a justiciable individual right; instead, it formulated an obligation for the state that was conditional on available budgetary resources. The Court also relied on cost-containment and cost-efficiency arguments when dismissing the submission under the right to social security. It emphasized that it was at the discretion of the legislator to draw limits to the health benefit package, and that the Constitution did not impose on the state any obligation to fully subsidize a certain health service or good.

Patients' attempts to challenge the constitutionality of laws imposing copayments were equally unsuccessful. In Decision 179/I/2007 the President of the Constitutional Court addressed a submission challenging the flat-rate visit fees and hospital daily fees applied between 2007 and 2008 for services included in the insurance package (see the discussion of these copayments in Subsection 8.2.2). Patients argued that such copayments violated the constitutional right to free health care and imposed a double burden on insured persons who were already required to pay insurance contributions. The Court found this submission unfounded and dismissed it, finding yet again that the constitutional right to health did not guarantee an individual right but formulated a state duty that provided a wide discretion for the decision maker.

8.3.2 *Other Mechanisms*

Beyond challenges in the Constitutional Court, individuals have tried to use other mechanisms to improve equitable access to health care. Those mechanisms include the Commissioner for Fundamental Rights – hereafter the ombudsman's

---

[75] Alkotmánybíróság (AB), MK.1996.(105) 54/1996. (XI. 30.), at 187.
[76] Alkotmánybíróság (AB), 517/B/2003. (XII. 12.).

office – where individuals have challenged copayments based on the constitutional right to health and to social security. The ombudsman's office was established in 1993, empowered to investigate complaints by citizens, conduct systematic investigations into violations of constitutional rights, and initiate general or particular measures for their redress.[77] Examples for such measures include, among others, initiating the review of rules of law at the Constitutional Court, submitting annual reports to parliament with recommendations and proposals for regulations or amendments, proposing amendments to laws affecting fundamental rights. Anybody whose fundamental rights may have been violated as a result of an action or omission by a public authority established by law can apply to the ombudsman.[78]

The challenges to copayments brought to the ombudsman's office have focused mostly on access to medicinal products, arguing that rules excluding certain products from the insurance package or imposing high copayments violated the constitutional right to health. Other issues concerned copayments charged for access to services provided within the HIF scheme, such as visit fees for outpatient services, including general practitioner care. The ombudsman's office has addressed these challenges by issuing recommendations to relevant authorities. It emphasized safeguarding the principle of equal opportunities in access to essential medicines and medical aids.[79] It has recommended to the Minister of Health to initiate the inclusion of certain medicinal products and medical devices in the insurance package and/or increase the share of subsidy. Examples include recommendations to include in the insurance package certain Alzheimer's disease medication,[80] include a follow-up treatment for Heine-Medin disease,[81] and increase the subsidy for a specific migraine medication (Imigran).[82] The Ministry of Health has followed some of

---

[77] Before January 1, 2012, there were four Parliamentary Commissioners in Hungary: one for Civil Rights with a General Deputy, one for Data Protection and Freedom of Information, one for the Rights of National and Ethnic Minorities and one for Future Generations. Starting January 1, 2012, their responsibilities have been taken over by the Office of the Commissioner for Fundamental Rights, the legal successor of the Parliamentary Commissioner for Civil Rights.

[78] 2011. évi CXI. törvény az alapvető jogok biztosáról [Act CXI of 2011 on the Commissioner for Fundamental Rights] (Hung.).

[79] Állampolgári Jogok Országgyűlési Biztosa, Beszámoló az Állampolgári Jogok Országgyűlési Biztosának és Általános Helyettesének 2006. Évi Tevékenységéről, [Parliamentary Commissioner for Civil Rights. Annual Report on the Activities of the Parliamentary Commissioner and the Deputy Commissioner for Civil Rights in 2006] (2006).

[80] Case No. OBH 5164/2002, Állampolgári Jogok Országgyűlési Biztosa, Beszámoló Az Állampolgári Jogok Országgyűlési Biztosának És Általános Helyettesének 2003. Évi Tevékenységéről, [Parliamentary Commissioner for Civil Rights. Annual Report on the Activities of the Parliamentary Commissioner and the Deputy Commissioner for Civil Rights in 2003] (2003).

[81] Case No. OBH 4243/1997, Állampolgári Jogok Országgyűlési Biztosa, Beszámoló Az Állampolgári Jogok Országgyűlési Biztosának És Általános Helyettesének 1998. Évi Tevékenységéről, [Parliamentary Commissioner for Civil Rights. Annual Report on the Activities of the Parliamentary Commissioner and the Deputy Commissioner for Civil Rights in 1998] (1998).

[82] Case No. OBH 4920/1998, Állampolgári Jogok Országgyűlési Biztosa, Beszámoló az Állampolgári Jogok Országgyűlési Biztosának és Általános Helyettesének 1999. Évi Tevékenységéről, [Parliamentary

the ombudsman's recommendations. For example, it decided to increase the subsidy of specific Alzheimer's disease medication (Aricept and Exelon) from zero to 50 percent. This has improved access to this treatment for 5,000 patients registered in Alzheimer's disease centers. The Ministry of Health also ensured coverage of follow-up treatment for patients suffering from Heine-Medin disease. Another example concerns the visit fee discussed in Subsection 8.2.2. Further to the recommendation made by the ombudsman during the process of drafting the law on visit fees, children younger than eighteen and full-time students were exempted from its application.[83] In addition, at the ombudsman's recommendation, a long-term care institution ceased to charge unlawful copayments for medical tests required to establish patient treatment plans and compensated the patients who had already incurred these copayments.[84]

In other cases, recommendations of the ombudsman have failed to initiate any change, for example in the case challenging high copayments for migraine medication (Imigran). In this case, the ombudsman concluded that the high copayments required from patients made access to treatment impossible, which violated the constitutional right to health. The Minister of Health decided, however, not to follow the ombudsman's recommendation to make this treatment more accessible by increasing the share of its subsidy. Another example is the refusal of the NHIFA to follow the recommendation of the ombudsman concerning reimbursement of travel expenses that prevented the parents of a child hospitalized in another city to visit him regularly. The NHIFA argued that the HIF was not obliged to cover all travel-related expenses of patients and their relatives.[85] Yet another case concerned access to a certain cancer treatment medicine: although the medicine at issue was known and used successfully in international medical practice, it was not granted marketing authorization in Hungary and was therefore excluded from the insurance package.[86] Based on recent research results, the physician of the patients concerned intended to use the medicine at issue for a condition for which it was not approved by the NHIFA. The NHIFA refused to grant approval, and the patients concerned did not get access to the medicine despite their willingness to pay for it. In this case,

---

Commissioner for Civil Rights. Annual Report on the Activities of the Parliamentary Commissioner and the Deputy Commissioner for Civil Rights in 1999] (1999).

[83] Állampolgári Jogok Országgyűlési Biztosa, Beszámoló az Állampolgári Jogok Országgyűlési Biztosának és Általános Helyettesének 2007. Évi Tevékenységéről, [Parliamentary Commissioner for Civil Rights. Annual Report on the Activities of the Parliamentary Commissioner and the Deputy Commissioner for Civil Rights in 2007] (2007).

[84] Case No. OBH 3316/1999, Annual Report on the Activities of the Parliamentary Commissioner for Civil Rights and Its General Deputy, *supra* note 82.

[85] Case No. OBH 1263/2005, Annual Report on the Activities of the Parliamentary Commissioner for Civil Rights and Its General Deputy, *supra* note 79.

[86] Case No. OBH 1655/2004, Állampolgári Jogok Országgyűlési Biztosa, Beszámoló az Állampolgári Jogok Országgyűlési Biztosának és Általános Helyettesének 2004. Évi Tevékenységéről, [Parliamentary Commissioner for Civil Rights. Annual Report on the Activities of the Parliamentary Commissioner and the Deputy Commissioner for Civil Rights in 2004] (2004).

the rights-based review applied by the ombudsman extended to the right to dignity and autonomy (personal and financial). The recommendation of the ombudsman emphasized that procedural debates concerning in-country registration of medicines were not supposed to lead to violation of these fundamental rights through a denial of care. The ombudsman argued that financial considerations did not justify the NHIFA's decision to limit and/or prohibit the use of medicines that were necessary and recommended by doctors. However, neither the Minister of Health nor the NHIFA followed that recommendation.

It is noteworthy that the ombudsman has proved to be an institution that is accessible to individuals and that is willing to undertake a mediating role between individuals and authorities in cases concerning access to treatment, medicinal products, and nursing services. The ombudsman has emphasized repeatedly the equity concerns linked to partial or total exclusion of services from the insurance package and high out-of-pocket payments. In particular, it has initiated negotiations with the NHIFA with the aim to promote a more patient-centered approach that could compensate for the rigid financial considerations dominating the NHIFA's decisions on subsidizing medicines and medical aids.[87] Nevertheless, one should bear in mind that recommendations of the ombudsman are not binding and thus do not have the strength of a court decision.

Another mechanism individuals formerly could use to challenge copayments was the Health Insurance Supervisory Authority (HISA). The HISA was created in 2007 and operated until September 2010 as a public body designated to strengthen consumers' rights within the HIF scheme.[88] Its responsibilities included:

1. protecting patients' rights;
2. providing information to the public on the health insurance system and health care providers;
3. overseeing the contracts between providers and the NHIFA and monitoring fulfilment of contractual obligations;
4. performing service quality control;
5. monitoring waiting times in selected procedures on the basis of provider reports;
6. conducting targeted inspections focused on issues of access and equity (i.e., management of waiting lists, respect for equal treatment, application of copayments, continuous availability of services, etc.).[89]

---

[87] Állampolgári Jogok Országgyűlési Biztosa, Beszámoló az Állampolgári Jogok Országgyűlési Biztosának és Általános Helyettesének 2002. Évi Tevékenységéről, [Parliamentary Commissioner for Civil Rights. Annual Report on the Activities of the Parliamentary Commissioner and the Deputy Commissioner for Civil Rights in 2002] (2002).

[88] 2006. évi CXVI. törvény az egészségbiztosítás hatósági felügyeletéről (Act CXVI of 2006 on Supervision of Health Insurance) (Hung.).

[89] Among other duties, the HISA created and operated a quality indicator system suitable for measuring, evaluating, and comparing/ranking the health care providers contracted. Results of the comparative assessment were published on a yearly basis.

Patients could submit complaints against health care providers operating within
the HIF scheme (i.e., contracted by the NHIFA) and/or against the NHIFA. In
addition, the HISA could investigate cases at its own instigation. It could call on
health care providers to fulfill their contractual obligations and terminate unlawful practices. Depending on the seriousness of the violation committed by the
provider, it could impose a fine and eventually call on the NHIFA to suspend or
terminate the financing contract with the provider concerned. The complaint procedure was designed in a way to ensure easy access: individuals were exempted
from any costs,[90] they could submit a complaint by several methods, and short
procedures with strict deadlines were ensured.[91] Minorities were entitled to use
their own languages. The HISA was not empowered to award compensation for
patients, but could advise patients with compensation claims to initiate civil lawsuits. Parties involved could request judicial review of the HISA's decisions. The
government disestablished the HISA in September 2010,[92] and its responsibilities
were divided among several other public institutions. Since September 2010, complaints related to health care services provided within the HIF scheme have been
addressed by the Hungarian National Public Health and Medical Officer Service.
Starting September 2012, a new patients' rights institution named National Center
for Patients' Rights, Children's Rights and Documentation[93] began to operate under
the supervision of the State Secretariat for Health. This institution is responsible for
examining patient complaints, informing patients and providers about health care
rights, and creating the institutional background for the operation of patient rights
representatives.

During its short time of existence, patients made extensive use of the HISA to
voice their dissatisfaction with access to health care services and goods within the
HIF scheme. Between March 2007 and May 2010, the HISA issued more than 1,300
decisions resulting from patient complaints and its own investigations.[94] Some of
these complaints challenged copayments. An analysis of the submissions reveals,
however, that patients used the HISA to challenge incorrect or unlawful practices
of individual health care providers rather than contest legal norms establishing
copayments or NHIFA decisions. Examples of issues include:

---

[90] Between July 2008 and August 2010, the HISA covered the costs of complaints that proved to be
unjustified. Costs of justified complaints were charged to the health care provider concerned.

[91] The time limit was established at thirty days with the possibility of the HISA's president to prolong it
once with additional thirty days. When other organizations were consulted as part of the investigation,
the period of awaiting the response was added to the originally set time limit.

[92] See 2010. évi LXXXIX. törvény egyes egészségügyi és szociális tárgyú törvények módosításáról (Act
LXXXIX of 2010 on Amendment of Certain Laws Concerning Health Care and Social Affairs).

[93] The Hungarian name of this new institution is Országos Betegjogi, Ellátottjogi, Gyermekjogi és
Dokumentációs Központ (OBDK).

[94] Complaints investigated and decisions issued were posted on the website of the HISA, http://www.
ebf.hu (website no longer available), for complaints see e.g. nn. 95–100.

1. incorrect or unlawful application of visit fees, hospital daily fees, and other copayments;[95]
2. failure of the provider to inform patients about the possibility to opt for services that do not require copayments;[96]
3. conditioning free choice of hospital doctors on unlawful copayment and other illicit rules in case of maternity care;[97]
4. inappropriate separation of financed and non-covered (supplementary package) services;[98]
5. equality in placement on waiting lists;[99]
6. postponement of necessary care motivated by lack/ shortage of financing.[100]

In response to such challenges, the HISA aimed at terminating unlawful practices of individual health service providers and preventing them from recurring.

Patients can also turn to the Equal Treatment Authority (ETA) when they face a violation of the equal treatment principle. This authority was established in 2004 as a central budgetary agency.[101] Its responsibilities include conducting self-initiated investigations with regard to observance of the equal treatment principle, initiating lawsuits (pursuant to the right of *actio popularis*), imposing fines or other sanctions if a violation is found, and commenting on draft laws, governmental decisions, and other instruments of public administration. Its decisions are subject to judicial review. Health care–related complaints submitted to the ETA have mainly related to discrimination in employment and education based on the person's health condition and disability. A number of cases also concerned equality in access to information on pharmaceuticals. A patients' rights organization has submitted several complaints challenging the failure of distributors of pharmaceutical products to provide information leaflets in Braille or an electronic format as required by visually impaired

---

[95] *See e.g.*, Case 773–5/HAT/JHF/2007 Egészségbiztosítási felügyelet (Ebf) [HISA] May 29, 2007; Case 145–5/HAT/JHF/2007 Egészségbiztosítási felügyelet (Ebf) [HISA] Apr. 6, 2007; Case 138–5/HAT/JHF/ 2007 Egészségbiztosítási felügyelet (Ebf) [HISA] Mar. 30, 2007; Case 26–10/ESZOLG/EF/ 2007 Egészségbiztosítási felügyelet (Ebf) [HISA] Mar. 30, 2007. The HISA decisions were posted on the HISA website, but the names of the complainants were deleted. The HISA was closed in 2010, and the decisions are no longer available online.

[96] Case 2511–6/HAT/JHF/2007 Egészségbiztosítási felügyelet (Ebf) [HISA] Oct. 29, 2007.

[97] Case 968–14/2010 Egészségbiztosítási felügyelet (Ebf) [HISA] Apr. 20, 2010.

[98] Case 2794–41/2009 Egészségbiztosítási felügyelet (Ebf) [HISA] Aug. 31, 2009; Case 494–20/2009 Egészségbiztosítási felügyelet (Ebf) [HISA] Jun. 15, 2009.

[99] *See e.g.*, Case 737–13/HAT/JHF/2008 Egészségbiztosítási felügyelet (Ebf) [HISA] Jul. 11, 2008; Case 985–7/HAT/JHF/2008 Egészségbiztosítási felügyelet (Ebf) [HISA] Mar. 20, 2008.

[100] Case 24–5/ESZOLG/EF/2007 Egészségbiztosítási felügyelet (Ebf) [HISA] Mar. 14, 2007; Case 172– 5/HAT/JHF/2007 Egészségbiztosítási felügyelet (Ebf) [HISA] Mar. 30, 2007; Case 379–3/ESZOLG/ EF/2007 Egészségbiztosítási felügyelet (Ebf) [HISA] Mar. 14, 2007; Case 2740–5/HAT/JHF/2007 Egészségbiztosítási felügyelet (Ebf) [HISA] Nov. 27, 2007.

[101] The Hungarian name of this authority is Egyenlö Bánásmód Hatóság. *See* 2003. évi CXXV. törvény az egyenlö bánásmódról és az esélyegyenlöség elömozdításáról [Act CXXV of 2003 on Equal Treatment and Promotion of Equal Opportunities], chap. V/A.

persons.[102] Further to negotiations mediated by the ETA, the patient rights' organization and distributors reached agreement on the issue. These cases have resulted in progressive outcomes through increasing equality in access to information on pharmaceuticals.

As shown above, there are several mechanisms in the Hungarian health system designed to address complaints of individuals concerning inequity in access to health care. Constitutional litigation has not been very successful because of the reluctance of the Constitutional Court to second-guess governmental decisions concerning health care organization and financing. The ombudsman has undertaken a mediating role between individuals and authorities in cases concerning equity in access to health care. In some cases, its intervention was successful and brought about progressive outcomes, but it is not guaranteed that authorities will always follow the ombudsman's recommendations. Other mechanisms such as the HISA only redressed violations of health care rights by individual service providers and did not review acts and decisions of authorities performing public services.

If an individual is unsatisfied with the response of these institutions, he or she can still opt for a civil lawsuit. Patients opting for extrajudicial settlement can also make use of the mediation service. However, individuals rarely challenge health equity issues in Hungarian civil courts. So far, health care–related lawsuits have largely concerned medical negligence cases based on delictual liability under the Hungarian Civil Code.[103] Nevertheless, medical negligence litigation has contributed to strengthening the right to health care and other patients' rights in Hungary. As show by an extensive analysis of medical malpractice litigation during the first half of the 1990s,[104] such litigation was an important contributing factor to the adoption of Act CLIV of 1997 on Health. This act codifies patients' rights and establishes institutions designated to enforce these rights, in particular the institution of patients' rights representatives.[105] Such representatives are responsible for assisting patients with access to rights information and enforcement. In case of violation of the right to health care and other patient rights, the representatives help patients formulate their complaints, submit complaints to the management and the owner of the health care facility, suggest remedies, and represent patients in procedures with the authorities concerned. Health care providers are obliged to operate an internal system that addresses patient complains. According to the 2002 report of the ombudsman, the number of complaints submitted to its office concerning the right to health has

---

[102] See Decisions No. 723/2008, 731/2008, 732/2008 and 733/2008 Egyenlö Bánásmód Hatóság (EBH) [Equal Treatment Authority] (Jun. 2008), available at http://www.egyenlobanasmod.hu/jogesetek/jogesetek#y2008.

[103] Judit Sándor, Gyógyítás és Ítélkezés. Orvosi "Műhiba" Perek Magyarországon [Medicine and Jurisprudence: Medical Malpractice Litigation in Hungary], (1997).

[104] Sándor, supra note 103.

[105] Sándor, supra note 45, at 73–74.

decreased significantly as a result of the work of patients' rights representatives who are equipped to address such complaints within the health care facility itself.[106]

8.3.3 *Challenging Informal Payments*

As discussed earlier, one of the most regressive elements in the Hungarian health care system is the persistence of informal payments. Despite their negative impact on equity, patients rarely challenge such payments. The burden is on the patient to prove that health care professionals asked for informal payments as a condition for providing the necessary services. In such cases, the law regards informal payments as illicit fees amounting to bribery and corruption, and criminal proceedings can be initiated against health care personnel accepting them. However, the law does not punish gratitude payments offered voluntarily by patients. In fact, the Hungarian Labour Code in force since July 2012 allows for employees to accept fees or gifts from third parties if the employer approves this in advance.[107] The management of health care institutions is thus allowed to approve the acceptance of gifts offered by patients to medical personnel if such gifts are voluntarily provided after the treatment. Unless the patient is able to prove that the treatment was conditional on payment of informal charges, it is unlikely his or her challenge will be successful.

The difficulties met by patients in challenging informal payments are illustrated by the relevant decisions of the HISA. The number of complaints about informal payments is very low: out of the 1,304 complaints investigated by the HISA between January 2007 and August 2010, only 3 were related to informal charges (all charged within the HIF scheme). In two of these cases, the treatment provider denied acceptance of informal charges and the HISA concluded that there was no evidence proving their receipt.[108] In the third case, the provider admitted acceptance of informal charges and justified it as a means to ensure trust in the relationship with the patient and her relatives.[109] The provider denied that provision and quality of services were by any means made conditional on receipt of informal charges. The HISA concluded its investigation by rejecting the complaint on the basis that there was no evidence proving that the services obtained were conditional in any way on informal payments. None of the HISA's decisions were submitted to judicial review by the complainants.

---

[106] Állampolgári Jogok Országgyűlési Biztosa, Beszámoló az Állampolgári Jogok Országgyűlési Biztosának és Általános Helyettesének 2002. Évi Tevékenységéről [Parliamentary Commissioner for Civil Rights. Annual Report on the Activities of the Parliamentary Commissioner and the Deputy Commissioner for Civil Rights in 2002] (2002).

[107] 2012. évi I. törvény a munka törvénykönyvéről [Act I of 2012 on the Labour Code] (Hung.), art. 52(2)-(4).

[108] Case 1177–1/2010 Egészségbiztosítási felügyelet (Ebf) [HISA] Feb, 15, 2010; Case 176–25/2009 Egészségbiztosítási felügyelet (Ebf) [HISA] Nov. 23, 2009.

[109] Case 574–15/2009 Egészségbiztosítási felügyelet (Ebf) [HISA] Jun. 5, 2009.

These cases reflect the fee-for-service character of informal payments (as opposed to voluntary expression of gratitude). They reveal that patients' main motivation was ensuring proper attention and care on behalf of medical professionals. Only one of the complaints challenged the fact that provision of services was conditional on informal charges. The other two complaints argued that despite the acceptance of informal charges, doctors failed to provide services of appropriate quality and effectiveness. These patients did not challenge the informal payment itself but complained about failure of doctors to provide proper care despite the informal payment. The complaints reveal that patients perceived informal charges as a necessary financial sacrifice expected by providers and a means to secure a "right to better and more effective treatment" within the HIF scheme. Informal payments persist and raise fundamental issues about patient-doctor relationship.

8.4 FINAL REMARKS

The Hungarian health system is a two-tier system composed of the public, compulsory HIF scheme and private, non-contracted providers. The latter operate alongside the public system and rely largely on out-of-pocket payments by patients who are not satisfied with the services provided within the HIF scheme and are willing and able to opt for a privately provided alternative.

The HIF scheme includes a comprehensive health package with a large share of services fully covered. Providers can charge copayments for a limited range of services established by law. Some pharmaceuticals and medical aids are fully subsidized, but others are only partly subsidized, and the share of copayments can be significant. A limited number of services are excluded from the benefit package (mainly non-curative interventions, nonmandatory vaccinations, and certifications not relevant to patient care). Opting out of the compulsory system is prohibited, but patients may purchase complementary private health insurance to cover copayments and/or services excluded from the benefit package. Consolidation of social health insurance in health care financing has been high on the political agenda but is hindered by persistent challenges. Failure of attempts to involve private actors and funding in social health insurance illustrates that a clear and coherent vision on the expected role of the market, the state, and patients in health care is yet to be developed.[110]

The Hungarian case illustrates that recognition of health care rights encompassing the idea of accessibility is not sufficient for ensuring equity if implementation of these rights is distorted by regressive elements like out-of-pocket payments. Informal payments are particularly regressive; they constitute a major challenge to equity by placing a proportionally higher financial burden on low-income groups. Informal charges widen the gap between the rich and the poor and strengthen the view that

---

[110] See also *supra* note 60, for the analysis of Orosz on the economic, political, and health policy factors that reversed the process of health care reforms initiated in 2006–2007.

access to appropriate health care within the HIF scheme is a commodity purchased by those who can afford it. Rights-based review and litigation has not yet meaningfully addressed the issue of informal payments. Because the burden of proof is on the patient, litigation is difficult and patients very rarely challenge informal payments.

Choice between health services provided in the HIF scheme and services available at non-contracted private facilities is as a privilege reserved for those who have the financial means to afford it. As ruled by the Constitutional Court, the right to health care is only an individual right within the context of the HIF scheme.[111] In other words, access to health care outside the public scheme is not a right, but a privilege won by those with financial means. The commitment of the health system to the principles of equity, universality, and accessibility is shaken by turning access to health care at private, non-contracted providers into a privilege enjoyed only by higher-income groups.

Despite the existence of constitutional rights to health and social security, constitutional litigation to date has not been effective in addressing equity issues in access to health care. The Constitutional Court has dismissed claims challenging the legitimacy of individual copayments and is reluctant to extend review of state decisions to those concerning the health package. The Court interprets the right to health care as constrained by budgetary considerations and leaves it at the discretion of decision makers to draw limits to health care coverage. The Constitutional Court decisions discussed in this chapter show that it is unlikely that state decisions concerning the health package are justiciable in constitutional terms.

The Hungarian context illustrates the importance of making the mechanisms of health rights enforcement accessible also to disadvantaged, low-income groups. Empowerment of such groups is crucial in ensuring that those most affected by limitations on health service coverage can voice their needs. One method of ensuring this is establishing rights enforcement institutions in health care that are easily accessible to individuals from lower-income groups. Examples discussed in the Hungarian context include the ombudsman's office, the institution of patients' rights representatives, and the (former) Health Insurance Supervisory Authority (HISA). These mechanisms ensure access for low-income groups by exempting complainants from procedural costs. Individuals have used these institutions to voice their dissatisfaction with copayments charged for health services and goods and other inequities. Authorities can promote access to these mechanisms by taking into account specific needs of vulnerable groups. This remains an important task for future health care reforms.

---

[111] Alkotmánybíróság (AB), MK.1996.(105) 54/1996. (XI. 30.), at 173.

9

Lending a Helping Hand

The Impact of Constitutional Interpretation on Taiwan's National Health Insurance Program, Health Equity, and Distributive Justice

Y. Y. Brandon Chen

INTRODUCTION

Taiwan's universal health care program – the National Health Insurance (NHI) – was launched in 1995. While it has enjoyed strong popular support,[1] the program has also stirred legal debates over the role of government and the scope of personal liberties. To date, Taiwan's Constitutional Court has issued six constitutional interpretations relating to the NHI.[2] Through these decisions, the Constitutional Court shaped the NHI's overarching philosophy by articulating an obligation for everyone, particularly the rich, to contribute to the program, and sowing the seeds for a constitutional right to health insurance, especially for the disadvantaged. As a result, the NHI was considered by some to have been transformed from a scheme that was purely social insurance by design to one with a social assistance flair,[3] thus enhancing its capacity to advance health care equity and distributive justice.[4]

---

[1] Jui-Fen Rachel Lu & William Hsiao, *Does Universal Health Insurance Make Healthcare Unaffordable? Lessons from Taiwan*, 22 HEALTH AFF. 77, 85 (2003).

[2] Article 78 of Taiwan's Constitution, *infra* note 52, bestows on the Constitutional Court the authority to engage in constitutional interpretation. Pursuant to art. 4 of the Constitutional Interpretation Procedure Act, *infra* note 59, Justices of the Constitutional Court have the power to decide "[m]atters concerning doubts and ambiguities in the application of the Constitution" as well as "the constitutionality of statutes or regulations." If a law or regulation is found in conflict with the Constitution, it is rendered invalid. The requests for constitutional interpretation can be brought by central or local government bodies, Taiwan's legislative assembly with endorsement from one-third of its members, a legal person whose constitutional rights have been breached and who has exhausted all other legal remedies, or judges at all levels who believe the law or regulation to be applied in a case is unconstitutional.

[3] CHEN YINGQIN (陳櫻琴), HUANG YUYU (黃于玉) & YAN ZHONGHAN (顏忠漢), YILIAO FALÜ (醫療法律) [HEALTH LAW] 376 (4th ed. 2007).

[4] For the purpose of this chapter, health equity refers to the pursuit of eliminating systemic health disparities that arise from socioeconomic differences such as race/ethnicity, sex/gender, and socioeconomic status. Distributive justice in health care, in comparison, describes the endeavor to achieve health equity through reallocation of society's burdens and benefits such that health resources are

The viability of a human rights–based strategy in achieving distributive justice and health equity is increasingly under scrutiny. For example, after examining the outcomes of bill of rights litigation in Canada, Israel, New Zealand, and South Africa, Ran Hirschl concluded that human rights have largely been conceptualized in individualistic, antistatist terms, and consequently they have played a minor role in wealth redistribution and equalization of life conditions.[5] Regarding the right to health specifically, both Donna Greschner and Aeyal Gross similarly observed a tendency for the adjudication of rights to focus on individual interests, potentially at the expense of collective considerations and social contexts.[6] As such, the Taiwanese Constitutional Court's dismissal of legal challenges based on individualistic rights, in favor of collectivist principles, represents an intriguing point of contrast for scholars. By examining the Taiwanese experience, this chapter hopes to illustrate the potential for a rights-based approach, when infused with collective values, to safeguard the public health care system and in turn facilitate progressive reallocation of health resources. Furthermore, this chapter urges the judiciary to adopt a broad understanding of the right to health, which embraces not only access to health care but also social determinants of health, in order to better achieve the goal of health equity.

9.1 OVERVIEW OF TAIWAN'S HEALTH CARE SYSTEM AND THE NATIONAL HEALTH INSURANCE

Before the establishment of the NHI, there were ten social insurance schemes in Taiwan, the largest of which were Labor Insurance, Government Employee's Insurance, and Farmer's Insurance. Under this patchwork of programs, more than eight million Taiwanese were reportedly without any health insurance, the majority of whom were children, adults older than sixty-five, and unemployed individuals.[7] In 1986, reacting to strong demands from the public and the opposition party, the executive branch of the Taiwanese government (i.e., the Executive Yuan) announced an agenda to implement a national health insurance system.[8] Ultimately, the National

---

collected based on ability to pay and distributed according to needs. Allocative decisions that facilitate such distributive justice are considered progressive in nature, whereas the converse – namely, a system of allocation where financial burdens of health are disproportionally placed on the less well-off – is deemed regressive.

[5] Ran Hirschl, Towards Juristocracy: The Origins and Consequences of the New Constitutionalism 146–148 & 150–151 (2d ed. 2007).

[6] Donna Greschner, Charter *Challenges and Evidence Based Decision Making in the Healthcare System: Towards a Symbiotic Relationship*, in Just Medicare: What's In, What's Out, How We Decide 42, 44 (Colleen M. Flood ed., 2006); Aeyal M. Gross, *The Right to Health in an Era of Privatisation and Globalisation*, in Exploring Social Rights: Between Theory and Practice 289, 298 (Daphne Barak-Erez & Aeyal M. Gross, eds., 2007).

[7] Tsung-Mei Cheng, *Taiwan's New National Health Insurance Program: Genesis and Experience So Far*, 22 Health Aff. 61, 63 (2003).

[8] *Id.*, at 63. *See also* Tung-Liang Chiang, *Taiwan's 1995 Healthcare Reform* 39 Health Pol'y 225, 226–29 (1997).

Health Insurance Act (NHI Act) was promulgated in August 1994 and the NHI was officially launched on March 1, 1995.[9]

Within a decade of its introduction, the NHI managed to reduce the proportion of uninsured individuals from 41 percent of the population to less than 1 percent, achieving virtually universal coverage.[10] Studies have shown that by 1996, the frequency of health services utilization among those previously uninsured had risen to a level on par with individuals already insured before the NHI.[11] Moreover, under the NHI, the poorest quintile of the population was found in 1998 to enjoy 1.8 times the amount of health benefits for each dollar of premium paid as compared to the richest quintile, suggesting relatively progressive reallocation of health resources.[12] Comparing the WHO's Fairness in Financial Contribution Index pre- and post-NHI, researchers have found that health care financing in Taiwan has become more equitable since the advent of the universal health care program.[13]

By design, the NHI is a government-run program with compulsory enrollment. As a single-payer scheme, the NHI is administered by the Bureau of National Health Insurance (BNHI), which collects premiums from the insured, employers, and the government, contracts health facilities to provide comprehensive health services to the insured, and reimburses providers based on a global budget approach.[14] In this section, I briefly review Taiwan's health care delivery system and the NHI's modus operandi.

9.1.1 Health Care Delivery System

According to 2012 statistics, there were 502 hospitals and 20,935 clinics across Taiwan, offering Western medicine, traditional Chinese medicine, and dental care.[15] Correspondingly, there were 40,000-plus physicians who practice Western medicine, more than 5,700 Chinese medicine doctors, and more than 12,000 dentists in the

---

[9] Quanmin Jiankang Baoxian Fa [NHI Act] (2010) (amended 2011) (Taiwan), QUANGUO FAGUI, *available at* http://law.moj.gov.tw. For the purpose of this chapter, references to specific provisions in the NHI Act concern the 2010 version of the law unless otherwise clarified.

[10] Simon Li, Legislative Council Secretariat, Healthcare Financing Policies of Canada, the United Kingdom and Taiwan 33, 36 (2006) (H.K.), *available at* http://www.legco.gov.hk/yr06–07/english/sec/library/0607rp02-e.pdf.

[11] Chiang, *supra* note 8, at 233. *See also* Lik Wang Chen et al., *The Effects of Taiwan's National Health Insurance on Access and Health Status of the Elderly*, 16 HEALTH ECON. 223 (2007).

[12] Tung-Liang Chiang, *Tackling Health Inequalities through Universal Health Insurance: Lessons from Taiwan, in* YILIAO QIONGREN BUZAIYOU (醫療窮人不再有) [NO MORE MEDICALLY INDIGENT] 105, 109–110 (2008).

[13] Lu & Hsiao, *supra* note 1, at 81.

[14] Cheng, *supra* note 7, at 64. *See also* Li, *supra* note 10, at 34.

[15] Dep't of Health, Minguo Yibailingyi Nian Yiliao Jigou ji Yiyuan Yiliao Fuwuliang Tongji Fenxi (民國101年醫療機構現況及醫院醫療服務量統計分析) [Statistical Analysis of Health Care Institution Status and Hospital Service Provision in 2012] 1 (2013) (Taiwan) [hereinafter DoH Report], *available at* http://www.mohw.gov.tw/cht/DOS/Statistic.aspx?f_list_no=312&fod_list_no=1602.

country.[16] While each health care facility on average serviced approximately 1,100 individuals, there were 2.5 medical practitioners (or 1.7 Western-style medical doctors) per 1,000 persons.[17] The majority of the health care facilities in Taiwan are privately owned, and physicians and dentists either work as salaried hospital staff or operate their own clinics.[18]

There are more than 160,000 clinic/hospital beds in Taiwan. While there are 3.2 acute care beds per 1,000 persons, a ratio comparable to the OECD median of 3.1, only 66.2 percent of these beds are occupied versus the OECD median rate of 75 percent.[19] This relatively low level of bed occupancy reflects excess capacity in Taiwan's health care system. In this environment, patients in Taiwan are found to generally experience short wait times, if any.[20]

9.1.2 *Health Care Financing*

Taiwan's health care delivery system is mainly financed by funds collected via the NHI,[21] of which more than 90 percent consists of insurance premiums.[22] By law, all Taiwanese residents, including noncitizens with valid residency documents, are required to enroll in the NHI.[23] The amount of premium payable by the insured roughly corresponds to one's monthly wage and the number of dependents.[24] Depending on the status and nature of their employment, insured persons may have portions of the premium paid by their employers and/or the government. For example, whereas self-employed entrepreneurs and their dependents are liable for all of the required contributions, employees of private companies pay only 30 percent of their premium, with the remainder paid by their employers (60 percent) and the government (10 percent). For low-income families, service personnel, and veterans, the government subsidizes 100 percent of their premiums.[25]

---

[16] *Id.*, at table 28.

[17] *Id.*, at 3, 5 & 8.

[18] Cheng, *supra* note 7, at 61–62.

[19] DoH Report, *supra* note 15, at 9, 13 & 21.

[20] Cheng, *supra* note 7, at 62 & 64.

[21] Yasushi Iwamoto et al., Policy Options for Health Insurance and Long-Term Care Insurance 9 (2005), *available at* http://www.esri.go.jp/jp/prj-2004_2005/macro/macro16/09–1-R.pdf.

[22] Li, *supra* note 10, at 40. Beside premiums, the NHI is funded by a portion of the social health and welfare surcharge imposed on tobacco and alcoholic products and by parts of the surplus from Taiwan's welfare lottery.

[23] NHI Act, *supra* note 9, arts. 10 & 11–1. However, pursuant to art. 11 of the NHI Act (2010), individuals who are imprisoned or detained as a result of criminal convictions are currently excluded from the NHI program. Following the 2011 amendments, these persons will be granted health coverage.

[24] Li, *supra* note 10, at 39.

[25] Bureau of National Health Insurance, National Health Insurance in Taiwan 2012–2013 Annual Report 16 (2011) (Taiwan) [hereinafter 2012–2013 Annual Report], *available at* http://www.nhi.gov.tw/Resource/webdata/13767_1_NHI_2012-2013%20ANNUAL%20REPORT.pdf.

Other than the NHI, private expenditures represent another significant financial source for Taiwan's health care system, although its proportion among the
overall health outlays has decreased after the NHI's implementation.[26] Generally,
Taiwanese patients could incur out-of-pocket expenses on at least three occasions.
First, as of June 2012, less than 8 percent of health facilities in the country did not
contract with the BNHI,[27] and if patients wish to obtain care from these establishments, they would have to purchase services privately except in time of emergency
where subsequent reimbursement from the BNHI is possible.[28]

Second, even when patients access NHI-contracted health services, they are
required to make various copayments. For instance, when seeking outpatient services, the insured are liable for copayments ranging from NT$50 (1 U.S. Dollar =
approximately 30 New Taiwan Dollars) to NT$450 depending on the nature of ser-
vices accessed, the type of health facilities visited, and whether or not the services
were obtained following referrals. For hospitalizations, the insured pay between 5
percent and 30 percent of the cost – up to a predetermined copayment ceiling –
depending on the length of the stay and the nature of the ward. Patients also make
an escalating copayment of up to NT$200 for prescription drugs based on the price
of the medication. Although these copayments are designed to deter the moral hazard of superfluous health resource utilization, they also impose regressive financial
burdens on lower-income groups and therefore discourage them from accessing
medically necessary services. To minimize such concerns, the NHI exempt the
insured from copayments (1) when seeking treatment for legally defined major illnesses and injuries, child deliveries, and certain preventive services; (2) if they live
in mountainous areas or on outlying islands, where health resources are relatively
scarce; or (3) if they are from low-income families.[29] Other than these prescribed
copayments, the *NHI Act* prohibits extra billing by NHI-contracted health providers
for insured services.[30]

Third, many Taiwanese hold private health insurance policies to supplement the
NHI. According to 2004 data, private health insurance accounted for up to 4 percent
of the funding for the country's health care system.[31] However, unlike in some
countries where private insurers purchase health services directly from providers on
behalf of patients, health insurance companies in Taiwan make cash payouts to the
insured in cases of illness. The insured are then free to put these payments toward
any uses they see fit, such as alleviating copayment burdens or upgrading to private

---

[26] Iwamoto et al., *supra* note 21, at 9. See also Tu-Bin Chu et al., *Household Out-of-Pocket Medical Expenditures and National Health Insurance in Taiwan: Income and Regional Inequality*, 5 BMC HEALTH SERV. RES. 60 (2005), *available at* http://www.biomedcentral.com/1472–6963/5/60.
[27] 2012–2013 Annual Report, *supra* note 25, at 22.
[28] NHI Act, *supra* note 9, art. 43.
[29] 2012–2013 Annual Report, *supra* note 25, at 20–21.
[30] NHI Act, *supra* note 9, art. 58.
[31] Iwamoto et al., *supra* note 21, at 9.

or semi-private rooms while hospitalized. Furthermore, it is possible for a person to hold multiple private health insurance policies. As such, to many Taiwanese policyholders, private health insurance functions as a form of investment.[32]

9.1.3 *Allocation of Health Care Resources*

Aside from out-of-pocket expenditures directly transferred from patients to practitioners, health care resources in Taiwan are primarily allocated to service providers through the NHI regime. Prior to the NHI's establishment, medical professionals were paid by the various social insurance programs on a fee-for-service basis. To better control health expenditure, however, the NHI is legally required to phase in a prospective global budgeting system[33] – a process completed in 2002.[34]

Under this global budgeting approach, the NHI has achieved some successes in managing ballooning health care expenditures.[35] While Taiwan's national health expenditure grew at an annual rate of more than 10 percent during the years immediately before 1995, the annual growth rate has since decreased to as low as 2.6 percent in 2010. According to 2011 data, Taiwan's total health care expenditure represented approximately 6.6 percent of its GDP and amounted to US$2,499 per capita.[36] In comparison, OECD countries devoted an average of 9.3 percent of their GDP to health spending in 2011, with per capita health expenditure averaging US$3,322.[37]

9.1.4 *NHI Benefit Package*

The range of health services covered by the NHI is reasonably comprehensive, ranging from ambulatory and inpatient care to prescription drugs and dental treatments.[38] However, pursuant to art. 39 of the NHI Act, some medical services and products such as addiction treatment, cosmetic surgery, orthodontics, preventive surgery, assisted reproduction procedures, sex change operation, over-the-counter medications, blood products (except in cases of emergency blood transfusion), human subject clinical trials, and non-curative medical devices are excluded from the benefit package.[39]

---

[32] Tsung-Mei Cheng, *Private Insurance in Taiwan: An Author Responds*, 28 HEALTH AFF. 1863, 1863 (2009).

[33] NHI Act, *supra* note 9, arts. 47–54.

[34] Cheng, *supra* note 7, at 71.

[35] *Id.*, at 71–72.

[36] Dep't of Health, Minguo Yibai Nian Guomin Yiliao Baojian Zhichu (民國100年國民醫療保健支出) [National Health Expenditure 2011] 8, 26 (2012) (Taiwan), *available at* http://www.mohw.gov.tw/cht/DOS/Statistic.aspx?f_list_no=312&fod_list_no=2655.

[37] OECD, HEALTH AT A GLANCE 2013: OECD INDICATORS 154–157 (7th ed., 2013), *available at* http://www.oecd.org/els/health-systems/Health-at-a-Glance-2013.pdf.

[38] Cheng, *supra* note 7, at 64. *See also* Chiang, *supra* note 8, at 230.

[39] NHI Act, *supra* note 9, art. 39.

In addition to comprehensive benefits, the insured also enjoy much freedom in choosing health care providers. In fact, irrespective of the nature or seriousness of their illness, the insured can seek treatment directly from secondary and/or tertiary care facilities without referral by primary care providers.[40] Insofar as an insured person is seeking services covered by the national insurance, an NHI-contracted medical institution is legally obligated to provide reasonable care based on its specialties and facilities.[41]

9.1.5 *Policy and Law Reform: Second-Generation NHI*

Notwithstanding some successes in managing ever-growing health care outlays, the NHI has been incurring budgetary shortfalls since 1998.[42] Such a financial imbalance has led the BNHI to raise the rate of insurance premium on multiple occasions and to phase in a number of cost containment measures, including a pay-for-performance system for the treatment of certain illnesses and a more rigorous drug pricing control mechanism.[43]

NHI's financial challenges have also prompted legal reforms. In January 2011, Taiwan's Legislative Yuan passed an amendment to the NHI Act, ushering in what is commonly referred to as the second-generation NHI.[44] One of the primary objectives of the reform was to diversify the NHI's revenue streams and thereby improve the vertical equity of its contribution structure. Under this new regime, the amount of NHI premiums paid by the insured is no longer determinable by one's wage alone. Non-salary sources of income that are often associated with the affluent – such as interest income, dividends, earnings from rental properties, income from professional practice, and employment remunerations in the form of bonuses – will also be taken into account.[45]

Moreover, a new NHI Supervisory Board will be tasked with adjusting the rate of NHI premium, reviewing the scope of insurance benefits, determining the amount and the allocation of the global budget, and interpreting NHI-related laws and regulations.[46] It is hoped that the new board, with both revenue-generating and cost-controlling capacities, will be well positioned to balance the NHI's budget. Other changes to the NHI include, inter alia, stiffer penalties for fraudulent insurance

---

[40] Cheng, *supra* note 7, at 64.
[41] NHI Act, *supra* note 9, art. 60.
[42] 2012–2013 Annual Report, *supra* note 25, at 29 (whereas the yearly increase of the program's revenue has averaged 4.87% since its inception, the program's expenditure has on average risen by 4.94% annually).
[43] Id., at 28, 32–37.
[44] Quanmin Jiankang Baoxian Fa [NHI Act] (2011) (Taiwan), QUANGUO FAGUI, *available at* http://law.moj.gov.tw.
[45] Id., art. 31.
[46] Id., art. 5.

claims,[47] improved transparency for NHI records,[48] promotion of the family physician system,[49] and greater support for the poor to meet their insurance premium obligations.[50] These amendments began taking effect in January 2013.[51]

9.2 CONSTITUTIONAL FRAMEWORK FOR THE ACCESS-TO-HEALTH DISCOURSE IN TAIWAN

Taiwan's Constitution specifies that the country is founded on the Three Principles of the People, namely it "shall be a democratic republic *of the people*, to be governed *by the people* and *for the people* [emphasis added]."[52] In particular, the philosophy of "a State for the people" pertains to social policies and calls on the government to facilitate distributive justice by adopting a welfare state.[53]

Accordingly, regarding health care, art. 155 of the Constitution stipulates that "[t]he State, in order to promote social welfare, shall establish a social insurance system. To the aged and the infirm who are unable to earn a living, and to victims of unusual calamities, the State shall give appropriate assistance and relief."[54] Article 157 further provides that "[t]he State, in order to improve national health, shall establish extensive services for sanitation and health protection, and a system of public medical service."[55] In the same vein, art. 10 of the Additional Articles of the Constitution instructs the government to "promote universal health insurance and promote the research and development of both modern and traditional medicines."[56] These constitutional provisions elevate the establishment of a national health care strategy, particularly a universal health insurance scheme, to the status of a fundamental national policy. In J.Y. Interpretation No. 472, to be discussed later in the chapter, the Constitutional Court confirmed that the NHI finds constitutional support in these articles.[57]

---

[47] *Id.*, art. 81.
[48] *Id.*, arts. 73, 74, 79 & 80.
[49] *Id.*, art. 44.
[50] *Id.*, art. 36.
[51] Stacy Hsu, *Activists Press for Readjustment of Insurance Threshold*, TAIPEI TIMES (Jan. 15, 2013), *available at* http://www.taipeitimes.com/News/taiwan/archives/2013/01/15/2003552574.
[52] Minguo Xianfa [Constitution of the Republic of China] art. 1 (1947) (Taiwan).
[53] *See generally* Yat-Sen Sun, The Manifesto of First National Congress of the Guomindang, Address to the First National Congress of the Kuomintang (Jan. 30, 1924), *reprinted in* Alan Lawrance, CHINA SINCE 1919 – REVOLUTION AND REFORM: A SOURCEBOOK, 23–24 (2004).
[54] Minguo Xianfa, *supra* note 52, art. 155.
[55] *Id.*, art. 157.
[56] Minguo Xianfa Zengxiu Tiaowen [Additional Articles of the Constitution of the Republic of China] art. 10 (2005) (Taiwan).
[57] Shizi Di 472 Hao [J.Y. Interpretation No. 472], 2005 SHIZI 508 (Const. Ct. Jan. 29, 1999) (Taiwan), *translated in* TAIWAN CONST. CT. INTERP., *available at* http://www.judicial.gov.tw/constitutionalcourt/EN/p03.asp.

Nevertheless, these fundamental national policy provisions are generally regarded as directive in nature. While they steer the government toward certain policy paths, public officials and legislators maintain considerable discretion in how and when these constitutional visions are to be realized. Moreover, unlike constitutional rights, such constitutional principles do not entitle citizens to legal remedies if the government fails to fulfill them.[58] According to the Constitutional Interpretation Procedure Act, constitutional remedies are only available to a legal person whose constitutional right has been breached.[59] Thus, Taiwan's Constitution does not prima facie bestow on citizens an actionable right to health.

9.3 CONSTITUTIONAL INTERPRETATIONS AND ACCESS TO HEALTH

So far, Taiwan's Constitutional Court has released six NHI-related constitutional interpretations, four of which have particular bearings on access to health.[60] This section will review these four judgments in turn.

9.3.1 J.Y. Interpretation No. 472: Compulsory Enrollment Policy

Article 11–1 of the NHI Act mandates that all qualified Taiwanese residents shall subscribe to the NHI.[61] To this end, the Act imposes on anyone who does not enroll in the program a fine of up to NT$15,000.[62] Furthermore, those who are registered in the program but fail to make premium contributions on time are subject to overdue charges after a brief grace period. Before the outstanding premiums and overdue fees are paid, the BNHI has the authority to temporarily suspend these persons' health insurance benefits.[63]

Similar policies requiring universal health insurance coverage have been adopted by other governments as a strategy to correct the problem of adverse selection. As

---

[58] Chen Chao-Zheng (陳朝政), *Jibenguoce Anli Fenqi* (基本國策案例分析) [*Analysis of Cases Respecting Fundamental National Policies*], *in* XIANFA TIZHI YU RENQUAN JIAOXUE: BENTU ANLI FENQI (憲法體制與人權教學:本土案例分析) [CONSTITUTIONAL STRUCTURE AND HUMAN RIGHTS EDUCATION: ANALYSIS OF DOMESTIC CASES] 245, at 251–253 (Li Ming-Yi (李銘義) ed., 2008).

[59] Sifayuan Dafaguan Shenlianjian Fa [Constitutional Interpretation Procedure Act] art. 5(2) (1993) (Taiwan), QUANGUO FAGUI, http://law.moj.gov.tw, *translated in* SIFAYUAN DAFAGUAN XIANGGUAN FAGUI [RELEVANT STATUTES FOR THE CONSTITUTIONAL COURT, JUDICIAL YUAN], *available at* http://www.judicial.gov.tw/constitutionalcourt/en/p07.asp.

[60] Beside the four constitutional interpretations examined here, Taiwan's Constitutional Court has issued two other NHI-related interpretations: J.Y. Interpretation No. 533, 2005 SHIZI 642 (Const. Ct. Nov. 16, 2001) and J.Y. Interpretation No. 550, 2005 SHIZI 686 (Const. Ct. Oct. 4, 2002). While the former outlined the dispute resolution procedure for the BNHI and its contracted health care facilities, the latter confirmed the constitutionality for the NHI Act to require local governments in Taiwan to subsidize the premiums of some of the insured like the central government does.

[61] NHI Act, *supra* note 9, art. 11–1.

[62] *Id.*, art. 69–1.

[63] *Id.*, art. 30.

explained by Colleen Flood, because it is often difficult to assess the actual risk of ill health of each insured person, health insurers tend to set their premiums based on the average risk of an entire community. Consequently, in an unregulated market, individuals who consider themselves as low risk relative to the community as a whole have an incentive to opt out of the insurance program. With their departure, it follows that the insurers will likely need to raise the premiums to better reflect the heightened risk of the remaining insurance pool, leading to a self-perpetuating cycle of ever-rising premiums and a progressively smaller and higher-risk insurance group.[64] By preventing policyholders from opting out, universal health insurance coverage ensures adequate risk pooling and hedges against adverse selection.[65] Therefore, the NHI's mandatory participation measures are essential to the program's long-term viability.

Nonetheless, much like recent debates in the United States over the so-called individual mandate under the Patient Protection and Affordable Care Act, the policy of compulsory enrollment encountered intense opposition during the NHI's legislative process,[66] and the controversy persisted even after the NHI was launched. Within months of the NHI's inauguration, two separate applications for constitutional interpretation were lodged by various members of the legislature. In one, the applicants argued that the legal duties owed by Taiwanese vis-à-vis the government were exhaustively enumerated in arts. 19 through 21 of the Constitution, namely the duties to pay taxes, to perform military services, and to receive education. The NHI's mandatory contribution policy, according to them, imposed on citizens a legal obligation beyond those constitutionally prescribed, and therefore was invalid.[67] In the other application, mandatory enrollment in the NHI was alleged to have violated the constitutional doctrine of legitimate expectation. That is, the applicants argued that the various social insurance schemes that existed before the NHI offered their insured more generous benefits with lower premiums, a policy standard that these beneficiaries had come to expect. If the NHI was unable to uphold such expectations, the applicants argued that it should only be extended to persons that were not hitherto insured and leave others to be covered by the former schemes.[68]

A third request for constitutional interpretation relating to the NHI's compulsory enrollment policy was submitted by Niu-Chuang Ltd. in 1997. Having failed to contribute its share of some employees' premiums, the private company was ordered

---

[64] Colleen M. Flood, International Healthcare Reform: A Legal, Economic and Political Analysis 17–19 (2000).

[65] Chiang, *supra* note 8, at 229. *See also* Cheng, *supra* note 7, at 64.

[66] Tsung-Mei Cheng, A Brief History of Taiwan's Individual Mandate, CNN (Mar. 28, 2012), *available at* http://globalpublicsquare.blogs.cnn.com/2012/03/28/how-taiwan-learned-to-love-the-individual-mandate/.

[67] Lifa Weiyuan Zhou Bo-Lun deng Wushier Ren Shengqingshu (立法委員周伯倫等五十二人聲請書) [Application by Fifty-Two Legislators Including Zhou Bo-Lun], J.Y. Interpretation No. 472, 2005 Shizi 508 (Const. Ct. Jan. 29, 1999) (Taiwan).

[68] Lifayuan Shengqingshu (立法院聲請書) [Application by the Legislative Yuan], J.Y. Interpretation No. 472.

by court to pay not only premium arrears but also overdue charges. In response, Niu-Chuang applied for constitutional interpretation and contended that the statutory requirement of NHI contributions and overdue penalties breached its right to private property guaranteed under art. 15 of the Constitution.[69]

In J.Y. Interpretation No. 472, the Constitutional Court responded to these three applications at once. With respect to the claim that the NHI's mandatory enrollment policy imposed an extra-constitutional duty, Grand Justices Wu and Su in their respective concurring decisions found that drafters of the Constitution did not intend to limit citizens' legal obligations to those expressly identified in arts. 19 through 21. Rather, in keeping with the rule of law, citizens have an obligation to observe any legislation whose enactment process, purposes, and effects are constitutional.[70] Thus, insofar as the NHI's various compulsory participation measures were held to be constitutional – as demonstrated later in the chapter – citizens have an obligation to comply with them.

Concerning whether the NHI breached the doctrine of legitimate expectation when it displaced preexisting social insurance schemes, the majority of the Court answered this query in the negative. It held that there was no violation of legitimate expectation in cases "where the legislative body, in consideration of the needs of social development, makes or amends the laws and changes various social insurance regulations so as to establish the social security system in conformance with the constitutional purposes."[71] In other words, as Grand Justice Wu elaborated in his concurring decision, the concern about legitimate expectation tends to arise when ex post facto laws adversely affect some interests on which certain individuals have come to rely. Given that the NHI Act was enacted prospectively in the public interest as mandated by the Constitution, the argument of legitimate expectation fell short.[72] Moreover, Grand Justice Sun added in his concurring opinion that if there were a legitimate expectation, the government would have been forced either to allow the coexistence of multiple social insurance schemes each with a different benefit package, or to cover all citizens under a single program that provides a benefit package on par with what the former plans did. Both options, however, would run a risk of unconstitutionality. While the former might prima facie contradict the principle of equality, the latter would likely pressure the government into raising NHI premiums, thus countering the constitutional goal of making health care financially accessible to all.[73]

---

[69] Niu-Chung Qiye Youxian Gongsi Shengqingshu (紐創企業有限公司聲請書) [Application by Niu-Chung Ltd.], J.Y. Interpretation No. 472.

[70] J.Y. Interpretation No. 472, *available in* Jieshi, 3–4, http://www.judicial.gov.tw/constitutionalcourt/uploadfile/C100/司法院釋字第四七二號解釋.pdf (Grand Justice Wu Geng, concurring); J.Y. Interpretation No. 472, at 8–10 (Grand Justice Su Jun-Xiong, concurring).

[71] J.Y. Interpretation No. 472 (English translation), para. 3 under Reasoning.

[72] J.Y. Interpretation No. 472 (Chinese), at 4–5 (Grand Justice Wu Geng, concurring).

[73] *Id.*, at 7, (Grand Justice Sun San-Yan, concurring).

The Court similarly dismissed the argument that the NHI's compulsory enrollment measures contradicted the protection over property rights. However, the
Court's analysis in this aspect centered not on whether a constitutional right had been
breached by relevant NHI provisions, but whether any rights violations – assuming
they existed – could be justified under a proportionality test. That is, according to
art. 23 of the Constitution, if a rights-abridging law can be found to achieve a constitutionally permitted purpose and the degree of its rights impairment is proportional
to the benefits to be gained, then it may nonetheless be deemed constitutional.[74] In
this case, the Court held that mandatory NHI subscription was necessary in light of
"considerations of mutual social support, risk-sharing and the public interest, and
therefore conform[ed] to the constitutional purpose of promoting national health
insurance."[75] Furthermore, the Court found that the resulting benefits to the public
welfare derived from the impugned statutory provisions outweighed any injuries to
private interests.[76] Thus, the constitutionality of the NHI's mandatory participation
policy was upheld.

The Constitutional Court's ruling contained an interesting caveat. According to
the majority of the Court, "to those who cannot afford to pay [NHI] premiums, *the
State shall give appropriate assistance and relief and shall not refuse to pay benefits*, in
order to fulfill the constitutional purposes of promoting national health insurance,
protecting senior citizens, the infirm and the financially disadvantaged [empha-
sis added]."[77] In other words, while the Court permitted the government to adopt
measures such as overdue charges, penalties, and temporary benefit suspension to
realize the constitutional objective of universal health coverage, it also recognized
that the same strategies might in fact heighten the financial burden and inaccessibil-
ity of health care for socioeconomically disadvantaged individuals. The government
would need to remedy these concerns for the NHI's compulsory enrollment policy
to pass the proportionality analysis.

As such, the Court seemingly imposed a constitutional obligation on the government to provide assistance to persons who cannot afford NHI premiums. This duty
arguably entailed a corresponding right for Taiwanese to access health insurance
despite their inability to pay. However, it is unclear what the constitutional basis for
such a right is. While the majority of the Court was equivocal in this respect, Grand
Justice Su reasoned in his concurring decision that insofar as health insurance constitutes a means of subsistence, its denial would contravene the right to existence
enshrined in art. 15 of the Constitution.[78] Even then, however, many questions

---

[74] *See* Shizi Di 551 Hao [J.Y. Interpretation No. 551], 2005 SHIZI 689 (Const. Ct. Nov. 22, 2002) (Taiwan).
According to the Court, in order to be saved by art. 23 of the Constitution, a rights-infringing law needs
to (1) have a constitutionally permissible purpose, (2) achieve its ends through a minimally intrusive
means, and (3) ensure the extent of rights violation is reasonably proportional to the intended benefits.
[75] J.Y. Interpretation No. 472 (English translation), para. 1 under Holding.
[76] J.Y. Interpretation No. 472 (Chinese), at 4 (Grand Justice Wu Geng, concurring).
[77] J.Y. Interpretation No. 472 (English translation), para. 1 under Holding .
[78] J.Y. Interpretation No. 472 (Chinese), at 10 (Grand Justice Su, concurring).

remain unanswered regarding such a right to health insurance. For example, what is the scope and nature of this right? Is it a positive right that allows citizens to demand some levels of health care protection, or is it a negative right that simply affords patients a defense when the government impedes their access to health insurance? Moreover, does the constitutional right to existence – following Grand Justice Su's line of reasoning – encompass a right to health at large beyond mere access to health insurance?

Despite these legal ambiguities, less than six months following the issuance of the Court's ruling, the legislature amended the NHI Act to expand public subsidies to low-income families' premiums as well as to discontinue overdue charges and benefit suspension for individuals unable to meet contribution requirements because of temporary financial difficulties.[79] The Employment Insurance Act introduced in 2002 further extends NHI premium subsidies to recently unemployed individuals and their dependents.[80] In 2003, another revision to the NHI Act enabled the establishment of a government fund that would allow persons experiencing financial hardships to access interest-free loans to pay their premiums.[81]

Overall, this decision displayed the Grand Justices' appreciation for the collectivist values underlying a universal health care system. By appealing to ideals like "mutual social support," "risk-sharing," and "public interest," the Court was able to link the NHI with the constitutional philosophy of distributive justice and to fend off legal challenges from individuals with vested interests, such as those who had been insured before the NHI's introduction and those who were relatively well-off. Furthermore, the progressivity of the NHI was enhanced by the Court's mandate that no Taiwanese are to be denied care because of their inability to pay insurance premiums. While the Court's decision left numerous uncertainties to be resolved, it arguably set a promising analytical stage for all future NHI-related constitutional challenges.

9.3.2 J.Y. Interpretations No. 473 and No. 676: Minimum Presumed Insurable Income

In both J.Y. Interpretations No. 473 and No. 676, the Grand Justices wrestled with the constitutionality of various NHI regulations that provided for the calculation of some beneficiaries' premiums based on a presumed minimum income.

Generally, pursuant to art. 21 of the NHI Act, the insurable income for most beneficiaries is determined by referring to a grading table published by the BNHI.[82]

---

[79] Quanmin Jiankang Baoxian Fa [NHI Act] arts. 8, 87–1, 87–2 & 87–3 (1999) (last amended in 2011) (Taiwan), QUANGUO FAGUI, *available at* http://law.moj.gov.tw.

[80] Jiuye Baoxian Fa [Employment Insurance Act] art. 10 (2002) (Taiwan), QUANGUO FAGUI, *available at* http://law.moj.gov.tw.

[81] Quanmin Jiankang Baoxian Fa [NHI Act] art. 87–2 (2003) (last amended in 2011) (Taiwan), QUANGUO FAGUI, *available at* http://law.moj.gov.tw.

[82] NHI Act, *supra* note 9, art. 21.

The insured population is first divided by the table into myriad income brackets based on actual earnings, and then every person in the same bracket is affixed with an identical amount of insurable income, which is used to compute NHI premiums. For example, according to the latest table, any person whose actual monthly wage is NT$18,780 or less is deemed to have an insurable income of NT$18,780, whereas anyone earning more than NT$175,600 monthly would have a deemed insurable income of NT$182,000.[83]

However, for some beneficiaries, insurable income is stipulated by various subsections in art. 41 of the Enforcement Rules of the National Health Insurance Act (NHI Rules) regardless of their actual earnings.[84] For example, business owners, independent practitioners (e.g., accountants, attorneys, architects, physicians, and dentists), and specialized technicians presumptively fall within the highest income bracket prescribed in the BNHI's grading table. Although the NHI Rules allow these individuals to rebut such an income presumption with proper evidence, they also provide that the insurable income of these beneficiaries must not fall below the highest amount of insurable income set out in a similar grading table used by the Labor Insurance program.[85]

Presumably, these provisions were adopted by the NHI both for the convenience of its administration and to hedge against the risk of insured persons evading their contribution responsibilities. Given that NHI premiums – especially before the second-generation NHI reform – were computed based strictly on one's regular payroll, individuals seeking to lower their NHI contributions could simply reposition their wages as another form of income (e.g., one-off bonuses, commissions, business revenues, etc.). By imputing a minimum insurable income to high-earning beneficiaries and those whose income is difficult to track, the NHI could theoretically minimize the problem of premium evasion, thus securing its revenue stream.

In 1997, a constitutional challenge against art. 41(1)(4) of the NHI Rules was launched by an independently practicing lawyer after her insurable income, originally assessed at NT$33,300, was upwardly adjusted to NT$36,300 because of the minimum income presumption and her subsequent administrative appeals were unsuccessful. The applicant argued that because the NHI Act itself did not mandate such a minimum presumed insurable income, the impugned regulatory provision – which derived its legal authority from the NHI Act – was invalid. Moreover, the applicant posited that her constitutional right to property was violated when she was

---

[83] 2012–2013 Annual Report, *supra* note 25, at 19.

[84] Quanmin Jiankang Baoxian Fa Shixing Xize [Enforcement Rules of the National Health Insurance Act] art. 41(2009) (Taiwan), Quanguo Fagui, *available at* http://law.moj.gov.tw.

[85] The Labor Insurance program provides workers with social insurance benefits in cases of disability, old age, and death. According to the current grading table, the maximum insurable income for calculating workers' Labor Insurance premiums stands at NT$43,900. *Labor Insurance*, Bureau of Labor Insurance (Jun. 4, 2013) (Taiwan), *available at* http://www.bli.gov.tw/en/sub.aspx?a=ElgXn8JyGf4%3d.

ordered to pay NHI premiums based on an imputed insurable income greater than her actual earnings.[86] Both arguments, however, were dismissed by a unanimous Constitutional Court in J.Y. Interpretation No. 473.

With respect to the applicant's first argument, according to the Grand Justices, art. 41(1)(4) of the NHI Rules was in fact in conformity with the legislative intention behind art. 21 of the NHI Act. The Court found that "[t]o attain fairness in terms of financial capability-based cost-bearing, the premium for the National Health Insurance, which is a type of social insurance, differs according to the income of the insured."[87] That is, the Court recognized that the NHI was established on the philosophy that the beneficiaries would contribute according to their ability. Grounded in this principle, the grading table mandated by art. 21 of the NHI Act was developed based on careful actuarial analysis that was meant to categorize the insured population per their approximate financial status and in turn simplify the NHI's premium calculation process. Similarly, minimum presumed insurable income was used by the NHI as a strategy to more easily estimate insured persons' financial capacity in keeping with the nature of their occupations. As such, there was no inconsistency between the two.

In terms of the applicant's allegation that art. 41(1)(4) of the NHI Rules violated her right to property, the Court was equally unsympathetic. Without much elaboration, the Court held that the impugned provision in the NHI Rules properly took into account "the occupation type of the insured" and therefore did not contravene "the purpose of property right protection."[88] Presumably, it was the Court's opinion that the minimum insurable income imputed to the applicant in this case, albeit imperfect, nevertheless appropriately correlated with her perceived economic status as an attorney. Based on the ability-to-pay principle, the applicant thus had a responsibility to contribute to the NHI accordingly.

Notably, unlike in J.Y. Interpretation No. 472, the Court did not resort to the proportionality analysis but found that there was no rights breach at all. The Grand Justices could have reached the same outcome had they held that the impugned provision violated the applicant's right to property but such a violation was justifiable in light of the government's objective to achieve administrative efficiency. In this counterfactual scenario, the constitutional guarantee of property rights arguably would resemble a classical liberal interpretation that views it as a shield against government takings. In contrast, by finding that there was no property rights infringement in the first place, the Court appeared to adopt a more communitarian perspective that

---

[86] Jiang Juan-Juan Shengqingshu (蔣娟娟聲請書) [Application by Jiang Juan-Juan], Shizi Di 473 Hao [J.Y. Interpretation No. 473], 2005 SHIZI 510 (Const. Ct. Jan. 29, 1999) (Taiwan). As a result of subsequent amendments, art. 41(1)(4) of the NHI Rules challenged in J.Y. Interpretation No. 473 corresponds to art. 41(1)(2) of the current version of the regulation.

[87] J.Y. Interpretation No. 473, *translated in* TAIWAN CONST. CT. INTERP., para. 1 under Holding, *available at* http://www.judicial.gov.tw/constitutionalcourt/EN/p03.asp.

[88] *Id.*

sees the NHI as common property that every member of the society would need to participate in and be entitled to.[89] In so doing, the Grand Justices arguably reaffirmed their reasoning in J.Y. Interpretation No. 472: to the degree that both the Constitution and the NHI were anchored in collectivist ideologies, legal challenges against the NHI grounded in individual liberties must give way.

In 2007, another constitutional challenge was launched against a different subsection under art. 41 of the NHI Rules. The applicants in this case consisted of some 1,500 persons from various professional unions, including farmhands, taxi drivers, delivery persons, in-home caretakers, and nannies. Pursuant to art. 41(1)(7), individuals like them who did not work steadily for one employer and therefore participated in the NHI through professional unions were automatically deemed as belonging to the sixth grade in the BNHI's grading table – thus ascribed an insurable income of approximately NT$20,000 – without any possibility of disproving such a presumption. As their counterpart did in J.Y. Interpretation No. 473, these applicants argued that, inter alia, the impugned regulatory provision not only lacked legal authorization from the NHI Act but also violated their property rights.[90]

In J.Y. Interpretation No. 676, the Constitutional Court responded to these claims. First, the Court held that art. 41(1)(7) of the NHI Rules targeted a particular group of beneficiaries whose income was often difficult to assess because their workload frequently fluctuated. The impugned provision, according to the Grand Justices, attributed a reasonable amount of insurable income to these beneficiaries in order to simplify premium calculations. Therefore, echoing its previous finding, the Court held that art. 41(1)(7) of the NHI Rules was indeed consistent with the legislative intent behind art. 21 of the NHI Act insofar as both aimed at facilitating NHI premium collection on an ability-to-pay basis.[91] In other words, the NHI Act legitimately authorized art. 41(1)(7) of the NHI Rules.

The Court further held that so long as art. 41(1)(7) of the NHI Rules imputed a realistic amount of insurable income to the applicants, the provision was per se consistent with the right to property. In this regard, the Court appeared to follow its ruling in J.Y. Interpretation No. 473. Nonetheless, the majority of the Court went on to find that because the relevant category of beneficiaries encompassed workers in a wide range of industries, whose business cycles were respectively influenced by a different set of socioeconomic factors, it was likely that these persons would sometimes actually earn less than the presumed minimum insurable income. In such circumstances, the government was ordered to adopt appropriate measures to

---

[89] Chen Ying-Ling (陳英鈴), Xianzheng Minzhu yu Renquan (憲政民主與人權) [Constitutional Democracy and Human Rights] 295–97 (2004).

[90] Shizi Di 676 Hao [J.Y. Interpretation No. 676] (Const. Ct. Apr. 30, 2010) (Taiwan), *translated in* TAIWAN CONST. CT. INTERP., para. 1 under Editor's Note, http://www.judicial.gov.tw/constitutionalcourt/EN/p03.asp. Under challenge in this case was art. 41(1)(7) of then NHI Rules, which, as a result of subsequent revisions, refers to art. 41(1)(4) in the current version of the regulation.

[91] *Id.*, para. 3 under Reasoning.

allow these beneficiaries to rebut the minimum income presumption, thus adhering to the goals of vertical equity and mutual support.[92] As such, in terms of judicial outcome, the majority decision in this case seemingly conflicted with the ruling of J.Y. Interpretation No. 473, which upheld the constitutionality of a similar minimum insurable income provision.

One plausible explanation for this inconsistency may lie in the differences between the beneficiaries targeted by the impugned regulatory provision in these two cases. Whereas art. 41(1)(4) of the NHI Rules – challenged by the applicant in J.Y. Interpretation No. 473 – concerns business owners and independent practitioners, art. 41(1)(7) relates to manual and semiskilled workers. As the former group tends to be in a better financial situation than the latter, it understandably faces more difficulty convincing the Court that it should be exempted from the minimum NHI contribution requirement. The large number of applicants involved in J.Y. Interpretation No. 676 may have further bolstered the persuasiveness of the argument that the income presumption in question was a crude appraisal of the actual financial status of the diverse group of individuals implicated. Thus, the outcomes of these two cases are reconcilable insofar as the Grand Justices seemed to have adopted a position that while more affluent members of the society *must* contribute to the NHI at least based on a minimum amount of presumed income, those who are less financially established *may* be exempted from similar contributory obligations when appropriate.

Viewed as such, I argue that the outcome of J.Y. Interpretation No. 676 effectively reiterates the Court's pronouncement in J.Y. Interpretation No. 472, namely that for individual who cannot afford to pay premiums, the state shall give appropriate assistance and relief. Therefore, it is arguably disappointing that the Court did not seize this occasion to answer some of the legal questions that arose from J.Y. Interpretation No. 472 regarding the government's obligation to provide NHI premium relief to underprivileged beneficiaries. In fact, the majority ruling in this latest case has prompted a new set of questions. What criteria did the Court use to determine whether the financial status of a group of beneficiaries genuinely warranted an exemption from the minimum insurable income presumption? Also, if the government is obligated to provide assistance to individuals who cannot afford their prescribed insurance premiums, is the government constitutionally sanctioned to increase the contribution required from other beneficiaries at the same time so as to preserve the fiscal health of the NHI? Had the Court clarified these uncertainties, it would have provided much needed guidance to the government when seeking to implement the ruling of J.Y. Interpretation No. 676. Instead, at the time of writing, it remains unclear how the legislature will address the issue relating to minimum presumed insurable income.

---

[92] *Id.*, para. 4 under Reasoning.

9.3.3 *J.Y. Interpretation No. 524: NHI Benefit Package*

J.Y. Interpretation No. 524 invited the Court to examine the scope of health services to which beneficiaries were entitled under the NHI. As mentioned, the NHI's benefit package is relatively all-encompassing. In contrast, some countries – Canada being a prime example – limit their public health coverage to certain types of medically necessary services such as physician and hospital care. Whereas these countries sometimes encounter the problem of "passive privatization" where advances in medical technology gradually shift the primary locus of health care away from institutional settings and therefore outside of the public realm,[93] similar issues have largely been avoided in Taiwan because of the breadth of services covered under the NHI. In fact, some commentators have credited the NHI's comprehensive benefit package for leveling the financial accessibility of the Taiwanese health care system.[94] At the same time, however, as technological progress in health care drives up medical expenditures worldwide, it is arguably impossible for the NHI with its limited budget to cover every medical procedure – especially those without proven cost-effectiveness – if the program is to remain fiscally sustainable. Consequently, it is understandable that the benefit package of the NHI cannot truly be comprehensive; some limits must be in place.

Most categories of health procedures and medical products not covered by the NHI are itemized in art. 39 of the NHI Act. While subsections 1 through 11 of the provision identify specific services to be excluded from the NHI's benefit package, subsection 12 prima facie authorizes the government to expand the list of non-covered items at any given time so long as adequate prior notice is served.[95] In addition, pursuant to art. 41(3) of the NHI Act, no public coverage is extended to any health procedures and pharmaceuticals examined by the BNHI ex ante and deemed as medically unnecessary.[96] At the time of J.Y. Interpretation No. 524, art. 31 of the Regulations for National Health Insurance Medical Care (NHI Regulations) also stipulated that coverage for any medical treatment involving "high-tech procedures" would require prior approval from the BNHI, effectively limiting the inclusion of such services in the NHI's benefit package.[97] Together, these legislative provisions afford the BNHI an expansive and unilateral discretion over which health care services are publicly funded. However, they appear to offer little guidance on how

---

[93] Colleen M. Flood & Tom Archibald, *The Illegality of Private Healthcare in Canada*, 164 CAN. MED. ASS'N J. 825, 829 (2001).

[94] Lu & Hsiao, *supra* note 1, at 80.

[95] NHI Act, *supra* note 9, art. 39.

[96] *Id.*, art. 41(3).

[97] Quanmin Jiankang Baoxian Yiliao Banfa [Regulations for the National Health Insurance Medical Care] art. 31(1995) (Taiwan), QUANGUO FAGUI, *available at* http://law.moj.gov.tw. Article 31 concerned in J.Y. Interpretation No. 524 was removed from the NHI Regulations pursuant to amendments made in 2000.

the BNHI should exercise its discretion. For example, medically unnecessary or high-tech procedures are never clearly defined. As such, it is perhaps not surprising that beneficiaries eventually launched a constitutional challenge against these statutory provisions.

In 1996, Mr. Tian-Tian Xie underwent a temperature-controlled radiofrequency catheter ablation surgery to correct his heart condition. After the treatment, he was billed NT$48,510 by the hospital for the cost of the catheter used in the operation. Mr. Xie subsequently requested to have this medical expense reimbursed by the BNHI but was unsuccessful. According to the Bureau, it considered the catheter in question a high-tech medical device, so its coverage under the NHI would have required prior authorization, which Mr. Xie failed to seek. When Mr. Xie appealed his case to court, however, it was found that, as the NHI Act only stipulated a medical services payment scheme between the BNHI and its contracted health care facilities, Mr. Xie as a beneficiary lacked the proper legal standing to seek reimbursement directly from the BNHI. Dissatisfied with the ruling, Mr. Xie then applied to the Constitutional Court for an interpretation on the validity of the NHI benefit-restricting provisions, including arts. 39 and 41(3) of the NHI Act and art. 31 of the NHI Regulations.[98]

The fundamental question to be addressed by the Constitutional Court in J.Y. Interpretation No. 524 was to what extent provisions in the NHI Act could authorize the government to restrict and alter the basket of services provided by the NHI. According to the majority of the Court, in order to "prevent the abuse of medical resources or to accommodate the developments in medical or pharmaceutical technology," the government understandably should be permitted to update the NHI's benefit package from time to time.[99] Nevertheless, whether the NHI Act directly conferred such authority on the government or did so via other delegated legislation, the authorizing provisions must be clear and definite to meet the constitutional standard of fairness. The majority of the Grand Justices reasoned that because the NHI had significant implications for "the welfare of all citizens," entitlements and/or obligations relating to the program must be clearly enunciated and all changes thereto needed to be foreseeable by the insured.[100]

Measured against this overarching principle, the majority decision found that art. 41(3) of the NHI Act and art. 31 of the NHI Regulations were unconstitutionally vague. On the one hand, these two provisions failed to explicitly delineate the criteria for assessing what constituted medically unnecessary or high-tech treatments. On the other hand, while both clauses demanded the insured to submit health services whose public coverage was uncertain to the BNHI for ex ante review, they

---

[98] Xie Tian-Tian Shengqingshu (謝添田聲請書) [Application by Xie Tian-Tian], Shizi Di 524 Hao [J.Y. Interpretation No. 524], 2005 Shizi 617 (Const. Ct. Apr. 20, 2001) (Taiwan).

[99] J.Y. Interpretation No. 524, *translated in* Taiwan Const. Ct. Interp., para. 3 under Reasoning, *available at* http://www.judicial.gov.tw/constitutionalcourt/EN/p03.asp.

[100] *Id.*, para. 2 under Reasoning.

were ambiguous as to what beneficiaries should do in cases of emergency where preapproval is unfeasible. As such, the government was ordered to amend these provisions accordingly within two years.[101]

The majority of the Court was equally concerned about the vagueness and the breadth of art. 39(12) of the NHI Act, which on its surface seemed to allow the government to exclude from the NHI's benefit package any treatments and drugs beside those already listed in subsections 1 through 11 of the same provision. In order for art. 39(12) to conform to the constitutional standard of clarity, the majority of the Court held that it must be interpreted narrowly to only permit the government to restrict medical services and products of the same nature as those identified in arts. 39(1) through 39(11), and these exclusions must be prospectively announced by the government.[102]

In dissent, Grand Justice Shi went further to hold that insofar as the insured had come to expect a certain level of benefits in return for premiums paid, such expectations should be protected by the constitutional right to property. Legislative provisions in question that granted the government open-ended and unilateral powers to remove health services from the NHI's benefit package were in breach of the insured's benefit expectations and therefore their property rights.[103] That is, Grand Justice Shi appeared to begin his analysis from the perspective that the insured were entitled to a predetermined basket of health services under the NHI, and as a result attempts from the government to subsequently remove certain procedures therefrom would prima facie be unconstitutional. On the contrary, the majority of the Court began its reasoning from the assumption that it was necessary for the government to scrutinize the content of the NHI's benefit package so as to assure the program's fiscal health, and therefore legislation that conferred such authority on the government was constitutional so long as it was prospective, clear, and concrete. Juxtaposing these two views, the majority decision was arguably motivated more by an aim to uphold the collective interest in the NHI's sustainability than by a desire to protect beneficiaries' individual rights. Viewed in this light, J.Y. Interpretation No. 524 was consistent with the spirit of other NHI-related constitutional interpretations discussed in this chapter.

Following J.Y. Interpretation No. 524, the legislature adopted a new approach to defining the NHI's benefit package. Under the second-generation NHI, the government will be required to regularly publish a reference list of all medical services and pharmaceuticals that are publicly covered. Whereas the task of developing such a list will be a collaboration among stakeholders, the BNHI is permitted to conduct an assessment on any new medical technology – by investigating its cost-effectiveness

---

[101] *Id.*, para. 4 under Reasoning.
[102] *Id.*, para. 3 under Reasoning.
[103] *Id.*, *available in* JIESHI, http://www.judicial.gov.tw/constitutionalcourt/uploadfile/C100/524.pdf (Grand Justice Shi Wen-Sen, dissenting).

as well as its impact on human bodies, medical ethics, and the fiscal health of the NHI – before it is added to the benefit basket.[104] Furthermore, the new NHI Act will require treatments that are characterized as high risk, expensive, or prone to misuse to be preapproved by the BNHI, but not in emergencies.[105]

9.4 CONCLUSION: MAKING A CASE FOR A CONSTITUTIONAL RIGHT TO HEATH

As one traces the Constitutional Court's jurisprudence relating to the NHI, the following five themes arguably emerge:

1. Since the NHI is founded on a set of fundamental national policies enshrined in the Constitution, any of its intrusions on personal interests would prima facie generate constitutional implications that require careful examination.
2. The design of the NHI as a compulsory program financed largely by a progressive payroll tax with significant public subsidies for the poor reflects constitutional values such as mutual support, risk-sharing, and vertical equity.
3. To the extent that the NHI represents a common property enjoyed by all members of society, it is not per se in conflict with the constitutional right to property. In fact, the government seemingly owes a public duty to defend the common interest in the sustainability of the program.
4. Even assuming that various contributory obligations mandated by the NHI and the government's tinkering with its benefit basket may be in breach of individuals' right to private property, they are constitutionally justifiable and saved by the proportionality analysis.
5. The government has a responsibility to ensure low-income individuals do not bear an undue financial burden under the NHI at least with respect to premium requirements.

Overall, the Constitutional Court has been able to draw on the collectivist orientation that permeates Taiwan's Constitution as a counterweight to legal challenges against the NHI motivated by personal liberties. To the extent that the NHI demonstrably enhances health equity, the Constitutional Court's rulings have not only protected such an accomplishment from individual attacks but also engendered even greater progressivity by, for example, ensuring underprivileged beneficiaries would receive proper government assistance with their premiums.

Nevertheless, these NHI-related constitutional interpretations are not free from criticism. While the Constitutional Court appeared to hint at a right to health insurance in J.Y. Interpretation No. 472 by prohibiting the government from denying health services to persons who are unable to pay their NHI premiums, the Court

---

[104] NHI Act (2011), *supra* note 44, arts. 41 & 42.
[105] *Id.*, art. 42.

was ambiguous regarding the legal basis, scope, and nature of such a right. Perhaps even more disappointing is the fact that when the opportunity arose more than a decade later, the Court failed in J.Y. Interpretation No. 676 to finally clarify these uncertainties and to unequivocally proclaim a constitutional right to health.

As a result, the access-to-health discourse in the Taiwanese constitutional context has remained largely reactive in nature. Lacking an expressly actionable right to health, individuals seeking to improve the accessibility and quality of health care under the NHI are denied an important legal tool to proactively challenge the NHI's insufficiencies. In contrast, as seen in this chapter, opponents of the NHI – particularly those standing to gain from the retreat of the program – have made several attempts at advancing their cause by resorting to the right to property. Although these legal claims have not yet enjoyed much success, supporters of the NHI are effectively at the mercy of the Constitutional Court each time such cases arise. Furthermore, regardless of the outcomes of these cases, by virtue of possessing the power to initiate constitutional claims alone, those opposing the public insurance scheme arguably hold the upper hand in setting the judicial agenda around health, which might explain to some degree the repeated attention from the Constitutional Court to NHI premium contribution requirements (versus other aspects of the NHI or the broader health policy).

The fact that one single facet of the NHI program has dominated the Taiwanese constitutional jurisprudence on health care is cause for concern. Notwithstanding numerous studies cited in this chapter affirming the NHI's contribution toward improving the overall financial accessibility of health care, other evidence suggests that intra-population health disparities remain significant in Taiwan more than a decade after the NHI's introduction, and that universal health insurance alone is unlikely to bridge these gaps.[106] One of the major contributors to health disparities in Taiwan is the uneven distribution of medical resources. Health care institutions and medical practitioners are concentrated in large cities, particularly in the northern region of the country.[107] In 2012, whereas each medical facility in the capital city of Taipei was responsible for treating 805 patients on average, its counterparts in Taitung and Hualien – two relatively rural counties located in eastern Taiwan – were responsible for 1,423 and 1,189 patients, respectively.[108] A recent study published by the Taiwan Association for Promoting Public Health found that such geographical differences in medical resources could account for nearly 36 percent of all deaths

---

[106] See e.g., Chi-Pang Wen, Shan-Pou Tsai & Wen-Shen Isabella Chung, *A 10-Year Experience with Universal Health Insurance in Taiwan: Measuring Changes in Health and Health Disparity*, 148 ANNALS INT'L MED. 258, 263 (2008).

[107] Victor Kreng & Chi-Tien Yang, *The Equality of Resource Allocation in Healthcare under the National Health Insurance System in Taiwan*, 100 HEALTH POL'Y 203 (2011).

[108] DoH Report, *supra* note 15, at 3.

in eastern Taiwan in 2010.[109] Insofar as unequal distribution of health resources signals a physical rather than an economic barrier to the health care system, it is questionable whether repeated judicial scrutiny over NHI contribution obligations alone will remedy this problem. A legal guarantee of health insurance coverage will be of little assistance to patients in rural Taiwan who lack accessible medical service providers in the first place.

As in many other countries, socioeconomic inequality is another source of health disparities in Taiwan.[110] For instance, the health status of Taiwan's indigenous peoples relative to that of the general population has historically been poorer. Studies have shown that because indigenous persons tend to have a lower level of education and therefore largely work in low-skilled, labor-intensive industries, they experience a significantly higher rate of unintended injuries and accidental deaths.[111] It is also observed that alcoholism, tobacco use, depression, and suicide are much more prevalent in the indigenous communities as they struggle with cultural identities and related social marginalization.[112] These health disparities have persisted under the NHI regime, even as policy makers work to improve the program's financial accessibility for the poor pursuant to the Constitutional Court's rulings.[113] On the one hand, even with the public health insurance, indigenous patients face greater physical and cultural-linguistic barriers when accessing the health care system than their non-indigenous counterparts, as many reside in Taiwan's mountainous regions where medical resources are scarce and not always culturally or linguistically appropriate.[114] On the other hand, as Norman Daniels explained, to the extent that health inequalities are socioeconomically influenced, their resolution will require measures beyond

---

[109] Yi-Chia Wei, Shu-Li Huang & Tsun-Wei Chang, *Report Shows Distribution of Health Resources Uneven*, TAIPEI TIMES (Oct. 16, 2011), *available at* http://www.taipeitimes.com/News/front/archives/2011/10/16/2003515867.

[110] Wen, Tsai & Chung, *supra* note 107, at 262–63. *See also* Kreng & Yang, *supra* note 108, at 204.

[111] Chen Qiu-Rong & Xie Man-Li, Institute of Occupational Safety & Health, Yuanzhumin Laogong Zhiye Zaihai Yufang Celüe Yanjiu (原住民勞工職業災害預防策略研究) [Research on Strategies to Prevent Workplace Injuries Facing Indigenous Laborers] (2007) (Taiwan), *available at* http://www.iosh.gov.tw/book/Report_Publish.aspx?P=1156.

[112] Tzu-I Tsai, *Nursing Partnerships in Indigenous Health*, 22 CONTEMP. NURSING 264 (2006).

[113] For example, between 1991 and 1993, at-birth life expectancy of indigenous men and women, respectively, was approximately 12 and 7.5 years shorter than that of men and women in the general population; in 2006, these life expectancy gaps were still 11 and 8 years. *See* statistics from: Chun-Tsai Hsu, *Do Aboriginal Adults Struggle to Be Involved in Health and Social Care Services in Taiwan? Perspective of Paiwanese Older and Disabled People*, Presentation at the 4th Annual East Asian Social Policy Research Network Conference (Oct. 20, 2007) at 3, *available in* EAST ASIAN SOCIAL POLICY, *available at* http://www.welfareasia.org/4thconference/Themes.html; COUNCIL OF INDIGENOUS PEOPLES, EXECUTIVE YUAN, 95&96 NIAN YUANZHUMINZU RENKOU JI JIANKANG TONGJI NIANBAO (95&96年原住民族人口及健康統計年報) [ANNUAL REPORT ON THE POPULATION AND HEALTH STATUS OF INDIGENOUS PEOPLES, 2006–2007] 18 (2009) (Taiwan).

[114] Meeting notes from Yuanxiang dao Dushi – Yuanzhuminzu Chengxiang Ziyuan Guanxi Xueshu Yantaohui ["From Indigenous Communities to Cities: Urban/Rural Resource Relations for Indigenous Peoples" Seminar] (May 28, 2010), TAIWAN INDIGENOUS PEOPLES RESOURCE CTR., *available at* http://www.tiprc.org.tw/seminar/2010/0528/section2.html.

those found within the traditional health sector.[115] Without a clearly established right to health that safeguards not only timely access to appropriate medical care but also just distribution of social determinants of health, indigenous peoples have limited legal recourse against systemic health inequities.

As observed by Rebecca Cook and Charles Ngwena, "[u]nless the right to health is inclusive, targeted and attuned to systematic inequality, it has little prospect of facilitating the achievement of substantive equality, especially for vulnerable groups."[116] Internationally, art. 12 of the International Covenant on Economic, Social and Cultural Rights (ICESCR) represents one of the most authoritative recognitions and comprehensive formulations of the right to health.[117] However, because Taiwan is not a member of the UN and therefore unable to become a signatory to the ICESCR, this human rights instrument has hitherto received negligible attention in health policy discourse. While the Constitutional Court has attained some successes in advancing distributive justice in health care by relying solely on constitutional principles, the time has come for it to explicitly recognize a constitutional right to health and bring Taiwan's human rights protection in line with international standards, if it wishes to remain an influential player in contributing to the country's health equity.

In 2009, Taiwan's Legislative Yuan enacted a groundbreaking law that officially gives domestic legal effect to the ICESCR and related general comments.[118] I urge the Constitutional Court to take advantage of this legislative momentum and to finally entrench a robust right to health in Taiwan's Constitution. Specifically, the Court must recognize a constitutional right to health that attends to the needs of socioeconomically disadvantaged groups. It must also ensure that the content of this right addresses not only access to health care but also the underlying determinants of health, thus allowing progressive reallocation of resources to permeate beyond the bounds of the NHI regime. If the Constitutional Court can continue to follow its remarkable jurisprudence and pay heed to collectivist principles, it is not unrealistic to expect such a rights-based strategy to have a transformative impact on both health equity and overall social justice in Taiwan.

---

[115] Norman Daniels, *Justice, Health, and Healthcare*, 1(2) AM. J. BIOETHICS 1, 6 (2001).

[116] HEALTH AND HUMAN RIGHTS, at xiv (Rebecca Cook & Charles Ngwena eds., 2007).

[117] International Covenant on Economic, Social and Cultural Rights, G.A. res. 2200A (XXI), 21 U.N. GAOR Supp. (No. 16) at 49, U.N. Doc. A/6316 (1966), 993 U.N.T.S. 3, art 12 entered into force Jan. 3, 1976.

[118] Gongmin yu Zhengzhi Quanli Guoji Gongyue ji Jingji Shehui Wenhua Quanli Guoji Gongyue Shixingfa [Act to Implement the International Covenant on Civil and Political Rights and the International Covenant on Economic, Social and Cultural Rights], QUANGUO FAGUI (2009) (Taiwan), *available at* http://law.moj.gov.tw.

PART III

Mixed Private/Public Systems

10

Health Rights at the Juncture between State and Market

The People's Republic of China

Christina S. Ho[*]

10.1 HEALTH SYSTEM IN CHINA

10.1.1 Basic Description: Public Delivery System in Name

Since 1949, the main components of the health care delivery system in China have remained nominally public. Most hospitals and clinics are "public service organizations" (*gong gong shiye danwei*), meaning that they are organized by government with state-owned assets and personnel enjoy salary, rank and, other protections akin to those of civil servants. Only 20 percent of all hospitals are organized using private capital, delivering only 5 percent of overall inpatient and outpatient visits, although this fraction is growing.[1]

The delivery system's functions, however, belie these formally public characteristics: health organizations subsist mainly on revenue they can generate from fees rather than from public financial support. Nearly 90 percent of hospital funding is from revenue generation,[2] and doctors' actual take-home pay depends in part on how much revenue they generate for their departments.[3] The funding source to cover those fees has been mostly private as well. Health coverage rates had been as

[*] Thanks to Bill Alford for introducing me to this project, and to Aeyal Gross and Colleen Flood for envisioning and realizing it. I am indebted to the other chapter authors from whom I have learned so much. I would also like to thank the participants of the Columbia Law School Center for Chinese Legal Studies Workshop on Works-in-Progress, in particular Benjamin Liebman, Mary Gallagher, Carl Minzner, Alex Wang, and Ji Li for their helpful feedback. Any errors are mine alone. I am grateful to Hansi Men for his excellent research assistance.

[1] *Fixing the Public Hospital System* 1 (World Bank, Working Paper No. 58411, Vol. 1, June 1, 2010), *available at* http://www.worldbank.org/research/2010/06/13240556/fixing-public-hospital-system-china-vol-1-2-executive-summary#.

[2] Shanlian Hu, *Universal Coverage and Health Financing from China's Perspective*, 86(11) BULL. WORLD HEALTH ORG. 819, 819 (2008).

[3] Xiaoyun Liu et al., *Does Decentralisation Improve Human Resource Management in the Health Sector? A Case Study from China*, 63 SOC. SCI.& MED. 1836, 1842 (2006).

low as 10–20 percent in the rural areas, but universal coverage has been promised as of March 2009, when the highest organs of political power in China announced a major reform plan described later in the chapter.

To properly characterize the "public" and "private" – or more accurately, state-allocated and market-allocated – elements of China's health system, one must first understand the recent history of its development.

After the Communist Revolution of 1949, China established a pure public delivery system staffed by "Barefoot Doctors" who had minimal medical education. Government and collective funds supported their services and livelihoods. From 1950 to 1980, the system slashed infant mortality and doubled life expectancy.

With the advent of market liberalization in the 1980s, China's central government capped the central subsidies backstopping health care. Local governments, now responsible for the solvency of these health centers, came to treat them as hybrid entities that could then charge fees to generate revenue.[4]

The central State Pricing and Control Bureau tried to keep core prices low while allowing markups for pharmaceuticals and other higher-technology items that arguably exceeded the basic level. Medical practice inevitably skewed toward these items, and overprescribing, not to mention cost growth, ballooned.

Patients' paid 20 percent of total health expenditures out of pocket in 1978, but shouldered 60 percent in 2001.[5] As in Hungary, discussed in Chapter 8 of this volume, cost barriers consisted not solely of explicit fees for treatment but also in the widespread practice of giving physicians red envelopes containing informal monetary payments ("hongbao") to gain favor or access.[6]

A multilevel health care services infrastructure exists throughout the countryside, with a corresponding tiered system in urban areas, but its operation is hampered by fee-based incentives. A village doctor anchors the rural "three-tier network,"[7] with a township-level community health center one tier up, followed by a county hospital. In addition, local governments license other health providers, and tertiary hospitals exist at provincial and national levels. For even simple outpatient matters, patients tend to crowd at the higher-level hospitals, to seek what they perceive to be higher-quality care.[8] Meanwhile, township health center beds stand empty. Because providers depend on fees for revenues and fewer patients seek care at lower tiers, China has struggled to encourage doctors to serve there. The doctors now working

---

4   *See* Christina S. Ho, *Health Reform and De Facto Federalism in China*, 8 CHINA INT'L J. 33 (2010).

5   Guojia Tongji Ju (国家统计局) [National Bureau of Statistics of China], Stat. Y.B. China 875 (2007).

6   Liu et al., *supra* note 3.

7   *See* William Hsiao, *The Chinese Health Care System: Lessons for Other Nations*, 41 SOC. SCI. & MED 1047, 1047 (1995); see also Social Development Division, Promoting Sustainable Strategies to Improve Access to Health Care in the Asian and Pacific Region, U.N. Doc, ST/ESCAP/2529 at 41–42, (Feb., 2009) [hereinafter Promoting].

8   *See* Qunhong Shen et al., The Imbalance Between Patient Needs and the Limited Competence of Top-Level Health Providers in Urban China: An Empirical Study 1 (Stanford Shorenstein Asian Pac. Res. Ctr., Working Paper No. 19, Nov. 2010), *available at* http://ssrn.com/abstract=1705694.

in rural communities often lack even a bachelor's degree in medicine, and health care workers who cannot be fired are sometimes dispatched to community health centers, exacerbating the quality deficit on the front lines.[9]

While the welfare of Chinese citizens has surged in a few short decades, many of the striking improvements in health status preceded the 1978 reforms.[10] Economic growth following these market reforms has increased income for millions of Chinese citizens, but public health gains in the post-reform period have arguably slowed compared to other countries,[11] even as inequality threatens to destabilize the Chinese socioeconomic landscape.[12]

One of the most pronounced axes of social stratification in China divides those who live in urban areas from those in rural ones. Urban residents earn more, thereby attracting better health services, and are more likely to have coverage through their employers.[13]

Agricultural workers lack institutional employers, but prior to 1978, they did have coverage through the collective prepaid cooperative medical system (CMS), which has deteriorated since. In 1976, 85 percent of rural residents were covered by the rural CMS system,[14] but by 2003, 80 percent were uninsured.[15] Since then, the government has taken steps to strengthen coverage in both urban and rural areas, as I explain later.

10.1.2 *Government Response*

To address this litany of problems, the central government has in the past decade not only continued to fund public delivery but also developed a four-part system of demand-side subsidies in the form of health coverage.

Under the New Cooperative Medical System (NCMS), rural residents pay an annual premium, originally 10 RMB (a little over US$1), matched by 10 RMB each from local and central government. The total government contribution rose to 280 RMB in 2013, even as average individual contributions reached 70 RMB in some

---

9 Xilong Pan et al., *Service Utilization in Community Health Centers in China: A Comparative Analysis with Local Hospitals*, 6 BMC HEALTH SERVICES RES. 93, 97 (2006).

10 *See, e.g.*, Therese Hesketh & Wei Xingzhu, *Effect of Restricted Freedom on Health in China*, 329 BRIT. MED. J. 1427 (2004); Ajay Tandon et al., *Inclusiveness of Economic Growth in the People's Republic of China: What Do Population Health Outcomes Tell Us?*, 23 ASIAN DEV. REV. 53 (2006).

11 Ajay Tandon et al., *supra* note 10.

12 Houli Wang et al., *Factors Contributing to High Costs and Inequality in China's Health Care System*, 298 J. AM. MED. ASS'N 1928, 1930 (2007).

13 Hassan H. Dib et al., *Evaluation of the New Rural Cooperative Medical System in China: Is It Working or Not?*, 7 INT'L J. HEALTH EQUITY 17 (2008) *available at* http://www.equityhealthj.com/content/7/1/17.

14 Jin Ma et al., *From a National, Centrally Planned Health System to A System Based on the Market: Lessons From China*, 27 HEALTH AFF. 937, 939 (2008).

15 Dib et al., *supra* note 13.

places.[16] Localities use these pooled resources to provide varying coverage. While the program was initially geared to providing financial protection to patients in the event of hospitalization or major illness, it now covers primary care. Pilot-tested in 2002, NCMS has now become national policy. Despite its voluntary nature, it now covers nearly the entire rural population.[17]

Starting from the late 1990s, Urban Employee Basic Medical Insurance (UEBMI) replaced prior coverage for government workers and employees of state-owned enterprises. Virtually all employers are in theory required to enroll their employees and retirees.[18] The total population that China aims to cover under UEBMI is 340 million. It is financed by joint contributions from employers, who typically contribute 6 percent of payroll, and employees, who contribute 2 percent. That funding is then divided, with half funding individual Medical Savings Accounts and the rest funding the Social Pooling Account for catastrophic health expenses.[19]

Coverage for "urban residents" – that is, the nonworking population – lagged initially, but China has now extended Urban Resident Basic Medical Insurance (URBMI), providing benefits resembling the NCMS program for rural residents.[20] Enrollment is voluntary, and government-matched contributions for each enrollee are weighted toward the more disadvantaged central and western regions of China.[21]

Finally, China provides Medical Assistance (MA) to pay premiums and cost sharing for vulnerable populations to participate in URBMI and NCMS. This program remains patchwork and is overseen by the Ministry of Civil Affairs rather than the Ministry of Health, hampering coordination.

Despite some efforts to address migrant workers, residence still defines the risk pools, underlining the continued localization in health care. However these programs do establish channels for increased central subsidization of health costs.[22] The

---

[16] *See* Weisheng Jisheng Wei Caizheng Bu Guanyu Zuohao 2011 Nian Xinxing Nongcun Hezuo Yiliao Gongzuo de Tongzhi (卫生计生委财政部关于做好2013年新型农村合作医疗工作的通知) [Circular of the Ministry of Health and Family Planning, and the Ministry of Finance on Implementing the New Rural Cooperative Medical Care in 2013] 2013 MOH Gaz.15 (September 5, 2013)(China).

[17] *The Path to Integrated Insurance Systems in China* 6 (World Bank, Working Paper No. 58412 Vol. 2, June 1, 2010), *available at* http://www.worldbank.org/research/2010/06/13240422/path-integrated-insurance-system-china-vol-2–2-main-report# [hereinafter *Path*].

[18] *Id.*, at 5.

[19] *Chinese Health Sector – Why Reform is Needed*, RURAL HEALTH IN CHINA: BRIEFING NOTES SERIES, no. 33232 (WB/EASHD), *available at* http://www.worldbank.org/research/2005/04/6217192/chinas-health-sector-reform-needed#.

[20] *See* Opinions of the Central Committee of the Chinese Communist Party and the State Council on Deepening the Health Care System Reform, CHINA INTERNET INFORMATION CENTER (Mar. 17, 2009), *available at* http://www.china.org.cn/government/scio-press-conferences/2009–04/09/content_17575378.htm [hereinafter *Opinions*].

[21] Path, *supra* note 17, at 6.

[22] Zhang Zongtang et al. (张宗唐) *Lianghui Tegao: Cong Wunian Gonggong Caizheng Zhichu Kan Minsheng Gaishan Jincheng* (两会特稿: 从五年公共财政支出看民生进程) [Special Report From the Two Meetings: A View of Improvement in People's Livelihoods From the Perspective of Five Year's Expenditures From the Public Treasury], ZHONGHUA RENMIN GONGHEGUO ZHONGYANG RENMIN

State Council committed an additional 850 billion RMB for the first three years of health reform,[23] ending the retreat in central financing that vexed previous decades.

Yet, without curbs on local revenue generation, providers still charge per service, retain profits, and induce demand to maximize those profits; the only difference is they now draw from a deeper pocket.[24] In response, the central government has encouraged localities to experiment with supply-side cost controls, including capitation, global budgets, and case-based bundles. China is continuing to refine implementation to address these developments. In March 2009, the government officially released its blueprint for comprehensive health care reform, although many of the components had already been widely implemented on a pilot basis. As a sign of the importance accorded to the health care reform agenda, the plans were jointly released by two of the highest organs of political authority in China: the Central Committee of the Chinese Communist Party and the State Council of the People's Republic of China.[25]

Leading up to the announcement of health reform, both leadership and public alike vigorously debated whether China should adopt a "government approach" or a "market approach" to health reform. The blueprint blended the two.[26] In what follows, I describe the mix of public and private characteristics of the system described by the reform plans.

The health care reform plans promise universal coverage by 2020, with five items for rapid implementation. Among the five is the achievement of 90 percent coverage through the four-part system described earlier, with the promise that the value of government financing would reach at least 200 RMB per person per year, since revised to 280.[27] The government has also prioritized the provision of a formulary of essential drugs, investments in primary health care delivery, greater parity between

ZHENGFU MENHU WANGZHAN (中华人民共和国中央人民政府门户网站) [The Chinese Central Government's Offical Web Portal] (Mar. 7, 2008), *available at* http://www.gov.cn/2008lh/content_913007.htm; *2009 Nian Zhongyang Caizheng Yusuan Biao* (2009年中央财政收入预算表) [2009 Central Finance Budget], *available at* http://www.mof.gov.cn/zhengwuxinxi/caizhengshuju/200903/t20090319_124155.html.

[23] *Implementation Plan for the Recent Priorities of the Health Care System Reform (2009–2011)*, CHINA INTERNET INFORMATION CENTER, *available at* http://www.china.org.cn/government/scio-press-conferences/2009–04/09/content_17575401.htm.

[24] Xinxing Nongcun Hezuo Yiliao Shidian Gongzuo Pinggu Zu (新型农村合作医疗试点评估组) [NCMS Pilot Site Work Evaluation Group], Fazhanzhong de zhongguo xinxing nongcun hezuo yiliao: xinxing nongcun hezuo yiliao shidian gongzuo pinggu baogao (发展中的中国新型农村合作医疗:新型农村合作医疗试点工作评估报告) [Chinese New Cooperative Medical System in Development, New Cooperative Medical System Pilot Site Work Evaluation Report] 169 (2006) [hereinafter *Work Evaluation*].

[25] Opinions, *supra* note 20.

[26] *See also* Christina S. Ho, *China's Health Care Reform: Background and Policies, in* IMPLEMENTING HEALTHCARE REFORM POLICIES IN CHINA: CHALLENGES AND OPPORTUNITIES 1 (Charles W. Freeman III and Xiaoqing L. Boynton eds., 2011), *available at* http://csis.org/files/publication/111202_Freeman_ImplementingChinaHealthReform_Web.pdf.

[27] The original goal was 120 RMB.

rural and urban public health services, and experimentation to pilot different models for public hospital financing and governance.

President Hu Jintao's choice of "the four separates" as the guiding slogan for health reform captures the core problem that the heath care reform plans seek to address. Hu's four separates refer to "separating for-profit from non-profit, government from enterprise, management from operation, and prescription sales from treatment." The fundamental challenge for China parallels the experience many developing countries face when transitioning away from a pure public-integrated government model. Consumer choice and the development of commercial alternatives have accompanied privatization of the health care system in some countries, but in China, private health sector actors are underdeveloped and continue to face significant barriers. Accordingly, the health care reform attempts to substitute for some of the functions that private actors might perform by fostering functional disaggregation within government. The much-maligned model of the past thirty years leveraged the relative separation of local governments from central control to unleash quasi-market actors with incentives to maximize profits. Because of the furor over that model and its inequities, the health care reform seeks new methods that curb the excesses of the previous system, while permitting the pluralism of functions that would otherwise have emerged with the development of private activity in the health sector.

The reform plans more clearly divide financing from delivery by embracing the third-party purchasing structure of the coverage system[28] and channeling the bulk of the 850 billion RMB to demand-side purchasing rather than supply-side subsidies.[29] The demand-side funds flow through specialized social insurance offices within the Ministry of Human Resources and Social Security (MOHRSS) system, rather than the Ministry of Health, enabling an intragovernmental disentanglement of payer from provider. The central government is encouraging even more separation by urging that these social insurance offices involve commercial insurers in carrying out some of their functions. Wraparound commercial insurance and other products are envisioned as supplements for those whose means and demands exceed the basic level.

The public hospitals pilots explore another separation strategy, by seeking a governance model that would give hospitals greater relative autonomy from the revenue-generating priorities of local government. However, this reform has been hobbled by unresolved questions. The blueprint fails to articulate a model for public hospitals, reverting instead to a process of experimentation.[30] On the one hand, the reforms

---

[28] Opinions, *supra* note 20, at Art. 6.

[29] Wang Shiling, *Zengliang! 8500 Yi Yigai Touru Xuanyi Xiao* (增量! 8500 亿医改投入悬疑晓) [850 Billion RMB Is All Additional Investment], 21st CENTURY BUSINESS HERALD (2009), *available at* http://www.chinahealthreform.org/index.php/publicdiscussion/8-media/891–8500.html. Some Chinese economists believed two-thirds of the 850 billion would fund demand-side subsidies.

[30] Guo Yan, *A Midterm Assessment of China's Health Care Reform, in* IMPLEMENTING HEALTH-CARE REFORM POLICIES IN CHINA: CHALLENGES AND OPPORTUNITIES 1 (Charles W. Freeman III

describe a vision of public hospitals as entities treated like and even competing with private hospitals. Yet the blueprint also encourages local governments to manage hospitals using top-down bureaucratic controls.[31]

The reform blueprint also retains central-local separation, all the more striking as local government autonomy fueled the reviled profit-driven health delivery system of years past. While central government will undertake some functions,[32] such as setting medical service pricing methods, provincial or municipal pricing bureaus retain significant authority, and will work with health and labor bureaus to approve recommended prices for basic medical services.[33] The recently passed Social Insurance Law, which codifies the four-part coverage scheme, also reflects deference to local autonomy. The law outlines basic benefit parameters but shuns specificity. Article 28 merely requires basic medical insurance to include drugs on the "essential medicines" formulary, diagnostic and clinical care, appropriate/medically necessary treatment, and emergency care. The government may in the future define these benefit categories further by regulation or simply allow local government determination.[34]

The local latitude to determine UEBMI and NCMS benefits has produced benefit packages of roughly three types.[35] Initially, the most common type consisted of inpatient insurance coverage alone with outpatient coverage restricted to certain priority diseases. The second type, offered in wealthier regions of the country, consists of insurance coverage for both inpatient and outpatient services, often reimbursing a percentage of health costs with a deductible and annual cap. A third type offers pooled financing for major expenses, such as inpatient costs, as well as some assistance for priority diseases, but otherwise addresses outpatient needs by providing an individual medical savings accounts to enrollees.[36] However, one benefit parameter – the content of the essential medicines formulary – has been well described by the central government. While so-called Part B drugs are subject to some flexibility, Part A specifies several hundred drugs that cannot be modified by local government.[37]

In sum, the recent history of China's health care sector shows that the pre-1978 government approach to health care delivery, possible under a system of centralized

and Xiaoqing L. Boynton eds., 2011), *available at* http://csis.org/files/publication/111202_Freeman_ImplementingChinaHealthReform_Web.pdf.

[31] Opinions, *supra* note 20, at Art. 9.

[32] *See, e.g., Id.*, at Art. 4, 5, 8 & 11.

[33] Opinions, *supra* note 20, at Art. 11.

[34] Shehui Baoxian Fa (社会保险法) [Social Insurance Law] (promulgated by the Standing Comm. Nat'l People's Cong., Oct.28, 2010, effective July 1, 2011) 2010 STANDING COMM. NAT'L PEOPLE'S CONG. GAZ. 620 (China), *available at* http://www.gov.cn/flfg/2010–10/28/content_1732964.htm.

[35] *See, e.g.,* World Health Org. [WHO], *Health Insurance System in China: A Briefing Note* (World Health Report Background Paper No. 37, 2010), *available at* http://www.who.int/healthsystems/topics/financing/healthreport/37ChinaB_YFINAL.pdf.

[36] Work Evaluation, *supra* note 24, at 169; Promoting, *supra* note 7, at 49.

[37] *See* Path, *supra* note 17, at 14.

government control, achieved a measure of health equity and quality. Shifting responsibility to localities pressured health care providers to behave as quasi-private profit maximizers and led to increasing inequality and dissatisfaction across China's health system.

The ongoing health reform effort in China offers an opportunity for China to adjust its course, and while it seems unlikely that China will, or even can, return to the pre-1978 model, some of the steps extending coverage and experimenting with purchasing and cost control incentives hold promise. Whether China can restore sufficient equity throughout the health system remains to be seen.

10.2 ROLE OF LAW: CHINA AND THE RIGHT TO HEALTH

China has long considered economic rights to be among its purported political values. Although it has yet to ratify the International Covenant on Civil and Political Rights (ICCPR), China has signed and ratified the International Covenant on Economic Cultural and Social Rights (ICECSR), presumably espousing the right to health as specified in General Comment 14.

However, international law without domestic incorporation cannot ground individual claims or judicial decisions. Chinese courts also lack the power of interpreting the constitution and striking down conflicting laws. That power instead resides with the National People's Congress and its Standing Committee, although it has never been exercised.[38]

Nevertheless, it is important to note that the Constitution mentions health and medicine in fairly prominent ways.[39] In describing various State roles, the Constitution declares:

> The state develops medical and health services, promotes modern medicine and traditional Chinese medicine, encourages and supports the setting up of various medical and health facilities by the rural economic collectives, state enterprises and undertakings and neighborhood organizations, and promotes sanitation activities of a mass character, all to protect the people's health. The state develops physical culture and promotes mass sports activities to build up the people's physique.[40]

Article 14 also includes "establish[ing] a sound social security system compatible with the level of economic development" among state duties.

---

[38] See Fu Yulin & Randall Peerenboom, *A New Analytical Framework for Understanding and Promoting Judicial Independence in China, in* JUDICIAL INDEPENDENCE IN CHINA: LESSONS FOR GLOBAL RULE OF LAW PROMOTION (Randall Peerenboom ed., 2010) [Hereinafter *Judicial Independence*].

[39] XIANFA art. 21 (1982) (China), *available at* http://english.people.com.cn/constitution/constitution. html.
    The 1978 Constitution, art. 50–51 and the 1954 Constitution, art. 93 contain similar language.
    See XIANFA art. 50–51 (1978) (China), *available at* http://www.e-chaupak.net/database/chicon/1978/ 1978e.pdf.
    See also XIANFA art. 27 (1975) (China), *available at* http://www.e-chaupak.net/database /chicon/1975/1975e.htm.

[40] XIANFA art. 21 (1982) (China).

Chapter II, which details the fundamental rights and duties of citizens, also mentions health. Article 42 concerns a citizen's right and duty to work, and declares that in relation to this right, "the State creates conditions for employment, [and] enhances occupational safety and health." Article 45 guarantees citizens the right to "material assistance when they are old, ill or disabled," and ascribes to the state a role in "developing social insurance, social relief and medical and health services that are required for citizens to enjoy this right."

Since the 1949 revolution, the People's Republic of China has had numerous constitutions. The specific formulation of the right to health as one of "material assistance" (*wuzhi bangzhu*) in the event of illness appears essentially unchanged in every single version. Meanwhile, Chinese civil law articulates the state's role in protecting health rights against tortious infringement by others.[41]

While private law and other laws stipulating duties of medical providers to their patients in treatment may not provide patients a health equity claim against the state, public dissatisfaction with the state's organization of the health sector is often manifested in patients' conflicts with health providers whose behavior clashes with their vestigial "public role."

China's new tort law, passed at the end of 2009, contains ten articles on malpractice, reinforcing patients' rights to a certain standard of behavior in the treatment context.[42] These articles supplement the 2002 regulation on medical accidents, providing administrative mechanisms supplementing civil litigation in determining provider responsibility for injuries suffered by patients.[43] In April 2011, China instituted a regulation imposing duties on health care providers to engage in adverse event reporting. In recent years, the Supreme People's Court and the prosecuting body in China have issued stern clarifications that kickbacks or other practices in medical treatment are subject to criminal laws on commercial bribery and corruption.[44] China thus employs civil, administrative, and even criminal laws to regulate providers' duties once they have entered into a treatment relationship.

A regime of laws regulating a patient's right to receive treatment is also developing, but faces grave implementation challenges.[45] China's Social Insurance Law, which took effect in July 2011, devotes nine articles to outlining the NCMS, UEBMI,

---

[41] Minfa Tongze (民法通则) [General Principles of the Civil Law] (promulgated by the Standing Comm. Nat'l People's Cong., Apr. 12, 1986, effective Jan. 1, 1987) 1986 STANDING COMM. NAT'L PEOPLE'S CONG. GAZ. 3, Art. 119 (China).

[42] Qinquan Zeren Fa (侵权责任法) [Tort Law] (promulgated by the Standing Comm. Nat'l People's Cong., Dec. 26, 2009, effective July 1, 2010) 2010 STANDING COMM. NAT'L PEOPLE'S CONG. GAZ. 4 (China), *translated in* http://www.procedurallaw.cn/english/law/201001/t20100110_300173.html.

[43] Yiliao Shigu Chuli Tiaoli (医疗事故处理条例) [Regulations on Handling Medical Accidents] (promulgated by the St. Council, Apr. 4, 2002, effective Sept. 1, 2002) ST. COUNCIL GAZ., May 30, 2002 (China), *translated in* http://www.gov.cn/english/laws/2005-07/25/content_16885.htm.

[44] Guanyu banli shangye huilv xingshi anjian shiyong falv ruogan wenti de yijian (关于办理商业贿赂刑事案件适用法律若干问题的意见) [Opinions regarding selected problems using law in managing criminal commercial bribery cases.], SUP. PEOPLE'S CT. GAZ., Nov. 20, 2008, at 8, *available at* http://www.law-lib.com/law/law_view.asp?id=270119.

[45] *See infra* Section 10.3.

and URBMI coverage systems. However, the law avoids detailing what these programs provide. Whereas employer coverage for employees is officially mandatory,[46] enrollment in the other two coverage programs is voluntary. Article 28 does require certain benefit categories,[47] but enforcement provisions are vague, promising only "punishment under law" to those who may try to defraud, embezzle or misuse the funds, underpay, or fail to finance or pay benefits in a timely manner.[48] The lack of detail on how those injured might pursue their complaints raises concerns that legal rights in the social insurance law may not translate easily into enforceable claims. China's history of administrative enforcement in education and pensions does not inspire confidence.[49] Moreover, Chinese courts must enforce their own judgments, so up to half of all civil judgments and arbitral awards are never enforced.[50]

Article 24 of the Professional Doctor's Law prohibits refusal to treat in emergency situations,[51] and Article 31 of China's hospital management regulations contain an emergency treat-or-transfer provision.[52] However, the enforcement section of the hospital regulations allows agencies to impose warnings or license suspensions, but does not independently provide for individuals to sue for administrative enforcement.[53] Otherwise, these laws contain no requirement to provide free care; indeed, Article 37 of the hospital regulations embraces fee charging, requiring hospitals to follow laws when setting charges. Articles 38 and 39 of those regulations require that provider institutions take on government assignments to support or assist the rural population, especially in the event of emergencies, accidents, epidemics, or other special circumstances. However, this language suggests health care as a good that the government should provide, not an entitlement that the individual can demand.

---

[46] However employers often hire workers on an informal or part-time basis to skirt the law.

[47] See *supra* Section 10.2 & nn. 34–37.

[48] See Shehui Baoxian Fa, *supra* note 34, at Chapter 11.

[49] See, e.g., MARK W. Frazier, *What's in a Law? China's Pension Reform and Its Discontents, in* ENGAGING THE LAW IN CHINA, STATE SOCIETY AND POSSIBILITIES FOR JUSTICE 113 (Neil Diamant, Stanley Lubman, and Kevin O'Brien eds., 2005); *see also* THOMAS E. Kellogg, *Courageous Explorers? Education Litigation and Judicial Innovation in China,* 20 HARV. HUM. RTS. J. 141, 151 (2008); Randall Peerenboom, *Economic and Social Rights: The Role of Courts in China,* 12 SAN DIEGO INT'L L.J. 303 (2011). [Hereinafter *Economic and Social Rights*].

[50] Randall Peerenboom, CHINA'S LONG MARCH TOWARD RULE OF LAW 287 (2002). [Hereinafter LONG MARCH].

[51] Zhiye Yishi Fa (执业医师法) [Professional Doctors Law] (promulgated by the Standing Comm. Nat'l People's Cong., June 26, 1998, effective May 1, 1999) 1998 STANDING COMM. NAT'L PEOPLE'S CONG. GAZ. 255, *available at* http://www.gov.cn/banshi/2005–08/01/content_18970.htm.

[52] Yiliao Jigou Guanli Tiaoli (医疗机构管理条例) [Regulations Governing the Administration of Medical Institutions] (promulgated by the St. Council, Feb. 26, 1994, effective Sept. 1, 1994) ST. COUNCIL GAZ., Mar. 17, 1994, at 84, *available at* http://www.gov.cn/banshi/2005–08/01/content_19113.htm.

[53] *Id.,* at art. 37(2) (China does have laws that allow individuals to challenge administrative decisions; however, these laws have practical limitations. For instance, Chinese courts will review the legality, and not the appropriateness of the administrative act, leading to very narrow and not particularly searching review by judges. THE LONG MARCH, *supra* note 50, at 420).

Any of these underlying health laws allow agencies significant discretion in determining proper enforcement, such that patients cannot easily leverage agencies for enforcement against providers. Unless the Social Insurance Law dramatically changes the landscape of judicial protection for individual beneficiaries, prospects are dim for an individual right to health care benefits and services grounded in Chinese positive law.

The norm of a right to equal health care access is invoked from time to time in social and academic discourse.[54] However, that aspiration derives not from a statutory or regulatory source, but instead from the generalized notion of health provision as a public duty, acknowledged in the Constitution and still present in the ostensibly public nature of the health care delivery system.[55]

10.3 LITIGATION AND OTHER MANIFESTATIONS OF GRIEVANCE

10.3.1 *Backdrop to Litigation in China*

Employing the aforementioned laws in litigation is difficult. Litigation is a relatively weak tool in China and arguably even less effective in realizing health claims compared to commercial rights. As one observer has noted, "courts have resisted the pressure to judicialize what are at bottom socioeconomic disputes arising out of the lack of an adequate welfare system."[56] The Chinese legal system does not technically recognize judicial precedent as a source of law, and Chinese courts are answerable to political bodies, local and national congresses, and ultimately Party organs. The structure of the Chinese judicial system allows adjudicative committees or other leaders within each court to supervise some judgments, introducing opportunities for external pressure. Court fees and rampant corruption render courts unavailable to many who seek justice. Additionally, judges' relatively low level of professional prestige diminishes their independence.[57]

For these and other reasons, alternatives to the judiciary, including mediation and arbitration, are quite popular. Chinese law provides for so-called administrative reconsideration procedures that the aggrieved can invoke without going to court.[58] Meanwhile, an administrative system with even older roots – the "letters and visits"

---

[54] *See, e.g.*, Wang Yue (王岳), Yishi Fa (医事法) [Medical Law] (2009).

[55] *Id.* at 49, 62.

[56] Economic and Social Rights, *supra* note 49.

[57] *See* Stephanie Balme, *Local Courts in Western China, in* Judicial Independence in China: Lessons for Global Rule of Law Promotion 154 (Randall Peerenboom ed., 2010).

[58] Xingzheng Fuyi Fa (行政复议法) [Law on Administrative Reconsideration] (promulgated by the Standing Comm. Nat'l People's Cong., Apr. 29, 1999, effective Oct. 10, 1999) 1999 Standing Comm. Nat'l People's Cong. Gaz. 225 (China), *translated in* http://www.lehmanlaw.com/resource-centre/laws-and-regulations/administration/administrative-reconsideration-law-of-the-peoples-republic-of-china-1999.html; *see also* Xingzheng Susong Fa (行政诉讼法) [Administrative Procedure Law] (promulgated by the Standing Comm. Nat'l People's Cong., Apr. 4, 1989, effective Oct. 1, 1990) 1989

system – enables petitioners to visit or write to administrative bureaucracies and their superior organs in the government for redress. All state entities in China, even courts, address letters and visits, the handling of which has traditionally been a matter of official discretion, more like clemency than the application of ascertainable rules through public reason.[59]

These alternative channels are used – and even preferred – in health disputes. The Ministry of Health has prioritized mediation in addressing medical disputes, and aims to improve the resolution of "letters and visits."[60] Apart from these complaint-based systems, China also relies heavily on top-down political-administrative methods such as the cadre-responsibility performance system, the national audit system, and the party discipline committees to keep officials in line.[61] Given the health care delivery system's formally public status, directly answering to government, mechanisms of political accountability have been at least as salient as any mechanisms for judicial accountability.

Perhaps the most effective form of accountability consists in resorting to extralegal channels, revealing the lack of confidence in courts. Indeed, health care has proven a hotspot for unrest.[62] Individual petitioners often protest at agency buildings until they receive some payout from the local government. These practices have become so widespread that the Chinese Ministry of Health has issued guidelines for a "Social Stability Risk Assessment Mechanism" regarding major health incidents.[63] These guidelines urge monitoring of public opinion and early responses to ward off disturbances. Taken at face value, this measure resembles efforts by governments to attune administration and policy to public opinion, although bypassing the signaling function of litigation. On the other hand, some fear that the government could exploit these guidelines to crack down on activists or "troublemakers."

STANDING COMM. NAT'L PEOPLE'S CONG. GAZ. 64, *available at* http://www.dffy.com/faguixiazai/ssf/200311/20031109195715.htm, *translated in* http://en.chinacourt.org/public/detail.php?id=2695.

[59] See Carl F. Minzner, *Xinfang: an Alternative to Formal Chinese Legal Institutions*, 42 STAN. J. INT'L L.J. 103 (2006).

[60] Weisheng Bu Guanyu Yinfa 2011 Nian Weisheng Gongzuo Yaodian de Tongzhi (卫生部关于印发2011年卫生工作要点的通知) [Circular of the Ministry of Health on Transmitting and Issuing the Notice on Key Points of 2011 Healthcare Work] (Jan. 26, 2011), *available at* http://www.moh. gov.cn/publicfiles/business/htmlfiles/mohbgt/s7693/201101/50509.htm (China) [hereinafter *Gongzuo Yaodian 2011*]; *see also* Carl Minzner, *China's Turn Against Law*, 59 AM. J. OF COMP. L. 935 (2011).

[61] Randall Peerenboom, *More Law, Less Courts: Legalized Governance Judicialization and Dejudicialization in China*, LA TROBE L. STUD RES. PAPER NO. 2008/10 (2008), *available at* http://papers.ssrn. com/sol3/papers.cfm?abstract_id=1265147.

[62] *See, e.g.*, Benjamin L. Liebman, *China's Courts: Restricted Reform*, 191 CHINA Q. 620, 622 (2007).

[63] Weishengbu Guanyu Jianli Weisheng Xitong Zhongda Shixiang Shehui Wending Fengxian Pinggu Jizhi de Zhidao Yijian (卫生部关于建立卫生系统重大事项社会稳定风险评估机制的指导意见) [Guidance of the Ministry of Health on the Establishment of Risk Assessment Regime of Social Stability for Major Issues in the Health System], 2011 MOH GAZ. 21 (China).

With these caveats and alternatives to litigation in China, one might wonder that anyone with a health grievance would go to court at all. However, litigation to secure health-related rights in China does exist, and I turn to that next.

10.3.2 *Cases and the Litigation Landscape*[64]

Setting aside the pending reforms, China's underlying laws do not appear to support aggressive litigation to obtain equitable access to health services. However, laws that are otherwise obliquely related to health access and equity are being used creatively to provide some benefits to individual patients in a system widely perceived to be failing the public. Absent genuine policy and structural change, litigation may simply stand in as an outlet for disgruntled individuals, albeit in a manner that deflects discontent away from the government toward other targets of grievance.

Media occasionally report on legal action in situations where individuals were denied care. For instance, in Henan province, a court held hospital officials criminally liable when a patient without identification or means of payment died because he was discharged improperly and left on the roadside in the winter to freeze to death.[65] However, an occasional case along these lines does not mark out a reliable pathway for claimant-led enforcement of the right to obtain health care.

Meanwhile, the outcomes of other types of health-related claims under commercial or employment-based insurance, malpractice, or antitrust might not at first glance promote health care access, yet seem to favor patients more than one might expect.

Contract suits against commercial insurers for denial of benefits are common. One typical case in 2003 held that, according to China's Insurance Law, exclusionary clauses are not effective unless the insured had actual notice of its content.[66] Another case reads the terms "third-party" and "passenger" in a manner such that the injured party was not subject to the restrictive benefit caps that applied to passengers.[67] In short, there are numerous cases that construe health insurance clauses in favor of the insured. Many of these cases arise under the Insurance Law, which only applies

---

[64] Although government urges courts to post judgments online, case reporting is still underdeveloped in China. This discussion is based on the health-related cases in Peking University's database, China Law Info, which, despite its flaws, is still the single most comprehensive electronic database of Chinese case. The discussion is also supplemented by news of cases reported in the media. Any cases described are for illustrative purposes only, as they have no formal precedential value.

[65] Song Wenzhi, Wang Yue (宋文志, 王岳), Weisheng Faxue (卫生法学) [Health Law Studies] 49 (2nd ed., 2008).

[66] *See* Chen Jiandang Su Zhongguo Renshou Baoxian Nanyang Fengongsi Baoxian Hetong An (陈建党诉中国人寿保险公司南阳分公司保险合同案) [Chen Jiandang v. China Life Insurance Co. Nanyang Branch] (Nan Yang Interm. Mun. People's Ct. of Henan Province Sept. 16, 2003) *available at* http://vip.chinalawinfo.com/case/displaycontent.asp?gid=117488906 (China).

[67] Zheng Kebao v. Xu Weiliang and Changxing Sub-branch Company of PICC Property and Casualty Company Limited (Huzhou City Interm. People's Ct. of Zhejiang Province Sept. 18, 2006) *available at* http://www.lawinfochina.com/display.aspx?lib=case&id=787 (China).

to those few and fortunate patients with commercial health insurance. Arguably the effect of these cases is to empower the relatively privileged, who can afford not only commercial insurance but also court fees and a lawyer to pursue these cases.

The aforementioned cases do not validate rights against a governmental party. All of the claimants are sued under well-specified contract and statutory provisions rather than grounding their claims in government-sponsored health coverage.

However, from media reports, there do appear to be at least a handful of cases involving employees or retirees suing government for reimbursement under their employment-based benefit plans. Without either the primary source material or a domain of cases against which to judge the representativeness these lawsuits, it is difficult to draw conclusions. Yet these cases are notable because, unlike the commercial insurance cases, they do involve individuals suing their local Bureau of Human Resources and Social Security. Plaintiffs in these cases often seek benefits under UEBMI; however, many present situations that are atypical. Indeed, one formerly employed individual sought not the enforcement of UEBMI, but rather compliance with a negotiated agreement to funnel payments relating to the bankruptcy of his former employer, a ball-bearing factory, into supplementary individual medical savings accounts.[68] Another case involved a highly honored retired cadre, whose benefits, along with those of Long March survivors, predated UEBMI. The court found, against the protests of the local Social Security bureau, that the retired cadre could sue the Social Security office administering UEBMI and other health approvals, even if the cadre's medical expenses are settled out of the separate funds earmarked by the county government directly.[69] In this instance, the Social Security bureau was liable, because the county tasked it with the professional technical role of handling claims and administering the drug formulary for some benefits outside UEBMI as well.

The rest of the cases I found through media reports were treated in a manner arguably similar to the treatment of contract claims against commercial insurers. Some of the cases turn on technicalities that the court seems willing, at least in some instances, to read in favor of the insured. For example, one case refused to uphold a Social Security Bureau in requiring original rather than copied receipts as

---

[68] Wei Weihu Yibao Quan Mingaoguan Yi Tuixiu Zhigong Yingde Xingzheng Susong An Taohui Shuofa (为维护医保权民告官 一退休职工赢得行政诉讼案讨回说法) [A retiree prevailed on an administrative action against the government for protection of his right to healthcare] Henan Renmin Wang (河南人民网) [Henan People] (March 17, 2008, 14:15:28), http://henan.people.com.cn/news/2008/03/17/275039.html.

[69] Shangsu Ren Lijing Xian Chengzhen Zhigong Yiliao Baoxian Shiye Chu Yin Shehui Baozheng Xingzheng Jifu Yian (上诉人利津县城镇职工医疗保险事业处因社会保障行政给付一案) [In re appellant Lijing Village Employee Health Insurance Bureau's case on administrative provision of social security benefits] (Dongying Interm. People's Ct. of Shandong Province Mar. 10, 2005), *available at* http://www.66law.cn/lawwrit/7128.aspx.

a condition of reimbursement.[70] The court protected the insured in another case, where the Social Security Bureau contended that the insured misrepresented her medical status upon enrollment by not disclosing her diabetes and was therefore ineligible for benefits. The court found no misrepresentation because the patient subjected herself to the full pre-enrollment medical exam required by the bureau.[71] On the other hand, the court does also enforce technicalities imposed by the social insurance office to deny reimbursement. One court upheld the social insurance office's denial of reimbursement when a bill was presented beyond the year-end deadline for claim submission.[72]

The existence of these cases does not necessarily suggest a route to greater equity in health access through litigation. These plaintiffs are relatively fortunate, enjoying the benefits of formal employment as part of the compensation they have earned through their privately negotiated employment relationship. One could speculate that their suits to claim on these benefits were reported by the press because these plaintiffs are more sympathetic for this very reason. Although it is hard to conclude that other cases involving unemployed plaintiffs do not exist, some of the news stories expressly emphasize the unusual if not unprecedented posture of these lawsuits that name the Social Security bureau as a defendant.[73]

Health care reform and the Social Insurance Law are more radical insofar as they provide health entitlements to the unemployed and the poor, with funding obligations imposed on government rather than as a duty of a third-party employer. The Social Insurance Law has only recently come into effect, and so far, no reported cases specifically cite health coverage rights under this new law. As others have noted in the context of education litigation, it took some time for courts to determine whether they should permit suits under the education laws as civil cases or administrative law cases, if at all.

Formally, one can seek administrative review and redress for a government decision denying an individual access to, or reimbursement for, services and treatments they believed they are due. China's Administrative Litigation Law (ALL),[74] passed

---

[70] Woguo Shouli Yibao Jiufen An Zai Huayin ShiYishen Chenai Luoding – Shebao Ju Baisu (我国首例医保纠纷案在华阴市一审尘埃落定－社保局败诉) [Our country's first health insurance case is decided in Huayin City – the health bureau lost the suit], Tianya Shequ (天涯社区) [Tianya Community] (Sept. 27, 2011, 17:05:00), *available at* http://www.tianya.cn/publicforum/content/news/1/224404.shtml.

[71] Zhuanggao Shebao Ju Shimin Yinghui Yibao Zige (状告社保局市民赢回医保资格) [City resident won back his qualification for health insurance in an action against the local bureau of social security], Tengxun (腾讯) [Tencent] (Aug. 20, 2006, 12:02), *available at* http://cq.qq.com/a/20060820/000094.htm.

[72] Zhebi Yiliao Fei Gaibugai Baoxiao? (这笔医疗费该不该报销) [Should all these medical expenses be reimbursed?], Yunan Laonian Bao (云南老年报) [Yunan Senior Citizens' Newspaper], *available at* http://www.ynlnb.cn/64/2653.htm.

[73] *See, e.g.*, Woguo Shouli Yibao Jiufen An Zai Huayin ShiYishen Chenai Luoding, *supra* note 70.

[74] Xingzheng Susong Fa (行政诉讼法) [Administrative Procedure Law], *supra* note 58.

in 1989, provides a channel for judicial review of such adverse administrative determinations. However, circumstances would have to be compelling for a court to decide against a local government, especially on an issue of any prominence. Many ALL cases have been filed since its passage, and a notable proportion of claimants have even managed to obtain relief under the law. However, the probabilities and prevailing incentives are such that the Chinese still dismiss the possibility of suing the government as an act of "throwing an egg against a stone."[75]

As discussed earlier, nominally "public" providers, such as hospitals, actually exhibit both public and private characteristics, just as suits against the local bureau of social security for employee benefits may be interpreted as trying to claim on entitlements given by third-party employers rather than by the government. Therefore legal action against hospitals may serve as a pressure valve for those who wish to vent their frustration with the health care system while not challenging the government directly. In a notable antitrust case,[76] a hospital was held in violation of China's competition laws for taking kickbacks from drug companies, a practice characteristic of the profiteering and overprescribing that has soured the public on health care providers. The hospital claimed in its own defense that it was not subject to the competition laws because it was a state entity, despite having to make up for insufficiencies in government-allocated funds through drug sales. The court held that regardless of the entity's ownership and legal structure, the market behavior of the hospital rendered it a "business operator" for the purposes of the antitrust laws. This case resulted in an administrative fine for the hospital, and did not necessarily produce greater health care access for the patients of Yichang City, where the provider was located. However, it may have had provided some retributive satisfaction by striking a blow against a hospital system that is perceived as corrupt.

Another category of health-related litigation concerns adverse events in medical treatment. These are disputes over the appropriateness or quality of health care provided, rather than cases of rights to health care services. However, these might also be instances where the hospital or doctor becomes a target for grievance instead of the true culprit – the state.

Reflecting hospitals' mixed public-private status, malpractice claims appear not just as civil cases but also in administrative law dockets. The administrative

---

[75] See Susan Finder, *Like Throwing an Egg at Against a Stone? Administrative Litigation in the People's Republic of China*, 3 J. CHINESE L. 10, 28 (1989); Kevin J. O'Brien & Lianjiang Li, *Suing the Local State: Administrative Litigation in Rural China*, 51 CHINA J. 75 (2004); but see THE LONG MARCH, supra note 50, at 400, where Peerenboom finds that up to 40% of administrative cases favor the plaintiff. However, because many cases are withdrawn and so many grievances are never formulated as cases, the matters that survive to final decision are highly skewed toward those which government is likely to lose.

[76] The Health Care Hospital for Women and Children of Yichang City v. The Administrative Bureau for Industry and Commerce of Yichang City (Yichang City Interm. People's Ct. of Hubei Province, November 21, 2000) (China) *available at* http://en.pkulaw.cn/display.aspx?id=133&lib=case&SearchKeyword=yichang&SearchCKeyword=.

regulations on medical accidents provide that if a medical injury exceeds a certain threshold of severity, or if the injured patient so chooses, the health bureau in conjunction with the medical associations in a given area should appoint a medical advisory committee to make an administrative determination of key issues relating to the matter. Then parties can use this determination in a civil suit, or can appeal in an administrative lawsuit for courts to review such a determination. The medical advisory committees, unsurprisingly, have tended to shield providers. In fact, a number of cases reveal plaintiffs complaining that the hospitals may enjoy protection when the health bureaus that appoint the committees are also the same ones to which they report.[77]

Without the health bureau advisory committee's identification of provider blame for the patient's injury, the plaintiffs have little chance of winning a malpractice claim. Despite these barriers, patients achieve a surprising degree of success in recovery. Benjamin Liebman, in his analysis of all malpractice-related cases in one jurisdiction, has observed that, perhaps to ward off unrest, courts will sometimes find other ways to grant compensation in "compromise" verdicts, even when medical review bodies have rejected provider responsibility.[78] Although loathe to directly contravene heath bureaus and their medical advisory boards by establishing substantive rights, courts on occasion press for favorable settlements, or find other, sometimes procedural bases for relief, such as wrongful modification of records by providers, or failure to report in prescribed situations or time frames.[79]

There are also structural reasons to doubt that litigation helps patients and citizens broadly. Litigation is resource-intensive, and lawyers who take impoverished or unpopular clients suffer financially or may even be relieved of their licenses or arrested.[80] Those clients who can access courts and achieve "compromise" verdicts or large settlements are those who can afford lawyers and court fees, including the sometimes unauthorized additional fees that courts charge.[81] Sometimes, even if clients pay well, lawyers are reluctant to sue government agencies, as they may depend on relationships with ministries and officials to obtain lucrative work in the future.[82] Litigation is limited by existing power relations, and it can contribute

[77] Cao Fengjun Yu Shenhequ Weishengju Bulüxing Yiliao Xingzheng Chexiao Zhize Jiufen Shangsu An (曹风军与沈河区卫生局不履行医疗行政撤销职责纠纷上诉案) [In re Cao Fengjun's Dispute with Shenhe District Health Bureau's Nonfulfillment of Its Obligation of Administrative Revocation] (Liaoning Shenyang Interm. People's Ct. May 12, 2006) (Chinalawinfo).

[78] *See* Benjamin L. Liebman, *Malpractice Mobs: Medical Dispute Resolution in China*, 113 COLUM. L. REV. 181 (2013).

[79] In article 56 of the Regulations on Handling Medical Accidents, there are a number of other duties to which sanctions may apply apart from an identification of fault in a medical accident, which is left to the medical review advisory boards. *See* Yiliao Shigu Chuli Tiaoli, *supra* note 43.

[80] THE LONG MARCH, *supra* note 50, at 343–393

[81] *Id.*, at 285.

[82] *Id.*, at 352 & 367.

to queue jumping for the powerful, or exacerbate a tendency in China to provide one-off solutions to those who insist on dispensation.

Lacking precedential value,[83] favorable decisions will not necessarily apply to like plaintiffs. The unusual ways in which health-related cases are sometimes handled, by settlement or by improvised court decisions to bypass unfavorable substantive determinations on medical fault, do not enable a class of similarly situated plaintiffs to benefit.[84] Observers have noted that "[a] striking pattern running through all Chinese ... policies is a preference ... for particularistic contracting over uniform rules. Party leaders ... design policies to allocate benefits selectively to particular units."[85] Various circumstances in China impede legal action that might mobilize similarly situated plaintiffs to coordinate their advocacy. For instance, under the ALL, an enforcement action against a particular individual or entity might be challenged, but the court cannot vacate the rule, thereby fragmenting the class of potentially interested persons who might collectively oppose the rule.[86] Class actions or group litigation are disfavored.[87] Bribery of judges is a sufficiently embedded practice to exacerbate the availability of one-off resolutions for those with wealth and connections at the expense of broader solutions benefiting all.[88]

Litigation over health rights exists, but it seems to function as a weak proxy through which individuals vent particular frustrations at the margins of the health care system when they cannot strike directly at the structures in need of reform. Without clear declarations of duties and entitlements from the policy and administrative arms of government, the judiciary in China is insufficiently empowered to delineate substantive obligations in health. However, courts can, in individual cases, play a role in holding parties to duties, including employment-based benefits that have been privately negotiated or articulated by other more powerful government organs.[89] During an era when health care actors were viewed as market participants, they could be held in court to market norms, including antitrust and contract obligations and some procedural ground rules like honest record-keeping and reporting. However, courts have been much less effective in holding state actors to account. It remains to be seen whether the new health care reform and social insurance law articulate new rights and duties sufficiently to enable courts to play a positive role in patrolling equity in the future, despite their inability to spearhead health equity in the past.

---

[83] *Id.*, at 286.

[84] *See, e.g.,* Li Li, *Strategies for Judicial Restraint in Chinese Group Action Cases: A Realistic Reaction to Judicialization* (Mar. 25, 2011), *available at* http://papers.ssrn.com/sol3/papers.cfm?abstract_id=1789564.

[85] Susan L. Shirk, The Political Logic of Economic Reform in China 150 (1993).

[86] *See, e.g.,* Albert H.Y. Chen, *Reflections on Administrative Law in China*, 6 Harv. China Rev. 66 (2010).

[87] *See, e.g.,* Li, *supra* note 84.

[88] Ling Li, *Performing Bribery in China: Guanxi Practice, Corruption with a Human Face*, 20 J. Contemp. China 1 (2011).

[89] The Long March, *supra* note 50, at 307.

In the meantime, this portrait of litigation in the health context as helping a few individuals at the expense of the broader public and privileging market allocation and private negotiation is consistent with other practices that have operated throughout the health system. Even the ubiquitous "red envelopes" given to doctors can be seen as an individual method of contracting around the ordinary rules and procedures of the health delivery system for more timely or higher-quality care.

10.4 HEALTH EQUITY AND THE JUSTICIABLE RIGHTS CONCEPTION IN CHINA

If litigation proves discouraging, what are the long-term prospects for equity in China's health system? Such equity has historically correlated more with the degree of central government commitment to health care than with the effectiveness of courts. Even as China has cracked down on rights activists and restricted the scope of action for lawyers in recent years,[90] certain measures of health care access and equity have improved. For instance, coverage has expanded, especially in rural areas,[91] reimbursement rates and utilization have increased,[92] and the ratio between rural and urban per capita health expenditures has narrowed since 2008.[93] A study shows that rural patients are now more satisfied with health care services generally than are their urban and suburban counterparts.[94]

10.4.1 *Strong Informal Norm Exists*

Availability, access, and other dimensions of health care equity may be difficult to advance through rights claims in courts. Yet China remains a country where some settled expectations of equity in health care exist, and where government feels pressure to address deviation from those expectations. Others have

---

[90] *See* Minzner, *supra* note 59.

[91] *See* Center for Statistic Information Ministry of Health, P.R. China, 2011 Nian Woguo Weisheng Shiye Fazhan Tongji Gongbao (2010 年我国卫生事业发展统计公报) [A public report on the statistic regarding the development of healthcare in 2011] (2012), *available at* http://www.moh.gov.cn/publicfiles/business/htmlfiles/mohwsbwstjxxzx/s7967/201204/54532.htm.

[92] Zuixin Shuju Yinzheng Yigai Chengxiao (最新统计数据印证医改成效) [Latest data shows that health reform is working], MINISTRY OF HEALTH OF THE PEOPLE'S REPUBLIC OF CHINA (May 13, 2011, 21:50:07), *available at* http://www.moh.gov.cn/publicfiles/business/htmlfiles/mohbgt/s6717/201105/51648.htm.

[93] WEISHENG BU (卫生部) (MINISTRY OF HEALTH), HEALTH STAT. Y.B. CHINA (2009), *available at* http://www.moh.gov.cn/publicfiles/business/htmlfiles/zwgkzt/ptjnj/200908/42635.htm.

[94] Weishengbu Tongji Xinxi Zhongxi (卫生部统计信息中心) [Center for Statistics and Information, MOH], 2008 Nian Disici Guojia Weisheng Fuwu Diaocha Baogao (2008年第四次国家卫生服务调查分析报告) [Analysis Report of Health Services Survey in China, 2008] (Feb. 27, 2009) *available at* http://www.moh.gov.cn/publicfiles///business/cmsresources/mohwsbwstjxxzx/cmsrsdocument/doc9911.pdf.

questioned whether these politically instantiated norms can or should be called rights.[95]

Leaving aside nomenclature, I contend that these norms exist, and seem to have driven a number of actions and statements by different parts of the Chinese state and society in previous decades. Bringing health care to the people was considered central to the achievements of the Communist Revolution.[96] The Chinese government has deliberately embraced the provision of health and economic rights and highlighted those efforts in China's Human Rights Plan.[97] Amid the growing inequality that has emerged since market liberalization, the Chinese political leadership has made the fostering of a "harmonious society," rather than mere economic growth, a political priority. Notably, health reform has been the centerpiece of this agenda to address social equity and stability.

As evident throughout the debate surrounding health care reform, the Chinese overwhelmingly see health care as a good that the government must in some measure guarantee rather than leave to the vagaries of market allocation. Accordingly, in his report during the 17th Congress of the Communist Party of China (CPC) in October 2007, President Hu declared that the guiding direction for reform would be the restoration of "public character and orientation" to the public health system.[98]

If litigation has not been particularly salient in either reflecting or pressing for greater realization of this norm, other modes of public accountability have stepped into the breach. These alternative channels, whether top-down administrative controls, social protest, or crude violence, may not always deliver relief for an individual aggrieved in the course of seeking health care services. However, they have succeeded in the manner arguably most important to promoting health equity: by prompting broad government action and policy change in the health system. The important actions throughout the brief history of health system development in post-revolutionary China – deploying health care workers, building hospitals and clinics, vaccinating the population, improving nutrition and sanitation, insurance risk-pooling, and using higher central matching rates to cross-subsidize coverage in poorer areas of China – were all allocated by community. Moreover, they were achieved through political and administrative, rather than distinctively judicial, action.

---

95 Carl Minzner, *Riots and Cover Ups: Counterproductive Control of Local Agents in China*, 31 U. Pa. J. Int'l L. 53 (2009).

96 *See, e.g.,* John Fairbank, The United States and China 446 (4th Ed., 1983).

97 Pittman Potter, *Dilemmas of Access to Healthcare in China*, 8 China Int'l J. 164 (Mar. 2010).

98 Hu Jintao (胡锦涛), Secretary General, Gaoju Zhongguo Tese Shehui Zhuyi Weida Qizhi Wei Duoqu Quanmian Jianshe Xiaokang Shehui Xin Shengli Er Fendou (高举中国特色社会主义伟大旗帜 为夺取全面建设小康社会新胜利而奋斗) [Hold High the Great Banner of Socialism with Chinese Characteristics and Strive for New Victories in Building a Moderately Prosperous Society in All], Report at the 17th Nat'l Cong. of the Communist Party of China (Oct. 15, 2007); *see also* Opinions, *supra* note 20.

In the most recent health care reform plans, China has continued to use administrative and policy tools, directly building more health care infrastructure and improving health care personnel quality and consultation relationships in the rural areas by administrative pairing of urban with rural hospitals. Approaches also include holding local officials to quantitative performance measures, such as the target enrollment of more than 90 percent of the rural residents in health coverage and the 280 RMB target for per capita NCMS government financing.

10.4.2 *Prospects for Justiciability of Health Rights*

The closer a defendant's ties to the government, the less likely it is that courts will favor the rights of the patient-claimants. In short, a greater public role in health in the near future may correlate with equity attributable to greater political accountability, but it may also be inversely correlated with judicial accountability.

However, health reform has the potential to change this dynamic in part because of the reluctance of the health reform plans to decisively embrace a government approach. China cannot turn back to the days of the barefoot doctor when the health sector was structured as a national commons. Market forces have been unleashed in the health sector; a global medical technology industry now exists. The recent health care reform, in its emphasis on "the four separates," aims to establish a configuration capable of fostering equity when the players in the heath sector have fragmented and multiplied. These changes increase the need for justiciability of health rights to safeguard equity in the future.

By strengthening third-party payer configurations, rather than direct supply-side subsidies, by encouraging nongovernmental hospitals, by establishing social insurance offices that contract with and function as professional claims processors and actuarial experts, and by experimenting with separation of ownership (often public) from governance and administration, China's ongoing health care reforms complicate the lines of accountability. Certainly, this trend may help correct the system's perverse incentives, but it also conveniently serves to diffuse blame for health system decisions away from the state alone. With the attenuation of direct bureaucratic controls, the need for litigation may grow. More intervening actors will contribute to health outcomes and their roles should be defined not by financial motives alone but by enforceable duties to patients.

Whether courts can advance equity by regulating the interactions of these actors and achieving the necessary pluralism of accountability depends on changing several conditions that have weakened the judicial role in the past. However, the prospects for these changes are mixed. On the one hand, the availability of courts and lawyers will still skew toward those with greater resources, and judges will still lack the independence and relative clout that would enable them to take on established interests, or allocate resources among competing policy goals. On the other hand, cases are more likely to be cast in ways that do not pit beneficiaries directly against core government actors. Furthermore, courts do seem capable of helping preserve or confirm existing rights around which there is significant consensus, and in the aftermath of a reform that achieves universal coverage, the political and administrative arms of the government will have more clearly established rights and duties regarding health access. Unfortunately, as described in Section 10.1, the central government organs seem to have deferred much of the definition of benefits to local governments, who retain significant leeway to structure coverage and therefore remain a potential source of inequity across the health system.

10.4.3 *One Cautionary Note*

If China's courts do assume an aggressive role in vindicating health rights, I would flag the emerging "vulgar" conception of health rights as an issue to monitor carefully. In this subsection, I discuss three features of this "vulgar" conception – its propensity for defining health care coverage by contribution rather than benefits, its overemphasis on pharmaceuticals, and its privileging of impersonal commodities over other less fungible care. These features are the legacy of China's radically marketized health system and should not be reinforced by courts.

Yet China's courts may be too weak to resist the oversimplification of health rights discourse. The political organs in China have – in the manner typical of China's cadre-responsibility system – defined the norm of equitable health in China in sharp quantitative terms that reinforce the defined contribution approach to health security.[99] An example is the framing of health care reform targets in terms of a fixed per capita subsidy. A strong health entitlement should not define merely how much money each individual can claim, but instead center on what treatment and quality of care each patient warrants, and how such decisions should be made.

Too many of China's new benefit designs, for employed urban residents and rural agricultural workers alike, take the form of individual savings accounts for benefits below the catastrophic threshold. If a medical savings account is aimed at catalyzing inter-temporal pooling (i.e., saving), it is not well suited to China's health care financing problems, as China already has such a high rate of household saving that economic policies have been aimed at boosting domestic consumer demand instead. Rather than lack of savings, the problem in China is the control of provider and system incentives. These are the targets of Chinese citizens' protests, and their grievances are not addressed by giving individual entitlements to a defined sum of money.

This penchant for savings accounts cuts against equity in the sense that it impedes risk pooling between the healthy and the well-off on the one hand and those who are ill or impoverished on the other. In Singapore, for instance, despite the relative

---

[99] *See* Winnie C. Yip & William C. Hsiao, *Medical Savings Accounts: Lessons From China*, 16 HEALTH AFF. 244, 250 (1997).

success of the MediSave program, the provision of individual allotments of money, even when those allotments can be used to purchase health insurance, has worked against pooling, and has disadvantaged women.[100]

Aggravating this tendency is China's constitutional history of formulating the right to health as one of "material support" in the event of illness. The path of least resistance for the Chinese government in the face of pressure to make good on individual health rights could lead to articulation of particular sums of money as the scope of any individual's entitlement. Already one sees this strategy at work, not only in the lawsuits where claimants succeeded, albeit only in enforcing their right to an individual savings account,[101] but also in the health care reform blueprint, which managed to steer away from commitments other than a promise that total government-matched contributions will reach a set amount, and a guarantee to a formulary of essential drugs. These "vulgar" targets are already being used to measure the performance of local officials in implementing health care reform. If litigation facilitates individual claims, there will be added pressure to partition the promise of health care reform into individuated sums. In theory, courts could try to steer the definition of health rights in a more nuanced direction, but past practice predicts that courts in China will defer to other arms of government in defining entitlements.

The real work of making health equitable is in responding to people's expectations and addressing their suffering. China's reliance on defined contribution sums that can be assigned to each individual as the measure of health provision aligns with a view of individuals autonomously satisfying their own fungible preferences, an impoverished conception of people's health needs. This view may seem congenial in a society where markets, and those whose interests are served by market methods of social ordering, are ascendant. It may also seem congenial to the state, which hopes to designate certain spheres as "autonomous" from government to absorb the blame for problems in the health sector.

However, a defined contribution strategy fails to protect against supplier-induced demand; it provides a superficial sense of microeconomic empowerment, while government disclaims responsibility for the macroeconomic forces in the health system. The history of China has shown that autonomous decision making, if based solely on profit incentives, can run terribly amok. The Chinese government cannot merely provide financing and abjure any role in solving systemic and collective action problems, such as medical inflation, or the "brain drain" of personnel from underserved rural areas. To meet patient needs and improve health care system performance, building quality and public confidence in the corps of health care professionals, especially in rural areas, is arguably more important than financing

---

[100] *See, e.g.,* Medical Savings Accounts: Lessons Learned from International Experience 15 (WB, Discussion Paper No. 52, 2002).

[101] *See* Wei Weihu Yibao Quan Mingaoguan Yi Tuixiu Zhigong Yingde Xingzheng Susong An Taohui Shuofa, *supra* note 68.

pharmaceuticals. Courts, however, are comparatively ill-suited to brokering these polycentric matters.

The overemphasis on pharmaceuticals in China's health care system can also be understood as a response to the pressure for crisp, tangible measures of health rights. Drugs consume nearly half of all health expenditures. Health reform could exacerbate this condition. Slated for implementation first was the list of essential drugs available to all, and the pharmaceutical formulary is the single benefit parameter that has been defined publicly and specifically. Access to medicines on the formulary enjoys a disproportionately greater measure of guarantee and will thus be more easily litigable in China than other components of health care.

The contours of health rights are notoriously difficult to delineate because they depend on "uncertainty, complexity and technology" in medical practice, and the "wide variability" of need.[102] Moreover, even in our age of biomedical science, doctors are pastors, ministering our psyches, as well as technicians administering evidence-based solutions.[103]

Health care is an expression of care and comfort that we lend to one another in the face of suffering and mortality, and it must be personalized accordingly. Since health care is profoundly non-fungible, the content of what one has a right to is usually left open-ended and determined not solely according to legal norms of comparability, or uniform commodified definitions. Often there is deference to civil society or experts, and residual room for ad hoc considerations.[104] Right now, courts in China produce one-off resolutions of heath care disputes, with inadequate regard for comparability and equality. But the opposite extreme, the vulgar application of cookie-cutter medicine and monetary valuations, ignoring the personalized judgment involved in a doctor-patient relationship, is also problematic. Can courts play a role that achieves equity with individualization?

Strong health rights, enforceable in courts, can be perfectly compatible with this respect for the heterogeneity and non-fungibility of values relevant to health decision making. Other considerations can temper abstract nondiscrimination norms when courts defer to professional judgment or administrative decisionmaking.[105] However, China lacks strong professional associations, active civil society, and administrative institutions that are embedded in and accommodate broad, participatory stakeholder discourse. I would worry for China's health care governance if it rushed headlong to embrace justiciability, without recognizing that a strong judicial role depends

---

[102] Mark Hall, *The History and Future of Health Care Law: An Essential View*, 41 WAKE FOREST L. REV. 347, 358 (2006).

[103] Mark Hall, *Making Medical Spending Decisions, in* HEALTH CARE LAW AND ETHICS 24 (Mark Hall et al., 7th ed., 1997).

[104] *See, e.g.,* local coverage determinations under the U.S. Medicare system. Barry Furrow et al., HEALTH LAW: CASES AND MATERIALS 777–81 (Barry Furrow et al. eds., 6th ed. 2009).

[105] Einer Elhauge, *Can Health Law Become A Coherent Field of Law*, 41 WAKE FOREST L. REV. 365, 371 (2006).

on a space for other norms and the granularity of health care decision making to flourish.

Strong health rights discourse captures the importance of accountability – currently deficient in China – in fostering health equity. However, borrowing from the cadre responsibility system with its top-down decision-making structure and numerical performance measures undercuts pluralism in accountability.[106] For multiple strands of accountability, China needs participatory decision making, even more than justiciability at this stage. More stakeholders need to sit on governance boards of hospitals or community insurance funds. The medical advisory boards in malpractice cases should include community representation. Medical providers should form stronger professional associations, formal and informal. Health agencies must engage in dialogue with all their stakeholders, especially patients and beneficiaries, and not just regulated industries. The recent crackdown and "turn against law"[107] suggest that courts are unlikely to be the fora for these conversations to negotiate competing norms among stakeholders, but if other state institutions led the way, courts could adopt their definitions.

Accepting that market forces will continue to feature somehow in China's health care system in the coming years, accepting that China's legal and civil society institutions will still be works-in-progress, I would argue that if China is to pursue court-based reforms to strengthen justiciability, it must first pursue institutional and possibly political reforms that allow for pluralism, participation, and civil society. In the best of all worlds, the recent health reforms with the introduction of third-party payers, multiple competing government actors, nongovernmental providers, and more extensive professional consultation relationships would create a space where these types of changes could emerge. In the worst-case scenario, these changes create opportunities for the privileged to contract around, or opt out from, general health care conditions.

With resilient flexible institutions for resolving disputes in particularized ways, allowing for heterogeneous norms, deep reservoirs of social capital, and strong professional ethics, it is possible to institutionalize rights that help the health system fulfill that pastoral role. But in China, these features are still weak compared to the galloping imperatives of economic growth. It is unquestionably insufficient for the norm of equity in health care provision to inhere in China's stated policies, yet for individual deprivations to be neither justified nor contestable. However, the challenge for those of us who hope to one day celebrate greater health justice in China is how to ensure that markets and rights do not combine to eclipse other values and bonds, reducing health to just another mean sum.

---

[106] I have argued for structures of pluralism in health care accountability in China elsewhere. *See* Ho, *supra* note 4; Ho, *supra* note 26.

[107] *See* Minzner, *supra* note 59.

11

The Role of Rights and Litigation in Assuring More Equitable Access to Health Care in South Africa

*Lisa Forman and Jerome Amir Singh**

INTRODUCTION

South Africa is a unique exemplar of the justiciability of health rights and their potential to reduce health inequalities. An enforceable right to access health care services was entrenched within its post-apartheid constitution, and the country's highest courts have enforced this right, most notably over access to antenatal HIV/AIDS drugs. At the same time, South Africa's two-tier health care system is highly inequitable, divided into a well-resourced private system meeting the needs of a wealthy minority and an under-resourced public system meeting the health needs of the country's poor majority. In line with this volume's overarching inquiry, this chapter explores the extent to which the constitutional health right has assisted in reducing these disparities. More specifically, and in line with the language of international human rights law, it asks to what extent the right has contributed to improving the availability, accessibility, acceptability, and quality of health care within and between the public and private health sectors.[1]

The chapter explores these questions through the framework used throughout this volume. First, it describes South Africa's health care systems. Second, it outlines the legal entrenchment and scope of the constitutional right to access health care services, and its impact on subsidiary legislation. Third, it discusses litigation over this and other health-related rights in the country's highest courts, focusing on several primary cases at the Constitutional Court. Finally, it analyzes the efficacy of this

* The authors are grateful for research and editorial assistance from Vanessa van den Boogaard, Shijia Cui, Angelica Reyes and Kelly Tai.

[1] This is the 'AAAQ' analytical metric for measuring the realization of article 12 of the ICESCR proposed by the UN Committee on Economic, Social and Cultural Rights (CESCR) in General Comment 14. See CESCR, General Comment No.14: The Right to the Highest Attainable Standard of Health, U.N. Doc. E/C.12/2004/4 (Aug. 11, 2000), *available at* http://www.unhchr.ch/tbs/doc.nsf/%28symbol%29/E.C.12.2000.4.En.

litigation in reducing the gross inequalities in health care access within and between the country's health care systems.

11.1 SOUTH AFRICA'S HEALTH CARE SYSTEMS

Health care in South Africa is provided in both the public and private sectors, with significant disparities in financial and human resources. The following section explores these systems by first describing the inequities of apartheid-era health care and subsequent government policy that has sought to resolve these inequities in the context of the broader challenge of achieving socioeconomic transformation. Second, it describes the current state of the public and private health care systems, the minimum levels of care defined in each, as well as methods of health care financing in each sector. Third, it outlines the efficacy of efforts to achieve equity in both health and the health care sector.

11.1.1 *Apartheid-Era Health Care and Post-Apartheid Transformation*

In 1994, South Africa transitioned from apartheid into a constitutional democracy premised on the realization of human rights and transformation of the inequities of the apartheid years. The African National Congress (ANC) government inherited a two-tier health care system, with a public sector financed through general taxation serving the majority of the population and a private sector funded primarily through medical aid schemes for the largely white minority.[2] Governance of these systems was highly chaotic, with poorly managed resource generation.[3]

The apartheid-era public health care system was highly inequitable, characterized by highly fragmented service delivery, insufficient rural facilities, and highly limited access to health care services for women, children, and farm workers.[4] It was racially fragmented into fourteen separate operating authorities, including ten Bantustan health departments, three "own affairs" health departments, and a national Department of Health.[5] The public system disproportionately favored urban tertiary hospital care over primary care: for example, in 1994, academic and other tertiary level hospitals received 44 percent of total health care expenditure, with only 11 percent of this expenditure directed to primary health care.[6] In contrast,

---

[2] Helen Schneider et al., *The Promise and the Practice of Transformation in South Africa's Health System* in STATE OF THE NATION: SOUTH AFRICA 2007, 290 (Sakhela Buhlungu et al. eds., 2007).

[3] *Id.* at 290.

[4] SOUTH AFRICAN HUMAN RIGHTS COMMISSION (SAHRC), 3RD ECONOMIC & SOCIAL RIGHTS REPORT SERIES, chap. 5 *Health Care and Health Care Services for Children* (2000), *available at* http://www.sahrc.org.za/home/21/files/Reports/3rd%20ER%20report%20chapter_5.pdf

[5] Schneider et al., *supra* note 2, at 290.

[6] *Id.*, at 291, quoting Diane McIntyre et al., HEALTH SECTOR EXPENDITURE AND FINANCE IN SOUTH AFRICA (1995); and Hoosen Coovadia et al., *The Health and Health System of South Africa: Historical Roots of Current Public Health Challenges*, 374 LANCET 817, 828 (2009).

the apartheid-era private system (which primarily provided tertiary care) received the majority of resources with 56 percent of total health care expenditure, while servicing only 23 percent of the population who had access to health insurance (called medical aid in the country) on the basis of their ability to pay.[7] The private sector also employed the vast majority of health care workers, with more than 85 percent of dentists and pharmacists and more than 60 percent of all doctors, psychologists, physiotherapists, and other allied health professionals in the private sector.[8]

The government's commitment to transforming the inequities within and between the public and private health care sectors has formed a substantial part of national health policy since 1994. This ambition formed part of the ANC government's broader policy imperative of transforming the broader socioeconomic inequalities resulting from apartheid-era rule.[9] This principled commitment was formalized as government policy in the 1994 Reconstruction and Development Program (RDP), adopted as an "integrated coherent socioeconomic policy framework,"[10] which aimed to build the country through key programs to meet basic needs, including through access to electricity, water, telecommunications, transport, health, education, and training.[11] The goals for the health sector advanced in the RDP were to achieve "a complete transformation of the national health care delivery system and all relevant institutions."[12]

In 1997, the government issued a "White Paper for the Transformation of the Health System in South Africa," which proposed increasing access to primary health care, creating a unified national system, developing a district health system, ensuring the availability of safe, good-quality essential drugs in health care facilities, and rationalizing health financing through budget reprioritization.[13] While the White Paper proposed implementation through the three levels of health government (national,

---

[7] Schneider et al., *supra* note 2, at 291, quoting McIntyre et al., *supra* note 7; Coovadia et al., *supra* note 7, at 828.

[8] Schneider et al., *supra* note 2, at 291, quoting McIntyre et al., *supra* note 6.

[9] The word "transformation" can be found in almost all ANC documents, many speeches of the ANC and government leaders, and most policy documents of the new democratic government. In government usage, transformation embraced a broad range of social, legal, and political change, including democratization and governance, transformation of the state machinery, economic transformation, and meeting social needs. *See* Gregory Houston & Yvonne G. Muthien, *South Africa: A Transformative State?, in* DEMOCRACY & GOVERNANCE REVIEW: MANDELA'S LEGACY 1994–1999, 37, 40 (Yvonne G. Muthien et al., eds., 2000).

[10] African National Congress, *The Reconstruction and Development Programme: A Policy Framework* (1994), *available at* http://www.polity.org.za/polity/govdocs/rdp/rdp.html

[11] Hein Marais, SOUTH AFRICA: LIMITS TO CHANGE – THE POLITICAL ECONOMY OF TRANSFORMATION 180 (1998).

[12] African National Congress, *supra* note 10, at para. 2.12.5.2.

[13] South African Department of Health, *White Paper for the Transformation of the Health System in South Africa*, SOUTH AFRICAN GOVERNMENT INFORMATION (April, 1997), *available at* http://www.info. gov.za/whitepapers/1997/health.htm

provincial, and local), it envisioned health districts as the major locus of implementation, where there would be an emphasis on the primary health care approach.[14] A comprehensive package of primary health care interventions would be universally accessible, with particular emphasis placed on reaching the "poor, the under-served, the aged, women and children, who are amongst the most vulnerable."[15] The primary health care approach emphasized maternal, child, and women's health services, focusing particularly on the rural and urban poor and on farm workers.[16]

The challenge of achieving equity was made considerably more difficult by the country's high levels of inequality, poverty, and unemployment. Despite being a middle-income developing country with a gross domestic product comparable to far higher income countries,[17] South Africa has one of the most unequal distributions of wealth in the world. Moreover, inequality in South Africa has worsened over the past decade, with the Gini coefficient increasing from 0.65 in the late 1990s to 0.72 in 2005–2006 (on the Gini index, 0 reflects perfect equality, 1 perfect inequality).[18] The poorest 10 percent of South Africa's population receive approximately 0.1 percent of total income, while the top 10 percent receive approximately 51 percent.[19]

In 1998, poverty levels were approximately 40 percent, unemployment levels were roughly the same, and many households experienced limited access to education, health care, electricity, and clean water.[20] Levels of poverty and unemployment have worsened since this time.[21] These declines have occurred in spite of South Africa's growing role as an economic power within the subcontinent. Despite

---

[14] Lisa Forman et al., *A Review of Nearly a Decade of Health Legislation, 1994–2003, in* SOUTH AFRICAN HEALTH REVIEW 2003/04 13 (Petrida Ijumba et al., eds., 2004).

[15] South African Department of Health, *supra* note 13.

[16] Forman et al., *supra* note 14.

[17] For example, in 2011, South Africa's rank on the UNDP's human development index (HDI) was 123, while its gross national income (GNI) per capita was US$9,469. In contrast, Serbia, which is ranked at 59 on the HDI, have GNI per capita of US$10,236, and Croatia, which is ranked 49 on the HDI, had a GNI per capita of US$15,729. *See* UNITED NATIONS DEVELOPMENT PROGRAM, SUSTAINABILITY AND EQUITY: A BETTER FUTURE FOR ALL, HUMAN DEVELOPMENT REPORT 2011, 127–128 (2011), *available at* http://www.gm.undp.org/HDR_2011_EN_Complete.pdf.

[18] John Ele-Ojo Ataguba & James Akazili, *Health Care Financing in South Africa: Moving Towards Universal Coverage*, 28 CONTINUING MED. EDU. 74 (2010). See also David Sanders & Mickey Chopra, *Key Challenges to Achieving Health in an Inequitable Society: The Case of South Africa*, 96 AM. J. PUB. HEALTH 73 (2006).

[19] Statistics South Africa, *Income and Expenditure of Households 2005/2006: Analysis of Results* (2008), *available at* http://www.statssa.gov.za/Publications/Report-01–00–01/Report-01–00–012005.pdf .

[20] Julian May, Poverty and Inequality in South Africa: Report Prepared by the Office of the Executive Deputy President and the Inter-Ministerial Committee for Poverty and Inequality 1 (1998), *available at* http://www.polity.org.za/polity/govdocs/reports/poverty.html.

[21] The current rate of unemployment is either 25% with a narrow definition that includes only those actively seeking work, or 37% with a broader definition that includes all who are not employed and are seeking work, as well as those discouraged from seeking work. *See* Coovadia et al., *supra* note 6, at 823; Stephan Klasen & Ingrid Woolard, *Surviving Unemployment Without State Support: Unemployment and Household Formation in South Africa*, 18 J. AFR. ECON. 1 (2009); Sanders & Chopra, *supra* note 18; Cally Ardington et al., *The Sensitivity of Estimates of Post-Apartheid Changes in South African*

the growth since 1994 of a black middle class and affluent sector, the vast majority of poverty remains concentrated among black South Africans.[22] These conditions pose tremendous challenges to achieving health care sector transformation and health equity more broadly, given the disproportionate influence of social conditions (rather than medical care) on population health.[23]

11.1.2 *The Public and Private Public Health Care Systems*

The immediate focus of health sector transformation was to create a unified public health system, and in 1994 and 1995, the government integrated the fourteen departments of health into a single central ministry and nine provincial departments of health.[24] The National Department of Health is responsible for determining overall national health policy and issuing guidelines for its implementation. The Director-General of the National Department of Health is responsible for promoting adherence to norms and standards on the provision of health care services.[25] The nine provincial departments of health are responsible for developing provincial policy in relation to national policy and the imperatives of public health delivery. They provide and manage health services at all levels. The provincial departments are also responsible for coordinating the funding and financial management of district health authorities.[26] Local government is responsible for rendering preventative and promotive health care and environmental health services (including supply of safe and adequate drinking water, sewage disposal, and refuse removal). Many local governments provide additional primary health care services,[27] reflecting the fact that local government boundaries are largely coterminous and contiguous with the

---

Poverty and Inequality to Key Data Imputations (CSSR Working Paper No. 106, 2005), *available at* http://www.sarpn.org.za/documents/d0001148/P1265-South_African_poverty_Feb12005.pdf .

[22] Paula Armstrong et al., *Poverty in South Africa: A Profile Based on Recent Household Surveys* (2008), *available at* http://www.ekon.sun.ac.za/wpapers/2008/wp042008/wp-04-2008.pdf; Krisela Steyn & Michelle Schneider, *Overview on Poverty in South Africa, in* Poverty and Chronic Diseases in South Africa: Technical Report 2001 1, 12 (Debbie Bradshaw & Krisela Steyn, eds., 2001).

[23] *See e.g.,* World Health Organization Commission on Social Determinants of Health, Closing the Gap in a Generation: Health Equity through Action on the Social Determinants of Health: Final Report of the Commission on Social Determinants of Health 1 (2008), *available at* http://www.who.int/social_determinants/thecommission/finalreport/en/index.html.

[24] Schneider et al., *supra* note 2, at 295.

[25] These responsibilities are specified in relation to specific areas including nutritional intervention, environmental conditions that constitute a health hazard, the use of human tissue, blood and blood products and gametes, sterilization and termination of pregnancy, genetic services, and any other matter than affects the health status of people in more than one province. *See* National Health Act 61 of 2003 §21.2.b.i-viii (S. Afr.).

[26] South African Government Communication and Information System, South Africa Yearbook 2009/10 288 (2009), *available at* http://www.gcis.gov.za/content/resource-centre/sa-info/yearbook/2009-10 .

[27] *Id.* at 294.

demarcation of health regions and districts in all provinces.[28] The country's public health care system has three tiers of hospitals: tertiary, regional, and district. The primary health care system (primarily nurse-driven in clinics) includes district hospital and community health centers. NGOs at various levels play a crucial role in health care and cooperate with the government's priority programs.[29]

By 2008, approximately 82 percent of the general population of almost 50 million was dependent on the public health care sector,[30] and within that population approximately 86 percent are black.[31] Poverty among black South Africans remains dramatically higher than that among whites (54.8 percent versus 0.4 percent).[32] These demographics indicate that the public health care system caters primarily to a poor black majority, and conversely, that poverty (and a consequent lack of employment-related health insurance) determines dependence on the public rather than private health care sector.

The private health care system comprises general practitioners, specialists, and private hospitals, which are unevenly distributed nationally: in 2008, 70 percent of private hospitals were in three of the country's nine provinces, with 38 percent in Gauteng province alone.[33] Private hospitals and specialists are the primary drivers of private health care spending (35 percent and 21 percent of private medical schemes' expenditure, respectively).[34]

The private health care system continues to receive the majority of human and financial resources (60 percent of total health care funding and 70 percent of the country's health care personnel), while meeting the needs of less than 20 percent of the population.[35] A further 21 percent of the population uses private health care on an out-of-pocket basis, primarily for primary-level care.[36] Since 1994, the spending gap between the public and private systems has increased[37] while the population being served by the private system has remained relatively static at around 8 million people.[38] Static enrollment results from the lack of affordability of medical aid

[28] South African Department of Health, *The District Health System in South Africa: Progress Made and Next Steps* (2001), *available at* http://www.doh.gov.za/docs/policy/dhsystem.html.

[29] South African Government Communication and Information System, *supra* note 26, at 294.

[30] Candy Day & Andy Gray, *Health and Related Indicators*, in SOUTH AFRICAN HEALTH REVIEW 2008 239, 249 (Peter Barron & Josianne Roma-Reardon, eds., 2008).

[31] The rest of the public-sector-dependent population are Coloured (3,425,000), Indian (781,000), and white (1,447,000). *Id.*, at 250.

[32] Armstrong et al., *supra* note 22.

[33] Coovadia et al., *supra* note 6, at 829.

[34] *Id.* at 827.

[35] Antoinette Ntuli et al., *HIV/AIDS and Health Sector Responses in South Africa – Treatment Access and Equity: Balancing the Act* (Equinet Discussion Paper No. 7, Sept. 2003), *available at* http://www.hst.org.za/sites/default/files/equinet7.pdf .

[36] Coovadia et al., *supra* note 6, at 826.

[37] Schneider et al., *supra* note 2, at 296.

[38] *Who We Are*, COUNCIL FOR MEDICAL SCHEMES (June 22, 2012), *available at* http://www.medicalschemes.com/Content.aspx?28 .

scheme coverage.[39] Private health care is primarily regulated and delivered via 105 medical aid schemes (of which only 30 were "open schemes" – accessible to anyone versus only those who are employed).[40,] The inequities within the private health care sector have prompted considerable government policy and regulation of medical aid schemes, including, most significantly, the proposed introduction of a National Health Insurance Fund, all of which are discussed in the following subsections.

11.1.3 *Financing the Health Care Systems*

South Africa has the highest per capita health care spending level (public and private) in Africa.[41] While this should provide sufficient funding to provide more than universal basic health care, the current distribution of spending between the public and private health care systems has not produced this outcome.[42] The post-apartheid public health care system is funded almost entirely by general taxation (which constitutes 40 percent of total health financing).[43] Roughly 80 percent of the health care budget is allocated by provincial governments after receiving an unconditional grant from central government, while the other 20 percent is a conditional allocation from central government to address the "spillover" problem drawing patients from other provinces that results from the concentration of secondary, tertiary, and teaching services within only a few provinces.[44] While primary health care is free in South Africa's public sector, and disabled people, children under the age of six, and pregnant women also enjoy free health care, the country's public sector levies different fees for people of different income levels for certain types of public health services. The fee structure is dependent on the outcome of a "means test."[45] Indigent patients

---

[39] David Harrison, *An Overview of Health and Health Care in South Africa 1994–2010: Priorities, Progress and Prospects for New Gains* 24 (A Discussion Document Commissioned by the Henry J. Kaiser Family Foundation to Help Inform the National Health Leaders' Retreat Muldersdrift, Jan. 2010), *available at* http://www.doh.gov.za/docs/reports/2010/overview1994–2010.pdf.

[40] SOUTH AFRICAN GOVERNMENT COMMUNICATION AND INFORMATION SYSTEM, *supra* note 26, at 294; Council for Medical Schemes, *supra* note 38.

[41] Ataguba & Akazili, *supra* note 18, at 75.

[42] Ataguba & Akazili, *supra* note 18.

[43] Claire Botha & Michael Hendriks, Financing South Africa's National Health System through National Health Insurance: Possibilities and Challenges (Colloquium Proceedings, 2008), *available at* http://www.hsrc.ac.za/Document-2623.phtml.

[44] South African Department of Health, Committee of Enquiry – Health Chapter, Inquiry into the Various Social Security Aspects of the South African Health System, part 5 (2002), *available at* http://www.doh.gov.za/docs/reports/2002/inquiry/.

[45] South Africa's fee structure program in the health sector is based on the results of a "mean's test," which entails a personal interview with the patient (or his/her caregiver/parent/guardian). This interview entails assessing the annual family income, patient's declared household income, and wage (if applicable). *See* Meng Qingyue et al., MEANS TESTING FOR TARGETING THE PEOPLE IN HEALTH PROGRAMS: A SYSTEMATIC REVIEW (Draft, April 2010) (Review report submitted to the Alliance for Health Policy and Systems Research), *available at* http://www.who.int/alliance-hpsr/projects/alliancehpsr_meanstesting_systematicreviewshandong.pdf.

receive free health care services (even services of a secondary or tertiary nature), whereas those deemed able to afford paying for services are charged. However, even the fees charged to paying individuals are highly subsidized and invoiced at point of service.[46] The inability of public hospitals to turn patients away makes such a billing system impractical. In reality, the public sector rarely, if ever, institutes legal proceedings to recover unpaid fees, as following up on so many unpaid accounts is costly and impossible to administer.[47] Patients who have private health insurance are not barred from the public sector. In fact, the public sector invoices medical schemes,[48] if applicable. As hospitals do not retain revenue they collect (all revenues collected go the provincial health budget), they have a reduced incentive to claim user fees or funds owed from medical schemes or related funds. In reality, many patients with health insurance access the public sector to prevent exhausting their coverage. This practice further strains the already overburdened public sector. The impending National Health Insurance system will likely change this state of affairs (see discussion later in the chapter).

The post-apartheid private health care system continues to account for the largest share of total health care financing, with remaining health care expenditure comprised of out-of-pocket payments by individuals without medical aid coverage in the private sector.[49] Despite these regressive out-of-pocket payments in the private system, health care financing overall is predominantly progressive, with payments as a proportion of income increasing with household income.[50] In South Africa, the richest 20 percent spends about 18 percent of their income on health care (via medical scheme contributions), whereas the poorest 20 percent spends approximately 5 percent.[51] Despite this overall progressive nature, health care financing is highly fragmented, and there is little or no pooling of funds to guarantee income and risk cross-subsidization and financial risk protection.[52] Moreover, financing within the private sector is highly regressive, with the poorest 20 percent of medical aid members contributing twice as much of their income compared to the richest 20 percent.[53] Membership in private health insurance systems is not mandatory, and as the use of

---

[46] South African Department of Health, *South African Health System: A Review* (2002), *available at* http://www.doh.gov.za/docs/reports/2002/inquiry/sahs.pdf.

[47] Id.

[48] Id.

[49] Ataguba & Akazili, *supra* note 18; Diane McIntyre et al., Shield Work Package 1 Report: A Critical Analysis of the Current South African Health System (2007), *available at* http://uct-heu.s3.amazonaws.com/SHIELD_WP1_only_report_SA_final.pdf; John Ataguba & Diana McIntyre, *Financing and Benefit Incidence in the South African Health System: Preliminary Results* (Health Economics Unit, Working Paper 09–1, 2009), *available at* http://uct-heu.s3.amazonaws.com/HEU_Shield_Report_FIA_BIA_SA1.pdf.

[50] Ataguba & McIntyre, *supra* note 49.

[51] Ataguba & Akazili, *supra* note 18.

[52] Id.

[53] University of Cape Town Health Economics Unit, *HEU Information Sheet: Health Care Financing: Who pays for health care in South Africa?* (2009), *available at* http://uct-heu.s3.amazonaws.com/wp-content/uploads/2009/10/IS4_heu_WhoPaysForHealthCare.pdf.

the public sector by privately insured individuals implies, there is no prohibition for those with private health insurance from accessing public health care.

Despite comparatively high levels of health care spending within the sub-Saharan African region, since 2000–2001, the health care sector share of the total government budget has declined, from 11.5 percent to 8.75 percent in 2010–2011.[54] This falls short of the 15 percent commitment made by African heads of state in the 2001 *Abuja Declaration on HIV/AIDS, Tuberculosis and Other Related Infectious Diseases*.[55] Health spending itself has been erratic: an initial period of increased expenditure from 1995–1996 to 1997–1998 was followed by stagnation and restrictions from 1998–1999 to 2000–2001,[56] which resulted in several major tertiary health care centers being shut down in the late 1990s.[57] These regressions in health care expenditure resulted from the government's adoption in 1996 of the neoliberal Growth, Employment and Redistribution (GEAR) strategy, which emphasized privatization, deregulation, rationalization of the public sector, and strict economic stringency in social spending.[58] GEAR effectively replaced the RDP, leading to the curtailment of social spending.

Health spending increased again after 2001 given economic growth, large conditional grants for HIV/AIDS, and efforts to revitalize public hospitals.[59] However, these increases have not kept pace with inflation, population increases, increased demands on the public sector (including an estimated 6.5 million new users since 1996), and the high (and incompletely compensated) cost that HIV/AIDS is exacting from the public system.[60] Moreover, significant geographical inequities continue to mark public health care sector spending,[61] despite the fact that the National Treasury allocates funds for health care to provinces using equity-based formulae.[62]

[54] Ataguba & Akazili, *supra* note 18, at 76.
[55] Organisation of African Unity, *Abuja Declaration on HIV/AIDS, Tuberculosis, and Other Related Infectious Diseases*, O.A.U. Doc. No. OAU/SPS/ABUJA/3, para. 30, 31 (April 24–27, 2001), *available at* http://www.un.org/ga/aids/pdf/abuja_declaration.pdf.
[56] Schneider et al., *supra* note 2, at 297.
[57] Patrick Bond, TALK LEFT WALK RIGHT: SOUTH AFRICA'S FRUSTRATED GLOBAL REFORMS 83–84 (2004).
[58] *See* African National Congress, *supra* note 10; African National Congress, *Reconstruction and Development Program: A Policy Framework* (1994), *available at* http://www.anc.org.za/rdp/rdpall.html; MARAIS, *supra* note 12, at 163–165.
[59] Schneider et al., *supra* note 2, at 297.
[60] Diane McIntyre, The Nature and State of Health Care Financing and Delivery in South Africa: Obstacles to Realizing the Right to Health Care (2004), *available at* http://www.tac.org.za/Documents/healthsystem/context.ppt; Mark Blecher & Stephen Thomas, Health Care Financing, in SOUTH AFRICAN HEALTH REVIEW 2003/04 269 (Petrida Ijumba et al., eds., 2004).
[61] Schneider et al., *supra* note 2, at 297.
[62] Annie Neo Parsons et al., *The Impact of Global Health Initiatives on Access to Antiretroviral Therapy in South Africa*, in SOUTH AFRICAN HEALTH REVIEW 2010 107 (Sharon Fonn & Ashnie Padarath, eds., 2010); AIDS Law Project: 2010/2011 Provincial health budgets (May 21, 2010), *available at* http://www.section27.org.za/wp-content/uploads/2010/05/Provincial-Budget-Analysis-BEMF-Meeting-2010-May-21.pdf; James Alm & Jorge Martinex-Vazquez, South Africa's Provincial Equitable Share:

While the GEAR-related spending restrictions of the 1990s relaxed in the 2000s, GEAR and its operational presence in the Public Finance Management Act are viewed as having an enduring impact on health care services, establishing cost containment as the de facto driver of everyday practice in the health system. Staying within budget remains the key preoccupation of managers, and this implicitly relegates equity and other dimensions of institutional change to secondary goals.[63]

11.1.4 *Prescribed Baskets of Services*

Several statutes and policies seek to ensure minimum levels of health care within both the public and private sectors. The 2003 National Health Act requires the National Minister of Health to ensure the provision of essential health services, including at least primary health care services, within the limits of available resources.[64] However, the Act does not define either the content of primary or essential health services, both of which are left to the discretion of the Minister of Health.[65] The National Health Act does, however, define mandatory free health care services to be provided by the state, clinics, and community health centers as including all health care services for pregnant and lactating women and children below the age of six years without medical aid coverage, free primary health care to people receiving occupational disease compensation without medical aid coverage, and free termination of pregnancy services to women.[66] Government has indicated that defining the content of an essential health care package will be a primary step in developing a National Health Insurance system (described later in the chapter).[67] In the interim, the 2000 Primary Health Care Package Plan, Standard Treatment Guidelines and Essential Drugs List guides the public health care sector in providing essential health care.[68]

The 1998 Medical Schemes Act provides guidance on an essential package of health care in the private sector. The Act prescribes a set of minimum benefits

An Assessment Of Issues And Proposals For Reform (Int'l Studies Progran, Georgia State University, Working Paper 09–04, March 2009), *available at* http://aysps.gsu.edu/isp/files/ispwp0904.pdf.

[63] Schneider et al., *supra* note 2, at 297.

[64] National Health Act 61 of 2003 §3.1.d. (S.Afr.).

[65] *See, e.g.*, National Health Act 61 of 2003 §§ 3.1 & 4.1(S. Afr.).

[66] National Health Act 61 of 2003 § 4.3.a-c (S.Afr.).

[67] SOUTH AFRICAN GOVERNMENT COMMUNICATION AND INFORMATION SYSTEM, *supra* note 26, at 290 ("With regard to the Basic Benefits Package, one of the key components of adopting an NHI system is defining the set of health care services that individuals and households would be covered for and how much it would cost the State to provide these services to the national population.").

[68] South African Department of Health, *The Primary Health Care Package for South Africa – A Set of Norms and Standards* (2000), *available at* http://www.doh.gov.za/docs/policy/norms/full-norms.html; South African Department of Health, *Standard Treatment Guidelines and Essential Drugs List for South Africa* (2008), *available at* http://www.kznhealth.gov.za/edlphc2008.pdf.

that ensure coverage on a range of services previously excluded by medical schemes, including "health care related to HIV associated disease; sexually transmitted disease; inpatient psychiatric care for three weeks; substance abuse and drug rehabilitation; attempted suicide; infertility and imminent death comfort care and pain relief."[69] The benefits were originally defined to include a list of 271 diagnosis-treatment pairs (DTPs) that included most emergency care, hospital-based care for life-threatening conditions, some urgent care of non-life-threatening conditions, maternity care, and palliative care for the terminally ill.[70] The benefits specifically exclude very high-cost or ineffective treatments, those for non-urgent, non-life-threatening conditions, as well as primary care services and out-of-hospital medicines related to the diagnosis-treatment pairs.[71] These benefits have been further defined through regulations and amendments to the Medical Schemes Act, which have added discretionary services and primary health care interventions (such as screening for breast and cervical cancer, hormone replacement therapy, and infertility treatment), the inclusion of primary care for the DTPs, care for twenty-six chronic conditions, antiretroviral therapies, and beta-interferon to treat multiple sclerosis.[72] These benefits will form the basis for an eventual National Health Insurance package.[73]

11.1.5 *Progress in Transforming Health and Health Care*

The government has made considerable gains in relation to health and health sector transformation in the eighteen years since 1994. In this time, 1,345 new clinics have been built (representing almost 40 percent of primary health care facilities),[74] and immunization rates of children increased from 63 percent in 1998 to 72 percent in 2002, greatly reducing measles and improving progress in eradicating poliomyelitis.[75] The government's free primary health care policy was extended in 1996 from pregnant and lactating mothers and children under six to cover primary health care services for everyone in the public health system without cost.[76] Government issued essential drug lists and standard treatment guidelines for primary and tertiary health

---

[69] Debbie Pearmain, *Impact of Changes to the Medical Schemes Act, in* SOUTH AFRICAN HEALTH REVIEW 2000 183, 197 (Antoinette Ntuli, et al., eds., 2000).

[70] Bettina Taylor et al., *Prescribed Minimum Benefits – Quagmire or Foundation for Social Health Reform?*, 97 S. AFR. MED. J. 446, 447 (2007).

[71] Id.

[72] *Id.*, at 447–448.

[73] *Id.*, at 447.

[74] Coovadia et al., *supra* note 6, at 828. *See also* Gavin Reagon et al., *The National Primary Health Care Facilities Survey 2003*, ix (2004), *available at* http://www.hst.org.za/sites/default/files/phc_survey04.pdf.

[75] Coovadia et al., *supra* note 6, at 828.

[76] SOUTH AFRICAN GOVERNMENT COMMUNICATION AND INFORMATION SYSTEM, SOUTH AFRICA YEAR-BOOK 2004/05 54 (2004), *available at* http://www.gcis.gov.za/content/resource-centre/sa-info/yearbook/2004–05.

care, which improved the availability of key drugs in the public sector.[77] A comprehensive legislative suite legalized abortion, controlled tobacco use, and regulated the health professions, occupational health and safety, and the private health sector.[78]

The government has allocated public resources more equitably between provinces as well, with per capita spending gaps declining from a fivefold difference in 1992–1993 to a twofold difference in 2005–2006.[79] A hospital revitalization program across the country has replaced equipment and facilities and constructed eleven district and regional hospitals and three new academic complexes.[80] From a human resources perspective, conditions in the public sector have marginally improved in the last decade. Between 2001 and 2007, the number of specialists in the public sector increased by 4 percent (from 3,619 in 2001 to 3,765 in 2007); the number of public sector medical specialists rose from 8.9 per 100,000 population in 2003 to 9.2 per 100,000 population in 2006, and the current national public sector specialist deficit stands at 2,590.[81]

These measures have not, however, managed to overcome serious and persistent deficiencies in the public health care sector, including highly uneven performance within and between provinces,[82] limited access to critical services such as antenatal care (available at only 50 percent of primary health care facilities),[83] and persistent inequities in health care access.[84] Approximately 30 percent of medical practitioners, 60 percent of nurses, and 15.5 percent of pharmacists are employed in the public health sector and yet they serve approximately 85 percent of South Africa's population.[85] The poor availability of health care workers, particularly in geographical areas with high poverty, has emerged as a major obstacle to improving access to health care.[86] The crisis is particularly dire in rural areas, which receive less than 3 percent of the total number of medical graduates each year.[87] Between 1996 and 2003, the availability of doctors and nurses within provincial health structures

---

[77] Coovadia et al., *supra* note 6, at 828.

[78] Schneider et al., *supra* note 2, at 296. *See* Forman et al. *supra* note 14 for more on this legislation.

[79] Coovadia et al., *supra* note 6, at 828.

[80] Harrison, *supra* note 39, at 18.

[81] Chris Bateman, *Academic Health Complexes Bleeding in 'No Man's Land'*, 100 S. Afr. Med. J. 17 (2010).

[82] Schneider et al., *supra* note 2, at 305.

[83] Candy Day et al., *Facilities Survey 2003: Selected Findings from the Fourth National Survey of Primary Health Care Facilities, in* South African Health Review 2003/04 339, 342–345 (Petrida Ijumba et al., eds., 2004).

[84] South African Human Rights Commission (SAHRC), The Right to Health Care, 5th Economic and Social Rights Report Series 2002/2003 15 (June 21, 2004), *available at* http://www.sahrc.org.za/home/21/files/Reports/5th_esr_health.pdf.

[85] Health Economics and HIV & AIDS Research Division (HEARD), *Human Resources for health in South Africa: A Needs And Gaps Analysis Of HRH In South Africa* (Nov. 2009), *available at* http://www.heard.org.za/downloads/human-resources-for-health–a-needs-and-gaps-analysis-of-hrh-in-south-africa.pdf.

[86] Schneider et al., *supra* note 2.

[87] HEARD, *supra* note 85.

declined by 24 percent and 16 percent, respectively.[88] By 2008, there was a 35.7 percent vacancy rate among medical practitioners and professional nurses within the public health care system,[89] caused by a growing population dependent on the public health care system, the extraordinary additional disease burden created by HIV/AIDS, the decreased training of nurses, and increased migration of health care workers.[90] A significant proportion of doctors have migrated into the private sector, with the total percentage of doctors working in that sector rising from 40 percent in 1980 to 79 percent in 2007.[91] Moreover, the inequitable distribution of financial and human resources between public and private health care systems persists.[92] By the end of 2009, overall, there was a shortage of 80,000 health professionals in the public sector.[93] This is despite government efforts, which include recruiting foreign medical practitioners and increasing salaries of health personnel.[94]

There has been similarly uneven progress in relation to health outcomes. South Africa experiences a "quadruple burden of disease" experienced only in the Southern African region, comprised of communicable disease (especially HIV/AIDS), non-communicable disease (including cardiovascular diseases associated with lifestyle factors), maternal, neonatal, and child deaths, and deaths from violence and injury.[95] These factors account for the major causes of death in South Africa, with HIV/AIDS by far the single largest cause of death (at 29.8 percent of all deaths).[96] Despite its middle-income status, South Africa has health outcomes worse than many low-income countries, and is one of only twelve countries where child mortality increased since the Millennium Development Goal baselines were set up in 1990.[97] Significant disparities in health remain between and within provinces, as well as between men and women.[98]

All major health indicators demonstrated regressive outcomes: life expectancy at birth fell from fifty-two years in 1997 to forty-three years in 2007,[99] and infant mortality and maternal mortality increased from 1998 to 2003.[100] The primary factor in this deterioration is the virtually unchecked growth of the nation's HIV/AIDS pandemic,

---

[88] Schneider et al., *supra* note 2, at 298.

[89] The vacancy rate is determined by the number of existing health sector posts that are vacant. *See* HEARD, *supra* note 85.

[90] Schneider et al., *supra* note 2, at 298–299.

[91] Coovadia et al., *supra* note 6, at 830.

[92] Schneider et al., *supra* note 2, at 290.

[93] HEARD, *supra* note 85.

[94] Id.

[95] *See* Coovadia et al., *supra* note 6; Debbie Bradshaw et al., *South African National Burden of Disease Study 2000: Estimates of Provincial Mortality*, SOUTH AFRICAN NATIONAL RESEARCH COUNCIL (2004), *available at* http://www.mrc.ac.za/bod/estimates.htm.

[96] Bradshaw et al., *supra* note 95.

[97] Coovadia et al., *supra* note 6, at 817–818.

[98] Coovadia et al., *supra* note 6, at 824–825.

[99] Harrison, *supra* note 39, at 6.

[100] SAHRC, *supra* note 85, at 25.

the largest in the world. From 1.8 million people infected in 1996, infection rates have soared to an estimated 5.24 million people in 2010 – around 10.5 percent of the population.[101] AIDS has become the single biggest cause of death, with 250,000 people dying in 2008,[102] and an estimated 1.2 million deaths from HIV/AIDS to date.[103] The public health care system has buckled under the impact of the HIV/AIDS epidemic and the overwhelming illness and death it has caused. It is notable, however, that since the introduction of a national mother to child transmission (MTCT) prevention program and national antiretroviral program, infant mortality has reduced and life expectancy at birth has increased.

Government's failures in advancing toward greater equity in health outcomes and the health sector result from what Hoosen Coovadia and colleagues argue is "a notable lack of progress in implementing the core health policies developed by the ANC, and some disastrous policy choices."[104] The Mbeki government's controversial AIDS policies, which denied access to any forms of antiretroviral treatment, are widely viewed as a tremendous governance failure, and as having contributed to the internal ousting of Mbeki in 2009 by Jacob Zuma, the current ANC and national president.[105] These governance failures were the target of the successful health rights litigation brought in 2002 and discussed in the next section.

11.2 LEGAL ENTRENCHMENT OF THE RIGHT TO HEALTH

In South Africa, health rights are primarily protected in the 1996 Constitution's Bill of Rights. The Constitution was adopted as a direct response to the violations and deprivations of apartheid. It adopts a model of constitutional supremacy, with all law and conduct inconsistent with the Constitution held to be invalid.[106] Human rights are at the apex of governance, with the Bill of Rights a "cornerstone of democracy"[107] applying to all law (including the common law) and binding the legislature, executive, judiciary, and all organs of state.[108] The Constitution's most prevalent commitment is to create an open and democratic state based on equality,

---

[101] Statistics South Africa, *Mid Year Population Estimates 2010*, statistical release P0302, 6 (2010), *available at* http://www.statssa.gov.za/publications/P0302/P03022010.pdf. The historical figure comes from South African Department of Health, *National HIV and Syphilis Antenatal Sero-Prevalence Survey in South Africa 2004* (2004), *available at* http://www.doh.gov.za/docs/reports/2004/hiv-syphilis.pdf.

[102] Statistics South Africa, *Mid Year Population Estimates 2009*, statistical release P0302, (2009), *available at* http://www.statssa.gov.za/PublicationsHTML/P03022009/html/P03022009.html.

[103] Rob E. Dorrington et al., The Demographic Impact of HIV/AIDS in South Africa: National Indicators for 2004 (2004), *available at* http://www.mrc.ac.za/bod/demographic.pdf.

[104] Coovadia et al., *supra* note 6, at 832.

[105] *See, e.g.*, William Mervin Gumede, Thabo Mbeki and the Battle for the Soul of the ANC (2007); Xolela Mangcu, To the Brink: The State of Democracy in South Africa (2008).

[106] S. Afr. Const., pmbl., §§1(c) & 2.

[107] S. Afr. Const., §7(1).

[108] S. Afr. Const., §§ 8(1) & (3).

dignity, and freedom:[109] a system of government antithetical to the violations of the apartheid state. In addition, the Constitution aspires to "improve the quality of life of all citizens and free the potential of each person.[110] In line with these objectives, the Constitution entrenches a range of justiciable social and economic rights, including rights to food, health care, water, social security, housing, education, and children's rights to basic social amenities.[111]

The Constitution entrenches a number of health-related rights, including the right to bodily integrity in section 12, children's rights to basic health care services in section 28(1)(c), and prisoner's rights to adequate medical treatment in section 35(2)(e).[112] The universal health right is contained in section 27, which also entrenches rights to water, food, and social security. This section states:

1. (a) Everyone has the right to have access to health care services, including reproductive health care . . .
2. The state must take reasonable legislative and other measures, within its available resources, to achieve the progressive realisation of each of these rights.
3. No one may be refused emergency medical treatment.

This focus on the provision of health care is a markedly narrower formulation than is the international human right to the highest attainable standard of health, which arguably incorporates broader public health responsibilities.[113] While section 27 focuses on health care access alone, the government's public health responsibilities are arguably influenced by its duties under the Constitution's broader range of socioeconomic rights to water and housing (which are themselves social determinants of health). However, this inferred responsibility aside, the Constitution makes no explicit provision for the government's broader public health responsibilities. Nor is the scope of the narrower right to access health care services explicit from the wording of section 27, which provides little indication of what is encompassed within the entitlement to health care services, nor does it provide the extent to which resource limitations and progressive realization could permissibly limit the state's duty to ensure access. Some guidance on the state's obligations is provided by the Constitutional mandate that the state must respect, protect, promote, and

---

[109] S. AFR. CONST., §§ 1(a), 7(1), 36(1) & 39(1)(a).

[110] S. Afr. Const., pmbl.

[111] S. AFR. CONST., §§27, 28 & 29, respectively.

[112] There is also a right to an environment that is not harmful to health or well-being in Section 24(a) of the Constitution.

[113] *See, e.g.,* Universal Declaration of Human Rights, December 10, 1948, G.A. Res. 217A (III), U.N. Doc. A/810 at 71, art. 25 (1948); International Covenant on Economic, Social, and Cultural Rights, Dec. 16, 1966, 993 U.N.T.S. 3, 6 I.L.M. 360, art.12.1 (1967); International Convention on the Rights of the Child, Nov. 20, 1989, 1577 U.N.T.S. 3, 28 I.L.M. 1448, art. 24.1 (1989); International Convention on the Elimination of Racial Discrimination, Dec. 21, 1965, 660 U.N.T.S. 195, 5 I.L.M. 352, art. 5.e.iv (1966); Convention on the Elimination of All Forms of Discrimination Against Women, Dec. 18, 1979, 1249 U.N.T.S. 13, 19 I.L.M. 33, arts. 11.1.f & 12 (1980); Convention on the Rights of Persons with Disabilities, 24 January 2007, U.N. Doc. A/RES/61/106.

fulfill the Constitution's rights.[114] Drawn from international human rights law, this typology implies a range of positive and negative duties with respect to each right.[115] Nonetheless, the Constitution does not define the precise content of these duties, and the task of interpretation falls to the government as well as the judiciary.

11.2.1 *Legislation Based on Section 27*

The South African government has passed a number of laws designed to realize the constitutional right to access health care services, as well as to redress inequities within and between the public and private health care system. The three most important of these are the 2005 National Health Act, the 1998 Medical Schemes Act, and a proposed National Health Insurance system.

In 2005, the government issued a long-awaited National Health Act that seeks to establish a national health system encompassing both the public and private health care systems, and providing "in an equitable manner the population of the Republic with the best possible health services that available resources can afford."[116] The preamble of the Act explicitly references a number of constitutional provisions, including the government's duty under section 27(2) of the Constitution to take reasonable legislative and other measures within its available resources to achieve the progressive realization of the right of the people of South Africa to have access to health care services, including reproductive health care.[117]

The objects of the National Health Act are explicitly framed in relation to the constitutional health right, including to protect, respect, promote and fulfill the rights of

- i) the people of South Africa to the progressive realization of the constitutional right of access to health care services, including reproductive health care;
- ii) the people of South Africa to an environment that is not harmful to their health or well-being;
- iii) children to basic nutrition and basic health care services contemplated in section 28(1)(c) of the Constitution; and
- iv) vulnerable groups such as women, children, older persons and persons with disabilities.[118]

---

[114] S. Afr. Const., §7.2.

[115] The duty to respect imposes a negative obligation to desist from interfering with people's enjoyment of rights; the duty to protect requires the state to prevent third-party interference with people's rights; and the duty to promote and fulfill describes the state's positive obligation to realize access. The notion of a typology of rights is widely acknowledged to have been developed by Henry Shue. *See* Henry Shue, BASIC RIGHTS, SUBSISTENCE, AFFLUENCE AND US FOREIGN POLICY (1980). It is applied in the context of health in General Comment 14.

[116] National Health Act 61 of 2003 §2.a.i-ii (S.Afr.).

[117] National Health Act 61 of 2003 pmbl. (S.Afr.).

[118] National Health Act 61 of 2003 §2.c.i. (S.Afr.).

The Medical Schemes Act of 1998 was passed with considerable equity ambitions, including prohibiting risk rating and member exclusions based on age, gender, and health status, and introducing a prescribed set of minimum health care benefits.[119] While the Act makes no explicit reference to section 27 of the Constitution, one of its primary objectives was to ensure equity of access to medical scheme membership and cross-subsidization between the elderly and young and between low and high earners.[120] The Act introduced key equity-seeking elements into the private health sector, including prohibiting unfair discrimination by medical schemes on the basis of race, gender, marital status, ethnic or social origin, sexual orientation, pregnancy, disability, and state of health, and introducing the already mentioned prescribed minimum benefit.[121]

In 2005, the Department of Health collaborated with private-sector stakeholders to publish a *Draft Charter on the Private and Public Health Sectors in the Republic of South Africa*. The Charter's purpose is to promote access, equity, and quality in health services within and between the public and private sectors,[122] and to bring ownership of the private health sector into black economic empowerment (BEE) processes.[123] BEE is a policy designed to enhance the economic participation of black people in the South African economy.[124] As Helen Schneider et al. suggest, "[t]he emergence of health sector BEE may signal a new policy era in which private sector interests are defended rather than controlled or regulated."[125]

A proposed National Health Insurance (NHI) system constitutes the most significant legislative effort to address the inequities between the public and private health sectors. The ANC had been considering a NHI system through various committees and working groups at least since 1994.[126] In February 2011, the Inter-Ministerial Committee (IMC) on NHI approved the proposed NHI policy,[127] which the Department of Health released as a comprehensive policy document in August 2011.[128] The

---

[119] Forman et al., *supra* note 14.

[120] Pearmain, *supra* note 69.

[121] Medical Schemes Act, §§24.2.e and 67.1.g. (1998).

[122] Harrison, *supra* note 39, at 25.

[123] The policy was adopted in 2007 in order to "de-radicalize" the South African economy and create a black middle class. The policy has had two phases: a first period from 1994 to 2002, typified by the empowerment of a few individuals, often with longstanding connections to the ANC, and a second phase coinciding with the passing of the 2003 Broad-Based Black Economic Empowerment Bill (B-B BEE) in light of criticism of the narrow focus of Empowerment. See Kate Law, "'The Wild West World of BEE': Black Economic Empowerment Reviewed, 11 SAFUNDI: J. S. AFR. & AM. STUD. 313, 314 (2010).

[124] See, e.g., Broad-Based Black Economic Empowerment, SOUTH AFRICAN DEPARTMENT OF TRADE AND INDUSTRY, available at http://www.dti.gov.za/economic_empowerment/bee.jsp.

[125] Schneider et al., *supra* note 2.

[126] See South African Department of Health, Government Notice 657 National Health Act (61/2003): Policy on National Health Insurance, 554 GOVERNMENT GAZETTE STAATSKOERANT, No. 34523, 12–15 (Aug. 12, 2011), available at www.doh.gov.za/docs/notices/2011/not34523.pdf.

[127] IMC Approves Proposed NHI Policy, BUANEWS (Feb. 15, 2011), available at http://allafrica.com/stories/201102160036.html.

[128] South African Department of Health, *supra* note 127.

enabling legislation for the NHI system is expected to pass in 2012.[129] The policy document articulates the primary objective of the NHI as being to "eliminate the current tiered system where those with the greatest need have the least access and have poor health outcomes."[130] The NHI system aims to "ensure that everyone has access to appropriate, efficient and quality health services."[131] The principles of the NHI system are explicitly human rights oriented, including: (1) the right to access in section 27 of the Constitution, (2) social solidarity, (3) effectiveness, (4) appropriateness, (5) equity, (6) affordability, and (7) efficiency.[132]

The policy document is explicit in regarding the constitutional motivation for the system: articulating reform of health care as an important step toward realization of the constitutional health right, with a key aspect that "access to health services must be free at the point of use and that people benefit according to their health profile."[133] Notably many of the other key principles closely resemble the acceptable, appropriate, and good-quality (AAAQ) framework (explicitly articulating affordability and appropriateness). The aim of the new system is to ensure that "all members of the population will be entitled to a comprehensive package of health services at all levels of care namely: primary, secondary, tertiary and quaternary with guaranteed continuity of healthcare benefits."[134] The NHI policy document is unclear on its principal funding mechanism, indicating that while pooled funds are from a combination of sources including the fiscus, employers, and individuals, the precise combination will be the subject of continuing technical work.[135] Nonetheless, a contribution to the NHI will become mandatory, and it is anticipated that the current medical aid system will transform into a top-up model.[136] The Department of Health indicates that there are plans to implement this system in three phases from 2012 over a fourteen-year period, with the first steps in 2012 initiated with a ten-district pilot scheme.[137]

11.2.2 *Litigation Regarding the Constitutional Right to Access Health Care Services*

Since the Constitution came into force in 1996, the right to health care has been the focus of three decisions before the Constitutional Court.[138] The following section

---

[129] *NHI to be passed in 2012: Motsoaledi*, TIMES LIVE (Feb. 22, 2011), *available at* http://www.timeslive. co.za/local/article928089.ece/NHI-to-be-passed-in-2012–Motsoaledi.

[130] South African Department of Health, *Government Notice 657, supra* note 127, at para. 50.

[131] *Id.*, at para. 1.

[132] *Id.*, at para. 52.

[133] *Id.*, at 52a.

[134] *Id.*, at para. 69.

[135] *Id.*, at para. 114.

[136] *Id.*, at paras. 125–126.

[137] *Id.*, at para. 160.

[138] This chapter focuses only on the Constitutional Court cases. There have, however, been other decided cases where the constitutional health right was only indirectly relevant. Several others never went to

focuses primarily on the first of these, as well as the *Grootboom* case on housing which is relevant to the interpretation of section 27.

The 1997 case of *Van Biljon & Others v. Minister of Correctional Services and Others* was one of the earliest socioeconomic rights cases to reach the courts.[139] Prisoners approached the Cape Provincial Division of the High Court claiming state-sponsored access to antiretroviral medicines, as part of prisoner's rights to adequate medical treatment at state expense.[140] The Court held that the state owed a higher duty of care to HIV-positive prisoners than to citizens accessing care in a provincial hospital, because prisoners lacked financial resources to access medical treatment.[141] The Court ordered that the state provide two of the applicants with antiretroviral medicines as prescribed.[142] The case had strictly provincial application.

As outlined earlier, racial disparities characterized health care in general in South Africa during apartheid. These disparities persisted under all circumstances, including emergency medical situations. During political rallies and demonstrations, doctors sent into townships to aid victims of police assaults and other injuries either feared arrest or were blocked from access to hospitals.[143] The National Medical and Dental Association (NAMDA) also provided evidence that many political prisoners who were beaten and tortured were never seen by district surgeons, and those who were examined felt that they had received inferior care.[144] Therefore, the right to access emergency medical care (section 27(3)) was an important inclusion in the Constitution.

The first case on section 27(3) reached the Constitutional Court in 1998. In *Thiagraj Soobramoney v. Minister of Health (Kwa-Zulu Natal)*,[145] Mr. Soobramoney approached the Constitutional Court after being refused renal dialysis by a state hospital that rationed treatment for patients with chronic renal failure unless they were also eligible for a kidney transplant. The Constitutional Court dismissed Soobramoney's claim, finding that the provincial hospital's failure to provide renal dialysis

judgment. For a discussion of these and other cases related to socioeconomic rights in South Africa, see Jonathan Berger, *Litigating for Social Justice in Post-Apartheid South Africa: A Focus on Health and Education, in* COURTING SOCIAL JUSTICE: JUDICIAL ENFORCEMENT OF SOCIAL AND ECONOMIC RIGHTS IN THE DEVELOPING WORLD 38 (Varun Gauri & Daniel M. Brinks, eds., 2008).

[139] Van Biljon and others v. Minister of Correctional Services and Others 1997 (4) SA 441 (C) (S. Afr.) [hereinafter Van Biljon]. *See also* B v. Minister of Correctional Services 1997 (4) SA 411 (C) (S. Afr.).

[140] S. AFR. CONST., §35.2e. South Africa's judiciary is comprised in order of authority of the Constitutional Court, the Supreme Court of Appeal, the High Court, and Magistrates Courts.

[141] Van Biljon, at paras. 50–51.

[142] *Id.*, at 61.

[143] *Sector Analyses: A.2: The National Medical and Dental Association, in* HUMAN RIGHTS AND HEALTH – THE LEGACY OF APARTHEID (Audrey R. Chapman & Leonard S. Rubenstein, eds., 1998), *available at* http://shr.aaas.org/loa/sector.htm.

[144] This association was one of the few in South Africa that included physicians who actively opposed the apartheid regime and unethical health policies of the government. *See id.*

[145] Thiagraj Soobramoney v. Minister of Health (Kwa-Zulu Natal) 1998 (1) SA 765 (CC) (S.Afr.) [hereinafter Soobramoney].

facilities for everyone with chronic renal failure was not in breach of the state's obligations under section 27(3). While Justice Chaskalson acknowledged the deplorable conditions and great poverty in which millions of South Africans lived, he argued that limited resources and the extent of demand meant that "an unqualified obligation to meet these needs would not presently be capable of being fulfilled," and that both the state's obligations and the corresponding rights themselves were "limited by reason of the lack of resources."[146] The Court considered that permitting claims for dialysis and similarly expensive treatments could prejudice all other health needs,[147] and indeed the government's ability to meet broader social and economic needs.[148] While the Court denied Soobramoney's claim, it indicated that "a court would be slow to interfere with rational decisions taken in good faith by the political organs and medical authorities whose responsibility it is to deal with such matters."[149] This statement seemed to indicate the Court's willingness to intervene where rationality and good faith were lacking.

In the 2001 case of *Government of the Republic of South Africa & Others v. Irene Grootboom & Others,*[150] the Constitutional Court heard claims from people living in an informal squatter settlement at Wallacedene in the Western Cape, who had been forcibly evicted by the state from land earmarked for low-cost housing. The claimants sued the government for housing, citing the right of access to adequate housing in section 26, and children's right to shelter in section 28(1)(c). In *Grootboom*, the Constitutional Court established the standard of reasonableness to assess state compliance with its socioeconomic rights obligations. The Court's judgment extensively interprets the limitations clause in section 26 of the Constitution, which is identical to that in section 27, providing extensive guidance on the progressive realization of socioeconomic rights.

In a decision delivered by Justice Yacoob, the Court indicated that while reasonableness was determined on a case-by-case basis, given great poverty and the constitutional commitment to equality, dignity, and freedom, the state's primary obligation was to act reasonably to provide the basic necessities of life to those who lack them.[151] The Court indicated that reasonableness required comprehensive programs, and that excluding a significant segment of society would be unreasonable, as would excluding the needs of the poor, given their reliance on the state for the basic necessities of life.[152] In seeking to ensure that the basic necessities of life were provided to all, the state had to focus, in particular, on the needs of the most vulnerable,

---

[146] *Id.* at para. 11.
[147] *Id.* at para. 28.
[148] *Id.* at para. 31.
[149] *Id.* at para. 29.
[150] Government of the Republic of South Africa and Others v. Irene Grootboom and Others 2000 (11) BCLR 1169 (CC) (S.Afr.) [hereinafter Grootboom].
[151] *Id.* at para. 24 & 44.
[152] *Id.* at para. 35 & 40–44.

especially the poor, and those experiencing urgent and desperate needs.[153] The court interpreted "progressive realization" in line with international law to require the state to take steps to realize the rights as expeditiously and effectively as possible, and that any deliberately retrogressive measures would need full justification in light of all the rights in the Constitution and available resources.[154] While progressive realization recognizes that full realization of everyone's right to access health care services is not always immediately possible, the Constitution's goal was that "the basic needs of all in society be effectively met" and this requires that "the state must take steps to achieve this goal."[155] Thus, "accessibility should be progressively facilitated," with legal, administrative, operational, and financial hurdles examined and, where possible, lowered over time.[156] Nonetheless, the Court recognized that the state could not be required to do more than available resources permit, and that while resources would determine the content and pace of realization, the government nonetheless should give adequate budgetary support to social rights, and plan and monitor efforts to meet all needs.[157] The Court found that national housing policy fell short of the government's constitutional duties, and declared that section 26 required a comprehensive program to realize the right of access to adequate housing that included reasonable measures to provide relief to those with no access to land, no roof over their heads, and living in intolerable conditions or crisis situations.

While the *Grootboom* decision was widely viewed as illustrating the feasibility of enforcing social rights, the Court's adoption of the reasonableness standard (together with its rejection of the minimum core concept) had commentators criticize it as creating an administrative model that simply required sensible priority setting rather than creating an individual right to particular services.[158] In light of the earlier *Soobramoney* decision and the broader inequities of the country's health care system, it remained unclear whether the Constitution's socioeconomic rights offered individuals approaching the courts any hope for alleviating deprivation.[159]

The Constitutional Court's most important decision on section 27 came in 2002 with *Minister of Health and Another v. Treatment Action Campaign and Others.*[160]

---

[153] *Id.* at para. 35 & 43.

[154] CESCR, General Comment 3, *The Nature of State Party Obligations*, U.N. Doc. HRI\GEN\1\Rev.1 para. 9 (December 14, 1990), *available at* http://www.unhchr.ch/tbs/doc.nsf/%28Symbol%29/ 94bdbaf59b43a424c12563ed0052b664?Opendocument, cited with approval in Grootboom, at para. 45.

[155] Grootboom, at para. 45.

[156] Id.

[157] *Id.*, at para. 32 & 68.

[158] Cass R. Sunstein, Social and Economic Rights? Lessons from South Africa, 11 CONST. F. 123 (2000); David Bilchitz, *Towards a Reasonable Approach to the Minimum Core: Laying the Foundations for Future Socio-Economic Rights Jurisprudence*, 19 S. AFR. J. HUM. RTS. 1 (2002).

[159] Joan Fitzpatrick & Ron C. Slye, *Republic of South Africa v. Grootboom / Minister of Health v. Treatment Action Campaign*, 97 AM. J. INT'L. L. 669 (2003).

[160] Minister of Health and Another v. Treatment Action Campaign and Others 2002 (5) SA 721 (CC) (S. Afr.) [hereinafter TAC].

The case took place amid a tremendous social battle over the government's refusal to provide any form of antiretroviral treatment for HIV/AIDS within the public sector. This refusal drew from President Mbeki's support for "AIDS denialism" that disputes that HIV causes AIDS and views antiretroviral drugs as toxic agents that are themselves the real cause of AIDS-related death.[161] Social contestation over the government's resolute refusal to provide treatment coalesced around its delays and active obstruction of public-sector use of Nevirapine, an antiretroviral drug with growing efficacy in preventing mother to child transmission (MTCT) of AIDS.[162] Boehringer Ingelheim, the manufacturer and patent holder, had offered the drug to the government at no cost for five years. Despite government refusals, the expansion of a national MTCT program was well supported among the media, public, and medical communities, motivated by national legal and political advocacy and growing protests among health care workers themselves that government policy interfered with their ethical duties toward patients.[163]

In August 2001, a group of NGOs and public-sector doctors led by the Treatment Action Campaign (TAC) instituted successful legal action in the High Court against the Minister of Health and Provincial Health departments. TAC argued that the state's delays and refusal to make Nevirapine available in the public sector breached section 27, as well as children's right to basic health services. The government appealed the case to the Constitutional Court, defending the reasonableness of its approach from the perspective of cost and efficacy.

The Constitutional Court found state policy to be unreasonable and held that excluding the drug in question in public health care facilities pending study results unreasonably denied a potentially life-saving drug to children born to mostly indigent mothers dependent on the state for their health care.[164] The Court focused on the grave suffering and limited survival prospects of these children, and stressed that the case was concerned with newborn babies whose lives might be saved by the administration of simple and cheap intervention, the safety and efficacy of which had been established, and which the government itself was providing in pilot sites in every province.[165]

---

[161] *See* Marjolein Harvey, *How Can a Virus Cause a Syndrome? Asks Mbeki*, ICLINIC ONLINE (Sept. 21, 2000), *available at* http://www.aegis.org/DisplayContent/?SectionID=370502; Mike Cohen, *Mbeki Questions HIV Testing*, THE ASSOCIATED PRESS, April 24, 2001; Edwin Cameron, *AIDS Denial and Holocaust Denial – AIDS, Justice and the Courts in South Africa*, 120 S. AFR. L.J. 525 (2003).

[162] Dhayendre Moodley, *The SAINT Trial: Nevirapine (NVP) versus Zidovudine (ZDV) + Lamivudine (3TC) in Prevention of Peripartum Transmission*, Abstract No. LbOr2, XIII International AIDS Conference, Durban, South Africa (July 9–14, 2000); Laura A. Guay et al., *Intrapartum and Neonatal Single-Dose Nevirapine Compared with Zidovudine for Prevention of Mother-to-Child Transmission of HIV-1 in Kampala, Uganda: HIVNET 012 Randomised Trial*, 354 LANCET 795 (1999).

[163] Editorial, *Government Should Provide Anti-Retrovirals*, THE MERCURY EDITORIAL, Dec. 6, 2002; Salim Abdool Karim et al., *Vertical HIV Transmission in South Africa: Translating Research into Policy and Practice*, 359 LANCET 992 (2002).

[164] TAC, at para. 79.

[165] TAC, at para. 71 & 72.

The Court applied several aspects of the *Grootboom* decision to section 27 and the provision of MTCT, holdings that programs must not ignore urgent needs nor exclude significant segments of society,[166] and that state policy in this case affected poor people who could not afford to pay for medical services.[167] In this case, the Court held that

> [children's] needs are "most urgent" and their inability to have access to Nevirapine profoundly affects their ability to enjoy all rights to which they are entitled. Their rights are "most in peril" as a result of the policy that has been adopted and are most affected by a rigid and inflexible policy that excludes them from having access to Nevirapine.[168]

The state's obligation was therefore to ensure that children were able to access basic health care services contemplated in section 28, particularly since this case concerned

> children born in public hospitals and clinics to mothers who are for the most part indigent and unable to gain access to private medical treatment which is beyond their means. They and their children are in the main part dependent upon the state to make health care services available to them.[169]

The Court found that government policy failed to meet constitutional standards because it excluded those who could reasonably be included where such treatment was medically required.[170] The Court not only declared the government's responsibility to devise and implement a comprehensive MTCT program within available resources, but also ordered it to remove, without delay, restrictions on the drug and make it available in the public sector, provide for training of counselors, and take reasonable measures to extend testing and counseling facilities throughout the public health sector.

One other section 27–related case has come before the court since the *TAC* decision, which illustrates the important role played by section 27 in the Court's approach to balancing private economic interests against public health needs. In the 2005 case of *Minister of Health & Another v. New Clicks South Africa (Pty) Ltd & Others*,[171] several pharmacy chains challenged the government's legislative efforts to create a national pricing system for medicines, which included a pricing committee, a single exit price for all medicines, and a fixed dispensing fee for pharmacists and dispensers of medicines. The Constitutional Court held unanimously that the

---

[166] TAC, at para. 68, quoting Grootboom, at para. 43 & 44.
[167] TAC, at para. 70, referencing Grootboom, at para. 35–37.
[168] TAC, at para. 78.
[169] TAC, at para. 79.
[170] TAC, at para. 125.
[171] Case CCT 59/04 Minister of Health & Another v. New Clicks South Africa (Pty) Ltd & Others 2005 (2) SA 311 para. 661 (CC) (S.Afr.) [hereinafter New Clicks].

Medicines Act permitted regulations to provide for price controls, including setting a single exit price for drugs into the health system.[172] While the court split 6-5 against the constitutionality of the dispensing fee, it nonetheless upheld the constitutionality of the regulations, holding that given the important constitutional purpose served by the pricing system of making medicines more accessible and affordable, the appropriate remedy would be to preserve as much of the scheme as possible.[173] It proposed instead that the curing of defects in the regulations through severance of certain words or through reading in of others.[174]

The Court repeatedly validated the importance of the purpose of the Medicines Act in enabling the government to fulfill its constitutional obligations under section 27.[175] The judges could find no equivalence between the pharmacists' interests and the public's health needs. Justice Ngcobo held that while "the interests of the pharmacists is a factor to be taken into consideration . . . they must yield to the interests of the general public."[176] The Court also made several dicta regarding section 27 that add new substantive content beyond the constitutional framework of reasonableness elaborated in the *Grootboom* and *TAC* decisions. For example, in several places the judgment confirmed that the right to health care services includes the right to access affordable medicines, which places a range of obligations on the state in relation to assuring affordability.[177] In particular, Justice Sachs held that "preventing excessive profit-taking from the manufacturing distribution and sale of medicines is more than an option for government. It is a constitutional obligation flowing from its duties under section 27(2)."[178] Justice Moseneke reiterated this sentiment saying that "[p]rohibitive pricing of medicine . . . would in effect equate to a denial of the right of access to health care."[179]

11.2.3 *The Use of Other Health-Related Constitutional Rights in Litigation*

While litigation focused on the right to health has been central to inspiring health reform in South Africa, other constitutional rights have also played an important role in realizing health equity in the country, including the right to bodily integrity.

---

[172] *Id.*, at paras. 13 & 14.
[173] *Id.*, at paras. 14–16.
[174] *Id.*, at para. 14 .
[175] *Id.*, at paras. 16, 84, 314, 514, 519 & 650.
[176] *Id.*, at para. 519.
[177] *E.g.*, *Id.*, at para. 514 and 704.
[178] Sachs further contended that the impact of inaccessible medicines on the poor in particular suggested state duties to take "special measures to assist those who are the most vulnerable to disease and, simultaneously the most lacking in resources." *Id.*, at paras. 659 & 651.
[179] *Id.*, at para. 706. Moseneke distinguished between availability and affordability of medicines, in that availability points to continued supply of medicines to ensure ready access, whereas affordability is an incident of access to essential drugs. Implicit in the requirement of affordable medicines is a pricing regime that does not render medicines out of the reach of most users and thereby frustrate access to quality health care.

Working conditions inside mines create a high-risk environment for tuberculosis (TB) transmission, resulting in part from silica dust exposure (which increases the risk of pulmonary TB, particularly in gold mines), as well as confined and poorly ventilated environments, which is conducive to TB transmission. It is therefore not surprising that miners in sub-Saharan Africa have greater incidence of TB than does any other working population in the world; their TB incidence is estimated to be as much as ten times higher than in the populations from which they originate.[180] Part of the reason why TB incidence is so high in South African mines is that mining companies have not implemented best-practice occupational health and safety standards in mines, and have had little incentive to do so. During the apartheid era, the legislature promulgated the Occupational Diseases in Mines and Works Act (ODIMWA),[181] which, unsurprisingly, favored the interests of white-owned mining companies over their predominantly black employees. The Act required mining companies to contribute a nominal monthly percentage of a mine worker's salary toward an occupational injuries and diseases compensation fund. Employees who suffered from occupational injuries or diseases were obliged to seek compensation from the fund, which often awarded inadequate compensation. All workers, including commerce and services, are entitled to seek compensation for their occupationally acquired diseases and injuries under Compensation for Occupational Injuries and Diseases Act (COIDA),[182] which provides for the possibility of increased compensation where the injury sustained or disease contracted results from employer negligence.[183] However, ODIMWA has no comparable provision, and mine workers are precluded from claiming compensation under COIDA by virtue of section 100(2) of ODIMWA.[184] Mining companies are also deemed indemnified against civil claims brought by their employees by virtue of section 35(1) of COIDA. As a result of these two provisions, mining companies had little incentive to markedly improve the working conditions of their workers.

Mankayi, an employee of mining company, AngloGold, exemplified the plight of such mine workers.[185] He argued that AngloGold negligently exposed him to harmful dusts and gases as a result of which he contracted TB and which caused chronic obstructive airways, which have rendered him unable to work as a mine

---

[180] David Stuckler et al., *Mining and Risk of Tuberculosis in Sub-Saharan Africa*, 101 AM. J. PUB. HEALTH 524 (2010).

[181] Occupational Diseases in Mines and Works Act 78 of 1973 (S. Afr.) [hereinafter ODIMWA].

[182] Compensation for Occupational Injuries and Diseases Act 130 of 1993 (S. Afr.) [hereinafter COIDA].

[183] *Id.* §56(1).

[184] ODIMWA, §100(2) reads: "Notwithstanding anything in any other law contained, no person who has a claim to benefits under this Act in respect of a compensatable disease as defined in this Act, on the ground that such person is or was employed at a controlled mine or a controlled works, shall be entitled, in respect of such disease, to benefits under the Workmen's Compensation Act, 1941... or any other law."

[185] Case CCT 40/10 Thembekile Mankayi v. AngloGold Ashanti Limited 2011 (3) SA 237 (CC) (S. Afr.) [hereinafter Mankayi].

worker or in any other occupation. Mankayi argued that he received inadequate compensation for his diseases under ODIMWA.[186] He sued AngloGold on the basis of his common law right to claim compensation for injuries suffered as a result of his employer's negligence,[187] arguing that there is no provision in ODIMWA excluding a common law claim. AngloGold argued that section 35(1) of COIDA[188] had the effect of extinguishing Mankayi's common law right to sue it for negligence. The South Gauteng High Court and Supreme Court of Appeals found in favor of AngloGold, and Mankayi appealed to the Constitutional Court, arguing that that he did not receive compensation in terms of the compensation law but in terms of the mining law, and that he should therefore be able to sue at common law. Further, he argued that such an extinction of his common law right violated his right to freedom and security of a person as enshrined in section 12(1)(c) of the Constitution: "everyone has the right to freedom and security of the person, which includes the right −... (c) to be free from all forms of violence from either public or private sources."

The Court held that that any person may claim the protection of the right to the security of the person and public and private entities alike must respect that right. The Court held that

> [the] right to security of the person is engaged whenever a person is subjected to some form of injury deriving from either a public or a private source. This is because the common law right to claim damages for the negligent infliction of bodily harm constitutes an effective remedy required by section 38 of the Constitution in order to protect and give effect to the section 12(1)(c) right.[189]

The Court concluded that given the singular risks of mining and its unique historical role in South Africa's wealth, there was "nothing irrational in preserving employees' common law claims against their employers in respect of ODIMWA-compensatable diseases." After noting these strong sentiments, the majority of the Court upheld Mankayi's rights and awarded costs against AngloGold. While the Court's ruling does not alter the compensation available to workers who fall within COIDA, it will have an impact on the health and safety of mining communities who are governed by ODIMWA.

---

[186] After being certified in 2004 as suffering from a compensatable disease, he received compensation of R16,320 (approximately $2,300) under ODIMWA. *See id.*, at para. 4.

[187] Mankayi claimed damages amounting to approximately R2.6 million (US$371,500). This comprised past and future loss of earnings of R738,147, future medical expenses of R1,374,600, and general damages of R500,000. *See id.*, at para. 2.

[188] COIDA, §35(1) states: "Substitution of compensation for other legal remedies.... No action shall lie by an employee or any dependant of an employee for the recovery of damages in respect of any occupational injury or disease resulting in the disablement or death of such employee against such employee's employer, and no liability for compensation on the part of such employer shall arise save under the provisions of this Act in respect of such disablement or death."

[189] Mankayi, at para. 16.

11.3 ASSESSING THE IMPACT OF THE LITIGATION ON HEALTH EQUITY

The *TAC* decision – the first case where the constitutional right to health was successfully enforced against the government – would appear, prima facie, to have contributed to greater health equity for people with HIV/AIDS. Here the Court enforced
section 27 against an unwilling government, breaking the back of its intransigence
on a deeply divisive social and political issue. The decision effectively ensured that
neither irrational science nor murky unstated rationales could continue to moti-
vate government policy on MTCT of AIDS.[190] Together with other pressures, this
case powerfully influenced how the government subsequently formulated its AIDS
treatment policies.

The Constitutional Court's order in *TAC* motivated government to establish a
national MTCT program, and by 2009, MTCT interventions were available in 95
percent of public facilities.[191] The program likely contributed to declines in child
mortality (which had increased from 50 per 1,000 live births in 1994 to 60 in 2005).[192]
The *TAC* decision and its outcomes also laid the groundwork for a national AIDS
treatment program, announced in 2003.[193] The national antiretroviral program has
increased its coverage from 133,000 people in 2005 (7 percent of people in need) to
920,000 people in 2009 (38 percent),[194] a figure roughly consistent with access rates
for antiretrovirals (ARV) throughout low- and middle-income countries.

The government planned to increase coverage to 1.4 million people by 2011–
2012.[195] Most significantly, national increases in life expectancy at birth (from 43
years in 2007 to 53.3 years in 2010) are attributed to the rollout of antiretroviral
medicines.[196] The *TAC* decision therefore illustrates the considerable power of an
entrenched constitutional health right to effect changes in government policies.

While not an entitlement to health care on demand, the *TAC* decision illustrates
how a successful claim under the constitutional health care right may secure, for
example, a critical health service for poor women and their infants. The court's elaboration of a reasonableness standard provides further guidance to the government in
realizing the right to access health care services. Applied to health, the reasonableness standard appears to legislate great equity in health by requiring the government

[190] Lisa Forman, *Justice and Justiciability: Evaluating Right to Health Jurisprudence in South Africa*, 27 J. MED. & L. 661 (2008).

[191] Statistics South Africa, Mid Year Population Estimates 2010, supra note 102.

[192] Harrison, *supra* note 39, at 6.

[193] South African Department of Health, *Operational Plan for Comprehensive HIV and AIDS Care, Management and Treatment for South Africa* (Nov. 19, 2003), *available at* http://www.info.gov.za/otherdocs/2003/aidsplan/report.pdf.

[194] Gavin Mooney & Lucy Gilson, *The Economic Situation in South Africa and Health Inequities*, 374 LANCET 858, 859 (2009).

[195] SOUTH AFRICAN DEPARTMENT OF HEALTH, ANNUAL REPORT 2008/09, *available at* http://www.doh.gov.za/docs/reports/annual/2009/sectiona.pdf.

[196] Statistics South Africa, *Mid Year Population Estimates 2009*, supra note 103, at 6.

to devise and implement comprehensive health policies to meet basic health needs and to take particular account of the poor and vulnerable, and of urgent and desperate needs. This is a powerful guarantee of accountable and responsive health care decision making, and the right and the reasonableness standard therefore appear to have served an important democratic function. Democracy was further served by the way the constitutional right and the Constitutional Court decision conferred a powerful social claim on poor and vulnerable people unfairly excluded from the benefits of public health care. *TAC* therefore illustrates how enforcing health rights can guide health policy, empower citizens to challenge health care decision making (itself an important democratic and civic outcome), and enable the judiciary to hold the executive and legislature to constitutional standards of health equity.

Nonetheless, the Court's emphasis on state duties to take reasonable measures to meet basic health needs (evident arguably in *Soobramoney* as well as *TAC*) underscores that the right does not in fact confer an individual entitlement to health care services. Certainly, it could be argued that the Court's identification of state duties to take reasonable measures to meet basic health needs implies a corresponding individual entitlement to basic health care services (roughly consistent with primary or essential health care). This is certainly the implicit position taken in *TAC*, as well as in the *New Clicks* decision, which explicitly articulates a duty to provide access to affordable medicines under section 27. While the cases may create these entitlements, it is equally apparent from the Court's decisions (and especially its rejection of the international law concept of the minimum core) that state duties regarding these rights remain limited by progressive realization within resources.

While *TAC* illustrates that claims to this limited entitlement to basic health care services can be successful, the Court's recent rejection of a claim for greater access to water illustrates that there is no inherent guarantee of even basic needs implicit within section 27. In *Mazibuko and Others v City of Johannesburg and Others*,[197] the Constitutional Court addressed for the first time section 27(1)(b)'s provision that everyone has the right to have access to sufficient water. The case concerned the lawfulness of a city project to address severe water losses and nonpayment in Soweto by installing prepaid meters to charge for water use exceeding 6 kiloliters per household (equating to 25 liters per person daily). Mrs. Mazibuko and four other Soweto residents challenged the sufficiency of 6 kiloliters and the lawfulness of installing prepaid meters. The Constitutional Court held that the government's duty was to take reasonable measures to progressively realize this right, and that the pertinent question was whether the city's policy was reasonable. The Court argued that implicit in the concept of progressive realization is that it will take time before everyone has access to sufficient water. While the Court affirmed the democratic

---

[197] Case CCT 39/09, Mazibuko and Others v. City of Johannesburg and Others 2009 (4) SA 1 (CC) (S. Afr.).

value of litigation on social and economic rights in achieving accountability, it concluded that it was inappropriate for it (and not the government) to quantify the content of sufficient water under this right. The Court therefore concluded that the policy was reasonable despite recognizing that 100,000 city households still lacked access to the most basic water supply.

This case raises real concerns about the Court's willingness to enforce the constitution's socioeconomic rights in any meaningful way against government policy. It certainly lends credence to critiques that the Court's approach to the Constitution's socioeconomic rights creates nothing more than an administrative entitlement to accountability, which does not guide state efforts to assure progressive realization and does not serve the key populations intended to be the beneficiaries of such rights.[198] The contrast between the *Mazibuko* and *TAC* outcomes may suggest that the Constitution's socioeconomic rights may only yield equitable outcomes in cases of extreme legislative noncompliance. The implication is that *TAC* is to some extent a best-case scenario for litigation of health equity outcomes, not simply because the case was successful but because the health care service in question was required to deal with a grave disease pandemic with severe impacts on population health. The severity of the health risk posed by the pandemic and the potential life-saving nature of the decision for millions of people significantly ratcheted up the stakes for the Court as well as the equity impacts of their decision. This may suggest that *TAC* perhaps illustrates only the potential for similarly grave cases to achieve similarly equitable outcomes.

The equality potential of the right is further undercut by implementation problems. After the *Grootboom* decision, the government's formulation and implementation of housing policy was troublingly slow; a year after the decision, there had been little tangible change in housing policy to cater for people in desperate and crisis situations.[199] The picture was considerably different in *TAC*, perhaps because of the power of domestic treatment advocates who effectively used the media to highlight implementation delays, and who also instituted contempt of court proceedings against a provincial premier for not implementing the decision.[200] The disparities in outcomes between the cases seem to suggest that social mobilization is necessary to ensure the implementation of the Court's decisions.

---

[198] See e.g., Theunis Roux, *Understanding* Grootboom – *A Response to Cass R. Sunstein*, 12 F. CONST. 41, 46 (2002); Sandra Liebenberg, *South Africa's Evolving Jurisprudence on Socio-Economic Rights*, 6 L. DEMOCRACY & DEV. 159 (2002). See also David Bilchitz, *Towards a Reasonable Approach to the Minimum Core: Laying the Foundations for Future Socio-economic Rights Jurisprudence*, 19 S. AFR. J. HUM. RTS, 1 (2002); Marius Pieterse, *Possibilities and Pitfalls in the Domestic Enforcement of Social Rights: Contemplating the South African Experience*, 26 HUM. RTS. QUART. 882 (2004).

[199] Kameshni Pillay, *Implementing* Grootboom: *Supervision Needed*, 3 ESR REV. 13 (2002).

[200] Mark Heywood, *Contempt or Compliance? The TAC Case after the Constitutional Court Judgment*, 4 ESR REV. 7 (2003).

The Constitutional Court's interpretation of the right to bodily integrity in the *Mankayi* case will likely catalyze and spur health and safety reforms in the mining industry, which historically has arguably neglected the health and safety of mine workers. In so doing, the Mankayi decision will, in the long run, facilitate health equity in the occupational context.

11.4 CONCLUSION

The South African experience illustrates how an entrenched constitutional right to health care can advance health equity well beyond litigation. This effect is evident in the formative role of the constitutional right in motivating a range of legislation and policy in South Africa to achieve greater equity within and between the private sector and the public sector, including the Medical Schemes Act, National Health Act, and the proposed National Health Insurance system.

The entrenchment of the constitutional right has therefore made the national pursuit of universal access to health care a constitutional obligation. This may serve to insulate this pursuit from the vagaries of political goodwill and historical circumstances that undermine national commitments to health equity only affixed in policy or subsidiary legislation (as the abandonment of the RDP policy illustrates).[201] An entrenched constitutional commitment to equitable health care provides a far more enduring guarantee, particularly given the way that the South African government's broader macroeconomic choices (through reducing health spending) have restricted the achievement of health equity.

However, these legislative outcomes are hardly likely to have been achieved by the entrenchment of a constitutional health right without a corresponding political commitment to achieving equitable outcomes in health and other sectors. In South Africa, this commitment was a core component of the ANC's historical platforms and government policies. The impact of the constitutional health right was thus aided by the fact that it resonates with existing policy imperatives. It may therefore be less likely that a constitutional health right could influence government policy in quite the same way where the right did not resonate with core social and/or political values. This contingent outcome may mean litigation is the primary legal mechanism individuals within countries with health rights can use to advance health equity, although this too requires a judiciary willing to enforce it effectively.

In South Africa, the constitutional health right, whether via litigation or legislation, has nonetheless had limited impact in remedying disparities between the public and private health care sectors or in significantly improving access to health care within the public sector outside of HIV/AIDS. This outcome may simply reinforce that a

---

[201] Lisa Forman, *Ensuring Reasonable Health: Health Rights, the Judiciary and South African HIV/AIDS Policy*, 33 J. LAW. MED. ETHICS 711 (2005).

health right, however effectively enforced, cannot substitute for effective leadership at all levels of health care. In this light, the new NHI system reflects the most important effort yet to address the country's health inequities, and it is notably rooted in human rights and social justice objectives. To this extent, its success will provide somewhat of a litmus test of the extent to which a constitutional health right contributes to the achievement of health equity in a riven and inequitable country.

12

Provision of Health Care Services and the Right to Health in Brazil

The Long, Winding, and Uncertain Road to Equality

Mariana Mota Prado*

INTRODUCTION

Since its creation in 1988, the Unified System of Health Care (*Sistema Único de Saúde*, SUS) – the Brazilian public health care system – has had important achievements, reducing inequalities by expanding coverage to a significant portion of the population and replacing a disease-focused approach with an integrated health care model. SUS is also characterized, however, by significant failures. Dysfunctional public hospitals largely contrast with very functional and efficient private hospitals and health care clinics that are only accessible to a quarter of the Brazilian population – those who can afford these services. In sum, while there has been some improvements, inequality still runs rampant between the public and private health care systems in Brazil.

There is no conclusive evidence that litigation of the right to health in Brazil is reducing these inequalities. Some claim that litigation is depriving the public system of valuable resources and allocating these to the treatment of patients who can afford private treatment, making matters worse. Others question this conclusion, claiming that litigation has also benefited the poor and has kept the public system in check. Indeed, a fierce academic and public debate is currently under way in an attempt to determine the dimensions, characteristics, and consequences of the right-to-health litigation in Brazil.

The chapter is structured as follows. In the first section, I present a description of the health care system in Brazil, indicating the significant achievements of SUS since its implementation in 1988, as well as some of its persistent failures. This section also briefly describes the private health care system. In the second section, I identify the constitutional provision protecting the right to health, the relevant statutory and regulatory provisions, and the most recent attempts to implement legal reforms in

* I am grateful to Joanna Noronha and Tatiana Cardoso for excellent research assistance.

the system. In the third section, I present the convoluted and inconclusive debate on right to health and access to health care litigation. Finally, I discuss recent proposals that could potentially deal with some of the problems discussed in the chapter.

12.1 THE BRAZILIAN HEALTH CARE SYSTEM

During Brazil's democratic transition, the 1988 Constitution established SUS as part of a complete overhaul of the health care system. Before 1988, public health care was funded by the Social Security system and offered only to workers in the formal sector.[1] After 1988, Brazil started to offer free health care to all citizens but nonetheless allowed the continuance of a supplementary private health care system. While all citizens can obtain free health care in the public system at no charge, many elect to use the private system for most (if not all) services. This private system is supplementary (not complementary) to the public health care system; in other words, those who have chosen to have private care can still use the public system.[2] The costs of supplementary private health are covered either directly by the patients or through individual or collective insurance plans (often paid by employers). This section mostly describes the inner workings of the public system, adding a brief explanation about the private systems at the end.

12.1.1 *The Brazilian Public Health Care System (SUS)*

The Brazilian public health care system is one of the largest in world. In principle it should be able to provide primary and secondary care and emergency and specialized services to the 190.8 million Brazilian citizens. In practice, almost 50 million citizens have opted out of the public system. Nevertheless, serving roughly 140 million people still makes it a very large operation.[3]

SUS was intended to create a more equitable health care system and it has helped improve some important health indicators in the country. Brazil has already achieved one target in the first of the United Nations' Millennium Development Goals (MDG): reduction in the number of underweight children by half. It is also on track to meet MDG number 4: two-thirds reduction in the mortality rate of children younger than five years.[4] SUS has also leveled off the number of new cases of

---

[1] Marta Arretche, *Toward a Unified and More Equitable System: Health Reform in Brazil*, in CRUCIAL NEEDS, WEAK INCENTIVES 155, 159 (Robert Kaufman & Joan Nelson eds., 2004).

[2] *Id.* at 155.

[3] Carlos Octávio Ocké-Reis, A Constituicao de Um Modelo de Atenção à Saúde Universal: Uma Promessa Não Cumprida Pelo SUS? [The Construction of a Modelo of Universal Health Care: An Unfilled Promise by SUS?], Texto para Discussão n. 1376, IPEA 10 (2009) (indicating, for example, that Brazil has the second-highest number of organ transplants in the world, just behind the United States).

[4] Sabine Kleinert & Richard Horton, *Brazil: Towards Sustainability and Equity in Health*, 377 THE LANCET 1721 (2011).

HIV/AIDS with an effective prevention and treatment system.[5] In addition, as a result of the implementation of a very effective system of preventive medicine (moving away from the curative model that prevailed before 1988), massive inoculation campaigns, and a system comprising community health agents and family doctors (*Programa Saúde da Família*), Brazil has made significant progress in its health indicators in the last decade. Infant mortality (per 1,000 live births) has decreased from 69.1 in 1980 to 47 in 1990, and reached 26.26 in 2004.[6] Similarly, life expectancy increased from 62.6 years to 66.6 and reached 71.6 years in the same period.[7]

Despite these achievements, there are still problems. In 2000, a World Health Organization (WHO) report on the performance of national health systems ranked Brazil 125th among 191 countries worldwide, and 28th among 33 countries in Latin America and the Caribbean region.[8] Moreover, some health indicators are not improving: the numbers available suggest that neonatal and maternal mortality rates changed little in the last decade, and worsened in 2004.[9] Considering that more than 90 percent of deliveries in Brazil take place in a hospital, this is a clear indicator that there are considerable problems with the hospital system.[10] In other words, Brazil has seemingly made great achievements in some areas of preventive medicine and primary care, but these achievements in primary care are not universal, and the same advances are not occurring in other areas of the public system. The next sections explore how these achievements and failures have come about.

12.1.1.1 Level of Investment in the System

There is much debate as to whether the problems of the system are caused by lack of investment or by inefficient allocation of existing resources. Those who argue that Brazil needs more health care investment emphasize that Brazil's investment in health per capita is lower than the investment made in developed countries. For example, in 2004, Brazil spent $1,520 (PPP dollars) per capita in health investments,

---

[5] Jane Galvão, *Public Health: Access to Antiretroviral Drugs in Brazil*, 360(9348) THE LANCET 1862 (2002); Francisco I. Bastos et al., Treatment for HIV/AIDS in Brazil: Strengths, Challenges, and Opportunities for Operations Research, 1 AID SCIENCE (2001), *available at* http://www.aidscience.org/ Articles/aidscience012.pdf; Carlos Passarelli & Veriano Terto Jr., *Good Medicine: Brazil's Multifront War on AIDS*, 35(5) NACLA REPORT ON THE AMERICAS 35, 35–37, 40–42 (2002); Fabienne Orsi et al., *Intellectual Property Rights, Anti-AIDS Policy and Generic Drugs: Lessons From the Brazilian Public Health Program, in* ECONOMICS OF AIDS AND ACCESS TO HIV/AIDS CARE IN DEVELOPING COUNTRIES: ISSUES AND CHALLENGES 109 (J.-P. Moatti et al. eds., 2003).

[6] *See* James Macinko et al., *Evaluation of the Impact of the Family Health Program on Infant Mortality in Brazil 1990–2002*, 60 J. EPIDEMIOLOGY & COMMUNITY HEALTH, 13 (2006) (arguing that Programa de Saúde da Família was a factor, but not the only factor in the decrease of infant mortality rates).

[7] Gerard M. La Forgia & Bernard F. Couttolenc, HOSPITAL PERFORMANCE IN BRAZIL: THE SEARCH FOR EXCELLENCE 22 (2008).

[8] World Health Organization, HEALTH SYSTEMS: IMPROVING PERFORMANCE, THE WORLD HEALTH REPORT 2000, 152 (Annex Table 1) (2000).

[9] La Forgia & Couttolenc, *supra* note 7.

[10] *Id.*

both private and public, while Canada spent \$3,173 and the United Kingdom \$2,560.[11] In contrast, those who argue that Brazil's primary problem is not levels of investment emphasize that the country's investment in health as percentage of GDP (7.9 percent in 2002) is higher than other Latin American countries (7.0 percent).[12] In 2004, this number increased to 8.8 percent, making Brazil comparable to OECD countries,[13] although behind Argentina (9.6 percent).[14] The problem, for them, is not *how much* is being invested, but the fact that the money is not being allocated in the most effective way.

Some argue that Brazil has a very inequitable allocation of health care resources. After separating public and private investments on health, Octavio Ferraz and Fabiola Vieira show that the numbers in the previous paragraph can be misleading. The public spending is just US\$822 per capita and accounts for only 4.7 percent of the GDP.[15] Indeed, the public share of total health spending in Brazil (45.9 percent) is lower than in most middle- (49.9 percent) and high-income countries (73.3 percent).[16] The public share of total health spending in Brazil is also lower than the Latin American average (47.8 percent).[17] This provides support for arguments that there should be more resources available for the public health care system.[18] However, the argument is not so conclusive if one considers that Brazil's per capita expenditures (PPP dollars) in the public system in 2002 (\$566) was comparable with the average health spending in upper-middle-income countries (\$611) and is higher than the average in Latin America (\$486).[19]

Considering the relatively high levels of health spending as percentage of GDP and per capita spending for countries at the same income level, some scholars argue that the problem is not the lack of resources or unequal distribution of resources, but how to make better use of the resources available: "Brazil is already a big spender – but only an average performer."[20] Indeed, comparing Brazil with other Latin American countries, it has higher child mortality rates (33 per 1,000 in Brazil, compared to 16 in Argentina, 10 in Chile, 12 in Costa Rica, 16 in Uruguay, and 6, each, in the United Kingdom and Canada).[21] Of course, there are other factors that determine

---

[11] Octavio Luiz Motta Ferraz & Fabiola Sulpino Vieira, *Direito a Saúde, Políticas Públicas e Desigualdades Sociais no Brasil: Eqüidade como Princípio Fundamental* [*Right to Health, Public Policies and Social Inequalities in Brazil: Equity as a Fundamental Principle*], 52 DADOS 223, 229 (2009).

[12] La Forgia & Couttolenc, *supra* note 7, at 24, table 2.4.

[13] Ferraz & Vieira, *supra* note 11.

[14] *See* WHO website, *available at* http://www.who.int/countries/en/.

[15] Ferraz & Vieira, *supra* note 11.

[16] La Forgia & Couttolenc, *supra* note 7, at 23.

[17] *Id.*

[18] *See, e.g.,* José Mendes Ribeiro, *SUS Evolution and Hospital Services Rationing*, 14 CIÊNC. SAÚDE COLETIVA 771 (2009).

[19] La Forgia & Couttolenc, *supra* note 7, at 24, table 2.4.

[20] *Id.* at 24.

[21] Ferraz & Vieira, *supra* note 11.

health outcomes, such as access to water and sanitation, education, and distribution of resources. Yet even controlling for these factors, some countries achieve better health outcomes than do other countries with the same level of expenditure.[22] This seems to imply that Brazilian investment in health care in general and in the public health care system in particular is less effective than it is in other countries. The argument is that the public system invests too much in hospitals, to the detriment of primary and preventive care; it allows numerous dysfunctional and badly managed hospitals to remain in the system, and it spends too much money on expensive medications (partly as a result of litigation).[23]

Part of the obstacles in increasing investments and improvement the management of the public health care system are related to the division of responsibilities within Brazil's federalist structure. SUS promoted a radical decentralization of health care services, transferring the responsibility of health care provision to local governments (municipalities), while the federal and state governments remained responsible for transferring resources to fund these services.[24] These decentralization reforms had wide public support,[25] and had important achievements, as noted earlier. However, there were still significant problems related to the lack of clarity about how much each level of government will invest in the system.[26]

In attempt to address this problem, the Brazilian legislature in 2000 approved a constitutional amendment setting how much (as a percentage of their total fiscal resources) each subnational unit of government (i.e., state and municipal governments) is obliged to contribute to health (12 percent for states and 15 percent for municipalities). As discussed in Subsection 12.2.4, it is expected that this amendment will increase further the level of investment in the system, and will make the

---

[22] La Forgia & Couttolenc, *supra* note 7, at 24.

[23] *See infra* Sec. III.

[24] *See* Ricardo Cesar R. Costa, *Descentralização, Financiamento e Regulação: a Reforma do Sistema Público de Saúde no Brasil Durante a Década de 1990* [*Decentralization, Financing and Regulation: the Reformo of the Public Health Care System in Brazil in the 1990s*] 18 REVISTA DE SOCIOLOGIA E POLÍTICA 49 (2002) for a detailed analysis of this decentralization process. *See also* João Yunes, *O SUS na Lógica da Descentralização* [*SUS under the Logic of Decentralization*] 13(35) ESTUDOS AVANÇADOS – USP 65 (1999).

[25] Edla Hoffmann, *Política de Saúde no Brasil: os (Des)Caminhos Pós-1980 Desafios ao Serviço Social* [*Health Policies in Brazil: The (Bad) Path after 1980 and the Challend to Social Service*], in O SOPRO DO MINUANO: TRANSFORMAÇÕES SOCIETÁRIAS E POLÍTICAS SOCIAIS – UM DEBATE ACADÊMICO 73 (Carlos Nelson Reis, ed., 2007). Costa, supra note 24, at 51–52.

[26] José Serra & José Rodrigues Afonso, *Federalismo Fiscal à Brasileira: Algumas Reflexões* [*Fiscal Federalism Brazilian Style: Some Reflections*] 6(12) REVISTA DO BNDES 6–7 (1999). Sol Gerson & Erika A. Araujo, *Ações Sociais Básicas: Descentralização ou Municipalização?* [*Basic Social Actions: Decentralization or Municipalization?*], 23 INFORME: SECRETARIA PARA ASSUNTOS FISCAIS 1,1 (2001); Áquilas N. Mendes & Suzana B. Santos, *Financiamento Descentralizado da Saúde: a Contribuição dos Municípios Paulistas* [*Financing the Decentralization of Health Care: The Contribution of Municipalities in the State of São Paulo*], 9 SAÚDE E SOCIEDADE 111, 113 (2000).

transfers from federal governments more reliable, as they have varied from administration to administration.[27] Whether it will achieve these outcomes remains to be seen.

12.1.1.2 Investment Inequalities: Expenditures Per Capita with SUS in Municipalities

One negative consequence of decentralization is regional inequalities. Decentralization forced numerous municipalities to take on the responsibility for providing health care services while lacking the necessary fiscal resources to do so effectively.[28] This implies that wealthier municipalities are naturally able to invest more than poor ones. Indeed, while Brazil has shown significant progress in aggregate health indicators, there are still significant regional disparities. Municipalities in the poorest regions in the country, such as Maranhão, Alagoas, Paraíba, and Rio Grande do Norte, have infant mortality rates similar to African countries (more than 100 deaths per 1,000 births). In contrast, some municipalities in the state of Rio Grande do Sul have infant mortality rates similar to the most developed Latin American countries, such as Chile and Costa Rica (15 deaths per 1,000 births).[29]

Since 1996, the federal government decided to use part of the federal transfers to reduce regional inequalities by providing more resources to poorer municipalities.[30] This has increased spending in poorer regions as a percentage of the population.[31] Indeed, in 2000, the spending on health care followed closely the population distribution in the country, with distribution of overall resources being directly proportional to the population.[32] Despite these efforts, the expenditures per capita with health care services still vary markedly between municipalities. To illustrate how significant these differences can be, a World Bank report compared the lowest and highest levels of expenditures in health care per capita in Brazil in 2002. The municipality

---

[27] Gastão Wagner Campos, *Reforma Política e Sanitária: A Sustentabilidade do SUS em Questão?* [*Political and Health Reforms: The Sustainability of SUS Under Siege?*], 12 CIÊNCIA & SAÚDE COLETIVA 301, 306 (2007). *See also* Osmar Bertoldi, IDEIAS PARA UMA METRÓPOLE SUSTENTÁVEL [IDEAS FOR A SUSTAINABLE METROPOLIS] 88 (2006); Marizete A. Silva, *Centros Colaboradores Para a Qualidade da Gestão e Assistência Hospitalares: Uma Experiência Inovadora* [*Collaborative Centers to Improve Quality of Hospital Management and Service Provision: An Innovative Experience*], in GESTÃO DE SISTEMAS DE SAÚDE 280, 304 (Celia Regina Pierantoni & Cid Manso de Mello Vianna, eds., 2003); Costa, *supra* note 24, at 53 (showing that the overall amount of investment in these two periods was roughly the same: in 1990–1992, US$6.5 billion; in 1993–1994, US$7.5 billion.).

[28] André Medici, O DESAFIO DA DESCENTRALIZAÇÃO: FINANCIAMENTO PÚBLICO DA SAÚDE NO BRASIL [THE CHALLENGE OF DECENTRALIZATION: PUBLIC FINANCING FOR HEALTH IN BRAZIL] 47 (2002).

[29] Arretche, *supra* note 1.

[30] André Medici, *Propostas para Melhoras a Cobertura, a Eficiência e a Qualidade no Setor de Saúde* [*Proposals to Improve Coverage, Efficiency and Quality of Services in the Health Sector*], in BRASIL: A NOVA AGENDA SOCIAL 23, 34 (Edmar Lisboa Bacha & Simon Schwartzman, eds., 2011).

[31] *Id.* at 35 (citing the Northeast region as an example).

[32] Arretche, *supra* note 1, at table 6.10.

of Parintins was spending R$45 (US$22.50) per capita on health care, whereas Porto Alegre was spending R$349 (US$175) per capita – a difference of 770%.[33]

Even if the system was effective in leveling overall resources, it would still not compensate for historical inequalities. For instance, since 1988, public primary health care has been concentrated in the poorest regions. The North and Northeast had a higher number of primary health care establishments per capita than the did the Southeast in 1998,[34] but lacked better and more specialized services. In contrast, these services were primarily concentrated in the South and Southeast regions.[35] These inequalities have persisted over time: SUS spending on hospital health care in 2001 was concentrated in the Southeast (44.6 percent).[36]

The problem of regional inequalities in health care provision is compounded by the fact that the richer municipalities are more likely to offer sanitation, better education, and welfare services that will address some of the primary causes of poor health. São Paulo, a wealthy municipality, offers public referral facilities within one hour's travel to the entire population and yet its neonatal mortality varies from 3 to 24 per 1,000.[37] This variation, along with variations in other health indicators, is associated with socioeconomic disparities, not access to health care.[38] This is yet another argument for a redistributive system of federal transfers that pays more attention to the wealth of municipalities.

One of the obstacles to account for regional inequalities is the complexity of the system of federal transfers to states, municipalities, and service providers under the SUS.[39] In very simplistic terms, the municipalities alone are receiving:

(1) automatic transfers to cover their expenditures with health on a per capita basis;

(2) transfers destined to service providers, according to criteria and terms defined by the federal government;

(3) transfers that operate as incentives to adopt some of the actions proposed by the federal government; and

(4) transfers that are destined to finance special programs as designed by the federal government.

---

[33] The same is true for states, but I focus the analysis on municipalities because the variations are more pronounced. World Bank, *Brasil – Governança no Sistema Único de Saúde (SUS) do Brasil:Melhorando a Qualidade do Gasto Público e Gestão de Recursos* [*Governance in the Brazilian Public Health Care System (SUS): Improving Quality of Spending and Management of Resources*], Relatório Nº. 36601-BR 25 (February 15, 2007), *available at* http://siteresources.worldbank.org/BRAZILINPOREXTN/Resources/3817166–1185895645304/4044168–1186326902607/19GovernancaSUSport.pdf.

[34] Arretche, *supra* note 1, at 161.

[35] *Id.*

[36] *Id.* at 182.

[37] La Forgia & Couttolenc, *supra* note 7, at 36.

[38] *Id.*

[39] *See* World Bank, *supra* note 33 for an excellent attempt to capture this complex web in a graph.

This list does not convey the complexity of the rules governing each of these transfers, but it explains why some municipalities receive significantly higher levels of federal transfers than do others, despite not being necessarily the ones that need the most resources.

Two programs were implemented in 2006 in an attempt to streamline this system: *Pactos pela Saúde* and *Programação Pactuada e Integrada.*[40] These programs adopt the same principles as the "block grants" in Canada and the United Kingdom.[41] However, as of 2012, the programs had not been fully implemented, as they depend on a network of service providers (*Redes de Saúde*) that does not exist yet.[42]

Another problem is corruption, that is, the federal transfers that are appropriated by local elites instead of being used to provide services to people who cannot afford private health care. There is no data to offer a comprehensive picture of the impact of corruption on the system, and how many resources are misappropriated through corruption since decentralization took place.[43] Despite these difficulties, the problem seems to be particularly acute in municipalities.[44] The idea that a significant portion of these resources is misappropriated in certain municipalities and not others (i.e., that levels of corruption are higher in some places) adds another layer of complexity to the inequality problems in the system.

12.1.1.3 Inequalities within the Services Provided by the Public Health Care System

As indicated in the Introduction to this chapter, Brazil has made significant progress in health indicators, with a very effective program of inoculation and primary medicine. These achievements, however, have not reached the entire Brazilian population who depend on the public health care system. Moreover, these achievements stand in sharp contrast to the provision of medium and complex services in Brazil. There is lack of access to, and unequal distribution of, hospital services.

Despite having the right to such services at no cost, patients often find a number of problems: public hospitals are often ill equipped and have longer waiting times than

---

[40] La Forgia & Couttolenc, *supra* note 7, at 8; Medici, *supra* note 30, at 33.

[41] Medici, *supra* note 30, at 33.

[42] *Id.*

[43] Sandro G. Peixoto et al., Descentralização e Corrupção: Evidência a Partir dos Programas de Atenção Básica de Saúde [Decentralization and Corruption : Evidence from Programs of Basic Attention to Health] (2010), *available at* http://www.anpec.org.br/encontro2010/inscricao/arquivos/000-8a8eb7c4cb64e13fe518c2ecc44ade13.pdf.

[44] OECD/OAS, Forum on Implementing Conflict of Interest Policies in the Public Service, Estudo de Caso: A Experiência do Brasil na Administração de Conflito de Interesses no Serviço Público [Case Study: The Brazilian Experience in Managing Conflict of Interest in the Public Service] 10 (2004).

does the private system.[45] As a consequence, those who do not have a private health care plan seek medical assistance less often.[46] The problems with public hospitals in Brazil also stand in sharp contrast with the state-of-the-art medicine practiced in specialized public hospitals, such as the Heart Institute in São Paulo. These facilities provide services of such high quality that patients who have private insurance seek treatment at these hospitals when they need specialized care.

What explains these discrepancies within the public system? Why has Brazil made such significant achievements in primary care but not in other areas? First, Brazil promoted an informal but significant decentralization process of primary health care in the early and mid-1980s, focused on prevention. The decentralization process was spearheaded by a strong social movement called the Sanitarist Movement (*Movimento Sanitarista*),[47] which advocated for comprehensive and redistributive health care. At least partially, the Sanitarist Movement succeeded: by the end of the 1980s, 98 percent of all primary health care establishments were public, and states or local governments managed 93 percent of them.[48] These changes had a positive impact on health indicators.[49] This was consolidated by the formal decentralization promoted by SUS. Between the implementation of SUS in 1988 and the mid-1990s, however, Brazil did not made significant progress in the provision of primary and preventive care because of macroeconomic instability, lack of clear planning, and a series of institutional uncertainties and political battles that have frozen any attempt to reform the system.[50]

In 1996, the government implemented two important programs: the Health Community Agents Program (*Programa de Agentes Comunitários da Saúde*) and the Family Health Program (*Programa Saúde da Família*).[51] Both established strong financial incentives for municipalities to provide preventive and home care, by directly linking financing with performance.[52] In the Family Health Program, financing is also partially contingent on population coverage.[53] In addition, in the same year, the

---

[45] Umberto Catarino Pessoto et al., *Desigualdades no Acesso e Utilização dos Serviços de Saúde na Região Metropolitana de São Paulo* [*Inequalities in Access and Use of Health Care Services in the Metropolitan Region of São Paulo*], 12 Ciência Saúde Coletiva 351 (2007).

[46] Id.

[47] Arretche, *supra* note 1, at 160. *See* Tulia G. Falleti, *Infiltrating the State: The Evolution of Health Care Reforms in Brazil, 1964–1988*, in Explaining Institutional Change: Ambiguity, Agency, and Power 38 (James Mahoney & Kathleen Thelen eds., 2010) for a detailed analysis of the movement's success despite the autocratic regime.

[48] Id. at 166–167.

[49] Id. at 180 & n. 19.

[50] Medici, *supra* note 30, at 28, 30. *See infra* Section 12.2 for a detailed description of the political dispute over NOBs.

[51] These were not the only programs, but they are two of the most important ones.

[52] Arretche, *supra* note 1, at 177. *But see* Judith Tendler, Good Government in the Tropics (1997) (offering an alternative account of the success of these programs).

[53] La Forgia & Couttolenc, *supra* note 7, at 48 n. 8.

federal government decided to create the Program for Primary Care (*Programa de Assistência Básica*), which guarantees per capita transfers to states and municipalities in order to secure the provision of primary care.

These reforms have increased the number of municipalities receiving direct federal transfers for provision of primary care from 144 in 1998 to 5,516 in 2002.[54] The programs – especially the Family Health Program – have also improved health indicators in families that have access to these services, in comparison with those that do not.[55] A great deal of this achievement is ascribed to the nonorthodox system of interdisciplinary care, where a team of health care professionals (general physicians, nurses, dentists, psychologists, and social workers) visit people in their homes, and focus their attention on the family, as opposed to the individual.

Coverage is limited, however, especially in urban areas. In 1998, less than 10 percent of citizens living in cities with more than 20,000 people had access to the program. This percentage increased to 60 percent in 2002 and 76 percent in 2006. In the same year, nonethless, larger cities still had a very low percentage of the population covered (34 percent).[56] Since 2006, the expansion of these programs and their impact have stagnated.[57] Currently, the Family Health Program is consistent, covering 60 percent of the population, and the Health Community Agents Program is covering roughly 50 percent.[58] This stagnation is connected with the inherent difficulties of reaching isolated rural populations.[59] Also, it is important to note that the program only provides services in rural areas and in slums. Most of the residents of urban areas do not have access to the program.

These achievements in primary care services stand in sharp contrast against secondary and tertiary care. This is owing largely to a combination of lack of funding and poor management. Nearly all public hospitals are directly managed by the government,[60] and this is perceived to be one of the reasons for inefficient use of resources. Indeed, the few autonomous units have better performance outcomes

---

[54] Medici, *supra* note 30, at 33.
[55] Mauricio Reis, Public Primary Health Care and Child Health in Brazil: Evidence from Siblings, IPEA (2009), *available at* http://mitsloan.mit.edu/neudc/papers/paper_314.pdf; Medici, *supra* note 30, at 41.
[56] Ricardo Bandeira, Programa Saúde da Família: Ele cresceu. Falta aparecer [Family Health Program: It grew. Now it Needs to Be Visible], 7(16) Diversa – revista da Universidade Federal de Minas Gerais (Nov. 2008), *available at* http://www.ufmg.br/diversa/16/index.php/universalizacao.
[57] Medici, *supra* note 30, at 41.
[58] *Id.* at 42.
[59] Id.
[60] "Known as direct administration (administração direita), this traditional public governance form follows rules specified in legislation, stipulating labor, procurement, financial, and budgetary processes for all public agencies – with decision making highly centralized and almost always happening "above the hospital" in government health bureaucracies. ... Typical of the Brazilian public sector, directly managed hospitals suffer from overstaffing, a distorted skill-mix of personnel, and little accountability for results. Not surprisingly, these hospitals perform poorly on most available measures, particularly related to efficiency." Gerard M. La Forgia & April Harding, *Public-Private Partnerships and Public Hospital Performance in São Paulo, Brazil*, 28 Health Aff. 1114, 1115 (2009).

than their nonautonomous counterparts.[61] Acknowledging this, in early 2007, the Ministry of Health proposed a bill to convert public hospitals directly managed by the government into independent foundations, incorporated under private law.[62] This bill was still pending review by the legislature at the time of this writing (January 2013).

Public hospitals are, however, only a partial concern, as privately run hospitals are the main providers of hospital services in the Brazilian public health care system. These hospitals account for 69 percent of the hospital beds in Brazil, 70 percent of hospital admissions, 59 percent of emergency procedures, and 54 percent of outpatient consultations.[63] This comes as no surprise, as privately run hospitals represent 65 percent of all hospitals in the country, while 35 percent of them are public hospitals (most of them municipal hospitals).[64] Of all private hospitals in Brazil, 70 percent deliver services to the public and the private sector.[65]

Despite the key role they play in the public system, private hospitals have received less public funding in recent years, and have consequently faced severe financial constraints. Recent reductions in the proportion of federal transfers going to private hospitals forced a number of private hospitals to drop out of the SUS system. Hospitals that are heavily dependent on public funding (such those run by philanthropic and religious organizations) have established their own private prepayment plans to capture private patients.[66] Public hospitals are also trying to capture private financing by selling services to private patients;[67] however, such arrangements are still very limited and highly controversial in Brazil.

Despite the differences, there is one problem in the provision of hospital services extremely relevant to both public and privately run hospitals in the public system: the excessive reliance on emergency rooms.[68] This seems to impose high costs on the public system. Patients use emergency rooms as a gateway to the public system, creating an incentive for local politicians to invest in emergency facilities instead of exploring more cost-effective ways of allocating resources. The result is that Brazilian hospitals spend more on emergency care (16 percent of their budget) than other countries. Canadian hospitals, for instance, spend 5 percent on emergency care.[69]

In sum, Brazil has made great achievements in increasing access to hospitals in the

---

[61] La Forgia & Couttolenc, *supra* note 7, at 7. *See also* La Forgia & Harding, *supra* note 60.

[62] Poder Executivo, Projeto de Lei Complementar P.L.P. 92/2007 [Congressional Bill P.L.P. 92/2007], Camara do Deputados, (July 13, 2007), *available at* http://www.camara.gov.br/proposicoesWeb/fichadetramitacao?idProposicao=360082; La Forgia & Couttolenc, *supra* note 7, at 8.

[63] *Id.* at 30.

[64] *Id.*

[65] *Id.* at 29.

[66] *Id.* at 33.

[67] *Id.* at 37 & chap. 5.

[68] I would like to thank Marcelo Monteiro, Doctor of the SUS, for calling my attention to this problem.

[69] La Forgia & Couttolenc, *supra* note 7, at 39.

past two decades, but significant reforms are necessary to promote more efficient use of resources within this system.

The exception is a handful of public hospitals in Brazil that are internationally renowned as centers of excellence in specialized areas such as spinal cord injuries, coronary surgery, and transplants. In contrast to other public hospitals, these islands of excellence have a relatively autonomous governance structure, and some of them are private nonprofit organizations operating under a management contract with the government. Often these hospitals are affiliated with universities and have an additional source of funds, the Ministry of Education, owing to their research activities.

These centers of excellence are one of the few resources of the public system used by those who have access to private health care. This raises a serious equity issue. Normally, these specialized hospitals are only available to a privileged minority who qualify for treatment according to their screening procedures.[70] Indeed, many middle- and high-income Brazilians covered by private insurance use specialized and high-complexity services, such as the ones offered in these institutions, imposing significant costs on the public system.[71] Legally, they (or their insurance plans) should pay for such procedures, but there have been numerous problems with enforcing this.[72] This creates a very regressive allocation of resources within the SUS system, with a privileged minority that can afford private health care consuming more resources per capita in the public system than the deprived majority who have SUS as their only health care provider.

12.1.2 *The Private Health Care System*

In contrast to its ailing public counterpart, the privately financed health sector in Brazil has been expanding since the 1990s.[73] The first elected government (President Collor, inaugurated in 1990 and impeached in 1992) reduced the budget allocated to the public health sector in an attempt to reduce governmental expenses. This was in pursuit of a neoliberal agenda of reducing the size of the state. Consequently, many private providers terminated their SUS contracts and started offering services to the private sector. The reduced budget, combined with the exit of the best private providers in the system, had a significant negative impact on the quality of services in the public sector.[74] This created a self-reinforcing cycle, where visible decline in

---

[70] *Id.*

[71] *Id.* at 18.

[72] *Id.* at 48 n. 4.

[73] *See* ANS, Regulação & Saúde: Estrutura, Evolução e Perspectivas da Assistência Médica Suplementar [Regulation & Health: Structure, Evolution and Perspectives of Medical Assistance in the Supplementary System] (2002), *available at* http://bvsms.saude.gov.br/bvs/publicacoes/regulacao_saude.pdf for a detailed overview.

[74] Lenaura Lobato & Luciene Burlandy, *The Context and Process of Health Care Reform In Brazil, in* RESHAPING HEALTH CARE IN LATIN AMERICA: A COMPARATIVE ANALYSIS OF HEALTH CARE REFORM IN ARGENTINA, BRAZIL AND MEXICO 79 (Sonia Fleury, Susana Belmartino & Enis Baris eds., 2000).

the quality of public provision of health care services created an increasing demand for private health care services, which was accompanied by increasing supply. This upward spiral for private health care was aided by a series of governmental incentives benefiting both consumers and suppliers of such services, such as tax deductions for those paying for private health care.

Approximately 25 percent of the population (around 40 million people) are now served by the private sector, yet it receives approximately 50 percent of the total resources invested in health care in the country.[75] In absolute terms, the per capita expenditure on private health care grew from US$36.30 to US$100.50 per month between 1980–1981 and 1990–1995, or about 177 percent. In contrast, public health expenditure grew only 6.6 percent.[76] From 1997 to 2009, per capita expenditure on private health care continued to grow.[77] In other words, a well-funded and high-quality private health care sector is available to those who can afford a private health care plan, who work for an employer who provides such a plan, or those who can pay directly for the services. As a consequence, the Brazilian health care system is very much divided along economic lines: low-income people have access to a health care system of significantly lower quality than that available to middle and upper classes.

As a result of increasing investment in private health care, a market for private health insurance plans has flourished, subsidized by income tax deductions to companies and individuals who decided to buy these plans. One estimate indicates that the number of beneficiaries between 1989 and 1996 increased from 30 million to 42 million people (roughly 30 percent of the population at the time), and the annual revenues of the sector increased from US$2.3 million to US$15 million.[78] As a result of this growth, insurance companies have now become the primary mechanism through which middle and upper classes have access to private health care. Indeed, the private health care system is financed equally by private insurers and household out-of-pocket spending, but the latter is mainly for drugs, medical supplies, and dental and eye care.[79]

Despite increasing demand for their products, insurance companies (which are often medical cooperatives) operated for many years in a relatively unregulated fashion, creating many abusive practices. For instance, they refused to insure people with preexisting conditions, increased the prices of the insurance plans according to age (which has made even the most basic plans very costly to elderly people), and denied reimbursement claims arbitrarily (resulting in the highest volume of consumer complaints of any sector in the Brazilian economy).[80] This situation was

---

[75] Ferraz & Vieira, *supra* note 11, at 7–8.
[76] *Id.*
[77] *Id.*; *See also* ANS, *supra* note 73.
[78] *Id.*
[79] La Forgia & Couttolenc, *supra* note 7, at 26.
[80] Costa, *supra* note 24, at 50–51.

partially remediated in 1998 via regulation and the creation of a regulatory agency for the sector; however, the latter has not been particularly effective in combating the powerful lobby of large insurance companies.[81] This has led many consumers to bring their claims to courts.[82]

12.2 LEGISLATING HEALTH CARE RIGHTS IN BRAZIL

12.2.1 *Constitutional Provisions*

The 1988 Brazilian Constitution establishes a right to health in two provisions. The first provision, Article 6, provides a relatively long list of social rights, which includes not only the right to health but also the right to education, food, employment, and shelter, among others. The second provision, Article 196, offers the two components of the right to health, namely:

(1) an array of factors that are likely to affect a person's health, such as access to clean water, sanitation, and nutrition; and
(2) medical care or health services.[83]

Indeed, article 196 establishes that the right to health "shall be guaranteed by means of social and economic policies aimed at reducing the risk of illness and other hazards and by the universal and equal access to actions and services for its promotion, protection, and recovery."[84]

The Brazilian Constitution has no progressive realization provisions and no limitations on the basis of available resources, unlike the Constitution of South Africa, for

---

[81] Louise Pietrobon, Martha Lenise do Prado & João Carlos Caetano, *Saúde Suplementar no Brasil: O Papel da Agência Nacional de Saúde Suplementar na Regulação do Setor* [*Private Health Care in Brazil: The Role of the National Agency of Health Care in Regulating the Sector*], 18 PHYSIS 767 (2008). See also Deborah Carvalho Malta et al., *Perspectivas da Regulação na Saúde Suplementar diante dos Modelos Assistenciais* [*Perspectives of Regulation of Private Health Care in light of Public Provision*], 9 CIÊNCIA SAÚDE COLETIVA 433 (2004).

[82] Daniela Batalha Trettel, PLANOS DE SAÚDE NA VISÃO DO STJ E DO STF [PRIVATE HEALTH CARE PLANS ACCORDING TO THE SUPERIOR COURT OF JUSTICE AND THE SUPREME COURT OF JUSTICE] (2010).

[83] Committee on Economic, Social, and Cultural Rights, *General Comment No. 14, The right to the highest attainable standard of health*, ¶12, 34, 36, 43, U.N. Doc. E/C.12/2000/4 (Aug. 11, 2000), reprinted in Compilation of General Comments and General Recommendations Adopted by Human Rights Treaty Bodies, U.N. Doc. HRI/GEN/1/Rev.6 at 85 (2003), *available at* http://documents-ddsny.un.org/doc/UNDOC/GEN/G00/439/34/pdf/G0043934.pdf?OpenElement (on Substantive Issues Arising in the Implementation of the International Covenant on Economic, Social and Cultural Rights [ICE-SCR]). *See also* Aeyal M. Gross, *The Right to Health in a Era of Privatization and Globalization: National and International Perspectives*, in EXPLORING SOCIAL RIGHTS: BETWEEN THEORY AND PRACTICE 289, 295 (Daphne Barak-Erez & Aeyal Gross eds, 2007).

[84] Constituição Federal [C.F.] [Constitution] art. 196 (Braz.): "A saúde é direito de todos e dever do Estado, garantido mediante políticas sociais e econômicas que visem à redução do risco de doença e de outros agravos e ao acesso universal e igualitário às ações e serviços para sua promoção, proteção e recuperação."

example.[85] On the other hand, there is much debate about the justiciability of these open-ended rights in the constitution. Indeed, a group of influential constitutional law scholars and judges believe that these provisions are simply "programmatic", that is, they only set up principles and goals for the Brazilian state, as discussed in Section 12.3.

In addition to recognizing the two components of the right to health, the Brazilian Constitution also establishes the provision of these rights as an obligation of the government (Article 196). The word "government" refers to all three levels – local, state, and federal governments – which have a joint responsibility in guaranteeing the right to health (Article 23, II).[86] This obligation extends to the provision of what the Constitution calls "full assistance" (*atendimento integral*) (Article 198, II), which means that the state obligations extend to *any* type of medical need; it is not restricted to a package of essential services.

The Brazilian Constitution also sets up the SUS structure and provides that it is funded by federal, state, and local governments (Article 198, para. 1). Despite this unified structure, the Constitution establishes a decentralized system (Article 198, I), suggesting that municipalities are responsible for delivering services (Article 30, VII). The specific responsibilities of each level of government were specified in a statute enacted in 1990, and modified numerous times by regulations enacted by the Ministry of Health, as discussed in greater detail later.

The private health care system is also present in the Constitution. Article 199 establishes a free market for private provision of health care services and authorizes the state to contract out health care services by hiring private providers to complement the services offered in the public health care system. In addition, the Constitution obliges the state to regulate, oversee, and control health care services provision by public and private entities (Article 197).

12.2.2 *Statutory Provisions*

While the constitutional provisions establish principles and the financing structure of SUS, the system is regulated by two federal statutes, known as the Health National Statutes (Laws n. 8080/90 and n. 8142/90), which aim at establishing a complex system of cooperation between federal, state, and local governments. These statutes explicitly define the responsibility of each level of government. The first statute, Law n. 8080/90, reinforces the constitutional provision indicating that the

---

[85] *See* Lisa Froman and Jerome Amir Singh in Chapter 11 of this volume.

[86] The joint responsibility has been affirmed by Brazilian courts, including the Brazilian Supreme Court. *See* STF. Acórdão. RE 271286-RS. Relator: Min. Celso de Mello, 11.09.2000, 2013–07, Diário da Justiça [D.J.], 24.11.2000, 101 (Braz.). ("O Poder Público, qualquer que seja a esfera institucional de sua atuação no plano da organização federativa brasileira, não pode mostrar-se indiferente ao problema da saúde da população, sob pena de incidir, ainda que por censurável omissão, em grave comportamento inconstitucional").

municipalities will be in charge of the provision of these services (article 7, XI and
article 18, I), and provides that the federal government will define and implement
health policies through the Ministry of Health (article 9, I). The Ministry of Health
is also responsible for coordinating the entire system, while promoting and supporting the decentralization of the services (Law n. 8080/90, article 16). The state
governments, in turn, must create the necessary conditions for municipalities to be
able to deliver health care services, and are the main health care provider where the
municipalities are not capable of delivering the services themselves (Law n. 8080/90,
art. 17).

Despite the constitutional provision obliging the state to regulate, oversee, and
control private health care services, such regulations were only recently enacted. A
bill to regulate private health care insurance plans was first approved in 1998 (Law n.
9656/98), and in 2000 another statute (Law n. 9.961/00) created a regulatory agency
(ANS – *Agência Nacional de Saúde Suplementar*, or National Supplementary Health
Agency) to oversee the sector and ensure that there is compliance with statutory
provisions.

12.2.3 *Ministerial Regulation*

The implementation of both National Health Statutes happened through ministerial
regulation, in the form of executive decrees named *Normas Operacionais Básicas*
(NOBs). NOBs regulate important aspects of the system, including decentralization
of health care services. The National Health Laws mandated automatic transfers from
the federal government to municipalities. However, the 1990s were characterized by
a fierce political battle between the federal government and municipalities about
how resources should be transferred (automatically or through negotiation), to whom
they should be transferred (directly to providers or to local authorities), and how their
use should be evaluated.[87] None of these details were specified in the statute. This
dispute led to a series of NOBs that tried to articulate the rules for transfers.[88] By
1993, 22 percent of the Brazilian municipalities, which were then 4,974 in total, had
accepted the decentralization norms.

Regulation has also governed pharmaceutical assistance programs for three
types of drugs: essential, high-cost, and strategic. For the first type of drug, the
Ministry of Health regularly publishes the National List of Essential Medicines
(Relação Nacional de Medicamentos Essenciais, RENAME), which follows WHO
guidelines.[89] Municipal and state governments, in turn, have discretion to develop

---

[87] Arretche, *supra* note 1, at 169–170.

[88] *See id.* at 170 for an historical overview of the system and the implementation of these norms.

[89] Ana Luiza Chieffi & Rita Barradas Barata, *Judicialização da Política Pública de Assistência Farmacêutica e Equidade* [*Judicialization of Public Policy for Pharmaceutical Assistance and Equity*],
25 Cadernos de Saúde Pública, 1839 (2009) (indicating that RENAME was expanded in 2002,
2006, and 2008).

their own lists, based on the RENAME and the specific needs of their populations. Municipal governments are responsible for distributing these essential drugs. The high-cost drugs, which are part of the exceptional medicine program, cover diseases such as Parkinson's, Alzheimer's, Hepatitis B and C, and chronic renal transplanted patients, among others. The list of high-cost drugs to be provided free of charge by SUS is defined by the Ministry of Health, and the states are responsible for distributing these drugs. Finally, the strategic drugs include diseases such as AIDS, leprosy, malaria, leishmaniasis, Chagas disease, and tuberculosis. The Ministry of Health not only establishes the list of diseases included in the "strategic" disease programs; it is also responsible for purchasing and distributing these drugs. These programs have been the focus of most of the litigation nowadays, as we discuss in Section 12.3.

12.2.4 *Constitutional Amendment*

In 2000, in an attempt to deal with the problem of lack of resources in the public health care system and the lack of certainty regarding the amount of resources available each year, a constitutional amendment (EC 29/2000) added further details to the constitutional provisions regarding SUS. The amendment included an obligation for federal, state, and municipal governments to allocate a minimum amount of fiscal resources to the public health care system.

A comparison of the investments in the sector in 2000 and 2004 reveals that after the amendment, the total amount of investment increased by 3 percent,[90] despite the fact that many states and municipalities have not complied with it.[91] One of the problems with this scheme, however, is that the already fiscally stretched municipalities contributed a significant portion of this increase (a 37 percent increase in municipal investments between 2000 and 2004).[92] The increased levels of municipal (and state) investment may help foster the necessary political autonomy that has been lacking in the system since its creation, but there are questions as to whether this scheme is sustainable without an increase of the tax base of the municipalities.[93]

While the amendment defines the "constitutional minimum" for states and municipalities (article 198, par.2 (II)), it also establishes that statutory provisions

---

[90] World Bank, *supra* note 33, at 4, table 1.1.

[91] *Id.* at 26. Folha de São Paulo, Estados Deixaram de Aplicar R$ 2 Bi na Saúde, Diz Governo [States Have Failed to Invest R$2 billion in Health, According to the Federal Government], CADERNO PODER (September 19, 2011), *available at* http://www1.folha.uol.com.br/poder/977272-estados-deixaram-de-aplicar-r-2-bi-na-saude-diz-governo.shtml.

[92] Ana Cecília Faveret, *A Vinculação Constitucional de Recursos para a Saúde: Avanços, Entraves e Perspectivas* [Constitutional Allocation of Resources to Health: Progresses, Obstacles and Future Perspectives], 8 CIÊNCIA E SAÚDE COLETIVA 371, 376 (2003).

[93] Maria Alicia D. Uga & Isabela Soares Santos, *Uma análise da progressividade do financiamento do Sistema único de Saúde (SUS)* [An Analysis of the Progressiveness of the Public Health Care System Financing], 22 CADERNOS DE SAÚDE PÚBLICA 1597, 1600 (2006).

will define the amount for the federal government (article 198, par. 2 (I)). In January 2012, the statute regulating federal contributions was enacted (Special Law n. 141/12).[94] The general expectation is that this will increase the total investment in the system, reduce the burden on municipalities, and reduce uncertainty vis-à-vis the level of resources available, increasing the reliability and predictability of the system. At the time of this writing (January 2013), it remained unclear whether these goals would be achieved.

12.3 RIGHT TO HEALTH LITIGATION IN BRAZIL

The Brazilian Constitution secures the right to health as one of its social rights (article 6), and establishes that every citizen has the right to universal medical care and the state has an obligation to provide it (article 196), as described earlier. These provisions have been litigated in Brazilian courts, but there is much uncertainty as to whether the right-to-health litigation in Brazil is addressing existing inequalities in access to health care or, in fact, deepening and reinforcing them. One factor that contributes to such uncertainty comes from the fact that individual litigation prevails (i.e., collective litigation is rare), and an individual action benefits only the claimants, instead of benefiting a class of patients with the same condition. This reduces the potential positive universal impact that litigation could have in the system. The other factor comes from the lack of comprehensive and conclusive data on who is using this individual litigation and who is benefiting from it. Some argue that middle and upper classes are using the right to health to obtain privileges from the state – such as provision of expensive medication – reducing even further the scarce resources available in the underfunded public health system. However, this finding is highly disputed, as I discuss in detail in the following subsections.

12.3.1 *Overview*

Most of the litigation around the right to health in Brazil is centered on the provision of medical care, despite the fact that the Constitution conceives of the right to health in much broader terms, including the right to clean water, sanitation, and nutrition. In recent years, there has been a significant increase in this type of litigation. For instance, the state of Rio de Janeiro went from practically no cases in 1991 to 1,144 lawsuits in 2002,[95] and this number increased to 2,245 cases in

---

94 Lei Complementar No. 141/12, de 13 de janeiro de 2012, Diário Oficial da União [D.O.U.] de 16.1.2012 (Braz.).

95 Ana Messeder, Claudia Osorio-de-Castro & Vera Luiza, *Mandados Judiciais Como Ferramenta Para Garantia do Acesso a Medicamentos no Setor Público: A Experiência do Estado do Rio de Janeiro, Brasil* [*Injunctions as Tools to Guarantee Access to Drugs in the Public Health Care System: The Experience of the State of Rio de Janeiro, Brazil*] 21 CADERNOS DE SAÚDE PÚBLICA 525, 527 (2005).

2005.[96] There has also been an increase in the total number of cases, up to 7,400, in the states of Rio Grande do Sul, Bahia, Pernambuco, Rio de Janeiro, and Goiás from 1995 to 2004.[97] Similar increases have been observed in the states of São Paulo and Santa Catarina.[98]

Octávio Luiz Motta Ferraz, an expert on the right to health in Brazil, ascribes this recent increase in the number of cases to the high success rates in this kind of litigation.[99] According to him, there is a high success rate for the litigant because Brazilian judges interpret articles 6 and 196 "as an entitlement of individuals to the satisfaction of all their health needs with the most advanced treatment available, irrespective of its cost."[100] Ferraz argues that this expansive interpretation of the right to health is now firmly established in the Brazilian judiciary: generally, an individual litigant must simply prove their health needs, as described in a doctor's prescription, were not met.[101] Other researchers, in contrast, argue that the increase in litigation in Brazil stems from the institutional problems in Brazil's pharmaceutical programs. For instance, a series of studies of the judicialization in the Rio de Janeiro state have shown that a faulty and unreliable supply of medication and treatment, combined with a confusing decentralized system, may be driving patients to courts. The lack of clarity about which level of government (federal, state, or municipal) is responsible for funding and procurement of medication makes it time consuming and costly to figure out the appropriate administrative venue to request access to medication/treatment. As a result, patients resort to courts.[102]

---

[96] Daniela Borges, Uma Análise das Ações Judiciais para o Fornecimento de Medicamentos no Âmbito do Sus: O Caso do Estado do Rio De Janeiro no Ano de 2005 [An Analysis of Judicial Claims for the Provision of Medication against SUS: The Case of the State of Rio de Janeiro in 2005] (2007) (master thesis, Escola Nacional de Saúde Pública Sérgio Arouca), *available at* http://bvssp.icict.fiocruz.br/lildbi/docsonline/get.php?id=1233.

[97] Florian Hoffman & Fernando Bentes, *Accountability and Social and Economic Rights in Brazil*, in COURTING SOCIAL JUSTICE: JUDICIAL ENFORCEMENT OF SOCIAL AND ECONOMIC RIGHTS IN THE DEVELOPING WORLD 100, 100–145 (Varun Gauri & Daniel Brinks eds., 2010).

[98] Octávio Luiz Motta Ferraz, Right-to-Health Litigation in Brazil: An Overview of the Research, presentation addressed at Universidad Torcuato Di Tella, Buenos Aires workshop: The Right to Health through Litigation? Can Court Enforced Health Rights Improve Health Policy? (April 15–17, 2009), *available at* http://papers.ssrn.com/sol3/papers.cfm?abstract_id=1426011.

[99] Octávio Luiz Motta Ferraz, *The Right to health in the Courts of Brazil: Worsening Health Inequities?*, 11(2) HEALTH & HUM. RTS. J. 33, 40 (2009).

[100] *Id.* at 33.

[101] *Id.* at 35.

[102] Vera Lúcia Edais Pepe et. al., *Caracterização de demandas judiciais de fornecimento de medicamentos "essenciais" no Estado do Rio de Janeiro, Brasil* [Characteristics of the Judicial Demands for 'Essential' Drugs in the State of Rio de Janeiro, Brazil] 26 CADERNOS DE SAÚDE PÚBLICA, 461 (2010); Borges, Danielle da Costa Leite & Maria Alicia Dominguez Ugá, CONFLITOS E IMPASSES DA JUDICIALIZAÇÃO NA OBTENÇÃO DE MEDICAMENTOS: AS DECISÕES DE 1A INSTÂNCIA NAS AÇÕES INDIVIDUAIS CONTRA O ESTADO DO RIO DE JANEIRO, BRASIL, EM 2005 [Conflicts and Deadlocks in the Judicialization of Demands for Medication : First Instance Opinions in Individual Claims Against the State of Rio de Janeiro, Brazil, in 2005], 26 CADERNOS DE SAÚDE PÚBLICA, 59 (2010). Messeder et. al., *supra* note 95.

Florian Hoffman and Fernando Bentes dispute Ferraz's claim regarding the basis for such decisions. In one of the most detailed surveys of the right-to-health litigation in Brazil,[103] based on data from five Brazilian states[104] and the superior tribunals, the authors question whether the right to health is so firmly established in Brazil. The cases in their survey indicate that courts tend to decide provision of medical care cases based on the right to life (article 5 of the 1988 Constitution) and not the right to health. Moreover, the understanding that the right to health will entitle an individual to judicial remedies is popular among young judges and at the trial level only. A traditional strand of jurisprudence, hegemonic in the older judiciary, sees the right to health as a programmatic right, too vague to be directly justiciable. The authors also indicate that higher courts adopt the view that social rights fall under the "progressive realization precept: the courts apply a viability reservation (*reserva de possibilidade*) in the context of existing economic and political realities."[105]

While there is disagreement regarding the constitutional basis for judicial decisions on litigation involving the provision of medical care, there is consensus around the fact that courts have been much more favorable to individual rather than collective claims. Most demands in health litigation in Brazil are individual claims to a specific drug or medical procedure.[106] This seems to be driven by the fact that courts are more open to these individual claims than to collective ones.[107] Brazilian courts have generally discarded arguments related to the negative impact of ad hoc judicial concessions on administrative due process and public policies as being of lesser importance than fundamental civil rights.[108]

It is not clear, however, for how long this will remain the prevailing attitude in the judiciary. Indeed, in April and May 2009, the Brazilian Supreme Court (STF) held a series of public audiences in connection with cases of access to medicines, inviting a number of academics, governmental officials, and civil society representatives to discuss right-to-health litigation and its impact on the health care system.[109]

---

[103] Hoffman & Bentes, *supra* note 96.

[104] The states analyzed were Bahia, Goiás, Pernambuco, Rio de Janeiro, and Rio Grande do Sul. The sample attempts to be representative of the Brazilian diverse regions, but one may question whether excluding the State of São Paulo skews the data because it is the wealthiest and most populated state in the country, and probably the place where most litigation takes place. Hoffman & Bentes, *supra* note 96.

[105] *Id.* at 126.

[106] *Id.* at 104, 122.

[107] *Id.* at 106.

[108] *Id.* at 114.

[109] Advocacia Geral da União, Audiência Pública no STF sobre o SUS [Public Audience at the Supreme Court on the Public Health Care System], Avdocacia General da União, *available at* http://www.agu. gov.br/sistemas/site/TemplateTexto.aspx?idConteudo=94850&id_site=722&aberto=&fechado (with oral presentations at the public audience); Audiência Publica: Principal [Public Audience: Main], Supremo Tribunal Federal (May 12, 2009), *available at* http://www.stf.jus.br/portal/cms/verTexto.asp? servico=processoAudienciaPublicaSaude (with expert witnesses and the documents submitted to the court by civil society organizations).

The audiences were followed by a decision in September 2009, where the Brazilian Supreme Court (STF) introduced public policy considerations in a judicial decision related to the right to health.[110] Given that the decision is not binding on lower courts, the *Conselho Nacional de Justiça* (CNJ), the oversight body for the judiciary, has issued guidelines along the lines of the decision, that is, advising courts to seek information with experts and consult with public administrators before issuing injuntions related to access to medicines. It has also asked them to grant only requests for medication that has been approved by the Brazilian authorities (ANVISA).[111] At the time of this writing, there did not seem to be studies assessing whether the Supreme Court Decision or the CNJ guidelines have changed the pattern of litigation or the behavior of courts.

12.3.2 *The Right-to-Health Litigation: How Regressive Is It?*

The great majority of individual health rights actions in Brazil are successful,[112] and the vast majority of those actions involve individual actions related to access to medicine.[113] For some, this could potentially be worrying: if access to justice is restricted to those who can afford litigation and are generally educated enough to be aware of their rights, than those who already have access to health care – the wealthy people who have exited the public system – may be the ones who are bringing claims to courts. Considering that only the individual claimants are benefiting from litigation, these suits do not bring any benefit to those who cannot bring their claims to court. If this is true, litigation favors and protects those that need the least protection (the wealthy ones) at the expense of an underfunded health care system.

Ferraz argues that this regressive system does exist in Brazil. He presents data showing that in the states of São Paulo and Santa Catarina, for instance, privately funded lawyers bring the majority of claims, which suggests that wealthy people are the ones using litigation.[114] In addition, studies of the judiciary and litigation practices

---

[110] Brazilian Supreme Court (S.T.F.), STA 175 AgR/CE-CEARÁ, Relator: Min. Gilmar Mendes, 17.3.2010, 076 Diário da Justiça eletrônico [D.J.-e], 30.4.2010, 70 (Braz.).

[111] Conselho Nacional de Justiça, *Recomendação n. 31, de 31 de Marco de 2010*, 61 Diário da Justiça eletrônico [DJ-e], 4 (April 7, 2010) (Braz.), *available at* http://www.cnj.jus.br/images/stories/docs_cnj/recomendacoes/reccnj_31.pdf.

[112] Hoffman & Bentes, *supra* note 96, at 107.

[113] Miriam Ventura et al., Judicialização da Saúde, Acesso à Justiça e a Efetividade do Direito à Saúde [Judicial Claims for Health Care Services, Access to Justice, and Effective Protection of the Right to Health], 20 Physis 77 (2010), *available at* http://www.scielo.br/pdf/physis/v20n1/a06v20n1.pdf; Eli Iola Gurge Andrade et al., *A Judicialização da Saúde e a Política Nacional de Assistência Farmacêutica no Brasil: Gestão da Clínica e Medicalização da Justiça* [Judicial Claims for Health Care Services and the National Policy for Pharmaceutical Assistance in Brazil: Management of Health Clinics and Medicalization of the Judiciary], 18(4-S4) REVISTA MÉDICA DE MINAS GERAIS 46 (2008).

[114] Ferraz, *supra* note 98, at 40 (showing that in the state of São Paulo, 74% of health services litigations were conducted by private lawyers; in the state of Santa Catarina, this number was 59%).

often indicate that Brazil has significant access-to-justice problems, and lower classes are often excluded from the judicial system.[115] Thus, it is not unreasonable to assume that at least a very substantial part of those who are bringing claims to the courts are those who can already afford private health care.

Hoffman and Bentes are more cautious than Ferraz is in rushing to the conclusion that litigation skews the distribution of public health care resources in favor of wealthier classes. Focusing on a different set of Brazilian states, the authors point out that a significant number of health cases are litigated by the public defense's office (*defensoria publica* – DP), which offers services to people who cannot afford lawyers. This calls attention to the fact that Ferraz's claim that most actions are brought by paid lawyers is based on the analysis of only two of the twenty-six Brazilian states. Thus, they resist the idea that lower classes are not benefiting at all from this type of litigation, although they acknowledge that there is no general and uniform policy on means testing to determine who should be able to have access to the public pro bono litigation systems (DP and *Procuradorias de Assistência Jurídica* – PAJ). As a result, there is no uniform response from the courts as to class differentiation.[116] Hoffman and Bentes also acknowledge that although publicly funded legal services represent a significant number of people (even though the number is still disproportionate to the size of the population), those who have access to it still do not stand on a comparable footing with wealthier litigants. Even if the results are the same, courts take much longer to issue opinions in state-funded litigation (such as DP or PAJ), compared to privately litigated cases.[117] Considering this delay, there is an access-to-justice problem here.

Finally, the authors are careful to indicate that not all litigation is against the public health care system: exceptions to coverage by private health insurance companies are the second most important subject of litigation based on the right to health care.[118] Of the cases in the authors' database, 85 percent are direct provision claims by individuals to the state. Another 13 percent are claims by individuals against private health insurance companies.[119] This means a significant number of the cases litigated did not divert public resources to those without need. In sum, we need further research to settle the contrasting claims presented earlier in this section. Currently, there is not a clear picture of who is in fact benefiting from this litigation in Brazil.

---

[115] Hoffman & Bentes, *supra* note 96 at 111.

[116] *Id.* at 142. *See also* João Biehl et al., *Between the Court and the Clinic: Lawsuits for Medicines and the Right to Health in Brazil*, 14 HEALTH & HUM. RTS. INT'L J. (June 12, 2012), *available at* http://www.hhrjournal.org/index.php/hhr/article/view/484 (providing further evidence that litigation in the state of Rio Grande do Sul between 2002 and 2009 have largely favored low-income people, and the majority of plaintiffs were represented by the public defense's office).

[117] *Id.* at 114.

[118] *Id.* at 117.

[119] *Id.* at 111.

It is also not clear whether this litigation is adding more money to the system, or simply depriving the system of the already scarce resources. Some claim that litigation is diverting funds from low-cost collective preventive care, such as vaccines, in favor of high-cost individualized treatment.[120] If this is true, the amounts are not insignificant.[121] Federal spending on judicially granted medicines rose from R$188,000 (US$90,000) in 2003 to R$26 million (US$13 million) in the first half of 2007. In the state of São Paulo, litigated medication consumed R$48 million (US$24 million) in 2004, out of an R$480 million (US$240 million) budget for medication (10 percent).[122] If money is indeed being diverted, there is a serious redistributive issue. Ferraz notes that the amount that the state spent complying with judicial orders benefited 35,000 people, when it could have used the same amount of resources to vaccinate 2–3 million children.[123] However, there does not seem to be conclusive evidence on whether litigation is increasing the total amount of resources available in the system or not.

A potential regressive impact would still be present even if litigation was increasing the total amount of resources available in the system, as these new resources are not always being allocated to high-priority areas. Instead, they are being spent on medications, and especially new medications tend to be of relatively high cost and little net health benefit.[124] In an attempt to deal with this, the Brazilian Supreme Court has issued a decision in 2009 establishing that courts should not promptly grant claims for benefits not already offered by the Brazilian public health care system (i.e., those not on the "official list" of medication/treatment approved by the government). Instead, in these cases, courts need to analyze the reasons why the medication or treatment required is not being offered. In doing so, courts should distinguish cases where the medication/treatment was simply not considered by the legislative or the executive branch from cases in which the government has considered the possibility and decided not to offer the medication/treatment. To justify this decision, the Supreme Court considered the fact that the state has limited resources and cannot finance every single claim presented before the courts. According to the Brazilian Supreme Court, if courts continue to order the government to fund

---

[120] Fabíola Sulpino Vieira & Paola Zucchi, *Distorções Causadas pelas Ações Judiciais à Política de Medicamentos no Brasil* [Distortions to Pharmaceutical Policies in Brazil Caused by Judicial Claims], 41 REVISTA DE SAÚDE PÚBLICA 214 (2007); Hoffman & Bentes, *supra* note 96 at 116.

[121] *Id.* at 114.

[122] *Id.* at 115.

[123] Ferraz, *supra* note 98.

[124] Petryna, Adriana, WHEN EXPERIMENTS TRAVEL: CLINICAL TRIALS AND THE GLOBAL SEARCH FOR HUMAN SUBJECTS (2009) (showing how pharmaceutical companies have covered litigation costs for sick patients suffering from rare diseases to secure access to costly treatments through the courts. In some cases, courts grant access to drugs that were not approved by Brazilian regulatory agency for the health care sector (ANVISA). In other cases, courts have required the state to pay for expensive experimental drugs, using funds from the Brazilian public health care sector to buy medication that still lacks clinical trials to test the product's efficacy).

claimed treatments, they will impair the functioning of the public health care system and have a negative impact on groups that depend on this system.

The Supreme Court decision, however, is not binding, and lower courts may follow it or not. If followed by lower courts, this decision is likely to have a significant impact on how courts handle health care cases. In 2006, three years before the decision, the percentage of medication/treatment granted by courts of law that were not included in the list of medications/treatment approved by the government was 77 percent for the state of São Paulo and 80.6 percent for the state of Rio de Janeiro.[125] This impact, however, is still uncertain. Daniel Brinks, for one, is optimistic about the possibility of this Supreme Court decision changing the nature of litigation in Brazil.[126] However, no significant changes have been observed so far, and academic studies have yet to analyze potential changes in the pattern of litigation in lower courts.

12.3.3 *The HIV/AIDS Litigation*

The claim that litigation of the right to health in Brazil is regressive is in direct contrast with the accounts offered regarding the litigation of HIV/AIDS medicine in Brazil. This litigation was led by NGOs in the 1990s and led not only to successful cases in courts but also to very influential structural reforms in the HIV/AIDS policy in the country.[127] These structural reforms included the incorporation of these NGOs within the public health system, where they help implement policies, encourage litigation in partnership with the Public Prosecutor's Office, and represent indigent claimants before courts.[128] The reforms also included a statute (Law No. 9313/96) that sets out the free distribution of antiretroviral drugs for HIV/AIDS patients. This shows that "litigation can work as a signalling mechanism for demand in new medicines, and, hence, for the expansion of an existing public policy."[129]

While NGOs dealing with HIV/AIDS health rights have been successful and influential in terms of public policy participation and change,[130] this NGO activism has not spread to other health sectors. Private attorneys, *Defensoria Publica*, and the Public Prosecutor's Office (*Ministério Público*) deal with most of the cases involving the right to health. Thus, although NGOs were important in the first right-to-health

---

[125] Pepe et al., *supra* note 102 (for Rio de Janeiro); Chieffi & Barradas Barata, *supra* note 89 (for São Paulo).

[126] D. M. Brinks & W. Forbath, *Commentary: Social and Economic Rights in Latin America: Constitutional Courts and the Prospects for Pro-Poor Interventions*, 89 Texas Law Review, 1943 (2011).

[127] Richard Parker, *Construindo os Alicerces para a Resposta ao HIV/AIDS no Brasil: O Desenvolvimento de Políticas sobre o HIV/AIDS, 1982–1996* [*Building the Foundations for a Response to HIV/AIDS in Brasil: The Development of Policies for HIV/AIDS, 1982–1996*], 27 Divulgação em Saúde Para Debate 8 (2003).

[128] Hoffman & Bentes, *supra* note 96 at 114.

[129] *Id.* at 137.

[130] *Id.*

litigation cases, related to HIV/AIDS, today they play a minor role in other areas.[131] One possible explanation for this is the "crowding-out effect" in legal culture and the institutional arrangements that set incentives favoring the Public Prosecutor's Office.[132] Another potential explanation is that there was sufficient civil society organization around the HIV/AIDS cause as part of a larger public campaign to change the image of AIDS as the "gay cancer." The fact that there was an identified and well-defined minority group fighting for recognition may have helped mobilize these NGOs in a way that is hard to replicate.

12.4 CONCLUSION

In Brazil, health indicators (e.g., infant mortality[133] and maternal mortality[134]) are strongly correlated with income levels, which are in turn correlated with other determinants of health, such as sanitation, nutrition, and educational levels. Thus, the first obstacle to reduce health inequalities in Brazil is poverty.[135] Nevertheless, there are other policies that can also reduce health inequalities without requiring nationwide redistributive programs, or macroeconomic policies that will guarantee a significant increase in the per capita of the population over a short period of time. These are the policies related directly to the health care system. The problem is that such reforms are also not easy to implement. Dealing with the inequalities described in this chapter would require a major crackdown on corruption at all levels of government, a significant restructuring of Brazil's fiscal federalism and system of transfers, and perhaps it might even include the need for a serious judicial reform. These reforms, however, are likely to face significant obstacles to implementation and even if they surpass these challenges, they are unlikely to produce effects in the short term. Thus, I constrain myself here to a list of less daunting – and perhaps more feasible – options related to improvements in the quality of heath care services in the public system. Here are three of them.

---

[131] *Id.* at 115.

[132] *Id.*

[133] Anna Maria Chiesa, Marcia Westphal & Marco Ackerman, *Doenças Respiratórias Agudas: Um Estudo das Desigualdades em Saúde [Acute Respiratory Diseases: A Study of Inequalities in Health]* 24(1) CADERNOS DE SAÚDE PUBLICA 55 (2008); World Health Organization (WHO), World Health Statistics 2007, *available at* http://www.who.int/gho/publications/world_health_statistics/whostat2007.pdf.

[134] Lenice Harumi Ishitani et al., *Desigualdade Social e Mortalidade Precoce por Doenças Cardiovasculares no Brasil [Social Inequality and Early Death Due to Cardiovascular Diseases in Brazil]* 40 REVISTA DE SAÚDE PÚBLICA 684 (2006); *Alaerte Leandro Martins, Mortalidade Materna em Mulheres Negras no Brasil [Maternal Mortality Among Black Women in Brazil]*, 22 CADERNOS DE SAÚDE PÚBLICA 2473 (2006); Ministério da Saude, SAÚDE BRASIL 2006: UMA ANÁLISE DA DESIGUALDADE EM SAÚDE [BRAZIL'S HEALTH 2006: AN ANALYSIS OF INEQUALITY IN HEALTH] (2006).

[135] Octávio Luiz Motta Ferraz, Saúde, Pobreza e Desigualdade [Health, Poverty and Inequality], Folha de S. Paulo (October 9, 2008), *available at* http://www1.folha.uol.com.br/fsp/opiniao/fz0910200809.htm.

First, Brazil should consider expanding its successful policies in preventive primary care to urban populations, specially low-income groups.[136] This could reduce the excessive use of emergency room as a gateway to the public system. Moreover, it is a relatively cheap and effective way to improve basic health indicators. If one considers the success of programs such as the Family Health Program, there could even be a case to make the program universal, including all families, regardless of income.

Second, the state of São Paulo had a few successful examples of public-private partnerships (PPPs) for hospitals.[137] These should be replicated throughout the country. The other alternative would be a complete overhaul of the system governing public and private hospitals in Brazil, which would be highly complex, risky, and probably politically unfeasible. PPPs, in contrast, would allow the government to invest in alternatives that have already proven fruitful and still can be further improved.[138] PPPs could allow for a progressive replacement of old and dysfunctional hospitals with more efficient and well-managed ones. Over time, this could culminate in a completely new and more functional system of secondary and tertiary care in Brazil.

Finally, more research is needed to map the actual impact of litigation of health care rights in the public health care system.[139] It is still uncertain who are the beneficiaries, what is the impact of this litigation on the public health care system, and what are the systemic and long-term consequences of these lawsuits. Until reliable information is available, it is impossible to formulate any policy proposal in this regard.

These are just three simple – but relatively feasible – reforms that could start reducing health care inequalities in Brazil. Most importantly, these are proposals that are currently being discussed and advocated in Brazil. Whether any of them is likely to be implemented in the near future, however, remains to be seen.

---

[136] Bandeira, *supra* note 56.

[137] La Forgia & Harding, *supra* note 60 at 1115.

[138] *See* Terceiro Setor e Parcerias na Área da Saúde [Third Sector and Partnerships in the Health Sector] (Paulo Modesto & Luiz Arnaldo Cunha Jr. eds., 2011) for a collection of articles discussing possible improvements and other alternative arrangements.

[139] In 2009, the Brazilian Supreme Court held a public audience in an attempt to collect all the evidence available. Many experts, government officials, and scholars have provided their opinions, based on the data available. This was followed by the creation of a working group to gather data, monitor the judicial claims, and propose reforms to the system. Conselho Nacional de Justiça, *Resolução n. 107, de 6 de abril de 2010*, 61 Diário da Justiça eletrônico [DJ-e], 9–10 (April 7, 2010) (Braz.). This system may generate more comprehensive data to allow researchers to better understand the impact of this litigation.

13

A Vision of an Emerging Right to Health Care in the United States

Expanding Health Care Equity through Legislative Reform

Allison K. Hoffman[*]

INTRODUCTION

When asked to write a chapter on how litigation has advanced a right to health in the United States, I responded skeptically, both because evidence of the existence of any such right is weak and the role of litigation in promoting its development is small at best. A snapshot of the U.S. health care system evinces the absence of even a more narrow right to health *care* – a guarantee of equitable access to basic medical care.[1] Instead, it reveals a fragmented picture of public and private financing that leaves many people lacking meaningful access to care.[2] More so, the places where hints of a right to health care appear in the United States are largely not the result of litigation, but rather a product of incremental legislative efforts to advance health care access, suggesting the more compelling story might be one of legislation.

[*] Assistant Professor of Law, UCLA School of Law. My gratitude to Devon Carbado, Scott Cummings, Daniel Dumont, Russell Korobkin, Sam Krasnow, Amy Monahan, Abigail Moncrieff, Steve Munzer, and Kathy Stone for comments on various drafts of this chapter and to Billy Herbert for excellent research assistance.

[1] The more expansive notion of a right to health implies state obligations to promote population health, through protections and entitlements, by addressing "preconditions" of health outcomes, such access to food, clean water, and sanitation, as well as medical care. Siri Gloppen & Mindy Jane Roseman, *Introduction: Can Litigation Bring Justice to Health, in* LITIGATING HEALTH RIGHTS: CAN COURTS BRING MORE JUSTICE TO HEALTH 1, 3–4 (Alycia Ely Yamin & Siri Gloppen, eds., 2011). Some suggest an even more expansive notion that requires attention also to social determinants of health, including education and housing. *See, e.g.,* for research on these "social determinants" Richard Wilkinson & Kate Pickett, THE SPIRIT LEVEL (2009) (examining the effect of income inequality on health); Michael G. Marmot, *Social Differentials in Health Within and Between Populations,* 123(4) DAEDALUS 197 (1994); Geoffrey Rose, *Sick Individuals and Sick Populations,* 14 INTN'L J. EPIDEMIOLOGY 32, 38 (1985); Peter Townsend & Nick Davidson, *Introduction, in* INEQUALITIES IN HEALTH: THE BLACK REPORT 13, 20–23 (Douglas Black et al. eds., 1982).

[2] *See* Allison K. Hoffman, *Oil and Water: Mixing Individual Mandates, Fragmented Markets, and Health Reform,* 36 AM. J. L. & MED. 7 (2010) for a description of fragmentation and its consequences.

Litigation to advance a right to health care has faced paralyzing constraints. Unlike in many other countries, where litigation increasingly plays a central role,[3] there is no overarching constitutional or statutory right to health in the United States to serve as a foundation for legal challenges. As further impediment, the U.S. Supreme Court has limited access to the courts and remedies for individual claims arising from statute or contract. Such structural barriers – legal, procedural, and political – have constrained the use of litigation to define or defend an American right to health care.

In light of these roadblocks, I consider whether legislative change may offer a better (albeit also problematic) pathway to expanding health care equity in the United States. Over the past fifty years, incremental, majoritarian (sometimes barely) legislative efforts have created what can be described as pockets of a right to health care for some populations, such as the elderly or "deserving poor." Now, I suggest, the 2010 health reform law, the Patient Protection and Affordable Care Act (PPACA),[4] offers a vision for an emerging, broader American right to health care, realized by blending the role of public insurance and private insurance and relying on both to achieve more universal, affordable access to health care. The Supreme Court, while previously not influential in advancing an American right to health care, has now played a central role by affirming PPACA's legal validity.[5]

Reflecting on the historical development of the U.S. health care financing system, the limited success of health care rights litigation, and the success of past legislative efforts, this chapter reveals two primary insights. First, it illustrates how and why the United States lies in vivid contrast to many other countries in this volume, where battles over health rights – defined narrowly or broadly – occur largely in the courts. Americans have been and will likely continue to be relatively more reliant on statutory advancement of health care rights. Second, it argues that, going forward, PPACA offers transformative potential for an American right to health care, by gradually redefining who does, and perhaps by implication who should, have access to health care, regardless of ability to pay. Whether this formal legal change will shape social consciousness is still unclear.[6] Early backlash to both the law and

---

3 Gloppen & Roseman, *supra* note 1, at 1–2 (describing the recent rise in health rights litigation globally).

4 Patient Protection and Affordable Care Act, Pub. L. No. 111–148, 124 Stat. 119 (2010) (codified as amended in scattered sections of 21, 25, 26, 29, and 42 U.S.C.) and Health Care and Education Reconciliation Act of 2010, Pub. L. No. 111–152, 124 Stat. 1029 (2010) (codified in scattered sections of 20, 26, and 42 U.S.C.) [hereinafter collectively referred to as "PPACA"].

5 Nat'l Fed'n of Indep. Bus. v. Sebelius, 132 S. Ct. 2566 (2012).

6 Legislation alters health care financing in ways consistent with a right to health care, by increasing affordable access to meaningful health care. Whether social consciousness will follow is more complex and controversial. I suggest several reasons why legislative change *might* offer the potential to shape social consciousness of a right to health care, without asserting that it *will*, a question beyond the scope of this chapter. *See* Catherine Albiston, INSTITUTIONAL INEQUALITY AND THE MOBILIZATION OF THE FAMILY AND MEDICAL LEAVE ACT 11–17 (2010), describing the academic debate on how law shapes social consciousness.

the Supreme Court decision raises doubts. Yet, past experience with incremental health reform in the United States offers some evidence that PPACA could provide the vision and foundation for an evolving American conception of a right to health care. If PPACA offers the best pathway to social change, supporters of a right to health care should be particularly invested in its success, even if they see its vision as flawed or incomplete.

As a preliminary matter, in this chapter, I focus on a right to health *care*. More precisely, I examine a right to health insurance, which usually – but not always – enables access to medical care.[7] This focus is admittedly and intentionally narrow. While there is rich debate among scholars[8] and international human rights bodies[9] on the advisability and meaning of a right to health, I do not intend to join this broader debate. Rather, I examine equitable access to health *care*, which most agree is a critical component of a right to health[10] and which lies at the heart of current controversies in law, policy, and politics in the United States. This right to health care demands equality of opportunity to access medical care but not necessarily equality of health outcomes, which requires well more than access to medical care.[11] I also do not intend to define what particular medical care is core to a right to health care, but I do illuminate how the design and regulation of health insurance implicitly asserts such definition.[12]

While circumspect about the future of PPACA and its ability to provoke broader social mobilization, my goal in this chapter is to show how it offers a transformative vision, and perhaps the most promising pathway in light of impediments to litigation, for an emerging right to health care in the United States.

---

[7] But see David Orentlicher, *Right to Healthcare in the United States: Inherently Unstable*, 38 Am. J. L. & Med. 326, 336–337 (2012).

[8] *See, e.g.*, Public Health, Ethics and Equity (Sudhir Anand, et al. eds., 2004); Norman Daniels, Just Health: Meeting Health Needs Fairly (2008); Allen E. Buchanan, Justice and Health Care (2009); Tom L. Beauchamp & Ruth R. Faden, *The Right to Health and the Right to Health Care*, 4 J. Med. & Phil. 118 (1979); William W. Fisher & Talha Syed, *Global Justice in Healthcare: Developing Drugs for the Developing World*, 40 U.C. Davis L. Rev. 581, 602–47 (2007); Martha C. Nussbaum, *Capabilities as Fundamental Entitlements: Sen and Social Justice*, 9(2–3) Feminist Econ. 33, 41 (2003).

[9] *International Covenant on Economic, Social and Cultural Rights* art. 12, G.A. Res. 2200 (XXI), 21 U.N. GAOR Supp. (No. 16), U.N. Doc. A/6316, art. 12 (1966) for the place where a right to health is anchored in international law recognizes the right "to the enjoyment of the highest attainable standard of physical and mental health"; *see* U.N. Econ. & Soc. Council, Comm. on Econ. Soc. and Cultural Rights, General Comment No. 14: The Right to the Highest Attainable Standard of Health, PP 38–42, U.N. Doc. E/C.12/2000/4 (2000) for discussion of article 12.

[10] Daniels, *supra* note 7, at 29–30.

[11] *See* Jennifer Prah Ruger, *Ethics of the Social Determinants of Health*, 364 Lancet 1092, 1092–1094 (2004) (contrasting an equality-of-opportunity approach, as advocated by John Rawls and Norm Daniels, and an equality-of-results approach, closer to Amartya Sen's vision).

[12] I have elsewhere discussed three competing models for allocative decisions. Allison K. Hoffman, *Three Models of Health Insurance: The Conceptual Pluralism of the Patient Protection and Affordable Care Act*, 159 U. Pa. L. Rev. 1873 (2011).

13.1 BEFORE PPACA: INSURANCE FRAGMENTATION AND
INEQUITABLE ACCESS TO HEALTH CARE

To understand attempts to improve health care equity in the United States, it is necessary to examine the roots of inequity in the current system, which has become fragmented into many, incommensurate sources of financing. This fragmentation occurred in two ways. First, market and historical processes together created a proliferation of sources and types of insurance, which I call structural fragmentation. Second, the legal standards among these types have diverged over time, which I call regulatory fragmentation.[13] The result is that some types of insurance are superior to others. Because not everyone can access all – or any – of these types, fragmentation has resulted in inequitable access to medical care among Americans, depending on how – or whether – an individual is insured.

13.1.1 *Structural Fragmentation*

The U.S. health care financing system is a maze of public and private insurance programs, each covering different services and items for different populations. The primary fissure is between public and private insurance. The major public health insurance programs, Medicare and Medicaid, were created in 1965, intending to cover only a limited subset of Americans. Subsequently, private insurance developed to fill in the picture and, in so doing, diffused political pressure to expand public insurance, while still not meeting the needs of many not eligible for public insurance.

Public insurance programs create what could be considered a weak statutory right to health care for about 90 million Americans, mostly in medically vulnerable populations,[14] by defining entitlements to membership in programs for financing medical care. These rights are weak, however, for several reasons. First, because they are statutory, these programs can be terminated or altered at any time by legislators and regulators. With regard to Medicaid, in particular, the Department of Health and Human Services can waive program requirements for state demonstration projects.[15] Second, while these programs guarantee qualifying individuals *financing* for certain health care services, they do not necessarily guarantee *access* to covered services if providers are not available and willing to participate in the programs.[16] Third, the public programs have limited enforcement mechanisms, making some statutory rights not individually enforceable, as discussed later in the chapter.

Several public insurance programs, together, constitute this weak right to health care for some Americans. Most significantly, in 1965, the U.S. Congress passed

---

[13] For in-depth examination of fragmentation, *see* Hoffman, *supra* note 2.
[14] Carmen DeNavas-Walt et al., U.S. Census Bureau, Current Population Reports, Income, Poverty, and Health Insurance Coverage in the United States: 2009, 71 tbl.C-1 (2010).
[15] 42 U.S.C. § 1315 (2012).
[16] *See infra* n. 133–135 & text.

legislation to establish Medicare,[17] a federal program to finance care for the elderly (generally those over sixty-five years old) and Medicaid,[18] a joint federal and state health care program for the poor and disabled. Other public programs include the State Children's Health Insurance Program (CHIP) for near-poor children, Indian Health Services (IHS) for American Indians and Alaskan Natives, and TRICARE and the Veteran Administration's (VA) program for active duty military personnel, veterans, and their families. These programs share characteristics found in social insurance programs in other countries, such as tax-based financing, broad risk spreading, and access to a range of benefits with limited cost sharing.[19] They are all publicly financed and pay for privately-delivered health care, except for the VA and IHS, where the delivery system is public as well. We could think of these programs as delineating who – including, for example, the elderly and deserving poor – deserves guarantees to medical care, even if unable to pay for it on their own.

In contrast, the U.S. private health insurance market, the source of coverage for 195 million Americans,[20] is not available to all, and lower-income or less healthy individuals are less likely to have access to private insurance.[21] The private market is itself split into three markets based on employee group size – referred to as "large group," "small group," and "individual" markets. The quality of coverage generally decreases and cost increases in this same order.

Most privately-insured Americans obtain large- or small-group employer coverage, where the employer has discretion over the design of this coverage.[22] This system of employer-sponsored insurance (ESI) became common in the mid-twentieth century as a work-related benefit and has become deeply entrenched since. While employers are not required to offer employees health insurance, many do because expenditures on health benefits are excludable from taxes for both the employer and the employee. The beneficial tax treatment means that health benefits have become a less expensive way to compensate employees; one dollar worth of health insurance costs employers approximately $.65 .[23] In addition, some employees, especially if salaried and higher-income, expect health benefits.[24]

---

[17] Social Security Amendments of 1965, Title XVIII, 42 U.S.C. § 1395 (1965).

[18] Social Security Amendments of 1965, Title XIX, 42 U.S.C. § 1396 (1965).

[19] *See* Richard B. Saltman, *Social Health Insurance in Perspective: The Challenge of Sustaining Stability, in* Social Health Insurance Systems in Western Europe 3 (Richard B. Saltman et al. eds., 2004) (characterizing social insurance in Western Europe).

[20] DeNavas-Walt et al., *supra* note 14, at 71. More than 250 million Americans are insured, some with both private and public coverage.

[21] Kaiser Family Found. & Health Research & Educ. Trust, Employer Health Benefits 2011 Annual Survey 48–50 (2011), *available at* http://ehbs.kff.org/pdf/2012/8345.pdf. [hereinafter KFF Employer Health Benefits: 2011].

[22] *Id.*, at 36; Katherine Swartz, *Justifying Government as the Backstop in Health Insurance Markets*, 2 Yale J. Health Pol'y L. & Ethics 89, 94 (2001).

[23] Jonathan Gruber, *Covering the Uninsured in the United States*, 46 J. Econ. Literature 571, 574 (2008).

[24] KFF Employer Health Benefits: 2011, *supra* note 21, at 34.

Not all private insurance is obtained through employers. Some workers lack access to ESI, either because they work for an employer who does not offer it – more frequently the case with smaller employers – or because they do not qualify for employee benefits due to contingent work status, including part-time and seasonal employment. Without access to ESI, individuals seek out coverage on the "individual market," purchasing a policy directly from a private insurer. About 8 percent of the non-elderly (about 18 million individuals) had individual market coverage prior to reform.[25] This market is more unstable and expensive, dollar-per-dollar, than group coverage, as explained later.

The remaining 16–17 percent of the total non-elderly population (about 50 million individuals) is uninsured and has limited access to medical care;[26] unless they can pay for it directly, they may only receive care in limited locations and circumstances, and, at times, at exorbitant costs. For example, the Emergency Medical Treatment & Active Labor Act (EMTALA) guarantees access to emergency services regardless of ability to pay.[27] However, if an uninsured person receives care in an emergency room and does not pay for it, the care is considered "uncompensated" at the point of service,[28] and the hospital may try to collect payment directly from the patient, resulting in bankruptcies for uninsured and underinsured Americans.[29] EMTALA could be understood as creating a limited right for all to access some care but with potentially very high costs.

In sum, U.S. health care financing has evolved into a system with many parts. In the public system, the least well off – the elderly and poor – benefit from a circumscribed statutorily created right to care. In the private system, those with ESI, who tend to be higher-income earners, have more comprehensive insurance coverage, but that coverage exists at the employer's whim. Many fall through the cracks between these two systems, left to rely on safety nets, such as EMTALA for limited access to care.

13.1.2 *Regulatory Fragmentation*

Structural fragmentation set the foundation for regulatory fragmentation – namely, regulatory inconsistency among the different insurance markets that exacerbated

25 Office of Health Policy, U.S. Department of Health and Human Service, The Regulation of the Individual Health Insurance Market (2008).

26 DeNavas-Walt et al., *supra* note 1414, at 22.

27 The Emergency Medical Treatment and Active Labor Act 2006, 42 U.S.C. § 1395dd (2006).

28 Hadley et al., *Covering the Uninsured in 2008: Current Costs, Sources of Payment, and Incremental Costs*, 27 HEALTH AFF. 399, Aug. 25, 2008, at 402, *available at* http://content.healthaffairs.org/content/27/5/w399.full.pdf+html.

29 David U. Himmelstein et al., *Marketwatch: Illness and Injury as Contributors to Bankruptcy*, HEALTH AFF. w5–63, Feb. 2, 2005, *available at* http://content.healthaffairs.org/content/suppl/2005/01/28/hlthaff.w5.63.DC1.

inequities in access to care, depending on the type of insurance coverage an individual has.

13.1.2.1 Regulation of Public Benefits and Eligibility

Public insurance covers a set of basic benefits for eligible populations that gives meaning to the entitlements created in these programs. For the two largest public insurance programs, Medicare and Medicaid, the federal government defines a floor of coverage. Above these baselines, benefits can vary based on what plan a beneficiary chooses or, for Medicaid, in which state the beneficiary lives.

Medicare covers basic medical services for most Americans older than sixty-five, including inpatient care, outpatient care, and, as of 2006, prescription drugs,[30] but generally does not cover routine dental or vision care or custodial long-term care. Most Medicare beneficiaries, unless low-income, face moderate out-of-pocket expenses for premiums, deductibles, coinsurance for hospital services, and copayments for outpatient services and prescription drugs. As a share of income, the median Medicare beneficiary's out-of-pocket spending increased from 12 percent in 1997 to more than 16 percent in 2006, even though 90 percent also hold private supplemental coverage to fill in gaps.[31]

Medicaid programs likewise build on a required core, albeit a thin one, of mandatory eligibility categories and benefits. Medicaid is funded by both the federal (i.e., national) and state governments. The federal government dictates which beneficiaries and benefits states must cover to receive federal matching dollars, above which the states have discretion. Prior to PPACA, Medicaid eligibility has been "categorical," meaning that federal rules require coverage of certain populations, including children under age six and pregnant women in households with incomes below 133 percent of the Federal Poverty Level (FPL), children age six to eighteen in households with income below 100 percent of the FPL, and certain categories of people with disabilities.[32] For reference, the 2011 FPL was US$22,350 for a family of four and US$10,890 for an individual.[33] Beyond these categories, states have had discretion to define eligibility, typically doing so sparingly. For example, in 2009, the eligibility threshold for the nonmandatory category of "working parents" ranged from below 17 percent of the FPL in Arkansas to below 215 percent of the FPL in Minnesota.[34] Many states do not cover childless adults at all.[35]

---

[30] Kaiser Commission on Medicaid and the Uninsured, MEDICAID: A PRIMER 5 (2010), *available at* http://www.kff.org/medicaid/upload/7334–04.pdf, [hereinafter MEDICAID PRIMER].

[31] Kaiser Family Found, MEDICARE CHARTBOOK, FOURTH EDITION 60 (2010).

[32] Kaiser Comm'n on Medicaid & The Uninsured, MEDICAID: AN OVERVIEW OF SPENDING ON "MANDATORY" VS. "OPTIONAL" POPULATIONS AND SERVICES (2005).

[33] HHS Poverty Guidelines, 76Fed. Reg. 3637–3638 (January 20, 2011).

[34] MEDICAID PRIMER, *supra* note 30, at 12.

[35] Id.

For most beneficiaries, states must cover certain mandatory services, such as hospital and outpatient services, laboratory and X-ray services, family-planning services, and comprehensive diagnostic and treatment services for children.[36] In addition, state Medicaid programs may and typically do offer "optional" services, including prescription drugs,which all states offer, dental services, and hospice services.[37] Eligibility thresholds and benefits thus define the reach and substance of the Medicaid entitlement, but it varies considerably among states. In other words, the meaning of the right to health care guaranteed by Medicaid is not static among enrollees.

13.1.2.2 Regulation of Private Benefits and Eligibility

Private insurance benefits and cost-sharing requirements have been less tightly prescribed, suggesting a less clear and consistent normative vision for private insurance. Regulation of private insurance is reserved to the states unless the federal Congress acts and expressly preempts state regulation,[38] which it has done several times to meaningful effect. For example, many employer plans are not subject to state regulation, because of the preemption language in the Employee Retirement Income Security Act of 1974 (ERISA),[39] a federal law enacted to enable large, multistate companies to administer employee benefits (mostly pensions) seamlessly across states. As interpreted by the courts, ERISA preempts most state regulation of employer plans, including all state regulation of "self-insured" employee benefit health plans,[40] where an employer retains risk of high expenditures, rather than buying a group insurance product from an insurer to transfer the risk of unexpected high expenditures to that insurer.[41] According to a recent estimate, 60 percent of all workers and 96 percent of workers in large companies are beneficiaries of self-insured plans and thus exempt from state insurance regulation.[42]

Employer plans, however, must comply with ERISA and other federal laws that aim to reduce discrimination and spread risk more evenly among employees, who together form the group risk pool. For example, the Health Insurance Portability and Accountability Act (HIPAA), a 1996 statue that amends ERISA, prohibits discrimination against individual members of a group based on an individual's health status or

---

[36] *Id.*, at 14. Some states offer an alternative "benchmark" plan for certain high-need beneficiaries. *Id.*, at 17.

[37] *Id.*, at 15.

[38] The McCarran–Ferguson Act of 1945, 15 U.S.C. §§ 1011et seq. (2006).

[39] Employee Retirement Income Security Act (ERISA) of 1974, 29 U.S.C. § 1144 (2006).

[40] ERISA, 29 U.S.C. § 1144 (2006); *See* Russell Korobkin, *The Failed Jurisprudence of Managed Care, and How to Fix It: Reinterpreting ERISA Preemption,* 51 UCLA L. Rev. 457 (2003) for review and critique of ERISA preemption.

[41] Most buy stop-loss coverage, transferring risk to a stop-loss insurer; yet, the law maintains the distinction, even if myth.

[42] KFF Employer Health Benefits: 2011, *supra* note 21, at 151, ex. 10.1.

history.[43] Furthermore, federal tax law also prohibits employers from discriminating in favor of more highly-compensated employees,[44] and other federal laws prohibit employers from discriminating against employees due to genetic information[45] or disabilities.[46] These laws effectively assert that access to health care should not differ on the basis of these characteristics, even in private markets. The prohibitions on discrimination, however, have limits in application because, apart from a few categories of mandatory benefits, employers can exclude whole categories of care if exclusions are based on actuarial principles and are not a "subterfuge for discrimination."[47]

The limited, mandatory benefits for employer plans include a minimum hospital stay after childbirth[48] and parity between mental health and substance use disorder benefits, on the one hand, and medical benefits, on the other, to the extent a health plan covers both.[49] Although many employers do choose to offer relatively comprehensive health benefits, doing so is discretionary. Thus, apart from these few mandated benefits, employers give meaning to the employer health plan, but once defined, equal protection principles attach.

HIPAA also requires insurers to issue coverage to any group who applies ("guaranteed issue")[50] and renew coverage in subsequent years ("guaranteed renewal"), ensuring all groups can get coverage, even if at high prices.[51] This means that all employers can obtain group plans and members of an employer group, regardless of health status, can participate on relatively similar terms in any plan their employer chooses to offer.

Those seeking coverage on their own in the individual market have had fewer guarantees and less access to healthy risk pools, prior to PPACA. States regulate, to varying degrees, the design and content of insurance policies, including, for example, mandating coverage of certain benefits.[52] While most states' laws include some substantive regulations of benefits, few regulate the pricing and issuance of coverage in the individual market. Only a small minority of states has extended HIPAA-like rules to the state individual market; six states require guaranteed issue and

---

[43] Health Insurance Portability and Accountability Act of 1996, Pub. L. No. 104–91, 110 Stat. 1936 (1996).

[44] 26 U.S.C. § 105(h) (2010).

[45] *See* Genetic Information Nondiscrimination Act of 2008, Pub. L. No. 110–233, § 101, 122 Stat 881, 883–88 (2008).

[46] Americans with Disabilities Act of 1990, 42 U.S.C. § 12112 (2012), 29 C.F.R. § 1630.4 (2010).

[47] Equal Employment Opportunity Commission, Interim Enforcement Guidance on the Application of the Americans with Disabilities Act of 1990 to Disability-Based Distinctions in Employer Provided Health Insurance, No. N-915.002 (June 8, 1993).

[48] 42 U.S.C. §300gg-25 (2012).

[49] 42 U.S.C. §300gg-26 (2012). Certain plans that cover under 50 employees or experience an increase in claims costs of over one percent as a result of compliance may be exempt.

[50] 42 U.S.C. §300gg-1 (2012) (guaranteed availability in the group market).

[51] 42 U.S.C. §300gg-2 (2012) (guaranteed renewability in the group market).

[52] *See generally* Amy B. Monahan, *Federalism, Federal Regulation, or Free Market? An Examination of Mandated Health Benefit Reform*, 2007 U. ILL. L. REV. 1361, 1365 (2007).

one-third of states limit the variability in premium prices allowed among insured.[53] The result is that individual-market insurers in most states can issue, decline, or differentially price insurance based on an individual's health (or perceived health) – a practice known as underwriting or "risk rating."[54] To the degree an insurer judges an individual as high risk, it has historically been allowed to subject the individual to high premiums or coverage exclusions (e.g., carve-outs of preexisting conditions or low benefit limits), or deny coverage, to the extent allowed by a state's laws.[55] Americans disagree on the desirability of risk rating, based on differing conceptions of which types of risks should be shared and which should be borne individually through higher premiums or coverage exclusions.

Underwriting is time consuming and expensive, resulting in high overhead costs that make the individual-market policies relatively more expensive than group-market policies.[56] In turn, many people cannot afford coverage or pay more than they would in group markets for the same level of coverage. One study reported that in 2005, nearly three in five adults who applied for coverage in the individual market did not buy it because they were denied coverage, quoted unaffordable prices, or had a health problem excluded from coverage.[57] In states with relatively unregulated individual markets, insurers reject as many as 30–40 percent of applicants.[58] Some who do obtain coverage in the individual and small-group markets are considered "underinsured."[59] Only one-third of those with individual market coverage rate their coverage as "excellent" or "good."[60]

The combination of structural and regulatory fragmentation has thus led to highly variable insurance coverage among Americans and no coherent vision of what an American right to health care might entail. In particular, those who must resort to the individual market, especially if perceived as high-risk applicants, are more likely to have poor or no coverage. U.S. law and regulation has thus created a fragmented system with no common baseline in which people in need of health care often fall through the cracks.

---

[53] Kaiser Family Foundation, 50 State Comparisons: Health Insurance & Managed Care, STATEHEALTH-FACTS.ORG (2012), *available at* http://www.statehealthfacts.org/comparecat.jsp?cat=7&rgn=6&rgn=1.

[54] *See* Donald W. Light, *The Practice and Ethics of Risk-Rated Health Insurance*, 267 JAMA 2503 (1992).

[55] *See, e.g.*, Melinda Beeuwkes Buntin et al., *The Role of the Individual Health Insurance Market and Prospects for Change*, 23 HEALTH AFF. 79, 81 (2004); Sara R. Collins et al., THE COMMONWEALTH FUND, SQUEEZED: WHY RISING EXPOSURE TO HEALTH CARE COSTS THREATENS THE HEALTH AND FINANCIAL WELL-BEING OF AMERICAN FAMILIES 3–4 (2006); Michelle M. Doty et al., *Failure to Protect: Why the Individual Insurance Market Is Not a Viable Option for Most U.S. Families*, July, 2009, at 1–3, *available at* http://www.commonwealthfund.org/~/media/Files/Publications/Issue%20Brief/2009/Jul/Failure%20to%20Protect/1300_Doty_failure_to_protect_individual_ins_market_ib_v2.pdf.

[56] *See* Gruber, *supra* note 23, at 574–575.

[57] Collins et al., *supra* note 55, at 4.

[58] *Id.*, at 21.

[59] Cathy Schoen et al., *How Many are Underinsured? Trends Among U.S. Adults, 2003 and 2007*, HEALTH AFF. w298–309 (2008), *available at* http://content.healthaffairs.org/content/27/4/w298.full.pdf+html.

[60] *Id.*, at 4.

13.2 THE LIMITED ROLE OF THE JUDICIARY IN DEFINING A RIGHT TO HEALTH CARE

Attempts to address these inequities through litigation have faltered in the face of structural barriers – substantive, procedural, and political. Because of these barriers, litigation has not played the role in defining or expanding health equity in the United States that it has in other countries. In fact, U.S. courts have largely rejected rights-based claims to health care.[61] Litigants have, however, had some limited success with contractual claims to remedy wrongful denial of covered benefits for eligible enrollees. These lawsuits serve to preserve the contractual status quo but do not markedly stretch the bounds of access to health care.

13.2.1 *No Constitutional Right to Health*

The American legal structure is one that in general favors negative rights – or liberties – and disfavors positive rights. A primary reason why litigation has not played a major role in defining or guaranteeing a right to health care is because the U.S. Constitution has no explicit right to health, nor have the courts read an implicit one. The Supreme Court, as part of its resistance to an expansion of welfare rights more generally, has declined to read a right to health into the substantive due process provision of the Fourteenth Amendment to the Constitution, a provision protecting against deprivations of life, liberty, or property.[62] In the 1960s and 1970s, many scholars and activists thought the court would interpret the Fourteenth Amendment to guarantee welfare as a fundamental right, which would have implied a guarantee of health care, at least for the poor, but such predictions never came to fruition.[63]

Quite the opposite has occurred. Over the past few decades, Supreme Court decisions have explicitly dismissed a state obligation to pay for or guarantee health care, even to indigent populations.[64] Even benefits under public insurance programs, such as Medicare and Medicaid, are not considered property for constitutional

---

[61] Nicole Huberfeld, *Bizarre Love Triangle: The Spending Clause, Section 1983, and Medicaid Entitlements*, 42 U.C. DAVIS L. REV. 413 (2008); Timothy Stoltzfus Jost, DISENTITLEMENT? 24–30 (2003). *But see* Abigail Moncrieff, *The Freedom of Health* 159 U. PA. L. REV. 2209 (2011) [hereinafter, Moncrieff, *Freedom*]; Jessie Hill, *The Constitutional Right to Make Medical Treatment Decisions: A Tale of Two Doctrines*, 86 TEX. L. REV. 277 (2007) [hereinafter Hill, *Constitutional Right*]; Jessie Hill, *Reproductive Rights as Health Care Rights*, 18 COLUM. J. GENDER & L. 501 (2009) [hereinafter Hill, *Reproductive Rights*].

[62] President's Commission for the Study of Ethical Problems in Medicine and Biomedical and Behavioral Research, Securing Access to Health Care: Volume One 33 (1983); Puneet K. Sandhu, *A Legal Right to Health Care: What Can the United States Learn from Foreign Models of Health Rights Jurisprudence?*, 95 Cal. L. Rev. 1151, 1162–1165 (2007).

[63] Jost, *supra* note 61, at 26.

[64] *See* Harris v. McRae, 448 U.S. 297, 311 (1980); Maher v. Roe, 432 U.S. 464, 469 (1977).

purposes and thus can be revoked.[65] Further, in some recent cases, the courts quashed claims of a right to access a particular medical service or item, regardless of the source of payment for care.[66]

The Supreme Court has, however, delineated a very limited guarantee to medical care for those in state custodial control, under the Eighth Amendment to the Constitution's prohibition of cruel and unusual punishment.[67] This right was recently reaffirmed in *Brown v. Plata*, where the court ordered California to reduce its prison population by nearly 25 percent because prison overcrowding prevented provision of necessary medical care and mental health care to inmates.[68] This narrowly defined right only attaches in circumstances when the state has first restrained the individual's liberty through incarceration or other means.[69]

In addition, the Supreme Court has recognized health-related liberties, such as the right to refuse treatment,[70] obtain contraception,[71] or have an abortion.[72] Several scholars argue these liberties, together, could be read to carve out a "negative" right to health that protects individuals from excessive government interference with health decisions,[73] but the court has never explicitly acknowledged such a right. Even if read in such a light, these negative rights do not create any governmental obligation to guarantee health care; quite the opposite, they guarantee freedom from government interference.

State constitutions, while gesturing at health care rights textually, similarly do not tend to create any broadly enforceable right to health care in application.[74] According to research by Professor Elizabeth Weeks Leonard, about one-quarter of state constitutions mention the importance of public health and welfare or the responsibility of the state to care for the indigent, insane, or incarcerated, but court

---

[65] Jost, *supra* note 61, at 28.

[66] Abigail Alliance for Better Access to Developmental Drugs v. von Eschenbach, 495 F.3d 695 (D.C. Cir. 2007) (declining a right to experimental drugs, even for the terminally ill); U.S. v. Oakland Cannabis Buyers' Coop., 532 U.S. 483 (2001) (declining a right to medical marijuana).

[67] Estelle v. Gamble, 429 U.S. 97, 104 (1977) ("deliberate indifference" to medical needs of prisoners violates the 8th Amendment); *see also* Youngberg v. Romeo, 457 U.S. 307, 315 (1982) (affirming extension of rights to involuntarily committed persons).

[68] Brown v. Plata, 131 S. Ct. 1910, 1928 (2011).

[69] DeShaney v. Winnebago County, 489 U.S. 189, 200 (1989) (declining to extend the right to child under state social services review, who was living with, and abused by, his father); Wideman v. Shallowford Community Hospital, 826 F.2d 1030 (11th Cir. 1987) (declining to extend the right to woman in a public ambulance who subjected herself to custody).

[70] Washington v. Harper, 494 U.S. 210 (1990); Cruzan v. Dir., Mo. Dep't of Health, 497 U.S. 261 (1990) (assuming, not affirming the right to refuse treatment).

[71] Carey v. Population Servs. Int'l, 431 U.S. 678, 687–689 (1977).

[72] Gonzales v. Carhart, 550 U.S. 124, 156–58 (2007); Roe v. Wade, 410 U.S. 113 (1973).

[73] *See* generally Hill, Reproductive Rights, supra note 5; Hill, Constitutional Rights, sup, e.g., Hill, Reproductive Rights, supra note 611; Moncrieff, Freedom, supra note 61 re, 12 U. PA. J. CONST. L. 1325 (2010).

[74] Elizabeth Weeks Leonard, *State Constitutionalism and the Right to Health Care*, 12 U. PA. J. CONST. L. 1325 (2010).

interpretation of these provisions has not construed them to confer a right to health care.[75] With no acknowledged positive constitutional right to health (or health care) at the federal or state level, litigants lack an overarching hook for legal claims to a right to health care.

13.2.2 *Limitations on Private Rights of Action*

The Supreme Court's cabining of private rights of action to enforce even contractual or statutory rights to medical care has further minimized the role of the courts.[76] This erosion of individual access to the courts, which has occurred beyond the sphere of health care,[77] has significantly limited health care litigation.[78]

For example, courts have limited Medicaid beneficiaries' standing to sue state agencies or officials for violations of the federal conditions of the Medicaid program.[79] Medicaid does not have a private statutory enforcement mechanism of its own.[80] Beneficiaries have relied primarily on 42 U.S.C. § 1983, a Civil Rights Act provision that accords a private right of action against government actors for "deprivation of any rights, privileges, or immunities secured by the Constitution and laws."[81]

Scaling back this practice, a 2002 Supreme Court decision, *Gonzaga University v. Doe*, narrowed the use of § 1983 to seek remedy for individual harms.[82] In *Gonzaga*, the Court barred individual § 1983 challenges for the violation of conditions of federal spending programs, under the theory that such conditions – set by the federal government for participating states to follow – do not create *individually enforceable* rights.[83] Applying *Gonzaga*, most federal courts of appeal have rejected the use of § 1983 suits by Medicaid beneficiaries for enforcement of certain Medicaid provisions,[84] including the so-called Equal Access Provision.[85] This provision requires states to pay providers reimbursement rates sufficient to enlist adequate provider participation in Medicaid with the stated goal of guaranteeing that

---

[75] *Id.*, at 1392–1393.

[76] See generally Huberfeld, *supra* note 61; Moncrieff, The Supreme Court's Assault on Litigation Why (and How) it Could be Good for Health Law, 90 B.U. L. Rev. 2323 (2011). [hereinafter, Moncrieff, Assault on Litigation].

[77] *Id.*; *see also* Erwin Chemerinsky, *Closing the Courthouse Doors to Civil Rights Litigants*, 5 U. Pa. J. Const. L. 537, 537–539 (2003) (describing ways the Rehnquist Court limited private rights of action).

[78] Huberfeld, *supra* note 61, at 447–448; Moncrieff, *Assault on Litigation, supra* note 76.

[79] Huberfeld, *supra* note 61, at 443–450.

[80] *Id.*, at 417.

[81] The Civil Rights Act of 1871, 42 U.S.C. § 1983 (2012); Maine v. Thiboutot, 448 U.S. 1 (1980) (articulating the use of § 1983 to challenge statutory violations).

[82] Gonzaga University v. Doe, 526 U.S. 273 (2002) (finding no individual cause of action to challenge the Family Educational Rights and Privacy Act, which protects the privacy of student education records).

[83] Huberfeld, *supra* note 61, at 434.

[84] *See* Moncrieff, Assault on Litigation, *supra* note 76, at 2333.

[85] Medicaid Act of 1965, 42 U.S.C. § 1396a(a)(30) (2012).

Medicaid patients have the same access to medical care as their privately-insured neighbors.[86] The appellate courts have reasoned that the Equal Access Provision establishes a contract between the federal government and participating states and does not create any individually-enforceable rights, as in *Gonzaga*.[87]

With § 1983 causes of action unavailable to challenge state Medicaid reimbursement policies, beneficiaries and providers have attempted novel approaches to expand health care rights via litigation.[88] After the state of California cut Medicaid provider reimbursement rates by 10 percent in 2008 to address a budgetary crisis, litigants claimed state reimbursement policies were inconsistent with Medicaid's Equal Access Provision, a federal law, and thus void under the U.S. Constitution's Supremacy Clause, which invalidates state laws in conflict with federal laws.[89] The Supreme Court recently remanded this case on other grounds, not reaching a decision on the standing issue but suggesting hostility to the Supremacy Clause arguments.[90]

As with public insurance, the Supreme Court has foreclosed many individual rights of action to remedy harms arising from private insurance practices. A 2004 Supreme Court decision, *Aetna Health v. Davila*, prevented enrollees in employer plans from suing insurers in state court for harms resulting from denials of coverage, by interpreting ERISA's provision on remedies (§ 502)[91] to preempt these state causes of action.[92] Those injured by utilization review activities – insurance company review of requests for medical treatment under a policy – can still seek remedy in federal court under § 502, but remedies under § 502 do not include compensatory damages for harms or punitive damages, as available under state law.[93] This means that if an insurer denies a benefit under an employer plan as not "medically necessary," and the insured, as a result, suffers serious injury or death, the only remedy is the cost of the denied medical care. This interpretation provides little counterweight to managed care companies' incentives to limit care to save money, if the worst that can happen in the subset of medical care denials actually challenged in court is that the managed care companies are later obligated to pay for denied benefits.

The one case in which both publicly and privately insured have recourse through litigation is to vindicate contractual claims if wrongly denied eligibility or medical items or services that are arguably within the scope of enumerated benefits. For

[86]   *Id.*

[87]   Huberfeld, *supra* note 61, at 447–448; Moncrieff, *Assault on Litigation, supra* note 76, at 2332–2333.

[88]   Douglas v. Indep. Living Ctr. of S. Cal., Inc., 132 S. Ct. 1204, 1207 (2012).

[89]   *Id.; see also* Sara Rosenbaum, *Equal Access for Medicaid Beneficiaries – the Supreme Court and the Douglas Cases*, 365 NEW ENG. J. MED. 2245 (2011).

[90]   Douglas v. Indep. Living Ctr. of S. Cal., Inc., 132 S. Ct.

[91]   29 U.S.C. § 1132(a) (2012).

[92]   Aetna Health Inc. v. Davila, 542 U.S. 200, 209 (2004).

[93]   29 U.S.C. § 1132(a)(1)(B)(2012).

example, beneficiaries can still bring § 1983 challenges for violations of Medicaid's "Reasonable Promptness Provision," limiting wait times to access covered services, and the "Minimum Services Provision," requiring states to provide beneficiaries services for which they are eligible, because both provisions have been interpreted as creating individually-enforceable rights.[94] Medicare beneficiaries have access to administrative appeals and, if they exhaust the administrative process and the amount in controversy is more than US$1,000, may challenge benefits or eligibility denials in federal court.[95] Such challenges, often seeking coverage of new technologies, drugs, and devices as "medically necessary," can unlock access to these items or services. However, more often than not they fail, as courts usually defer to Medicare and Medicaid administrators' determinations.[96] Finally, for services that are not already covered, an individual may seek a "national coverage determination," a decision by the Secretary of Health and Human Services to add coverage of a new item or service to Medicare benefits.[97]

For private plans, even though members of an employer plan cannot sue their insurer to remedy harms from utilization review, they can still challenge a benefits denial and, if successful, gain access to wrongfully-denied benefits. First, they can bring a suit under § 502, as discussed earlier; however, courts are highly deferential to plan administrators, as they are to Medicare administrators.[98] Second, most states also have state external review statutes that require an independent review of plan utilization review decisions.[99] The Supreme Court determined these statutes survive ERISA § 502 preemption,[100] on the logic that reviews do not replace § 502 as the sole remedial provision; the court reasoned that decisions of external reviewers are only enforceable through a § 502 claim in federal court, in which the independent review serves as evidence.[101] PPACA attempts to reinvigorate and expand the reach of independent external reviews, by requiring that all health plan decisions be subject to a *binding* independent external review.[102] Nonetheless, even if universal and binding, these external reviews provide, at best, access to benefits arguably covered within the terms of plan benefits.

In sum, the Supreme Court has limited private rights of action and remedies so that litigation is available only to vindicate contractual rights to covered medical care. Courts rarely expand access to health care beyond the explicit terms of coverage and generally do not hear cases attempting to challenge systemic barriers to care, such

---

[94] Huberfeld, *supra* note 61, at 445–447.
[95] 42 U.S.C. § 1395ff (b) (2012).
[96] Jost, *supra* note 61, at 36, 40–41.
[97] *Id.* at 40.
[98] *Id.* at 42.
[99] *See* generally Karen Politz et al., Kaiser Family Foundation, Assessing State External Review Programs and the Effects of Pending Federal Patients' Rights Legislation (2002).
[100] Rush Prudential HMO v. Moran, 536 U.S. 355 (2002).
[101] *Id.* at 384. *See also* Korobkin, *supra* note 40, at 528.
[102] PPACA § 1001, 42 U.S.C. § 300gg-19 (2012).

as low reimbursement rates. Thus, litigation can affirm the status quo and perhaps stretch it a bit, under broad interpretations of medical necessity, but it rarely pushes the bounds of access to health care beyond contractual terms.

13.3 A RENEWED OPPORTUNITY FOR A RIGHT TO HEALTH CARE THROUGH HEALTH REFORM

In light of the constraints on litigation, legislation is proving a more successful pathway for an evolving right to health care in the United States. Starting with the creation of Medicare and Medicaid, continuing with the federal and state regulations that increase risk pooling and thus promote more equitable access to care among members of a group health plan, discussed earlier, and most recently with PPACA, legislation has offered incremental steps toward a more robust notion of a right to health care. Each statute defines a new baseline for guarantees to medical care. With the initial statutory suggestion of a more ambitious baseline, some portion of the public often recoils but then, over time, largely adjusts to the new conception. For example, while Medicare was only slightly more favored than not at its passage, it is now one of the most popular U.S. social welfare programs with 90 percent approval ratings.[103] At a time when Americans agree on little, most support Medicare and the notion that the elderly *should* have affordable access to good health care.[104]

PPACA offers an opportunity to advance a more expansive baseline conception of a right to health care for the non-elderly in two main ways. First, PPACA attempts to increase access to insurance by regulating private insurance markets so that they serve social ends and by expanding public coverage. Second, once coverage is more universal, it aims to make it meaningful, by more tightly regulating the content of all health insurance – public and private. Embodied in this expansion of coverage and benefits is an implicit conception of what risks should be shared more collectively. In other words, PPACA redefines who should have a right to care and the core of what this right must contain.

13.3.1 *Expanding Access*

PPACA's central goal is to make insurance available and affordable for many of the 50 million uninsured Americans, which can be seen as supporting a right to access

---

[103] Ninety percent of Americans support Medicare and nearly 90% support Social Security. Taylor Humphrey, *The Harris Poll: Medicare, Crime-fighting, Social Security, Defense – the Most Popular Federal Government Services*, Harris Interactive (January 14, 2010), *available at* http://www.harrisinteractive.com/NewsRoom/HarrisPolls/tabid/447/ctl/ReadCustom%20Default/mid/1508/ArticleId/257/Default.aspx.

[104] Support may not ensure survival, as evinced by vice-presidential candidate Paul Ryan's proposal to dismantle the Medicare program.

health care through insurance for most Americans.[105] One key way PPACA actualizes this goal is by is regulating private insurance, in particular the individual market. PPACA's regulation of the individual market for health insurance eliminates many of the mechanisms insurers previously relied on to select healthier applicants and limit risk pooling. For example, PPACA requires that insurers must issue coverage to all applicants ("guaranteed issue")[106] and prohibits them from excluding coverage of preexisting conditions.[107] Further, it prohibits most discrimination in pricing based on health status, by limiting the factors on which premiums for a policy may vary to only four: age (allowing variation up to a ratio of 3:1); geography; family size; and tobacco use status (allowing variation up to a ratio of 1.5:1).[108] Permitting continued rating on these factors suggests a right to health care is not absolute and that smoking or living in an area with expensive care, for example, could qualify this right. These rules, however, make individual-market policies more universally accessible and affordable, by requiring more even distribution of health risks among all individually insured, as has been the case previously for members in a group plan. PPACA also attempts to make it easier for people to find and purchase these newly-regulated private policies, by directing establishment of a state-based system of "exchanges" for individuals and small groups.[109]

In conjunction with easing access, the law requires that most Americans carry health insurance, through a provision that has become known (and loved or hated) as the "individual mandate."[110] The individual mandate requires all Americans carry "minimum essential coverage," defined as the level of coverage provided by most employer and exchange plans, or else pay a "shared responsibility payment" – a tax penalty, the amount of which is determined based on income but cannot exceed the average price of a bare-bones insurance policy on the exchange.[111] Some are exempted from the mandate and penalty for reasons including religious objection or affordability, defined as when premiums cost more than 8 percent of household income.[112] Nonetheless, the mandate will prevent adverse selection, or the tendency of healthier people to opt out of buying coverage, which might otherwise increase under PPACA because new guaranteed issue and community rating requirements enable them to buy coverage later with impunity if their health worsens. The mandate nudges both healthy and sick to buy coverage, thus diversifying risk pools and moderating premiums. The mandate can be thought

---

[105] It also addresses health care delivery and public health infrastructure. *See* Howard K. Koh & Kathleen G. Sebelius, *Promoting Prevention Through the Affordable Care Act*, 363 New Eng. J. Med. 1296, 1296–1297 (2010).

[106] PPACA § 1201, 42 U.S.C. § 300gg (2012).

[107] *Id.*

[108] *Id.*

[109] *Id.* § 1311(b), 42 U.S.C. § 18031(b) (2012).

[110] *Id.* § 1501, 26 U.S.C. § 5000A (2012).

[111] *Id.*

[112] *Id.*

of as requiring all Americans take part in this evolving system, some simply by financing care for others in their risk pools who are less lucky or healthy than they are.

Furthermore, to make coverage affordable for lower-income individuals, PPACA offers two solutions. First, it creates federal premium subsidies on a sliding scale for private insurance purchase by those who earn up to 400 percent of the Federal Poverty Level and do not have access to either Medicaid or an "adequate" and "affordable" employer plan.[113] Second, in order to cover the lowest-income Americans, PPACA expands eligibility for Medicaid to individuals earning up to 133 percent of the FPL, regardless of their age, health status, or family status, beginning in 2014,[114] growing this existing pocket of a right to health care for the poor to more people. The Congressional Budget Office initially predicted this Medicaid expansion would include about 17 million additional enrollees by 2021,[115] but subsequently lowered its estimates by about 6 million because of the Supreme Court decision on the Medicaid expansion, discussed later in the chapter.[116]

13.3.2 *New Mandated Benefits and Cost-Sharing Limits*

In addition to making insurance more accessible and affordable, PPACA creates new substantive requirements for covered benefits and policy terms, especially in the individual market but also to some degree for Medicare and Medicaid. These requirements give meaning to this expanded right to health care, creating a more consistent baseline of coverage among all insured. In essence, PPACA implicitly asserts what is substantively core to an American right to health care.

PPACA's coverage regulations do not apply uniformly to all insurance plans but should nonetheless address the greatest sources of current variability in benefits among different types of plans. For example, as part of the compromise necessary to enact the law, plans in place before September 23, 2010 are considered "grandfathered"[117] and exempted from certain PPACA regulations so long as they make only limited changes to existing benefits and cost-sharing structures.[118] But it is

---

[113] Adequate is defined as actuarial value of at least 60% and affordable is when the employee's share of premium cost is under 9.5% of income. PPACA § 1401, 26 U.S.C. § 36B (2012) (providing for "premium tax credits"); *id.* § 1402, 42 U.S.C § 18071 (2012) (providing for "cost-sharing reductions").

[114] *Id.* § 2001, 42 U.S.C. § 1396a(k) (2012).

[115] Statement of Douglas W. Elmendorf Director of Congressional Budget Office, *CBO's Analysis of the Major Health Care Legislation Enacted in March 2010* 18 (March 30, 2011) [hereinafter CBO 2011 ANALYSIS], *available at* http://cbo.gov/sites/default/files/cbofiles/ftpdocs/121xx/doc12119/03-30-healthcarelegislation.pdf.

[116] Estimates for the Insurance Coverage Provisions of the Affordable Care Act Updated for the Recent Supreme Court Decision, CONG. BUDGET OFFICE (July, 2012) [hereinafter CBO 2012 ESTIMATE] at tbl. 1, *available at* http://cbo.gov/sites/default/files/cbofiles/attachments/43472-07-24-2012-CoverageEstimates.pdf.

[117] PPACA § 1251, 42 U.S.C. § 18011 (2012).

[118] *Id.; See also* Preservation of Right to Maintain Existing Coverage, 45 C.F.R. § 147.40 (2010).

expected that many plans will relinquish grandfathered status over time and become bound by more of PPACA's regulations.[119]

One key substantive policy is a new floor of mandated benefits for non-grandfathered health plans sold in the individual or small-group markets. These "Essential Health Benefits" (EHBs) include categories such as emergency services, mental health and substance use disorder services, prescription drugs, and rehabilitative services and devices.[120] New Medicaid enrollee plans must also cover EHBs.[121] Large group and self-insured employer plans are not required to cover EHBs,[122] but given that most of these plans already do cover them, the regulations in effect align other plans with these large group policies.[123]

In addition, all non-grandfathered health insurance plans must cover certain preventive care without any cost-sharing obligations, such as screenings for breast, cervical, and colorectal cancer or alcohol-misuse and tobacco-use counseling. First-dollar coverage can be understood as defining certain services as so central to a right to health care that insurance must cover them in full to ensure everyone equal access.[124] As of March 2011, PPACA also eliminated copayments for certain preventive services for Medicare and Medicaid beneficiaries.[125] PPACA is expected to result in first-dollar coverage of preventive services for about half of all Americans by 2013, and more over time as plans relinquish the grandfathered status.[126]

Finally, the law restricts the total cost sharing a plan might impose on an insured in order to avoid erosion of insurance plan value through cost shifting. The law caps annual out-of-pocket limits for *all* private health insurance policies.[127] These caps are set at the dollar value limits in the tax code for allowable out-of-pocket spending for high-deductible health plans,[128] which are US$6,350 for individual and US$12,700 for family coverage in 2014.[129] In addition, PPACA prevents certain health plans from imposing annual or lifetime spending limits on

---

[119] Interim Final Rules for Group Health Plans and Health Insurance Issuers Relating to Coverage of Preventive Services Under the Patient Protection and Affordable Care Act, 75 Fed. Reg. 41,726, 41,732 (July 19, 2010) (estimating the number of people in grandfathered plans) [hereinafter Interim Final Rules for Preventive Services].

[120] PPACA § 1302, 42 U.S.C. § 18022(b)(1) (2012). The Secretary of Health and Human Services must define which benefits must be covered under each of these broad categories.

[121] *Id.* § 2001, 42 U.S.C. § 1396a(k)(1) (2012).

[122] *Id.* § 1201, 42 U.S.C. § 18022 (2012).

[123] PPACA § 1302, 42 U.S.C. § 18022(b)(2)(A) (2012).

[124] *Id.* § 1001, 42 U.S.C. § 300gg-13 (2012); *see* Interim Final Rules for Preventive Services, *supra* note 119, at 41,741–41,743; Koh & Sebelius, *supra* note 105, at 1296–1297.

[125] PPACA §§ 4104–4108, 42 U.S.C §§ 1395–1396 (2012); *see also* DeNavas-Walt et al., *supra* note 14, at 71 tbl.C-1 (reporting that 93 million Americans had public health insurance in 2009).

[126] Seventy-eight million in non-grandfathered plans plus 90 million publically insured will initially be covered.

[127] PPACA § 1302(c), 42 U.S.C § 18022(c) (2012).

[128] *Id.*; I.R.C. § 223(c)(2)(A)(ii) (2011).

[129] Internal Revenue Bull., Rev. Proc. 2013–25, IRS, (2013).

EHBs.[130] Finally, all plans offered by an insurer participating in a state exchange must have at least a 60 percent actuarial value with respect to EHBs, even for policies sold by that insurer outside of the exchange,[131] meaning that the plan must pay on average for 60 percent of total spending on EHBs covered under a policy. These restrictions on out-of-pocket spending ensure that insurance coverage will indeed finance a significant part of covered benefits so that beneficiaries will be able to afford and access medical care, even in cases when their medical needs are intensive.

All of these changes, together, redefine private markets as a situ for realizing more equitable access to medical care. The law requires that private insurance policies be widely available, reasonably priced, and high-value, and then provides subsidies for low-income enrollees to buy them. As was previously the case for public insurance, private insurance will take on more of the characteristics found in social insurance programs of other countries, such as tax-based financing, broad risk spreading, and access to a fairly rich range of benefits with limited cost sharing.[132] With greater similarities between the functions and characteristics of public and private coverage, the lines between and the goals of each may start to blend – both in effect and perhaps in the public's imagination. Both become key parts of a plan to guarantee a more equitable right to health care among Americans.

13.3.3 *Limitations of PPACA*

PPACA attempts to accomplish a significant expansion in health care equity, but it falls short in several respects. As noted earlier, even PPACA's provisions that serve to reshape private market coverage apply to only some policies and some benefits. In addition, PPACA ensures access to insurance, not necessarily to medical care, and could result in shortages of available physicians to treat the newly insured,[133] as occurred in Massachusetts after the state enacted a similar coverage expansion in 2006.[134] Medicaid enrollees might have particular difficulty accessing care if providers, especially specialists, increasingly refuse to care for patients because of low reimbursement rates.[135]

---

[130] PPACA § 1001, 42 U.S.C. § 300gg-11 (2012). "Grandfathered" plans are subject to the lifetime limit rule but not the annual limit rule. Self-funded plans are subject to both.

[131] PPACA § 1302, 42 U.S.C § 18022(d) (2012) (describing levels of coverage available on an exchange).

[132] Saltman, *supra* note 19, at 3.

[133] Suzanne Sataline & Shirley S. Wang, *Medical Schools Can't Keep Up*, WALL ST. J. (April 12, 2010), *available at* http://online.wsj.com/article/SB10001424052702304506904575180331528424238.html.

[134] Robert Pear, *Shortage of Doctors an Obstacle to Obama Goals*, N.Y. TIMES, April 26, 2009, at A1; MASSACHUSETTS MED. SOC., PHYSICIAN WORKFORCE STUDY – 2009, 2–3 (Sept. 14, 2009), *available at* http://www.massmed.org/AM/Template.cfm?Section=Research_Reports_and_Studies2& CONTENTID=31511&TEMPLATE=/CM/ContentDisplay.cfm.

[135] *See, e.g.*, Joanna Bisgaier & Karin Rhodes, *Auditing Access to Specialty Care for Children with Public Insurance*, 364 NEW ENG. J. MED. 2324 (2011) (finding more appointment denials and longer wait times at specialty clinics for children with Medicaid or CHIP, as compared to privately insured).

Finally, the reform does not realize a universal right. The Congressional Budget Office (CBO) estimates the law will insure about 30 million more Americans within a decade; yet, millions will remain uninsured.[136] Future uninsured are estimated to include about one-third "unauthorized immigrants," who are ineligible for Medicaid or subsidies through the exchanges, one-quarter of individuals eligible for Medicaid who do not enroll, and those who are exempted from or choose not to comply with the individual mandate.[137] Despite these limitations, PPACA does take a significant step toward defining a vision for an emerging, albeit not fully realized, right to health care.

13.4 TESTING THIS VISION FOR AN EMERGING RIGHT TO HEALTH CARE IN THE COURTS OF LAW AND PUBLIC OPINION

Unsurprisingly, in light of the way PPACA alters the distribution of health resources and challenges basic assumptions of private market ordering, the law has prompted early backlash and challenges in both the court of public opinion and courts of law. PPACA has by no means captured the American imagination yet (and may never do so). From the time of passage through implementation of the law, no more than half of Americans has viewed the reform favorably,[138] although most of its policies, when viewed individually, are highly popular.[139] Some commentators went as far as to blame PPACA for the Democratic Party's loss of majority control of the House of Representatives in the 2010 midterm Congressional elections, which occurred shortly after its passage;[140] even if only partially true, such claims reflect the perception of strong negative reactions to the law.

13.4.1 *Legal Challenges*

For the law to have any chance of having a longer impact, it first has to withstand legal challenges. Ironically, in light of the past insignificance of courts in shaping a right to health care in the United States, the courts took on a critical role in the case of PPACA: either ratify or veto PPACA's vision of an emerging right to health care. The Supreme Court had the final word and chose to ratify it (mostly).[141]

---

[136] CBO 2012 Estimate, *supra* note 116, at tbl. 1; CBO 2011 Analysis, *supra* note 114, at 18.
[137] CBO 2011 Analysis, *supra* note 115, at 1–2.
[138] *May Kaiser Tracking Poll: Views of Health Reform Law Remain Unchanged*, THE HENRY J. KAISER FAMILY FOUNDATION (May 25, 2011), *available at* http://healthreform.kff.org/en/scan/2011/may/may-kaiser-health-tracking-poll-views-of-health-reform-law-remain-unchanged.aspx.
[139] Michael J. Saks, *What Do Polls Really Tell Us About The Public's Views of The Affordable Care Act?*, HEALTH AFF. BLOG (September 21, 2012), *available at* http://healthaffairs.org/blog/2012/09/21/what-do-polls-really-tell-us-about-the-publics-view-of-the-affordable-care-act/.
[140] *See, e.g.*, Jonathan Weisman, *Loyalty to Obama Costs Democrats*, WALL ST. J., September 30, 2010.
[141] Nat'l Fed'n of Indep. Bus. v. Sebelius, 132 S. Ct. 2566 (2012).

The pieces of the law under assault were, not surprisingly, the Medicaid expansion and the individual mandate, two foundational policies for setting new baselines.[142] In fact, the individual mandate is often referred to as the "lynchpin" of the private insurance market reforms because of its role in preventing adverse selection and creating more heterogeneous risk pools, as discussed earlier.

The challengers claimed that these two provisions of the law were enacted without proper congressional authority. The states' challenge to the Medicaid expansion succeeded in part. Under a "coercion and commandeering" theory, half of the states claimed that PPACA's Medicaid policies placed untenable conditions on the states.[143] The Supreme Court has held in the past that Congress can condition states' receipt of federal funds so long as the conditions are unambiguous and do not rise to the level of compulsion.[144] The states claimed the requirement for a state to cover all individuals up to 133 percent of the FPL or lose *existing* Medicaid funding rises to the level of compulsion.[145] In other words, they claimed states had no choice but to expand their programs.

Although the expansion and new enrollees will be mostly federally funded (90–100 percent in the first decade), it does place burdens on the states, particularly given how thinly stretched states' budgets have been throughout the recent recession. Most importantly, to qualify for federal expansion funding, PPACA requires states to maintain pre-reform eligibility standards ("maintenance of effort").[146] Furthermore, it requires a state to pay its higher pre-PPACA matching share for enrollees who had been eligible under old rules but had not previously enrolled. Finally, the federal share of expansion funding could decrease over time, leaving states responsible for a growing share of the costs.

In a decision surprising to many, the Supreme Court agreed with the states' arguments, striking the provision of the law that would strip states of existing federal Medicaid funding if they failed to expand eligibility to 133 percent of FPL. No lower federal court had found these arguments compelling. Even a conservative judge dismissed the Medicaid claim as having "simply no support."[147] Nonetheless, the Supreme Court found the fact that states would lose all existing funding if opting against the expansion to rise to the level of compulsion.[148] The remedy, however, was mild in terms of impact on PPACA overall. The court simply struck the provision that said that states that failed to expand would lose current federal funding, leaving the rest of the expansion and related conditions

---

[142] CBO 2011 ANALYSIS, *supra* note 115, at 18.

[143] Florida *ex rel.* Bondi v. U.S. Dep't of Health & Human Servs., 780 F. Supp. 2d 1256 (N.D. Fla. 2011).

[144] South Dakota v. Dole, 483 U.S. 203 (1987).

[145] *See* I. Glenn Cohen & James Blumstein, *The Constitutionality of the ACA's Medicaid-Expansion Mandate*, 366 NEW ENG. J. MED. 103 (2012).

[146] PPACA § 2001, 42 U.S.C. § 13966(y)(2)(A) (2012).

[147] *See* Florida *ex rel.* Bondi v. U.S. Dep't of Health & Human Servs., 780 F. Supp. 2d.

[148] Nat'l Fed'n of Indep. Bus. v. Sebelius, 132 S. Ct. at 2603.

intact.[149] The result is that states can keep their current programs and decline federal money for expansion or expand in compliance with all of the conditions in the law and get the federal expansion funding. Because of the high value of the federal matching dollars, most states are expected to expand eligibility eventually,[150] despite early decisions to the contrary.[151]

Also unexpected by many, the individual mandate survived completely unscathed.[152] Furthermore, its survival turned on a different legal argument and court majority than anticipated. The challengers – uninsured individuals, a federation of small businesses, and twenty-six states – asserted that Congress did not have the authority under its enumerated powers to compel individuals to buy insurance they would not have otherwise purchased. In contrast, the Administration argued that Congress had the power under its authority (1) to regulate interstate commerce ("Commerce Clause" power), (2) to use means necessary and proper to carry out enumerated powers, and (3) to tax and spend for the general welfare.

Most observers thought if the mandate survived, it would be based on the Commerce Clause power, which was the argument favored by lower federal courts, scholars, and commentators, as well as explicitly asserted by Congress in the text of PPACA as the grounds for its authority.[153] The Commerce Clause power provides that Congress can regulate activities when it has a "rational basis" to conclude that the activities "taken in the aggregate, substantially affect interstate commerce."[154] The plaintiffs argued that the Commerce Clause power does not allow Congress to regulate *inactivity*. That is, an individual's decision *not* to purchase insurance is not activity contemplated by the Commerce Clause's legislative reach. The lower federal courts came to mixed decisions on this argument.[155]

In a decision surprising to many, based on lower court decisions and general buzz, the court rejected the Commerce Clause argument,[156] agreeing with the plaintiffs' inactivity/activity distinction, but found the mandate constitutional under Congress's taxing power.[157] To come to this decision, the court had to find that the mandate, which was called a "penalty" in PPACA, is in fact a tax. It did so based on the fact

---

[149] *Id.* at 2607.

[150] CBO 2012 Estimate, *supra* note 116, at 9–11.

[151] Michael Muskal, *Texas Rejects Two Pillars of New Federal Healthcare Overhaul*, LOS ANGELES TIMES (July 9, 2012, 12:24 PM), *available at* http://www.latimes.com/news/nation/nationnow/la-na-nn-texas-rejects-federal-healthcare-20120709,0,5870338.story.

[152] Amy Bingham, *Health Care Games: The Odds Are Not in Obamacare's Favor*, ABC NEWS (June 26, 2012), *available at* http://abcnews.go.com/Politics/OTUS/health-care-games-odds-obamacares-favor/story?id=16652833#.T_vl9fVKU1Q.

[153] PPACA § 1501(a), 42 U.S.C. § 18091 (2012).

[154] Gonzalez v. Raich, 545 U.S. 1, 22 (2005).

[155] *See* Brad Joondeph, *Update on Coons v. Geithner*, ACA LITIGATION BLOG (July, 2012), *available at* http://acalitigationblog.blogspot.com/ for summary of litigation in federal courts.

[156] Nat'l Fed'n of Indep. Bus. v. Sebelius, 132 S. Ct. at 2591.

[157] *Id.* at 2598; *see* Jack M. Balkin, *Tax Power: The Little Argument That Could*, CNNOPINION (June 30, 2012), *available at* http://www.cnn.com/2012/06/28/opinion/balkin-health-care/.

that the mandate is directed at taxpayers, and the enforcement mechanism occurs through the tax system, to the dismay of some Democrats who for political reasons resisted the characterization of the mandate as a new tax.[158]

Not only was the legal reasoning unexpected, but the makeup of the majority also came as a surprise. Many anticipated Justice Kennedy to cast the deciding vote;[159] Chief Justice Roberts instead played this role, joining with the four liberal Justices to uphold the mandate, despite his own conservative leanings. Although it is impossible to know why Roberts upheld the mandate, some posit he was balancing a long-term strategy to erode Congress' Commerce Clause power with a short-term desire to protect the institutional integrity of the Supreme Court, which might have been compromised if it overturned a major social reform law in a seemingly political decision. Regardless of his motivation, the Court affirmed a law that serves to expand more meaningful insurance coverage to more than 30 million more Americans.

Thus, the Supreme Court, which has historically played little role in defining or defending a right to health care, has now validated a law that envisions a much broader conception of a right to health care in the United States. This law – for both normative and political reasons – divided the Court in charged and unexpected ways. Yet it survived, perhaps foreshadowing a similar battle ahead in the court of public opinion. Professor Jack Balkin asserted that the Court affirmed a new social contract, legitimating the most major change in U.S. social policy by Congress in decades.[160] The open question is whether Americans will eventually accept and perhaps even embrace this social contract.

13.4.2 *An Opportunity to Build Consensus in the Court of Public Opinion*

Formal law, even if validated by the Supreme Court, does not necessarily lead to a change of consciousness among Americans, but it does redefine the status quo and offer a different way to think about insurance institutions. If the law survives continued legal challenges throughout implementation, political calls for repeal, and Americans' current ambivalence, as discussed later, it has the potential to begin to reshape public conceptions about the appropriate level of access to medical care for all Americans.

In particular, PPACA, over time, could change what Americans expect from private health insurance. In the past, private insurance, especially in the individual market, operated so that market forces allocated access to medical care on the basis of

---

[158] *Id.*

[159] Greg Stohr, *Kennedy's Pivotal Vote Focuses on Freedom as Court Ruling Looms*, BLOOMBERG (June 14, 2012), *available at* http://www.bloomberg.com/news/2012-06-14/kennedy-s-pivotal-vote-focuses-on-freedom-as-court-ruling-looms.html.

[160] Jack M. Balkin, *The Court Affirms Our Social Contract*, THE ATLANTIC (June 29, 2012), *available at* http://www.theatlantic.com/national/archive/2012/06/the-court-affirms-our-social-contract/259186/.

ability and willingness to pay. PPACA redefines private insurance so that it becomes a locus for more affordable and meaningful coverage and thus asserts that health insurance markets are fundamentally different than other private markets.

In light of these transformative changes to the private insurance system and the expansion of public coverage, it is possible that Americans might embrace – or at least accept – the idea that public and private insurance can and should work together to ensure greater heath care equity. PPACA asks all Americans to adopt and participate in a system of financing where those who need medical care can access it. This law could help develop a new norm of universal access to care and broader sharing of health resources, as commonly exists in countries with universal coverage.[161] The universal social insurance programs of Medicare and Social Security have only become more popular over time as Americans see the benefit of such programs for themselves, friends, or family members.[162] PPACA creates the structure for a solidarity-based system of heath care financing for all Americans. The question is whether the public consciousness will grow to accept this solidaristic norm and support a notion of sharing of health resources more collectively or whether, conversely, the law will face sustained backlash that could erode support for health solidarity. My hope is that it will create a slow evolution toward the former over time. Of course, even if it succeeds in doing so, as many of the other chapters of this book illustrate, universal access invites second-order problems, including managing costs and contentious battles over allocation of resources (i.e., rationing).

13.5 CONCLUSION

Even though Americans lack strong ground on which to make legal claims to a right to health care, legislation, including PPACA, has advanced the development of this right. PPACA establishes a structural and conceptual foundation for a broader sharing of health resources. In a country where a fragmented insurance system has resulted in inequitable access to medical care, and where private insurance excluded millions, private insurance might ironically become a strong thread in a more solid fabric of equitable coverage. PPACA's regulation of private insurance recasts it as a market supporting a social mission so that health insurance – public and private alike – can become a foundation for greater health care equity. If enduring, the law has the potential to shape how Americans experience and conceptualize health care rights and the role of public and private insurance in supporting such rights.

To many, the reform is too modest. Some will remain uninsured or underinsured. Even with insurance, some Americans might lack access to health care. And costs

[161] Saltman, *supra* note 19, at 3.
[162] *See* Humphrey, *supra* note 103 and accompanying text.

will continue to rise, putting increasing pressure on the system. Although clearly not the end of the story, PPACA is nonetheless an important chapter, outlining a vision for an emerging American right to health care. The question remains whether public consciousness will follow this vision and whether Americans might eventually espouse widespread support for a right to health care.

14

The Legal Protection and Enforcement of Health Rights in Nigeria*

Remigius N. Nwabueze

INTRODUCTION

A few statistics underscore the poor state of health and health care in Nigeria and the importance of the search for ways to protect health rights there. According to the Nigeria Demographic and Health Survey 2008, the infant mortality rate in Nigeria is 75 deaths per 1,000 live births, and the under-five mortality rate is 157 deaths per 1,000 live births.[1] This is worse than previous figures, which were already poor.[2] Only 39 percent of women gave birth with the assistance of a skilled provider; the maternal mortality ratio in Nigeria is 545 deaths per 100,000 live births; and 29 percent of children twelve to twenty-three months old did not receive any childhood immunizations.[3] Worse still, annual budgetary allocations to health care have remained at less than 5 percent of the gross domestic product,[4] and health infrastructure in Nigeria is in a general state of dilapidation. These statistics not only paint a gloomy picture of health care in Nigeria, but also highlight its potentially negative effect on Nigeria's development: a healthy nation is a wealthy nation, confirming the aphorism "health is wealth."[5] Health and development are mutually reinforcing values;[6] the WHO's Report of the Commission on Macroeconomics

* I am grateful for the insightful suggestions of colleagues that read the draft of this chapter, particularly Prof. Hazel Biggs, Dr. Ed Bates, and Dr Caroline Jones, all of the School of Law, University of Southampton. Any error or omission is mine.
1 Nigerian Population Commission, NIGERIA DEMOGRAPHIC AND HEALTH SURVEY 2008 (2009).
2 Michael Reid, *Nigeria Still Searching for Right Formula*, 86 BULL. WORLD HEALTH ORG. 663 (2008).
3 Nigerian population commission, *supra* note 1.
4 Reid, *supra* note 2, at 664.
5 World Health Organisation, MACROECONOMICS AND HEALTH: INVESTING IN HEALTH FOR ECONOMIC DEVELOPMENT 21 (2001).
6 "Health" and "health care" are used interchangeably in this chapter to refer to both medical care and other determinants of good health, although elsewhere I explored the more encompassing meaning of the former, and its unreachable depths, compared to the latter: Remigius N. Nwabueze, *Health Care*

and Health has observed that "health brings the capacity for personal development and economic security in the future. Health is the basis for job productivity, the capacity to learn in school, and the capability to grow intellectually, physically, and emotionally."[7]

Thus, African countries anxious to join the league of industrialized nations should willingly develop, embrace, and implement programs and policies designed to ensure the availability of adequate health infrastructure and supply of health services. For instance, the WHO's Report of the Commission on Macroeconomics and Health also observed that the "heavy burden of disease, and its multiple effects on productivity, demography, and education, have certainly played a role in Africa's chronic poor performance."[8]

Nigeria appreciates the dynamics of the health-development intermix; it also favors a broad conception of health, encompassing both access to health care and services and also the background conditions of good health, such as clean drinking water, sanitation, adequate nutritious food, and a clean environment.[9] Nigeria's Revised National Health Policy recognizes that "health and access to quality and affordable health care is a human right."[10] Thus, the Nigerian Constitution provides for a mix of rights to health and health care services, although such rights as articulated are not justiciable. I return to these issues in Section 14.2.2 of this chapter.

The National Health Bill 2011 intends to fill enforcement gaps in the protection of health rights. The Bill establishes a National Health System empowered to provide "for persons living in Nigeria the best possible health services within the limits of available resources"[11] and to "protect, promote and fulfil the rights of the people of Nigeria to have access to health care services."[12] This statutory enforcement of the right to health has yet to become law and, even if enacted, is conditional on the availability of resources. Given the absence of a statutory framework for the right to health, the analysis that follows focuses on the relevant constitutional provisions.

Given the centrality of health to the development of a country like Nigeria, and the dysfunctional state of health care infrastructure and services in Nigeria, one might expect the panoply of health-related guarantees under the Constitution would spur widespread litigation. Despite the non-justiciability of such rights, as argued in Section 14.3, indirect enforcement is possible through the right-to-life guarantee. However, social mobilization in favor of litigating health rights is lacking.

Law Curriculum and Scholarship in Canada, USA and England: Lessons for Nigeria, 44 L. TEACHER 32 (2010).

[7] WHO, *supra* note 5, at 21.

[8] *Id.* at 24.

[9] Aeyal M. Gross, *The Right to Health in an Era of Privatisation and Globalisation: National and International Perspectives, in* EXPLORING SOCIAL RIGHTS: BETWEEN THEORY AND PRACTICE 295 (Daphne Barak-Erez & Aeyal M. Gross eds., 2007).

[10] Federal Ministery of Health: Abuja, Revised National Health Policy 4 (2004).

[11] National Health Bill (2011), § 1(1)(c).

[12] *Id.* at § 1(1)(e).

Furthermore, even if a social movement resulted in constitutional or other legal challenge to allow the enforcement of health care rights, there are other barriers to such litigation. For example, dilatory judicial procedures,[13] the restrictive rules on standing to sue (*locus standi*), the stultification of adjudication on substantive rights by unnecessary and prolonged interlocutory appeals,[14] and the material poverty of potential health litigants all negatively affect the prospects of health rights litigation.[15]

As this is a book about health care rights, which addresses right-to-health litigation, it may seem at first blush that Nigeria has little to contribute. Indeed, legal analysts often despair at the dearth of health-related litigation in Nigeria. For example, toward the end of his analysis on the judicial enforcement of socioeconomic rights in Nigeria, Chidi Odinkalu lamented that there "is inadequate material for any serious quantitative analysis and the jurisprudence ... hardly profits rigorous analysis."[16] Nevertheless, there are a few cases in Nigeria that involve health concerns, such as those in which an accused person used their ill health to sustain an argument for bail in criminal proceedings,[17] as well as custodial cases in which prisoners alleged that their ill-health rendered their continued incarceration without treatment unjustifiable.[18] Given that these cases were primarily concerned with the enforcement of the claimants' civil and political rights, they are only tangential to the enforcement of a constitutional right to health. In essence, there is not a single reported Nigerian judicial decision that squarely raises the constitutional issue of the right to health. However, in view of the analyses in Sections 14.2, 14.3, and 14.4, the potential for such litigation exists. Thus, this chapter proposes to evaluate the prospects for health-related litigation in Nigeria and to assess its likely effects. The next section examines some of the features of health care system in Nigeria by exploring the organization and financing of health care in Nigeria. Section 14.3 examines the legal architecture of health rights in Nigeria by looking to the tier of government with constitutional responsibility for health care in Nigeria, and the constitutional

---

[13] Remigius N. Nwabueze & Polycarp C. Okorie, *Flexibility of Damages for Conversion and Detinue*, 17 Afri. J. Int'l & Comp. L. 102 (2009).

[14] Bakare v. African Continental Bank Ltd., [1986] 3 NWLR (Pt. 26) 47, 58–59 (SC) (Nigeria) (per Aniagolu, JSC).

[15] Prado also notes that poverty significantly inhibits health rights litigation by the poor in Brazil: *see* Chapter 12 in this volume. *See also* Tunde I. Ogewowo, *Self-Inflicted Constraints on Judicial Government in Nigeria*, 39 J. Afr. L. 46 (2005).

[16] Chidi A. Odinkalu, *The Impact of Economic and Social Rights in Nigeria: An Assessment of the Legal Framework for Implementing Education and Health as Human Rights*, in Courting Social Justice: Judicial Enforcement of Social and Economic Rights in the Developing World 219 (Varun Gauri & Daniel M. Brinks eds., 2010).

[17] Fawehinmi v. State, [1990] 1 NWLR (Pt. 127) 486 (Nigeria); Abacha v. State, [2002] 5 NWLR 761 (Nigeria); Ojuwe v. Federal Government of Nigeria, [2005] 3 NWLR 913 (Nigeria).

[18] Festus Odafe v. Attorney-General of the Federation, [2004] FHC/PH/CS/680/2003 (Nigeria), (unreported judgment of Justice R.O. Nwodo delivered on February 23, 2004, on file with the author); Ishmael Azubuike v. Attorny-General of the Federation, [2004] FHC/PH/CS/679/2003 (Nigeria), unreported judgment of Justice R.O. Nwodo. These cases are examined later.

recognition of health rights. In the absence of extant health-related litigation in Nigeria, Section 14.4 evaluates the prospects for such litigation in Nigeria by examining the protection and enforcement of health rights under the African Charter (as domesticated in Nigeria), and the right-to-life guarantee under the Nigerian Constitution. The final section concludes this chapter by emphasizing the urgency of the need for measures to protect health rights in Nigeria, as well as highlighting the justification for a constitutional approach to health rights in Nigeria.

14.1 ORGANIZATION AND FINANCING OF HEALTH CARE AND THE NIGERIAN NATIONAL HEALTH INSURANCE SCHEME

Before political independence in 1960, the organization and financing of health care in Nigeria was unsurprisingly colonial in nature; the system was urban-centered and focused on curative services for the personnel of the colonial administration.[19] Health care services for the rest of Nigeria were nascent to nonexistent (particularly in rural areas)[20] and focused on avoiding the spread of infectious disease. While it has launched various policy initiatives since 1960 to establish a more egalitarian health system, post-independence Nigeria has effectively inherited the colonial model of health based on privileged access to care.[21]

The organization and financing of health care in Nigeria reflects the country's federal political system based on three tiers of government – federal, state, and local.[22] Local governments are responsible for the provision of primary care and administer local dispensaries; state governments provide secondary care through public hospitals; and the federal government concentrates on tertiary care through university teaching hospitals and is responsible for the formulation of health policy for the whole country.[23] In addition, traditional healers and for-profit and licensed private health care organizations provide a significant amount of health care services: they currently account for 60–80 percent of health service provision in Nigeria.[24]

Nigeria's layered structure of health care organization and financing has been criticized as cumbersome. Public health expert Sally Hargreaves has remarked that

---

[19] Ralph Schram, A HISTORY OF THE NIGERIAN HEALTH SERVICES (1971).

[20] Israel O. Orubuloye & John C. Caldwell, *The Impact of Public Health Services on Mortality: A Study of Mortality Differentials in a Rural Area of Nigeria*, 29 POPULATION STUDIES 259 (1975).

[21] Ogoh S. Alubo, *Power and Privileges in Medical Care: An Analysis of Medical Services in Post-Colonial Nigeria*, 24 SOC. SCI. MED. 453 (1987).

[22] Michael C. Asuzu, *The Necessity for a Health Systems Reform in Nigeria*, 16 J. CMTY MED. & PRIMARY HEALTH CARE 1, 1 (2004).

[23] Federal Ministery of Health: Abuja, *supra* note 10.

[24] Hyacinth E. Ichoku & William M. Fonta, *The Distributional Impact of Healthcare Financing in Nigeria: A Case Study of Enugu State* 3 (2006) (PMMA Working Paper No. 2006–17, 2006); David Johnson, DFID Health Systems Resource Centre Country Health briefing Paper: Nigeria 3 (2000) (DFID's paper, on file with author).

Nigeria's health care system "results in chaotic coordination and communication, poor accountability, and considerable disparities throughout the country."[25] However, while Hargreaves accurately describes the current health system in Nigeria, this has not always been the case.

The 1980s witnessed the glorious days of the Nigerian health care system.[26] At that time, diagnosis and treatment of diseases at all levels of health care were rendered practically free of charge,[27] and prescriptions were also filled without charge.[28] Patients only had to pay out of pocket for prescriptions that were not available at the hospital or local dispensary, and such cases were few. It was a period that was reasonably free of fake drugs and the pharmaceutical scandals that came to characterize the Nigerian health care sector after 1985.[29] There was, however, a one-off nominal registration fee, although even the poor could afford it. This sort of "public health insurance system" that prevailed up to the early 1980s was not the result of any statutory requirement; it was rather the outcome of a deliberate and benevolent health care policy involving significant budgetary allocations to the health sector. In short, the public health care system was established and financed with government subsidies. As Ogunbekun observed: "subsidies made up as much as 90% of the revenue of public health institutions for most of the 1970s and the 1980s, a situation which was encouraged by the 'free health care' policies pursued in many states of the federation during the period from 1979 to 1983."[30] Thus, ironically, before all the talk of constitutional rights to health care, Nigeria had a well-performing health care system that has since atrophied.

Health care crises in Nigeria set in with the economic recession and implementation of International Monetary Fund and World Bank-styled structural adjustment programs in 1986.[31] The health care sector took a battering, witnessing a significant

---

[25] Sally Hargreaves, *Time to Right the Wrongs: Improving Basic Health Care in Nigeria*, 359 LANCET 2030, 2031 (2002).

[26] Idris Mohammed, ACADEMICS, EPIDEMICS & POLITICS: AN EVENTFUL CAREER IN PUBLIC HEALTH, 42–45 (2007).

[27] Orubuloye and Oni observed that in "keeping with the philosophies adopted by the various pre- and post-independence plans, modern health facilities were expanded and treatment at public health facilities was until 1984 free for those under 18, all government workers and their families; and highly subsidized for the rest of the population." Israel O. Orubuloye & Jacob B. Oni, *Health Transition Research in Nigeria in the Era of the Structural Adjustment Programme*, 6 HEALTH TRANSITION REV. 301, 302 (1996). Ogoh S. Alubo, *The Promise and Limits of Private Medicine: Health Policy Dilemmas in Nigeria*, 16 HEALTH POL'Y & PLANNING 313, 314 (2001) also observed: "At the time (1971–1980), free medical services, including food for hospitalized patients, were provided in public hospitals."

[28] Alubo, *supra* note 21, at 456.

[29] Some of the poisonous drug scandals, in which many Nigerian children died, involved adulterated paracetamol syrup and chloroquine phosphate injections: Ogoh S. Alubo, *Death for Sale: A Study of Drug Poisoning and Deaths in Nigeria*, 38 SOC. SCI. MED. 97 (1994).

[30] Ibukun O. Ogunbekun, *Which Direction for Health Care in Nigeria?* 6 HEALTH POL'Y & PLANNING 254, 255 (1991).

[31] Orubuloye & Oni, *supra* note 27, at 303–304; Ogunbekun, *supra* note 30; JOHNSON, *supra* note 24.

reduction in government health spending,[32] increases in user fees, and the introduction of high user fees where none existed previously.[33] In contrast to the universal public health care of the 1970s and early 1980s, about 70 percent of health care payments in Nigeria are currently made out of pocket.[34] Given that only 0.03 percent of the population is covered by private health insurance, this creates significant accessibility problems for the poor.[35] Moreover, Ichoku and Fonta argue that exorbitant user fees under the current system can be financially ruinous for some families, using funds needed for other essentials, and pushing families into poverty.[36]

Worse still, per capita health expenditure in Nigeria is only US$8 and "secondary health care facilities are in a prostrate condition."[37] Facilities and equipment at tertiary care centers are outdated and in decrepitude.[38] The very poor state of facilities and standard of care at public-sector clinics has brought utilization rates to an unprecedented low.[39] So bad is the situation that the mother of a sick child remarked: "[A]lthough treatment was expensive (in private hospitals) . . . taking the kids to the government hospitals is like giving them the death sentence."[40] Similarly, S. Ogoh Alubo has observed that the prevalence of fake and adulterated drugs have made Nigeria's public hospitals "veritable transit camps to the mortuary."[41] As in Brazil,[42] the collapse of the public health care sector led to the explosion of private health care facilities and medical practices in Nigeria.[43] However, inefficiency and weak regulation have compromised the quality of care in the private health sector as well.[44] Absent an alternative and efficient public health care system, therefore, those who can afford it, especially the political class, seek medical treatments abroad.[45]

---

[32] Averaging 1.6–1.9 of total expenditure of the government in the first four years of the structural adjustment program (1986–1990). *See* Ogubekun, *supra* note 30.

[33] Ogunbekun, *supra* note 30, at 256.

[34] Lloyd A. Amaghionyeodiwe, *Government Health Care Spending and the Poor: Evidence from Nigeria*, 36 INT'L J. SOC. ECON. 220, 223 (2009).

[35] Ichoku and Fonta, *supra* note 24, at 3–4.

[36] *Id.* at 14–16. *See also* Israel O. Orubuloye et al., *The Impact of Family and Budget Structure on Health Treatment in Nigeria*, 1 HEALTH TRANSITION REV. 189, 205 (1991).

[37] Federal Ministry of Health: Abuja, *supra* note 10, at 2.

[38] Un Economic and Social Council Commission on Human Rights, QUESTION OF THE VIOLATION OF HUMAN RIGHTS AND FUNDAMENTAL FREEDOMS IN ANY PART OF THE WORLD: SITUATION OF HUMAN RIGHTS IN NIGERIA 52 (1999).

[39] Johnson, *supra* note 24, at 3.

[40] ASSOCIATED PRESS, Nov. 21, 1994, quoted in Orubuloye & Oni, *supra* note 27, at 304. While the quoted observation was made in 1994, the situation is very much the same as shown by the recent analysis of Amaghionyeodiwe, *supra* note 34.

[41] Alubo, *supra* note 29, at 102.

[42] Prado, *supra* note 15.

[43] Ichoku & Fonta, *supra* note 24, at 3.

[44] Ibukun Ogunbekun, Adenike Ogunbekun & Nosa Orobaton, *Private Health Care in Nigeria: Walking the Tightrope*, 14 HEALTH POL'Y & PLANNING 174–181 (1999). A more scathing analysis of the private health sector in Nigeria is provided by Alubo, *supra* note 27.

[45] Davidson Iriekpen, *Nigeria: How Bad Can the Health Sector Be?*, THIS DAY, April 13, 2010 (page unknown).

Low budgetary allocations for health care reflect endemic corruption in the country and an embarrassing misplacement of national priorities. For instance, in 2010, the governor of Central Bank of Nigeria lamented that 25 percent of the total expenditure of the federal government was spent as the administrative costs of lawmakers who constitute only a tiny fraction of the population.[46] Similarly, the Special Rapporteur for the UN Commission on Human Rights observed that health care constituted only 4.9 percent of the federal government's total budget in 1998, compared to 9.8 percent allocated to defense, and that "resources which should have been employed in improving the health, living and education standards of the people and furthering their socio-economic rights have been diverted by corruption."[47] Unsurprisingly, the World Health Organization (WHO) ranked Nigeria's overall health system performance at 187th out of 191 member states.[48] Challenges in the Nigerian health care system are exacerbated by the globalization of health care labor market.[49] Emigration of Nigerian-trained health professionals to the developed countries of Europe and North America has negatively affected the already dysfunctional and underfunded health care system in Nigeria.[50] In 2004, for instance, estimates put Nigeria as the sixth-largest supplier of nurses to the United Kingdom and the fifth-largest supplier to the United States.[51]

In 1999, in contrast to the nonstatutory and government-subsidized public health care that flourished in the 1980s, the government established a system of health insurance as the mode of financing health care in Nigeria. With the aim that the new system would arrest further deterioration in the Nigerian health care sector and improve the delivery of health care services,[52] the National Health Insurance Scheme (NHIS) was created and established by legislation.[53] Plans for the NHIS, however, had existed as far back as 1990.[54] The NHIS is similar to many of the social

---

[46] Olalekan Adetayo et al., *25% Annual Overhead Cost Spent on Lawmakers – Sanusi*, PUNCH, Nov. 30, 2010 (page unknown).

[47] UN Economic and Social Council Commission on Human Rights, *supra* note 38, at 53–56.

[48] World Health Organisation, World Health Report (2000).

[49] Paul F. Clark, James B. Stewart & Darlene A. Clark, *The Globalization of the Labour Market for Health-care Professionals*, 145 INT'L LABOUR REV. 37 (2006), noting that the "globalization of the health-care labour market has had a profound effect on the ability of many national health-care systems to deliver vital services to their citizens. The most dramatic impact is being felt in the least developed nations, where there has been a tremendous increase in emigration."

[50] *Id.* at 49.

[51] James Buchan & Julie Sochalski, *The Migration of Nurses: Trends and Policies*, 82 BULL. WORLD HEALTH ORG.587 (2004); Donna Kline, *Push and Pull Factors in International Nurse Migration*, 35 J. NURSING SCHOLARSHIP 107 (2003); Clark, Stewart & Clark, *supra* note 49, at 43–44.

[52] Editorial (Health Insurance Report), *Repositioning the National Health Insurance Scheme (NHIS) for Effective Take-Off: From Policy to Action*, 7 HEALTH INSURANCE REPORT 1, 2 (2005).

[53] National Health Insurance Scheme Act (2004) Cap. (N42) (Nigeria) (while the Act was enacted in 1999, the scheme became operative in 2005).

[54] Ogunbekun, *supra* note 30, at 259–260. NHIS was even traced back to 1962 by Ireh Iyioha, *Medical Negligence and the Nigerian National Health Insurance Scheme: Civil Liability, No-Fault or a Hybrid Model?* 18 AFR. J. INT'L & COMP. L. 46, 49 (2010).

health insurance schemes that exist in Europe, relying on regulation of not-for-profit and/or for-profit insurers to ensure affordable insurance for all (see Chapter 7 in this volume). The objectives of the NHIS are to

(1) ensure access to high-quality health care services;
(2) protect families from the burden of large medical bills;
(3) control the rise in the cost of health care services;
(4) ensure equitable distribution of health care costs among income groups;[55]
(5) maintain a high standard of health care delivery services;
(6) ensure efficiency in health care services;
(7) improve and harness private-sector participation in the provision of health care services;
(8) ensure adequate distribution of health facilities in Nigeria;
(9) ensure equitable patronage of all levels of health care; and
(10) ensure the availability of funds to the health sector for improved services.[56]

The Act establishes a Governing Council to administer and manage the scheme[57] and provides for the registration of health care providers and health maintenance organizations (HMOs).[58] Services covered by the scheme include:

(11) defined curative care;
(12) prescription drugs;
(13) diagnostic tests;
(14) maternity care for up to four live births for every insured person;
(15) preventive care (including immunization, family planning, prenatal and postnatal care) consultation with defined specialists;
(16) hospital care;
(17) eye examination and care (excluding eye test and spectacles); and
(18) a range of prosthesis and defined dental care.[59]

Funding for the scheme comes from the contributions of employers (including the government), employees, and voluntary contributors (including self-employed people and rural dwellers).[60] Employees contribute a percentage of their salaries, which the employer deducts from their wages and pays to the relevant HMO.[61] Under current NHIS guidelines, employees contribute 15 percent of their basic salaries, and

[55] National Health Insurance Scheme Act (2004) Cap. (N42), § 5(a–d).
[56] *Id.* § 5(e–j).
[57] *Id.* § 2.
[58] *Id.* § 18, 19.
[59] *Id.* § 18(1)(a–h).
[60] *Id.* at N42, § 16–17.
[61] *Id.* at § 16(2).

two-thirds of that 15 percent are contributed by employers.[62] The federal government is, however, "responsible for payment of the contributions in respect of members of the Armed Forces, the Nigerian Police Force, Nigerian Customs Service, Nigerian Immigration Service, Nigerian Prisons Service and such other deferral uniformed services as the Minister may . . . specify."[63]

Despite some progress, the NHIS has so far failed to achieve its objectives. The NHIS is not mandatory – employers are not required to provide coverage to their employees and presently the NHIS only covers 3 percent of the population.[64] The NHIS also discriminates against people whose contributions are not government-funded, for example unemployed or self-employed rural dwellers.[65] This provokes the objection that the NHIS is significantly elitist.[66] Equally, the NHIS is neither universal nor comprehensive, and limits care to the list of essential drugs and diagnostic tests approved by the NHIS, so that patients must completely pay out of pocket for health care services not on the list.[67] Underenrollment in the NHIS stems partly from the unwillingness of states to join the program, presumably to avoid employers' contributions under the scheme: so far, only two (Bauchi and Cross River States) out of the thirty-six states of the federation have joined the NHIS.[68] All of these shortcomings mean that the NHIS has failed the tripartite test of breadth, depth, and height of coverage identified by the WHO as the fulcrum of any universal health coverage.[69]

14.2 LEGAL ARCHITECTURE OF HEALTH RIGHTS IN NIGERIA

14.2.1 *Constitutional Responsibility for Health Care in Nigeria*

Despite the complexity of health care financing in Nigeria, it is still necessary to identify the seat of constitutional responsibility for health, at least in order to properly

---

[62] See Felicia N. Monye, *An Appraisal of the National Health Insurance Scheme of Nigeria*, 32 COMMONWEALTH L. BULL. 415 (2006).

[63] National Health Insurance Scheme Act (2004) Cap. (N42), § 44.

[64] Wole Oyebode, *Pharmacists Fault NHIS Implementation*, THE GUARDIAN, Nov. 2, 2010 (page unknown); Gabriel Enogholase, *Nigeria's Health System Ranks 197 of WHO's 200 Nations – NHIS*, Vanguard, October 28, 2010 (page unknown), observing that "4.5 million enrolees are now accessing their healthcare through the Scheme." Nigeria's population is estimated to be 150 million.

[65] Monye, *supra* note 62, at 427.

[66] Reuben Abati, *Nigeria's Problematic Health Insurance Scheme*, THE GUARDIAN, Jan. 17, 2010 (page unknown), observing: "Without any doubt, the NHIS over which so much air has been split is a programme for the elites. Providing a non-discriminatory, broad-based healthcare opportunity for all Nigerians should be the overriding objective."

[67] Iyioha, *supra* note 54, at 51.

[68] Abati, *supra* note 66.

[69] The World Health report 2008, Primary Health Care: Now More Than Ever, WHO, 25–28 (2008). *See also* The World Health report, Health System Financing: The Path to Universal Coverage, WHO (2010).

inform litigants contemplating judicial enforcement of their health rights, as well as locating the appropriate authority against which activists might mobilize for the realization of health rights. In despair on this point, the Revised National Health Policy observed that "the 1999 Constitution fell short of specifying what roles the various levels of government must play in the national health care delivery system."[70]

Nigeria operates a Presidential Constitution (1999) that entrenches a federal system of government and involves, among other things, the distribution of legislative powers between the federal and state governments.[71] Under section 4(2) of the Constitution, the federal government, through the National Assembly, can legislate on all matters listed in part one of the second schedule to the Constitution, otherwise known as the Exclusive Legislative List. The federal government also shares legislative competence with the states in relation to matters listed in part two of the second schedule to the Constitution, otherwise known as the Concurrent Legislative List. Under section 4(7) of the Constitution; any matter not included on the Exclusive Legislative List and the Concurrent Legislative List falls within the exclusive legislative sphere of the states.[72] Thus, residual matters, logically more numerous than the enumerated legislative items on both the Exclusive and Concurrent Legislative lists, are left for the exclusive legislative competence of the state governments through each state's House of Assembly.[73]

Neither the Exclusive nor the Concurrent Legislative list mentions health specifically.[74] Logically, therefore, health should be a residual matter within the legislative competence of the states. Thus, the House of Assembly of a given state should have exclusive legislative authority over health matters, such as access to care and medical treatment. However, certain provisions and interpretations of the Constitution create ambiguity on this question. For instance, item 68 of the Exclusive Legislative List gives the National Assembly exclusive legislative competence over matters "incidental and supplementary to" those specifically mentioned on the list.[75] These specific matters include drugs and poisons, immigration, insurance, nuclear energy, prisons, labor, and quarantine, all of which have significant health implications. Accordingly, the National Assembly can legislate on health issues arising from these specific (legislative) items as an incidental exercise of its express powers.[76] A good example of health legislation emerging as an incidental exercise of power over

---

[70] Federal Ministry of Health: Abuja, *supra* note 10, at 50.
[71] Nigeria has thirty-six states and a Federal Capital Territory.
[72] Of course, conflict between the federal and state government in relation to the Concurrent Legislative List is mediated through the famous doctrine of covering the field.
[73] In *Attorney-General of Ogun State v. Attorney-General of the Federation*, [2002] 2 NCLR 116 (Nigeria), the Supreme Court held that the National Assembly has no power to make law on residual matters.
[74] Federal Ministry of Health: Abuja, *supra* note 10, at 50.
[75] In *Balewa v. Doherty*, [1963] 1 WLR 949 (Nigeria), a case originating from Nigeria, the Privy Council narrowly interpreted the phrase "incidental and supplementary" powers, so that it should not be taken to give rise to a separate and independent power of legislation.
[76] *Id.*

a non-health subject matter is item 17(a) of the Concurrent Legislative List, which authorizes federal legislation on issues relating to labor and health of employees, interstate commerce, and transportation.[77] In other words, health legislation might arise from the exercise of federal powers over labor or employment issues. Moreover, if one gives a robust interpretation to item 60(a) of the Exclusive Legislative List, which grants the federal government powers for "the establishment and regulation of authorities for the Federation or any part thereof – to promote and enforce the observance of the Fundamental Objectives and Directive Principles contained in this Constitution," then the reach of the federal government into health care grows considerably.[78]

14.2.2 *Constitutional Recognition of the Right to Health*

The Constitution's most explicit provision on the right to health care in Nigeria is section 17(3)(d), which guarantees "adequate medical and health facilities for all persons." However, falling as it does under Chapter Two of the Constitution, it is nonjusticiable.

Chapter Two – the Fundamental Objectives and Directive Principles of State Policy – was borrowed from the Indian Constitution (1948) and made its debut in the 1979 Constitution.[79] Although Chapter Two is nonjusticiable,[80] its provisions may be relied on as interpretive tools in constitutional debates.[81] Furthermore, the appalling statistics around access and health outcomes, discussed earlier, inspire a search for a means by which to give teeth to Chapter Two.

The argument in favor of the traditional approach to health as a constitutional issue is that health care requires the allocation of scarce resources and this justifies its status of non-justiciability.[82] However, arguments based on insufficient resources

---

[77] Under item 17(a) of the Concurrent Legislative List, the Federal government could make laws for Nigeria or any part of it with respect "to the health ... of persons employed to work in factories, offices or other premises or in inter-State transportation and commerce including the training, supervision and qualification of such persons."

[78] Such a robust interpretation was given to the provision by the Supreme Court of Nigeria in Attorney-General of Ondo State v. Attorney-General of the Federation, [2002] 9 NWLR (Pt. 772) 222 (Nigeria). For strident criticism of this decision, *see* Ben O. Nwabueze, THE JUDICIARY AS THE THIRD ESTATE OF THE REALM 169–204 (2007).

[79] It has also been retained in chapter two of the current Nigerian Constitution (1999).

[80] Archbishop Okojie v. The Attorney-General of Lagos State, [1981] 2 NCLR 337 (Nigeria); Badejo v. Federal Minister of Education, [1990] LRC (Const.) 735 (Nigeria).

[81] Ben O. Okere, *Fundamental Objectives and Directive Principles of State Policy under the Nigerian Constitution*, 32 INT'L & COMP. L. Q. 214, 223–225 (1983). *See also* Damisha v. Speaker, House of Assembly, Benue State, [1983] 4 NCLR 625 (Nigeria).

[82] For instance, FEDERAL REPUBLIC OF NIGERIA, REPORT OF THE CONSTITUTION DRAFTING COMMITTEE CONTAINING THE DRAFT CONSTITUTION, 1 Lagos: Federal Ministry of Information (1976), observed that "by their (Fundamental Objectives and Directive Principles in Chapter Two of the Constitution) nature, they are rights which can only come into existence after the Government has provided facilities for them. Thus, if there are facilities for education or medical services one can speak of the 'right' to

are not to be exaggerated. Commentators have observed, among other things, that corruption and kleptocracy, rather than limited resources, are to blame for the inadequate health services in Nigeria.[83]

Interestingly, the Supreme Court of Nigeria has begun to develop a window of enforceability for the provisions of Chapter Two of the Constitution (including the right to health). Thus, in *Attorney-General of Ondo State v. Attorney-General of the Federation*, the Supreme Court adopted a liberal construction of the Constitution which suggests that a relevant federal legislation could make Chapter Two provisions enforceable:

> As to the non-justiciability of the Fundamental Objectives and Directive Principles of State Policy in Chapter 11 of our Constitution, section 6(6)(c) says so. While they remain mere declarations, they cannot be enforced by legal process but [it] would be seen as a failure of duty and responsibility of State organs if they acted in clear disregard of them. . . . But the Directive Principles (or some of them) can be made justiciable by legislation.[84]

This suggests that the right to health under Chapter Two of the Constitution is indirectly justiciable, that is, by means of executing legislation. Thus, should the federal government pass legislation providing for needed insurance, medical infrastructure, and such like, it is possible that such legislative provisions may be interpreted through the lens of Chapter Two so as to bolster health rights.

14.3 FRAMEWORKS FOR PROTECTING AND ENFORCING THE RIGHT TO HEALTH

The preceding analysis indicates that there is no direct and justiciable right to health under the Nigerian Constitution, a deficiency exacerbated by the absence of legislation providing access to universal and reasonably comprehensive health care. This section attempts to fill the gap by analyzing possible strategies for litigating and enforcing health rights in Nigeria. One of the possible strategies is to deploy the African Charter on Human and Peoples' Rights as a basis for articulating health rights in Nigeria. Another strategy, which has found favor with Indian courts, is to embed the right to health within the right to life, which is enforceable under the Nigerian Constitution. This section concludes by examining a few recent cases in Nigeria that have followed the latter approach.

such facilities. On the other hand, it will be ludicrous to refer to the 'right' to education or health where no facilities exist."

[83] Obiajulu Nnamuchi, *Kleptocracy and Its Many Faces: The Challenges of Justiciability of the Right to Health Care in Nigeria*, 52 J. Afr. L. 1–42 (2008); Shedrack C. Agbakwa, *Reclaiming Humanity: Economic, Social, and Cultural Rights as the Cornerstone of African Human Rights*, 5 Yale Hum. Rts. & Dev. L. J. 177, 188–191 (2002).

[84] *See* Attorney-General of Ondo State v. Attorney-General of the Federation, [2002] 9 NWLR 382 (Nigeria) (SCN, per Uwaifo, JSC).

14.3.1 *Right to Health in Nigeria through the African Charter*

The African Charter on Human and Peoples' Rights (the African Charter or Charter) was developed as a regional response to egregious human rights abuses perpetrated by some post-independence African political leaders.[85] The Charter also sought to remedy the non-prioritization of human rights in the Organization of African Unity (OAU) (an organization since replaced by the African Union in 2002).[86] OAU members adopted the African Charter on June 27, 1981, and it entered into force on October 21, 1986.[87] Without reservations, Nigeria domesticated the Charter by enacting the African Charter on Human and Peoples' Rights (Ratification and Enforcement) Act.[88] Unlike most international human rights instruments, which bifurcate civil and political rights on the one hand and socioeconomic rights on the other,[89] the African Charter adopted an integrated approach to human rights protection.[90] The right to health under the African Charter is guaranteed in Article 16:

> 1. Every individual shall have the right to enjoy the best attainable state of physical and mental health.

> 2. State Parties to the present Charter shall take the necessary measures to protect the health of their people and to ensure that they receive medical attention when they are sick.

On account of the generality and fluidity of Article 16, and other rights protected under the African Charter, B.O. Okere, a Nigerian legal scholar and expert in international human rights law, doubted not only the "immediacy of enjoyment of these rights" but also "the efficacy of these provisions. These socioeconomic rights are purely exhortatory, resembling the Fundamental Objectives and Directive Principles of State Policy under the Nigerian Constitution."[91] With respect to the

---

[85] Oji U. Umozurike, THE AFRICAN CHARTER ON HUMAN AND PEOPLES' RIGHTS (1997) [hereinafter Umozurike, THE AFRICAN].

[86] Gino I Naldi, *Future Trends in Human Rights in Africa: The Increased Role of OAU?*, in THE AFRICAN CHARTER ON HUMAN AND PEOPLES' RIGHTS: THE SYSTEM IN PRACTICE 1986–2000 1–35 (Rachel A. Murray & Evans Malcolm eds., 2002); Ben O. Okere, *The Protection of Human Rights in Africa and the African Charter on Human and Peoples' Rights: Comparative Analysis with the European and American Systems*, 6 HUM. RTS. Q. 141, 142–145 (1984); Chidi A. Odinkalu, *Analysis of Paralysis or Paralysis by Analysis? Implementing Economic, Social, and Cultural Rights under the African Charter on Human and Peoples' Rights*, 23 HUM. RTS. Q. 327 (2001).

[87] African Charter on Human and Peoples' Rights, adopted June 27, 1981, O.A.U. Doc. CAB/LEG/67/3/Rev. 5, reprinted in Report of the Secretary General on the Draft African Charter on Human and Peoples' Rights, O.A.U. Doc. CM/1149 (XXXVII) (Annex I1) (1981); 21 I.L.M. 58 (1982).

[88] African Charter on Human and Peoples' Rights Act (Ratification and Enforcement) (1990) Cap. 10.

[89] Peter Cumper, *Human Rights: History, Development and Classification*, in HUMAN RIGHTS: AN AGENDA FOR THE 21ST CENTURY (Angela Hegarty & Siobhan Leonards eds., 1999).

[90] For analysis of right to health under major international human rights instruments, *see* Gross, *supra* note 9.

[91] Okere, *supra* note 86, at 174.

right to health, there are concerns about its conceptualization, the procedures for its enforcement, and its constitutional status in Nigerian domestic law. While the following analysis attempts to flesh out these objections, it should be noted at the outset that domestic litigation on the African Charter is relatively infrequent.[92] However, as observed by Frans Viljoen, the handful of domestic cases in Nigeria under the African Charter nevertheless provides the strongest judicial expression of the impact of the Charter on domestic legal systems.[93]

14.3.1.1 Conceptual Ambiguity

The first objection is that the sheer open-endedness of Article 16 creates problems for judicial enforcement.[94] However, the sting of this objection is significantly diluted by the analysis of the African Commission on Human and Peoples' Rights in the famous case of *Social and Economic Rights Action Centre (SERAC) v. Nigeria*, in which the African Commission welcomed the "opportunity to make clear that there is no right in the African Charter that cannot be made effective."[95] In that case, the complainant alleged that the Nigerian government violated several provisions of the African Charter, including Article 16, as a result of Nigeria's oil exploration activities and repressive military operations in the Niger Delta region, which is inhabited mainly by the Ogoni people. Exploration of the oil reserves in the Niger Delta and several military incursions in the area (to quell civilian opposition to the degradation of Ogoniland resulting from the exploration) created a complete state of devastation, as well as severely contaminating the environment of the Ogoni people, including their water, fish, and land. Thus, the complaint alleged wide-ranging violations of the rights of Ogoni people under the African Charter.

In *SERAC*, the African Commission confronted the argument that socioeconomic rights under the Charter, including Article 16, lack definable minimum core obligations that are susceptible to immediate enforcement. Thus, it observed that "social and economic (rights) – generate at least four levels of duties for a state that undertakes to adhere to a rights regime, namely the duty to respect, protect, promote and fulfil these rights."[96] These core minimum duties involve both negative and positive dimensions.[97] For instance, while the "duty to respect" entails negative forbearance by the state from interference with the enshrined rights, the

---

[92] F. Viljoen, *Application of the African Charter on Human and Peoples' Rights by Domestic Courts in Africa*, 43 J. AFRI. L 1–17 (1999).

[93] *Id.* at 7.

[94] Stanley Ibe, Beyond Justiciability: Realising the Promise of Socio-economic Rights in Nigeria, 7 AFRI. HUM. RTS. L.J. 225, 229 (2007); Agbakwa, supra note 83, at 193.

[95] Social and Economic Rights Action Centre (SERAC) v. Nigeria, [2001] 1 AFI. HUM. RTS. RPTS., at 60, 73. Note, however, that the judgment of the African Commission is not binding on parties to the Charter.

[96] *Id.* at 66.

[97] *Id.*

"duty of protection" is a positive obligation on the state, through legislation and other effective measures, to protect right-holders against other subjects. This may include the creation and maintenance of a framework or environment conducive to the exercise of Charter rights. Similarly, just as the "duty to promote" relates to measures undertaken to maximize the enjoyment of Charter rights, such as the promotion of tolerance and the raising of awareness, the "duty to fullfil" speaks to the expectation on states to create machinery for the actual realization of Charter rights. Thus, *SERAC* established Article 16 as more than purely aspirational, giving it a definable and minimum core obligation that is immediately enforceable in Nigeria.

14.3.1.2 Lack of Domestic Enforcement Framework

The second objection to the African Charter relates to the absence of any special procedural framework for the enforcement of its provisions in Nigeria. Counsel for the State latched onto this "lacuna" in *Nemi v. State*.[98]

However, the Supreme Court had previously declared in *Ogugu v. State* that the African Charter is enforceable in Nigerian High Courts through the relevant High Court Rules.[99] The Supreme Court in *Ogugu* rejected the defendant's argument that "because neither the African Charter nor its Ratification and Enforcement Act has made a special provision . . . for the enforcement of its human and people rights within a domestic jurisdiction, there is a lacuna in our laws for the enforcement of these rights."[100] Thus, the Supreme Court held that the domestication of the African Charter entailed that "the enforcement of its provisions like all our other laws fall within the judicial powers of the courts as provided by the Constitution and all other laws relating thereto."[101]

In *Abacha v. Fawehinmi*, the Supreme Court (per Ogundare JSC), went further to hold that the Fundamental Rights (Enforcement Procedure) Rules – that is, the procedural framework for the enforcement of civil and political rights – might be used to enforce the provisions of the African Charter in Nigeria.[102] Similarly, in *Oruk Anam L.G. v. Ikpa*, the Court of Appeal held that the African Charter is enforceable in Nigeria through the process of originating summons.[103] Consequently, all arguments relating to the procedural inapplicability of the Charter in Nigeria appear untenable.

---

[98] Nemi v. State, [1996] NWLR (Pt. 452) 42 (SC) (Nigeria) – Bello CJN however held that since the Charter had become part of Nigeria's domestic law, the enforcement of its provisions fell within the judicial powers of the courts as provided by the Nigerian Constitution.
[99] Ogugu v. State, [1994] 9 NWLR 1, 27 (Nigeria).
[100] *Id.* at 26.
[101] *Id.*
[102] Abacha v. Fawehinmi, [2000] 6 NWLR 228, 293–294 (Nigeria).
[103] Oruk Anam L.G. v. Ikpa, [2003] 12 NWLR 558 (Nigeria).

14.3.1.2.1 STATUS OF AFRICAN CHARTER IN NIGERIAN DOMESTIC LAW The last, and probably most significant, obstacle to the enforcement of health rights in Nigeria through the African Charter concerns the constitutional status of the Charter in Nigeria. In other words, granted that the Charter is domestically enforceable in Nigeria in relation to health rights, does it rise to the level of a constitutional norm? If the Charter has constitutional character, some significant consequences would follow; for instance, it would be a basis for challenging restrictive or unfavorable health legislation. Furthermore, constitutional status for the Charter in Nigeria would spur demands for a positive right to health care.

The Supreme Court of Nigeria considered some of these issues in the important case of *Abacha v. Fawehinmi*.[104] In that case, a detainee under a military decree that ousted the jurisdiction of courts to question detentions ordered by the military government (as was common during the military dictatorship in Nigeria) argued that the jurisdiction of the court to entertain his case under the African Charter was unaffected by the provisions of the decree. To decide this issue, the Supreme Court had to consider the status of the African Charter in Nigeria's hierarchy of laws. Ogundare JSC observed:

> No doubt Cap. 10 (the legislation that domesticated the African Charter) is a statute with international flavour. Being so, therefore, I would think that if there is a conflict between it and another statute, its provisions will prevail over those of that other statute for the reason that it is presumed that the legislature does not intend to breach an international obligation. To this extent I agree with their Lordships of the Court below that the Charter possesses "a greater vigour and strength" than any other domestic statute. But that is not to say that the Charter is superior to the Constitution.... Nor can its international flavour prevent the National Assembly, or the Federal Military Government before it [to] remove it from our body of municipal laws simply by repealing Cap. 10. Nor also is the validity of another statute [to] be necessarily affected by the mere fact that it violates the African Charter or any other treaty, for that matter.[105]

The first part of the preceding quotation emphasizes the strength and preference accorded the African Charter compared to domestic legislation, but the remainder of the quotation embodies limitations and exceptions that dilute that emphasis. On this basis, it is likely that the African Charter is not a constitutional norm. Second, and consequently, it is not a norm of validity, in the sense of having potential to invalidate other statutes. Third, the legislature could simply repeal the Charter through appropriate legislation. Moreover, *Abacha v. Fawehinmi* implies that the African Charter is inferior to a decree:[106] Ogundare JSC held that the Charter was

---

[104] Abacha v. Fawehinmi, [2000] 6 NWLR 228, 293–294 (Nigeria).
[105] *Id.* at 289.
[106] Designation of laws enacted by the ruling military government in Nigeria.

applicable in that case only because a relevant decree did not effectively suspend it.[107] In his dissenting judgment, however, Belgore JSC (as he then was) observed that the decree in question effectively suspended both the African Charter and Chapter Four of the Constitution, at least by implication. Otherwise, the African Charter would "have run counter to the Decree of the Military which in essence makes the Charter void."[108] While the majority in *Abacha v. Fawehinmi* was prepared to accord the African Charter a pride of place in the Nigerian legal order, it did not elevate the Charter to the status of a constitutional norm. As domestic legislation, therefore, the Charter offers a veritable platform for demanding health rights in Nigeria, but the Charter does not impose a constitutional duty on the government concerning health care.

14.3.2 *Right-to-Life Guarantee Embeds Right to Health*

The right to life is guaranteed under section 33(1) of the Constitution: "Every person has a right to life, and no one shall be deprived intentionally of his life, save in execution of the sentence of a court in respect of a criminal offence of which he has been found guilty in Nigeria." In addition to the exceptions to this right outlined by section 33(2),[109] the saving clause of section 33(1) clearly shows that the right to life is not an absolute guarantee.[110] Obviously, the right to life is rarely meaningful in the absence of background conditions of good health, such as clean drinking water, sanitation, adequate nutritious food, clean environment, and access to health care and services.[111] Thus, at the international level, article 12(2) of the International Covenant on Economic, Social, and Cultural Rights recognizes that the right to health goes beyond the provision of medical services and encompasses the conditions necessary for life to flourish:

> The steps to be taken by the States Parties to the present Covenant to achieve the full realization of this right shall include those necessary for:
>
> (a) The provision for the reduction of the stillbirth-rate and of infant mortality and for the healthy development of the child;
> (b) The improvement of all aspects of environmental and industrial hygiene;

---

[107] Abacha v. Fawehinmi, [2000] 6 NWLR 228, 292 (Nigeria), particularly Iguh, JSC, at 304.

[108] *Id.* at 299.

[109] Section 33(2) Nigerian Constitution (1999): "A person shall not be regarded as having been deprived of his life in contravention of this section, if he dies as a result of the use, to such extent and in such circumstances as permitted by law, or such force as is reasonably necessary – (a) for the defence of any person from unlawful violence or for the defence of property; (b) in order to effect a lawful arrest or to prevent the escape of a person lawfully detained; or (c) for the purpose of suppressing a riot, insurrection or mutiny."

[110] Kalu v. State, [1998] 13 NWLR (Pt. 583) 531 (Nigeria).

[111] Gross, *supra* note 9, at 295.

(c) The prevention, treatment and control of epidemic, endemic, occupational and other diseases;
(d) The creation of conditions which would assure to all medical service and medical attention in the event of sickness.

With judicial creativity, it is possible to adopt an interpretive approach to section 33 of the Constitution that is sufficiently purposive and expansive to also encompass protections for health. Nigerian courts have not taken this route so far, and the major cases on right to life focus on the constitutional validity of a death sentence.[112] However, the suggested approach potentially yields formidable protections for health rights in Nigeria. Regrettably, Nigerian courts have at times held that the right to life merely protects physical existence.[113]

Arguably, the innovative interpretation of section 33 involves minimal judicial activism, because the Nigerian Supreme Court has declared a liberal and purposive approach as the mantra of its constitutional interpretation.[114] In this regard, the Indian constitutional experience is uniquely exemplary for Nigeria, not only because the Fundamental Objectives and Directive Principles of State Policy in the Nigerian Constitution was, as explained earlier, extracted from the Indian Constitution,[115] but also because the Indian Constitution, like its Nigerian counterpart, made the Fundamental Objectives and Directive Principles of State Policy non-justiciable.[116]

In contrast to Nigeria, however, Indian courts have held that the right to life under the Indian Constitution encompasses protection for the background conditions of good health, as well as ensuring access to required medical services.[117] The philosophy that animates Indian judicial activism in the enforcement of socioeconomic rights was explained extrajudicially by the former Chief Justice of the Indian Supreme Court, P. N. Bhagwati: "We in India are trying to move away from formalism and to use juristic activism for achieving . . . 'social justice'. Let me make clear that the objective for which we are trying to use juristic activism is realization of social justice."[118] As concerns the right to life, specifically, Bhagwati opined that this "expanding right has encompassed, through a process of judicial interpretation . . . the right to live with basic human dignity."[119] Similarly, Shylashri

---

[112] Kalu v. State, [1998] 13 NWLR (Pt. 583) 531 (SC) (Nigeria).
[113] Ezeadukwa v. Maduka, [1997] 8 NWLR 635 (CA) (Nigeria).
[114] The most definitive statement of this principle is Nafiu Rabiu v. Kano State, [1980] 8–11 SC 130 (Nigeria) (per Sir Udo Udoma, JSC, at 148–151, and Idigbe, JSC, at 195).
[115] India Const. Part IV.
[116] India Const. Part IV, art. 37.
[117] Sheetal B. Shah, *Illuminating the Possible in the Developing World: Guaranteeing the Human Right to Health in India*, 32 VAND. J. TRANSNAT'L L. 435 (1999).
[118] P. N. Bhagwati, *Judicial Activism and Public Interest Litigation*, 23 COLUM. J. TRANSNAT'L L. 561, 566 (1985).
[119] *Id.* at 567. Some of the relevant cases that support this extra-judicial proposition include: F C Mullin v. Union Territory, (1981) 2 S.C.R. 516, 523 (India); Parmanand Katara v. Union of India, A.I.R. 1989 S.C. 2039 (India); CESC Ltd. v. Subhash Chandra Bose, A.I.R. 1992 S.C. 573 (India); Paschim Banga Khet Mazdoor Samity v. Sate of West Bengal, (1996) 3 S.C.J. 25 (India).

Shankar and Pratap B. Mehta observed that "using the notion of a right to life with dignity, judges expanded the ambit of health to include physical, social, and mental well-being and aimed at the policy goals of a healthy environment, nutrition, and socioeconomic justice."[120] A similar approach in Nigeria will not only enliven the equivalent constitutional guarantee in Nigeria; it will also do away with the judicial restriction of the right to life to issues of death penalty and the sustenance of mere animal existence. Recent trends show that Nigeria is already inclining toward the Indian approach.

14.3.2.1 Reinterpreting the Right to Life in Nigeria

Reverberations of the Indian approach are already noticeable in some unreported decisions of High Courts in Nigeria. In *Jonah Gbemre v. Shell Petroleum Development Co. Nigeria and 2 Ors*,[121] for instance, the applicants, members of the the Iwherekan community in Delta State of Nigeria, complained that flares from the defendant's oil and gas explorations were injurious to their health and environment, and caused food insecurity. They alleged a violation of their fundamental rights under the Nigerian Constitution (sections 33 – life, and 34 – dignity of human person) and the African Charter (Arts 4, 16, and 24). Interestingly, the applicants specifically sought a declaration that the right to life protected under section 33 of the Nigerian Constitution, as well as the right to the dignity of the human person guaranteed under section 34 of the Nigerian Constitution, "includes the right to a clean poison free, pollution free, and healthy environment."[122] The Court accepted this expanded conception of the right to life, observing that "these constitutionally guaranteed rights (right to life and right to the dignity of human person) inevitably include the right to clean, poison-free, pollution-free healthy environment."[123] The Court proceeded to hold that the "actions of the . . . respondents in continuing to flare gas in the course of their oil exploration and production activities in the applicants' community is a gross violation of their fundamental right to life (including healthy environment) and dignity of human person as enshrined in the Constitution."[124] This is a radical departure from the narrow approach to right to life adopted by appellate courts in Nigeria.[125] While there appears to be no extant appeal in *Gbemre*, the flurry

---

[120] Shylashri Shankar & Pratap B. Mehta, *Courts and Socioeconomic Rights in India*, in COURTING SOCIAL JUSTICE, *supra* note 16, at 154.

[121] Jonah Gbemre v. Shell Petroleum Development Co. Nigeria and 2 Ors, [2005] Suit No. FHC/B/CS53/05 (Nigeria) (unreported judgment of the Federal High Court of Nigeria, Benin Division, delivered on 14 November 2005) – on file with the author.

[122] *Id.*

[123] *Id.* Although this case does not consider the issue of whether the Constitution is applicable to a private entity, Shell was probably presumed to be a state actor because the federal government has an interest in its operations in Nigeria. For a detailed analysis of the problem (horizontality), *see* Remigius N. Nwabueze, *Securing Widows' Sepulchral Rights Through the Nigerian Constitution* 23 HARV. HUM. RTS. J. 141–155 (2010).

[124] *Id.*

[125] For instance, Ezeadukwa v. Maduka, [1997] 8 NWLR 635 (CA) (Nigeria).

of litigation expected to follow in its wake (instituted by other oil communities in Nigeria) has also not materialized. Although *Gbemre* goes against the tenor of appellate decisions on the right to life, it is possible to rationalize it on different grounds. For instance, in none of the current (reported) appellate decision on the right to life was the court specifically asked to extend the meaning of the right to life to include the protection of health and background conditions of good health. Furthermore, reported appellate decisions on the right to life in Nigeria have not explicitly denied that the right to life requires the protection of health. Regrettably, the Court in *Gbemre* did not engage in this type of analysis and distinctions, nor did it seriously discuss the meaning and scope of the right to life under the Nigerian Constitution. Nevertheless, the intuition of the Court is right and its conclusion is justifiable on the premises adumbrated earlier in the chapter. In effect, *Gbemre* creates opportunities for the judicial enforcement of health rights in Nigeria through the right to life.

A similar approach was taken by the Federal High Court (Port Harcourt Division) in *Azubike v. Attorney General of the Federation and 3 Ors.*[126] In that case, the applicants were convicts on death row awaiting their executions. They argued that supervening mental retardation rendered their continued incarceration unconstitutional. Thus, they alleged that their continued detention on death row in a state of mental incapacity violated their right to human dignity under section 34 of the Constitution, as well as their right to medical treatment under the Prison Act 1972.[127] While the Court observed that there was no significant evidence or proof to sustain the applicant's claim under section 34 of the Constitution, it nevertheless held that the applicants were entitled to appropriate medical and psychiatric treatment under the Prison Act. Consequently, the court observed that "clearly the Applicants are suffering from various grades of mental disorder and regardless of the fact that they are condemned, by the provisions of Prisons Act s.7 and s.8 they are entitled to be treated and have a right to good health and life until the sentence is executed."[128]

While the Court did not expressly invoke the right-to-life guarantee in this case, the preceding quotation suggests that the relevant provisions of the Prison Act and the order of the Court in that regard are justified by the constitutional protection of health through the right-to-life guarantee.

Again, in *Festus Odafe v. Attorney General of the Federation and 3 Ors,*[129] the Federal High Court was asked to determine whether the continued detention of prison inmates awaiting trial, who were diagnosed with HIV/AIDS but had no access to medical care, amounted to torture, cruel, and inhuman treatment under section 34 of the Constitution. Nwodo J accepted the argument that the applicants'

---

[126] Azubike v. Attorney General of the Federation and 3 Ors, [2004] Suit No. FHC/PH/CS/679/2003 (Nigeria) (unreported judgment of Justice R.O. Nwodo delivered on Feb. 23, 2004, on file with the author).

[127] Nigerian Prison Act (1990) Cap. 366. (Nigeria).

[128] Azubike v. Attorney General, [2004] Suit No. FHC/PH/CS/679/2003, 16 (Nigeria).

[129] Festus Odafe v. Attorney General of the Federation and 3 Ors, FHC/PH/CS/680/2003 (Nigeria).

section 34 rights, and also their rights under article 16 of the African Charter, which guarantees access to medical treatment for the applicants, were violated by their deprivation of medical treatment for HIV/AIDS. Of more interest for this chapter, however, is the Court's assessment of applicants' argument that their continued detention in prison without access to health care for their HIV/AIDS condition violated their right to life under section 33 of the Constitution. Beyond the observation that "this submission is too simplistic to uphold," it is not easy to comprehend Nwodo J's reasoning on this point. In any event, his outright dismissal of this fundamental point is quite unjustifiable. Remarkably, Nwodo J held that applicants' complaint regarding lack of access to health care for their HIV/AIDS condition was justified by article 16 of the African Charter (right to health) and the Prison Act (requiring medical treatment for prisoners); however, he held that the defendant did not violate the applicants' right to life under section 33 of the Constitution. In other words, a situation of illness, short of death, does not amount to a violation of the constitutional right to life:

> The Applicants I agree have a right to life; however, the fact [is] that the Applicants are in the custody of the 2nd and 4th Respondents awaiting trial and suffering from illness. The 2nd to 4th Respondents are under a duty to provide medical attention for them; failure to do so is a non-compliance with the provisions of s.8 Prison Act and Article 16 of the African Charter on Human and Peoples Right. *The nature and detailed consequences of the virus is not placed before the court for me to arrive at the conclusion that the non-compliance is an infringement of their right to life. In other words, that if treatment is provided they will live; if not provided they will die.* This is for an expert in the medical area concerned to tell the court and there is no expert evidence before me.[130] (emphasis added)

In the emphasized portion of the preceding quotation, it is evident that Nwodo J relapsed into the traditional analytical model for right to life in Nigeria; that is, a constitutional guarantee limited to the protection of mere physical or animal existence, infringed only by the occasion of death or imminent death. Regrettably, Justice Nwodo's observation is in dissonance with the expansive view on right to life that the Court in *Gbemre* adopted.

14.4 CONCLUSION: WHY THE NEED TO PROTECT AND ENFORCE HEALTH RIGHTS IN NIGERIA?

The health statistics highlighted in the Introduction of this chapter show that questions of access and health inequalities in Nigeria are serious and compel the search for solutions, including whether litigation of a right to health could be a positive force for change. Although the Constitution accepts both the social determinants of health and health care itself as important governmental objectives, it prima facie

---

[130] *Id.* at 12.

provides no ability for patients to enforce these rights. However, there is hope from both international law and international precedent. For instance, Article 16 of the African Charter could protect health rights in Nigeria, and with judicial creativity, Nigerian courts could expand the right to life to include protections for health rights, as per the approach in India.

However, we must ask, why constitutionalize or seek enforceable health rights in Nigeria? After all, as the other chapters in this volume show, none of developed nations such as Canada,[131] the United Kingdom,[132] or the United States[133] protects the right to health on a constitutional basis, yet their citizens and residents enjoy a relatively high standard of health care.

There are two responses to this criticism. First, no legislation in Nigeria provides anything that approximates to universal, comprehensive, and accessible health care for Nigerians. Thus, the right to health is not secured even on a statutory basis. As the Section 14.2 shows, the NHIS is not performing satisfactorily, and the National Health Bill 2011 is yet to pass into law. In any event, the Bill establishes only a progressively realizable and highly resource-dependent right to health. In fact, provision of health care under the Bill depends on the discretion of the government, rendering health care a product of state beneficence.[134] The analysis in Section 14.2 shows that the state is unlikely to exercise its discretion for the benefit of Nigerians, for reasons ranging from corruption to lack of political will. In the same vein, Leslie London warns against a move away from the discourse of health as a right to reframing it as mere service delivery, noting that such "reframing of health away from its nature as a socio-economic right strips health policy-making of its inherent elements of power and the contestation that goes with the recognition of power."[135] Thus, the government needs a push in the form of a judicially enforceable (constitutional) right to health. Whether the government will obey a relevant order of the court is another matter that merits a separate chapter.[136] Suffice it to say that governmental disobedience of court orders is not uncommon in Nigeria.[137] The key point is that the Constitution must fill gaps created by the non-statutory protection of health rights in Nigeria.

---

[131] Flood (Chapter 3 in this volume).

[132] Newdick (Chapter 4 in this volume).

[133] Hoffman (Chapter 13 in this volume).

[134] Of course, this will fall short of the immediately enforceable and minimum core obligations on health imposed by Art 12 of the ICESCR and Art 16 of the African Charter as interpreted by SERAC's case, *supra* note 95.

[135] Leslie London, *What Is a Human Rights-Based Approach to Health and Does It Matter*, 10 HEALTH & HUM. RTS. 65, 71 (2008).

[136] For instance, Gloppen observed that "affirming rights at the formal level does not necessarily bring changes on the ground. To realistically assess the accountability potential of health rights litigation, we need to know to what extent the judgments are accepted and implemented and under what circumstances litigation brings changes to health systems and policies"; Siri Gloppen, *Litigation as a Strategy to Hold Governments Accountable for Implementing the Right to Health*, 10 HEALTH & HUM. RTS. 21, 22 (2008).

[137] *See, e.g.*, Ojukwu v. Governor of Lagos State, [1986] 1 NWLR (Pt. 18) 621 (Nigeria).

Second, despite the return to civil rule in 1999, there is no democratic account-ability or political legitimacy in Nigeria.[138] Elections are rigged.[139] Referring to the 2003 elections in Nigeria, Lewis observed that there was abundant "evidence of large-scale rigging, fraud, and intimidation in many parts of the country. Observers noted numerous instances of unqualified voters; ballot-stuffing or theft; failure to deliver materials to opposition wards; intimidation by party thugs, vigilantes, or police; falsification of tally sheets and declaration forms."[140] Absent electoral accountabil-ity, therefore, elected political officeholders and leaders do not feel any obligation toward the public.[141] This partly explains the wide scale and institutionalized cor-ruption in Nigeria. For instance, the Special Rapporteur of the UN Commission on Human Rights observed that just a tiny fraction of stolen funds recovered from a for-mer military Head of State in Nigeria (General Sani Abacha) was twice the budget of four big federal ministries in Nigeria (including health and education).[142] This political situation will not lead to an adequate and efficient health system without a constitutional obligation. Thus, Leslie London was right to observe that a human rights approach to health carries the advantage of "defining who is a rights holder, who is a duty bearer, and what the nature of the obligation is, allows a much clearer opportunity to establish accountability (typically of government) for the realization of rights and creates a range of mechanisms to hold government accountable."[143]

Similarly, although Gloppen opined that there was "inadequate knowledge base for assessing the accountability potential of health rights litigation,"[144] he acknowl-edged a general view that such litigation is effective and offered some analytical tools for measuring the impact of health rights litigation.[145] Therefore, while I do not argue that a constitutional guarantee of health rights is the best way to ensure availability of and access to a universal and comprehensive health system, it does provide a platform for social mobilization and a basis for legal claims.

---

[138] Stephen M. Omodia, *Elections and Democratic Survival in the Fourth Republic of Nigeria*, 3 J. PAN AFR. STUD. 35–42 (2009); Afro Barometer, Performance and Legitimacy in Nigeria's New Democracy 1–14 (July, 2006) (unpublished manuscript, on file with author).

[139] Karen E. Ferree, *The Social Origins of Electoral Volatility in Africa*, 40 B.J. POL. S. 759, 767 (2010); Michael Bratton, *Second Elections in Africa*, 9 J. DEMOCRACY 51–66 (1998); a less pessimistic view of elections in Africa is projected by STEFFAN I. LINDBERG, DEMOCRACY AND ELECTIONS IN AFRICA (2006).

[140] Peter M. Lewis, *Nigeria: Elections in a Fragile Regime*, 14 J. DEMOCRACY 131, 141 (2003).

[141] Barometer, *supra* note 138, at 11.

[142] Economic and Social Council Commission on Human Rights, *supra* note 38, at 57–62.

[143] London, *supra* note 135, at 68.

[144] Gloppen, *supra* note 136, at 32.

[145] *Id.* at 21–36.

15

Litigating the Right to Health in Venezuela

A *"justiciable"* (?) *Right in the Context of a Deficient Health Care System*[*]

Oscar A. Cabrera and Fanny Gómez[**]

INTRODUCTION

In 1998, Venezuela began a major process of social and political transformation with the election by popular vote of President Hugo Chávez,[1] who won by a wide margin, and the adoption of the 1999 Constitution by a constitutional assembly created by popular referendum. Despite the robust substantive social provisions contained in this Constitution, including a constitutional right to health and its correlative state's obligations, an effective realization of the right to health has not been achieved. This is in part attributable to a deficient, underfunded, non-regulated and non-coordinated public health system. Considering the results yielded by health-related litigation, particularly since 2004, it is unlikely that litigation will have an impact in addressing the deficiencies of the public health system.

In 1999, Venezuela's highest court handed down a decision that would pioneer the adjudication of social and economic rights. The now extinct Supreme Court of Justice[2] ordered the Ministry of Health to provide universal access to treatment to all persons living with HIV in the country, and, although compliance with this and other HIV-related decisions that followed has been deficient, the ruling was very

[*] The authors wish to acknowledge the invaluable editorial support and research assistance of Carlos A. Herrera and David Mielnik. The authors also wish to thank Colleen Flood, Aeyal Gross, and Marcelo Rodríguez for their feedback and comments on earlier versions of this chapter. All the mistakes and omissions remain our own.
[**] Her contribution appearing in this volume reflects only her views and those of the coauthor and not those of the IACHR or the Organization of American States.
[1] On March 5, 2013, Venezuelan Vice President Nicolás Maduro announced that President Hugo Chávez had passed away after a long battle with cancer. This article examines the situation of health care and health rights litigation during the past fourteen years of Venezuelan constitutional history.
[2] The 1999 Constitution of the Bolivarian Republic of Venezuela, which entered into force in March 2000, substituted the Supreme Court of Justice with the Supreme Tribunal of Justice.

progressive.[3] In 2004, the Supreme Tribunal of Justice (TSJ) had the opportunity of continuing on this path as a regional reference in economic and social rights adjudication, similar to what the Colombian Constitutional Court did four years later.[4] Instead, a pro-government majority of justices in the Constitutional Chamber of the TSJ handed down an extremely narrow interpretation of the right to health. In a constitutional claim (*amparo*), plaintiffs argued that the failing public health care system, and in particular lack of availability and deficient quality of public health care facilities, goods, and services, amounted for a violation of fundamental rights, including the right to health. Against the international progressive trend, the TSJ determined that public policies are not subject to judicial review. As we examine in this chapter, this decision may hinder the impact that litigation may have on reducing inequities and improving health outcomes. Litigation in areas such as access to treatment for HIV, health care services for children with congenital heart defects, and interruption of public health services have sought to contribute to health equity by addressing issues of availability, accessibility, and quality. However, in most of these cases, implementation by public health care entities involved remains a challenge.

A considerable number of judicial decisions regarding health do not address the merits of the matter. Nonetheless, they highlight the deficiencies of the system in areas such as quality of public health care facilities, goods, and services, as well as access to information and the state's obligation to produce reliable statistics on basic health indicators. Litigation concerning health rights has not been sufficient to offset the failures of health care in Venezuela, which stem from systemic structural problems. On this note, the vast majority of complaints received by the Office of the Public Defender (Ombudsperson) in 2010 regarding the public health care system relate to availability, accessibility, and acceptability.[5]

A fragmented, underfunded, and underregulated public health care system continues to be at the root of the problems associated with the delivery of health care in Venezuela. Government expenditure on public health has been generally low. The health care system has undergone successive back-and-forth radical reforms that, far from fostering the government's ability to address the most pressing public health problems, have undermined its capacity to fulfill many of its obligations related to the right to health. The disintegrated and poorly coordinated health care

---

[3] TSJ, Politico-Administrative Chamber (SPA), Cruz Bermudez et al. v. Ministerio de Sanidad y Asistencia Social (MSAS), Decision No. 915, File No. 15789 (July 15, 1999) (Venez.), *available at* http://www.ghhrdb.org/judgments/Cruz%20del%20Valle-Venezuela-1999.pdf.

[4] Constitutional Court (C.C.), Precautionary Measures: Manuel José Cepeda Espinoza, Judgement T-760/08 (July 31, 2008) (Colom.); Alicia E. Yamin, Oscar Parra-Vera & Camila Gianella, *Judicial Protection of the Rights to Health in Colombia: An Elusive Promise?, in* LITIGATING HEALTH RIGHTS: CAN COURTS BRING MORE JUSTICE TO HEALTH? 103 (A. E. Yamin & S. Gloppen eds., 2011); *see also* Oscar A. Cabrera & Ana S. Ayala, *Advancing the Right to Health Through Litigation, in* ACHIEVING THE HUMAN RIGHT TO HEALTH, chap. 5 (José M. Zuniga & Lawrence O. Gostin eds., 2013).

[5] Defensoría del Pueblo, Republica Bolivariana de Venezuela, Informe Anual 2010 [Yearly Report 2010], (March, 2011) (Venez.), *available at* http://www.defensoria.gob.ve/dp/phocadownload/userupload/publicaciones/informes_anuales/DdP_Informe_Anual_2010.pdf.

system is aggravated by the absence of a law regulating it. More than thirteen years have passed without the state enacting a comprehensive health act or executing a coherent, lasting public health policy. In this context, the Venezuelan government has been unable to provide services that are affordable, of quality, and accessible, and has also failed to have adequate prevention and promotion health programs and plans.[6] The administration's attempt to address these deficiencies has been through "social missions." Although social missions have considerably reduced the health equity gap, at least in the delivery of primary health care, they have serious structural challenges stemming from their conceptualization. These include their inability to tackle the underlying issues, the duplication of efforts, lack of integration with the existent public health system, their political imprint which challenge sustainability, as well as the reduced availability of facilities, goods, and services.

In this chapter we start by providing information on the main features of the health care system in Venezuela, examining the structure of the system as well as statistical data. This background will inform the legal sections that address not only the constitutional and statutory regulation of the right to health but also health rights–based litigation. In order to provide an accurate assessment of the current state of health rights litigation in Venezuela we also address overarching issues related to the independence of the judiciary, and its effect on health rights adjudication.

15.1 MAIN FEATURES OF VENEZUELA'S HEALTH CARE SYSTEM

15.1.1 *Available Statistics: Basic Health Indicators and Expenditures on Health*

In 2011, Venezuela's population was 27,227,930 people.[7] In terms of the basic health indicators, the World Health Organization's (WHO) 2011 *World Health Statistics Report* shows Venezuela is behind the WHO Americas Region Averages (RA).[8] In detail, life expectancy at birth was 78 years for females and 71 for males (RA: 79/73); adult mortality for both sexes was 146 (92 for females and 196 for males) per 1,000[9] (RA: 125 for both sexes). Child mortality was once substantially lower than the RA (during the 1990–2005 period: 30 per 1,000 live births vs. a RA of 40), but as the regional indicator fell to 18 deaths per 1,000 live births in 2010, Venezuela has not gone any further than that and is now on par with the RA.[10]

---

[6] Provea, Informe Anual, Situación de los Derechos Humanos en Venezuela [The Situation of Human Rights in Venezuela] (Oct. 2010 – Sept. 2011) (Venez.), *available at* http://www.derechos.org.ve/informes-anuales/informe-anual-2011.

[7] Instituto Nacional de Estadística, Republica Bolivariana de Venezuela, *Resultados basicos*, XIV CENSO NACIONAL DE POBLACIÓN Y VIVIENDA 2011, (Aug. 9, 2012) (Venez.), *available at* http://www.ine.gob.ve/documentos/Demografia/CensodePoblacionyVivienda/pdf/ResultadosBasicosCenso2011.pdf.

[8] World Health Organization (WHO), WORLD HEALTH STATISTICS 2011, *available at* http://www.who.int/whosis/whostat/EN_WHS2011_Full.pdf.

[9] *Id.* at 52.

[10] *Id.* at 70.

In terms of the availability of health care facilities, goods, and services, Venezuela has a small health care workforce, with 19.4 physicians per 10,000 people (RA: 22.5) and, more dramatically, only 11.3 nurses per 10,000 inhabitants (RA: 61.5).[11] Also, the number of hospital beds per 10,000 inhabitants has declined from 13 in 2007 to 11 in 2009.[12] According to the WHO, Venezuela's total expenditure on health care as a percentage of the GDP has oscillated between 5.4 percent and 6 percent in the past ten years.[13] In 2008, the administration announced the creation of a special fund through which oil revenues surplus would finance the health care system up to the point where total expenditure constituted 10 percent of the GDP (such spending is yet to be attained).[14] Compared to other countries in the region, Venezuela spends a low percentage of total expenditure on health care in relation to its GDP: for example, in 2008, the total expenditure on health care was 5.4 percent of the GDP, while the RA for the same year was 12.6 percent.[15] In OECD countries, the average of total expenditure on health in relation to GDP was also significantly higher: 8.5 percent for 2008.[16] In per capita terms, the government's expenditure on health care in Venezuela was only US$307 for 2008,[17] whereas countries in the region were well above: Argentina: US$757, Brazil: US$385, Chile: US$479, Colombia: US$434, Cuba: US$473,[18] and Uruguay: US$619.[19]

15.1.2 *Venezuela's Health Care System*

Venezuela's health care system can be described as a "mixed national system," comprising three subsystems: (1) a public system; (2) a social health insurance system, combining mostly public funding and employees and employers contributions; and (3) a privately financed sector.[20] Given the sources of funding, Venezuela's health care system would be most accurately described as a two-tiered – public and a private – system, because the social security subsystem is mostly publicly funded.

[11] *Venezuela (Bolivarian Republic of) Statistics Summary (2002 – present)*, WHO, *available at* http://apps.who.int/gho/data/node.country.country-VEN?lang=en.
[12] *Id.*
[13] *Id.* (Total expenditure on health as a percentage of GDP. However, government expenditure on public health increased by 65% for the year 2011). *See also* Situación de los Derechos Humanos en Venezuela, *supra* note 6.
[14] Situación de los Derechos Humanos en Venezuela, *supra* note 6, at 160.
[15] Venezuela (Bolivarian Republic of) Statistics Summary (2002–present), *supra* note 11 (total expenditure on health as a percentage of GDP).
[16] *Id.* (Observed data: Average of total expenditure on health). Out of the total expenditure on health in Venezuela for the year 2008, public expenditure accounted for 44.9% – the RA being 49.4%. In turn, expenditure on social security represented 31.4% of total expenditure on health for 2008, while the average for the region of the Americas was 29% for that same year.
[17] WHO, World Health Statistics 2011, at 135.
[18] *Id.* at 129.
[19] *Id.* at 135.
[20] María Helena Jaén et al., Costo de la Salud en Venezuela [The Price of Health in Venezuela] 28, 46 (2006) (Venez.).

15.1.2.1 The Public Health Care System: Structure and Functioning

The Venezuelan public health system has a complex functioning structure. The system has three sources in charge of administering and providing health care in the country: (1) the Ministry of Health, (2) other state institutions, and (3) state-financed "social missions" directed to provide primary health care.

The Ministry of Health provides most of the funding for the public health system, and it has twenty-four offices in different states in Venezuela,[21] fifteen of which are characterized by the government as "decentralized."[22] The ministry works as a decentralized health care system with hospitals and outpatient centers (*ambulatorios*).[23] Venezuelan states receive funding for health care from the federal government through the national budget and through the general allocation of funds to states, as the Constitution mandates (article 85), from which each state directs a percentage to health care. States also receive funding directly from the Ministry of Health.[24]

Following an unsuccessful attempt to centralize the health care system in 1987,[25] Venezuela reversed course in 1989 and began a process of decentralization in many areas, including health care. This process led to the enactment of the 1989 Decentralization and Transfer of Public Competencies Act.[26] This resulted in the transfer from the federal government to state governments of a variety of health care functions, including the delivery of public health services and the coordination of the

---

[21] Ministerio del Poder Popular para la Salud, Gobierno Bolivariano de Venezuela, Memoria 2008, [Memory 2008] (Feb. 2009) (Venez.), *available at* http://www.ovsalud.org/doc/MEMORIAMPPPS2008.pdf.

[22] These fifteen decentralized states in terms of health care are: Aragua, Mérida, Táchira, Lara, Monagas, Nueva Esparta, Carabobo, Sucre, Trujillo, Anzoátegui, Apure, Yaracuy, Bolívar, Falcón and Zulia. *See also* Ministerio del Poder Popular para la Salud, Gobierno Bolivariano de Venezuela, Memoria 2011 [Memory 2011] (Jan. 2012) (Venez.), *available at* http://www.derechos.org.ve/pw/wp-content/uploads/Memoria-2011MPPS.pdf.

[23] Pan American Health Organization (PAHO), División de Desarrollo de Sistemas y Servicios de Salud, *Perfil del Sistema de Servicios de Salud de la República Bolivariana de Venezuela* [A Profile of the Health Services System of the Bolivarian Republic of Venezuela], *in* PROGRAMA DE ORGANIZACIÓN Y GESTIÓN DE SISTEMAS Y SERVICIOS DE SALUD, 5 (2nd ed., 2001) (Venez.).

[24] *Id.* at 5; *see also* María Helena Jaén, EL SISTEMA DE SALUD EN VENEZUELA: DESAFÍOS [THE HEALTH SYSTEM: CHALLENGES] 37 (2001) (Venez.).

[25] The reform process of the health system in Venezuela began in 1987 with the adoption of the National System of Health Act providing for the centralization of health care services. *Ley Orgánica del Sistema Nacional de Salud*, OFFICIAL GAZETTE No. 33.745 (June 23, 1987) (Venez.). This legislation sought the gradual integration over the course of ten years of the Ministry of Health and all government agencies in charge of health care in the country (*see infra* the IVSS, the IPASME, the IPSFA), as well as a process of reform of this ministry. However, owing to a variety of factors, including political instability, there was little political will for reform and to implement the changes required by this act. Marino J. Gonzalez R., *Reformas del Sistema de Salud en Venezuela (1987–1999): balance y perspectivas* [Reforms of the Health System in Venezuela (1987–1999): Balance and Perspectives], NACIONAL UNIDAS CEPAL – SERIE FINANCIAMIENTO DEL DESARROLLO 111 (June, 2001) (Venez.), *available at* http://www.eclac.org/publicaciones/xml/0/7110/lcl1553e.pdf.

[26] *Ley Orgánica de Descentralización y Transferencia de Competencias del Poder Público*, Official Gazette No. 4.153(E) (Dec. 28, 1989) (Venez.).

efforts to secure appropriate nutrition. Following the 1999 major overhaul with the new Constitution, several bills have been put forward attempting to regulate the system. In 2007, President Hugo Chávez announced a new reform of the health care system,[27] calling on the centralization of the health care system. This clearly contravenes the 1999 Constitution, which established that the state would be responsible for creating a decentralized health care system. This back-and-forth approach on the centralization and decentralization has had a profound negative effect on the public health care system. Not only the scarcity of resources but also – and specifically – the unequal and inefficient distribution of those scarce resources are the defining features of contradictory health care policies on centralization/decentralization. The Venezuelan public health care system has been characterized as "fragmented, poorly coordinated, excessively centralized and inequitable,"[28] and as "disintegrated and incoherent . . . [with] grave deficiencies in its institutional design."[29] These criticisms remain valid to the present day.

The public health care system is also underfunded. The absence of a fair and adequate budget affects not only the capacity of the government to provide adequate health care to the population but also the quality of the services provided.[30] The Office of the Ombudsperson has received recurrent complaints relating to the lack of adequate medical equipment and medicines,[31] insufficient number of health care providers and medical staff, inadequate health care settings denial of medical care, and a limited availability of specialized services for treating the most vulnerable populations.[32] Also, as examined, Venezuela's public health care system suffers from grave deficiencies in budget and allocation of resources. An inefficient public care health system forces those who can afford it to go to the private health care system for certain services.[33]

---

[27] AFP, *Chávez Anuncia Centralización del Sector de Salud en Venezuela* [*Chávez Anounces Centralization of the Health sector in Venezuela*], EL UNIVERSO (April 24, 2007, 16:31), *available at* http://www. eluniverso.com/2007/04/24/0001/14/C26982B6F2EE4D3A9F53A2491662DB8D.html.

[28] Antonio J. Trujillo, *Petro-State Constraints on Health Policy: Guidelines for Workable Reform in Venezuela*, 67 HEALTH POL'Y 39 (2004).

[29] Jaén, *El Sistema de Salud en Venezuela*, *supra* note 24, at 36.

[30] PROVEA Informe Anual, Situación de Los Derechos Humanos en Venezuela [The Situation of Health Rights in Venezuela] 40 (Oct. 2004 – Sept. 2005) (Venez.), *available at* http://www.derechos. org.ve/pw/wp-content/uploads/06_alimentacion.pdf.

[31] Desiree Prieto, AFP, Gobierno y ciudadanos buscan superar escasez de medicinas en Venezuela [Government and Citizens Seek to Overcome Shortage in Medicines in Venezuela], GLOBOVI-SION.COM (June 20, 2012, 01:42:45), http://globovision.com/articulo/afp-gobierno-y-ciudadanos-buscan-superar-escasez-de-medicinas-en-venezuela. There is a severe shortage of medicines. In this regard, the government announced in July 2012 the creation of Farmapatria, a network of pharmacies that will offer medicines at 40% of the cost in private pharmacies. Detractors of this initiative indicate that this measure will not be effective because it does not address the shortage of medicines on the market.

[32] Defensoría del Pueblo, Informe Anual 2010, supra note 5.

[33] In 2005, 45% of the complaints by patients in the public sector reveal that patients must attend the private sector for "laboratory tests, x-rays, CAT scans and electrocardiograms." In 2005, 364 complaints

Several public entities finance, regulate, and provide health services. These public institutions are the Ministry of Health, the Venezuelan Institute of Social Security (*Instituto Venezolano de Seguridad Social*, IVSS),[34] the Institute of Social Security of the Ministry of Education (IPASME), the Institute for Social Security of the Armed Forces (IPSFA), and the states' governments.[35] Additionally, the Ministry of Justice finances health care in penitentiary centers and the Ministry of Urban Development finances the construction of health centers.[36]

The government is also directly involved in the delivery of primary health care through "social missions." These are state-financed programs created by the executive to address deficiencies in the delivery of social services, including health care. The "missions" main objective is reaching the poorest sectors of the population, traditionally overlooked by previous administrations.[37] The most relevant social mission concerning the delivery of health care is called *Misión Barrio Adentro* (delivering mostly primary health care services),[38] but there are other social missions that provide health care services.[39] The state oil company PDVSA directly finances all these missions, including *Misión Barrio Adentro* (*Barrio Adentro*).[40]

---

in 97 public hospitals were filed concerning issues such as shortage of basic and surgical materials, closure of operating rooms, and inadequate and poor supply of foods for patients. PROVEA INFORME ANUAL 2004–2005, *supra* note 30, at 128, 136. By 2010, the number of complaints had risen to 486. PROVEA INFORME ANUAL, SITUACIÓN DE LOS DERECHOS HUMANOS EN VENEZUELA [THE SITUATION OF HEALTH RIGHTS IN VENEZUELA] , 173 (Sept. 2009–Dec. 2010) (Venez.).

[34] The IVSS is a centralized and independent entity that runs the social security system in Venezuela through the financing and provision of health services in hospitals and outpatient centers. PAHO, *Perfil del Sistema de Servicios de Salud de la República Bolivariana de Venezuela*, *supra* note 23, at 5. The IVSS delivered health services to 57% of the population in 1997. Basic Health Indicator Database, PAHO (2011), *available at* http://www.paho.org/English/DD/AIS/cp_862.htm (select Venezuela).

[35] JAÉN, EL SISTEMA DE SALUD, *supra* note 24, at 36.

[36] PAHO, Perfil del Sistema de Servicios de Salud de la República Bolivariana de Venezuela, *supra* note 23, at 5.

[37] Other missions focus on other social aspects such as education, land tenure, indigenous peoples, environment, and housing, among others. Embassy of the Bolivarian Republic of Venezuela to the United States, *Fact Sheet: Social Missions in Venezuela* (Nov. 12, 2009), *available at* http://venezuela-us.org/live/wp-content/uploads/2009/08/socialmissionsinvenezuela-12.11.09eng.pdf. *See also* Inter-American Commission on Human Rights (IACHR), OEA/Ser.L/V/II., Doc. 54, ¶ 1045 (Dec. 30, 2009), *available at* http://www.cidh.oas.org/countryrep/Venezuela2009eng/VE09.TOC.eng.htm.

[38] This social program was meant to be implemented in three phases: Barrio Adentro I (BA-I), Barrio Adentro II (BA-II), and Barrio Adentro III (BA-III). BA-I, launched in 2003, was in charge of delivering primary health care through health centers in communities; BA-II was launched in June 2005 with the main objective of establishing 600 comprehensive diagnostic centers, 30 high-technology centers, and 600 Rehabilitation Centers. It was reported that this goal was only 50% accomplished in 2007. BA-III was launched with the main objective of modernizing 33 public hospitals. As of 2007, it was reported that this process had only reached 3 hospitals. *See* Yolanda D'Elia & Luis Francisco Cabezas, Las Misiones Sociales en Venezuela [The Social Missions in Venezuela], 11 (May 2008) (Venez.), *available at* http://www.ovsalud.org/doc/Las_Misiones_Sociales_en_Venezuela.pdf.

[39] *Misión José Gregorio Hernández* (focusing on providing health services for persons with disabilities), *Misión Niño Jesús* (created to provide prenatal maternity care), *Misión Milagro* (eye surgery needed for health reasons, mostly removal of cataracts), and *Misión Sonrisa* (dental health).

[40] PAHO, Misión Barrio Adentro: The Right to Health and Social Inclusion in Venezuela 12 (July 2006), *available at* http://www.paho.org/English/DD/PUB/BA_ENG_TRANS.pdf.

According to the Ministry of Health, the first phase of implementation of *Barrio Adentro* (BA-I) reached 17 million people – a government estimate of 63 percent of the population.[41] However, Datanálisis, an independent survey company, reports that at its best (2004) BA-I reached 7.2 million people or 30 percent of the population.[42] Since 2007, *Barrio Adentro* has deteriorated: many centers have closed, and the number of health care professionals working there declined.[43] In September 2009, President Chávez declared a nationwide sanitary emergency when it was reported that out of 4,298 primary health care facilities that were part of *Barrio Adentro*, 2,149 had been abandoned and 1,119 were only working part time.[44] When interviewed, the Minister of Health identified "excessive centralization" as the main problem affecting the government's health plan.[45] Also, former health ministers published an open letter listing some of the causes contributing to *Barrio Adentro*'s collapse, which include: dissatisfaction within the communities because of obstacles in access and the lack of quality of the services provided; the 65 percent reduction, in 2008, of the budget available to all twenty-one social missions; the worsening of the conditions of the health care facilities because of lack of maintenance; the lack of articulation of *Barrio Adentro* within the National Health System, which resulted in efforts and resources duplicated and inefficiently allocated; and the general lack of transparency in the allocation and management of the resources.[46]

Regarding the overall effectiveness of *Barrio Adentro*, the Inter-American Commission on Human Rights (IACHR), noted that "although civil society organizations have recognized the contribution of *Misión Barrio Adentro* to expansion of the medical ranks in the poorest sectors, the IACHR was informed that such efforts have not sufficed to offset deficiencies in the public health system."[47] The social missions delivering health care services, especially *Barrio Adentro*, are criticized because they have fragmented the public health system even further by establishing a parallel system for the supply and delivery of health care services.[48] Also, the political imprint attached to these social missions is a major threat to their effectiveness,

[41] D'Elia & Cabezas, *supra* note 38.

[42] *Id.* at 8.

[43] PROVEA Informe Anual, Situación de Los Derechos Humanos en Venezuela 136–37 (Oct. 2008–Sept. 2009) (Venez.); *see also* IACHR, Democracy and Human Rights in Venezuela, (2009), *available at* http://www.cidh.oas.org/pdf%20files/VENEZUELA%202009%20ENG.pdf. (indicating that this decline dates back to 2005).

[44] PROVEA Informe Anual 2009–2010, *supra* note 33, at 163; *See also*, IACHR, *Democracy and Human Rights in Venezuela*, *supra* note 43, ¶1043.

[45] PROVEA Informe Anual 2009–2010, *supra* note 33, at 163.

[46] *Id.* at 9.

[47] IACHR, Democracy and Human Rights in Venezuela, *supra* note 43, ¶1041.

[48] Regarding *Barrio Adentro*, the IACHR has expressed concern: "It thus appears . . . that services provided by the different stages of Barrio Adentro involvement do not replace services rendered by ambulatory health clinics and regional and national hospital centers but operate instead in parallel to them, sometimes at a deficit. This causes duplication of efforts and public expenditure in the health sector. The Commission has noted concern that such fragmentation proves an obstacle to effective health care delivery." IACHR, *Democracy and Human Rights in Venezuela*, *supra* note 43, ¶1039.

which makes the services offered very vulnerable, as well as diverting resources from an overarching public policy in these areas, including health care.[49]

15.1.2.2 The Social Security System

In the public health care system, the social security system of Venezuela is constituted by government-owned and -operated federal hospitals, as well as hospitals owned and run by the Venezuelan Institute of Social Security (IVSS). This system is mainly available to the working population. The Social Security System in Venezuela is conceived as a subsystem within the public health system; the IVSS is mainly financed by the federal government and supplemented by workers and employers through mandatory payroll taxes. In recent years, however, the financial sources for this system have primarily come from the federal government. Workers' and employers' contributions to social security are very low. In 2009, for instance, it was reported that only 37.2 percent of workers contributed to the social security system.[50]

15.1.2.3 The Private Health Care System

The private health care system in Venezuela comprises institutions and health care professionals who receive funding from private sources, such as prepaid medicine plans,[51] surgery and maternity insurance (*Hospitalización, Cirugía y Maternidad*, a specific form of private insurance offered by employers), and, most frequently, out-of-pocket payments by patients. Services in the private system are mostly provided by for-profit private clinics – *clínicas*.[52] There are also some state-managed institutions that receive private sources of income, for example from patients with private insurance.[53]

---

[49] D'Elia & Cabezas, *supra* note 38, at 14.

[50] PROVEA Informe Anual 2009–2010, *supra* note 33, at 203.

[51] Prepaid health care has become increasingly popular in Venezuela, as it constitutes a cheaper alternative to the considerably higher costs of private insurance. There are two major types of prepaid health care services in Venezuela: full plans, which cover all expenses; and partial plans, which cover only certain services and require patients to incur extra costs when using the services. Jaén, Costo de la Salud, *supra* note 20, at 49.

[52] Marino & Gonzalez, *supra* note 25; *see also* Jaén, Costo de la Salud, *supra* note 20, at 46. Private health care expenditure statistics related to different health insurers. In the late 1990s and in the years 2000 and 2001, *out-of-pocket* expenditure represented an average of 88% of private expenditure on health. In 2003, *out-of-pocket* payments accounted for no less than 92.6% of the private expenditures on health. The latest figures available, according to the 2011 World Health Observatory data, show a level of *out-of-pocket payments* accounting for 89.5% of the private financing in 2008. From 1999 to 2008, private *prepaid plans* (i.e., a form of contract-based health insurance covering some variable expenditure in exchange for a regular fee) represented between 3.3% and 4.1% of the private expenditure on health. In 2003, private *prepaid plans* constituted only 4.5% of the private expenditure on health. *See Venezuela (Bolivarian Republic of) Statistics Summary (2002–present)*, *supra* note 11 (out-of-pocket expenditure as a percentage of private expenditure on health, private prepaid plans as a percentage of private expenditure on health).

[53] Marino & Gonzalez, *supra* note 25.

When compared to other countries, Venezuela has a significantly higher percentage of private expenditure on health care in relation to the total expenditure. For the year 2010, private expenditure on health care in Venezuela accounted for 55.1 percent of the total expenditure on health, while the average in Latin America and the Caribbean was 42.9 percent, and the average for OECD countries was much lower (27.5 percent).[54] In the same year, out-of-pocket payments in Venezuela represented 89.5 percent of total private expenditure on health, while the average in Latin America and the Caribbean was 78.8 percent and the average in OECD countries was only 19.5 percent.[55] The financial burden of private expenditure has a significant impact on Venezuelan households.[56]

According to the Pan-American Health Organization (PAHO), in 1997, 65 percent of the Venezuelan population had *some* kind of health insurance.[57] By 2011, PROVEA[58] reported that approximately 70 percent of the population had no insurance.[59] The private sector possesses a significantly higher amount of resources, and the services it provides are considered the best-quality health services available in Venezuela. This essentially means that access to a better care in Venezuela (or one that at least satisfies minimum standards of quality) is contingent on the capacity to pay for such services.

The private health care system in Venezuela shows how the proliferation of a largely unregulated and more profitable private sector affects the public health care system. For instance, in Venezuela most medical schools are in public universities, which are mainly financed by the government and mostly free of charge to students. Upon graduation, physicians move on to the private sector without any limitation or restriction; thus the public cost of educating and training doctors is largely lost when their training is complete. The deficit of medical professionals has been one of the most enduring problems for the public health system. Physicians working only for the private system reportedly account for roughly 58 percent of such deficit (the remaining 42 percent corresponds to doctors moving to a different country).[60] The Venezuelan Medical Federation (FMV) has estimated a loss of about 50 percent of the medical personnel in public hospitals (roughly 10,000 medical professionals).

---

[54] *Venezuela (Bolivarian Republic of) Statistics Summary (2002–present)*, *supra* note 11 (citing private expenditure on health care as a percentage of total expenditure on health care).

[55] *Id.* (citing out-of-pocket expenditure as a percentage of private expenditure on health care).

[56] PROVEA Informe Anual 2009–2010, *supra* note 33, at 172.

[57] Basic Health Indicator Database, *supra* note 34 (providing information on the Health System), *available at* http://www.paho.org/English/DD/AIS/cp_862.htm; *See also* Jaén, El Sistema de Salud en Venezuela, *supra* note 24, at 37.

[58] The Programa Venezolano de Educación-Acción en Derechos Humanos (PROVEA) is an NGO specialized in the defense and promotion of economic, social, and cultural rights. The NGO's aim is to fully guarantee the execution of human rights and respect for the rule of law in an active and democratic societal framework. *Mision, Vision, y Objetivos Generales*, PROVEA (2012), *available at* http://www.derechos.org.ve/provea/misionvision-y-objetivos-generales/.

[59] PROVEA Informe Anual 2009–2010, *supra* note 33, at 162.

[60] *Id.* at 173.

According to the FMV, a constant wave of professionals resigning their positions started in 2005 given "the low salaries, the indefinite suspension of collective contracts, the pauperized working conditions which threaten life and health of the admitted professionals, and the insecurity within the medical facilities to which professionals are held subject on a daily basis."[61] Another example of resources shifting from the public to the private sector is when the government hires private health care services as an employment benefit for employees in the public sector.[62]

However, recent efforts have been put forward aimed at regulating prices at the private sector. President Chávez announced in June 2011 that he was going to look into imposing sanctions on private clinics for charging excessive fees for their services, as well as into irregularities by private insurance companies.[63] Two days later five private clinics and private insurance companies were fined by the Venezuelan Consumer Protection Agency (Indepabis).[64] On July 21, 2011, eleven state-owned institutions formed an alliance aimed at regulating the costs that private clinics charge state employees. This alliance, following a study of costs, established a set of limits on the fees charged by private doctors and clinics. Also, on June 16, 2011, the Ministry of Health issued a resolution freezing the prices of private clinics for three weeks. This measure was dictated in the context of a decree law[65] *Decreto-Ley sobre Costos y Precios Justos,*[66] aimed at regulating goods and services, costs, and prices of private economic entities. In November 2011, four private clinics signed an agreement with the alliance of state entities, bringing down their prices for state employees by approximately 40 percent.[67] This measure by the executive and other regulations of the private sector by the legislative and judicial branches, however, has little to no impact on reducing the health equity gap, given the small percentage of the population who have access to private health care. Moreover, one could argue that these measures increase the equity gap by reducing the burden on

---

[61] *Id.*

[62] *Id. See also* La reforma de salud de Venezuela: Aspectos Políticos e Institucionales de la Descentralización de la Salud en Venezuela [The Health Reform of Venezuela: Political and Institutional Aspects of the Health Decentralization in Venezuela] (Jorge Díaz Polanco Ed., 2001) (Venez.).

[63] PROVEA Informe Anual, Situación de Los Derechos Humanos en Venezuela 154 (2010–2011) (citing Presidente Chávez Pidió Investigar Irregularidades en Clínicas y Seguros Privados [President Chávez Asked to Investigate Irregularities in Clinics and Private insurances] AVN (June 12, 2011), *available at* http://www.avn.info.ve/node/62405.

[64] *Id.* at 155 (citing Indepabis Multó a Varias Clínicas y a Empresas de Seguros en Caracas [Indepabis Fined Various Clinics and Insurance Companies in Caracas], AVN (June 14, 2011), *available at* http://www.avn.info.ve/contenido/indepabis-mult%C3%B3-empresas-seguros-y-cl%C3%ADnicas-caracas.

[65] Constitution of the Bolivarian Republic of Venezuela, arts. 74, 236(8). Under Venezuelan law, the executive may dictate decree laws (decretos-ley), which have the force of a law passed by the National Assembly.

[66] This decree law creates a Superintendencia de Costos y Precios, an entity in charge of enforcing these policies.

[67] PROVEA Informe Anual 2009–2010, *supra* note 33, at 154–157.

people with high income who can afford to pay for health care services in the private sector.

The inefficiency of the public health care system directly impacts on the status of health and access to health care by the lower socioeconomic sectors. An inefficient, fragmented, poorly coordinated, and underfunded public health care system has a direct impact on the enjoyment of the right to health, in all its components. In part stemming from the lack of regulation, facilities, goods, and services are not available, the vast majority of the population does not have access, in particular since efficient quality services provided by the private health care system are not affordable, and facilities, goods, and services in the public sector are not of quality. As seen, the government's attempt to address these structural issues is temporary, has proven unsustainable, and faces great issues regarding availability of services.

15.2 CONSTITUTIONAL AND STATUTORY REGULATION OF THE RIGHT TO HEALTH IN VENEZUELA

15.2.1 *A Progressive Constitutional Protection of the Right to Health*

While the 1961 Constitution's health-related provisions were limited to one article referring to the state's general obligation to oversee the provision of health care (article 76), the 1999 Constitution not only strengthened the definition, extent, and content of the right to health but also specifically defined state's obligation regarding health care and the right to health. The Constitution establishes that health, as a fundamental social right, is a responsibility of the state, which, in turn, must guarantee it as a part of the right to life. All persons have the right to protection of health and the duty to participate "actively in its promotion and protection" (article 83). The community has both the right and the duty to participate in the decision-making process in relation to the planning, implementation, and control of policies in public health institutions (article 84). The constitution prohibits the privatization of existing health care assets and services (article 84). The state is responsible for the financing of the public health using internal revenue, contributions to the social security system,[68] and other sources established at statutory level. Although article 85 provides for the state to guarantee "a health budget such as to make possible the attainment of health policy objectives," it does not explicitly establish that the state's policy objectives should accord with internationally accepted standard of the highest attainable standard of health. The state is responsible for regulating public and private health care institutions.

---

[68] The Constitution has a socially progressive provision on social security. CONSTITUTION OF THE BOLIVARIAN REPUBLIC OF VENEZUELA, art. 86. This provision was interpreted by the Tribunal Supremo de Justicia [TSJ or Supreme Tribunal] in 2011. TSJ, SC, López, Abreu Raúl y otros seeking review of the decision, Decision No. 1771, File No. 11–1279 (Nov. 28, 2011) (Venez.), *available at* http://www.tsj.gov.ve/decisiones/scon/noviembre/1771–281111–2011–11–1279.html.

The 1999 Constitution explicitly establishes the decentralization of the health care system and that it shall be under the control of the federal[69] and municipal governments (article 178). However, the Constitution remains silent in regards to the state's health care responsibilities. Recent attempts by the administration to centralize the public health care system infringe the constitution calling for a decentralized (and participatory) health system governed by "the principles of gratuity, universality, comprehensiveness, equality, social integration and solidarity" (article 84).

The Venezuelan government has signed and ratified the International Covenant on Economic, Social and Cultural Rights (ICESR), and according to the Venezuelan Constitution, international human rights treaties become part of domestic law immediately upon ratification. Moreover, international human rights treaties that provide higher standards of protection than domestic law are to be considered by courts as hierarchically superior to domestic law, even above the Constitution itself (articles 19 and 23). The Venezuelan government is arguably bound to implement these treaties. Thus, implied in the Constitutional provisions regarding the right to health is an aim to achieve the standards set forth in the ICESR and other international human rights instruments.[70] As discussed in this chapter, these strong constitutional protections of the right to health have not necessarily translated into better access to health care or an effective enjoyment of the right to health by Venezuelans.

15.2.2 *Statutory Protection of the Right to Health: A Thirteen-Year Delay in Regulating the Constitutional Provision of the Right to Health*

For the past thirteen years, the National Assembly has been discussing several versions of a health bill that had to be enacted within two years of the entry into force of the 1999 Constitution. These bills have proposed at least five different versions of a prospective health care system.[71] Among these proposed bills, the Health and

---

[69] Health-related competencies of the Federal Government are the (1) governance and organization of the Social Security System, (2) national policy and legislation in the field of health, among others, and (3) health policies and services. *See* CONSTITUTION OF THE BOLIVARIAN REPUBLIC OF VENEZUELA, art. 156.

[70] On this note, Venezuela has recently shown unwillingness to comply with its international human rights obligations. In 2008 and 2011, the TSJ handed down decisions explicitly declaring the inapplicability of binding rulings by the Inter-American Court of Human Rights, alleging a violation of Venezuelan sovereignty, in clear violation of its international human rights obligations and the Constitution. TSJ, CC, Action reviewing constitutionality of decision rendered by I/A C.H.R., Decision No. 1939, File No. 08–1572, (Dec. 18, 2008) (Venez.), *available at* http://www.tsj.gov.ve/decisiones/scon/Diciembre/1939-181208-2008-08-1572.html; TSJ, CC, Action reviewing constitutionality of decision rendered by I/A C.H.R., Decision No. 1547, File No. 11–1130 (Oct. 17, 2011) (Venez.), *available at* http://www.tsj.gov.ve/decisiones/scon/Octubre/1547-171011-2011-11-1130.html.

[71] PROVEA Informe Anual, Situación de Los Derechos Humanos en Venezuela, 167, 168 (Oct. 2005–Sept. 2006) (Venez.).

National Public Health System Act,[72] proposed by the Health Ministry, was approved by the National Assembly "in first discussion" in December 2004.[73] The legislature must still approve it "in second discussion," and the executive must promulgate it before it enters into force. The reform proposed in this bill points at strengthening the role of the central government in steering the health care system. It is a form of centralization within an overall decentralized structure, allowing states, through local health authorities, to manage their own health care systems within the general directions set by the central government. This is consistent with late President Chávez's announcement in 2007 of a centralization of the health care system, but violates the decentralization provisions in the Constitution.

The 1998 Health Act[74] (which is currently in effect) precedes the 1999 Constitution, which introduced a significant reform in Venezuela's health care system. This Health Act establishes the general framework for the administration of health care services at the national, states, and municipal levels, including the powers of the Ministry of Health and those reserved to the local authorities. As of March 2013, the National Assembly has yet to adopt a new health act that is in accordance with the 1999 Constitution. This delay clearly violates the Constitution, which established that this law should be enacted within two years of the entry into force of the Constitution.[75] The Ombudsperson has requested the National Assembly to enact a Health Bill.[76] Without a law regulating the health care system in light of the new constitution, there is still no national public health care system that is coherent, clearly establishing competencies and obligations.[77] We discuss this legislative void in the next section, as it has been subject to litigation.

As examined earlier, according to the Constitution, the state must regulate both public and private health care institutions. In July 2010, the National Assembly passed the Insurance Activity Act, which aims at regulating forty-eight private insurance companies.[78] However, the impact on the poorest sector of the population is limited. The vast majority of the population does not have the economic means to buy insurance or access the private health care sector.[79] These regulations of the private sector by the different branches of government, as previously described, may actually

---

[72] National Assembly of Venezuela, Proyecto de Ley de Salud y Sistema Público Nacional de Salud [Project of Health and National Health System Act], *available at* http://www.asambleanacional.gob.ve/noticia/show/id/192.

[73] Approval process of bills usually requires two different discussions at the National Assembly, commonly referred to as "first discussion" and "second discussion."

[74] *Ley Orgánica del Sistema Nacional de Salud*, OFFICIAL GAZETTE No. 36.579 (Nov. 11, 1998) (Venez.).

[75] *See* Constitution of the Bolivarian Republic of Venezuela, "temporary provisions."

[76] PROVEA INFORME ANUAL 2009–2010, *supra* note 33, at 318.

[77] PROVEA INFORME ANUAL 2010–2011, *supra* note 63, at 152.

[78] *See Ley de la Actividad Aseguradora*, OFFICIAL GAZETTE No. 39.481 (Aug. 5, 2010) (Venez.) (citing Official Gazette Extraordinary No. 5.990, July 29, 2010).

[79] PROVEA INFORME ANUAL 2009–2010, *supra* note 33, at 159 (noting that 68% of the population and 78% of the poorest sector of the population do not have any form of insurance, whether public or private, and less than 30% of the population has the economic means to access private medical centers).

contribute to widening the health equity gap, as it arguably lessens the economic burden of the higher socioeconomic classes, who can afford private health care.

15.3 LITIGATION OF HEALTH CARE RIGHTS IN VENEZUELA

In Venezuela, there are two legal actions that are usually used to litigate health rights and health care–related issues. The *Amparo constitucional* (*amparo*) is a constitutional action seeking protection from a violation or threat of violation to a fundamental right enshrined in the Constitution. *Amparos* can be filed against public or private actors, and can also be used to challenge the constitutionality of laws and regulations. Because of the subject matter and urgency of the issues addressed through *amparos*, such cases should be examined with urgency by courts and with prevalence over any other type of legal action. The Constitutional Chamber of the TSJ, created by the 1999 Constitution, has the final say in constitutional *amparos*, and it also serves as the higher instance of judicial review of government acts (exercising a concentrated control of constitutionality of laws, regulations, and government acts).[80] The purpose of an *amparo* is to restore the situation of a person whose rights have been violated to the state prior to when the violation took place.

Ordinarily, when seeking to repeal an act or omission by the administration, *amparos* do not proceed when there are other adequate legal actions available to plaintiffs, such as the request for an annulment of the act via the *contencioso-administrativo* jurisdiction (the jurisdiction called to review acts by the public administration). An exception to this rule is available when resorting to the ordinary legal action would not remedy the situation effectively and timely, given the urgency of a matter. We argue that in health-related cases, the TSJ has contradictory jurisprudence in determining what constitutes urgency. As will be examined, in a 2012 decision on a request for information on the distribution of expired medicines from Cuba in the Venezuelan market, the TSJ considered that this was not an urgent matter that would merit an *amparo*, whereas in 2002, the TSJ had considered the closing of the night shift of a medical center urgent enough to merit an *amparo*.[81]

The other action regularly used in this type of litigation is the constitutional action for the protection of collective or diffuse interests. This claim is presented before the Constitutional Chamber of the TSJ on behalf of a group of people or the general

---

[80] *Ley Orgánica de Amparo sobre Derechos y Garantías Constitucionales*, OFFICIAL GAZETTE No 34.060 (Sept. 27, 1988) (Venez.), which predates the creation of the Constitutional Chamber by the 1999 Constitution, but which was interpreted by the TSJ in a 2000 decision. TSJ, SC, Emery Mata *Millán v. Ministerio del Interior y Justicia Ignacio Luis Arcaya*, Decision No. 01, File No. 00–0002 (Jan. 20, 2000) (Venez.), *available at* http://www.tsj.gov.ve/decisiones/scon/Enero/01–200100–00–002.htm.

[81] Cf. TSJ, SC, Carlos Correa, et al., v. Public Ministry of Health, Decision No. 805, File No. 12–0355 (June 18, 2012) (Venez.), *available at* http://www.tsj.gov.ve/decisiones/scon/Junio/805–18612–2012–12–0355.html; TSJ, SC, Vilma Mariela Peña Linares, et al., v. Venezuelan Institute of Social Security (I.V.S.S.), Decision No. 1280, File no. 00–2305 (June 12, 2002) (Venez.), *available at* http://www.tsj.gov.ve/decisiones/scon/Junio/1280–120602–00–2305%20.htm.

population based on "collective interests."[82] Claimants of these actions must have legal standing, that is, they must be affected by the situation that originates the action. It is deemed very positive and useful for guaranteeing persons from lower socioeconomic sectors access to justice, who otherwise would not be able to do so.

15.3.1 *Independence of the Judiciary*

A review of the litigation regarding health rights cannot begin without first considering the issue of the undermining of the independence of the judiciary in Venezuela. In the past decade, Venezuela has been criticized by NGOs and international monitoring human rights bodies, which have severely questioned the independence of the judiciary. Critics argue that the passing of legislation aimed at packing the TSJ with pro-government justices in violation of the established procedure,[83] the high percentage of provisional judges coupled with an irregular process aimed at giving them tenure,[84] recent TSJ jurisprudence questioning the separation of powers,[85] and statements by the TSJ president are all key factors threatening the independence of the judiciary.[86]

---

[82] The *acción por intereses colectivos y difusos* has been interpreted and defined by the TSJ, Declaration No. 7703, File No. 00–24074 (Oct. 30, 2000) (Venez.), *available at* http://jca.tsj.gov.ve/decisiones/2002/abril/025-24-00-24074-2002-872.html.

[83] In 2004, a simple pro-government majority at the National Assembly passed the Organic Law of the Supreme Tribunal of Justice, which allowed for expanding the number of justices from twenty to thirty-two to ensure a pro-government majority. The Inter-American Commission stated that this law enabled the executive branch to manipulate the 2004 election of justices. IACHR, ANNUAL REPORT OF THE INTER-AMERICAN COMMISSION ON HUMAN RIGHTS, para. 161 (2003). Five years later, the IACHR affirmed that the law "continue[d] to have an impact on the independence of the judiciary up to the present, in that the [TSJ], made up of a pro-government majority, has subsequently appointed and removed hundreds of judges in the rest of the judicial system, without holding open public competitions for their selection." IACHR, *Democracy and Human Rights in Venezuela, supra* note 43, at ¶ 201; IACHR, ANNUAL REPORT OF THE INTER-AMERICAN COMMISSION ON HUMAN RIGHTS, chap. V, para. 180 (2004); *See also* Human Rights Watch, A Decade Under Chavez: Political Intolerance and Lost Opportunities for Advancing Human Rights in Venezuela (2008), *available at* http://www.hrw.org/sites/default/files/reports/venezuela0908web.pdf.

[84] Judicial tenure is a guarantee of judicial independence. Provisional judges can be removed freely without a previously established proceeding. Venezuela had approximately 80% of provisional judges, especially in 2000–2004. From 2005 on, the process for giving them tenure was not an open public competition. The number of provisional judges was decreased to approximately 44% at the end of 2008. Reveron Trujillo v. Venezuela, Inter-Am Ct. H.R. (ser. C) No. 197, paras. 79, 106, (June 30, 2009) (Venez.), *available at* http://www.corteidh.or.cr/docs/casos/articulos/seriec_197_ing.pdf; *see also* IACHR, *Democracy and Human Rights in Venezuela, supra* note 43, paras. 180 & ff; Chocron Chocron v. Venezuela, Preliminary Objection, Merits, Reparations and Costs, Inter-Am Ct. H.R. (ser. C) No. 227, (July 1, 2011) (Venez.), *available at* http://www.corteidh.or.cr/docs/casos/articulos/seriec_227_ing.pdf.

[85] TSJ, CC, Rafael Badell Madrid y otros, recurso de nulidad, Decision No. 1049, File No. 04–2233 (July 23, 2009) (Venez.), *available at* http://www.tsj.gov.ve/decisiones/scon/julio/1049-23709-2009-04-2233.html.

[86] Luisa Estella Morales, President of the TSJ, stated on behalf of all public powers: "Our institutionalism is so embedded ... that one public power [the Executive] represents each one of the other public

A case that exemplifies the interference of the executive with the judiciary concerned a suit brought by an organization of physicians claiming that a government agreement with Cuba on contracting Cuban physicians for *Misión Barrio Adentro* (as mentioned earlier, one of the key government health care policies implemented by President Chavez's administration) violated several rights, including to life, health, and physical integrity. It was argued that foreign professional credentials for the practice of medicine in Venezuela were legalized without proper recertification. The First Court of Administrative Disputes, composed of five judges and in charge of reviewing the acts of the administration, handed down a decision on August 2003 in the *Barrio Adentro* case, requesting that the foreign doctors be substituted by Venezuelan doctors or by foreign doctors who met the legal practicing requirements.[87] Three days later, President Chávez stated on national television that this judgment would not be complied with because it was an outrageous decision made by judges of the opposition, and that there was "a lot of excess fabric to be trimmed in the judicial branch."[88] On October 2003, the three judges who ruled on this matter against the government were removed through a disciplinary proceeding that violated their due process rights, including the right to be tried by an independent tribunal. The grounds for dismissal were that they had committed an inexcusable judicial error regarding another matter.[89] The two judges, who dissented in the *Barrio Adentro* case, retired and were appointed a year later as justices to the Supreme Tribunal of Justice.[90] Notably, these two judges had voted along with the other three judges in the matter in which the inexcusable judicial error was committed. This case reached the Inter-American Court of Human Rights – the highest

powers. And of course, your direction . . . your concept of the Republic is what constitutionally inspires the development of our activities. . . . President: . . . Here are all your institutions, and we are, above all, firmly moving forward with the responsibilities that have been given to us, which we will never betray, not now, not ever." Luisa Estella Morales, President of the TSJ, *see* video uploaded by Vivetelevision *Chávez, Sabemos que Dios Tiene Para Ti un Propósito Grande*, YouTube (July 2011), *available at* http://www.youtube.com/watch?v=kfvLQB-i8Xg&feature=player_embedded.

[87] First Court of Administrative Disputes (CPCA), Federación Médica Venezolana v. Recurso Contencioso Administrativo de Nulidad [Venezuelan Medical Federation v. Administrative Act Issued by the Colegio de Médicos de Caracas), Decision No. 2727, File No. 03–2852 (Aug. 21, 2003) (Venez.), *available at* http://jca.tsj.gov.ve/decisiones/2003/agosto/025–21–03–2852–2003–2727.html.

[88] Apitz Barbera et al. (First Court of Administrative Disputes) v. Venezuela, Inter-Am. Ct. H.R. (ser. C) No. 182, Preliminary objections, merits, reparations and costs, para. 115 (Apr. 6, 2006), *available at* http://www.corteidh.or.cr/docs/casos/articulos/seriec_182_ing.pdf.

[89] *Id.* at 147–148.

[90] As of March 2013, Justice Evelyn Marrero Ortiz is the president of one of the chambers of the Supreme Tribunal of Justice (for her biography, *see* Evelyn Marrero Ortiz, Tribunal Supremo de Justicia [2013], *available at* http://www.tsj.gov.ve/eltribunal/magistrados/EvelynMarrero.shtml) and Justice Luisa Estella Morales Lamuño is currently the president of the Supreme Tribunal of Justice (for her biography, *see* Luisa Estella Morales Lamuño, Tribunal Supremo de Justicia [2013], *available at* http://www.tsj.gov.ve/eltribunal/magistrados/luisamorales.shtml). Apitz Barbera et al. ("First Court of Administrative Disputes") v. Venezuela, Inter-Am. Ct. H.R. (ser. C) No. 182, Preliminary objections, merits, reparations and costs, para. 201, (Aug. 5, 2008), *available at* http://www.corteidh.or.cr/docs/casos/articulos/seriec_182_ing.pdf.

regional court for examining human rights violations committed by states in the region – which ruled that the facts of the case evidenced a clear exertion of pressure on the court.[91] The Inter-American Court, however, decided that it did not have enough proof to assert the lack of independence of the judiciary beyond the facts of the case.[92] Also, the arrest and prosecution of a judge following a decision against government interests in 2009[93] has had a devastating impact on the independence of the judges, who now not only fear disciplinary proceedings or dismissals but also imprisonment.[94]

Litigation relating to health care occurs in this context of strong indicia of lack of independence of the judiciary. Public trust in the judiciary as exerting the necessary checks and balances is threatened. Also, the current administration has been denounced for exerting great pressure, including criminal prosecution, on human rights defenders, NGOs, and civil society organizations perceived as criticizing the government. Such actions have taken a toll on human rights advocacy,[95] creating a chilling effect, which could affect future litigation regarding health care policies.

As will be examined, the vast majority of claims filed against other branches of government, whether the executive or the legislative (composed by a pro-government majority), have either been ruled out at the preliminary stages for procedural reasons, have been dismissed, or declared without merits. A minority of decisions have been ruled in favor of plaintiffs and against public entities in charge of delivery of health care. However, these have been very specific and limited to HIV (based on a precedent established back in 1999), on children with congenital heart defects, and one decision – very limited in reach – regarding the provision of services in a small public health center. The most important overarching 2004 decision on an *amparo* – with potential serious consequences for the subsequent litigation of economic and social rights – was based on collective interests and called for a judicial review of state budget

---

[91] *See* Apitz Barbera et al. (First Court of Administrative Disputes) v. Venezuela, Inter-Am. Ct. H.R. (ser. C) No. 182, preliminary objections, merits, reparations and costs, para. 136 (Aug. 5, 2008). The Inter American Court noted "the removal came after the highest Government authority [President Hugo Chávez] said all the victims were 'coup-plotters.'"

[92] *Id.* at ¶ 108.

[93] Another important case, which calls into question the independence of the judiciary, is the arrest in 2009 of Judge Afiuni, who authorized the conditional release of a banker and critic of President Chavez. His release was ordered because he had been in pretrial detention well beyond the legal limit. Immediately after issuing the decision, Judge Afiuni was arrested. The following day, President Chavez called her a "bandit" and asked that she be imposed the maximum penalty established by law – thirty years. She was later charged with corruption, abuse of power, and favoring evasion of justice – allegations unsubstantiated by prosecutors. Human Rights Watch [HRW], Tightening the Grip: Concentration and Abuse of Power in Chavez's Venezuela 31 (July 2012), *available at* http://www.hrw.org/sites/default/files/reports/venezuela0712webwcover.pdf.

[94] International Bar Association, Distrust in Justice: The Afiuni Case and the Independence of the Judiciary in Venezuela 9 (April, 2011), *available at* http://www.ibanet.org/Document/Default.aspx? DocumentUid=CE82F018–221F-465B-81CD-2C4E1669A2EE; *see also* HRW, Tightening the Grip, *supra* note 93, at 42.

[95] HRW, Tightening the Grip, *supra* note 93, at 42.

and public policies on health care. However, as we examine in the following section, this case was dismissed by a pro-government Constitutional Chamber of the TSJ.

15.3.2 Decisions by Theme

Some of the decisions regarding health care and the right to health handed down by Venezuelan courts in recent years are discussed in this section.[96] Cases pending a final decision on the merits, for example on tobacco control[97] or on health topics not directly relevant to the analysis developed in this paper,[98] have been omitted. Cases have been arranged by the themes as follows: access to antiretroviral therapy

---

[96] The review of the decisions included is not exhaustive, but rather illustrative.

[97] Pending a decision on the merits, there is a tobacco control case that was been declared admissible at the preliminary stage of proceedings by the TSJ in a 2008 decision. The case concerns an action on diffuse and collective interests presented by the Venezuelan Federation of Consumers against the Ministry of Health and the National Assembly, arguing that failure by the National Assembly to implement article 8 of the WHO Framework on Tobacco Control on the protection from exposure to tobacco smoke in enclosed public places was a violation of their rights to health, life, and a clean environment. In its October 2008 decision, the TSJ, on preliminary grounds, admitted the claim, ruling that the state has the duty to oversee the correct compliance of social interest activities benefiting the common good. TSJ, SC, FEVACU et al., Decision No. 1587, File no. 08–0520 (Oct. 10, 2008) (Venez.), available at http://www.tsj.gov.ve/decisiones/scon/Octubre/1587–211008–08–0520. htm. See also Decision to notify two tobacco companies that were admitted as interested third parties in the proceedings, TSJ, SC, Decision No. 1615, File no. 08–0520 (Dec. 5, 2012) (Venez.), available at http://www.tsj.gov.ve/decisiones/scon/Diciembre/1615–51212–2012–08–0520.html. As of March 2013, however, a decision is pending on the merits. It is relevant to mention that the Ministry of Health adopted an important resolution on March 2011, prohibiting tobacco consumption in closed spaces and on public transportation. Ministry of Health, Resolution No. 030, OFFICIAL GAZETTE No. 39.627 (March 2, 2011) (Venez.).

[98] Decisions relating to medical malpractice, contentious objection, and state's regulation of materials used for breast implants, for example, have been omitted as they do not contribute to the health equity gap discussion. On malpractice: in October 2010, a decision by the TSJ, changing its previous jurisprudence in malpractice cases, indicated that medical doctors affiliated with private clinics could be financially responsible for malpractice. TSJ, SPA, Arteaga, María de los Santos y otros v. IVSS, Decision No. 01010, File 2004–1496 (Oct. 19, 2010) (Venez.). On contentious objection: the TSJ examined the case of a twelve-year-old adolescent with leukemia who needed a blood transfusion, but whose mother requested an injunction arguing that it was against their religion as Jehovah's Witnesses. The Tribunal ruled that patients could not object to treatment when no other alternative treatment is available; viewing that his right to life was at stake. TSJ, SC, Pérez Carreño, Yolima v. Consejo de Protección del Niño y del Adolescente del Municipio Libertador, Decision No. 1431, File No.07–1121 (Aug. 14, 2008) (Venez.), available at http://www.tsj.gov.ve/decisiones/scon/agosto/ 1431–140808–07–1121.htm. On implants used for breast augmentation: in June 2012 the TSJ ordered the recall of PIP (Poly Implant Prothèse), which had been used for breast augmentation cosmetic surgeries in Venezuela from June 2007 to April 2010, affecting thousands of women. The TSJ also ordered doctors to remove the ruptured implants free of charge, and requested the Ministry of Health to keep a database with the information of the affected women. These implants, of French fabrication and available at lower costs, were manufactured with silicone not apt for the human body, intended to be used in the manufacturing of mattresses, and with lower quality standards rupturing seven years earlier than advertised, and, arguably, causing severe, devastating, and irreversible health problems. TSJ, SC, Ombudswoman et al. v. Galaxia Médica, C.A. et al., Decision No. 790, File No. 12–0526, (June 6, 2012) (Venez.), available at http://www.tsj.gov.ve/decisiones/scon/Junio/790–6612–2012–12–0526.html.

(ART) for persons living with HIV; justiciability of the right to health; regulation of the health care system; inadequate access to health care and lack of medical equipment; access to information on public health; private health care systems; and states' regulation of pharmaceuticals.

15.3.2.1 Access to Antiretroviral Therapy and Associated HIV Treatments

One of the most important health-related decisions in Venezuela's recent history was *Cruz Bermudez et al.*, a 1999 decision by then-Supreme Court of Justice grant-ing universal access to ART and associated HIV treatments. The case was not only significant due to the topics discussed, but also extremely important for human rights litigation of social and economic rights in general. The petition was brought before the courts based on the 1961 Constitution, which, as examined, did not guar-antee the right to health as onerously as did the 1999 Constitution. Notwithstanding, the Court found the right to health to be fully justiciable. In its decision, the Supreme Court, acknowledging the close link between the right to life and the right to health, ordered the Ministry of Health (1) to provide medicines to people living with HIV; (2) to cover the cost of blood tests for patients to obtain ART and other treatment for opportunistic infections related to HIV; (3) to develop policies and programs in the field of treatment and assistance for HIV-positive patients; and (4) to reallocate the budget accordingly in order to comply with the Court's mandate.[99] Thereafter, the Ministry of Health issued a resolution aimed at preventing vertical transmission and ensuring availability of ART.[100]

There has been further litigation – at both federal and state levels – regarding access to treatment for persons living with HIV, under the new 1999 Constitution. For example, in 2001, a group of persons living with HIV filed an *amparo* against the IVSS, alleging that it had failed to supply treatment for HIV and other opportunistic diseases with the frequency that was medically required. The TSJ decided in favor of the plaintiffs, ruling that the omissions by the IVSS were a violation of the right to health, a threat to the right to life, as well as a violation of the right to enjoy the benefits of scientific and technological progress, among others. The TSJ ordered the IVSS to provide a regular and consistent supply of ART and other drugs to treat opportunistic diseases, as well as to cover tests-related expenses. Also, following a request by the plaintiffs in this regard, the TSJ established that this decision would benefit all persons living with HIV who were in the same situation (those who legally qualified for social security and who had required of the IVSS to provide treatment

---

[99] TSJ, SC, Cruz Bermudez et al. v. Ministerio de Sanidad y Asistencia Social (MSAS), Decision No. 916, File No. 15789, (July 15, 1999) (Venez.), *available at* http://www.ghhrdb.org/judgments/Cruz%20del%20Valle-Venezuela-1999.pdf. *See also* Mary Ann Torres, *The Human Right to Health, National Courts, and Access to HIV/AIDS Treatment: A Case from Venezuela*, 3 CHI. J. INT'L L. 105 (2002).

[100] Ministry of Health, Resolution No. 292, OFFICIAL GAZETTE No. 37.009 (Aug. 7, 2000) (Venez.).

and to cover expenses related to tests), and that the IVSS could not allege lack of resources to justify lack of compliance.[101]

In another case, a regional court in the state of Zulia[102] ordered the state health care system and the state agency in charge of sexually transmitted infections (STIs) and HIV to ensure that health care rights are guaranteed to all persons living with HIV in that state. The plaintiffs had argued that approximately 2,000 persons living with HIV were receiving irregular treatment under degrading conditions. The center was located near a dumpsite and a water sewage. Plaintiffs claimed that there had not been any citizenry participation regarding the location of the center. The court held the state has to guarantee citizenry and any interested party a right to participation in any decision taken by the Regional Health System of the State of Zulia along with the state entity on STIs and HIV. This would be the only way, the court stated, to guarantee fully developed educational, preventive, and informed policies, which are key to guaranteeing an integral treatment for persons living with HIV and STIs.[103]

Regarding the implementation of decisions concerning free universal access to ART for persons living with HIV, the Venezuelan government affirms ART is in fact available to the public at no cost, but admits the process to obtain the treatment after a diagnosis needs adjustments.[104] It has been argued that neither ARTs nor materials needed to conduct HIV testing are easily available in Venezuela.[105] Provea also reports that the government has not fully complied with more than twenty decisions handed down by the TSJ on HIV-related matters.[106]

15.3.2.2 Justiciability of the Right to Health

The Medical Federation of Venezuela (FMV) filed an *amparo* on collective interests, requesting the TSJ to order the Ministry of Health and the IVSS to ensure sufficient resources to tackle deficiencies in public hospitals, including lack

---

[101] TSJ, DC, López, Glenda y otros v. Instituto Venezolano de los Seguros Sociales (IVSS) s/ acción de amparo, Decision 487, File 00–1343 (April 6, 2001) (Venez.), *available at* http://www.escr-net.org/usr_doc/Lopez_and_Glenda_Final_Sentence.doc.

[102] Zulia has the second-largest city in Venezuela, Maracaibo.

[103] Juzgado Superior en lo Civil y Contencioso Administrativo de la Región Occidental, AMAVIDA v. Sistema Regional de Salud de la Gobernación del Estado de Zulia y otro, Decision No. N/A, File No. 8846, (Aug. 3, 2005) (Venez.), *available at* http://www.stopvih.org/pdf/Sentencia_Participacion_Comunitaria_VIH_SIDA_Zulia_Venezuela.pdf.

[104] Informe Nacional relativo a los avances en la implementación de la Declaración de Compromisos sobre VIH/SIDA (2001) y Declaración Política sobre VIH/SIDA (2006) (Enero de 2008 – Diciembre de 2009)[National Reort on Progress in the Implementation of the Declaration of Commitment on HIV/AIDS (2001) and Political Declaration on HIV/AIDS (2006)], 165–166 (March 2010) (Venez.), *available at* http://www.unaids.org/en/dataanalysis/knowyourresponse/countryprogressreports/2010countries/venezuela_2010_country_progress_report_es.pdf.

[105] PROVEA Informe Anual 2010–2011, *supra* note 63, at 182.

[106] *Id.* at 183.

of medical materials and equipment, which severely impaired adequate access to health. The 2004 decision handed down in this case has been (rightfully so) criticized for undermining the justiciability of economic, social, and cultural rights.[107]

The TSJ ruled against the FMV and dismissed the *amparo*, holding that (1) the justiciability of economic, social, and cultural rights is only feasible when there is an actual, well-defined, and legally significant relation between the persons entitled to the right and the alleged violation of such right, and that such relation does not exist in the case of public policies; (2) the provision of medical equipment and materials is a political activity and therefore can only be controlled through political means – not through the judiciary – given that, according to the Court, there was no concrete violation of the right to health; and (3) the Constitutional Chamber of the Supreme Court was not the appropriate organ for controlling the state policies on economic, social, and cultural rights. The adequate public entity for raising such a claim is the Office of the Ombudsperson.[108]

The TSJ failed to address the connection between the right to health and the right to life, as the previous Supreme Court of Justice had done in 1999 in *Cruz Bermudez et al.*, which had viewed the right to health as justiciable, thereby granting ART to all persons living with HIV. Arguably, following this 2004 decision, violations of economic, social, and cultural rights through government inaction are not subject to judicial review. This regressive decision affects the impact litigation may have in improving health outcomes, as the judiciary can – and arguably does, in other countries – play a significant role in improving health equity by reviewing government health policies.

15.3.2.3 Regulation of the Health Care System

Civil society organizations argue that the thirteen-year delay in enacting a health care law has created serious problems in the health care system, stemming from, among other reasons, lack of adequate health care personnel, lack of equipment in medical centers, and a deteriorated infrastructure, which severely affect patients and health care providers.[109] Thus, in July 2009, a group of NGOs filed an unconstitutionality action before the TSJ against the National Assembly challenging this legislative

[107] PROVEA Informe Anual, Situación de Los Derechos Humanos en Venezuela, 398 & ff 40 (2003–2004) (Venez.).

[108] TSJ, SC, Federación Médica Venezolana v. Ministra de Salud y Desarrollo Social *et al.*, Decision No. 1002, File No. 02–2167 (May 26, 2004) (Venez.), *available at* http://www.tsj.gov.ve/decisiones/scon/Mayo/1002-260504-02-2167%20.htm. Contrast with a previous decision in April 2001, in which the TSJ established that the right to health is a positive or enforceable right. TSJ, SC, López Glenda et al. v. IVSS, Decision No. 487. File No. 00–1343 (Apr. 6, 2001), *available at* http://www.escr-net.org/sites/default/files/Lopez_and_Glenda_Final_Sentence.doc.

[109] *Ley Orgánica de Salud Ya!*, PROVEA (July 22, 2011), *available at* http://www.derechos.org.ve/2011/07/22/omision-legislativa/.

omission.[110] On February 26, 2013, the TSJ ruled against the plaintiffs and found the National Assembly was not at fault. The TSJ, while highlighting the importance of the protection and recognition of the right to health, ruled that – in contrast with legislation on indigenous' peoples, education, and borders, for which there were specific mandates in said provision of the Constitution – the 1999 Constitution did not specifically requested the National Assembly to legislate on health care; rather, it was a general mandate to legislate "on all subject matters related to" the Constitution, within the two-year framework.[111]

Regarding the recent centralization efforts by the government, the Venezuelan state of Táchira filed a complaint against the Ministry of Health arguing that its actions for "boosting the health system" exceed its competence according to the constitution, which established a decentralized health care system. In its 2012 decision, the TSJ, in a decision arguably favoring a centralization of the health care system, held that the federal state has competence to monitor and diagnose health care systems in the different Venezuelan states.[112]

15.3.2.4 Inadequate Access to Health Care and Lack of Medical Equipment

Several *amparos* have been filed against the Ministry of Health and the IVSS regarding the lack of adequate medical services or care in the public health care system, and although the TSJ has not gone into the merits of all these claims, they evidence the deficiency in medical services as perceived by patients.[113] In a merits decision,

---

[110] *TSJ Admite Acción de Inconstitucionalidad Contra la Asamblea Nacional Presentado por Organizaciones de Derechos Humanos*, PROVEA (June 7, 2010), *available at* http://www.derechos.org.ve/2010/06/07/tsj-admite-accion-de-inconstitucionalidad-contra-la-asamblea-nacional-presentado-por-organizaciones-de-derechos-humanos/.

[111] TSJ, SC, Provea et al. (Acción de Inconstitucionalidad por omisión legislativa de la Asamblea Nacional), Decision No. 83, File no. 09–0897 (Feb. 26, 2013) (Venez.), *available at* http://www.tsj.gov.ve/decisiones/scon/Febrero/83–26213–2013–09–0897.html. The relevant provision of the Constitution reads: "The National Assembly, within the timeframe of two years will legislate on all subject matters related to this Constitution. Priority will be given to organic laws on indigenous' peoples, education and borders."

[112] TSJ, SPA, Procurador General del Estado de Táchira y otro v. Ministerio del Poder Popular para la Salud, Decision No. 00016, File No. 2010–0774, (Jan. 18, 2012) (Venez.).

[113] TSJ, SPA, Hernández Zerlini, Illier Jhoyne y otro v. IVSS, Decision No. 865, File No. 2010–0744 (June 29, 2011) (Venez.), *available at* http://www.tsj.gov.ve/decisiones/spa/junio/00865–30611–2011–2010–0744.html declared the claim void. TSJ, SC, Julio Sosa Branger, et al. v. IVSS, writ of *amparo*, then later writ of appeal, Decision No. 1664, File No. 11–1090 (Nov. 28, 2011) (Venez.), *available at* http://www.tsj.gov.ve/decisiones/scon/noviembre/1664–21111–2011–11–1090.html, declared extemporaneous. A case was brought before the TSJ regarding the health-related problems caused to patients, medical personnel, and hospital staff stemming from a toxic accident that occurred in a hospital in the state of Aragua in 1993. Although the SPA of the TSJ partially decided in favor of the plaintiffs, ordering the IVSS to pay damages in this case and to prioritize treatment and care for those affected, an appeal by the IVSS to the SC resulted in a July 2010 decision by the SC to void said decision and order a retrial. *Intoxicados Hospital La Ovallera*, PROVEA (Jan. 17, 2010), *available at* http://www.derechos.org.ve/2010/01/17/intoxicados-hospital-la-ovallera-aragua/.

the TSJ ordered the IVSS to reverse its decision to stop night shift health care services at a health center, thereby guaranteeing the non-interruption of services.[114] Children's hospital J.M. de los Ríos provides services to a great number of children with different complex conditions, including congenital heart defects; however, care is not always delivered effectively. In 2000, various NGOs filed a writ of *amparo* against the Caracas municipality, claiming violations to the right to life and health and requesting the court to order the development and execution of a plan to ensure adequate and timely medical care. The 2001 court's judgment recognized a violation to the rights to health and life of more than 500 children afflicted with heart-related conditions.[115] In August 2001, the agencies involved signed an agreement in accordance with the court's decision.[116] Although not all agreements reached with the government have been complied with, the case made it possible to identify children with congenital heart disease as a vulnerable group requiring special measures by the state.[117]

15.3.2.5 Access to Information on Public Health

Two *amparos* regarding access to information on health filed by NGOs against the Ministry of Health in 2009 and 2012 were dismissed at the preliminary stage for procedural reasons. Although these do not address the merits of the complaints, they highlight deficiencies regarding the state's obligation to produce information needed to comply with its obligations,[118] including the constitutional obligations vis-à-vis the right to health. Since 2007, the Ministry of Health has failed to make health data available on a regular basis necessary. This information is needed to assess the health system outcomes and develop evidence-based policies. There are mainly two categories in which data has not been regularly provided. One such set of data is the official statistics on mortality and morbidity. The other is the weekly national epidemiology reports (*boletines epidemiológicos*), which was delayed by

---

[114] TSJ, SC, Vilma Mariela Peña Linares et al. v. I.V.S.S., Decision No. 1280, File No. 00–2305 (June 12, 2002) (Venez.), *available at* http://www.tsj.gov.ve/decisiones/scon/Junio/1280–120602–00–2305% 20.htm.

[115] Tribunal de Protección del Niño y del Adolescente de la Circunscripción Judicial del Área Metropolitana de Caracas, Sala IV de Juicio, CECODAP, ACCSI y PROVEA v. Alcaldía Metropolitana de Caracas, File No. 3174 (July 16, 2001) (Venez.).

[116] See agreement signed between several NGOs and state agencies, *Suscriben Acuerdos por el Derecho a la Salud y a la Vida de los Niños con Cardiopatías Congénitas* (Aug. 27, 2001), *available at* http://www.derechos.org.ve/pw/wp-content/uploads/acta_compromiso1.pdf.

[117] Tribunal de Protección del Niño y del Adolescente de la Circunscripción Judicial del Área Metropolitana de Caracas, Sala IV de Juicio, CECODAP, ACCSI y PROVEA v. Alcaldía Metropolitana de Caracas, File No. 3174 (July 16, 2001) (Venez.).

[118] On the right to access to information and states' obligations under international human rights law to produce and gather information needed to fulfill its human rights obligations, *see* Office of the Special Rapporteur for Freedom of Expression, Inter American Commission on Human Rights (IACHR), THE INTER-AMERICAN LEGAL FRAMEWORK REGARDING THE RIGHT TO ACCESS TO INFORMATION (2009).

as many as five years at one point in 2010.[119] While it is unclear why morbidity-mortality statistical information was not made public, it was the Minister of Health that directly resolved not to publish the epidemiological reports because of an alleged political and destabilizing misuse given to this information.[120] This prompted two NGOs to file a joint writ of *amparo* before the Constitutional Chamber of the TSJ in 2009. They argued that failure by the state to make this information promptly and readily available is a violation of the right to health, to petition, and to access to information.[121] In June 2010, the newly appointed health minister publicly committed herself to publishing the requested data in a timely manner on the ministry's website; however, her promise was not kept.[122] A decision declaring this claim inadmissible was handed down by the TSJ on July 9, 2010, indicating the legal remedy adequate for challenging this omission was direct litigation against the state before the *contencioso-administrativo* jurisdiction, and not the *amparo* (constitutional jurisdiction).[123]

In March 2012, several NGOs filed another *amparo* before the TSJ against the Health Ministry, owing to its failure to respond to a request for public information, which sought access to information concerning irregularities in the medicines coming from Cuba and being distributed in Venezuela (mostly the distribution of expired medicines). This suit was based on a recommendation and reports issued by the *Contraloría General de la República*[124] to the Ministry of Health, concerning irregularities in the acquisition and distribution of medicines of Cuban origin.[125] On June 18, 2012, the TSJ declared it inadmissible, alleging that the plaintiffs failed

---

[119] Midolis Ramones Servet, *Más de Cinco Meses de Silencio Epidemiológico*, PANORAMA, June 8, 2010, at C-6; PROVEA INFORME ANUAL 2009–2010, *supra* note 33, at 180.

[120] PROVEA INFORME ANUAL 2009–2010, *supra* note 33, at 158.

[121] *Espacio Público y Provea introducen Amparo contra el Ministerio de Salud*, ESPACIO PÚBLICO (Oct. 30, 2009), *available at* http://www.espaciopublico.org/index.php/noticias/134-derechos-humanos/2030-espacio-pco-y-provea-introducen-amparo-contra-el-ministerio-para-la-salud.

[122] PROVEA INFORME ANUAL 2009–2010, *supra* note 33, at 181 (citing Ministra de Salud, Eugenia Sader: Boletín epidemiológico estará a la vista de todos. Ultimas Noticias, 26.06.10. pág. 4).

[123] TSJ, SC, Espacio Público & Provea (Constitutional writ of *amparo* against Ministry of Health), Decision No. 697, File no. 09–1238, (July 9, 2010) (Venez.), *available at* http://www.tsj.gov.ve/decisiones/scon/Julio/697–9710–2010–09–1238.html.

[124] The Contraloría General de la República is an autonomus entity with a constitutional mandate, which serves the state and the Venezuelan people, in the process of controlling, regulating, and demanding accountability in the administration of public funds. Contraloría General de la República, *available at* http://www.cgr.gob.ve/.

[125] ONG Demandan a la Ministra de Salud por No Informar Sobre Medicinas Vencidas [ONG Sue the Health Minister for not Reporting about Expired Medicines], ESPACIO PÚBLICO (March 19, 2012), *available at* http://www.espaciopublico.org/index.php/noticias/134-derechos-humanos/2286-ong-demandan-a-la-ministra-de-salud-por-no-informar-sobre-medicinas-vencidas; Organizaciones de DDHH demandan a Ministerio de Salud por irregularidades en medicinas importadas [HR Organizations Sue the Ministry of Health about Irregularities in Imported Medicines], ESPACIO PÚBLICO (March 19, 2012), *available at* http://www.espaciopublico.org/index.php/noticias/1-libertad-de-expresi/2311-organizaciones-de-ddhh-demandan-a-ministerio-de-salud-por-irregularidades-en-medicinas-importadas.

to demonstrate that the alleged irregularities, including the distribution of medicines past their due date could be tantamount to irreparable harm, making it the basis for an *amparo*.[126] Also, with a similar line of reasoning to the case mentioned before, the TSJ held the adequate legal remedy was a motion before the *contencioso-administrativo* jurisdiction.

15.3.2.6 Private Health Care Systems

In 2003, the TSJ declared the inapplicability of a provision of a 2002 tax law that levied an 8 percent tax (*Impuesto al Valor Agregado* – IVA, equivalent to the Value Added Tax or VAT) on all medical, dental, surgery, and hospitalization services provided by private entities. Such tax was deemed incompatible with "the superior value of justice proposed by the new constitutional model," and the constitutional provision that the state has to guarantee quality health care services to all, without discrimination. The Tribunal stated that the public health care sector is deficient, to the point that the different health centers have exceeded their capacity and lack equipment and medicines needed to provide efficient services, which has left a large section of the population with no choice but to resort to the private sector.[127] This was deemed unfair by the TSJ, especially to lower socioeconomic sectors, which poses threat to the right to equality and nondiscrimination. Similar to the analysis made earlier with respect to measures from the executive and the legislative to control prices and private insurance companies, the impact of this decision is limited in reducing the health care equity gap (and arguably can actually increase the equity gap), as the vast majority of Venezuelans do not have access to the private health care system.

---

[126] TSJ, SC, Carlos Correa, et al. v. Ministra Del Poder Popular Para La Salud, Decision No. 805, File No. 12–0355, (June 18, 2012) (Venez.), *available at* http://www.tsj.gov.ve/decisiones/scon/Junio/805-18612–2012–12–0355.html; *see also* Sala Constitucional del TSJ declaró inadmisible acción de amparo contra la Ministra del Poder Popular Para la Salud [TSJ Constitutional Chamber Declared Inadmissible the Injunction Against the Minister of Health], PROVEA (June 20, 2012), *available at* http://www.derechos.org.ve/2012/06/20/sala-constitucional-del-tsj-declaro-inadmisible-accion-de-amparo-contra-la-ministra-del-poder-popular-para-la-salud/; TSJ Declara Inadmisibile Amparo por Solicitud de Información al MPSS [TSJ Declared Inadmisible the Injunction Requesting Information to MPSS], ESPACIO PÚBLICO (June 25, 2012), *available at* http://www.espaciopublico.org/index.php/noticias/1-libertad-de-expresi/2385-tsj-declara-inadmisible-amparo-por-solicitud-de-informacion-al-mpps. Other *amparos* have been submitted requesting access to information that should be made publicly available by state entities. For example, Provea presented an *amparo* against the director of the National Program on Mental Health because of a written and oral denial to a request for information made in July 2009, on the statistics of cases of mental health in Venezuela for 2009. It is noteworthy that this information was provided to PROVEA by this institution following the *amparo* presented against it. PROVEA INFORME ANUAL 2008–2009, *supra* note 43, at 138.

[127] TSJ, SC, Fernando José Bianco Colmenares v. Venezuela, Decision No. 1505, File No. 03–0124 (June 5, 2003) (Venez.), *available at* http://www.tsj.gov.ve/decisiones/scon/junio/1505–050603–03–0124%20.htm.

15.3.2.7 State's Regulation of Pharmaceuticals

In February 2002, Bayer, Pzifer, and twenty-two other pharmaceutical companies filed a suit challenging the constitutionality of two articles of the 2000 Medicines Act.[128] These articles required pharmaceutical companies to make medicines available in individual quantities (individual presentation), and that all medicines that enter the country had to be clinically tested. The plaintiffs argued that these restrictions imposed an excessive economic burden on pharmaceutical companies, as well as that they represented violations of the rights to health and to freely exercise economic activity. In its 2006 decision, the TSJ ruled against the plaintiffs, arguing that the Constitution established that economic activity can be limited due to health and that no foreign drug can be distributed before its safety and effectiveness are reviewed. Also, that the Medicines Act was enacted to guarantee access to medicines in quantities that could be affordable to lower socioeconomic classes.[129]

15.4 CONCLUSIONS: IMPACT OF LITIGATION ON THE RIGHT TO HEALTH

The lack of independence of the judiciary has become the main element hindering any potential impact that health rights litigation may have on advancing the right to health and improving health outcomes. In order to assess Venezuela's fulfillment of the right to health, the judiciary would need to critically evaluate government policies and actions or omissions. As examined earlier, the 2004 TSJ decision concluding that certain components of the right to health are nonjusticiable may prevent the judiciary from evaluating health policies. More importantly, this closes the door for litigation to tackle structural problems and deficiencies within the health care system, and limits health rights litigation to a much narrower dimension by only entertaining individual cases related to access to medicines and services. Although such individual cases can have broader implications on the fulfillment of the right to health, their impact tends to be more limited. In this context, we identified two positive decisions issued by Venezuelan courts in recent years addressing deficiency of health care services. One concerned the interruption of the night shift in a local health center and the other one addressed deficiency in health care services at the most important children's hospital in the capital. These decisions are important in terms of ensuring availability and quality of health care services and goods, with a potential reach well beyond the plaintiffs who filed the cases. In addition to that,

---

[128] The two articles that the plaintiffs sought to be repealed were Article 51 and 66 of said Act. *Ley de Medicamentos*, OFFICIAL GAZETTE No. 37.006 (Aug. 3, 2000) (Venez.).

[129] TSJ, SC, Bayer S.A, et al v. Ley de Medicamentos (arts. 51 y 66), Decision No. 1107, File No. 2002–0404 (May 26, 2006) (Venez.), *available at* http://www.tsj.gov.ve/decisiones/scon/Mayo/1107–230506–02–0404.htm.

decisions regarding ART for persons living with HIV have had an impact on reducing the health care equity gap. They have helped advance the right to health by ordering ART to be made available, accessible (in particular physical accessibility and nondiscrimination), acceptable, and of quality.[130] However, the government has not yet fully complied with or implemented these decisions. Finally, another positive judicial development comes from a state court (Zulia). This decision sets an important precedent regarding participation of citizens in health policy making. As we can see, there have been progressive decisions on access to ART after the enactment of the 1999 Constitution. Notably, HIV-related litigation has been limited to addressing issues related to access to goods and services, and in the context of individual cases (cases with more limited impact to advance policy reform). Moreover, the somewhat progressive HIV-related case of 2001 was decided by the Supreme Tribunal prior to the entering into force of the 2004 Organic Law of the Supreme Tribunal of Justice, which allowed for expanding the number of justices from twenty to thirty-two to ensure pro-government majority. This 2004 law marked the actual change in the composition of the TSJ and it has been regarded as the starting point for the undermining of the independence of the judiciary. Finally, the Zulia case (state level) is a progressive decision taken after 2004, but it is a state-level ruling (not a TSJ decision), with more limited reach and not constituting a binding precedent.

As examined, the Venezuelan health care system is unregulated, underfunded, and deficient, which directly affects the fulfillment of the right to health. Attempts by government to provide better access to primary health care, although signifying an improvement for lower socioeconomic sectors, cannot tackle the underlying structural problems. Civil society organizations and individuals have sought to remedy some of these structural deficiencies through litigation, without much success. The lack of independence of the judiciary is a key problem in limiting the role that health right litigation can have in improving health outcomes. This is evidenced by the February 2013 decision, in which the TSJ ruled that after thirteen years of delay in enacting a National Health Law, the National Assembly was not at fault (although the 1999 Constitution clearly establishes a two-year period for adapting the legislative framework to the new Constitution).

In 1999, even before the landmark South African decision in *Minister of Health v. Treatment Action Campaign* (2002), the Supreme Court of Venezuela started making significant progress on health rights adjudication and overall justiciability of socioeconomic rights. This progress came to a halt in 2004, when the new TSJ drastically limited its role by excluding public health policies from judicial review. This shift seems to be influenced by the lack of independence of the Judiciary. It is not easy to anticipate whether this trend will continue, but it seems clear that

---

[130] Committee on Economic, Social, and Cultural Rights, *General Comment No. 14, The right to the highest attainable standard of health,* ¶12, 34, 36, 43, U.N. Doc. E/C.12/2000/4 (Aug. 11, 2000).

the current TSJ is reluctant to challenge and review government action. Cases are not decided – they are dismissed on procedural grounds – but even in the cases in which the merits are examined, decisions tend to be narrow and usually supporting the government's actions. In conclusion, in the current scenario, in which both the Venezuelan health care system and the Judiciary have structural systemic problems, it is unlikely that litigation will significantly advance the fulfillment of the right to health.

16

Right to Health

Addressing Inequities through Litigation in India

Anand Grover, Maitreyi Misra, and Lubhyathi Rangarajan

INTRODUCTION

The right to health in India has been shaped by international law, its constitutional mandate, and judicial interpretation. Judicial review has enabled superior courts not only to fill in gaps in legislative and executive action but also to innovate and give content and form to the right to health.

Public health and the health care system in India, examined in Section 16.1, though improving in parts, has a lot of shortcomings. India is lagging behind its targets for Millennium Development Goals (MDGs). Prevalence of non-communicable diseases (NCD) is on the rise. The health care system in India has not been able to tackle these issues, partly because of low health care spending. However, it must be kept in mind that India has a constitutional as well as international obligation to guarantee the right to health, which by implication will require higher domestic spending to secure the right to health and its underlying determinants. These obligations are examined in Section 16.2. Although the government has formulated public health policies informed, at times, by equity, parliament has yet to enact a comprehensive law on the right to health. In such a situation, the judiciary has read the right to health into the fundamental right to life and continuously shaped the right to health. The judiciary not only has played a critical role in providing indicators regarding right-to-health obligations of the state, but has at times directly and immediately brought about policy change within the state, as we examine in Section 16.3. However, the judiciary cannot be expected to urge the state into action at each hurdle. We conclude by emphasizing on need for a comprehensive law, passed by parliament, recognizing the state as the primary duty-bearer and crystallizing the state's mandatory obligations along the framework that the judiciary has already set up.

16.1 HEALTH AND THE HEALTH CARE SYSTEM IN INDIA

India is a developing, lower-middle-income economy with an estimated annual growth rate of 6.88 percent.[1] However, India's spending on health care, as a percentage of its GDP, for the 2007–2011 period was lower than most countries belonging to the same income group such as Swaziland, Ghana, Guatemala, and Uzbekistan.[2] The 2011 census revealed India's population at approximately 1.2 billion, having grown by almost 181 million since 2001. The gender ratio has been historically negative, with only a marginal improvement in the last decade, and is now at 940 females per 1,000 males.[3] Poor health outcomes for women are a result of the culturally disadvantaged position of females in India, which has led to their poor socioeconomic status.[4] A cultural preference for male children has led to high rates of female feticide in India, which prompted the government to ban prenatal diagnostic techniques to determine the sex of the fetus under the 2002 amendment of the Pre-Conception and Pre-Natal Diagnostics Act 1994.

16.1.1 *Burden of Disease*

Indirect contributors to disease causation in India are low socioeconomic status, illiteracy, and poverty.[5] At the clinical level, lack of and inadequate health care, unskilled medical personnel, and low community awareness regarding the public health care system contribute to an already failing public health system. Communicable and non-communicable diseases are on the rise in India, and the public health care system needs to be geared to accommodate increasing number of people within the system. Communicable diseases, maternal, perinatal, and nutritional disorders are responsible for 38 percent of deaths in India.[6]

---

[1] Planning Commission of India, *Data for Use of Deputy-Chairman Planning Commission* (2012), *available at* http://planningcommission.nic.in/data/datatable/0904/comp_data0904.pdf.

[2] *Total Health Expenditure (% of GDP) 2012*, WORLD BANK (2013), *available at* http://data.worldbank.org/indicator/SH.XPD.TOTL.ZS.

[3] Planning Commission of India, *State-Wise Sex Ratio (Female per 1000 Males) in India {As per 1951 to 2011 Census}* (May 18, 2011), *available at* http://planningcommission.nic.in/data/datatable/1705/final_123.pdf.

[4] 36% of adult females are malnourished. *See* Ministry of Health and Family Welfare, Government of India, Annual Report to the People on Health 36 (2011), *available at* http://mohfw.nic.in/WriteReadData/l892s/6960144509Annual%20Report%20to%20the%20People%20on%20Health.pdf.

[5] According to the Planning Commission poverty had declined to 29.8% in 2009–2010. *See* Government of India Planning Commission, Press Note on Poverty Estimates 2009–2010 (March 2012), *available at* http://planningcommission.nic.in/news/press_pov1903.pdf. However, this figure is highly disputed.

[6] Ministry of Health and Family Welfare, Government of India, ANNUAL REPORT TO THE PEOPLE ON HEALTH 13 (2010).

Malaria is a major endemic disease in India according to the World Malaria Report, 2011.[7] In 2010, 66 percent of all reported cases of malaria in the world were from India.[8] HIV/AIDS is also an area of concern. The average national adult prevalence of HIV/AIDS is estimated to be 2.5 million people.[9] Prevalence of TB and deaths attributable to TB, including multi-drug-resistant TB, has also seen resurgence in India. More than 300,000 people die from TB every year in India,[10] and 4.6 percent of people living with TB have HIV as a comorbid infection.[11] With $100 million being incurred as debt annually by persons living with TB, 100,000 women living with TB being stigmatized and ostracized, and 300,000 children permanently discontinuing schooling because of a family member living with TB, the Revised National TB Control Programme faces enormous challenges.[12]

India also struggles with a high prevalence of NCDs, which accounted for approximately 53 percent of all deaths in 2010.[13] India has the largest number of people with diabetes in the world, and prevalence of Type 2 diabetes increased from 3 percent in 1970 to 12 percent in 2000.[14] In the last four decades, coronary heart diseases have seen a twofold increase in rural areas and a sixfold increase in urban areas.[15] In the same time frame, tobacco-related cancers were responsible for 42 percent of male and 18.3 percent of female cancer deaths.[16] India's increasing burden of NCDs can be attributed to high rates of smoking and tobacco use, occupational risks, and poor living conditions.[17] Moreover, demographic and economic transitions, migration, and rapid urbanization have been identified as socioeconomic determinants of the rising prevalence of NCDs. The need for treatment of NCDs has caught the attention of the state only recently, and the government has now set up the National

---

[7] World Health Organization, WORLD MALARIA REPORT 66 (2011).

[8] *Id.* at 66.

[9] Planning Commission of India, Report of the Working Group on Disease Burden for the 12th Five Year Plan (2011), *available at* http://planningcommission.nic.in/aboutus/committee/wrkgrp12/health/WG_3_1communicable.pdf.

[10] *Core Programme Clusters Communicable Diseases and Disease Surveillance: Tuberculosis*, World Health Organization Country Office for India (2010), *available at* http://www.whoindia.org/en/section3/section123.htm.

[11] S.P. Agarwal & L.S. Chauhan, Tuberculosis Control in India (2005), *available at* http://tbcindia.nic.in/pdfs/Tuberculosis%20Control%20in%20India-Final.pdf.

[12] *Id.*

[13] NCD Country Profiles: India, World Health Organization (2011), *available at* http://www.who.int/nmh/countries/ind_en.pdf.

[14] K. Srinath Reddy et al., *Responding to the Threat of Chronic Diseases in India*, 366 THE LANCET 1744, 1744 (2005).

[15] *Id.*

[16] Rajesh Dixit et al., *Cancer Mortality in India: A Nationally Representative Survey*, 379 THE LANCET 1807, 1811 (2012).

[17] Monika Arora et al., *Multi-Sectoral Action for Addressing Social Determinants of Non-Communicable Diseases and Mainstreaming Health Promotion in National Health Programs in India*, 36(5) INDIAN J. OF COMMUNITY MEDICINE, 43, 44 (2011).

Cancer Control Program and the National Programme for Prevention and Control of Diabetes, Cardiovascular Diseases and Strokes.[18]

16.1.2 *Millennium Development Goals (MDGs)*

Improving maternal health, reducing child mortality, and combating HIV/AIDS, malaria, and other diseases are the three health MDGs. The MDGs are a set of goals (indicators) that countries set for themselves in 2000, and which are to be achieved by 2015. Eradication of extreme poverty and hunger is, along with the other MDGs, an underlying determinant of health. According to the MDG indicators – a report card reflecting a country's development in, primarily, public health spheres – India needs to improve its public health outcomes. Although poverty levels have fallen, India will miss its MDG target of reducing poverty levels to 18.5 percent[19] of the total population by 2015. Malnutrition and child health is also an area of concern in India. According to the MDG for child health, India should reduce the proportion of underweight children below the age of three to 26 percent, but the actual figure still hovers at 33 percent.[20] In 2010, the infant mortality ratio (IMR) was 47, the neonatal mortality ratio was 33, and the under-five mortality ratio was 59 per 1,000 live births, respectively.[21] Maternal mortality ratio (MMR), albeit reduced, was estimated to be 212 per 100,000 live births between 2007 and 2009.[22] It is predicted that India will fall short of the goal set for MMR. Similarly, although infant mortality has seen a reduction, India will still fall short of its goal of 26.67 per 1,000 children by 2015.[23] Though adequate funds are disbursed at a provincial level, poor implementation of policies and lack of accountability impedes progress in achieving MDGs.[24] To achieve the public health targets set by the MDGs, India must build on existing health facilities and develop strategies to provide health care services to all regions and people, especially the vulnerable and marginalized sections of society.

---

[18] *Id.* at 47.

[19] Ministry of Statistics and Programme Implementation, Millennium Development Goals: States of India Report 2010, xii (2011), *available at* http://mospi.nic.in/mospi_new/upload/MDG_2010_18oct11. pdf.

[20] *Id.* at 4–5.

[21] Census Commissioner of India, Estimates of Mortality Indicators in Sample Registration System Statistical Report (2010), *available at* http://www.censusindia.gov.in/vital_statistics/srs/Chap_4_-_2010. pdf.

[22] Ministry of Home Affairs Office of Registrar General, India, Sample Registration System, Special Bulletin for Maternal Mortality in India 2007–2009 (June, 2011), *available at* http://www.censusindia. gov.in/vital_statistics/SRS_Bulletins/Final-MMR%20Bulletin-2007-09_070711.pdf.

[23] UN Resident Coordinator's Office, MDGs, United Nations in India (2011), *available at* http://www. un.org.in/_layouts/UNDP/MDG.aspx.

[24] Newsroom, Achieving MDGs in India: Elimination of Inequalities and Harnessing New Opportunities for Implementation of Policies and Programmes, UNDP (Sep. 8, 2010), *available at* http://content. undp.org/go/newsroom/2010/september/achieving-mdgs-in-india.en.

16.1.3 *India's Health Care System*

According to the Indian Constitution, health and the health care system fall under the domain of state governments rather than the federal government. However, the central government also contributes to policies and makes financial contributions.

India has a complex mixed health care system, with the state-run health care system operating in parallel with the private health care system. India currently lacks universal health coverage, although it is under consideration.[25] The public health care system, though in theory accessible to all, lacks adequate number of health care professionals, which limits accessibility and quality. It is estimated that currently the public sector provides only about 20 percent of actual health care services.[26] Low spending on health care and shortage of health care professionals are acknowledged as impediments to a good public health system in India.[27] Though public health services are heavily subsidized and in some cases are free, low spending and capacity issues plague state-run services. On the other hand, private health care expenditure, which remains largely outside state control, stood at 3.3 percent of GDP in 2011, whereas central government expenditure amounted to around 1 percent.[28] Moreover, the private health system is concentrated in urban areas and provides mainly secondary and tertiary facilities. Preventive facilities are mostly provided by the public health care system; 90 percent of immunizations and 60 percent of prenatal care are provided by the public sector in India.[29]

Lack of universal coverage for health results in out-of-pocket payments (OOP) and has continuously been pushing people in India into poverty. Dissatisfaction with the quality of care in the public sector might also be a reason for individuals who are poor to seek care in the private sector, which relies heavily on OOP.[30] In 2004–2005, about 39 million people were pushed into poverty because of OOP.[31] The percentage of people who are unable to afford and access the health care system in India is substantial, especially because most health care facilities are located in

[25] Planning Commission of India, High Level Expert Group Report on Universal Health Coverage for India (2011), *available at* http://planningcommission.nic.in/reports/genrep/rep_uhc0812.pdf. [hereinafter: Universal Health Coverage for India].

[26] Stephen M. Sammut & Lawton R. Burns, Meeting the Challenges of Healthcare Needs in India: Paths to Innovation, 9(2) Insight 5, 5 (2007), *available at* http://www.isb.edu/isb/File/ISBInsight_Volume9Issue2-Media.pdf.

[27] Planning Commission of India, Faster, Sustainable and More Inclusive Growth: An Approach to the Twelfth Five Year Plan, India Environmental Portal 8 (2011), *available at* http://www.indiaenvironmentportal.org.in/files/file/An_approach_to_the_twelfth_five_year_plan_Draft_report_Planning_Commission_2011.pdf.

[28] Universal Health Coverage for India, *supra* note 25, at 23.

[29] David H. Peters & V. R. Muraleedharan, *Regulating India's Health Services: To What End? What Future?* 66 Soc. Sci. & Med. 2133 (2008).

[30] Y. Balarajan, S. Selvaraj & S. V. Subramanian, *Health Care and Equity in India*, 377 The Lancet 505, 509 (2011).

[31] *Id.* at 505.

urban areas; 84 percent of hospital beds are in urban areas, yet 75 percent of the population resides in villages.[32] Even though India produces the cheapest medicines in the world, a WHO World Medicine Report found that it has the largest number of people (649 million in 2004) lacking access to essential medicines.[33] Thus, within India's health care system, high-quality health care goods, services, and facilities are neither accessible nor affordable for a large section of the population.

A high-quality health care system includes and requires a well-functioning primary health care system. The Indian National Health Policy, formulated periodically, establishes the primary health care system as the responsibility of the government.[34] Primary health care is delivered mainly through state-run primary health centers where each center serves between 20,000 and 30,000 people in rural and urban areas, respectively.[35] Human resource and infrastructural challenges plague the effective delivery of health services, which cannot cope with an increasing population. As of 2001, India required 26,022 primary health centers, while at least 880 vacancies for doctors need to be filled in the current centers.[36]

16.1.4 *Future Prospects*

In the latest Five Year Plan, covering the period between 2012 and 2017, the total public health expenditure by the central and state governments as proposed by the Planning Commission is 2.5 percent of GDP[37] (though the global average for middle-income countries is approximately 5 percent).[38] Nonetheless, this is an increase in public expenditure over the previous Five Year Plan, which was around 1.4 percent.[39] In addition to the planned increase in public expenditure, there are other positive developments. For example, the polio eradication program has been successful. From close to 800 polio cases in 1998, India reported zero polio cases in 2012 and was removed from the WHO list of polio-endemic countries.[40] According to official data, under the National AIDS Control Program, approximately 380,000 million people living with HIV (PLHIV) were being treated at antiretroviral treatment centers in association with the National AIDS Control Organisation, a

[32] Ravi Duggal, The Private Health Sector in India: Nature, Trends, and a Critique 11 (2000).

[33] Amit Sengupta et. al., Economic Constraints to Access to Essential Medicines in India, at 1(2008), *available at* http://www.healthpolicy.cn/rdfx/jbywzd/gjjy2/yd/yjwx/201002/P020100227571385215688.pdf.

[34] Ministry of Health and Family Welfare, National Health Policy 2002 (India) (2002), *available at* http://www.mohfw.nic.in/NRHM/Documents/National_Health_policy_2002.pdf.

[35] Ministry of Health and Family Welfare, Report of the Working Group on Public Health Services (including Water & Sanitation) for the Eleventh Five-Year Plan (2007–2012), 29 (Sept., 2006), *available at* http://planningcommission.nic.in/aboutus/committee/wrkgrp11/wg11_rphfw1.pdf.

[36] *Id.* at 30.

[37] Newsroom, *supra* note 24, at 7.

[38] World Bank, *supra* note 2.

[39] Newsroom, *supra* note 24, at 87.

[40] India Taken Off Who's List of Polio Endemic Countries, WHO (2013), *available at* http://www.searo.who.int/entity/immunization/topics/polio/polio_summit_india/en/index.html.

central government-established body.[41] However, nearly 55–60 percent of PLHIV in India are co-infected with TB, making it a leading cause of death.[42] In response, the government established the National Framework for Joint HIV/TB Collaborative Activities to strengthen a cross-referral system.[43] Further the central government has established the National Rural Health Mission (NRHM), which pays special attention to maternal, infant, and primary health care.[44] One of the policies under NRHM provides prenatal and postnatal care to below-poverty-line pregnant women to incentivize deliveries in health care institutions. To increase hospital usage by people living below poverty line, the *Rashtriya Swasthya Bima Yojna* (RSBY), an insurance scheme, was adopted to provide hospitalization coverage up to Rs. 30,000 ($ 551.40) per annum.[45] These schemes promote a more equitable health system by concentrating on the poor and vulnerable sections of society, such as women and PLHIV.

Although schemes such as RSBY exist, their impact is diluted because of corruption and lack of accountability. The evaluation report by the Planning Commission of India for the Integrated Child Development Scheme, for instance, acknowledges that in 2008–2009, approximately 59.7 percent of funds were siphoned off from reserved funds.[46] Thus, while steps are being taken in the right direction, what is still conspicuously lacking is comprehensive legislation placing a positive duty on the state in respect of the right to health, and which provides for independent monitoring and auditing mechanisms to enhance transparency in collection, allocation, and utilization of public funds.

16.2 INTERNATIONAL AND DOMESTIC OBLIGATIONS OF THE STATE WITH RESPECT TO THE RIGHT TO HEALTH

16.2.1 *International Obligations*

India has ratified a number of international instruments with health as an explicit right,[47] including the International Covenant of Economic, Social, and Cultural

---

[41] National AIDS Control Organization: Department of AIDS Control, Annual Report 2010–2011, xi (2011), *available at* http://www.nacoonline.org/upload/REPORTS/NACO%20Annual%20Report%202010–11.pdf.

[42] UNGASS India, Country Progress Report, 53 (2010), *available at* http://www.unaids.org/en/dataanalysis/knowyourresponse/countryprogressreports/2010countries/india_2010_country_progress_report_en.pdf.

[43] *Id.* at 54.

[44] National Rural Health Mission, Ministry of Health and Family Welfare (Mission Document (2005–2012)), *available at* http://www.mohfw.nic.in/NRHM/Documents/Mission_Document.pdf.

[45] Ministry of Labour and Employment, About Us – What Is RSBY?, Rashtriya Swasthya Bima Yojna (2012), *available at* http://www.rsby.gov.in/about_rsby.aspx.

[46] Program Evaluation Organization Planning Commission Government of India, Evaluation Report on Integrated Child Development Services (2011), *available at* http://planningcommission.nic.in/reports/peoreport/peo/peo_icds_vol1.pdf.

[47] India is party to the following international law instruments, which also deal with the right to health of particular groups of people: *International Covenant on Economic, Social and Cultural Rights*, G.A. res.

Rights (ICESCR), which India acceded to on July 10, 1979. The ICESCR imposes an obligation to "recognize the right of everyone to the enjoyment of the highest attainable standard of physical and mental health" under Article 12. The General Comment 14 of the Committee on Economic, Social, and Cultural Rights[48] (General Comment 14) in its elaboration of the right to health mentions that states are mandated to respect, protect, and fulfill the right to health. The right has been interpreted as including underlying determinants of health such as the right to food, housing, work, education, human dignity, life, nondiscrimination, equality, privacy, and access to information.[49] Four essential elements have been identified as integral to the right to health: availability, accessibility, affordability, and quality of all health facilities, goods, and services. The right to health includes freedoms and entitlements. It also includes the principles of adequate progress and non-retrogression, participation, transparency, accountability, and monitoring as well as proportionality, that is, when limiting the right to health of an individual the least restrictive alternative must be applied where several types of limitations are available. Unlike civil and political rights, the right to health – an economic and social right – is progressively realizable and is dependent on available resources. However, certain obligations, including nondiscrimination, are to be realized with immediate effect. Similarly, core obligations, such as ensuring access to health facilities, goods, and services on a nondiscriminatory basis, are minimum conditions and are non-derogable.

As India is a dualist state, international law needs to be incorporated in Indian law through an Act of parliament to have domestic legal validity. Traditionally, obligations arising out of international law were not enforceable in municipal courts in India unless backed by legislation.[50] In the event of a conflict between domestic law and international law, the former would prevail.[51] The Supreme Court in *Vishaka v. State of Rajasthan*,[52] however, substantially altered this

---

2200A (XXI), 21 U.N. GAOR Supp. (No. 16) at 49, U.N. Doc. A/6316 (1966), 993 U.N.T.S. 3, *entered into force* Jan. 3, 1976; *Convention on the Elimination of All Forms of Discrimination Against Women*, G.A. res. 34/180, 34 U.N. GAOR Supp. (No. 46) at 193, U.N. Doc. A/34/46 (1979), 1249 U.N.T.S. 13, *entered into force* Sept. 3, 1981 [hereinafter: CEDAW]; Convention on the Rights of the Child, G.A. res. 44/25, Annex, 44 U.N. GAOR Supp. (No. 49) at 167, U.N. Doc. A/44/49 (1989), *entered into force* Sept. 2.

[48] *International Covenant on Economic, Social and Cultural Rights*, G.A. res. 2200A (XXI), 21 U.N. GAOR Supp. (No. 16) at 49, U.N. Doc. A/6316 (1966), 993 U.N.T.S. 3, *entered into force* Jan. 3, 1976;Committee on Economic, Social, and Cultural Rights, *General Comment No. 14, The right to the highest attainable standard of health*, para. 12, 34, 36, 43, U.N. Doc. E/C.12/2000/4 (Aug. 11, 2000), reprinted in Compilation of General Comments and General Recommendations Adopted by Human Rights Treaty Bodies, U.N. Doc. HRI/GEN/1/Rev.6 at 85 (2003), *available at* http://documents-ddsny. un.org/doc/UNDOC/GEN/G00/439/34/pdf/G0043934.pdf?OpenElement.

[49] *Id.* para. 3.

[50] Birma v. State of Rajasthan, A.I.R. 1951 Raj. 127 (India); Civil Rights Vigilance Committee, Bangalore v. Union of India, A.I.R. 1983 Kant. 85 (India).

[51] V/O Tractor Export, Moscow v. Tarapore and Co. and Anr., A.I.R. 1971 S.C. 1 (India).

[52] Vishaka v. State of Rajasthan, A.I.R. 1997 S.C. 3011 (India).

position. The case concerned a woman who was raped while at work. India had ratified Convention on Elimination of Discrimination Against Women,[53] but it had failed to transform its obligations into domestic law. Nonetheless, and in the absence of contrary domestic law, the Supreme Court invoked provisions of CEDAW to hold the state liable for failing to put in place laws protecting women from discrimination and gender-based violence at the workplace. The Court reasoned that as the state had a constitutional obligation to promote international law,[54] and as international law was not at odds with constitutionally guaranteed fundamental rights, it could be read into domestic law to enlarge and strengthen constitutional guarantees and fill any vacuum left unattended by domestic law. This jurisprudence is extremely relevant in right to health litigation, because there is no comprehensive federal domestic health legislation and the state legislation in place has many gaps into which can be read obligations sourced in international law. As we demonstrate later in the chapter, international obligations under the right to health have since been called on with increased frequency to hold the state and its instrumentalities accountable for failing to respect, protect, and fulfill the right to health.

16.2.2 *Constitutional Obligation*

In India, the Constitution is the supreme law and all other laws are subordinate to it. Fundamental Rights, akin to civil and political rights, enshrined in Part III of the Constitution, are negative covenants against state legislation or action and are enforceable by courts. Socioeconomic rights are enshrined as Directive Principles of State Policy (Directive Principles) contained in Part IV of the Constitution and are intended to promote an equitable social order. Although not enforceable by any court, the Directive Principles are fundamental in the governance of the country, and it is the duty of the state to apply these principles in making laws. Even though there is no explicit fundamental right to health in the Constitution, the state has an obligation to improve public health, under Part IV, in Article 39 (e) (right to health of workers) and (f) (right to health of children) and Article 47 (obligation of the state to improve public health). Further, as we discuss later in the chapter, the right to health has been read in as part of the right to life under Article 21.

The constitutional scheme in India follows the doctrine of separation of powers. The Constitution envisages, and India does have, a strong and independent judiciary. Courts are empowered to test the validity of statutes against fundamental rights and review state action.[55] They can strike down constitutional amendments if they

---

[53] India ratified CEDAW on June 25, 1993.
[54] INDIA CONST. art. 51(c).
[55] The Supreme Court and High Courts have writ jurisdiction for the enforcement of fundamental rights or any other purpose (judicial review). *Id.* at art. 32, 226.

breach the basic structure of the constitution[56] or if they infringe fundamental rights.[57]

It was in *Francis Coralie Mullin v. The Administrator, Union Territory of Delhi,*[58] a case involving facilities to be provided to a prisoner, that the Supreme Court tore apart the artificial barrier between civil and political rights and socioeconomic rights. It reinterpreted Article 21, which provides that "no person shall be deprived of his life or liberty except by procedure established by law" – a classical civil and political right and a negative covenant – into a positive obligation on the state. The Court used dignity as the fulcrum and held that a prisoner's dignity meant that she was entitled to the bare necessities of life, save and except those which could not be provided in a prison. Following on the heels of the *Mullin* decision, the Supreme Court has judicially embedded the right to health, along with a number of other social and economic rights, within the fundamental right to life.

16.2.3 *Statutory Obligations*

Within the domestic framework, and apart from constitutional obligations, a number of laws and policies exist that regulate India's health and health care system. As background it is relevant to remind the reader that as a matter of constitutional propriety, the central government is precluded from legislating on certain subjects, such as public health and sanitation, and hospitals and dispensaries, which fall under the domain of state governments. However, if two or more states want the center to legislate on such a subject, the central government can do so. In such a scenario, the legislation is not automatically binding on other states. The other states can choose not to use the central law, instead regulating through their own state laws. This is why the health care sector (both public and private) may be differentially regulated in states.

One of the biggest hindrances in the quality of health care provided in India is a severe lack of enforceable regulation and oversight mechanisms. For instance, although the Consumer Protection Act 1986 covers deficiency in service and medical negligence, there is a conspicuous lack of a body of laws establishing rights, duties, and available remedies between recipients of services and service providers and health care workers. An important aspect of a well-functioning health care system, health financing also falls outside the purview of regulation and is seen as falling

---

[56] Kesavananda Bharti v. State of Kerala, A.I.R. 1973 S.C. 1461 (India); Minerva Mills v. Union of India, A.I.R. 1980 S.C. 1789 (India). Judicial review is part of the immutable basic structure of the Constitution.

[57] Golaknath v. State of Punjab, A.I.R. 1967 S.C. 143 (India); Kesavananda Bharti v. State of Kerala, A.I.R. 1973 S.C. 1461 (India). Constitutional amendments have subsequently been struck down: Minerva Mills v. Union of India, A.I.R. 1980 S.C. 1789 (India); Chandra Kumar v. Union of India, A.I.R. 1997 S.C. 1125 (India).

[58] Francis Coralie Mullin v. The Administrator, Union Territory of Delhi, A.I.R. 1981 S.C. 746 (India).

squarely within the four corners of government policy. Moreover, the private sector, which accounts for almost 80 percent of outpatient visits in the country,[59] is also largely unregulated, although cases regarding medical negligence and deficiency of service can be brought against doctors in private clinics and hospitals.

With respect to the health care system, The Clinical Establishments (Registration and Regulation) Act 2010 partially regulates the private sector by imposing minimum requirements of space and infrastructure for the effective functioning of all medical establishments. Additionally, it imposes a duty on all doctors to provide emergency health care but fails to monetarily compensate them for it. The Act came into effect this year after multiple legal challenges on the ground that it hinders the autonomous functioning of private practitioners.[60] However, the Act has been adopted by only a few states.

The public health system and public health are regulated to a certain extent through laws, but these laws are not sufficient in terms of the ground they cover. These laws also do not approach the public health system or public health from a rights-based perspective. Therefore, they lack requirements of right to health such as the obligation of the state to make available accessible, acceptable, and quality health facilities, goods, and services, which are extremely important for a successful rights-based approach to health.

For example, The Epidemic Diseases Act 1897, a federal law, controls and aims to prevent the spread of dangerous epidemic diseases by delegating necessary powers to state governments. This is due to geographical and other indicators that aggravate a disease in a particular province, requiring specialized prevention and control techniques. In addition, state (provincial) enactments impose duties on local authorities to ensure that standards of public health are met through consistent intervention. However, this Act also omits requirements of the right to health such as nondiscrimination and the right to autonomy and community participation in the decision-making process.

Regulation of drugs in India is under the Drugs and Cosmetics Act 1940, which establishes the Central Drug Standards Control Organization (CDSCO) as the functioning authority. Drug prices in India are the cheapest in the world, because there was no product patent protection until 2005 when India became TRIPS compliant. A report by the Parliamentary Standing Committee on Health and Family Welfare[61] in 2012, however, exposed the "skewed priorities and perceptions of CDSCO"[62] in

---

[59] Peters & Muraleedharan, *supra* note 29, at 2135.

[60] R Ramachandran, Public Health Crisis, Frontline 4 (July 13, 2012), *available at* http://pay.hindu.com/ ebook%20-%20ebfl20120713part1.pdf.

[61] Rajya Sabha Secretariat, Department-Related Parliamentary Standing Committee on Health and Family Welfare, 59th Report on The Functioning of the Central Drugs Standard Control Organisation (CDSCO) (2012), *available at* http://164.100.47.5/newcommittee/reports/EnglishCommittees/ Committee%20on%20Health%20and%20Family%20Welfare/59.pdf.

[62] *Id.* at 9.

contributing to drug regulation. The report states that CDSCO has been favoring the drug-manufacturing industry over the public interest. It also reveals a collusive nexus between drug manufacturers, medical professionals, and government authorities in the approval of new drugs. The report comments on the wide discretionary powers of the CDSCO and indicates a severe lack of accountability in the decision-making process, which could have a detrimental effect on public health.[63]

In response to its international obligation under the Framework Convention on Tobacco Control and domestic obligation to promote public health, India passed, in 2003, the Cigarettes and Other Tobacco Products (Prohibition of Advertisement and Regulation of Trade and Commerce, Production, Supply and Distribution) Act (COPTA). The purpose of the Act is to prohibit the advertisement of, and to provide for the regulation of trade and commerce in, and production, supply, and distribution of, cigarettes and other tobacco products.

The Medical Termination of Pregnancy Act, 1971 (MTP Act), along with the Pre-conception and Pre-natal Diagnostics Techniques Act, 1994 (PCPNDT Act), deals with the right to reproductive health of women. The object of the MTP Act is to regulate abortions, making the consent of the pregnant woman paramount. The PCPNDT Act prohibits sex-selective abortion in order to prevent female feticide and to provide stronger protection of the woman's right to reproductive health. The Draft HIV/AIDS Bill and the Draft National Health Bill are currently being pushed for enactment to introduce a rights-based approach to public health. The National Health Bill, if passed, would for the first time statutorily recognize the right to health in India, including specific obligations of the central as well as the state government to respect, protect, and fulfill the right to health. The HIV/AIDS Bill would ensure statutorily enforceable rights for people living with HIV/AIDS in India. It would specifically prohibit discrimination against people living with HIV/AIDS even within the private sector. Both Bills will strengthen and take forward the existing judicially created framework of rights and duties in India.

16.3 THE ROLE OF THE JUDICIARY IN FORMULATING THE RIGHT TO HEALTH

Against the backdrop of insufficient statutory obligations and nonbinding constitutional obligations of the state, courts have been an important actor in providing a structure to right to health obligations of the state and spurring the health rights movement in India. To facilitate realization of fundamental rights, the Supreme Court devised the concept of public interest litigation (PIL). Originally PIL was fashioned out of the need to promote the rule of law and facilitate access to justice. In conjunction with Directive Principles of State Policy, PIL was conceived as a

[63] *Id.* at 37.

vehicle to initiate socioeconomic change[64] and allow litigants seeking social and economic justice to challenge legislation and executive measures on behalf of a vulnerable, disadvantaged community while doing away with prerequisite procedural measures. PIL is still used by NGOs advocating for the rights of the disadvantaged, but strong private interests also have begun to further their interests through PIL in the disguise of fundamental rights claims.[65] For instance, in *Malick Brothers*,[66] the Supreme Court characterized public interest actions as those redressing public injury and required for enforcing public duties. The Court dismissed the case as it related to matters benefitting an individual rather than society.

In what follows we use a selection of cases to trace the development of the right to health. We have chosen cases that reflect the landmarks and milestones in the developing jurisprudence of the right to health in India. We first discuss the right to access affordable medicines and treatment in India. This issue is of special significance in India because of its link with the socioeconomic status of the country. As a result of low health care spending and high out-of-pocket expenditure, health financing issues, which we deal with next, go to the heart of India's crumbling health care system. The high cost of treatment in the country and the lack of universal health coverage also highlight the problems related to affordability of health care. Rights related to and arising out of the right to health, such as nondiscrimination, the right to reproductive health, and the right to employment of PLHIV are looked at subsequently. Rights to employment and nondiscrimination have been chosen to illustrate the treatment of public health vis-à-vis the individual right to health. The right to reproductive health also has special importance in India owing to the culturally vulnerable situation of women. Lastly, we take a brief look at the treatment of public health in relation to tobacco use and its treatment by the courts.

16.3.1 *Access to Medicines and Treatment*

The state's obligation to provide access to medicines was addressed by the Supreme Court in *Vincent Panikurlangara v. Union of India*.[67] In a PIL objecting to the sale of drugs that had been banned by the state, the Court stressed the need to ensure access to high-quality medicines at affordable rates. Although the Court admitted that it did not have the requisite expertise to measure the far-reaching implications of banning medicines, it called for rigorous monitoring of the manufacture and sale of drugs, and for implementing measures to prevent harmful drugs from entering the market.

---

[64] PIL was first referred to in Hussainara Khatoon and Ors v. Home Secretary, State of Bihar, Patna, A.I.R. 1979 S.C. 1360 (India).
[65] Malick Brothers v. Narendra Dadhich, (1999) 6 S.C.C. 552 (India).
[66] *Id.*
[67] Vincent Panikurlangara v. Union of India, A.I.R. 1987 S.C. 990 (India).

The Court endorsed the reasoning employed by the Supreme Court in *Mullin* that the right to life, as all other fundamental rights, derived its meaning from Directives Principles, which urged the state to create just and humane conditions of work and to secure the health of workers. The Court added another component to it by linking the right to life with the state's obligation to improve public health under Article 47 of the Constitution. It formulated the obligation of the state as creating a system to ensure that for every treatable illness, the patient must be able to access the relevant medicine. It mentioned that the state's obligation extended to making useful drugs available in abundance at reasonable price so as to be within the common person's reach and in doing so highlighted the importance of affordability and availability – issues related to access to medicines and treatment, which were so recognized only much later in General Comment 14. In order to convert the obligation to improve public health from a constitutional ideal to a reality, the Court urged the state to read even non-enforceable constitutional obligations as imperatives and recommended the formulation of a national policy that would promote universal access to quality and affordable medicines.

The Court has on many occasions enforced the state's obligation to improve public health from the lens of access to health care facilities, goods, and services. Access to affordable medicines and treatment is one of the issues where the Court has consistently highlighted the link between the state's duty to improve public health and the right to health and life. Recognizing the importance of making medicines economically accessible, the government is putting in place policies to promote generic medicines in the market and to make generic medicines available free of charge to users of the public health care system.

In *Pt. Paramanada Katara v. Union of India*, the Supreme Court addressed the issue of governmental failure to provide timely emergency medical care.[68] In this case, an accident victim was not permitted to be treated at the hospital closest to the accident site, but was referred to another hospital for fear of tort liability. Sadly, given the time taken to travel from one hospital to the other, the victim died. Referring to the Code of Medical Ethics, which makes it a doctor's duty to provide emergency care without exception, the Court urged doctors to provide emergency care without apprehensions regarding legal proceedings that may follow in a medico-legal case. To reduce the apprehension of doctors, the Court urged the law enforcement agencies as well as courts to not require the services of doctors, in medico-legal cases, such as road accidents, unless necessary. It emphasized the fact that any law or state action preventing the discharge of obligations cast on the medical profession would be unsustainable and called for a simplification of medico-legal cases to avoid loss of lives caused by procedural requirements imposed by law. Although the Court did not explicitly address the right to health, it placed

---

[68] Pt. Paramanada Katara v. Union of India, (1989) 3 S.C.R. 997 (India).

emphasis on the value of human life and sought to balance legal requirements with a doctor's anxiety regarding legal procedures.

The right to emergency medical care was stressed again by the Supreme Court in a case of refusal to treat a patient in *Paschim Banga Khet Mazdoor Samiti v. State of West Bengal.*[69] Once again the constitutional obligation of a welfare state to make available and ensure adequate and high-quality health care facilities as a component of the right to life was underlined as a mandate rather than an unenforceable obligation of the state. The Court held that failure by a government hospital to provide treatment to a person results in violation of the person's fundamental right to life. Further, the Court held that violation of a fundamental right required the government to provide adequate compensation to the victim. With specific reference to emergency medical care, the Court laid down guidelines to create a coordinated network of hospitals, which would ensure that each hospital has information about where to best refer a patient. Notably, the Court held that the obligation of the state to provide medical aid to preserve human life could not be disregarded because of financial constraints of the state.

Similarly, the Delhi High Court tested accessibility of health care in the private health care sector against the right to life and the now related duty of the state to promote public health in *Social Jurist, A Lawyer's Group v. Government of NCT.*[70] Private specialty hospitals were provided land by the state at concessional rates on the condition of setting aside a percentage of beds for the poor. It was found that some hospitals violated this contractual condition. By linking the right to life to a co-relative duty of the state to improve public health, the Court held that access to and quality of health care could not be "rendered nugatory by inaction or inadequate action on the part of the State."[71] The Court made it clear that it was the state's duty to ensure that terms and obligations under the contract were being complied with. While tying the state's responsibility to promote public health with the right to life, the Court held that this responsibility does not end with the state but extends to all those "placed at an advantageous situation because of the help or allotment of vital assets,"[72] such as land. The Court issued directions to the hospitals to comply with the terms of their agreement with the government. Additionally, it evolved a procedure for referral of patients from government hospitals to these super-specialty private hospitals. It ordered a special committee to be constituted to ensure the directions of the Court were being followed.

In *KS Gopinath v. Union of India,*[73] a PIL, the Karnataka High Court examined the constitutionality of a pharmaceutical policy in the context of price control of essential drugs against the right to equality and the right to life. The Essential Commodities

[69] Paschim Banga Khet Mazdoor Samiti v. State of West Bengal, (1996) 4 S.C.C. 37 (India).

[70] Social Jurist, A Lawyer's Group v. Government of NCT, (2007) 140 D.L.T. 698 (India).

[71] *Id.* at para. 1.

[72] *Id.* at para. 94.

[73] KS Gopinath v. Union of India, (2003) 1 K.C.C.R. 269 (India).

Act 1955 empowers the state to control the price at which essential commodities may be bought or sold to secure their equitable distribution and availability at fair prices. The offending policy sought to exclude essential drugs from price control based on two major criteria supplemented by market research: mass consumption of the drug and absence of sufficient competition in such drugs. Before analyzing the policy, the Court stated that courts should not strike down policy decisions as a rule. According to the Court, public policy can be tested only against illegality and unconstitutionality. The state argued that the policy was in keeping with India's obligations under the WTO as it liberalized the economy. However, the Court, while upholding the fundamental right to health, deemed that "[a]bundant availability on a continuous basis, at reasonable prices, of essential, life-saving and prophylactic medicines of good quality is the cornerstone of any [p]harmaceutical policy."[74] It held that the consideration of sales turnover as an element of price regulation was unreliable and insufficient. As some essential drugs would be unable to reach the sales turnover threshold under the policy, essential medicines would fall outside price regulation and would therefore be susceptible to increase in prices. The Model List of Essential Drugs by WHO also had not been taken into account by the policy makers. The policy was struck down as arbitrary and against public interest as it prevented equitable accessibility of essential life-saving drugs.[75]

In *Novartis AG v. Union of India*,[76] the Madras High Court linked issues of patentability of pharmaceuticals to that of access to medicines in the country. With India becoming TRIPS compliant in 2005, product patents were introduced within the legal regime. However, the amended provision, Section 3 (d) of the Patent Act 1970, establishes certain qualifications for patentability and disallows patents for known substances unless the known substance displays enhanced efficacy. To prevent ever-greening, new forms of known substances that do not prove enhanced efficacy from those in existence are not eligible for patents under the section. Novartis challenged this provision as unconstitutional, unreasonable, and incompatible with TRIPS. Novartis argued that the efficacy criterion was arbitrary due to a lack of

---

[74] *Id.* at para. 16.

[75] In an unreported case, the Supreme Court directed the government to "consider and formulate appropriate criteria for ensuring that essential and lifesaving drugs do not fall out of price control and further directed [*sic*] to review drugs which are essential and lifesaving in nature . . . " *See* Draft National Pharmaceuticals Pricing Policy (Nov. 15, 2011), *available at* http://pharmaceuticals.gov.in/mshT2810/FTY2.pdf, which mitigates these concerns to a certain extent.

[76] Novartis AG v. Union of India, (2007) 4 M.L.J. 1153 (India). The decision is currently under appeal in the Supreme Court of India, *see* SLP (Civil) Nos. 20539–20549 of 2009. Novartis appealed the order of the IPAB in the Supreme Court of India. However, the appeal was dismissed on April 1, 2013. The Supreme Court rejected Novartis's patent on the drug. It held that Novartis's drug did not fulfill the requirements of Section 3(d) of the Patent Act, and therefore could not be patented in India. The Court established the path for making drugs more affordable and accessible while at the same time upholding the patent regime in India as one that awards genuine inventions. See Novartis AG v. Union of India, Civil Appeal Nos. 2706–2716 of 2013, Court – Supreme Court of India, Date of Judgment – 1 April 2013.

guidelines on the meaning of "significant efficacy." The Court rejected the argument on the ground that the meaning of efficacy was well understood by people of science. Interpreting section 3(d) as a measure to promote access to medicines and public health, the Court observed that the section allows cheaper and generic versions of drugs to enter the market. In keeping with the constitutional notions of an equitable social order, the Court upheld the amendment while pronouncing the need to make cheaper drugs available. By ensuring that pharmaceutical companies were unable to patent non-efficacious new forms of known drugs, the Court bolstered efforts by the state to encourage competition between generic and brand name drugs to counter high medicine prices. The Court reiterated the state's constitutional obligation to provide good health care by ensuring easy and affordable access to life-saving drugs. Implicitly, the Court seems to have established a consensus with precedents discussed earlier, on ensuring that private companies do not exploit the constitutional ideal of a democratic health system in a bid to become profitable.

The Supreme Court rejected fiscal and capacity-related concerns as reasons for denial of health care to PLHIV in a PIL, *Sahara House v. Union of India and Ors.*[77] Although the National AIDS Control Organization (NACO) maintained its commitment to treatment and prevention of HIV/AIDS, it continued to put restraints in its ART regimen. Until the decision in *Sahara*, second-line treatment was available only to those people who had undergone first-line treatment in treatment centers registered with the NACO. On the Court's direction, the NACO, lawyers for the respective parties to the suits, persons living with HIV/AIDS (PLHA), and the government consulted with each other and decided that second-line treatment would be extended to all PLHA regardless of whether their first-line treatment was in a private or public hospital registered with the NACO or whether they were put on irrational or rational treatment regimen. The Court endorsed the mutually taken decision of the petitioners and respondents. In a first for universal access to health care for PLHA, second-line ART was required to be provided to all who required it in a phased manner to make treatment universally available at the earliest time.[78] In recognizing that members of the community, in this case PLHA, must necessarily be involved in decisions impacting their right to health, the Court implicitly affirmed the importance of a participatory and democratic approach in forwarding the right to health.

16.3.2 *Health Care Financing*

The Supreme Court has reviewed administrative actions or omissions by state-run establishments in areas of health financing in relation to the availability, accessibility,

---

[77] Sahara House v. Union of India and Ors., Unreported Judgment, 2010 S.C. (India).
[78] The Supreme Court directed the parties to the case and NACO to resolve the issue through mutual consultations, with the overriding condition that all PLHIV who needed second line ART must receive it.

and quality of health facilities, goods, and services. The following discussion sheds light on repeated failures of the state to live up to benefits guaranteed by it under various government policies. It also displays the need to have a comprehensive, consistent, and justiciable law on the right to health as opposed to policies, which the government can change without any checks.

In *State of Punjab v. Mohinder Singh Chawla*,[79] the Supreme Court examined a government medical reimbursement policy for government employees and pensioners. The respondent employee sought reimbursement for hospitalization and treatment, including the bill for hospital room rent, at an empanelled private hospital. Upholding the respondent's claim, the Court held the right to health to be an integral part of the right to life and directed the state to reimburse the respondent for the full amount incurred due to hospitalization, including the hospital room rent.

The Court addressed issues of economic affordability and availability of quality health care services by correlating the state's duties under the policy, to provide reimbursements, with its constitutional obligation toward ensuring the right to health. The Court held that under the right to health, the state had a duty of "to bear the expenditure incurred by the Government servant,"[80] by providing reimbursements. The Court's treatment of the case, however, did not lead it to formulate a legal principle on accessibility issues. By viewing the case as one involving duties owed to only one individual, as opposed to duties toward society, the Court missed an opportunity to expound principles that would have led to a deeper analysis turning on both the accessibility and the quality of health care facilities, services, and goods within the right to health. As a result of this restricted approach, the Court subsequently trumped the right to access quality health care facilities with the economic limitations of the state in a subsequent case, *State of Punjab v. Ram Lubhaya Bagga*.[81]

In *Ram Lubhaya Bagga*, the Supreme Court looked to balance financial constraints of the state with its obligation to improve public health by facilitating access to quality health care facilities, goods, and services in a private hospital. The reimbursement policy, which was at issue in *Mohinder Singh Chawla*, had been reformulated to exclude certain private hospitals from the list of empanelled hospitals. The respondent, a government employee eligible for the reimbursement policy, sought full reimbursement of his medical expenses incurred in a hospital that was empanelled under the old policy but had been excluded when the policy was reformulated. The Court held that the policy of medical reimbursement was an attempt by the state to make health care services accessible and available and was in furtherance of its obligation to improve public health. The Court, however, justified the new restrictions on reimbursement by holding that "[n]o

---

[79] State of Punjab v. Mohinder Singh Chawla, (1997) 2 S.C.C 83 (1996) (India).
[80] *Id.* at para. 2.
[81] State of Punjab v. Ram Lubhaya Bagga, (1998) 1 S.C.R 1120 (India).

right [could] be absolute in a welfare state."[82] The obligation to improve public health, the Court held, was subject to Article 41 of the Constitution, which recognizes duties of the state under Directive Principles as being subject to the state's "economic capacity and development." Distinguishing this case from *Mohinder Singh Chawla*, the Court held that as the policy had been reformulated, the respondent employee could not claim benefits under the old policy. The Court limited the right to access of quality treatment based on the state's alleged financial constraint.

Although resource constraints are recognized even by the ICESCR (the right to health is to be progressively realized), the Court's unquestioned acceptance of the state's argument is problematic. A right-to-health approach would have led the Court to recognize the retrogressive element in the new policy. Retrogression is contrary to the principle of progressive realization and the right to health. Progressive realization entails that the state cannot roll back existing benefits and policies. Moreover, as the Court looked at resource constraint as a restriction on the enjoyment of the right to health, it should have subjected the state's claim to strict scrutiny. The Court did not look into the validity of a policy, which excluded previously available choices. The Court paid no attention to the requirements of the right to health, and revoked the utility of *Mohinder Singh Chawla*'s decision. As in *Mohinder Singh Chawla*, the Court did not go beyond looking at the issue on an individuated basis. However, since *Mohinder Singh Chawla* and *Ram Lubhaya Bagga*, the court has consistently upheld individual medical reimbursement claims.[83]

The Supreme Court, however, looked at an aspect of health care financing as part of the broader issue of economic equality in *Life Insurance Corporation of India v. Consumer Education and Research Centre*.[84] The petitioner (LIC – a state-run corporation) floated an insurance policy aimed at a particular economic class. People with salaries lower than the minimum stipulated income and people in occupations other than the specified categories of occupation were excluded from this policy. The respondent, in a PIL, challenged the policy as being in violation of the right to life (Article 21) and right to equality (Article 14) under the Constitution.

The Court held that the policy unreasonably limited the availability of life insurance to only the economically affluent and had the "insidious and inevitable effect of excluding lives in vast rural and urban areas."[85] The Court ruled that it offended the right to equality and equal protection and to socioeconomic justice. Relying on Article 25 of the UDHR (right to health) and Article 7 of the ICESCR (right to social security), the Court held that the actions of the state were to be directed toward the

---

[82] *Id.* at para. 8.
[83] C. Nagamuthu v. State of Tamil Nadu and Ors., (2006) 2 M.L.J 747 (India); Prithvinath Chopra v. Union of India, (2004) 74 D.R.J 175 (India).
[84] Life Insurance Corporation of India v. Consumer Education and Research Centre, (1995) Supp (1) S.C.R 349 (India).
[85] *Id.* at para. 57.

establishment of a socialist welfare state. The Court deemed it unreasonable for the state to exclude people based solely on their salaries and occupation when offering the policy to the general public. Thus the offending clause in the contract was struck down. The Court extended its logic requiring all insurance policies issued by any authority to be informed by public interest.

The Court took the opportunity to read the right to social justice (which includes social security) into the right to life in order to extend the policy's benefits to a larger section of the population. The furtherance of an egalitarian social order even in transactions that apparently belong to the domain of private commercial law, as opposed to those within the public law sphere, was entrenched by the Court. It looked at the far-reaching implications of the exclusionary policy in *LIC* as compared to the policy in *Ram Lubhaya Bagga* and *Mohinder Singh Chawla*, which was scrutinized without factoring in its right-to-health implications.

Litigation is expensive – both in terms of money and time – and the individual claims litigated in *Ram Lubhaya Bagga* and *Mohinder Singh Chawla* do very little to address the health challenges and outstanding access issues we canvassed in the first part of this chapter. What is vastly preferable is that the Court looks into issues with the intention of expounding broader legal obligations of the state, rather than enforcing obligations only in respect of specific individuals.

16.3.3 *Nondiscrimination*

Jurisprudence of the courts in matters of discrimination against PLHIV has changed from subordinating the fundamental rights of PLHIV to the interests of the larger public good to recognizing that the rights of PLHIV are not antithetical to public health measures of the state.

In *Lucy D'Souza v. State of Goa and Ors*,[86] the Bombay High Court (Goa Bench) upheld a law providing for isolation of PLHIV to control the spread of HIV. In balancing competing interests, the Court regarded the fundamental rights of a person – in this case, a PLHIV – to be subordinate to public interest and held that individual rights must give way to public interest. The Court held evidence-based treatment and nondiscrimination as principles suited to an "ideal" world but not "practical in life."[87] Considering AIDS a "foreign invasion" and Goa (the state to which the provision was applicable) a "well-known international tourist spot," and therefore at high risk for AIDS, the Court found "nothing surprising or objectionable" in such legislation. The Court regarded isolation as fulfillment by the state of its duty to improve public health under Article 47 (Directive Principles) of the Constitution. In the face of its limited medical knowledge, the Court left it to legislative wisdom to decide on the ways to prevent the spread of HIV. This was despite scientific evidence

---

[86] Lucy D'Souza v. State of Goa and Ors., A.I.R. 1990 Bom. 355 (1989) (India).
[87] *Id.* at para. 10.

presented that decried the use of isolation as a method of treatment or prevention. Although this law was upheld, the offending provision was later omitted primarily as a result of advocacy by civil society.[88]

The insistence on viewing the interests of PLHIV as competing with public health was reinforced in *Mr. X v. Hospital Z*[89], even as some rights of PLHIV were recognized. The marital union of a PLHIV was called off after a doctor revealed to the PLHIV's prospective wife his health status, causing him to be socially ostracized. The Supreme Court affirmed the duty of a doctor to keep a person's health information confidential to prevent stigmatization and discrimination in society. After looking at medical ethics in the United Kingdom and India, the Court also upheld the exception that when a specific and identifiable person was at risk of getting infected, the doctor owed a higher duty to inform such a person of the risk they could be exposed to, "regardless of the patient's own wishes." However, in its ultimate analysis, based on constitutional jurisprudence, the Court created a hierarchy of rights rather than looking at rights in a continuum. The Court pitted the right to privacy and confidentiality of a PLHIV against the right to health of a person likely to be affected by nondisclosure. In a "clash of two fundamental rights" the Court upheld the one that allegedly promoted public interest and morality. Disregarding the requirement of consent of the PLHIV, the Court viewed the rights involved as distinct opposing claims. An approach with consent in the foreground would have required the Court to look into issues regarding consensual disclosure or advocating preventative practices, as has been done in some jurisdictions,[90] and the subsequent flow of information. The Court also failed to consider the principle of least restrictive alternative[91] in the context of disclosure of information, where it could have imposed a duty on the PLHIV to inform his prospective spouse or indulge in protected sexual intercourse only. Instead it suspended the "right to marry" for PLHIV for fear of transmission.[92] The Court also did not address confidentiality in the context of third-party disclosure to unknown persons, which took place in this case.

The Court further buttressed its reasoning in *Mr. X v. Hospital Z* by referring to penal provisions regarding criminal transmission of diseases.[93] In viewing the rights of PLHIV and the state's duty to promote public health as mutually exclusive, the Court in fact negated the very ideal it sought to protect.

---

[88] Goa Public Health (Amendment) Act, No. 13 of 1995.

[89] Mr. X v. Hospital Z, A.I.R. 1999 S.C. 495 (1998) (India).

[90] *BT v. Oei*, [1999] N.S.W.S.C. 1082 (Austl.); Reisner v. Regents of the University of California, 37 Cal.2d 518 (Cal.,1995); *Harvey v. PD*, [2004] N.S.W.C.A. 97 (Austl.).

[91] Tarasoff v. Regents of the University of California, 17 Cal. 3d 425 (Cal., 1976).

[92] Subsequently in 2002, the Supreme Court modified its order and held that its observations regarding the suspension of the "right to marry" in the course of the illness were unnecessary.

[93] Indian Penal Code No. 45 of 1860, PEN CODE § 269 & 270 penalize the intentional spreading of infectious diseases with imprisonment and/or a fine.

In the space of almost a decade, courts have grappled with the complex issues surrounding PLHIV. A breakthrough occurred when the Delhi High Court ruled in *Naz Foundation v. Union of India*,[94] a pathbreaking judgment on the rights of the lesbian, gay, bisexual, and transgender (LGBT) community. The Court attacked issues of prejudice and stigma, as well as equality and discrimination, within the framework of constitutionally recognized fundamental rights and freedoms. The case arose out of a PIL against S.377 of the Indian Penal Code, 1860, which penalized "carnal intercourse against the order of nature" (anti-sodomy law). The PIL challenged the constitutional validity of the section in that it criminalized consensual sexual acts between adults in private, including between same-sex adults. The Court read down the section and held that "insofar [the section] criminalizes consensual sexual acts of adults in private [it] is violative of Articles 21, 14 and 15 of the Constitution."[95]

Pertinently, contradictory arguments by two governmental bodies were presented. The Ministry of Home Affairs argued for the retention of S.377 primarily on grounds of public morality and curbing sexual offenses. The Ministry of Health and Family Welfare, however, stated in an affidavit that criminalizing homosexuals denied them access to safe treatment options and prevention techniques due to their fear of being penalized. Evidence presented by NACO showed that S.377 was hampering their efforts to curb the spread of HIV/AIDS and provide treatment to homosexuals living with HIV. The offending section drove PLHIV underground thus making them inaccessible to public health workers. Unlike in earlier cases, the Court integrated a rights-based approach to public health grounded in Articles 21, 14, and 15, which we turn to discuss more fully now.

16.3.3.1 Article 21 – The Right to Life and Protection of a Person's Dignity, Autonomy and Privacy

The Court regarded human dignity as constitutionally protected and as resting on the "recognition of the physical and spiritual integrity of the human being."[96] This included the right to be free from arbitrary interference in one's privacy, family, and home as enunciated by Article 12 of the Universal Declaration of Human Rights. Sexual orientation as an expression of one's personality was accorded the dignity, protection, and recognition that for so long had not only been denied to it but had been seen as a criminal state of being. Therefore, the Court rejected the argument that decriminalizing homosexuality would defeat the "compelling state interest" of public health. The Court held that S.377 criminalized a person's "core identity solely on account of his or her sexuality"[97] and was therefore an infringement on

---

[94] Naz Foundation v. Union of India, (2010) Crim.L.J. 94 (2009) (India).
[95] *Id.* at para. 132.
[96] *Id.* at para. 26.
[97] *Id.* at para. 48.

a person's dignity and life under Article 21. In another departure from its earlier stance, the Court acknowledged the importance of promoting evidence-based treat-ment. It agreed that retention of S.377 to promote public health was contrary to scientific and professional understanding of homosexuality and rejected the argument that homosexuality was the cause for the spread of HIV. Relying on NACO's affidavit, it held that "no scientific study . . . [recognized] any causal connection existing between decriminalization of homosexuality and the spread of HIV/AIDS."[98] Instead it reasoned that since criminalization furthers stigmatization, it prevented people from accessing treatment. The fear of being penalized prevented homosexuals from revealing themselves thereby staying beyond the reach of HIV/AIDS intervention and prevention programs. It therefore held that the section acted as an impediment to India's obligations under Article 21 of the Constitution and Article 12 of the ICESR as elaborated in General Comment 14.

16.3.3.2 Article 14 – The Right to Equality and Equal Protection of Law

For equality before law to be effective, the Court deemed it necessary to treat people differently according to their different circumstances. S.377 prevented this as it discriminated against homosexuals as a class and subjected them to harassment. Moreover, the rationale of public morality as a justification for S.377 was unrelated to the intended object of S.377, namely curbing the spread of HIV/AIDS. Stressing the need for creating a nondiscriminatory and enabling environment, the Court rejected all arguments supporting the continued criminalization of homosexuality; central to this was a replacement of public morality with constitutional morality informed by the rights to equality, life, privacy, freedom of expression, and freedom from discrimination.

16.3.3.3 Article 15 – Prohibition of Discrimination on Grounds of Religion, Race, Caste, Sex, or Place of Birth

The Court was of the opinion that any law that discriminated against vulnerable groups based on an expression of personal autonomy would be subject to "strict scrutiny," especially if the law affected "protective discrimination" seeking to further the interests of vulnerable groups. S.377 was held to be in violation of Article 15 (right against discrimination on the grounds of sex) because the state's "moral disapproval" of homosexuality was offensive to the constitutional tenets of equality and nondiscrimination. It held sexual orientation to be an integral part of a person's identity and equivalent to "sex" in Article 15.

The Delhi High Court in *Naz* broke free of earlier precedents and refused to defer to the legislature. It did not presume the validity of a criminal provision

---

[98] *Id.* at para. 72.

as the Supreme Court had done in *Mr. X v. Hospital Z*. It did not shirk from examining scientific evidence as the Bombay High Court had done in *Lucy D'Souza*. It examined the cause, purpose, and effect of the impugned provision to hold that criminalization of homosexuality was an anachronism in India's constitutional morality, and in doing so underscored the undesirable effect criminalization had on a person's dignity, life, and health, as well as on public health.

16.3.4 *Right to Health for Women*

As mentioned in the Introduction to this chapter, access to necessary health care in India is particularly problematic for women. Courts have examined not only the normative content of the right to health, such as the right to autonomy vis-à-vis the right to health, but have also scrutinized procedural requirements, which play a part in the successful realization of the right to reproductive health of women.

In *Suchita Srivastava and Anr. v. Chandigarh Administration*,[99] the Supreme Court delved into the right to reproductive health, including the right to abortion, of women, particularly those with mental illness. The survivor was raped in a state-run institution, which resulted in her pregnancy. As she was "mentally ill," the state argued for the termination of her pregnancy, even though the woman had refused an abortion. Abortion in India is regulated by the Medical Termination of Pregnancy Act, which allows abortions in certain cases and requires the consent of the woman as an essential condition except in the case of "mental retardation," where the consent of her guardian is a prerequisite.

Looking at the legislative wisdom of the MTP Act, the Court recognized a woman's qualified "right to abortion." Reading this qualified right with the right to life, the Court held the right to reproductive health to be a dimension of liberty within the right to life of a woman. Expanding on the idea of the right to reproductive health, the Court held that reproductive choices such as "right to refuse participation in sexual activity or alternatively the insistence on use of contraceptive methods" should be made available to a woman. Rejecting any "compelling state interest" in these choices, the Court held that a pregnancy could be terminated only on the grounds mentioned in the MTP Act. The state argued that because mental retardation of the woman was one of the grounds for termination under the MTP Act, it could assume *parens patriae* jurisdiction and replace the woman's decision with its own. The Court rejected this argument and held that mental "illness" was not analogous to mental "retardation." Therefore, the doctrine of *parens patriae* was misplaced in this case. In its argument the Court relied on the report of the committee of experts set up to determine the severity of the survivor's mental illness, which indicated that she was capable of raising a child. It also found that resource concerns (regarding care of the woman and her child) were no reason to terminate the pregnancy of a woman.

---

[99] Suchita Srivastava and Anr. v. Chandigarh Administration, (2009) 14 S.C.R. 989 (India).

Even though the judgment was undeniably progressive, it nonetheless detracted from the right to reproductive health of women. Before holding that a woman's privacy and dignity should be respected, the Court validated the notion that "termination of pregnancy has never been recognised as a normal recourse for expecting mothers."[100] This implied a qualification to the woman's right to reproductive health. Because of this qualification – based, one suspects, on underlying presumptions about the nature of a fetus as one with life as well as the traditional role imposed on women – the Court let slip the opportunity to untie a woman's right to reproductive health with traditional and societal expectations.

The Supreme Court has also had a recent opportunity to review the Pre-Conception and Pre-Natal Diagnostic Techniques Act 1994, including the amendment made in 2002 regarding prohibition of prenatal diagnostic techniques to determine the sex of the child. This Act had remained unimplemented by governments five years after the legislation had been passed. The Act was intended to check a cultural preference for a male child by prohibiting prenatal sex determination and female feticide. In *CEHAT v. Union of India and Ors*,[101] the Court, in a series of six orders, issued directions to the central and state governments to create public awareness around the practice of prenatal sex determination and selection, and to implement the PCPNDT Act. The Court linked the objective of the Act – prevention of female feticide – to discrimination against women and the girl child. The Court lay down a framework within which the PCPNDT Act was to be implemented, including periodic reporting by the authorities regarding the status of implementation. In *Vinod Soni v. Union of India*,[102] the constitutionality of the PCPNDT Act was challenged as being in violation of the right to personal liberty as it allegedly prevented a woman from exercising her right to reproductive health under Article 21 of the Constitution. Upholding its constitutionality, the Bombay High Court held that personal liberty could not limit the "coming into existence of a female or male foetus which shall be for nature to decide."[103] In reaching its conclusion, the Court regarded the fetus as having life. It held that the Act was enacted to further the "right of every child to full development."[104]

There are a number of rights and issues that the Court seemed to have analyzed in reaching its conclusion. The ultimate aim of the Act is to promote gender equality in India by recognizing that gender discrimination against women starts from the conception stage. Therefore, the Court's ruling is progressive in the sense that it recognizes and enforces the purpose of the Act. However, the Court, in its reasoning, undoubtedly steps into unchartered territory by basing its analysis more on the life of the fetus rather than the ethical implications of sex-selective abortions. A comment

[100] *Id.* at para. 11.
[101] CEHAT v. Union of India and Ors, (2001) 5 S.C.C. 577 (India).
[102] Vinod Soni v. Union of India, (2005) Crim.L.J. 3408 (India).
[103] *Id.* at para. 8.
[104] *Id.* at para. 6.

on the right to life of a fetus only curbs the reproductive right of a woman vis-à-vis unwanted pregnancies.

The Delhi High Court had the occasion to adjudicate on the issue of the right to health of pregnant women in the context of prenatal and postnatal health in *Laxmi Mandal v. Deen Dayal Harinagar*.[105] The case concerned central government policies, which provided perinatal and prenatal care and nutrition to women and newborn children to promote institutional deliveries. This case highlights the need for responsive and efficient state-run bodies to provide services such as counseling, cash assistance, medicines, and food guaranteed by the state under various policies and the necessity of addressing the underlying determinants of health, particularly for the most vulnerable sections of society. Establishing links between the rights to health, life, and food, the Court held that the "right to food [is] integral to the right to life and right to health."[106] With regard to the right to life of women and children, the Court held that it included "the right to health, reproductive health and the right to food,"[107] and it further characterized the right to health as the right to access government facilities and to receive a minimum standard of treatment and care.

In the absence of explicit domestic right-to-health obligations on the state, the Court in *Laxmi* took recourse to international law (ICESCR, General Comment 14, CEDAW and the CRC) to situate the policies within a framework of legal obligations and provide a right to health rationale for the policies. The Court's analyses borrowed heavily from international instruments, especially General Comment 14, to substantiate its arguments on the right to health of women and children. Consequently, the Court directed the state government to compensate the victims by providing them with monetary assistance under the applicable schemes. Borrowing from the ICESCR, the Court mentioned that the state was under an "obligation of conduct" as well as an "obligation of result." Further, it held that the state may have discharged its obligation of conduct by putting in place policies forwarding the right to health, but directed the state to bolster reporting and accountability measures and reduce bureaucratic requirements to fulfill its obligation of result.

16.3.5 *Public Health and Tobacco Use*

In *Murli Deora v. Union of India and Ors*,[108] the Supreme Court looked to implement the Cigarettes and Other Tobacco Products (Prohibition of Advertisement and Regulation of Trade and Commerce, Production, Supply and Distribution) Act 2003 (COPTA). In this judgment, the court focused on the ill effects of smoking on public health and hinged its analysis on the need to protect the right to life of

---

[105] Laxmi Mandal v. Deen Dayal Harinagar, (2010) 172 D.L.T. 9 (India).
[106] *Id.* at para. 19.
[107] *Id.* at para. 27.
[108] Murli Deora v. Union of India and Ors, A.I.R. 2002 S.C. 40 (2001) (India).

nonsmokers. Consequently, it issued directions to governments to ban smoking in public places. Although the Court did not mention it, its analysis stemmed from the obligation of the state to improve public health. In *Crusade against Tobacco v. Union of India and Others*,[109] the Bombay High Court required licenses for eateries with a smoking area to incorporate special conditions and requirements. In an act reminiscent of *Vishaka v. State of Rajasthan*, the Court formulated guidelines which eateries have to abide by if they want licenses. It directed the authorities to suspend licenses where the conditions were not being followed stringently. The Court sought to regulate, instead of banning, smoking in public places vis-à-vis public health in a way that would not inconvenience nonsmokers in the restaurant.

16.4 CONCLUSION

India does not have the right to health stated explicitly in its Constitution. Notwithstanding, the Supreme Court of India, after dissolving the difference between Fundamental Rights and Directive Principles, has evolved a right to health under the rubric of the right to life, with positive obligations on the part of the state. Continuously evolving health-related litigation has given structure and substance to the right to health.

Although we claim that overall a right to health is constantly evolving in Indian jurisprudence, its evolution has been problematic, with many positive cases being offset by cases that retreat from the otherwise progressive agenda. For example, although cases such as *Mr. X v. Hospital Z* were instrumental in bringing about a change to the rights of PLHIV, another case, *Mohinder Singh Chawla*, failed to elucidate a right-to-health principle. Moreover, the danger of individual claims is that they may end up claiming disproportionate resources, as has happened in some of the Latin American jurisdictions. For example, in Brazil (which is discussed more fully by Mariana Prado in Chapter 12 of this volume), it has been claimed that individual claims privilege those who have the capacity to access courts over the rest of the population, and that instead of reducing health inequity, individual litigation claims may increase it.[110] In contrast, public interest litigation (PIL) is able to address bigger issues on a larger scale. PILs on issues such as availability of quality medicines in *Vincent Panikurlangara* and universal access to medicines and treatment for PLHIV in *Sahara House* have advanced the right to health of all people, by extending the relief given by courts to everyone and by making inroads into traditional jurisprudence, as was the case in *Naz Foundation*. As we discussed

[109] Crusade against Tobacco v. Union of India and Others, PIL No.111sxu 2010 Bom. (India), *available at* http://tobaccocontrollaws.saforian.com/litigation/decisions/in-20111005-crusade-against-tobacco-v.-uni.

[110] Octavio Luiz Motta Ferraz, *The Right to Health in the Courts of Brazil: Worsening Health Inequities?* 11(2) HEALTH & HUM. RTS.: AN INT'L J. 33 (2009), *available at* http://www.hhrjournal.org/index.php/hhr/article/view/172/256.

in this chapter, PILs dilute the requirement of standing, and thereby dissociate the availability of relief from the ability and capacity of individuals to claim relief. Of course, this is not to say that all PILs have resulted in immediate change; however, they have helped in developing the right-to-health jurisprudence and in steering the state toward formulating and implementing more equitable policies. In *Sahara House*, for example, the Court's endorsement urged the state into action to roll out second-line treatment for all people living with HIV regardless of whether they had followed the first-line treatment regimen.

Health-related litigation, however, has not fully addressed important challenges relating to the efficient and effective allocation of financial resources, whether in terms of challenging the government's decision to invest such relatively low amount of public money into health care or the failure to prioritize investments in primary health care infrastructure. Although courts have been cautious in upholding arguments of financial constraint and economic capacity forwarded by the state, they have looked at questions of budgetary allocations as falling within the domain and authority of policy and lawmakers. However, it could be argued that health-related litigation might be indirectly affecting state spending on health care. For instance, universalizing access to second-line ARVs in *Sahara House* will effectively lead to higher state spending on ART.

The right to health in practice in India has not been realized inasmuch as the state has not always been the primary actor in furthering the right. It had, many times, to be nudged and aided by Courts and the civil society. The time has now come when these positive developments need to be recognized, guaranteed, and furthered by legislation, framed on the principles of participation of all stakeholders. The National Health Bill and the HIV Bill should be passed in order to further strengthen the right to health in India. An explicit recognition of the right to health – which has already been grounded in the right to life – would enable people to demand that a national strategy, in conjunction with quality health care facilities, services, and goods, be made available and accessible.

Conclusion: Contexts for the Promise and Peril of the Right to Health

Colleen M. Flood and Aeyal Gross

HUMAN RIGHTS AND HEALTH CARE: A HAPPY MARRIAGE OR IRRECONCILABLE DIFFERENCES?

As discussed in the Introduction to this volume, since the 1990s we have witnessed a surge of interest in the application of human rights to health and health care issues, including a growth of health rights litigation. But has this marriage of human rights and health care been a happy one? This book has explored the role of health rights in legal, socioeconomic, cultural, and political contexts, offering a comparative perspective on the role that law and human rights play in access to health care.

Legal advocates for this approach, of course, hoped that human rights would be an important tool in battling discrimination and advancing equal access.[1] In this book we have critically assessed whether it has played this role either directly (through courts) or in a larger, normative sense. In this latter regard, the rise of health rights is not solely a legal development – it also reflects a changing philosophical outlook on the state's obligations to the individual, as well as a changing understanding of the economics of health care (e.g., concerns about the efficacy of free-market allocation of health care).

In philosophical terms, social rights represent a revolution in the long-standing liberal conception of rights. In classical liberalism, rights are articulated as restrictions on the state's power that, in Locke's articulation, prohibit it from denying a citizen's life, liberty, or property.[2] In this tradition, rights mostly confer a negative duty on the state not to act, and are not only devoid of any distributional potential, but – to the

---

[1] The questions of equality and access are addressed in detail *in* Committee on Economic, Social, and Cultural Rights, *General Comment No. 14, The right to the highest attainable standard of health*, ¶12, U.N. Doc. E/C.12/2000/4 (Aug. 11, 2000) [hereinafter: General comment 14].

[2] John Locke, SECOND TREATISE ON GOVERNMENT (1690). For a discussion of this understanding of rights, *see* Daphne Barak-Erez & Aeyal Gross, *Introduction: Do We Need Social Rights? Questions in the Era of Globalisation, Privatisation, and the Diminished Welfare State*, *in* EXPLORING SOCIAL RIGHTS: BETWEEN THEORY AND PRACTICE 1, 1–3 (Daphne Barak-Erez & Aeyal Gross eds., 2007).

contrary – may entrench existing economic relationships.[3] The rise of social rights in the twentieth century, including the right to health (especially as articulated in Article 12 of the International Covenant on Economic, Social, and Cultural Rights), led to a rethinking of human rights in general as encompassing positive obligations[4] and having distributive consequences,[5] bringing to the fore the ideological nature of the division of the rights into two sets.[6]

Thus, the theoretical promise of a human rights framework is to advance an egalitarian approach to distributive justice in allocating health care resources. By this we mean that a human rights approach, in theory, supports public finance and access to health care on the basis of need as opposed to ability to pay,[7] which is a requirement of equity and substantial equality in health care.[8] Implicit in this approach is that health is a "right" rather than a "commodity,"[9] given its "overriding importance" as a precondition to our participation in democratic, economic, and civil life, and more broadly "our feelings of wellbeing, security, comfort and ultimately happiness."[10] Inequalities in health constitute inequalities in people's capacity to function,[11] which differentiates health from other goods.[12] Jennifer Prah Ruger, building on the work of Amartya Sen, emphasizes the injustice of disparities in human capability resulting from ill health to argue in favor of universal health care as a means to minimize the risk of infirmity and foster human development.[13] In a similar vein, Norman Daniels points to how health inequities undermine people's capacity to function as free and

---

[3] The classic critique pointing to this was Karl Marx, On the Jewish Question (1958) (1844).

[4] *See* Sandra Fredman, Human Rights Transformed: Positive Rights and Positive Duties (2008).

[5] Barak-Erez & Gross, *supra* note 2, at 2–4.

[6] *Id.* at 8.

[7] On the importance of this dimension of access to health care, *see* Colleen Flood, International Health Care Reform: A Legal, Economic, and Political Analysis 27 (2003).

[8] The relationship between the concepts of "equality" and "equity" in this context is complex. Dahlgren and Whitehead argue that "health inequalities count as inequities when they are avoidable, unnecessary and unfair." *See* Göran Dahlgren & Margaret Whitehead, Policies and Strategies to Promote Social Equity in Health (Institute for Future Studies, Working Paper No. 14, 2007), *available at* http://www.framtidsstudier.se/wp-content/uploads/2011/01/20080109110739filmZ8UVQv2wQFShMRF6cuT.pdf. However, as Yamin notes, "There is no consensus as to what is avoidable, unnecessary, and unfair": *see* Alicia Ely Yamin, *Shades of Dignity: Exploring the Demands of Equality in Applying Human Rights Frameworks to Health*, 11 Health & Hum. Rts.1, 9 (2009). For the purpose of discussions here, we propose that both equality (understood as substantive equality) and equity share in the basic idea of health justice addressed in the text, which requires that access to health be based on need and not ability to pay. For a discussion of the complexities of the concept of equality in the context of health rights, *see id.*

[9] Aeyal Gross, *The Right to Health in an Era of Privatisation and Globalisation: National and International Perspectives, in* Exploring Social Rights, supra note 2, at 289, 291–292.

[10] Flood, *supra* note 7, at 27.

[11] Sudhir Anand, *The Concern for Equity in Health, in* Public Health, Ethics, and Equity 15, 17–18 (Sudhir Ahmed, Fabienne Peter & Amartya Sen eds., 2004). *See also* Amartya Sen, *Why Health Equity in Health, in* Public Health, Ethics, and Equity 21.

[12] As Anand notes, inequalities in health, nutrition, and health care offend us much more than inequalities in clothes, furniture, motor cars, or boats. *See* Anand, *id.* at 17.

[13] J. P. Ruger, *The Moral Foundation of Health Insurance*, 100 Q. J. Med. 53 (Jan. 2007).

equal citizens.[14] There is a strong link between social inequalities and health[15] – generally, the poorer we are, the sicker we are.

Apart from arguments in political philosophy that support treating health care as a right and not a commodity, there are also arguments in economics that underscore failings in health care markets, thus justifying government intervention. Market failures include the following factors: first, uncertainty about our health needs (will we be unlucky enough to get cancer or not?);[16] second, demand for many kinds of health care services does not decrease in response to rising prices ("inelastic demand");[17] and finally, health care providers generally have much more information than patients, thus negating the usual free-market assumption of perfect information (an "information asymmetry" exists between health providers and patients) as to the real costs and benefits of different treatments.[18] These economic factors combined with social justice factors[19] point to treating health care as a right *for all* and not a mere commodity for those with means. This conception of health care – as a right and not a mere commodity – becomes even more important given the need to resist the pervasiveness of neoliberal ideology and policies, which tends to drive toward the distribution of health and health care as if it were a kind of consumer good.[20]

However, while social rights can potentially contribute to transforming human rights thinking and have an effect on civil rights, they may also be subjected to the classical structure of rights. The concern is that the classical structure of rights, notably its individualized focus, may undermine the distributional potential, making the rise of social rights – and as we shall see, specifically health care rights – a Pyrrhic victory. This is especially poignant given that on one hand, social rights still struggle to stand on equal footing with civil and political rights,[21] but on the other hand, the very nature of rights-based reasoning may limit their distributional effects. Additionally, the risk remains that rights analysis will address only the "tip of the iceberg."[22] By this we mean that efforts to establish health care rights may merely

---

[14] Norman Daniels, JUST HEALTH: MEETING HEALTH NEEDS FAIRLY 14 (2008).

[15] *See* Norman Daniels, Bruce Kennedy & Ichiro Kawachi, *Health and Inequality, or Why Justice Is Good for Our Health*, *in* PUBLIC HEALTH, ETHICS, AND EQUITY 63.

[16] *See* Flood, *supra* note 7, at 28.

[17] The inelastic nature of demand means that people will continue to buy health insurance and services even when very expensive, and the demand for services is relatively unresponsive to changes in price. *See id.* at 19.

[18] *See id.* at 23–25.

[19] *See* Daniels, Kennedy & Kawachi, *supra* note 15, at 63.

[20] See Sue McGregor, *Neoliberalism and Health Care*, 25 INT'L J. CONSUMER SERVICES 82 (2001); DaniFilc, *The Health Business Under Neo-Liberalism: The Israeli Case*, 25 CRITICAL SOC. POL'Y 180 (2005); Paul O'Connell, *The Human Right to Health in an Age of Market Hegemony*, *in* GLOBAL HEALTH AND HUMAN RIGHTS: LEGAL AND PHILOSOPHICAL PERSPECTIVES 190 (John Harrington & Maria Stuttaford eds., 2010).

[21] Barak-Erez & Gross, *supra* note 2, at 6–7.

[22] On rights as dealing with merely the "tip of the iceberg," *see* David Kennedy, THE DARK SIDES OF VIRTUE: REASSESSING INTERNATIONAL HUMANITARIANISM 32 (2004).

divert attention away from real political and social change necessary to address substantive inequalities,[23] and worse, rights discourse may be co-opted in a way that subverts equitable access.[24] The latter risk is attributable to the individualist nature of rights. Making individual demands on the state, whether demands that the state act or instead that attempt to restrict it from acting, may actually serve to give the clout of rights to individual claims, in ways that obscure distributional questions.[25]

To explore this concern we must analyze who brings the actions enforcing health care rights, what the nature of those actions are, whether or not claims are successful, and the distributional impact of judicial decisions in the short and long term. Is health care rights litigation focused on expensive but not particularly effective drugs and procedures? If litigants win access to expensive drugs and procedures, does this divert resources from other needy areas, or are more resources somehow added, and if so, from where? Is health rights litigation successful in challenging regressive developments such as copayments and two-tier systems that embed inequities? Is litigation being used to attack governmental attempts at greater progressivity, such as in the ultimately unsuccessful attack on the recent expansion of health insurance to millions in the United States (dubbed Obamacare by the media)[26] or the upcoming constitutional challenges to one-tier Medicare in Canada? In addition, we need to consider that the recognition of a right to health care may result in an undue emphasis on medicalization over social determinants of health, such as education, nutrition, and housing, which can have a far greater impact on health.[27]

Attempts to specify the content of the right to health care are complicated by the ever-changing nature of health care systems, which are structured around priority setting within limited resources, amid growing demands and expectations (the latter being the result, inter alia, of technological and demographic changes[28]). Can abstract human rights concepts illuminate a path through this flurry of changing variables and competing priorities? How can human rights within this framework

---

[23] Barak-Erez & Gross, *supra* note 2, at 16–17.

[24] For a discussion of how in the United States resorting to rights discourse with its individualist bent may, in the context of public health, entail risks of co-opting the right to health to the detriment of sound public health policies, *see* Peter D. Jacobson & Soheil Soliman, *Co-opting the Health and Human Rights Movement*, 30 J. L. MED. & ETHICS 705 (2002).

[25] See Aeyal Gross, *Is There a Human Right to Private Health Care?*, 41 J. L. MED. & ETHICS 138 (2013).

[26] Allison Hoffman, Chapter 13 in this volume.

[27] On "medicalization," *see* Benjamin M. Meier, *The World Health Organization, the Evolution of Human Rights, and the Failure to Achieve Health for All*, in GLOBAL HEALTH AND HUMAN RIGHTS, *supra* note 20, at 163. On social determinants, *see* Audrey R. Chapman, *The Social Determinants of Health, Health Equity, and Human Rights*, 12 HEALTH & HUM. RTS. 17 (2010); WHO Commission on Social Determinants of Health Final Report, Closing the Gap in a Generation: Health Equity through Action on the Social Determinants of Health (2008), *available at* http://whqlibdoc.who.int/publications/2008/9789241563703_eng.pdf.

[28] See Alicia Ely Yamin, *Power, Suffering and Courts: Reflections on Promoting Health Rights through Judicialization*, in LITIGATING HEALTH RIGHTS: CAN COURTS BRING MORE JUSTICE TO HEALTH? 333, 353 (Alicia Ely Yamin & Siri Gloppen eds., 2011).

advance mutual social dependence while at the same time guaranteeing individual protection?[29] How can a rights-based approach deliver justice in individual cases while at the same time reckoning with the overall needs of the community?[30] What does rights analysis actually achieve in this sphere; who litigates, who benefits, and how does health rights litigation affect the overall equity of the system?[31]

LOOKING AT RIGHTS LITIGATION

What factors produce a harmonious marriage between health care systems and human rights litigation? We have found a huge degree of variability in satisfaction within the union. Some of this satisfaction/dissatisfaction is inherent in the nature of the institutions involved (e.g., the adversarial nature of the courtroom, the individualistic nature of rights, the preference for negative as opposed to positive rights) and some of it is contextual to the design of the health care system and the history, culture, law, and economics of the country in question. We follow here in the footsteps of previous research projects that have explored the role of social rights in legal systems around the world,[32] and specifically consider two that looked at the role of courts and litigation in guaranteeing the right to health.[33] In spite of differences between these projects and ours, we all share the observation that the role of rights in health care varies across countries and is contingent on a number of contextual factors. In what follows we elucidate the factors we found to be of special relevance. Our discussion follows the typology set out in the introduction, dividing the countries under study into three categories based on their health systems.

(i) *National Tax-Financed Health Systems*

First, let us begin with some conclusions regarding national tax-financed health systems that are part of this volume, namely Canada, the United Kingdom, Sweden,

---

[29] For a discussion of some of these questions, *see* Harvard Law School Human Rights Program & François-Xavier Bagnoud Ctr. for Health and Human Rights, Economic and Social Rights and the Right to Health: An Interdisciplinary Discussion Held at Harvard Law School in September, 1993 (1995), especially the contribution of Martha Minow at 2–5.

[30] *See Health* in Andrew Clapham & Susan Marks, INTERNATIONAL HUMAN RIGHTS LEXICON 197, 207 (2005); Dianne Otto, *Linking Health and Human Rights: A Critical Legal Perspective*, 1 HEALTH & HUM. RTS.273, 277–279 (1994).

[31] See Siri Gloppen, *Litigation as a Strategy to Hold Governments Accountable for Implementing the Right to Health*, 10 HEALTH & HUM. RTS.21 (2008); Oscar A. Cabrera & Ana S. Ayala, *Advancing the Right to Health through Litigation, in* ADVANCING THE HUMAN RIGHT TO HEALTH RIGHTS 2 (Jose M. Zuniga, Stephen Marks & Lawrence Gostin, eds., 2013).

[32] *See, e.g.*, Malcolm Langford, SOCIAL RIGHTS JURISPRUDENCE: EMERGING TRENDS IN INTERNATIONAL AND COMPARATIVE LAW (2008).

[33] Litigating Health Rights, *supra* note 28; COURTING SOCIAL JUSTICE: JUDICIAL ENFORCEMENT OF SOCIAL AND ECONOMIC RIGHTS IN THE DEVELOPING WORLD (Varun Gauri & Daniel M. Brinks eds., 2008).

and New Zealand. Notwithstanding changes under way in some of these systems, they remain (relatively) robust in their commitment to redistribution, from the healthy to the sick and from the wealthy to the poor. Moreover, governments of these countries are often able to leverage their monopsony power as "single payers" to contain health care costs/prices – easing pressure on the system by comparison to other models. Despite having well-established public systems, in these countries there is generally no judicially enforceable right to health care. However, all of these countries, in which health care was and still is considered a governmental service, are today facing the challenges of growing demands on one hand (stemming from the technological and demographic changes, and also from the wish of individuals to buy better or quicker access to health care) and diminished capacity and/or willingness to provide on the other hand. These pressures heighten the need for prioritization, rationing, and selectiveness in listing decisions. In turn, individuals in these systems are increasingly seeking to bring challenges to prioritization and listing decisions through various legal means (for example, through administrative law and international law) but also through political means. When they do so through litigation, it is without a constitutional framework that explicitly recognizes a right to health care, and is limited in its scope – though mention of the right to health may enter the discourse, reflecting the influence of global and regional norms. We discuss these challenges in more detail later in the chapter.

More generally, one can contrast this group of national tax-financed systems – where public health systems developed as part of the modern welfare state – with our third category of countries, mixed public/private systems, that generally are far less well resourced, have comparatively much higher rates of private financing, and are much more likely to have enshrined constitutional rights to health care. As we discuss further in this chapter, in those latter countries, frequently the right to health has been inserted into newly enacted (mostly post-1989) constitutions, and in some cases was embedded as part of a transition to democracy, with the aspiration that a rights framework would expedite the establishment of a more equal welfare state.

In Sweden, as Anna Sara Lind writes in her chapter,[34] health care rights legislation sets a framework within which regional and local governments are granted considerable freedom to organize and prioritize health services. Health rights as such are not justiciable by individuals. The irony is that Sweden – a country without any articulated set of health care rights or litigation related thereto – has one of the most robust commitments to redistribution of all the countries included in this volume. However, Sweden has recently embraced a much greater role for private for-profit delivery within the public system. This raises concerns that, over the longer term, this increased profit motive will test Sweden's commitment to solidarity, by inviting increased private finance and skewing the system toward meeting market demand as opposed to meeting the health needs of the population on an equitable basis.

---

[34] Anna-Sara Lind, Chapter 2 in this volume.

Further, the Swedish model (as with the Dutch system discussed later) must now meet challenges from international law, as it has ratified the European Convention on Human Rights and Fundamental freedoms (ECHR), requiring compliance with the ECHR and related case law. Additionally European Union (EU) laws have loosened restrictions on Swedish patients accessing care in other EU countries, allowing those with the means to avoid wait time queues and other rationing constraints. Over time the test will be whether Sweden can balance a focus on individual wants and needs of patients, as demanded increasingly by European law and private interests, with an overall commitment to social solidarity.

New Zealand too has little in the way of a formal articulation of rights, but a handful of cases have arisen under New Zealand's Bill of Rights and through administrative law. Jo Manning's discussion[35] of these cases highlights the intersection of court challenges and political movements. She contrasts how comparatively well-off individuals have successfully employed the judicial process as part of a social mobilization process, while more vulnerable individuals have had no similar success. She argues the Herceptin case[36] – concerning access to a very expensive breast cancer drug – illustrates how "whoever screams the loudest" wins the day, for although the court itself did not grant patients a substantive remedy, protest surrounding the case successfully rallied political support for the drug's inclusion on the national formulary on the terms demanded.[37] In sharp contrast is the *Shortland*[38] case, involving access to dialysis on the part of a patient who was a Maori, elderly, and poor, for whom the legal challenge was unsuccessful, resulting in his subsequent death. There was no resulting mobilization in protest galvanizing political action to save the patient's life. The reader may notice here some factual similarities with the South African case of *Soobramoney*[39] – which also concerned access to dialysis – but of course, New Zealand is a much wealthier country, calling into serious question the legitimacy of this kind of "tough choice."

Canada has a written constitution explicitly guaranteeing certain individual rights. Canada's Charter of Rights and Freedoms includes a guarantee of life, liberty, and security of the person, but to date this has not been interpreted as including a right to (public) health care. Instead, most successful health rights challenges are grounded in "negative rights," challenging government restrictions on individual liberty, for example to access medical marijuana, abortion, and safe-injection sites. Consequently, as Flood explains,[40] constitutional challenges to date have done little

---

[35] Joanna Manning, Chapter 1 in this volume.
[36] Walsh v Pharmaceutical Management Agency [2010] NZAR 101 (HC) (N.Z.).
[37] Herceptin was already in the national formulary, but the claimants wished it to be funded for a much longer course of treatment than the funder (Pharmac) was prepared to cover. Pharmac did not think there was sufficiently robust clinical evidence supporting a longer course of treatment.
[38] Shortland v Northland Health Ltd. [1998] 1 NZLR.433 (CA) (N.Z.).
[39] Thiagraj Soobramoney v. Minister of Health (Kwa-Zulu Natal) 1998 (1) SA 765 (CC) (S.Afr.).
[40] Colleen M. Flood, Chapter 3 in this volume.

or nothing to meaningfully expand or improve access within the public health care system (as, for example, even if constraints on abortion are liberalized, there is as yet no corresponding right to public coverage for, or accessibility of, abortion services). *Eldridge*,[41] the case concerning access to translation services for deaf patients, is the only case where plaintiffs successfully litigated a positive right to a health service under the s. 15 equality provisions (finding that sign language translation services must be provided in hospitals, to ensure that deaf patients have equal access to care). But again underscoring the importance of the interaction between the judiciary and political decision making, notwithstanding this win in court, across Canada there is still very little provided in terms of translation services for the deaf. In contrast, as in New Zealand, there are cases where health rights litigants have walked away empty-handed from the courts, but litigation helped draw attention to an access issue and galvanized public support. For example in the case of *Auton*,[42] middle-class parents of autistic children lost their challenge under the Charter's equality guarantee, demanding access to treatment for autistic services, but under public pressure, provinces across the country have moved to fund this care. Overall, Flood argues that health care rights litigation has done little to advance equality of access to health care within Canada, let alone to equalize broader social determinants of health.

Two upcoming cases will truly test whether litigation of health care rights in Canada proves regressive or progressive. One is a constitutional challenge following on the heels of the *Chaoulli* case, the successful 2005 challenge to a Quebec law restricting the sale and purchase of private health insurance.[43] This new challenge seeks to overturn *all* laws that inhibit a flourishing parallel private tier, thus enabling those with means to bypass waiting lists in the public system, and potentially allowing all physicians to bill whatever they wish for services rendered to private payers, while retaining their status within the less-lucrative public system as a fallback option. If this case is successful, it will be a significant step toward a much higher level of private finance and a retrograde step for equity and access within Canada. Simultaneously, another constitutional challenge is looking to reverse the federal government's decision to delist refugee claimants from certain countries (Hungary, Mexico) from *any* coverage for health care services. A loss for the plaintiffs in this latter case would cast further doubts on the progressivity of rights litigation in the Canadian context; it would appear the pursuit of individual rights is destroying rather than upholding a commitment to equality and social solidarity in health care.

A much more promising portrait of the interaction of the courts and the health care system emerges from experience within the United Kingdom's National Health Service (NHS). Notably, it is the only country in the category of national tax-funded

---

[41] Eldridge v. British Columbia (Att'y Gen.), [1997] 3 S.C.R. 624, para. 64 (Can.).

[42] Auton v. British Columbia(Att'y Gen.), [2004] 3 S.C.R. 657 (Can.).

[43] Chaoulli v. Quebec (Attorney General), [2005] 1 S.C.R. 791 (Can.).

health systems where individualized petitions seeking access to new types of care (mostly new drugs and devices) have resulted in courts developing general criteria to inform future decision makers and judges. As detailed by Christopher Newdick,[44] decision making must adhere to principle of procedural fairness, and consider only relevant factors as set out in the framework, such as the nature of illness, evidence of the treatment's overall effectiveness, the extent and likelihood it will work in this patient, extent of improvement it might be expected to provide, the absolute cost of treatment, numbers that may benefit, and relevant cost and effectiveness by comparison to other effective treatment. These criteria require a priority-setting system under which hard choices will have to be defended, with scrutiny becoming especially stringent where the decision seriously affects a citizen's health.

As Newdick shows, those criteria have been incorporated into policy through the NHS "constitution." Further, the courts also showed "sympathy" to claims for "exceptional" cases. This framework for priority scrutiny and the extent to which courts will put policy decisions under the microscope perhaps strikes a balanced marriage, offering robust protections for individual health care rights while at the same time acknowledging that public decision makers must balance priorities within limited resources.

It is important to note that the United Kingdom's approach emerged in the context of administrative law rather than in the application of constitutional rights to health care. Perhaps it is this frame of legal analysis that allows a better balance between the overall goals of social solidarity and individual patient rights, because inherent within administrative law is a requirement that a court consider the extent to which it should be deferential to governmental decision making. As we argue further later – whether in the context of a system with constitutional rights to health care, statutory rights, or within general administrative law – reasonableness can play a central role as a standard by which to judge decisions concerning access to new services or drugs. Similarly, when it comes to large structural issues – concerning, for example, whether individuals receive coverage at all, and issues of copayments that detrimentally impact vulnerable populations – judges should not shy away from reviewing these decisions on a standard of reasonableness. We return to this issue later.

(ii) *Social Health Insurance (SHI) Systems*

From National Health Insurance systems, let us now turn to Social Health Insurance (SHI) systems (within which we include managed competition systems). Although it is not inherent in their design, SHI systems do overall seem to allow or generate a greater role for private finance than do National Tax-Financed Systems. This may be partly the result of the involvement of third parties as insurers – who may

---

44 Christopher Newdick, Chapter 4 in this volume.

be less averse than government is to imposing out-of-pocket charges on patients. Moreover, a number of SHI systems around the world have recently privatized their management/insurer functions (shifting from not-for-profit sickness funds to regulated private health insurance) as part of managed competition reform. These recent reforms are difficult to unpack from the perspective of overall equity and the public/private perspective, for while on the one hand they often represent an expansion to universal health insurance, on the other they may involve privatization of the management of the insurance function (e.g., from nonprofit social insurers to regulated for-profit insurers).

We see that in SHI countries, not only may health care rights be encapsulated in statute but also the insurance contracts between the fund/insurer and an individual may provide a basis for claiming rights to health care. SHI systems have formal decision-making processes to determine the list of goods and services covered for every citizen by the relevant universal insurance plan. What we see in these countries is that the legal structure of the health care system itself – with its emphasis on a defined package of benefits that are part of a contract of insurance – frequently provides the conditions conducive to litigation of health care rights.

In Colombia, as discussed by Everaldo Lamprera,[45] the introduction of a managed competition system was part and parcel of an effort to establish universal access. As mentioned, this kind of reform is quite common and, on the one hand improves equity by achieving universal coverage but, on the other hand, raises concerns by achieving this expansion through reliance on regulation of private health insurance. In Colombia's case, reliance on insurance delivery ultimately precipitated health care right claims, as private insurers (Health Promoting Entities or *Entidades Promotoras de Salud* [EPS]) frequently failed to provide services that were mandated as part of the publicly funded universal basket. Further litigation was triggered when expensive and life-saving drugs were not included within the basket.

These problems in access, combined with three further factors, resulted in a tsunami of litigation that eventually threatened the very survival of the universal scheme: first, a constitutional right to health care was inferred from general provisions in the constitution; second, *tutelas* offered an inexpensive forum for exercising the constitutional right to health; and third, the court issued a decree that government officials immediately pay for the cost of the treatment ordered as part of a *tutela* claim or risk being found in contempt of court. Colombia thus might first appear a utopia for proponents of health human rights, with easy access to the justice system and reliable enforcement of outcomes. But this is arguably a mirage, for as Lamprea discusses, the result is that the universal plan is required as a result of *tutela* claims to cover all services and goods and cannot say "no" and thus cannot negotiate prices (with drug companies, hospitals, physicians, and other providers) and keep costs down.

---

[45] Everaldo Lamprea, Chapter 5 in this volume.

Here then we see a more general problem: if health rights are treated as unconditional and not limited by resource capacity, this can put an unsustainable burden on public insurers and undermine their ability to act as a wise steward of public resources through negotiating prices or resisting patent extensions and so forth. Colombian courts have recently taken steps to achieve greater balance between individual rights and the larger societal interest. These steps have been crystallized in the Constitutional Court's ruling T-760 of 2008,[46] which approached the issue from an overall policy perspective – that is, focusing on underlying factors driving right-to-health litigation and not only on the individual cases that reach the court – and ordered the government to implement policy aimed at de-incentivizing the growth of litigation. Such policy includes the establishment of universal health coverage, the unification of the baskets of health services, and the implementation of a new financial scheme for the delivery of health services. Time will tell whether the Colombian judiciary is sufficiently attuned to the structure and dynamics of an evolving health system to strike the right balance. It is notable that, thanks to ruling T-760 and to the follow-up process triggered by the Court after 2008, the Colombian government in 2013 passed health care reform through Congress. The reform, among other things, declares that the right to health is the touchstone of Colombia's health system and restructures the financial scheme for the insurance and delivery of health services.

In Taiwan, attempts to provide universal health insurance as in Colombia were made under the auspices of the managed competition model. However, unlike Colombia, in Taiwan there is no equivalent to a *tutela* action or an actionable individual right to health care. In fact, in Taiwan other constitutional rights (e.g., property rights) have been employed to challenge the legitimacy of attempts to achieve universality through mandates to purchase health insurance. Here we see a resonance with similar challenges to the recent expansion of health insurance ("Obamacare") in the United States. In Taiwan, the Constitutional Court to date has upheld the mandate to buy private health insurance in order to ensure universal access and the overall constitutionality of the national insurance scheme, noting it is based on mutual support and risk sharing. However, Y. Y. Brandon Chen expresses concern that the supporters of the system are at the mercy of the Constitutional Court each time such a claim arises.[47] In Taiwan, we can conclude that the court has shielded governmental attempts to advance equity, but to date the right to health has not acted as a sword to further an equity agenda.

As in Taiwan and Columbia, Israel's SHI system also blurs the divide between old conceptions of public and private, albeit in a different way. In Israel, the SHI scheme underwent reforms in 1995, resulting in insurance premiums now being paid directly to the government rather than to regulated nonprofit sickness funds. We normally

---

46 *See* Corte Constitucional [C.C] [Constitucional Court], octubre 21, 2011, Auto 226/11 (Colom.), *available at* http://www.corteconstitucional.gov.co/T-760–08/Autos%20genericos/AutosGenericos.
47 Y. Y. Brandon Chen, Chapter 9 in this volume.

associate this level of public control with greater progressivity, but as Aeyal Gross discusses in his chapter, in Israel this centralization has allowed the government to implement a series of neoliberal measures including onerous copayments that severely challenge accessibility for the poor.[48]

In response to court challenges, the Supreme Court of Israel has generally acted to shield government policy, be it regressive or progressive. Thus, on the one hand, the court has largely rejected claims against the state with respect to the noninclusion of services or categories of individuals in the scheme, and against copayments. On the other, it has rejected petitions against government measures designed to protect the public system from private incursion. Similar to Taiwan, where a government takes a progressive step, a court is likely to defend this from attack, but the court is (1) far less likely to insist on equity-enhancing measures resisted by the government and (2) more likely to protect government initiatives that are regressive, such as copayments. There may be some softening on the part of Israeli courts, however, and a recent decision holding that the government had acted unreasonably in its protracted failure to update the "health cost index" that determines the budget for the health services basket is promising.[49]

Another promising development is that, while refraining from expanding the health services basket generally, Israeli courts have held that the sickness funds must exercise discretion in exceptional cases. In a series of cases from recent years, the labor courts have been developing jurisprudence, later incorporated into a Ministry of Health directive, about the considerations that "exceptions committees" within the sickness funds must take into account. These will include (1) objective considerations regarding the requested treatment such as the international experience with it and its proved efficiency; (2) subjective considerations such as previous treatments given to the patient, and whether there are considerations that bar treatments normally indicated for their situation; and (3) broad budgetary considerations, in accordance with the principles of equality, which must have a concrete basis.[50] These developments, while not identical to those taking place in the United Kingdom, are in many regards similar and attest to what we may call a "middle way" between blanket deferral to prioritization and rationing decisions made by the state on one hand and a tendency to broadly accept any individual petition on the other hand.[51]

---

[48] Aeyal Gross, Chapter 6 in this volume.

[49] HCJ 8730/03 Macabee Health Services v. Minister of Finance, para. 54 (June 21, 2012), Nevo Legal Database (by subscription) (Isr.).

[50] NLC 575–09 Macabee Health Services v. Dahan, para 24 (Jan. 6, 2011), Nevo Legal Database (by subscription) (Isr.), currently under review, see HCJ 5438/11 Macabee v. Minister of Health (pending) (Isr.).

[51] Recall that in the United Kingdom, the courts developed criteria that apply to individualized petitions seeking access to new types of care (mostly new drugs and devices), and additionally allowed for "exceptional" cases. In Israel, the courts' criteria were developed within the context of the "exceptions" themselves, but the definitions of "exceptional cases" in the Israeli case law seems to be broader in a way that makes the judicial development of criteria in the two countries comparable.

The Dutch health care system discussed by André den Exter[52] is long-standing, with a formal scheme first established in 1941. In recent decades it too has experienced a radical transformation, from an SHI model (albeit with a portion of the population covered by private health insurance) to a managed competition model achieving universal coverage. Again this raises the double-edged sword of reform being progressive in the sense of achieving a universal scheme but regressive in the sense of allowing a much greater role for private insurers/providers, albeit in a regulated environment. The Dutch case study is also of interest for here we see patients turning to international and EU law to claim access to treatments that local insurers have not yet covered. As a result of European Court of Justice case law, Dutch patients are entitled to coverage for treatments deemed effective by *international medical science*.[53] This could mean that where a certain treatment has been sufficiently tested by international science, the health insurer would not be able to refuse authorization on the grounds that it is not presently provided in the Netherlands (for a fuller discussion of the exceptions to this principles, see Chapter 7). Here again we see the double-edged sword of rights: while national insurers (whether public or private) sometimes need to be pushed to cover new and promising treatments, there is a risk of their being pushed too far, as the global pharmaceutical industry invests heavily in the medicalization of life, promoting the "need" for highly priced drug therapies. This industry is not generally required to demonstrate the efficacy or cost-effectiveness of any drug relative to existing treatments and therapies. While the promise is that these developments will allow access to technologies that states fail to provide, the risk is then that appeal to global norms via international law will exacerbate costs, skew priority setting, and put greater pressure on domestic commitments to social solidarity.

Finally, the case of Hungary provides an exception to our claim that the structure of SHI/managed competition systems seems to spark associated health care litigation. Here, as discussed by Mária Éva Földes,[54] courts acknowledge that "rights" to health are really goals to aspire to and heavily constrained by governmental budgets. They have so far showed no desire to peer into decisions on health care coverage, and state decisions on the health care basket are not deemed justiciable in constitutional cases. Perhaps this in part reflects Hungary's legacy as a state-socialist regime and its transition toward democracy. Although self-defined as a SHI model, Hungary is relatively unusual as there is one central fund albeit with regional branches, administered by the National Health Insurance Administration. Consequently, the

---

[52] André den Exter, Chapter 7 in this volume.
[53] Case C-157/99, Geraets-Smits v. Stichting Ziekenfonds VGZ and Peerbooms v. Stichting CZ Groep Zorgverzekeringen, 2001 E.C.R. I-5473; Case C-385/99, Müller-Fauré v. Onderlinge Waarborgmaatschappij OZ Zorgverzekeringen and Van Riet v. Onderlinge Waarborgmaatschappij ZAO Zorgverzekeringen, 2003 E.C.R. I-4409.
[54] Mária Éva Földes, Chapter 8 in this volume.

Hungarian system resembles a national tax-financed agency in the sense of only having a single payer; this may partly explain the far more deferential approach Hungarian courts take to judicial review, akin to that of the courts in national tax-financed systems. But regardless of the approach of domestic courts, as in the United Kingdom and the Netherlands, Hungarian decision makers may find themselves forced to cover different kinds of therapies as a result of decisions by the European Court of Justice. We return to the theme of the impact of international law and global norms later in the chapter.

(iii) *Public/Private Systems*

Unlike our previous two categories that are all high-income countries (with the exception of Colombia), those in our final category of public/private systems are all middle-income countries (with the exception of the United States, which is really in a category of its own). All countries have a mixture of public and private finance, but in this category of public/private systems, the private sector is much more extensive and the public system is poorly financed. This is evident in the fact that the percentage of public funding of the national expenditure on health is lower than that of the countries in the previous two categories, with the percentage of private expenditure accordingly higher.[55] Of the three groups of countries in our analysis, this public/private group is the most diverse both in terms of the wealth of its systems (Nigeria vs. the United States) and the justiciability of health care rights (China, with no justiciable rights vs. South Africa with a constitutional right to health care and for many of the determinants of health such as housing).

A few trends are apparent in this category: (1) in some countries courts have opened the door to massive numbers of individualized petitions, with some critics arguing that this leads to "telescopic" judgments that distort the prioritization and rationing processes (Brazil and Colombia); (2) in other countries, collective cases have arisen that consider structural problems, South Africa being a prime example (the TAC case), and India demonstrating the potential of public interest litigation rather than individualized petition; (3) in other countries in this category – China,

---

[55] Other than China, where it is 52.5%, the percentage of public expenditure on health in all the countries in this category is less than 50%, with India being the lowest at 30.3%. In contrast, in the other two categories, public expenditure ranges between 57.5% (Taiwan) and 84.1% (United Kingdom). See Health expenditures *in* WHO, World Health Statistics 2012, 134, table 7, *available at* http://www.who.int/healthinfo/EN_WHS2012_Full.pdf. For Taiwan, which is not included in the table, *see* Minguo Jiushijiu Nian Guomin Yiliaobaojian Zhichu (民國99年國民醫療保健支出), Dep't of Health (Jan. 5, 2012) (Taiwan), *available at* http://www.doh.gov.tw/CHT2006/DM/DM2_po2.aspx?class_no=440&now_fod_list_no=12040&level_no=2&doc_no=83068.

Nigeria, and, to some extent, Venezuela – lack of judicial independence makes courts ineffectual.

As our authors highlight, some countries in this category have enshrined health care as a constitutional right in an attempt to accelerate redistributive and access goals, and to cut a transformative path. A prime example here is South Africa, which in its post-apartheid constitution explicitly entrenches a right to health (as well as other social rights such as housing) to challenge the monumental gap in access between the rich and the poor.

The Treatment Action Campaign case (TAC) in South Africa[56] is often celebrated as demonstrative of the true power of a health human rights approach. There, the Constitutional Court of South Africa interpreted the constitutional right to health to require the government address mother-to-child transmission of HIV in public clinics. Although the case was undoubtedly a breakthrough, Lisa Foreman and Jerome Amir Singh take a more nuanced approach to the success of the TAC case and highlight that while the decision did mobilize improvements, this was very much part of a larger political dynamic.[57] They note how social mobilization was necessary both to bring this case to court and to ensure the implementation of the decision. In fact, it has been argued that litigation played a subordinate role to social mobilization in the TAC's accomplishments.[58] Thus a constitutional right to health care played a role, but political commitment was also necessary – a theme that resonates through a number of our chapters. The TAC case also points to how the lines may be sometimes blurred between petitions for specific services and broader policy petitions. While the claim was for a specific service, the decision had a larger policy effect on government's approach to decision making, as it was part of a broader challenge to AIDS denialism and government inaction, grounded in grassroots mobilization. Addressing a much more individualized claim, in Soobramoney,[59] the Constitutional Court showed deferral to the hospital's decision regarding rationing for renal dialysis, pointing to how defining the content of a right must engage with the question of resources and the need to defer to rational decisions made in good faith.

In Brazil and Venezuela, as in South Africa, litigation over access to HIV/AIDS medicines not only resulted in courtroom successes but also generated important reforms on the ground. However, as Mariana Prado discusses in her chapter,[60] recent

---

[56] Minister of Health and Others v. Treatment Action Campaign and Others 2002 (5) SA 721 (CC) (S. Afr.).

[57] Lisa Forman & Jerome Amir Singh, Chapter 11 in this volume.

[58] William Forbath, *Cultural Transformation, Deep Institutional Reform, and ESR Practice: South Africa's Treatment Action Campaign, in* STONES OF HOPE: HOW AFRICAN ACTIVISTS RECLAIM HUMAN RIGHTS TO CHALLENGE GLOBAL POVERTY 51, 87 (Lucie White & Jeremy Perelman eds., 2011).

[59] Thiagraj Soobramoney v. Minister of Health (Kwa-Zulu Natal) 1998 (1) SA 765 (CC) (S.Afr.).

[60] Mariana Mota Prado, Chapter 12 in this volume.

litigation in Brazil has been controversial, with many arguing that the proliferation of individual petitions based on the right to health is distorting the allocation of resources. In this regard Brazil stands with Colombia as a case where the existence of a huge volume of litigation on the part of individual litigants raises the concern that pursuit of rights has resulted in a hyper-individualized approach. This question of who litigation benefits remains controversial. In sharp contrast is Venezuela where, as Oscar Cabrera and Fanny Gómez discuss,[61] a newly constituted court retreated from the initial jurisprudence interpreting a constitutional right to health care. Cabrera and Gomez express concern that the newly created Supreme Tribunal of Justice is "pro-government," lacking the independence needed to demand accountability under the right to health. Here, the interrelationship of politics and law spills over into the very judicial-making enterprise itself, rendering the right to health care largely nugatory.

A number of important decisions in the Indian system have come about as a result of public interest litigation. By definition, such decisions will result in a larger benefit for the public than petitions on the part of individual patients for new drugs or devices. In India, the state's obligation to improve public health is part of the Directive Principles of the constitution, but the right to health care has been "read in" as part of the right to life, and is understood to entail positive obligations for the state. However, notwithstanding a few significant decisions, many issues are not addressed in litigation, and enormous access and equity problems persist within the Indian health care system. India offers a challenging case in thinking about the role of health human rights: it has a universal system, but it is impoverished. Human rights litigation, grounded in the right to life, is playing an important role, but these judicial nudges pale in comparison to the scale of need and the health care problems that must be addressed.

This then raises the question of what happens when the right to health rings hollow even when the fundamentals (i.e., universal coverage) are in place. What role should courts play in spurring higher levels of overall investment in an inadequate public health care system? Anand Grover, Maitreyi Misra, and Lubhyathi Rangarajan[62] argue for coverage of a minimum core of care for all citizens, but it is unclear what combination of legal and political forces are needed to achieve this. It is also unclear whether the courts are equipped to determine a minimum core; missteps here may inappropriately divert resources to health care from other important needs such as clean water, safe food, education, housing, and so forth. Thus, in India, a constitutional recognition of the right to health care in and of itself does not seem to have the potential to transform a poor health care system.

Litigation does not play any important role in Nigeria, due to lack of social mobilization, legislation, and constitutional rights, combined with an absence of

---

[61] Oscar Cabrera & Fanny Gómez, Chapter 15 in this volume.
[62] Anand Grover, Maitreyi Misra & Lubhyathi Rangarajan, Chapter 16 in this volume.

democratic accountability and political legitimacy. Remigius Nwabueze[63] calls on Nigerian courts to act proactively to realize health care rights, employing, for instance, Article 16 of the African Charter on Human Rights and People's Rights, and arguing that with judicial creativity, Nigerian courts could expand the right to life to include protections for health rights, as per the approach in India. He argues that judicialization of health care rights could cut through failures in democracy and to provide a platform for social and political mobilization. The experience from India again suggests, however, that enforcement of rights to health care on their own are unlikely to be transformative and litigation must be synergistic with political, cultural, and economic forces.

While Nwabueze has hopes that a right to health care in Nigeria could prove transformative, in the context of China, Christina S. Ho[64] points to risks if courts do assume an aggressive role in vindicating health care rights: this may result in a tendency to limit health care insurance to what an individual has contributed (medical savings accounts) rather than to ensure pooling and sharing of risk; to an overemphasis on pharmaceuticals; and to a tendency to privilege impersonal commodities over less fungible care. Given a blank template to develop a right to health care, Ho argues it should emphasize primary and preventive care and caring services over discrete treatments and drugs. Ho's thesis here poses a challenging puzzle: How can we craft a health human right that duly prioritizes public health? And would articulating a health human right in this fashion be appropriate in countries with much higher levels of national wealth? In other words, a health human right needs to be flexible to be just, adjusting to needs and resources over space and time, while resisting forces seeking to commercialize and exploit the public desire to fund a fair base for all.

The United States is a unique case given the outlier status of its health system, characterized by enormous wealth alongside great disparities in access. However, the Obama reforms nudge it from being a system located in this public/private group more toward the category of SHI/managed competition. The Patient Protection and Affordable Care Act in the United States requires most of the country's legal residents to obtain health insurance, provides subsidies for low-income enrollees, and imposes penalties on mid-to-large-size employers if they fail to offer health care benefits.[65] With full implementation, an additional 31 million Americans will have the security of health insurance.[66] The scale of this achievement, as discussed by Allison

---

[63] Remigius N. Nwabueze, Chapter 14 in this volume.

[64] Christina S. Ho, Chapter 10 in this volume.

[65] Patient Protection and Affordable Care Act, Pub. L. 111–148, 124 Stat. 119 (2010) (codified in scattered sections of 42 U.S.C. & 26 U.S.C.).

[66] Letter from Douglas W. Elmendorf, Congressional Budget Office Director, to the Honorable Harry Reid, Senate Majority Leader, Table 3 (March 11, 2010), *available at* http://www.cbo.gov/ftpdocs/113xx/doc11307/Reid_Letter_HR3590.pdf.

Hoffman,[67] brings home that, to a large extent, litigation of health care rights can only ever have a modest impact compared to democratic and political reforms that establish and solidify universal health insurance. Litigation of health care rights may, however, be used to help ensure the reasonableness of decision making once that universal base is established, and inhibit governmental attempts to regress from a standard of solidarity once established.

REFLECTING ON OVERALL THEMES

Building on the comparative works of Gauri and Brinks,[68] Yamin and Gloppen,[69] and other authors who have written more generally on social rights,[70] we too find it difficult to draw hard and fast conclusions about the role of rights; their impact is contextual and dependent on a number of interrelated factors. Moreover, it is still too premature to parse out the weight and interaction of the relevant factors, as robust social science has not yet been done (and may be infeasible) that locates cause and effect. Nonetheless, as a result of this comparative work, we can refine our understandings and draw out insights to orient future research and lines of inquiry. Unlike the previous comparative projects that looked into the implementation of the right to health and its enforcement by courts, our study includes both "developed" and "developing" countries, reflecting a variety of health and legal systems. The typology dividing the countries under study into three categories based on their health care systems allows us to reflect on the differing roles of rights in these different categories. Notwithstanding context-specific and contingent factors, and variations in the outcome of rights litigation across countries, there are clear differences in the role of the right to health among the three categories of countries we discussed:

1. A lack of recognition of a constitutional or otherwise enforceable right to health care is apparent in established democracies that are high-income countries with relatively strong, predominately tax-financed health systems. In these countries rights were traditionally not "needed," as these are modern welfare states where health was part of policy. Individuals may turn to courts to put their grievances through when faced with prioritization and rationing, but courts are usually unlikely to offer substantive remedies given the lack of recognition of the right to health. However, EU law has opened new channels for litigation in some of these countries. Moreover, forces pushing for privatization may mean that

---

[67] Allison K. Hoffman, Chapter 13 in this volume.
[68] Courting Social Justice, *supra* note 33.
[69] Litigating Health Rights, *supra* note 28.
[70] *See, e.g.,* Langford, *supra* note 32; Kathering G. Young, Constituting Economic and Social Rights (2012).

more individuals in these systems look to litigate health care rights to ensure access.

2. Rights play a more significant role in SHI/managed competition systems (which are mostly high-income countries) where decisions or decision-making processes concerning the defined basket of benefits may be subject to judicial review. Some of the significant litigation in these countries is directed at the (regulated) insurers/providers rather than the state.

3. In middle-income countries with big gaps between a poor public health system and a rich private one, we are most likely to find an express constitutional right to health care, or that the right to health care is inferred from other constitutional provision. In some of these countries, constitutional rights were included as part of the transition to democracy and as an attempt to address huge inequities that previously existed, for example as result of apartheid in South Africa.

We elaborate on these topics later in the chapter, also drawing some conclusions from our sample of sixteen countries of where courts are tending to intervene as opposed to not, and argue that courts should often be taking a different approach, that is, intervening in some situations where they are not and showing more restraint in other cases. For example, we see that in many systems and contexts, especially in some of the Latin American countries we reviewed[71] and a number of European countries where EU law prevails, courts tend to be more ready to intervene on an individual application, for example to a new drug or therapy. We contend that in this domain courts should exhibit more restraint and be very cautious about second-guessing decision makers who are striving to balance community needs with individuals needs/wants within a universal, public system. On the other hand, across different systems, courts tend to be reluctant to intervene in larger policy questions, particularly those directed to the structure of the system.[72] We argue that courts should be more willing than they presently are to scrutinize policy measures that are retrogressive, and push systems toward a commitment to universal, public health care that secures access on the part of those most in need. We argue for this not because courts can replace policy decisions, but rather because we see a role for courts in holding governments to a standard of rationality and reasonability and ensuring that governmental decision making adheres to human rights standards, as discussed later.

---

[71] A similar finding on Latin America is made in Yamin and Gloppen's research; *see* OttarMastad, LiseRakener & Octavio L. Motta Ferraz, *Assessing the Impact of Health Rights Litigation: A Comparative Analysis of Argentina, Brazil, Colombia, Costa Rica, India and South Africa, in* LITIGATING HEALTH RIGHTS, *supra* note 28, at 273, 286–288.

[72] Brinks and Gauri also observe that it is harder to secure and realize a collective rather than individual remedy. Daniel M. Brinks & VarunGauri, *A New Policy Landscape: Legalizing Social and Economic Rights in the Developing World, in* COURTING SOCIAL JUSTICE, *supra* note 33, at 303, 305.

To structure our analysis here, we hark back to themes we asked our contributors to explore: (1) variations in the impact of rights depending on their mode of enactment (international, constitutional, statutory and de facto, and international law); (2) the relationship between the impact of rights, justicability, and access to justice; (3) whether litigation of health human rights inappropriately skews resources; (4) the interaction of law and politics in determining the full realization of health human rights; and (5) our overall conclusions regarding litigation of individual rights as opposed to more structural claims and some thoughts on how to better strike a balance between individual needs and the larger societal interest.

(i) *What Kinds of Rights Have the Greatest Impact?*

Let us begin with the issue of the impact of different kinds of rights. We explored four broad categories of rights: first, constitutional rights that directly provide for health and health care; second, constitutional rights such as the right to life, security or dignity that are interpreted as including a right to health care; third, statutory/contractual rights as we sometimes see in SHI/managed competition models; and finally, de facto or political rights where there is no legal right to health but a dominant political discourse and set of policies that has effectively ensured a fair and universal health care system.

We conclude that the decision of whether to adopt a rights-based approach, and the modality of rights instrument chosen, is not exogenous to the health system in question. A country's historical context and stage of development will partly determine the structure of its health care system, and these factors in turn determine its approach to health rights.

National tax-financed systems are found in high-income countries with relatively strong, predominately tax-financed health systems. These countries do not (generally) have constitutional rights to health care or statutory statements regarding individual rights to health care. Individuals may turn to courts to put their grievances through when faced with prioritization and rationing, but courts are usually unlikely to give substantive remedies. In part this is owing to the fact that a rights framework is, arguably, not so obviously needed, as universal and public health care systems have evolved through political and cultural processes over the course of the twentieth century. It bears emphasizing that decision-making processes (for rationing etc.) are more centralized in national tax-financed systems, and in principle are subject to democratic accountability. These factors, respectively, lead to heightened concern about courts' institutional competence and the democratic legitimacy of judicial review. These factors militate against a rights-based approach and robust judicial review.

In contrast, concerns about accountability are attenuated with SIH/managed competition systems, where there is a much greater reliance on arm's length insurers and increasingly on regulated private health insurers. The institutions and legal instruments at work here – for example, contracts of insurance and lists of insured services (the boundaries of which are frequently contested)[73] – more readily invite judicial scrutiny.

Finally, in our very diverse category of public/private systems (which are made up, apart from the United States, of middle-income countries), there are big gaps between a poor public health system and a rich private one, but we are far more likely to find an express constitutional right to health care, and/or the right to health care is inferred from other constitutional provisions. In some of these latter countries, such constitutional rights have been included as part of the transition to democracy and amount to an attempt to address huge inequities that previously existed, for example, as a result of apartheid in South Africa. But in assessing the impact of litigation in these systems, it is important that we avoid, as it were, mistaking the trees for the forest. From a social justice perspective, court victories expanding coverage for individuals or groups within the public system are overshadowed by this larger cleavage between poorly financed public systems and well-financed private systems. To date, there is scant evidence that health rights advance equity *across* the public and private systems that operate in parallel in these countries.

In terms of the impact of rights depending on the source of law, we did see in a number of European countries that international law and conventions are having an impact. On the one hand, individuals have been able to find relief by turning to European human rights law and EU law, especially the latter. On the other hand, regional and international law in this regard can result in the imposition of "global" standards that may not be sufficiently reflective of the resources of the health care system in question. The danger of a health rights approach may be that rights are rarefied and divorced from local contexts, straining the ability of public insurers to sustain a public system. Multinational pharmaceutical companies and the manufacturers of devices have much to gain by having their products adopted into public insurance schemes in a manner that reduces the ability of the public payer to negotiate a reasonable price.

(ii) *Impact of a Rights Approach: Justiciability and Access to Justice*

Judicial policy is a major factor, affecting the impact of health care rights in various ways. First there is the issue of justiciability. State obligations couched merely as governmental objectives or aspirations, as in China and Hungary, may prove

---

[73] *Cf.* the discussion of the relationship between providers and recipients of health care, as contrasted to the relationship between recipients and the state on one hand and the state and providers on the other hand, suggested by Gauri and Brinks. Gauri and Brinks describe those as "private obligations," and while we see them as actually often having a "public" nature themselves, we join in the assessment that it is important to look at these relationships in the study of health rights; as we discuss in the text, significant litigation occurs in this context. Varun Gauri and Daniel M. Brinks, *Introduction: The Elements of Legalization and the Triangular Shape of Social and Economic Rights*, COURTING SOCIAL JUSTICE, *supra* note 33 at 1, 11.

meaningless in the absence of judicial enforcement. For example, the Hungarian constitution (since January 2012) includes a new social security provision, replacing rights language with the much weaker language of aspirational goals. It may be that over time these nonjusticiable commitments by government will have a normative sway that drives progressive change, but it is also possible that the words may remain mere symbolic tokens to improving access to health care.

Second, and related to the former issue, is a concern about judicial impartiality: if a court is not sufficiently independent of government, then it may be the case as claimed in Venezuela that even a forcefully written constitutional right to health will be rendered hollow.

The third issue concerns access to justice and the extent to which barriers to justice result in litigation being pursued by those with means as opposed to those, objectively, in the greatest need. Our comparative analysis has shown that justiciable rights can have an enormous impact if litigants are able to readily access the courts through, for example, elimination of procedural barriers (see, in particular, Colombia and Brazil). Although, as discussed further later, more litigation is not necessarily better; it is reasonable to conclude that individual litigation (as opposed to structural litigation) cannot *possibly* be progressive where barriers to justice are insurmountable for those in greatest need. With respect to the actual cost of litigation, representation by public lawyers and NGOs may be a partial solution. Even when many barriers to litigation have been removed – as in Brazil and Colombia – some argue that it is primarily the middle class and the wealthy that avail themselves of rights litigation. However, as Mariana Prado argues in her chapter on Brazil, if some litigation is carried out by public defense lawyers, this may in fact benefit those with lower incomes.

Moreover, even if litigation directly benefits the middle class, it is of course possible that over time, the impact of litigation will "trickle down" to benefit lower socioeconomic groups. This might occur, for example, if litigation spurs greater transparency, accountability, and overall reasonableness in rationing decisions at a systemic level. However, it is also possible that litigation will result in a distortion of resources toward expensive new technologies and drugs, and away from primary and preventive care that would most benefit the poor.

(iii) *Whether Rights Litigation Inappropriately Skews Resources*

As mentioned, a high volume of litigation does not necessarily mean that those most in need are having their rights adjudicated upon, or that the overall litigation of health rights is progressive. This point relates to a theme thoroughly explored in this volume, namely whether rights litigation can undermine the fair allocation of limited resources. This risk is heightened if, as evidenced in Brazil and Colombia, rights litigation is not anchored to some extent within a consideration of resources and the need to ensure the sustainability and ongoing commitment to a system of redistribution. The flip side of this, however, is that there are dangers too from having *no* rights articulated and thus virtually no judicial oversight of governmental decision making. For example, in developed countries with well-established health care systems, the absence of rights de jure to health may prove problematic as pressure to privatize compromises existing systems of redistribution (Canada and Israel), and the politics of the day changes as wealthy Baby Boomers seek access to more health care in a timely way, while opposing the public investments needed to maintain universality. But also in such contexts, the effects of recognizing a right to health would depend on the interpretation it is given, and the extent to which this interpretation incorporates distributive (rather than individualistic) notions of the right.

We argue that there is a "halfway house" between realizing every individual claim and refusing to acknowledge a right to health at all (a topic to which we return later in the chapter). However, we note here the concern that such an approach can at best be a very incremental spur to meet egregious inequity as we see in countries like South Africa, Nigeria, and India. Countries with impoverished public health care systems will not find that a right to health and associated litigation will in and of itself transform a poorly performing system. Thus it is important that we be modest about what can be achieved through rights and appreciate that whatever a court decides has to be refracted through political processes.

(iv) *The Intersection of Law and Politics*

This concept that rights have to be refracted through political processes has two components. The first is that to understand the impact of litigation, one has to look past the point of the court decision itself and see how it has been interpreted through political and social practices. It is clear that social mobilization and political follow-up[74] are crucial for petitions to truly succeed.[75] In this regard we have seen cases whose implementation is lacking (Canada, Venezuela), but also cases where petitioners lost the battle in court but won the war as a result of politics responding to public concerns (Canada, Israel, New Zealand).

Secondly, rights often need to be refracted through a political lens in a more foundational sense – taken out of the judicial box altogether, and advanced directly in the political sphere. For example, Paul Farmer points to the need to rethink health and human rights in a way that will not pin all hope on legal battles, but rather shift the paradigm to one of political solidarity and, pragmatically, to the provision of services for those in need. Farmer says the real transfer of money, food, and drugs is needed rather than more litigation.[76] This is especially noteworthy given

[74] On the importance of follow-up, *see also id.* at 19–20.
[75] *See* Forbath, *supra* note 57.
[76] Paul Farmer, Pathologies of Power: Health, Human Rights, and the New war on the Poor, chap. 9, 213 (2003); *see also* Paul Farmer & Nicole Gastineau, *Rethinking Health and Human Rights: Time for a Paradigm Shift*, 30 J. L. Med. & Ethics 655 (2002).

that the right to health, and especially constitutional rights, are mostly recognized in countries with impoverished public health systems. Moreover, there is a danger that the rhetoric of rights can be employed to dampen the political movements needed to make a positive change. In this regard, Lucie White reflects on a "health rights campaign" on which she worked with students from the United States and a West African university. She expresses concern that protests over injustices in health will be framed in muted legal concepts like "progressive realization" and "reasonableness" at the price of keeping their passion in line. In her words, human rights consciousness could train people in very poor areas to think of themselves "as good, liberal, rights-consuming subjects as they watched their children die."[77] If rights in the context of health care are not to be "more façade than fact,"[78] we not only need an egalitarian concept of rights, supported by broad social mobilization. We must also realize that rights discourse will often run against problems that are too big for the judicial branch alone, which, in Hamilton's famous articulation, has "no influence over either the sword or the purse."[79] We are not saying that litigation is completely ineffective here, but rather that the potential impact of rights pales in comparison to the scale of the problem.[80]

(v) *Individual Claims vs. Structural Claims and Striking a Balance between the Individual and Society*

Our comparative review has revealed at least two different kinds of claims that may be advanced under the right to health care. The first is an individual claim for a particular treatment not offered under an established coverage scheme (e.g., due to cost concerns or doubts about effectiveness). The second kind of challenge is structural in nature, testing the balance between public/private systems, or challenging systemic inequities caused by, for example, copayments or an overall lack of coverage. What we see from our comparative review is that courts in some countries are more comfortable intervening in individual claims than in structural challenges. We argue, however, that the opposite approach would be preferable: courts should be more reluctant to intervene with respect to individualized claims for new drugs

---

[77] Lucie White, *"If You Don't Pay, You Die": On Death and Desire in the Postcolony, in* EXPLORING SOCIAL RIGHTS, *supra* note 2, at 57, 72.

[78] *See* David P. Fidler, INTERNATIONAL LAW AND INFECTIOUS DISEASES 218 (1999).

[79] THE FEDERALIST No. 78 (Alexander Hamilton).

[80] On the promises and limits of right in this context, *see also* Gross, *supra* note 9, at 336–339. *See also* Forbath's discussion of the TAC litigation and of how TAC did not bring to courts its broader claim for a national ARVT plan, but instead chose the public political sphere as the arena for that, even if the constitutional court was an important "partner" in their campaign: Forbath, *supra* note 57, at 87. *See* more generally Jeremy Perelman & Lucie E. White, *Stones of Hope: Experience and Theory in African Economic and Social Rights Activism, in* STONES OF HOPE, *supra* note 57, at 149, discussing robust social rights practice that uses litigation but does not privilege it, engages multiple public actor in every domain of state power, and engages both private and state actors.

and technologies, and when they do, their aim should be to ensure that the decision is reasonable, reflects a fair process, and accords due consideration to all (and only) relevant factors. Conversely – and perhaps counterintuitively given the conventional view that courts should not muddy their hands with larger policy decisions – we argue that courts should take a close look at structural changes that threaten universality and equity.

Turning first to individualized petitions, we can identity three general approaches to adjudication: (1) outright rejection, on grounds that rationing decisions fall within the purview of government (Hungary); (2) opening the door widely to individualized petitions, at the risk of causing stress and distortions in overall allocations of care (Colombia and Brazil); (3) a middle route of administrative review for reasonableness, which sets strict criteria about when courts should intervene, licensing intervention where the decision maker has not followed a fair process, and/or where the decision is found to be substantively unreasonable (e.g., it overestimated the systemic costs of providing a given service, or it failed to account for relevant considerations and was partly grounded in irrelevant considerations).

We see this third route being favored in the United Kingdom, Israel, and South Africa, and in a single New Zealand case, as well as some movement in this direction by the Brazilian Supreme Court. This kind of judicial approach resonates with the "accountability for reasonableness" framework first put forward by Norman Daniels,[81] calling for a deliberate and transparent process for priority setting. The judicial process itself is deliberative in character and thus can foster accountability for reasonableness on the part of those charged with safeguarding access to health care: it requires the parties to bring evidence and reasoned arguments to the courts; it requires the courts to provide reasoned arguments for its decision; and the presence of dissenting arguments fosters public discussion.[82]

In common law countries where judgments have precedential value, this model may not only create precedents that will be followed for the specific technology, but also create criteria (as has been the case in the United Kingdom and Israel) that authorities will work by, thus providing clearer guidance about what will and will not be covered in the future and diminishing the need for expensive and protracted litigation. We posit that some form of review for priority-setting and rationing decisions is a reasonable compromise between rejecting any challenge to rationing decisions, or, alternatively, accepting them all on the basis of the unique and special nature of health care needs. Reasonableness review, anchored in the

---

[81] Daniels, *supra* note 14, at 103–139. Daniels argues that the rights of individuals to have certain needs met in the context of health are specified only as a result of a fair, deliberative process aimed at meeting population health needs fairly, and that the right to health can yield entitlements only to those needs that we can reasonably try to meet. *Id.* at 146; *see also* Norman Daniels & James E. Sabin, Setting Limits Fairly: Learning to Share Resources for Health (2d ed., 2008).

[82] Keith Syrett, Law, Legitimacy, and the Rationing of Health Care: A Contextual and Comparative Perspective, chap. 5, 120, 154–156 (2007).

notion that access to health care is a *right*, can be used to drive transparency, accountability, and fairness in the decision-making process.

Reasonableness is admittedly an open-ended concept, and the mode of judicial review we are discussing here has taken different forms in different countries, with varying levels of deference to government decisions. In Israel, for example, as Aeyal Gross shows, the Supreme Court has taken a very deferential position when reviewing principled government decisions over whether or not to cover certain services. At the same time, the labor courts have opened a "back door" to stricter judicial scrutiny, focused on criteria that sickness funds must consider when addressing "exceptional" cases. Reasonableness has also drawn criticism in the South African context, for failing to provide principled criteria, leading to decisions that are not adequately justified and deflecting the focus from urgent interests of deprived populations.[83] As a more robust criterion of judicial review, David Bilchitz suggests a focus on the "minimum core," requiring that health care systems attend to the basic needs of the most vulnerable, with the strictest level of scrutiny applied where this minimal threshold is not met.[84] Recall that, as we discussed in the Introduction to this volume, states are required under international law to provide for "core obligations" regarding the right to health, meaning they must ensure at the very least a minimum essential level of the right, including, for example, primary health care.[85]

However, we side with Lisa Forman who argues that "reasonableness" is consistent with the "minimum core" and would only be inconsistent if "bald scarcity arguments were allowed to limit state actions designed to meet the basic needs and priority health interests of the poor"[86] and justify denials of care. But the reasonableness standard need not entail such deference. As the *TAC* ruling demonstrates, the reasonableness standard can be construed in a manner that functionally replicates the minimum core approach, forbidding policies that violate people's equal dignity.[87] The desired effect here is careful judicial scrutiny of decisions that deny or impede access to care for vulnerable populations; whether this is achieved pursuant to a reasonableness or minimum core standard, or some combination of the two, remains a matter of debate between us.[88] We also note that many of the issues concerning

[83] David Bilchitz, Poverty and fundamental rights: The justification and enforcement of socio-economic rights 135–177 (2007). For a discussion of similar critiques, *see* Lisa Forman, *What Future for the Minimum Core? Contextualizing the Implications of South African Socioeconomic Rights Jurisprudence for the International Human Right to Health, in* Global Health and Human Rights, *supra* note 20, 62, at 74 and references therein.

[84] Bilchitz, *id.* 83, at 208, 234.

[85] General Comment No. 14, *supra* note 1; Forman, *supra* note 83.

[86] Forman, *supra* note 83, at 74–75.

[87] *Id.*

[88] As it happens, the authors themselves disagree on the optimal approach. Flood holds that the reasonableness standard – crucially prioritizing the health needs of vulnerable populations – renders the minimum core standard largely redundant. The two standards may diverge in circumstances of extreme scarcity, as reasonableness might allow shortcomings in the minimum core; but Flood's view

the effect of policies on poor populations are apparent not so much in individual petitions but rather in litigation concerning broader policy decisions that we discuss later, where indeed judicial review should ensure that governmental choices do not worsen inequality.

A reasonableness standard would include some limited mechanism to accommodate patients with unique medical needs. This is in keeping with idea that we consider not only the abstract "general other" (as required from an ethics of justice and rights) but also the specific "concrete other" (as required from an ethics of care and responsibility),[89] bearing in mind that the general design of the health care system may not always be able to address exceptional individual needs. This approach has been taken in the United Kingdom and Israel where, as mentioned earlier, courts set criteria for exceptions. These developments complement the review of general decisions about the provisions of services, allowing courts to consider whether individuals should receive coverage for specific therapies not covered by the general scheme. For example, reasonableness will require a fair process for patients who, owing to conflicting medical conditions, cannot safely use the standard insured treatment and thus need access to a more expensive treatment not normally insured. However, we underscore that review for "exceptions" must be limited to cases where there is robust medical evidence about the efficacy of the therapy in question, and

---

is that the reasonableness standard provides better guidance even here, in countenancing that competing social needs (e.g., education, poverty) may justify shortfalls of the minimum core. Gross, while also acknowledging the overlap, would prefer that courts employ *both* standards: generally relying on the reasonableness standard, but applying the minimum core standard when adjudicating severe deprivations of essential health care.

[89] The terms are borrowed from Seyla Benhabib, Situating the Self: Gender, Community, and Postmodernism in Contemporary Ethics 102–148 (1992); *see also* Gross, *supra* note 9. Benhabib herself follows on Carol Gilligan's work on the importance of ethics of care and responsibility as an addition to the ethics of care and justice. Actually, Gilligan's classic research dealt with access to medications: in it two children were asked to save one of Kohlberg's moral dilemmas, in which a person deliberates whether it is proper that he should steal a medicine which he cannot afford but which he needs in order to save his wife's life. Gilligan illustrates the ethics of justice by an approach that constructs this dilemma as a clash between the value of property and the value of life, and prefers the right to life. The ethics of care is illustrated by an approach that looks at the issue as one of an ongoing relationship, and seeks a solution that will give a proper hearing to all the parties, and thus requests that the husband and the pharmacist deliberate the matter to find a solution. *See* Carl Gilligan, In a Different Voice: Psychological Theory and Women's Development (1993). But in the cases we are discussing, the attempt to convince the "pharmacist" usually already failed, and thus courts have to decide. When they hold for patients, they do it out of an ethics of justice and rights, but this is combined with an ethics of care and responsibility, which requires us to look at the concrete person beyond the formal rules. The "exceptions" mechanisms may be considered as a forum that can combine these approaches, the ones of a general conception of justice with a perspective of care and responsibility toward the specific case. It is following Gilligan's work that Benhabib addresses the need to regard both the "general other" (as required from an ethics of justice and rights) and the "concrete other" (as required from an ethics of care and responsibility). Whereas regarding the "general other" requires us to examine each person in an abstract way, regarding the "concrete other" requires us to regard each person based on his needs and concrete circumstances.

should be allowed to take its cost into account, for otherwise claims of exceptionality could undermine the "big picture" decision-making process. Moreover, to do otherwise would be to play into the hands of large pharmaceutical companies and others only too happy to make the most of a keen desire on the part of the patients for any hope of cure and the political liability of governments who are portrayed as hard-hearted in denying funding, regardless of price.

Let us now turn to consider our second category of litigation, namely that which challenges structural features of a health system, for example the balance between public and private health insurance, or the levying of copayments. Judicial engagement with these kinds of challenges raises the concern that courts lack the institutional competence to intervene in questions of policy and, moreover, that their interference on these matters is antidemocratic. Concerning question of institutional competence, structural challenges may be more complex than individual claims for drugs, devices, or services, as a court's decision with respect to a structural challenge will have system-wide implications (although the cumulative and precedential effect of individualized decisions may eventually result in structural change). Moreover, decisions on the part of courts in structural challenges may be more difficult to enforce, as courts frequently lack the institutional capacity to monitor and follow up on system-directed reforms. Thus judgments will only be effective if backed by social mobilization.

On the other hand, there is a very clear evidence base that speaks to the importance of universal health care and the benefits of a collective commitment to equity in health care provision. Given the overriding and universally accepted importance of health and health care at both domestic and international levels, we argue that it is past time for courts to acknowledge health care as a human right, and take available opportunities to nudge and push governments to ensure a reasonable standard of health care for all and in particular to vigilantly eliminate barriers to care for the poor.

In our comparative review, there have been cases in various countries (Colombia, Canada, Taiwan, the United States, and Israel) where courts have ventured into more structural features of health systems, but the effect of these judgments has admittedly been mixed. In Colombia, the courts have attempted to spur broad health reform – rectifying a problem partly created by a tsunami of health rights litigation – by ordering the government to work toward the universal health coverage, harmonize the baskets of health services offered, and implement a new financial scheme for the delivery of health services. In Canada, the court's foray into structural issues opened the door to further privatization of the Canadian system. In Taiwan and the United States, the courts have upheld new legislative mandates to purchase health insurance as a bridge to universal access. In Israel, the court upheld policies that aimed to protect the public system, and criticized the lack of a proper update mechanism for the cost of the health services basket, but also rejected petitions challenging increased privatization. From our comparative review we see, then, that courts are usually more willing to serve as a "shield" than a "sword," protecting government initiatives that are rights enhancing but declining to overturn regressive governmental policy. The expectation for advocates of health care rights is that they will be used as a sword, not a shield. We agree that courts have a greater role to play in these structural cases.

First, it is important that courts be vigilant that rights discourse does not actually become *part of* the processes of privatization and commodification[90] rather than a tool to restore equity. To counter this we need to embrace a notion of rights that incorporates principles of substantive equality.[91] As Daniels suggested, we may claim a right to health care only if it can be harvested from an acceptable general theory of distributive justice or from a more particular theory of justice for health and health care, which would tell us which kinds of rights claims are legitimate.[92] Moreover, this general distributive scheme must prioritize access for those most in need.[93] Thus "rights" claims should be rejected where they threaten structural components buttressing universal access (e.g., assertions of a "right" to opt out of public plans).

Further, courts may on occasion need to act as a sword rather than merely a shield. This is particularly so when governmental policy under review is regressing from previous standards of universality and distribution. For example, we would claim that governmental policy promoting a new system of copayments should be closely scrutinized by courts, given that copayments are generally a burden for the most vulnerable. It may be the case that governments can justify such retrograde steps on the basis of falling revenues, but the court should demand robust justification rather than duck the question in deference to policy makers' authority. Moreover, in such cases, and generally when scrutinizing policy questions, courts should also ensure that policy changes do not violate equity by creating disproportionate burdens on the poor and by enlarging, rather than reducing, gaps in accessibility. General Comment 14 may come handy here with its AAAQ criteria (availability, accessibility, acceptability, and quality), which may be useful to scrutinize policy, especially in regard to whether or not it advances equal access.[94]

In sum, we argue that wherever possible, courts should both protect and assist the democratic process of establishing universality, equal access, and reasonable coverage for health care. Courts must be cognizant of resource constraints, but this should not close off judicial inquiry into government efforts to provide universal health care. Once a country has a universal health care system, courts should continue to test the reasonableness of government decision making about what is covered or not covered while allowing for an "exceptions" mechanism based on

---

[90] Or, in other words, "part of the problem"; *see* KENNEDY, *supra* note 22.

[91] *See* Morton J. Horwitz, *Rights*, 23 HARV. C.R.-C.L. L. REV. 393 (1988).

[92] Daniels, *supra* note 14, at 15 (2008).

[93] See Leslie London, *Human Rights and Public Health: Dichotomies or Synergies in Developing Countries? Examining the Case of HIV in South Africa*, 30 J. L. MED. & ETHICS 677 (2002).

[94] General Comment No. 14, *supra* note 1. *See* our discussion in the Introduction, *supra* in this volume.

robust evidence. Moreover, the adjudication of a health care right must be guided by a commitment to solidarity, universality, and substantive equality, scrutinizing whether decisions adhere to rights and equality or whether they do the opposite by taking retrogressive measures, putting an unfair financing burden on the poor, reducing equality, and curbing accessibility.[95] One's right to health should be viewed as a relational right[96] and interpreted in the context of a larger societal commitment to a reasonable standard of access to health care for all. Further, courts should, as we have seen in the United Kingdom, set standards for decision making to ensure that decision making is fair, transparent, and accountable. Courts may not have the institutional capacity or expertise to make individual determinations about what to cover and what not to cover, but they do have something to contribute in objectively ensuring best practices in the way decisions are taken.

There is, we feel, a new fragility in many established public health care systems, and many countries have embraced market-like reforms within their universal systems. These developments will constantly test societal consensus about what is just in terms of coverage and the balance between the individual and the community. A health human rights framework must be flexible, for as societies grow wealthier, reasonable expectations of access and coverage grow as well. At the same time we must recognize there are enormous global pressures to fund all health care, all services, and to pay very high prices for drugs and treatments that often of very limited effectiveness. One danger with a rights approach is that it can reinforce the latter process, thus exacerbating the difficulties governments have in running fair and efficient health care systems. Consequently, courts need to be very careful when second-guessing governmental decision making in this regard. On the other hand, we recommend careful judicial scrutiny of initiatives that are unequivocally reductions in equity and access.

---

[95] *See* General Comment No. 14, *supra* note 1.

[96] On relational rights, *see* Jennifer Nedelsky, Law's Relations: A Relational Theory of Self, Autonomy, and Law (2011). *See also* Being Relational: Reflections on Relational Theory and Health Law (Jocelyn Downie & Jennifer J. Llewellyn eds., 2011).

Index